The Pain of Confinement

Jimmy Boyle was born in 1944 in the notorious Gorbals in Glasgow. He was in and out of remand homes and borstals from the age of thirteen until, in 1967, he was sentenced to life imprisonment for murder. Solitary confinement, brutality from all quarters and prison riots became the new way of life 'inside', as he chronicled in his first book, *A Sense of Freedom*. The setting up of the Special Unit in 1972 was to change his life.

His personal growth in this oasis of humanity within the walls of Barlinnie Prison and his skill as a sculptor are now well known. He was finally released in November 1982, since when he and his wife have been involved in social work. He takes a radical approach to community problems, tackling them at street level; hence his involvement with the problems of heroin abuse and homeless teenagers.

Jimmy and Sarah Boyle are soon to open The Gateway Exchange for ex-prisoners and others in need of help. It will employ the principles of the Special Unit, using art in a broad sense as its central theme.

He was consultant to Granada TV for three documentaries on heroin, has lectured to law students and talked in schools. The full and useful life he leads is a testimony not only to the Special Unit but to Jimmy Boyle himself.

JIMMY BOYLE

A Sense of Freedom

The Pain of Confinement

Prison Diaries

LOMOND BOOKS
36 West Shore Road, Granton,
EDINBURGH, EH5 1QD

A Sense of Freedom first published 1977 simultaneously by
Canongate Publishing Ltd and Pan Books

The Pain of Confinement first published 1984 by
Canongate Publishing Ltd

This combined edition published 1995
for Lomond Books by Pan Books
an imprint of Macmillan General Books
25 Eccleston Place, London, SW1W 9NF
and Basingstoke

Associated companies throughout the world

ISBN 0 330 34757 8

Copyright © Jimmy Boyle 1977, 1984

The right of Jimmy Boyle to be identified as the
author of this work has been asserted by him in accordance
with the Copyright, Designs and Patents Act 1988.

All rights reserved. No reproduction, copy or transmission
of this publication may be made without written permission.
No paragraph of this publication may be reproduced, copied or
transmitted save with written permission or in accordance with
the provisions of the Copyright Act 1956 (as amended). Any
person who does any unauthorized act in relation to
this publication may be liable to criminal prosecution
and civil claims for damages.

1 3 5 7 9 8 6 4 2

A CIP catalogue record for this book is available from
the British Library

Printed and bound in Great Britain by
Cox & Wyman Ltd., Reading, Berkshire

This book is sold subject to the condition that it shall not,
by way of trade or otherwise, be lent, re-sold, hired out,
or otherwise circulated without the publisher's prior consent
in any form of binding or cover other than that in which
it is published and without a similar condition including this
condition being imposed on the subsequent purchaser.

A Sense of Freedom

Introduction and Dedication

Writing this book has been a difficult and very painful experience as it has meant not only opening my own thoughts and experiences to the reader, but revealing a private and personal part of my family life. This includes my mother, children, brothers and other relatives, all of whom are hard working, decent people, and most of whom have never had any trouble with the police. These are what I would call the invisible victims of the offender and the offence.

The issues raised in the book are not peculiar to the city of Glasgow, but are part of a very serious worldwide pattern that is escalating to an alarming degree. From a personal viewpoint, the salient and most alarming factor is that the age of the person involving himself in crime is getting younger and the offence more serious.

I entered this world with the innocence of every child; had dreams of being a fireman, train driver, superman, along with the fantasies that are part of childhood. What went wrong? I do hope that laying open my thoughts and experiences as I felt them at the time will make a positive contribution to a better understanding of the problem. Personal experience has led me to believe that the pattern of my own life in crime is analogous to the vast majority involved in it.

In anticipating any criticism and debate that may arise as a result of the contents of this book, I would like to make it clear that my position is such, unlike that of other authors, that I won't be able to take part in them, though I would dearly love to. It is not meant as a deliberate or calculated indictment on any particular section of society; that would be too simplistic a view. It would be nearer the truth to say that the book is an indictment on the whole of society, and I have no hesitation in placing myself amongst that number.

In writing the book in a manner that expresses all the hatred and rage that I felt at the time of the experiences, especially the latter part, I have been told that I lose the sympathy of the reader and that this isn't wise for someone who is still owned by the State and dependent on the authorities for a parole date. The book is a genuine attempt to warn young people that there is nothing glamorous about getting involved in crime and violence. I feel that the only way any real progress can be made in this direction is through having a better understanding of it and the only way this will be achieved is by putting our cards on the table, and this I've tried hard to do. I don't feel that sympathy or popularity contests have anything to do with it.

It is appropriate that the proceeds from this book should go to the issue that it is highlighting. I have asked that my royalties should be used to set up a Trust Fund to help kids in the socially deprived areas in the West of Scotland. So anyone who buys this book will be making a contribution.

There are a number of people that I owe my survival to; and many that have reached out and touched me. I won't name them as they know who they are. It is to them that I am tempted to dedicate this book, but won't. Instead, I dedicate it to my two children, not only because I am their father, but more importantly, they are symbols of the future. A future that is in *our* hands.

Jimmy Boyle
Special Unit, Barlinnie.

Part One

I

I don't think it's good enough for me to say that I was born in the Gorbals, in May, 1944, and leave it at that. Perhaps it's all I can say, but who am I? I don't really know who I am. The one thing I am certain of is the womb I came from. And if it were possible for one to choose the womb that one was conceived in, then this is the one I'd have chosen. My Mother, Bessie, was in many ways too good for this world, and the more I got to know the world the more I believed this.

When I was born my Mother already had two sons, Tommy and Pat — aged four and eight respectively. My father's name was Tommy. From birth to the age of five my memories are vague snatches of a complete family living in a room-and-kitchen in an old Gorbals tenement building. Throughout this period certain memories remained with me that were connected with the physical and spiritual feeling of the house, such as the big coal fire that was always burning in the kitchen, which was a very small room though it managed to hold the table where everyone ate; the cooker, some furniture, and my parents' bed which sat in a recess. The kitchen was where most things were done, and everyone would sit around the fireplace talking. The fireplace played a principal role in our home as it did in most homes in the district. My father would stand in front of it with his hands behind his back, and this is one of the few memories I have of him. On a Saturday night my mother would get the tin bath out from under the bed and fill it with water to bathe all three of us, one after the other. This was a time I always disliked. Saturday was also the night that my parents' friends and relatives would come up to our house with "carry-outs" to drink and have a party.

We would be put to bed in the small room while the adults sang songs and danced, but once they started getting mellow with the booze we would get out of bed and mix with them, asking them for money while they were in this happy frame of mind. Parties and people being what they are they would either finish in a fight, or with everyone embracing each other.

The room of our house was where we three boys slept. There

was a fireplace in the room but it was rarely used as we couldn't afford it; there were also other pieces of furniture, including a large wardrobe that held the whole family's clothes. Our bed was in a recess with Pat and Tommy sleeping at the top of it and me at their feet to give us more room. I think sleeping with Pat was a good preparation for the tough life ahead because he was the worst sleeper in the world. All through the night he would nip me with his fingers if I moved near his part of the bed, and he would do this instinctively at the slightest infringement onto his area. Other times he would kick, and being the youngest, I had to accept it, though at the time I always resented it and wanted a bed of my own.

Sunday morning was always the essence of family life in our house as Mother would get us all up and made ready for chapel which was at the corner of our road, Sandyfaulds Street. Mother took us all down, giving us a ha'penny each for the collection plate. Leaving chapel was a great occasion as everyone used to eye everyone else up to see what they were wearing, and to see who was there. If anyone had a new suit or new clothes of some kind then they always wore them to chapel. People stopped and talked in the street after mass to gossip, and there was a very close community feeling at such times. From there, Pat, my eldest brother, was sent to the nearby newsagents to buy the Sunday newspapers — no *News of the World* permitted. Mother, Tommy and I returned to the house where she began the breakfast. The Sunday breakfast surpassed all others, as it was ham, eggs, black pudding and potato scones. This was a ritual repeated throughout the district in most homes on a Sunday morning. While Mother was preparing this Tommy would be breaking sticks for the fire, while I was grudgingly getting coal from the bunker, which meant that I had to wash my hands for the second time that morning. By the time the fire got going, breakfast would be ready so we would all sit around the table and wire in. I can't remember my father sitting down with us but somehow I imagine he got his breakfast in bed as my Mother seemed that sort of woman. Immediately after the meal Mother would clean up and prepare for the Sunday dinner which usually took her the rest of the morning and afternoon, while we kids went down the streets to play.

The Gorbals was full of old tenement buildings three storeys high, each floor containing three houses. Two of the houses were one-room-and-kitchen, the other in the centre was a single end (one room). The toilet was on the stairway, shared by the three families on each landing. The door of these toilets usually had no locks, which meant that the user had to sit on the seat with one hand holding the door so that none of the neighbours would come rushing to use it only to find someone sitting there — a common occurrence. The toilets were always in a terrible state which meant that during the daylight hours one could sit doing the toilet with a view onto the backcourts and see what was going on there. This was okay so long as the wind wasn't blowing.

The backcourts and streets were our playgrounds, the backcourts in particular playing a significant part in the Gorbals sub-culture. In these backs there were old washhouses — brick shelters — which, like most things in the district, had fallen into disrepair and were no longer used for the purpose for which they were built. However, they did make ideal gang huts. The backs had at one time been sectioned off, so much space to so many houses, but the metal railings and stone dykes that had acted as partitions were now either completely obliterated, or had large gaps torn in them so that the inhabitants could use the gaps as a passageway. This meant that there were two routes to a destination: through the backs, or by the street. People in a hurry took the back way as it was quicker, but more dangerous, and I don't mean in a criminal sense but in an environmental one, as the backcourts always had large puddles of black muddy water that one would have to navigate. There would always be one adventurer who would create a passage over the large puddle for those using this route. Improvisation was at its best then, as bricks from the nearby torn dykes would be dotted across the muddy water so that the traveller could step from brick to brick and make a safe journey. With practice one became adept at this and in fact the backcourt route became a busy thoroughfare. The middens were another characteristic of these backs. They were brick shelters with four bins for the householders to put rubbish in. These middens were nicknamed "midgies". There was a distinction between the midgies in our own backs to the ones in the "toffy" backs which we called "lucky didgies". The reason they acquired this name was due to a Gorbals "industry" of searching middens in the middle class areas for anything they threw out that could be used or sold.

Middle or Upper class people were "toffs" and sometimes disposed of articles that were of good quality, with damaged parts that were repairable, children's toys in particular. Groups of us, usually with the arse torn out of our trousers, snot running from our noses and filthy, would head for Queens Park, a "toffy" district, to rake the lucky didgies. These people were so toffy that they had even locked doors in their closes to prevent strangers getting into their backcourts! When a group of us went out midgie raking there was always an agreement to share any "lucks" found. We would overcome the locks on the close doors by going up the stairs to the first landing, opening the window, climbing out and dropping the fifteen feet or so to the ground. From there we would climb the iron railing or stone dyke to the neighbouring midgie, and repeat this till we struck gold or were chased by the householders who were disgusted to find scruff such as us polluting their midgies. It was amazing what we found: toys the like of which we had never seen. Anything which could be used was like gold to us, although we never restricted ourselves just to toys. But I am digressing from our backs in the Gorbals.

While "Ma" was making the Sunday dinner all the kids would be playing in the backs and there were various favourite games. Up to the age of five, my pals and I would get lumps of wood and sail them in the muddy puddles and play at boats, using stones to throw at each other's boats if the game happened to be warships. We would also get spoons and dig holes in the ground, not building castles or anything in particular but just digging hole after hole and I guess this was why the backs were all muddy and full of puddles.

One kid from the next close to me added to the attraction of digging holes as he would swallow all the worms we found. When he was around we would all dig like little Navvies and give them to him. All of us would gather round as he would drag it out and make it a big deal before taking the worm in his mouth and chewing it up. He had a very bad burn mark on his face which was a source of ridicule, and he was rejected by most of us until we discovered his appetite for worms. When it got back to his mother she would be on the look out, and catching sight of her son surrounded by us all looking, open-mouthed, while he dropped a big "blood-sucker" into his mouth, she would scream at the top of her voice and come charging downstairs, but by that time we would have made off. The kids in my brother Tommy's age group would always be lighting fires in the backs at night. Everyone would go off to collect fuel for the fire, finding toilet-doors or floor-boards from empty houses. On the whole the kids immediately older than us would reject us as they felt they were men, though in reality they were aged eight to ten.

The midgies held one of the other favourite pastimes of the dark, and that was rat-catching. The Gorbals was full of rats and they were a feature of the place and could be seen often on the stairways as one went up to the house at night. They were in many of the houses, but the backcourts were full of them and in particular the midgies. The first rule of rat-catching was, if you wore long trousers, to tuck the bottoms into your socks in case the scampering rats ran up your trouser-leg, as there were lots of rumours of this having happened. It would start with a couple of kids going to the midgie where rats would be foraging amongst the rubbish for food. One kid would pull the bin out and this would panic the rats into rushing out. The rest of us would be waiting to hit them with whatever weapon we happened to have, or with our boots. As the group went from midgie to midgie we grew in number, which meant that before long a large group of kids were going from back to back, some carrying dead rats on the end of sticks. There were times when this group would have a maximum crowd and that was when a mongrel dog called Laddie was with them. This dog was a sort of legend in the Gorbals and in fact went on to win Corporation medals for the number of rats it had killed. No-one really owned it and it used to wander the district. It had a place of pride amongst the locals, yet most of them were scared to let it lick them because of the rats it had killed. When Laddie was out rat-catching it was a pleasure to see him in action. He would catch one rat, throw it in the air snapping its neck and without stopping to see if it was dead run and kill the next. We would go into all the midgies and old wash-houses but the supply of rats was inexhaustible and the ones that the kids killed had no effect whatsoever in improving the situation. The rats were just like everyone else, fighting for survival. It was a common sight to see big cats, sitting on hot ashes that had been thrown out while rats, some as big as the cats, moved around the cats almost as though they didn't exist. As one used the back route at night time the squeak of fighting rats was a familiar sound.

Another backcourt game was dyke jumping. This was a game where kids would jump over a large gap, from one part of the dyke to another, the height from the ground being considerable. It was a prestige game and in many ways very dangerous; inevitably there were a lot of accidents, sometimes resulting in broken limbs but this game was usally reserved for the older kids of about nine or ten. Most streets had a good jumper so there was plenty of competition between kids.

There was also the "Bogie", which was a plank of wood with two halves of a roller skate nailed to each end and a wooden apple box nailed on top which we leaned on so that we could push it up and down the street. Usually one "Bogie" was owned by a handful of kids so it was a case of shots each. The streets were always busy with a multitude of kids playing street-games, and we would play until the early hours of the morning. The Gorbals streets had their own warm blend of character that was very comforting to the locals. In most cases the conditions were that of gross deprivation with buildings that were crumbling around them, but in a funny sort of way the closeness of the community compensated for the material deficiencies. The women of the district would either lean out of their windows or, if the weather was good, take chairs down to the streets to sit and gossip about anything and anyone. I remember when I was about four my Ma called me over to a group of neighbours sitting and standing around the close-front saying "Let Cathy hear you speak proper", and I, all blushing and trying to hide behind my Ma, would finally be persuaded to say "My name is James", and they would all have a good laugh. Everyone was very familiar with each other and we kids were out and in each other's houses as though they were our own. There was a tremendous community spirit about the Gorbals people and this extended to all things fortunate and unfortunate that occurred in our lives.

Although the architectural structure of the old buildings may have encouraged a sort of closeness, I think the dominant factor for this unity was that everyone was in the same boat, and didn't have two pennies to rub together. The physical surroundings were bad, but that wasn't the fault of the inhabitants. Each householder did their bit to keep the place as clean as possible, taking turns to clean the stairs and if someone was sick then a neighbour would always do the sick person's turn. The houses were as clean as circumstances would allow. If someone in the street died, the neighbours would go round the street houses collecting money in a bedsheet to help the family meet the costs of the burial. Though people couldn't afford much they would usually try to contribute something. From the extreme circumstance of a death to the simple need of borrowing a cup of sugar, help was always at hand.

Sandyfaulds Street was a strange one as two cultures thrived within the one place. All the buildings were identical, but of the fifty or so close-mouths, three were different because the people in them were "toffs", and in a way there was a resentment even amongst the kids from our closes against those who stayed in them, to such an extent that we wouldn't even rake their midgies for "lucks". The exterior of their part of the building was no different from that of ours. The difference lay in the interior, as their windows were always beautiful with a fresh appearance about them, nice curtains, coloured glass, bright paint making the houses look very warm and cosy, like palaces. The close-mouth was always clean, with white chalk running up the sides and it smelled of fancy disinfectant when washed. It was really a sharp contrast from the houses in the rest of the street, though they weren't rich enough to have doors on their closes to prevent strangers getting into their back courts. The kids in these three closes kept together when playing and none of them ever played with us in the poorer closes. However, this didn't bother us as our parents called them "half-boiled toffs", and when clustered around the closes at night our mothers used to gossip about them, mimic their proper accents and laugh at them. None of the mothers from the toffs' closes ever stood around gossiping late into the night nor, for that matter, did they lean out of their windows to talk to each other; there seemed to be a hollowness about them. Their kids were always clean as new pennies with their hair combed neatly and their nice clothes, with stockings pulled up to the knees, a clear sign of a toff. Most of them were in the Boy Scouts or the Cubs and wore the uniforms. Even at this early age I remember feeling inferior to the lot that stayed in those closes, as though there was this strange feeling that they never really belonged in the district in the first place, and in fact most of them were waiting on the first chance to move out to a better area.

Another street game was catching "Hudgies". This meant jumping on to the tail of cars and lorries as they slowed to turn the corner and jumping off as they slowed down again to turn the corner at the top of the street. Those of us who were too young for this would hang on to the back of the much slower horses-and-carts that were on their way to the nearby stable. This was really great fun though usually the driver would get off and chase us up the road, if he was sober. If we were hungry I would go into the back and shout up to the kitchen window, asking my Ma for a piece'n-jam (sandwich with jam in it) and if any of my pals were with me then they got one too. This shouting for a piece was a common occurrence throughout Glasgow. The same applied to meal times, if I happened to be playing with one of my pals and his mother shouted him into the house for his meal then usually I would be shouted in too. This happened with most families unless things were so bad that the food just wasn't there. There were various ways we kids would make cash, and one was to go for messages to the shops for neighbours for a few pence, or a couple of empty bottles that could be traded for cash. There were certain neighbours that were favourites to go messages for, simply because they gave the really good "bungs". Another way of making cash was to go round the doors in the nearby streets asking for empty beer bottles. The best day for this was a Monday, after the regular weekend parties. We would get tu'pence on the return of each bottle so it was profitable, particularly if the boozing had been heavy. The times when the competition was thickest was at the Glasgow Fair, and the New Year. Then we would take bags or large sacks and go round the doors filling them up as early as possible before the others got there. Some of the publicans put a special stamp on the labels of their beer bottles and would only take their own back, so there were all sorts of moves afoot to tear the labels where the stamp should have been or improvisations to fake a stamp.

Hallowe'en was another favourite time as we would all get done up, the favourite make-up being soot from the chimney and hundreds of little Al Jolsons would be seen going around. We would turn our jackets inside out or put our shirts on back to front and crash into pubs to sing for money. The older kids would get us younger ones to do it, take the cash and get us some sweets. At this early age we were almost professional beggars: we would stop strangers in the street, act very distressed, and say we had lost our car fare home. More often than not they would give it to us, though some people would offer to take us home and that was a sign for taking off. Most of us had relatives who were very fond of us — a favourite aunt or uncle — who would give us a few pence when we went to their houses. Usually they stayed at the other end of the district or out of it altogether, so we didn't go up too often or a good thing would be spoiled.

When I was four my Ma had another baby, a boy, and he was named Harry. I can't remember it too clearly but do recall being told, no doubt after constant enquiry, that he was found in a cabbage patch and that was the only explanation I was given as to how he came to be in the house. At the age of five I started school at St Francis' infants' school that was in our street, attached to the chapel. There are only a few memories of this, one being my first day when all of us kids were crying our eyes out and refusing to let our mothers leave. Most of my pals were in the same class though some of them went to the nearby Protestant school. But even all these familiar faces didn't stop us crying on that first day.

It was shortly after this that disaster struck our family and changed the whole pattern of our family lives, as we had known it. My father died in his late thirties. I've tried hard to remember him and shall describe the memories I have. He would stand in front of our kitchen fire with his back to it, and on one of these occasions I was in the tin bath in front of the fire on a Saturday night, and can vividly remember him kissing my Ma. On another occasion I remember owning a massive racing car that he got me, but for some reason it was taken away and I was told it was away to the garage for repairs. That was the last I saw of it. Once he took my brother, Pat, into the room and leathered his arse with a slipper after catching him skipping into the Paragon picture house without paying. When he came out, leaving Pat in the room screaming, he told us we would get the same if we did anything wrong like that. I can always remember being taken to the motor cycle speedway racing by him and being bought a rosette — for some reason or other I connect this with Hampden football park. Just shortly before he died I came out of the infants' school at three o'clock and caught a hudgie on the back of a passing horse and cart. I was clinging to it quite happily as it headed in the direction of my close when I was kicked on the backside. It was my father who was with some pals and as I ran away they all laughed.

I can vividly recall waking up one morning and finding this man lying beside me covered in bandages like a mummy, with bloodstains seeping through the dressings. To this day I don't know if it was my father or one of his pals, but one thing I do know is that something terrible had happened the previous night with my father and his pal getting badly injured. I can remember on another occasion my father struggling violently to reach up to a shelf in the small lobby to get a parcel, but being restrained by others in the house, and somehow a vague recollection connects this parcel to a gun. These are the total memories I have of my father, though I did hear plenty about him in later years as he was much talked about and respected by the older men in the district and even the present day guys who knew him have a good word for him.

Usually in a criminal environment there are the cliques who are the good thieves and those who are the "heavies", the fighters. But in my father's time there was a particular clique who were thieves and heavies, and my father was one of these. They were good money getters, and in particular, safe blowers. This was known in the district and respected in its own way. One memory that I have is getting a biscuit tin of "smash" — silver coins, florins, and half-crowns — from my father and his pals. The few of us shared it amongst ourselves. It probably came from a robbery that was particularly fruitful so that after sharing the paper money they would give the smash to the kids of the house they were in to divide amongst themselves. The incident when the injured man was in a mummified condition in our bed was, in fact, a notorious incident in the district that led to a series of shootings. A rival gang had waylaid my father and one of his pals in a dark, quiet lane in the next street to ours. They really worked them over and as a result they were taken to hospital, but on regaining consciousness they immediately signed themselves out, hence me finding one of them in our bed. The reason why this is all so vague is that the old folks didn't talk to us kids about such things, one only knew what one overheard or saw with one's own eyes.

I was kept off school the day my father was buried and a neighbour's son from my class at school was also kept off to keep me company. I distinctly remember kneeling at the coffin to say some prayers before he was taken away, and laughing with my pal simply because I didn't know what it was all about. Had I known what was ahead for me I'd have cried my heart out. I remember returning to school with my pal next day and telling the kids in my class that we had smuggled ourselves into the boot of the hearse and had gone to my father's burial. The truth was that I was never allowed to go to the graveyard, but somehow this fantasy stayed very strong within me and remains vividly clear to this day.

After my father died our life style didn't immediately change much. All my father's friends came to see my Ma and helped her in any way possible, but as time went on they got fewer and fewer, though many kept in touch. Those very close to Ma were my Aunt Peggy, my Ma's sister, and my Ma's pal, whom we called Aunt Maggie. It became apparent to Ma that she would have to get a job to keep the house and four boys going. This meant a change in our routines. She got a job cleaning tram cars which meant that Pat, my eldest brother, took over the house-cleaning and chores, and Tommy gave him a hand. My job was to look after Harry, who was at Nursery by this time so I had to collect him from there every day. Before we got used to this Ma had to give up the tram cleaning, and took a part-time job till eventually she worked from 5.30 a.m. till 8 a.m. which meant she was home to get us out to school, and from there go to a big house and clean it out. Lastly she went to a Jew's house from 4.00 p.m. till 9.00 p.m. to do cleaning, and help look after a senile old guy in the house while the rest of the family were at their businesses.

With Ma away most of the time we soon took to the streets and lived there all the time. I would collect Harry from the Nursery and supposedly take him home but we would wander all over the place or go to our Aunt Peggy's — she was very much a second Ma — and get something to eat. Sometimes we would go home but if we had been raking midgies, which was usually the case, and attempted to go into the house carrying all our "lucks" then Pat would have a fit and chase us for our lives. He would have spent hours getting the house spotless for Ma coming home and if we came in bringing loads of rubbish and dirtying the place then she would say he never cleaned it, so he was very possessive of the house. If he did let us in then he was very strict and would make us sit in the one chair and do nothing more energetic than read.

Most days Harry and I would stand at the close-mouth peering down the street to where the trams passed, and wait expectantly for the familiar figure of Ma, who would usually be carrying a message bag filled with food. The Jewish woman that Ma worked for was aware of our domestic situation and would give her any food that she had left over. Most of it was kosher, but it was all the same to us, and to this day I still have an affection for Jewish food, Bagels, Egg Loafs, pickled herrings and so on. When we saw Ma's figure in the distance we would both run like the clappers towards her, passing the warm, comfortable windows of the three toffy closes. There were nights when it was as cold as ice but we would stand at the close-mouth waiting to see if Ma was coming, or if it was foggy, we would go down to the car stop and stand waiting. Then when she came, we would take the bag from her and carry it, all the time asking what was in it. She would ask us every night why we weren't waiting in the house and we would always put the mix in for Pat saying he wouldn't let us in. The truth was that Pat would, but he had this very effective habit of nipping us if we made one wrong move, so it was better staying out of it. Anyway the streets had a magnetic effect on us. The nightly ritual of getting into the house and around the fire while we unloaded Ma's bag of goodies was great, and while we did this she would make us a meal. Tommy, of course, was very much a street child and he would be out wandering the streets with his pals and doing the things that kids at his age did. Ma would be worn out by the time she got home and instead of being able to sit down and put her feet up, would have to prepare our meal and then do all the washing up afterwards. We would do small bits here and there but only when told to, because on the whole we were not thinking at that age.

On a Saturday morning Harry and I would get up and go down to the Shan shop at the bottom of our street, and keep a place in the enormous queue, giving Ma time to visit shops to get the things she wanted there. The Shan shop was a Co-op store that sold fresh spoils sent over from the nearby Co-op Bakery and it was very popular as people would come from all over to get the cheap, fresh food. They gave out big bags of broken buns for a penny and we used to get someone at the front of the queue to get us a bag and we would do them all in while waiting our turn.

The local playing park for our part of the Gorbals was the Caledonia Road graveyard and this was the favourite playground on Saturdays when there was no school. It was a disused graveyard, nicknamed "gravey", but next door to it was one that was still being used. During the day and the nights when it was still daylight our parents would send us up to the "gravey" to play out of the road, so there would be lots of the kids from the district up there at any one time, even though one had to climb a wall about eight feet high to get in. We did this by stopping a passer-by and asking him for a lift up which he usually gave. Once up we would sometimes throw clods of grass at the passers-by. We would play hide-and-seek amongst the gravestones, and there were times when the older kids would try toppling the taller stones over and we would all stand watching. There was this big funny hollow reed which grew up there and looked just like rhubarb: it always grew thickest around the graves and all of us used to eat it. To this day I haven't a clue as to what it was, but it can't have been bad anyway.

I remember we decided to build a tarzan-type gang hut in one of the gravey trees and we went looking for tools. One of the guys knew where we could get swords and bayonets to help build our hut, so he took us to Commercial Lane behind Lawmoor Street police station. The idea was to get up to the open back window and put our hands in. On top of a locker were lots of weapons, that had been either confiscated or found. One of the kids would clasp his hands making a foothold for another to climb onto. The one on top would then feel about, to get whatever he could. The first trip went very smoothly and we stole two really good bayonets. We made our way back to the gravey to start building our hut all chuffed and excited, certainly not thinking of it as stealing, just good fun.

No one stayed in the gravey when it was dark. The "Fiddler" was the only one who did this. He was rumoured to be an old man who used to go into the graveyard to play his fiddle at his wife's grave each night, so before it got dark everyone would scamper. But first we would hide our bayonets in the next door gravey amongst the flower pots — nothing was sacred. The tarzan hut idea didn't last too long as one of the big boys building it fell off the tree and broke his leg. It so happened he was the best dyke jumper in the street. There was a terrific atmosphere in the gravey, it was like a jungle with lots of big weeds and plenty of cover for playing games and it was all free and easy with no adult interference. We could make-believe all we wanted and I had a personal subconscious way of identifying those that belonged there, by whether they had no arse in the seat of their trousers or patches. I don't know why this was but it's a memory that stays with me, just as I remember having a distrust for grown men who wore gloves — even in the middle of winter.

The best nights of the whole week in our district were Friday and Saturday at pub closing time. It was a sort of occasion as all the women would be looking out of their windows for the pubs coming out. This was when all the fights took place and it was great fun watching them, the funny part being that there was hardly ever a policeman in sight at this time. One of the best fighters in our street was a guy called Big Ned and he was always fighting although he didn't always win. He was always drunk on these nights and after a fight would stumble up the street with all of us kids following him, and when he got to the chip shop he would take us in and buy us bags of chips without paying the man for them and this really delighted us because mostly when we hung around the chip shop door the same man would kick our arses and tell us to get away from his shop. We used to love it and always looked on this as an honour when Big Ned singled us out. We all idolised him. There would be occasions when Big Ned used to mess his opponents up very badly, and in some cases they were seriously hurt, but the following morning he would walk down the street and people who had seen the fight the previous night, would chat away to him as though nothing had happened. In a sense this was socially acceptable and no one ever made a big deal over it.

On Friday nights the men came home from their work and went straight into the pub with their mates, as most of them had just been paid, and those who had no jobs were taken for a drink by their pals. The Gorbals must have had more pubs per head than any other district in Glasgow, as there was one at almost every corner. On Friday kids would be at the pub doors, sent there by their mothers to tell their fathers to come home with the wages before they drank most of them. There were occasions when wives went to the pubs to hunt down their men and rescue the income, but on the whole this was considered an affront to the husband. Men filthy from their work would be swilling down beer and spirits like nobody's business. Large groups of men stood and sat at bars talking, arguing and singing till nine o'clock when the last call was made. All of us kids stood outside the pub door listening and looking in, and most of all taking in this man's world. At time up there would be orders of "carry outs" (drinks bought to take home) and the men would stagger outside to the pavement with them, and congregate there, reluctant to part company and go home.

Just prior to the last call, women in the houses overlooking any pub would go to their windows to look out, and we kids would run to the corner of Sandyfaulds Street and Rutherglen Road as that was the most advantageous point giving us sight of seven pubs. From their we would usually see where the action was taking place. Extremities were the norm on such occasions as drunkards would be on the pavement outside the pub doors, some with their arms round each others' necks singing songs well out of tune, and alongside them would be two or three others rolling around the ground in a drunken fight, in some cases with blood all over the place.

On one particular Friday night during the summer months there were the usual crowds outside the pubs but we sensed trouble in the air. It was still daylight when two of the men who were well known in the district, started arguing. The next thing to happen was that one pulled out a revolver and shot the other in the arm. The injured ran man away through a lane and we followed him. For us it was a scene straight from a movie, seeing this guy through drink and gunshot stagger along the road and up to his house. We then ran back to the pub to find some of the other men still leaning on each other singing drunken songs as if nothing had happened. The guy with the gun had disappeared. This particular incident had an unreal quality about it for me. As shootings weren't an every day occurrence, I expected it to be a main talking point, and to cause some local reaction but there was none. I even began to think I had imagined it until years later, when I asked the guy who was shot and he confirmed it. The message that came home to me even at this early age, rightly or wrongly, was that people talk or gossip about drunken and daft fights throughout the week but when two heavies like that fight then people leave it alone and mind their own business.

This was the highlight of our week, going to the pubs at closing time to watch the fights, and there is no doubt that everyone else enjoyed it too. The men, no matter how drunk, would be like homing pidgeons and always find their way. Some would stagger up the street with arms out-stretched, singing to their hearts' content, and the women hanging out their windows either encouraging them or shaking their heads and rólling their eyes at the drunken character making an ass of himself. From closing time onwards till the early hours of the morning, one would see steady streams of drunks wending their ways home, and of course we endeavoured to cash in on this. We would approach them and ask for money, and would either get it or a mouthful of curses, but that was all in the game. There would be the regular characters returning from the boozers full to the gunnels, and one of these who stayed in our street and was looked on with great affection was a guy named Dan Noble. Every time he was drunk he would stagger up the street shouting at the top of his voice "D.N. Dan, my name's Dan, Dan Noble". Sometimes he would throw in that he didn't give a fuck for anybody, and Dan would start this cry from the minute he left the pub till he fell into bed. He would stagger up the middle of the street with the stray dogs following him, barking and adding to the din. Dan would take over the street and any passing cars would have to make way for him while occasionally one of the onlooking women would shout for him to go away to his bed. The best laugh was that when he was sober Dan was a quiet wee man who didn't bother a soul. The way people looked at it was that Dan, who was a widower, worked like hell all week to keep his family and this was his way of letting loose, and as he wasn't bothering anybody then good luck to him.

2

My family situation began to deteriorate and my father's absence began to be felt as Ma was beginning to find things very difficult — this would be in 1951 when I was seven years old. The authorities turned off the electricity as we couldn't pay the bill and things were bad all round as our relatives and neighbours were all feeling the pinch. St Francis Chapel had a poor box and I can remember me and my brother Tommy going to the Franciscan priest there to ask for money to pay for the light. They were usually very good at helping those in need but things were so bad that they had emptied their poor box giving the money to others. Instead they gave us two big candles to use in the house and we took them home. The image of us sitting around in the dark all feeling very sad isn't the impression I want to give here, as the truth was that to us kids living in candle-light was fun a lot of the time as we would use the darkness and shadows to make up games, though it must have been terribly difficult for my Ma as she was working like hell and things were getting worse instead of better. One of the few luxuries she had was sending us down for a loose Woodbine. The shopkeeper would open a five-pack of Woodbines as they sold a lot of them in singles to people who couldn't afford to buy more.

When I was about eight I managed to get a job selling coal briquettes from a barrow and got five bob a week for it — including tips. Tommy also managed to get a few bob, selling fish from a barrow. We only worked on a Saturday when there was no school, but these few bob extra helped Ma and were added to the mere pittance that she got from her three part-time jobs. For clothes we would go to the State hand-out people that we called the Parish. I'm pretty vague about its official name but this is as I remember it. It was in the city centre and they used to give out big hairy suits and hairy underwear, but best of all, enormous tackety boots. I was constantly aware of a deep feeling of shame about going to the Parish as it was only the poorest that went there and the people in charge treated us like dirt. I remember that Ma would always get in a state at such times and to add to her embarrassment she knew we hated going because the clothes that one got there were their own stamps of identification as anyone could, at a glance, identify Parish clothes. However, once at the Parish we would play outside with the other kids who were there for the same reasons as us. The Parish was located on, or next to, a very steep hill, and this we loved for when we got our Parish boots on, the big tackety ones, we would go outside and slide down the pavement. One particular guy serving behind the counter was always on the look-out for this so we would get the kids who had never been there before to go first so that the guy would come rushing out of the door and clip him on the ear then return to shout at our parents about it while we continued to slide. He would tell our parents that if this continued he would stop handing out the clothes and this would result in rare old arguments.

Amongst the kids at the Parish the atmosphere was great as we were all the same and knew it. Then we had to go home and I knew that my brothers felt as I did — inferior. There were lots of families in the district who got free clothing from the state but there was a great deal of teasing and taunting from the other kids about it, and the same went for "free dinners". This was set up for kids whose parents couldn't afford to pay for a meal or were dependent on the state for upkeep. Every Monday morning the teacher would call out the kids who were going to the dinner school for their meal and those who paid for it were called first to pay their moneys and get their tickets and then the teacher would call out the free tickets and the remainder of us would trail out.

In my class at school there was this kid who used to sit next to me and he was well dressed but a friend of mine. The point is we both shared the same desk and there was a strong smell of shit. Naturally all the fingers (those not holding noses) were pointed straight at me and my Parish clobber. There would be days when the smell was so strong, that I would suspect the clothes of giving out the sour smell and I would race home, take them off and give the crutch of my pants a thorough sniffing. All kidding aside I really did have a bad complex about this, until one day in the school playground, with the smell at its height, one beautifully observant kid pointed to the legs of my deskmate and there was the shit running down his wee legs and over the top of his stockings. Honestly I could have kissed him, I felt so happy as the burden of my own complexes vanished completely. When playtime was over the teacher ordered my deskmate to stand where he was and as we left he still stood there almost as though he was stuck to the corner as I bounced all the way to the classroom. I always wondered why the teacher hadn't tracked him down before. After this the poor guy was nicknamed "Smelly" and the name stuck with him for some time.

There was plenty of teacher power in the schools in those days with us not being allowed to speak unless spoken to. My teacher at St Francis was a very frightening female whom I never liked as she would beat the hell out of us at the slightest whim. She was a nice looking woman too, but that side of it didn't interest us at that age. If you did something that she didn't like then she would get hold of us by the hair or the pullover and swing us about the class like an Irish navvy swinging a pick. There would be the occasional time when someone would threaten to bring up their Ma to her but that was the furthest it went. Although it was a working class school there were kids in my class that I thought were toffs as they were always nicely dressed, and seemed to be the cleverest. Whenever teacher asked a question theirs would be the first hands to shoot up and they would answer it immediately. They were a bunch of kids who always played together during the play interval and after school. I personally felt that I was very stupid at school, and mixed this with an overpowering feeling of inferiority due to my circumstances. At one time I wanted to be an Altar boy (a child who serves the priest while he is serving the mass) in our chapel but this was at a time when our family circumstances were at their worst, economically and otherwise. Besides my boots, all I had was a big pair of wellies and altar boys needed sandshoes. But apart from this, for some reason or other, these toffy guys seemed to be the ones picked every time.

The reality of the educational side was that never at any time during my primary school attendance did I ever want to do well at my lessons for some very simple reasons. From Primary school there were two schools that the kids in my class could go to after the qualifying exams. One was St Bonaventure's (Bonny's) a junior Secondary, and the other was Holyrood, which we called the toffy school. Now my aim from the minute I went into the primary school was to attend Bonny's, as that was where my older brothers and other kids from my street had gone so I had already made my mind up that this was where I was going. This meant that there was no incentive for me to go anywhere else and anyway going to Holyrood meant the expense of paying for a uniform so there was no way that this could happen. Therefore it would be Bonny's for me. Expenses aside, the dominating factor that made me always want to go there was that everyone in my street went to Bonny's. Bonny's was for our kind and I knew I'd be happier there. I can still remember the day when they read out the results of the qualification exams, with Smelly and I nearly crapping our breeks, no doubt he did, in case we passed with a high mark and were sent to Holyrood. So, idiots that we were, we rejoiced in failing the exams. If I had been honest then I would have had to admit to a certain feeling deep down of wanting to pass. The strange thing, or should I say obvious thing, was that there were no surprises at exams. Those that wanted to go to Bonny's went, and those that wanted Holyrood went, so on the whole were we superficially satisfied.

There is one thing that perhaps I should make clear here and that is that these kids that I call toffs were not really. It was just a fact that in this vast socially deprived area where poverty was rife, they were fortunate to have had fathers who had good paying jobs that could keep the family clothed reasonably well. The truth of the matter was that they also had next to nothing but by our standards they seemed to have plenty and the way we judged them was on the way they were clothed, their behaviour and usually the money they had to spend. For instance, we, the scruffs, would take our play-piece into school and just before the bell rang for playtime we would stick the sandwich under our arses and heat it up as well as flattening it to make it look bigger. These other guys didn't do this sort of thing. Even within this class of scruffy kids there was this feeling of inferiority and discrimination that no outside observer would have noticed as there was never any open hostility amongst us, it was just that each kept to his own group as if by some natural instinct.

There was an instance when one of these toffy guys was knocked down by a car and a group of us were sent by the teacher to visit him while he lay in bed at home a few streets from us, in a house which was on a par with the toffy ones in my street. We sat around the bed looking at him like idiots with his father there. I asked for a drink of water and went to get one, but as I stuck my head under the tap and turned it on to drink straight from it, the father let out a loud scream and leapt from his chair as though someone had stuck a pin in his arse. He dragged me away from the tap as though it were about to suck me up and then proceeded to lecture me on the finer points of hygiene and the beasties that wait up taps to jump down the throats of people who drink straight from it. He then made me drink from a nice glass. This is the one thing that I really hated about these people, the way they tended to exaggerate everything to show that they were different. For the rest of the visit he gave us all school lessons, and I couldn't get out quick enough as it was almost as bad as school. The kid in the bed wasn't only suffering from the accident but from his father as well.

After school we would play all the street games of football, headers, kick the can, K.D.R.F. (Kick-door-run-fast). This game involved going to the third flat of a close and kicking every door on the way down with all the people opening the doors after you'd gone to see who was there. But some people were aware of the game so when they saw that it was K.D.R.F. they would run to the window with a pan of water and throw it over us as we came out of the close. We would go to districts away on the other side of Glasgow just walking as far as we could, sometimes getting lost, but always finding our way home. It was all great fun. On a winter's night there would always be some of us grouped round one of the sweet shop windows playing Guesses — this was to choose the name of a sweet and give the others the initial (i.e. C.B.? — Candy Balls) and we would pass hours playing this game. It didn't matter what time of night it was and every mother had the same problem and that was getting us into the house as we always wanted to stay out, even though it was the early hours of the morning and there would be replies of "Aw Ma, just five minutes."

As bad as my circumstances were, I was always aware of others much worse off than me and I can mind a pal of mine with eleven of a family all staying in the one single room. With all of us we didn't say how crowded it was as we just lived that way accepting it without question. The resignation to the conditions and the ignorance were probably the biggest sins of all.

The big day came when I was sent to my new school. It was a great feeling to be going to Bonny's as it made me feel all grown up to mix with lots of the tough guys in the district that we looked up to. New kids entering Bonny's were thrown over the walls by the older guys as an initiation ceremony. There were two walls, each about six feet in height, one of which had a drop of about fifteen feet and the new kids were lifted up and thrown over them. Some kids would be thrown over the wall with the six feet drop and others over the fifteen feet drop but it all depended on whether the older guys caught you nearer one or the other. Trust me to go over the higher of the two. I didn't hurt myself — the fear hurt more than anything. The older guys used to split us into groups and hold "dummy fights" and all of this was frightening. In a way this was when the age of innocence was lost. There seemed to me to be a more serious side to life now and going to Bonny's brought this out because in the school one was "judged" on one's fighting ability. Watching gang fights and drunks brawl was something that was fun and that we, as kids, played no part in; but now in Bonny's I felt very close to physical violence as there were lots of fights going on. This is far away from the atmosphere of the previous infants schools, where the feeling had been that neither you nor the school mattered as you were too young. Although from this early age I had helped steal bayonets from the police station, some fruit and chocolate from shops, we had not thought it really criminal. Certainly I was aware that it was wrong but there was a feeling that it didn't count then, much in the same category as catching hudgies and playing in the gravey, or raking midgies, most of which were frowned on but tolerated, simply because there was nothing more for us to do. I am certainly not for one moment suggesting that parents in the Gorbals condoned their kids in crime for that wasn't the case, in fact their part in the community probably kept down the number of crimes and accidents in the area. The sub-culture amongst the kids was such that the petty "crimes" mentioned were socially acceptable. Yes, their parents would give them a good thumping if caught, and yes we would go out and do it again after the beating because not only was it something to do but there was no money.

One feature of the Gorbals sub-culture was that the men in the district who were put on pedestals by us, and in many ways idolised, were the likes of Dan Cronin. Although he was dead by the time I was six years old he remained very much alive locally being almost a legend in the Gorbals for his fighting abilities. There was Danny O'Neil who ran the local Shebeen — a place that sold illegal booze after pub hours — and Paddy Slowey who was by now replacing the legendary Dan Cronin as one of the great street fighters. There were times when other guys in the district would steal all sorts of gear and sell it to almost everyone at cheap prices, and these were just things that were a regular part of our lives. It wasn't a case of me thinking these men were bad for I didn't, never at any time, nor was it only the kids who looked up to them but a great many of the adults also. It was a great thing for us to see these men even if they were only standing about the street. We were always aware of their presence and would put on acts for them so that we would be noticed.

There was a guy in our street called Big Jim who was not one of our hero figures but typical of our district nevertheless. He would be fighting most weekends. In every sense his behaviour was a part of our lives and he would fight nine Fridays out of ten and walk away, then get up in the morning and go about his normal business like everyone else. However, one time out of the ten Big Jim would be caught fighting and, when reported in the press, be held up as a monster, when in reality the most that was said in the district about him would be along the lines of: "You would think he would grow up", or "He should meet a nice lassie and settle down". If he was sent to prison then everyone would be asking after him.

As kids we were always looking for adventurous things to do, like putting a rope round the branch of a tree in the gravey and swinging on it, or jumping from dykes that had sharp metal railings beneath us. There was this great thirst for adventure and I know that this was what had me first stealing from shops. I can remember the first time I stole. It was a bar of chocolate and I did it more as a challenge than out of need. There were times when my pals and I would steal soap or something else that was of no use to us, and no sooner had we stolen it than we would throw it away. At the same time each of us was a "good boy" to our parents, as we would run all the messages and try to do things to help the domestic situation, or the neighbours for that matter. We didn't tell our mothers what we did, especially me, as my Ma would have kicked up hell, but the point was that none of us saw anything very bad in it.

I do remember the first occasion that we stole money. It was a winter's night and I was with two other pals. Two of us cop-watched while the other stole cash from a van driver's pocket. Once we were safely away, my pal started dividing the money up but I refused to take any as I was terrified and classed this as real stealing as distinct from what we had been doing in the past. However, I let them pay me into the movies after they had shared the money between them. In all, it amounted to about thirty shillings which was more money than I had ever seen — so I allowed them to buy me sweets and ice cream with it as this was quite acceptable to my conscience. Halfway through the film I started to regret not having taken anything and by time-up I was making noises to the effect that they should give me something. By this time a lot of it had been spent; but I did get half-a-crown which I was very happy with.

It was never hard after this experience. As for the police, we were always aware of them and basically mistrusted them as one was always being told that they would come to take you away. There were only two cops that were familiar to me by name in those early days. One was a beat cop who was known to all the kids as Foxy and the other was a detective called Goodall, who was pretty notorious in our district. Foxy was the one that we watched for as he used to use all sorts of tricks to catch us playing football after school; tricks such as taking his hat off and putting it under his coat then sidling up the street to catch us. He was strongly disliked by us all and counter measures would be taken by posting lookouts who would shout "Foxy" whenever he came in sight. This guy would take playing in the street very personally and he had the same thing about anyone loitering on the street corners. The other cop, the detective Goodall, was a different kettle of fish. Although I was only a youngster, he was very well known to me by name, though I had never even seen him. Goodall was spoken of with fear.

All of the kids from my class in St Francis who had qualified for Bonny's were put into the same class there and we were joined by others from neighbouring schools. I was about twelve at the time. Right from the start I had the feeling that things were for real here. All the ruffians were in the same class in the toughest school in the district. There was another school in the district for the Protestants called Adelphi and this also was a very tough school, but it so happened that Bonny's held most of the guys with the "reputations". However, if you went to either of these schools you had to be able to look after yourself both physically and mentally. There was a thing known as "hard men's walks" of which we were all aware and having just arrived at Bonny's we would all try to adopt a walk that was suitable to us. It must have been funny to see us, still in short trousers, swaggering up to school with these exaggerated walks.

The dominant gang in the district, which mostly originated at Bonny's, was the Cumbie, which took its name from the central street in the area — Cumberland Street. There were two Cumbie gangs: The Big Cumbie and the Wild Young Cumbie. To put the picture straight, the Big Cumbie was made up of silly pricks who were what we called toffy guys and who did nothing to merit their being called a gang. They had a history of some really good fights in other districts like Calton or Bridgeton, but at no time did I ever see them fight and throughout my time they didn't do anything that counted, so they were reckoned to be a pretty impotent bunch. Now the Wild Young Cumbie were a different matter, as they were a force to be reckoned with in the Glasgow world, and they were the ones that most of the kids looked up to in our school.

Things at home had improved by this time as my older brother Pat had a labouring job and Tommy had taken a plumbing apprenticeship in a local shop — a luxury that couldn't be afforded but Ma gave Tommy every encouragement and was proud to have a son serving his time as an apprentice — the university of our world. Ma still worked her three part-time jobs. She seemed to be addicted to them, but the reality was that though two brothers were working, Ma still couldn't afford to give her jobs up.

My oldest brother Pat was exceptionally bright and very talented. He was like me in features, but that's where the resemblance ended as he had a great head on his shoulders and by some means or other found he could play the piano and was really out of this world at it. The music he loved was classical, to play or listen to and this alone was very unusual. He managed to get an old piano and would sit playing it for hours. There was a part of me that loved this and wanted to take lessons from him, but there was another part that hated it as the music was "toffy" and I would get very embarrassed when any of my pals came up to the door for me to find Pat playing this classical music. He was also a talented sketcher and could draw anything in a very life-like way, as could my brother Tommy. But Pat was different as he was on a very high level, one that was alien to us. Tommy was different again and very much a Gorbals kid doing all the things that most of us did. Because of her jobs Ma had grown terribly old before her time. The household tasks had been passed on to Harry and me, with the eldest two now at work, but there was never much to do as no-one was ever in the house and Ma would always clean it when she came in. All that was to be done was to put the fire on for them coming in and I would get Harry to do this as I was caught up in the street activities and would be fully involved with what I was doing there.

In the class at school some of us knew each other and some didn't, but it was very much a new experience for all of us except the teacher who gave me the impression that he had had enough of the class of his previous term, and was therefore going to be master of this one. I say this because he immediately gave us a lecture on the school "hard men", going on to describe all the moves that we would try and ended his lecture by saying he was the only hard man here. We would all look knowlingly at each other, giving sniggers, while he rambled on, as we had heard similar things from similar people.

I went about with three guys from my previous class. We had never gone about with each other before but now we became friends in and out of school. They were Padge Gallagher, Johnny Boris, and a guy called Tam, all of whom stayed in the district. In the beginning we would go round to play at the Molls Mire, which was a big piece of industrial waste ground behind the school. There were lots of places to explore there, and though there would be times when other classmates would join us, mostly it would be just us four. We would play all the ordinary games and we would make a team for going round the lucky didgies sometimes leaving school to go straight to the toffy district to rake them. Eventually we ended up going into shops and stealing cakes or sweets and although I can't remember how this first started I do know that it wasn't by design. We found it exciting and soon we were deliberately stealing, going into the shops on the way home to take whatever we could. One technique was to go into the shop with a penny, wait in the queue, while the shopkeeper was busy serving others, and lift whatever was near us in the way of "good eats".

At school it became known to the other classmates that we were going "knocking" and some of them would want to come. This is how we became the identifiable toughs of our class. We always made an agreement that whatever we stole we halved, or divided equally amongst ourselves and in this way we became the guys with plenty of sweeties and things that the other kids didn't have and this was a good feeling. Of course there were the others who would come with us and do no stealing but take some of the stolen goodies and some started going on their own as the stealing habit was spreading. By this time we were becoming known to the shopkeepers en route to and from the school so we had to move on to greener pastures. We had no wish to give it up for fear of being caught. We had now come to like it and the gains that it brought, and we pursued our new pastime with full energy. There were occasions when we were caught lifting cakes by the shopkeeper and would be chased out but on the whole we were very successful by our standards. We would fill our pockets with biscuits and cakes and walk along the street eating them till we got sick then throw the remainder at each other. It was a natural progression from cakes to more expensive things.

In the classroom our crowd, with me as their leader, became noticeable as the baddies, and the teacher would let us know this in a roundabout way. When one of us got the belt there would be remarks passed by the teacher such as "How hard are you now?" but this was just accepted as a challenge to be met by a determination on our part not to show any weakness or emotion. But there were times when we couldn't help it as they would lay the strap on heavily for us. The teacher would always talk to us in a familiar fashion as though he knew just what we were up to, but we knew that he only talked in this way so that we wouldn't think him an easy mark or take him for a mug. In an odd sort of way we regarded this as a form of condonation of what we were doing. This was something that I always felt very strongly about lots of adults, and even cops that I came in touch with. None of them ever made me feel that they wanted me to be any different to how I was.

At playtime everyone would crowd into the toilets and smoke cigarettes and some of the older boys would even, on occasions, drink wine, but although the toilet was always full of smoke, no-one seemed to notice. There would be many fights but we, as the youngest group, would never be involved in these and would only watch on. Most of the talk would be about the Cumbie gangs with everyone pretending that they knew the leaders personally. Some of the kids would say that the leader of the Cumbie was their big cousin so that no-one would hit them, and in fact the leaders were held in such high regard that this con trick would always work because no-one was ever brave enough to challenge it. On seeing the power it gave him the "pretender" would automatically acquire the reputation of a good fighter, which he would make the most of.

On a Monday, Wednesday and Friday after school there would be a big rush as most kids would head for the lucky didgies, or go round the doors of the houses in the district for empty bottles, all in the hope of getting sixpence each. There was a picture house in Cumberland Street round the corner from where I lived and it had a rule on those three nights that the first sixty kids under fourteen would get in for a tanner, hence the mad rush. This was an unbelievable scene as the kids would get the money, by hook or by crook, and would all be queueing up and it was pandemonium with all sorts of fights to get in among the first sixty. The adults round about would stand watching the sight of all these kids trying to get in and really it must have made fantastic entertainment for them. The two door-keepers were brave guys, especially when their counting got to the fifty mark as that's when the panic really struck the remainder. The picture hall was out of this world because, for starters, no one could hear the movie for us screaming at each other. The seating was of sturdy church-like benches made of wood and, if it was raining, water poured in at certain parts of the hall. There was the occasional rat scampering about the feet of the patrons.

If we happened to miss the first sixty, or if we could only get the price for one of us, then one would go in and when the movie had started he would creep over to the exit door and lift the iron bar and a crowd of us would flood in. There was the odd occasion when we would skip up to the balcony but this was real luxury. One time we pissed over it onto the people below. I remember my Ma and Aunt Maggie taking about nine of us kids to the Paragon one night and we were all sitting on our best behaviour watching this movie, with the place so silent that a pin could be heard dropping, when this enormously fat woman in front of us let out a great big fart and we kids broke into laughter, and so did our parents and the people around us. The laughter went on and on until the big fat woman got up and left. We all used to go to the matinee each Saturday afternoon and this was the big treat. Harry and I used to wear our Parish trench-coats that were coloured black and buttoned right up to the neck. A woman outside used to sell whelks and make a roaring trade so we would all go in with bags of them. All the kids would eat the whelks by taking the centre out and throwing the shell at those sitting in front. After watching the matinee trailers and cartoons, we would all come out, Harry and I with our coats like capes, buttoned only at the neck, running with hands in the air as though we were flying, very much in the superman tradition, the other kids being Roy Rogers.

St Francis' school had a boys club two nights a week and kids from the district could go there to take part in sports and games to keep them off the street. I went to it and gave it a try but I really wasn't much of a football man and although I did put some effort into it there was always this feeling of being trapped, though I could never really explain what this meant at the time. In many ways it was very like school, which I detested, and there was always the feeling that I was being talked "down" to by the guys who ran it, who for some reason or other would take every high spirited action as a direct challenge to them. There was one guy who had been a boxer in his army days and lived on this reputation. He constantly reminded us of this in a very subtle, intimidating sort of way. I had always possessed a great deal of energy and the routine of this club wasn't able to contain it. For instance, the club was pretty small (the games area that is) and if there were between thirty or forty boys present split into five-a-side football teams this meant that the playing teams would take up all the space while the rest sat on benches or window ledges. During the time that I had to sit on the window ledge while the teams played I was wrestling about with some others and I smashed two windows while jumping all over the ledge. The guy in charge of us didn't like it and I was barred from going back again.

There was no way that I could explain myself, I didn't know how. How could I explain nervous energy when I hadn't even heard of it before? So what if a few windows are broken? Surely the logical step would have been to leave it broken and to let me experience the consequences of it when the wind blew in on a winter's night. If I, or any of the others, had complained of cold then the practical disadvantages of breaking windows could have been pointed out. Eventually the club lost its true purpose as it barred guys like me from coming in when in fact we should have been the ones to be stopped from leaving at any cost. It then became a meeting place for nice kids who weren't prone to trouble anyway, and it looked as though the guys running it were after a quiet time as they became pretty selective. It wasn't nice to be barred and there were nights when we would go round and stand outside the door and try to get back in. Sometimes we would sneak in and try to hide amongst the other kids but the place was so small that we would soon be seen and thrown out. Eventually being thrown out like this became a prestigious thing for us, though it wasn't at first. Inevitably I got fed up hanging around the club doorway and went back to the streets where I met some old pals from my school.

During the early months of Bonny's I consolidated my friendship with Padge, Johnny and Tam. We were now going around together all the time and the stealing from shops became a big part of our existence. We extended it to the weekends and would go out to shops in other districts on the Saturday when shopping was a busy time and we could really plunder. By now we were lifting more expensive materials, household goods in particular, all of which would be sold to people in the district. We had no shortage of "fences" for buying the stuff that we stole, usually at around the half-price mark. The streets in the Gorbals were always very dark on winter nights as there were only gas lamps lighting the area, which could have a frightening effect on people not used to them. But to those of us who were accustomed to them the streets held a warmth. At nights groups of us would roam about moving aimlessly from street to street. There was nothing much to do but someone would usually find something for a laugh or out of devilment.

It was on one such night that one of the guys with me took a run at a shop door and kicked it, a little too hard, for the door flew open and seeing this we all ran away down the dark street in case anyone had seen us. From a safe distance we looked back and could see that no-one had heard it or come out so we debated going back. Some were for it and some were against, but everyone was in a state of scarey excitement and I went back with a few others. On reaching the shop door I looked in at the darkness and very slowly moved in, always expecting someone to come pouncing on top of me. I was followed by a couple of others who left the last one cop-watching. A constant nervous dialogue took place between me and the cop-watcher, asking him if it was alright. The shop was a Babieswear one and sold lots of kids' clothes. I was very scared while in the building but at the same time I had this wonderful feeling of excitement at being in a shop with the goods completely at my disposal. There was this constant duality of feeling with a strong fear on one side and a good feeling of challenge on the other. We were only in the place minutes but in that time had jumped over the counter and taken boxes of goods without looking to see what they were, as there was too much panic and excitement. We took as much as we could carry and then ran to join the others who hadn't come, then on to an old washhouse to see what we had. The kids who stayed outside the shop were now wishing they hadn't for we shared the spoils amongst those of us who had gone in. We had no problem getting the goods sold, as everyone who had a child would have bought them if they had had the chance, so it all went very easy for us this first time and the success of the venture made us feel we were "big time".

Up until this, all we had done was shop lifting and as we had become adept at this and felt on pretty safe ground, with full confidence in our abilities, we then began to turn more to the actual breaking-in to shops. While shoplifting we would have competitions to see who had the best "nerve", to see who could steal the best and most valuable article without being seen. There was something adventurous about entering a shop, watching the assistant move, waiting till he was in a certain position then, with as swift a movement as possible lift whatever was the target. Now that I was into shopbreaking the feeling was that bit more exciting, and far more rewarding financially, with a whole store full of goods within one's grasp.

Certainly we didn't give up shoplifting altogether but concentration was more on our night time activities of breaking and entering. With the money gained from the Babieswear shop I bought a hacksaw and set out one night to break into another shop which meant congregating round the back window and sawing through the metal bars while someone stood outside cop-watching. A basic rule was to always have a cop-watcher while the rest were doing the necessary. Cutting metal bars takes a bit of doing when one is trying to be quiet about it as the rasping of the saw becomes exaggerated in the mind, so sweaty hands and bodies were a part of breaking in. This second shop was a Painters and Decorators and once we had gained entry it was a case of having to crawl along the shop floor, as the front was brightly lit, to get to the till where the money was kept. At this stage we didn't realise that most shopkeepers leave psychological cash in the till. This is petty cash for thieves like us to settle for and make off with, rather than ransack the place and in this case it worked because we took only the cash and a blow-lamp and some paint. The knowledge that we could now break into any shop we wanted was really something. When it got round the class in school that we were "screwing" shops the other kids had me and my pals on pedestals and this boosted our egos. The fact that we got practically no financial gain from our second job meant nothing as the important thing was the actual success of getting into the shop. By now I was recognised as leader of the thieving gang and also, for some reason or other, as being the best fighter, even though I hadn't struck a blow at anyone, but this didn't bother me as I loved to accept anything like this.

After school there would be lots of kids wanting to come stealing with me as they thought my pals and I were getting lots of money. Many were stealing in twos or threes, but we were the ones getting most money and the ones with *nerve*, so all the kids stealing at school wanted to be with us. The competition between me and my pals at stealing was really something and it was this strong competitive spirit that made us the best in the school. But despite it being an added honour to have the best nerve in our clique, there was still the rule of dividing equally all that we stole. Johnny, who was the smallest and the fastest, and on the whole gamer than the rest of us, had the best nerve, but only by a shadow.

As well as our activities becoming known to our fellow pupils they were also well known to the teaching staff and they would let us know this in front of everyone with remarks such as, "Some of the class will end up in the Bar-L prison" (Barlinnie). This, in itself, was a sort of prestigious thing, and seemed to give us a form of identity, because when they made these remarks in a general way we would all give each other knowing looks as though to confirm who they were aiming it at. Although there was a lot of dodging school, we were all regular attenders in the early months. But as time went on various tactics and techniques were used to excuse us from school. The ordinary inconspicuous kid could afford to dodge it without making elaborate excuses but the well known ones like me had to be doubly wise to get away with it. There was usually some woman about who would write a note for me with an explanation for my absence to take into the teacher as though it had come from my mother. Of course there were times when I was caught as were my pals.

Whenever we dodged school we would go out stealing from shops and off lorries, knowing full well that the following day when we returned the teacher would give us six of the best but that didn't matter to us. On such occasions the teacher would give us the belt in front of the girls' class. Of course he only did this with our crowd and it was his way of putting us down so as to show us up in front of the girls, hoping we would cry and at the same time showing the girls how tough he was in his treatment of us. The anomaly of this was that the whole exercise appealed to us as it let us impress the girls and frustrate the teacher who would be disappointed at getting no satisfaction from our tough façades. We would be determined to take it like men even though it hurt like hell and save our pain for the minute we got outside the door.

The one comforting factor we could support each other on was that the teachers were all bastards and we hated them. This, of course, was my pupil point of view and there were exceptions to this. There was one particular man who was teaching us technical drawing but who had a predilection for talking at great length about the hard men who had passed through his hands at school.

This guy would always digress from the official subject matter to go on about his personal experiences with the hard men of the Gorbals and we would all sit loving it. So with this in mind it was all a matter of individual teachers and how to handle them for they ranged from those who didn't really care to the complete authoritarian personality. I never got on with any of the teachers at school and most of my pals were in the same boat. There was a void between teacher and pupil and that was it. By the age of twelve and a half there was a feeling that the teachers had given us up for lost.

In contrast to this, three of us, including two other classmates, Padge and Joe Regan, took an early morning milk delivery job in a toffy district. All the week through we would get up very early, me along with my Ma at 5 a.m., and deliver the milk round the door steps and finish at 8.30 a.m. We got 25/- for it and would make an extra few bob in tips. I really enjoyed this very much as there was something nice about the world at that time of the morning. The idea of working and bringing money into the house was very important to me, as it was me paying my way. There was also the fact that Ma was completely worn out and needed all the help she could get. The only way I could help was to work as there was no way that she would take anything from me that was stolen. I usually made school at nine in the nick of time, eating my breakfast on the bus, which was normally a roll and a pint of the firm's milk. Of course no one could be told about the job because at this time there was a scare on about kids working without permits, which was all new to me but it was a fact so the teachers weren't to know about the work. One day the woman who employed us told me that I couldn't come back as she could get into trouble for giving me work. I think she was using this as an excuse to get rid of me as she had already told me that she wasn't worried about the permit issue. Anyway, from there I got another job delivering messages on a bicycle to big toffy houses in a district where I had previously raked the midgies. It was only a temporary thing but I liked it and was sorry when it ended.

3

In about 1957, when I was 13 years old, a new machine was put into operation. It was a chewing gum machine and the distributors put them on shop front doors and walls so that passers-by could purchase gum. There must have been a big sales drive, for they were put on lots of shops throughout the district. It was a penny for a packet and, for every fourth one, a free pack was given. These machines made a fortune as everyone was using them, but their accessibility was very tempting to us who roamed the street. We decided to break into them and wrenched one off the wall, taking it into one of the backs to force it open, but opening it under these circumstances was too much work as there was no means of leverage. However, from this primitive method of wrenching the whole machine off the wall, we developed a technique that was very simple and effective and that was to put a metal spike up the spout where the gum came out and to force the front off, open the money part and take the cash along with the remaining gum. All the kids in the school would get free gum from us but the worst of it was that the method, once it became known, was too easy, and lots of kids were doing them. If someone in the school had a pocketful of pennies then he was sure to have done a machine the previous night. With this competition we would go out at night and sometimes break into four or five machines, one after the other, till the time came when the company refused to repair them as they must have been losing too much cash, so it was a case of hunting at nights for a surviving machine. The pennies that I got from them would be put into an old nylon stocking and stashed up the room chimney. There was never a fire there so there was no reason for anyone to go near it.

One night we were out screwing machines and it was one of those dark winter evenings. Just as we were taking the cash from the machine two uniformed cops came upon us and we scattered, the six of us, all from the school. As we belted along Cumberland Street with cops well behind with no chance of catching us, a kid who knew us was coming in the opposite direction and not seeing the cops behind us shouted asking where we were going. On seeing the cops he shut his mouth and started walking as he had before. But it was too late, the cops had seen him attempting to speak to us and as there was no chance of them catching us, they stopped and caught hold of the kid and questioned him. Meanwhile, we split the cash and went home and I was all washed, had my pennies up the chimney and was in bed with my brothers when the cops came in the early hours of the morning; they were detectives.

My Ma let them in and woke me up and the butterflies started going in my stomach when I saw who they were. They told me that they had three of my pals in the squad car downstairs and named them saying that they had admitted doing the machines. With this I gave them the pennies I had up the lum and my Ma just couldn't believe it. The look on her face was that of astonishment, but I was absolutely petrified at the sight of the cops. They told me to get dressed as they were taking me away. My Ma, who had done her best for me, was saying things like, "Oh no", and asking the cops not to take me. What would happen to me, she asked, and they said that I would be taken to a Home tonight, and all the things about the cops taking me away to a Home were the threats that had been said over and over again by most adults and here it was coming true. I left the house crying and on reaching the squad car was met with wails from Padge, Johnny and Tam who were howling the car down, and from my close they drove us to the Police Headquarters with us repeatedly asking them to let us go and we would never do it again. We were charged in the police office and locked in a room till a van was ready to take us to the Remand Home. While in this room we were so terrified that we didn't dare even speak to each other and when questioned by the cops we admitted to every machine we had done giving them the details of each. There was no tough façade on my face now, or the rest, as we were only four wee boys who were terrified at the thought of being put away.

A police van drove us to Larchgrove. The squad car and the police van had the same very distinctive scent. There was this smell of fear in them that I have always connected with police uniforms and vehicles, this sense that is more of a feeling than a smell, but it's there. It was in the early hours of the morning when we drove up to the front door of Larchgrove, which is in Glasgow, and the thing that hit me, even then, was the newness of the place. We cowered in the doorway waiting for it to open and when it did we found the entrance to be gleaming, absolutely spotless, with brass or chrome doorplates gleaming and a strong smell of disinfectant. These places have a smell of their own. The screw that took charge of us on entry didn't really see us. We didn't exist. His way of communicating was to point in the direction, without looking at us, and shout in a crisp, clear voice what we were to do, and we did it. Being in such a state of fear and confusion we stumbled, faltered and fell in the rush to do as he said. He was a giant of a man who neither smiled nor allowed any other expression to enter his face which I could tell from the glances I stole at him whenever a movement forced me to look his way.

We were made to strip off all our clothes and we were then taken to a big square that seemed to be the centre spot of the place. The man lifted a big bucket that stood in the square and taking a stick from it he slapped this thick white gooey stuff on the end of the stick onto our hair and ordered us to rub it in which we did with great enthusiasm in the hope of pleasing him. Each of us were given a shower and a locker to put the home clothes in. He led us to the dormitories where the beds were and the sound of crying children permeated the place, silenced only by the shout of "shut up" from the screw, but on hearing the crying we four broke into loud sobbing that couldn't be subdued because we were terrified out of our wits and I kept asking for my Ma, over and over again. I was put into a dormitory with three other strangers all my own age. I lay saying to myself as I cried that I would never do it again and how sorry I was for doing it. I'll never forget that first night nor the boy in the next bed who seemed to be crying in his sleep or was too afraid to open his eyes, but my own personal pain was tremendous as this was the first time I had been away from the house. The whole thing was terrifying for me, I was physically shaking with fear and didn't dare sleep in case something happened. I honestly couldn't believe what was happening to me. I wanted my Ma.

At six in the morning a man came walking along the corridor ringing a big bell and shouting for everyone to get out of bed and make them up. This I did along the with others, following their every move, as I hadn't a clue what was to be done, and everyone made their way to the toilets and spray room or the big room where the lockers stood. Everyone had to get ready as the screws stood about shouting at anyone who seemed to be slow in doing so. I was amazed at the ease with which some of the kids were taking it, almost in a confident manner as though they knew what they were doing and had been there for some time yet it was incomprehensible to me that anyone could have been there in that place for any length of time. I was too terrified to speak to anyone, as were many of the others, but there were some kids who even laughed as they were dressing. When we were dressed, everyone was hurried along to the big square we had been in before. There must have been about sixty kids in all and everyone was dressed in khaki short trousers, a shirt and a pair of sandshoes. The screws were all dressed in civilian clothing and made us all stand to attention in complete silence until it was time to march to breakfast. If, on the way, someone made the slightest noise we were about-turned and taken back to the square to wait till we were ready to go in silence and this determined whether breakfast would be hot or cold.

That first morning we were turned around twice and although I heard no one making a noise, I was still incredulous at the thought of someone having the nerve to do so and angry that they should, as I felt this might make things worse for me. After breakfast those of us who were to make court appearances were taken away to be put into our own clothing and made ready for the police van which was coming for us. The screw told us to leave the Home clothes in a neat bundle as we might be coming back. The thought of this almost knocked me over. We all looked at each other with trembling lips. Of course I knew that my Ma would take me home once I had seen her; I prayed to God that she would.

Once back in the Police Headquarters where the court was to be held, the detectives came and took the four of us out of the cell and started joking about how busy we had been keeping them with all the work that went into investigating the break-ins. Of course we had told them everything and had cleared their books for them. From here we were taken to a make-shift cell that was used as the fingerprint department and these very tall men in brown coats took our fingerprints, and from there to another make-shift cell that was converted into a photography room to take mug shots of us, and in this way I went officially into the police files. These two things were mind blowing experiences and added to the seriousness for me. The people doing this were taking it all for granted and herding us about like sheep as though they had been doing it all their lives; whereas I was in a stupefied state, doing things I was told in a very nervous fashion, always afraid that I would bring the wrath of the cops down on me. When I went into the courtroom which was filled with people, I saw my Ma and felt that little bit better as I knew that she would help me. The parents of the four of us were allowed to come across and stand immediately behind us while the hearing proceeded. It was very short and sweet with the four of us being remanded for four days in Larchgrove, and we were escorted by the Police out of the room. It all happened so quickly that we were in the cell again before we realised what was happening. The thought of returning to the Remand Home was worrying me very much as the few hours I'd spent there had been enough and I only wanted to go home and I'd never get in trouble again. But taken back we were.

Larchgrove Remand Home is on the East end of Glasgow and sits in a large estate that has a wall around it. Kids who get into trouble go there up to the age of sixteen and from that age onrwads they go to Barlinnie Prison. Kids can lie on remand for nearly four months awaiting trial. When found guilty, they can be sent back to Larchgrove to serve sentences, the maximum being 28 days, so as well as a Remand Home it is also a Detention Centre where kids are sent for punishment. For misbehaving in the place the punishments range from extra scrubbing of floors to being locked in solitary, or to corporal punishment which takes the form of a thick leather strap over the buttocks. Discipline reigned supreme in Larchgrove and each person in there had to maintain a high standard. I felt very much at the mercy of the screws, as I'm sure everyone else did. Everything they said went, and was law. After breakfast in the morning the kids were split up into groups with one screw taking charge of so many and each of us were given a bucket and scrubber and cloth. The whole morning was spent scrubbing the floors and the scrubbing had to be very thorough because if it wasn't everyone in that group had to go back to the beginning and start over again. I was in such a daze with the whole experience I just scrubbed till I was told to move on as I was scared to do anything without being told. In the afternoon, after lunch, we were put into a small yard for exercise, and from there back to scrubbing the walls and cleaning the brasses. It was no wonder the place was absolutely gleaming, and had this constantly new look about it: the screws wanted to see their faces in everything and see them they did. Nothing was left untouched or uncleaned.

At four o'clock we were made ready in the big square for the evening meal and put through the marching procedure. The dining hall is upstairs and I'll never forget this meal as I was seated next to a window from which I could see buses travelling along the Edinburgh Road. At five o'clock lots of men and women came out of the Olivetti Typewriter factory across the road. It was a winter's night with lights on and I felt as though someone had torn the heart from me, as here were all these people going home to sit at the table near a fire and eat. To go Home! The sight of this hurt me very much. I thought of how, later that night, Ma would come home and make a meal for my brothers. It was terrible to see all these people walking about free, and so I always tried to avoid sitting near a window in Larchgrove. After the meal we were taken to the dormitories and made to sit there while some of the screws went for their meals. At seven o'clock that night my Ma came up, as that was visiting time. It was great to see her and I sat so close to her, almost on her knee and kept asking her what would happen to me and could she get me home? She kept asking me if I was all right and I just implored her to get me home and I would never get into trouble again. Lots of kids had visits and most of them looked very much as I did. When they called "time-up" I wanted very badly to crawl back up Ma's womb and stay there.

After the visit we were lined up in the Big Square and had the white ointment slapped onto our hair. We were then given a shower and put to bed. This was the daily routine, except visits were only allowed every second night. There was no acting in a tough manner now. I was what I was, just a little boy.

After four days of this we were taken to court and given two years probation each. It was pure bliss to walk out of the court with my Ma, with all of us kids repeating again the words that we had been saying those past four days, that we would never get into trouble again and this we promised while our parents assumed that we had learned our lesson. My Ma told me to keep away from the others or I'd just get into trouble and the other parents told their kids the same. I was told that I was to come straight home after school and stay in, as I was on probation now and had to take great care or I'd be taken away again, so I said I'd adhere to this and anything else as long as I never had to go back to that place. She had to go straight off to work, but was obviously delighted to have me back in the house. Everyone else was out at work or in school and I was so glad to be back in the house; it seemed like years since I had been there as so much had gone on during the last four days.

The following morning it was back to school and on the way there I met some of my classmates who questioned me about the experience of Larchgrove. By the time I had reached the school the fear of it was fading and I was responding to their questions boastfully, so that before very long I was giving a completely fictitious account of my experience and how I had handled it in a manly way. There was no talk of tears and heartbreak or the pain I had felt. In many ways I was believing what I was saying about how confident and unafraid I had been. When I told them this I was thinking of the few kids who were very confident about the Remand Home, those who had been in many times before and were used to it. All four of us were in the same class and our experience was the talk of the class, and school. Our reintroduction to the class was made by the teacher remarking that four of our friends were with us again and that he hoped they had learned a lesson. Just the previous day the four of us had been terrified out of our wits, but here we were, one day later, putting up fronts and acting the toughies. Even to each other there was this denial that we had been scared and we began to make-believe about things that we knew just weren't true.

However, for a week or so after school time I would return to the house and stay in till Ma came home at nine o'clock, and I would have the fire on and the house tidied as best I could. My pals had parents who were home so they were kept in the house after school, but mine was purely a self discipline thing as Ma was out at work. There didn't seem much use in sitting in the house alone, so, with this in mind, it was back to the streets, though I made sure I was home for Ma coming in. Harry was old enough to get about himself with his own pals now, so there was no need for me to look after him.

The reality of me keeping away from my pals was nonsensical because we met each other all the time through school and doing messages or playing in the street, so we still went about with each other but made sure our parents didn't see us. Although each of our parents maintained that their son was good and that the others had got him into trouble, this just wasn't true. There was no individual to blame for leading us.

Being on probation meant that I would be under supervision for two years, with a man, the Probation Officer, paying periodical visits to the house to speak to me and find out how I was getting on. He was a large man with an intimidating sort of way about him and it was very odd having him in the house as it made everyone feel they were under supervision, and I felt very guilty as it had been my behaviour that had brought this man into our lives. Whenever he came we felt that he was observing everyone and looking the house over and the atmosphere of the house would seem to change when this "intruder" entered. While he was in everyone would put on a front and Ma would run around getting him tea and trying to be nice to him. His visits were only once a month but even then it was too much. There were quite a lot of people, adults too, on probation in our district so he would have lots of clients, but as everyone was keen to avoid him, an early warning system would go round when he was in the district. This used to happen as well when the GPO were around with their vans for licences or when the debt man was looking for his cash. So whenever he came into the area word went round and people refused to answer the door. After some time he would get fly to this and come through the backs, or when it became very bad he sent letters demanding our presence at his office, but this was better as it kept him out of the house.

One of the kids in our district got a television and though he was the sort of toffy kind of kid his telly endeared him to us and he found himself with more friends than he had ever had in his life. It was the first telly in the street and everyone would try to get him to take them up to his house to watch a programme. We would all be on the look out for him and really he wallowed in this new found popularity. I often wondered how he coped with the situation when tellies became more common. One day he took a crowd of us up to his very nice house when his mother and father were out working. He had this grandfather, a grumpy old man who used to moan continuously, but this time he slept on a chair while we all sat in front of him watching "Bill and Ben the Flower Pot Men". It was fantastic, except that the old guy woke up and started shouting and hitting those nearest to him with his stick. We just moved out of reach and continued watching while this old guy continued to shout; but we were glued to the telly and wouldn't budge.

Another guy in our class at school who was a bit of a nonentity also became everyone's friend because of a domestic phenomenon — a bath. He had moved to a new house and it had a bath in it. The house was in a fringe district of the Gorbals called Oatlands which was quite toffy — very middle class we thought. They were houses that had good lucky didgies which we didn't hesitate to rake. Word soon got round about the bath and one day after school we persuaded him to take us along to see it. He had a lovely house with venetian blinds on the windows. It was very impressive as were the other houses around it. He showed us the bathroom and we all wanted a bath but his mother came in which put an end to that. However, we did get one another day. I thought how great it must have been to live in a house that one could bathe and shit in.

Things in school were returning to normal as our parents had got over the shock of our being inside, so we were now officially going around together again. At night we would concentrate on raising money to go to the pictures and one of the ways we did this was to go round the fruit shops collecting the empty wooden boxes, breaking them up into bunches and selling them round the doors for firewood. We sold them cheaper and bigger than the shops so the sales were good. At night we would sit in the old wash-house in the back for hours, using it as a gang hut. We used candles to light it up and those of us who were Catholics would get a Protestant pal of ours, who stayed downstairs from me, to go into the chapel and steal candles for the gang hut as they were too scared to do it.

The chapel had a hold over us, in a curious way, and it was the same going to Confession. No matter what sins had been committed, after telling the priest there was this extraordinary feeling of being pure. Religion played a dominant part in the life of our district: the Catholics and the Proddies, Celtic and Rangers football teams. I was never very strong on this, maybe due to not having any great love for football, where all the discrimination seemed to stem from. Also, some of my best pals were Protestants. There was the annual thing of going on St Patrick's Day from our school down to the local Proddy school, grabbing anyone we could and asking "Are you a Billy, a Dan or an old tin can?" If he was a "Billy" he was tossed in the air because that meant he was a Protestant, if he was a "Dan" he was okay as that was Catholic, and though the "old tin can" meant neither, since everyone seemed to mention the latter anyway, they got thrown up too. Though this was more a carry-on than a religious thing with me, for others it was the real thing as Billys were bluenose bastards. The Proddies would do the same and so it was a case of give a little — take a little. In general the real religious bigots were among the grown-ups.

About this time I decided to go into business along with my pals, Johnny, Padge and Tam. We were to use a barrow as transport to sell coal briquettes around the neighbouring districts. We would have to do this on Saturdays, when we had a break from school. There was a family in the Gorbals who hired out barrows to anyone wanting to go out with rags or coal. We went to Coal Hill, a yard in the Gorbals where trains bring in coal for the merchants to load up. We were naive enough to think that the merchants would give us briquettes without payment and let us pay up after we'd sold them, but on seeing us, they chased us away. Obviously they looked on us as daft wee boys, but we didn't see ourselves as such. Eventually we gave up trying to get the coal legitimately and decided to steal it. There was a guy with a big store a couple of streets from me and he sold firewood and coal briquettes and the place was loaded with them. We decided it would be a very simple matter to break into it. We broke the padlock on the store door and took boxes of briquettes, making trip after trip to get them, and so it was back to thieving only months after being released from Larchgrove. When Saturday came we were all up early and out on the streets with the barrow and coal shouting "Coal Briqueeeettttteess" and we would tramp round the streets shouting our lungs out selling them at 2/6d. a dozen. We sold them all and it was good fun but we had no money at the end of it as we spent it all as we earned it on hot pies and peas, having about four lunch times in all. At the end of the day we gave the barrow away to the kids in the street to keep instead of taking it back — we had given a phoney name anyway.

One day we decided to run away and make our fortunes, so the four of us jumped a train and ended up in Edinburgh with a few bob in our pockets. We wandered round the city looking it over and went into a railway yard late at night and climbed into an open wagon that was covered with a tarpaulin. We got underneath and had all started singing and carrying on when a torch shone in — it was a cop. He took us out and we ended up in the police station where they took our names and put us in a cell for the night. The cell had a big fire with a guard over it, far different from the Glasgow ones and much cosier. In the morning they gave us a stick of Edinburgh rock for our breakfast and that's the truth. The cops told us our parents had been notified and they put us on the Glasgow train where they asked a man to see that we were okay on the journey. Fool that he was he took the responsibility. By the time we got to Glasgow the man was a nervous wreck as we were running all over the place. It was Sunday morning and as soon as our parents met us on the station we were slapped for running away, but they then took us into the station cafe and bought us breakfast, so it was okay. As usual we were told that we had to stay in at nights but as always we knew that they would have to let us out sometime.

The fear that Larchgrove held for us had completely vanished and I was now out stealing much worse than I had ever done. Now that I was experienced in the game the emphasis was on stealing goods that could be sold for money, only taking stuff to eat when I was hungry. Things like electric shavers and transistor radios which had just hit the commercial market were a good steal as people would buy them, also clothes for kids and adults. Whatever was the fashion, we would get it. Our own fences were plentiful. At New Year we would concentrate on booze, whisky in particular, as it would go as fast as it was stolen. The best targets were lorries delivering to the local pubs. We watched till the guy went into the shop with his load, then we would walk over, lift a case and walk off in full view of everyone around. It would be done so casually that most people would think nothing of it and those who did would just give a wry smile. I was only thirteen and all sorts of adults would be looking for me to remind me that they would buy any cheap Scotch that I got, as people got frantic for it at that time of year. On one particular occasion I had just lifted a case of Scotch from a lorry, having taken my jacket off to look like a delivery boy, walked away with it through the backs and was just crossing the next street, when this guy with a horse and cart selling coal (in the middle of the street) saw me and asked if I was selling it and when I told him I was he took six bottles from me then and there. I had known him just to see before but obviously he had heard of me, so this was typical of the way things went.

Women who wanted nylons or men's shirts for their husbands or boyfriends, would ask me if I had any. Our "fence" wasn't some mastermind Fagin who sent us out to steal or exploited us by buying the stolen articles. It was just ordinary people who took the stuff from us as they probably couldn't afford to pay the full price. If it wasn't me that was selling stolen gear then it would be any number of others, as there was this sort of unofficial "underground" market for stuff and usually anything could be bought at half price or well below that. There was a great deal of excitement about it and I had this pal who had fantastic patter and he would chat up shop owners to buy the gear from us. He was really good and got the best of prices for me. Stealing and selling the gear was good as it gave me a sort of identity; people knew that if they wanted things they could come to our crowd and we would usually find a way.

4

I became very interested in pigeons, not the racing kind, but show pigeons and there seemed to be a fever gripping a few of us over them. We would buy what birds we could from the money we made from stealing, but that wasn't enough so we started stealing them and to do this we would break into pigeon huts all over Glasgow and bring them home. I got quite a notorious name amongst pigeon flyers in the district for having lots of stolen birds. I used to keep them in the loft above the house and they would make a terrible noise but the neighbours would say nothing about that as they were only too glad to see me keeping out of trouble; little did they know. Eventually I had to give it up because, whenever birds were stolen, men from all over Glasgow would come to my door knocking asking for their birds, even when I hadn't got them. One of my pals was still keen on the bird flying and knew an easy pigeon hut to screw in the Oatlands, so one night three of us went up to it and broke in. The hut was empty but while we were there the cops came and chased us, catching us all.

We were charged and taken through the whole admittance procedure finding ourselves back in Larchgrove the following day. The hatred of the place returned the minute the police caught us and I was sick at the thought of going back there and very frightened. After being fingerprinted and photographed we were taken to court and sentenced to 14 days Detention for breaking into an empty hut. The routine was the same, as were my feelings about the place: the scrubbing, the discipline, the occasional thumping from the screws. My Ma was shattered when she came up to see me and I told her the same as I did the last time I was in, that I wouldn't get into trouble again and really all she could do was believe me.

Near the end of this period of detention the screws selected me to go with four older guys of about sixteen to a farm to get manure for the Larchgrove garden. Some of the farm workers offered me cigarettes, I didn't smoke so I took them for the others. It was a great trip as we went by lorry along the Edinburgh Road and getting the cigarettes was a small victory, as the big guys were chuffed with them, saying I was a great wee guy. At night everyone would lie in bed and listen for the loud steps of the Headmaster of the place as he walked from his office to the big square. He had metal tips in his shoes and the sound of him walking on the stone floor could be heard all through the Home. Corporal punishment was always given out at night, after everyone had been put to bed, and no-one ever knew who was to get it so we would lie there listening for the name to be shouted. The place was in silence, with no-one daring to even whisper. On this particular night my name was called out. It was a bolt out of the blue and I stiffened with fear, unable to budge. My name was called again, "Boyle". I slid out of bed, the fears inside me reflected on the faces of the others, all of them feeling the pain with me, wondering if they would be next.

On reaching the Big Square the screws all stood in silence as I came along in my pyjamas. The Head accused me of bringing cigarettes into the Home when I had known they weren't allowed. I made a feeble attempt to deny it, but was so surprised at him knowing that I then admitted it. He had this big leather belt in his hands and it was so stiff that it stood out straight. He told me to bend over but I was too terrified to move. He repeated the order but I honestly couldn't move so he put his hand in his pocket, pulled out a sweet (obviously he had experienced this sort of thing before) and threw it on the floor telling me to pick it up. As I bent down to do so he hit me full force across the arse and I yelled and the tears flowed down my cheeks. I stood with my arse against the wall refusing to turn round and crying louder hoping he would give up but he shouted for me to turn round and bend over. All the while the others were lying in bed listening to this. Finally he told the screws to hold me and with me screaming all the while, he proceeded to belt me. For refusing to obey him by not turning round, he put me in the strong cell for the night. The following morning I was let out to join the others and they told me that two of the older guys had been caught smoking and had given my name. My arse was sore for days.

I truly suffered with other kids who got the belt in the nights to come as each stroke could be heard throughout the place. The anomalous situation was that those of us who received the belt were looked up to by the other kids in the place even though they had heard each of us crying our eyes out at the time. I had cried loudly and unashamedly when getting the belt because it really was sore, just as it was to every kid who received it. One could hear stories of kids afterwards boasting how they had never cried and I also took part in this boasting, yet we had all heard each other.

Thankfully the day of release came and it was a Saturday at 6 p.m. Our parents were there to meet us at the door. I was glad to see my Ma and she gave me the usual lecture. In our world there wasn't much cuddling or embracing of parents, as that was too sissy, so when we first saw our parents it was just a big hello and then the lectures came. I was overjoyed to be out and sincerely meant it when I told my Ma that I would never get into trouble ever again. I told her this again and again, and with my whole heart and soul this was what I meant. Why, when feeling like this did I return time and time again? I never wanted to get into trouble and there were times when this feeling was passionately strong, not only in me but in all of us, though we would only admit this to each other when caught, because when we were out in the streets what we were doing seemed so natural. I always felt very inarticulate when I was a kid and could never talk to people like teachers or those who were part of the authorities. My probation officer used to have to drag every word out of me even though it was very meaningless stuff. It was different with my own people in the district as I would talk away naturally with them. Certainly there were lots of kids in the Gorbals who had never been in trouble and lots of them had gone about with me at one time or another. The difference was that although they had taken part in the mischief, unlike us, none of them had been caught.

When we got out of Larchgrove we left the thieving again and after school resumed the practice of going over the Mollsy to play at various games, wrestling and dummy fighting. It was at this time that we decided to become a gang and set about thinking up a name for it. We came up with the "Skull Gang", so we all got white skulls painted on the back of our leather jerkins, which caught on so that lots of kids wanted to join us. It wasn't really a fighting gang but just a group of us who were going around together playing at various games. It all started innocently enough. As the leather or imitation leather jackets were the rage, with backs painted, everyone was all for it. One kid came up to us and asked me if he could join our gang and I told him he would have to go through an initiation ceremony, after school. He agreed to do this. At first I meant it as a joke but during the class period some of us were whispering about what to do. After school hours we all went up the Mollsy with the kid who wanted to join us. Each of us were trying to outdo the other with outrageous suggestions for initiation tests. Finally, as we were walking over the railway bridge, a spot where lots of trains slow down to come in or leave the nearby depot, I told him to drop off the bridge onto a moving train and everyone backed me up on this. So the guy waited with us until a train came along at a reasonable speed then he climbed over the parapet and dropped the fifteen feet or so into the open wagon of the train which by then gathered speed and went in the opposite direction from the depot. We ran to the other side of the bridge and there was his little head over the rim of the truck shouting that he couldn't get off, and we were in stitches laughing and shouting for him to send us a postcard. I think he ended up in Motherwell or some place like that but it certainly gave us laughs for some time to come.

At nights it was a case of back to playing in the streets at various games, and by this time some girls were going around with us and we would feel them up. It was about this time when I had my first girl and it was a glorious knee-trembler in the back, with cats and rats running about. After it I can remember going home and wondering if my Ma would be able to tell from my face that I had had it. The first thing I did when I walked into the house was to look in the mirror but I looked just the same. For some reason or other I thought I'd look different. Sometimes when I went home Ma would be in the house and she would be worrying because my brothers hadn't come home. I would tell her that they were out playing and she used to say that she didn't worry too much about me as she knew I could look after myself.

There wasn't much money about but the shops in the area used to cater to the people in the district. For instance, one of the chip shops, "Greasy Peters", would sell a penny's worth of scrapings — that was the fine bits of batter and potato from the chips and fish. Lots of us would go in and get these and buy a burnt hot roll from the bakers and put the scrapings onto the roll. One shopkeeper used to sell penny packets of currants with candy balls and she made a fortune from this so that when she died the cops found a large sum of money in her shop. Another shop sold penny Vantas, which was a small bottle of coloured water that was meant to be ginger. There was "Dirty Maggies", where the kids could go and swap comics. Her shop would be piled high with them but always well away from reach, as experience had taught her that we would rather swipe them than buy or swap. Most of the shops in the district gave "tick" and this was worked out by people going down to the shop during the week and getting food on tick and paying it back on the Friday or Saturday when the wages came into the house. However, the old favourite was "John the Pawns" — the pawnshop — and the Monday would see queues of great length outside the place. People would have big brown paper-wrapped parcels under their arms to put the man's suit into Uncle John's and the same people could be seen in the same queue on the Friday waiting to lift the stuff that had been pawned on the Monday and this would go on week after week. Most of these shops were small and very dirty with little lighting in them, but everyone would know where to go. A stranger in the district would find it difficult to believe that the shops were open as they seemed very dark and ill used. One could go into the fruit shops and buy chipped fruit. The fruiterer would cut the bad part off and sell the remainder to us so that nothing was wasted. The same could be done in the bakers for broken biscuits or the day-before's left-overs as these were sold at a cheaper price. There was Paddy's Market in the Bridgegate which would always be full of people in to buy cheap clothes. My Aunt Peggy had a stall selling old clothes that they had been out hawking for. She would always give us clothes out of the "bag" so if I needed trousers my Ma would ask Peggy if there was anything decent in the "bag". The bag was the name for the bundle she carried when out hawking.

There were lots of gangs in Glasgow and this seems to have been the case since I can remember. In the Gorbals alone there were the two "Cumbie" gangs, "The Beehive", "The Hammer", "The Dixy", "The Valley", "The Clatty Dozen", "The Skull", "The Stud", "The Kay", also one or two others that I can't recall. But gangs were very much a part of the place and it was the done thing to join one. Up to this point I had avoided gang fights and preferred watching the many that took place. "The Skull", the gang that I led, were basically a stealing gang and a group that went around together. However, one night as we were hanging around the street corner in a group in Lawmoor Street, a gang of guys from down the street approached us and asked us to help them out against a mob from another district who were coming over to fight them that night. This mob from down the street didn't have a gang name but they were pretty wild and their leader was Mad Owny, who was feared amongst us, so although we wanted to keep our distance, at the same time it was very difficult to turn them down because they may have taken offence. But they had made us feel good by asking us to fight with them. They were slightly older than us and more experienced and we all went to their wash-house ganghut and they gave us lots of weapons and I was given a metal knuckleduster that was very heavy and could do plenty of damage. There were butterflies in my stomach while waiting on the gang coming to fight but inside myself I was saying that I would just act the part and not hit anyone, though my biggest thought was on the fear that I might be injured, so I was both frightened and excited.

Owny's gang had plenty of girls going around with them and there was a lot of showing off in front of them about how we would use the knife or the knuckleduster. As the night wore on, and there was no sight of the opposition, Owny's pals started getting a bit restless and messing us around to show off to the girls, so by this time we were wondering what we had let ourselves in for. Eventually it was decided that this other mob weren't going to show up so one of Owny's boys decided that we should have a "dummy fight", with their gang against ours; having been on the brunt of it all night, I didn't like the smell of it. This "dummy fight" was to take place where we stood, about a hundred yards from Lawmoor Street police station, in the middle of the street, but as the streets were so dark the cops could have been a hundred miles away for all the difference it made. The "dummy fight" started with Owny coming for me with his heavily metal-studded leather belt and fear more than gameness made me strike at him with the knuckleduster and very hard at that, so almost immediately the "dummy fight" was for real. I burst Owny's head and he started shouting that the fight was only for fun — he was taking fright at the ferocity of my blows. Within this very short period of time I was able to see Owny wasn't so tough after all and when the others also saw this they stepped back a bit and my pals became the confident ones, though a shakey confidence it was. It was amazing the transformation that took place. Owny could beat all of his pals physically and because I had just beaten Owny they thought that I could beat them. The relief of not getting beaten up myself and the total surprise that it was turning into a victory, was enough to fill me with an enthusiasm that was circulating the group. Owny was even saying that I was "crazy" and the rest were reiterating what he was saying; so although it was only minutes after the "dummy fight", we were talking about having a fighting gang with me as the leader. We were all for it and I was very excited and chuffed at the idea of being classed as a good fighter and loved it when they said I was crazy as this is meant as a compliment within our culture. All this adulation was going to my head, with all the birds hanging around, and I was loving it. The ironic thing is that before I hit Owny, I was very scared and when actually striking him it was only through fear, that and nothing else. But just like the Larchgrove experience when I was very afraid, the adulation and kudos that came my way were easy to succumb to after the event. That night I went home feeling great and could hardly sleep for thinking of this new victory. Next morning it was all over the school, everyone there seemed to be talking about it.

From then on we would all meet at night and run around the streets shouting gang slogans and playing around. We would go around the gravey a lot, but about this time there was a big scare going about that a madman was terrorising kids in there. It was said that a man with a cape and big iron teeth was roaming about. After school time there would be literally hundreds of kids from all over the district going to the gravey wall and climbing up. Some of us would take a few steps inside the gravey and shout that we had seen the madman and everyone would scatter and run. This went on for over a week and very soon got out of hand as kids were terrified. The Press came on the scene and it so happened that across the street was a small shop that sold fruit, vegetables and comics and some of the comics were horror ones. The Press immediately jumped on this as being the cause and before anyone knew what was happening there was a loud cry for the banning of comics. There was also a decision to put an iron railing on top of the wall round the gravey to keep kids out and this was done, so although the bigger kids could still climb it, the gravey as a playground went out of action.

Owny's gang had plenty of experience of breaking into places and thieving, having been at it longer than us. One of these methods was known as "grafting", which was finding a shop with an empty house next to it or above it and making a hole in the roof or through the wall and going in that way. There was plenty of scope for this as the Gorbals was part of a redevelopment scheme. Lots of kids at our school were being rehoused in housing schemes in Castlemilk, Garthamlock and Drumchapel. Some of our neighbours were also being moved. Many people resisted this strongly and my Ma was one of them. However, some of my classmates and pals who had been moved were still attending school and travelling to and fro to play with their old pals. No-one seemed to like the new housing schemes.

But to get back to the shopbreaking, all these movements meant that there would often be empty houses next to shops full of goods. When we went out to break into them we would carry a Brace and Bit, a chisel and a hammer, as these tools would take us through bricks and wooden floorboards. Another thing was the using of a stout plank of wood between the bars on the windows of a back shop to force the metal bars apart. At first we couldn't believe it would work, but when we saw that it did we would go round bending bars for the fun of it. The graft was the safest and best as we could cut the floorboards of a house and, using a rope, drop to the floor of the shop below. At least two of us would go down the rope, clean out the goods that we knew we could get "fenced" and pass them up to those above. This meant that a cop passing on his rounds could be checking the doors and see nothing amiss. Our cop watcher would have warned us of his movements and we would sit in the shop very quietly listening to him pulling the locks and checking the back door, if there was one, and passing on. Once he was well away we would continue our work. There was real excitement about this sort of thing and I really loved it. Of course there was an element of fear, the fear of getting caught, which was always present.

By the time I was fourteen I had been doing lots of breaking into shops and warehouses and fighting with other gangs but I was finally caught for screwing shops and given twenty eight days detention in Larchgrove. Padge and Johnny were with me again but this time I found it different. I wasn't afraid of it as I had been before. I knew the system and how to work it and although I disliked it every bit as much it held no fear for me now. I was going in amongst people that I knew, for instance the screw knew my name and asked what I was in for and at the same time I knew them and how each one liked me to behave and I would handle it that way. The screws knew that we three had been there before and would give us jobs that were cushy but that needed kids who didn't have to be watched all the time. I was put in the kitchen and would sneak into the food store and steal large bars of cooking chocolate for my pals and myself and they would get the perks from their jobs, so we had a better time. Although we were still very much into the disciplinary scene, by this time we could do our scrubbing and make our beds square without any bother. The screw that would give you a cuff on the lug was avoided so that it was usually the new kids that got it. The difference was that I was now one of the confident ones and every morning when new kids would come in looking as frightened as I had once been, it made me think how it was good knowing the ropes. My Ma would come up to see me and I would tell her that I was never coming in again and I really believed this, and so did Ma. I caught on to the fact that if I wore a mechanical smile and was subservient to the screws then I would skate through the 28 days and this is what happened. No doubt I hated doing this but it was how one got out and I was cute enough to see that this was what they wanted. On Sunday they would take us to chapel at St John's Approved School, that lay in the same grounds, and during mass I was able to see some of my pals who had been going around with me there and other friends I had made in the Remand Home. The place was full of old faces I had known.

After discharge from Larchgrove I was back at school the next day and each time I came home from the place I was put on a higher pedestal in the class and school by all the other kids and most of the teachers left me alone as I was looked on as a real troublemaker. I was left with a year to do in school but there was nothing to justify my being there as lessons were secondary to everything else that went on. The funny thing was that until about this period I had been a pretty mild pupil, and though I had a bit of a carry on I was always manageable and afraid of the teachers. At this time I was still wearing a leather jacket and an army belt with metal studs hammered into it and the trend was to see who could undo his belt the quickest to use in a fight and most of the kids were pretty quick at this and would pass the time practising.

We had this big teacher who talked just like a man in the street, a very rough one, in comparison to teachers as we knew them. One day in class he lifted his foot, put it on the desk of a pal of mine and leant on his knee as he continued to speak to us and the next thing he knew, we were all in stitches laughing at him as the sock he had on was full of holes. We thought this hilarious as it was one thing for us to have holes in our clothes but not the teacher! Anyway this big teacher took offence at our laughter and pulled out one of the boys and was about to strap him. The boy was Johnny, and I told him to leave him alone and swore at him. By this time he was really angry and he left Johnny and came for me. I stood there like Billy the Kid, and tried to loosen my belt to get it off and hit him but, unlike the other times, it wouldn't come so I ran away with this big teacher chasing me around the class, and just at this time the bell rang and everyone scampered out leaving me getting chased around the class with him calling me all the little bastards of the day and me trying like fuck to get the belt loosened, but it wouldn't come. When he did get me he pounded the shit out of me and at that moment the cleaner came in to clean the classroom and the teacher turned to tell her to get the Headmaster, but she took one look at me and said she was calling the police as my face was in a bit of a state. I managed to get away from him but by that time my lip and nose were burst and a black eye was on the way. All the kids were looking in the classroom window and when I got out they cheered me. There was no way I could lose. Due to the state of my face I had to tell my Ma, so the next morning she took me to see the Headmaster and after a long discussion it was all forgotten and I was allowed a few days off.

By this time we were drinking wine in the toilets and smoking. Another gang had sprouted up in the school and we would fight with each other and one time I sat in class with a bayonet down the side of my trouser leg as a fight was looming with the other gang. I ended up fighting with the leader of the gang and he pulled a flick knife on me during the fight — which was supposed to be a fair one. A "Square-Go" is one where the fists, head and feet are used, but no weapons. When this guy pulled out the flick knife it was one of my pals who saw it and shouted to me and I got it off him and kicked it to my pal but the Headmaster came in and caught us, taking both of us to stand outside the door of his room. While there, we never spoke but the other guy's face was in a mess and mine was okay. All the girls had to walk past the Headmaster's room to get to their classes and it was good to watch them seeing his face and asking if I had done it, with their teachers shouting at them for speaking to us. The other guy was looked on as the best fighter in the school so this was a big victory for me and I loved it. We stood there for some time until the police came, which surprised me as it had been a fair fight. They let the other guy go and the two uniformed cops took me between them and walked me all the way to Lawmoor Street Police Station. I walked past neighbours who asked me what was wrong and I shouted that it was okay and that nothing was wrong. The cops said I was to be sent away and they left me in a small room for a couple of hours but then they let me go and nothing further happened.

By this time Johnny Boris was sentenced to an Approved

School, and a new kid, Johnnie Crosby, who had just come out of one, joined our class. Johnnie's uncle had been sentenced to death and reprieved so this was a big talking point for us and he joined our gang. There was a lot of coming and going in the school at this time due to the new housing development. Some of my pals who used to come down to our district at nights after moving house started making new pals up there and from this there grew more gangs; some of which became rivals of ours.

Meanwhile my reputation was expanding amongst the kids of my age, and with the police who were keeping a close eye on me. Our group took up street fighting more seriously though we still did the odd bit of stealing. This meant that we would meet and go to other parts of the district and fight rival gangs. At nights we would all be standing around the corner when someone would say that members of a rival gang were nearby and we would go for them, just like that and they did the same with us. There would be frequent meets to have a full gang fight but these took place very seldom as by the time we had made arrangements the cops would usually be on the spot though there were times when we would be fully into it before they arrived. All sorts of weapons were used: knives, hatchets, bayonets, and swords, but they were for show rather than for use. The main rival gang to us in the Gorbals was "The Stud" and we fought continually and went for each other individually when we met on the street. Eventually there was an arrangement made for me and the leader of the "Stud" to fight each other on a one-to-one basis. The fight was to be on the "Stud" territory, in a place called "The Raw", a piece of waste ground that had once held houses which had since been knocked down. It was a "Square Go" and by the time we had got there the place was filled with people from all over the district. The area was in complete darkness, with everyone squeezing around us to see what was going on, so there was little space left to fight. Anyway we went ahead and flew at each other but the minute both of us rolled on the ground everyone started booting the two of us. The boots were from each of our supporters trying to help us, but thank Christ someone called that the cops were coming and this scattered everybody and we made off. If they hadn't called out, the chances are that the two of us would have been kicked to death. I spent days looking for guys who had kicked me but it was hard trying to find out as they had all been at it.

Not long after this the "Stud" began to fall away and we went looking for greener pastures. By now it was all a case of getting a reputation and this was only gained through fighting other gangs. We started fighting the gangs in Castlemilk, some of whom had been our pals and part of our old gang, but they became as much against us as we them. We beat them without any bother. All during these fights no one was badly hurt as they were only boys' fights, till one hot summer's night in a desolate part of the district we had a fight with a gang in Govanhill, which is a fringe district of the Gorbals. Most of the guys in the gang there came from the Gorbals and we all knew each other pretty well. All of us were armed to the teeth and I had a butcher's knife, the others had their own weapons. As the two gangs came into sight of each other they broke into a run throwing bottles as they came. This usually broke the groups up and we met and fought the individual who was nearest. I was fighting this guy who had a hammer that kept bouncing off my head and during the struggle we ended up in the closemouth with me on top of him. I hacked the butcher's knife into his face and slashed him, the skin parted and the blood started pouring over both of us. Between the blood coming from him and from my head, we were covered in it. On seeing us most of the others took fright and bolted but we were each helped by our pals.

This was the first time I had slashed anyone and really I didn't feel any remorse or pity for the guy as my head was sore and cut and I was cursing that I didn't give him worse, with my pals telling me not to worry as we would get him again. Certainly I had hit Owny with the knuckleduster but that was different as this time I had gone out to fight with a weapon intending to use it. The reason that I didn't feel any sorrow was that all the other fights had prepared me for this and I was actually looking forward to using the weapon as were the others. In the other fights I hadn't slashed or hurt anyone seriously although we boasted amongst ourselves as though we had. So when it did happen it wasn't just an idle boast and in fact it lent credibility to the earlier boasts and fantasy tales that we had been spreading. Another aspect that, for me, made slashing all the more a proper action was the injuries I suffered myself, a couple of gashes and bumps on the head from the hammer blows. They were a great prize in a strange sort of way because they let the others see that the victory was all the more deserved. It didn't take that incident long to circulate the district and other gangs outside. Within days I was a force to be reckoned with and some kids were saying that I was as "mad as a brush." There was a sort of hero worship about all of this and I was placed on a higher pedestal by all my own gang, but like reputations in other fields, you've got to deliver the goods otherwise you're in trouble.

By this time I was becoming pretty well known in the Gorbals as a thief and a fighter and the older guys in the district would use us to carry out what we thought were important tasks. For instance there was the Shebeen runner who put us to good use. His Shebeen was run from an ordinary house in Lawmoor Street and each weekend he would stack it full of cheap wine and other booze. It would open after the pubs closed during the weeks, but the bulk of the business was at the weekends when all the parties would be taking place. He would get the booze at wholesale prices then sell it for more than the retail prices, therefore making a good profit. The rumours would fly about frequently that he was paying the cops off and locally this was felt to be true as his Shebeen was only 100 yards from the cop station. We would make some cash for standing about and telling strangers looking for the Shebeen how to find it. Taxidrivers would bring clients, and prostitutes would bring American sailors and ordinary "johns" to it for booze. If they didn't know where his Shebeen was we would refuse to direct them till we got more cash out of them and this would always work. Some of them were only too glad to give it to us as they were usually in need of a drink.

It was great watching the Shebeen owner move about, as if he was a mini Al Capone, with a big black car and the usual henchmen. They would get all their booze from the pub at the corner and we were fascinated watching them load up. They had cases and cases of booze and it was incredible to see all this being done with no one saying a word. It was as though they were a law unto themselves. Occasionally there would be a fight in the Shebeen but never as many as one would expect in such a place. There was lots of singing and yanks screwing the brass nails (prostitutes) in the closes nearby which we used to watch. Lots of local people used the Shebeen and they could get tick but only if their names were good. The local men also used to play Pitch and Toss at the street corners, which was tossing pennies in the air and betting whether they landed heads or tails. There was a banker who would hold the cash and do the betting and the local men would play this through the week. We would be told to cop watch for this and it was always good for a few bob bung from the men. We would approach the winner afterwards and tell him we had been cop watching and a good bung would be handed out. Sometimes we would shout that the cops were coming when they weren't, and they would scatter taking all the heavy cash with them, leaving the small change lying on the ground and we would jump over and pick it up, but we could only do this occasionally. However, on the Saturday and Sunday there was a big Pitch and Toss held in the Moll's Mire, run by the Shebeen owner. This was the big daddy as there would be lots of money changing hands; most of the men from the district went there, in fact men came from all over Glasgow. There was no way we could get to cop watch this, the adults did it, but it was rumoured that the cops were paid not to come near though on occasions they made a token gesture.

Some of the local safe blowers blew a safe in a Post Office and took lots of postal orders and the stamp to ramp them with. In order to get rid of them they got some of us together and asked us to go into the local shops to change them, giving us so much from each one. This meant a lot of money for us by any standards. Each night after we had been out cashing them we would go into the local pub and pay them the cash. They would buy us a pint and this was fantastic sitting there in the pub at fourteen drinking. The publican would say nothing as they were all pals which was good for us as we could now go into the pub. It was great for us to walk home from school at lunch time and go straight into the pub with other kids from the school looking on. All week we would go out stealing, save up for the weekend and sit in the pub buying the older people drink and putting it back ourselves, although a few pints would have us full to the gunnels. Before we were allowed into the pubs we would buy cheap wine and go into the backs and sit round a fire drinking it or in someone's house if none of the adults were in. We would hold parties with girls and have fun getting drunk out of our minds.

Boozing became a big thing for us and when we got drunk we would do crazy things like smashing shop windows and fighting. I would waken in the morning wondering what I had done the night before and go round to my pals and find that they were in the same state. From there we would walk along the street and see windows smashed in the shops and would then recall that we had done it. Sometimes it was so bad that I wouldn't even remember. Now any booze that we stole we kept for our own parties unless it was an excessive amount. Our stealing was now for booze money and there would be times when we would be going into school with a hangover and bleary eyes. Kids at fifteen would try to bluff their way into the pubs and be turned back and we would be sitting there a year younger, getting away with it. These were the things that I and my pals valued most. The things that I would do in drink were unbelievable. I went round to the Big Cumbie and challenged them to fight and had the shit kicked out of me by one of them for being a cheeky wee bastard. The situation got so bad that all of us were going around becoming near-alchoholics at the age of fourteen. The pitiful side of it all is that never at any time did I get the least pleasure from drinking. I really didn't like the stuff, but drinking was the done thing so I did it. All my life the men of the district had hung around the local pubs. The pub was where it all happened, and this was the good thing about being in with the right people as you could always get that bit more. At the night's end we would fall out of the pub with the drunken men and women.

The worst thing about breaking into shops at night and stealing goods was having to sell them as it meant taking another risk selling the stuff, so it was much better to get the cash whenever possible. About this time I hit on another seam and that was breaking into the shops during their lunchtime closing hour. The owners would lock the front door putting a token lock on, as they would only be gone for an hour or so and who would break into the shop in broad daylight? We would and we did. This was really good as we would spend our school lunch time walking around looking at the shops usually knowing which ones would be going for their lunch. We would watch till they had gone and wait till the street was vacant for a good stretch. It didn't matter if people were a good distance up the street for all they would see was a kid running and kicking the wall, or what looked like the wall from their vantage point and how many times have we seen this happening? I would go in and clear the till and search around as some shopkeepers usually kept cash hidden in biscuit tins or other hidey holes. The tills were usually packed with money and I would load it into my pockets and fill a bag with cigarettes or any other easy selling articles and walk out. The money to be made at this was really tremendous when comparing our other hauls. Usually we would go back to school with about ten pounds each in our pockets, a great feeling as this was a lot of money for us.

I remember the first time I scored during a dinner hour break-in, we got over ten pounds. It was a rainy day, the sole of my shoe had a big hole in it and my sock was soaking wet. All afternoon I thought about getting another pair of shoes but how could I wear them into the house as Ma would see them and kick up hell if she thought I had been out stealing. At four o'clock I took this guy in my class with me to the cobbler shop in Rutherglen Road. He always had shoes for sale that had been in for repair but hadn't been picked up by the owners who couldn't afford to pay. I made a deal with this pal in my class that I would buy him a pair of these, as he too had holes in his, if he would come home with me so I could use him as my alibi. He agreed so I told my Ma that this guy's Mother had given me the shoes and he confirmed this. Ma gave the shoes a thorough going over and when she saw that they weren't new, she accepted it. I had to go to such lengths with schemes such as this to fool Ma, otherwise she just wouldn't have it. So there was I with plenty of money and a good pair of shoes asking myself, "What more did anyone want?" Apart from booze, we spent the money on paying everyone into the movies and smoking the cigarettes that we stole and though I didn't smoke I would puff twice from a cigarette and throw away the remainder. We really felt prosperous at such times but no sooner was it there than it was gone. Easy come, easy go. One time after a few rapid lunch time raids the cops came up to the school with a witness as we were lining up to go into the classes. The cops took the witness round everyone in the school to see if she could identify the raiders and passed me by with a lot of the money in my pockets. After this scare we cooled it for a while.

It was about this time that I got really desperate and with a few pals wearing balaclavas went into some of the local shops and held them up. In one shop the woman told us she had no money; we opened her purse and a holy medal was in it so we all ran out not bothering to take the cash from the register. We got nothing from the four shops that we tried to hold up as it was real desperado stuff and with the masks off all the shopkeepers knew us. However, all of us were arrested by the detective Goodall and put on an identification parade. When the witnesses came in to pick out the raiders we called them by their names and they us, asking what we were doing there. This was a close call so we decided to put an end to that one.

Just before leaving school I could see that no one was interested whether I stayed or left so I took the latter course and went looking for a job. I went to a lemonade factory and they employed me. When they asked for my insurance cards I said I would get them soon. Of course I knew that when starting a job one gets about three weeks grace before the cards are demanded. I went round the shops with a lorry taking the crates in behind the counter and while doing so I would take what I could and smother it in the crates of empty bottles that I was taking out. My favourite "steal" was small packets that held £10 in silver and I would always be on the lookout for these and get a couple as well as other goods. The driver was a suspicious bastard, but he was also a lazy one and his downfall was caused by sitting in the back shop eating or drinking tea. I had this job five days and looted almost every shop I went into. On the Friday the driver went into a cafe for his tea and left me out in the van; I was standing on the back of it. I knew where the driver kept all all his smash collected from the lemonade sales, so when some guys came along that I knew I told them to steal it. When he noticed it missing later he questioned me but I denied it, so he went to Lawmoor Street Police office to report it while I sat outside. That night I lifted my wages getting about two pounds odd, but I was laughing as I had been scoring all week. If they came near me then I would say I was too young to work. On my way back to school one morning I saw the same driver delivering lemonade to a shop and he stared at me, but he had another van boy.

At fifteen I left school and in every way it was like leaving prison. I had no regrets. I felt a real sense of freedom. There was a dance held for those leaving but it was made plain that we weren't welcome. That was okay by us as none of us wanted to go anyway. It was great to be finished with the dump. For the last few months I had been going around with this girl, who would cop watch for us at night while we screwed and fought. She was sixteen, and after school she would come up and wait at the gate for me. There would be no more of that now as I was no longer a child.

The school didn't have a very good success story as I continued to meet guys from my class in prison.

My Class

Johnny — Approved School, Borstal, Prison and now serving Life Imprisonment.
Andy — Borstal, Prison and Life Imprisonment
Johnnie C. — Various institutions, Prison and Life Imprisonment.
Padge — Various institutions and a long term prison sentence.

There are at least four other kids from classes younger than me serving life sentences. All of these listed were for separate charges of murder in different parts of the country. There are lots serving sentences of varying lengths. But there is always that bond of being Bonny's boys and we look back on our times there as having been fun. My vision of a future when I was leaving didn't stretch very far as my only ambition was to get a job so that I could buy a new suit. All I could think of was a labouring job, as a trade was a luxury and the money was too small. I had done nothing at school and found it hard to be articulate. It was easier to stand and nod or shrug my shoulders than to talk.

All of this led to me taking a job with the *Evening Times*, a Glasgow newspaper. The job was about all I could get and about all I wanted as it meant delivering the newspapers as van boy. The good point for me was that in between rounds I would go to the shops not far away, as it was in the city centre, and steal. By this time I had a good seam worked out. I would go to the shop, usually a large one, with an old classmate and give him my jacket and I would roll up my sleeves. I had stolen a key to the display windows which fitted lots of them as they seemed to be standard. I would pick an appropriate moment and enter as though I worked in the shop and was doing my work. The space outside the window would be filled with customers looking at some of the goods that I was in fact stealing, but they would never guess. I would take what I wanted and leave locking the window behind me. I would go back to work and complete my round then sell whatever I had stolen that particular day. The job was easy and so was the stealing so I was quite happy with my lot. Now in the paper jobs it's all slack till printing time when the papers are parcelled and ready for delivery and then the rush is on. This particular day, I was at the railway station and missed the run and this upset the guy who was my immediate boss and we had a clash. He wasn't a bad guy but I didn't fancy him much and I became a bit awkward. Then he had a go at me one day and that was it. I was unemployed.

I went back to gang fighting and full-time stealing. Most of us from the school still went around together and by this time I was well established as a good fighter amongst my own group. Whenever any of us got caught out stealing the golden rule was to say nothing and plead not guilty and the rest of us would get bail money. A few of our pals got caught and the rest of us went out stealing to raise the bail money. We stole lots of gear and sold it and I went round the guys' parents giving them the dough to help with the bail, or to get them some food while they were in. I went to one of their houses and the mother took me in, but not long after the step-father came in and he didn't know me. During the conversation we had, he started talking about Boyle who had led their son astray. His mother, standing there with a fistful of readies, was holding her face at her man's bloomer. I just got up and walked away and laughed like hell when I got outside the door. If it had been me I could imagine my Ma saying the same thing. There was always a great deal of loyalty amongst us in that respect.

It was around this time, while breaking into shops, that I stole my first safe. We had taken the complete set of bars from the back shop window and decided to lift the small, but very heavy safe out. When moving it from under the counter and turning it over, the cash inside the safe rattled and this gave us great delight. Though we hadn't a clue how to open it we decided to take it as the sound of the cash was just too much to resist. After getting it out of the shop window we put it onto an old pram and wheeled it to a back-court in Lawmoor Street where we tried to open it with hammers and chisels. While struggling with it to get it into better positions the money rattled and this in turn brought the householders to their windows. We pulled iron railings out of the fence nearby and attacked the metal box with these, the noise bringing more spectators to their windows. One man threw us a heavy hammer to try to open it with but it was all in vain. As the night passed into morning we decided to call a halt putting it in the nearby midgie and covering it with ashes then going home to bed.

I felt very tired but it was a rich sort of tiredness with the money in the safe, feeling as though it were in my pocket. We didn't touch it during the day time but spent the time speculating on the contents and what we would do with it. The more we speculated the higher the sum got as we all forgot that it had come from a wee store; but we lived on these day-dreams and they were good while they lasted. It's very difficult to try keeping anything a secret in our district, so by afternoon it seemed as though everyone knew about it and other kids were asking us for a look. Some mothers, on hearing it, didn't let their sons out that night; but it was in vain, as a night's sweat was all we got and each of us were thoroughly frustrated with it. Spectators threw suggestions thick and fast but to no avail. We even carried the safe up three flights of stairs and dropped it over onto the back but the ground was all mud and it sank a good deal into the ground leaving the safe unmarked. The rattle of cash was enough to keep us at it, but we had to return it to another midgie for the night and no sooner had I got to sleep when I was awakened by one of my pals as the men were emptying the midgies. So we went round and started throwing stones at them and they ran away to get the cops as we were stopping them from doing their job. While they were doing this we had the safe in the pram and wheeled it to a safe midgie. On one occasion we wheeled it past the Police Office, on the other side of the street.

The next day I went to this guy who was a safeblower and asked him to open it and he gave me instructions to take it to the "Raw" and he would get it. That night we made the meet and he came in a big car, took me away with it and into a house. He had hardly got it into the house when within a few minutes he had the back of the safe torn off and was extracting the contents. I watched, fascinated at how easy he had made it. There was £90 odd and we split it up, giving him a good whack for opening it. By the time I had divided it between the rest of us there wasn't much. Had we worked like we did for Wimpeys they would probably have given us more. However, to look at the bright side I now had the know-how to open a safe and had made another good contact. Most of these guys like to know kids who can shut their mouths and the experience was good. The safe incident was looked on as quite an event and everyone thought we were loaded: they of course were working on the same assumption as I had been, that nobody puts a little drop of cash in a safe, that's where all the big cash is kept.

Two days later I was picked up by the cops — detectives — and as I walked into the squad room one of them told me to take a good look — he was referring to a safe with the back torn open but I played dumb and gave him a quizzical look. The two detectives in charge of the case had been onto me since I was a kid so we knew each other. They had this crazy act where one would be the baddy and the other the goodie with the big melting warm heart. It was very difficult not to laugh at them as they went through this routine. The baddy would always go through this taking-off-the-jacket-meaning-business routine while his partner would restrain him and offer me a cigarette. This would go on and on with them throwing in that they had my fingerprints on the safe but I said nothing, till they eventually put me out. I used to wonder why they went through this routine over and over again till it struck me that it may have been worked with others, but even so, why continue it with me whey they had tried it so often and it had failed? By now I was smart for all the games the cops played and followed the golden rule of saying nothing till I had seen my lawyer. I didn't really hate the cops at that time, although I was certainly very wary and in some cases frightened of them. They were by now the recognised enemy and the less one had to do with them the better.

Although only fifteen I was drinking quite openly in the pubs and mixing with older criminals, listening to them talk of their exploits and in some cases their dealings with the police, how the police planted evidence on them and told lies when giving evidence in court against them. All of this I would listen to and nod as though believing it but there was this innocence that made me not believe it deep down. I had the odd thump from cops, but I also had the odd thump from teachers and a gaffer, among many others. Any dealing I had with the police was of a superficial nature, whereas these guys were on a more intense level. So the innocence was still there in me and I wasn't aware of the politics of crime — the real politics. These older guys had been where I was yet to go and had the experience that I was yet to gain.

So apart from my own petty clashes with the cops, I was also gaining through the experiences of others. I can remember the case of a drunk guy being lifted on Hogmanay by two beat police. There was a crowd round them trying to persuade the cops to let the man go saying some of them would take him home. There was obviously a lot of feeling from the people as New Year is an emotional period when everyone likes to be in their own home. However, the cops weren't going to let the man go so a struggle started between the crowd and the cops with one of the police going for assistance and leaving the other to watch the drunk. The remaining cop said that we were to wait till his mate had gone out of sight and then he would let him go. There was no doubt that he was frightened. It was on such occasions that I began to get to know the cops. I looked at them the way most people do, with a basic mistrust, but then I had had that bit more personal experience than most.

Around this time the "Wild Young Cumbie" were very active, getting involved in lots of heavy fighting scenes and were getting the name of being the best fighting gang ever to come out of the Gorbals, both collectively and as individuals. Some of them were involved in a big fight that was reminiscent of a wild west saloon brawl in the Gorbals and there was a big court trial afterwards where John McCue, Artie Austin, and three others were involved and all given sentences. John — 4 years and Artie — 18 months. The Press made a big deal of it and labelled John as the leader. The fact was that another guy was the leader. This was all part of the image-building process of the Press. All of us younger kids would pore over these newspapers and the press coverage only confirmed the years of adulation that we had given them. Being in the papers was a great thing to us. All of the kids that went about with me idolised these guys so when they were jailed and put out of the way we saw fit to change the name of our gang from the "Skull" to the "Cumbie". Our activities on the gang scene became more intense. I was intent on making a name for myself, and the only way this could be achieved was by violence. There seemed to be plenty of rewards for the gamest guy, and I was intending to be him. Certainly the punishments were pretty severe but when living this existence it is difficult to think about getting caught so this didn't really enter into it.

Violence now entered our thieving and when we broke into a place it would be done quite openly by walking up to the premises, smashing the window, jumping through and loading up with what we wanted to take. If any good citizen tried to stop us we would face up to him, but almost every time we did it unheeded. The dialogue and rumour that went on about the gangs was what gave us, as individuals, a boost; so the more daring or cheeky the event, the bigger the impact. The same thing went for gang fights as the one giving out the most stitches got the reputation. It also made others think twice before coming near you. When anyone did come for you, it was usually the real thing with no messing about, so there was a dangerous side to it, but I must have accepted the risks because that's the path I trod. This sort of attitude was held in almost every gang. There were times when we would talk about losing our "nerve" or "bottle" and this was a great fear amongst us.

Some kids that had gone about with us had fallen away to get a job or go with a girlfriend. This to us, was "chickening out" which was something we didn't want to do and which we were afraid of. I would frequently "test" my nerve, setting myself tasks which would usually take the form of stealing. My Ma used this old pram for taking her house washing to the "steamy" (washhouse). One night I borrowed it and went to a small pub, jemmied the front door, went in and took lots of booze, loaded it onto the pram and got away. We used to hang around this old guy's house with girls and so I took the load of booze up there where all my pals were and surprised them with the drink and we all had a party. This was looked on as being really game, but most important, these were things that I used to do to prove to myself that I hadn't lost my "nerve". The old guy whose house we used would get very drunk and we would be lying on the floor with the girls and he would shout to me (he was an old sailor) to clear the deck and we just laughed. We found that lots of older guys would hang around us as they were sure to get booze; but usually they were the weaker ones. They were district characters with fantastic lines in patter and they would tell us stories of how they did lots of depredation (dep as we called it). The important thing for us was that these guys were putting our names about to the older guys in the district making us known to them, so it was all part of climbing the ladder into the real criminal world.

5

My lone journeys of testing myself came to an abrupt end when I stole a cash box of money from the Carnival during the Glasgow Fair Holiday and on the way out a squad car with detectives who knew me pulled up and spoke to me on a routine questioning thing, searched me and found the cash box. So once again I was inside. I went through all the old familiar procedures and ended up in Larchgrove. Then there was a court appearance where I was put on remand for Approved School Reports. The reports proved positive as I was assessed as eligible for Approved School and sentenced for an indefinite period which meant up to three years. This shocked me even though I had expected it, but the reality was far worse than I had ever imagined. I felt as I did the very first time I had ever been arrested. My Ma was in court crying, and so was I at the thought of going away for three years.

I was taken by car to St John's Approved School, barely fifty yards from Larchgrove. I was left standing by the front door for some time until a man came along, took my name and one or two other particulars, then left me. Much later, as though by accident, a guy who I knew came along and to his surprise found me standing there, so he took me to change my clothing. The place seemed empty as these were the only two people that I had seen in the two hours I had been there. As I walked along the corridor quizzing him I looked over the surroundings in trepidation. Coming in the opposite direction was an old guy in robes and as we drew near him, he reached forward and pulled me to him and struck me full on the head with something hard, watching as I fell back. Not one word was uttered between us. This was my introduction to St John's. I was then told that the old man was one of the staff and that he had hit me with a billiard ball.

I was given the school uniform to wear, a green shirt and a pair of trousers, by an old tailor who had bomb shells and hand-grenades all over his desk which he apparently collected. Such was my introduction to the place. This approved school was run by a team of religious Brothers who wore black cassocks. The place was not only for kids like me who got into trouble, but also for other kids who didn't get into trouble but were in the place for "care and protection". Most of these boys had been in orphanages all their lives but when they became too old and foster parents couldn't be found for them they were put into St John's. There were some kids who had done the full three years period but these were exceptional cases. The common period of stay was fourteen months, though a great percentage went straight to Borstal from there. My first few days there were hellish as I hated the place and wanted to get out of it very quickly. The fact that I met plenty of old friends meant nothing. I was intent on running away at the first possible chance and kept telling them this but they just said that everyone feels the same when they first come in but I would get used to it. The action of the old guy hitting me meant nothing to them as this sort of thing happened all the time and obviously they were used to it. They were right, within a few days I had settled down somewhat.

In the morning we would get up, make our beds, then go downstairs to the toilets where everyone would wash. There were about a hundred and fifty boys in the place and we would all wash at the sinks then line up and be marched to the chapel where mass would be said with everyone closing their eyes for sleep more than for prayer. After mass everyone was marched downstairs for breakfast and prayers which were said before and after the meal. We would then be lined up in the big yard and taken to our particular workshop. I was put in the joiners as a few of my pals were there and they said I was to come with them. At lunchtime it was back to the dining hall and while we were saying prayers the meal would be put on the table. I'll never forget my first meal. The time between meals was pretty lengthy and there was always talk about being hungry, so that while the prayers were being said two kids seated on the opposite side of my table leant forward, one of them spitting in his own dinner and the other extracting his false teeth from his mouth and placing them on top of his meal. I watched puzzled and laughed at it thinking it was a joke, but later on I found out that they were recognised as being the weak ones and therefore more likely to have their meals eaten by the others. This prevented that from happening. It was just a survival tactic.

After lunch it would be back out to the yard for football then back to work. Work ended at 4.30 p.m. at which time we were all lined up for a shower. There was a big communal shower section where about twelve boys could shower at a time and one of the Brothers would stand looking in, ordering us to wash our necks or something else. From there it was to the dining hall for the evening meal, after which the rest of the evening was our own. The school had a swimming pool in it which was the favourite attraction for everyone.

Kids came to the school from all over Scotland. It was a senior approved school which meant it took boys in from the age of fifteen upwards. There were a number of civilian staff but they were usually the workshop instructors though some would come in at nights to supervise. There were a number of Irish matrons who did the cooking and the laundry and they stayed in the buildings as did the Brothers. There was one night watchman, he too was a civilian. The system was such that kids who were in for a certain length of time would be allowed to visit their homes on Saturdays and Sundays. When kids didn't return it was often said that it was because of mass rather than anything else, as the prayers that were said in that place were unbelievable and really put me off the Catholic religion which was already coming out of my ears. The only kids that went home at the weekends were those who were within travelling distance, anyone who lived beyond Edinburgh had to stay in. The ones in for care and protection had no homes to go to, but those of us with homes would be able to take one of these kids home for the day so that he could have a day out at a friend's house and get a good meal. So for this reason the kids from Glasgow and Edinburgh had the advantage and those from far away would try to keep in the good books.

The kids from the smaller towns and villages in the outlying districts would look up to the city kids, as did those from the orphanages. Most of the talk during the working hours and the recreation periods was centred around crime, as we from the cities would be impressing those from the small towns. When one of these kids went out with a city boy to his home for a meal it was often the first time he had ever been in the city so he would be easily impressed. The Gorbals had a bad reputation, so they would be afraid but also fascinated by going there. The approved school must have been like a university of crime for these kids, as they learned more and newer techniques from it than anything else. But this went for the city boys too as we were making new contacts in other districts so it was exciting all round. The orphanage kids, who had no previous criminal inclinations, were soon up to their necks in stealing, some of them getting put to Borstal from St John's for committing crimes while there. Stealing was new and exciting to them and they would go out on Saturdays and Sundays to enjoy the adventure of it all. It gave them a sense of independence as they didn't need to ask others for handouts all the time. The approved school gave us 2/6 a week, which was for the work we did. They used to march us all down to the State picture house on the Saturday afternoon for the matinee and our seats would be segregated from the kids that stayed in the Shettleston area. There was always sure to be kids running away under the darkness of the film.

After the initial shock of entry I soon hardened and became very much a part of it, trying to gain a position in the only way I knew possible, by violence. Certainly I polished the floors along with everyone else and did my bit as all new boys do, but eventually I asserted myself and sat back while the weak put their shoulders to the wheel. Bullying was commonplace and was very much a part of what the approved school was all about and the same could be said of homosexuality. These two activities were rife within the place and it was through them that one asserted one's position. It was either that or be on the receiving end. It was a very tough place and every kid had to be tough to survive in it from the official and the unofficial stand-point. For sleeping arrangements the boys were split into dormitories, there being four dorms in all, each holding from twenty to forty beds. One nightshift man, who was on constantly, moved between the dorms and his own office which meant that we hardly saw him. This would allow us to sit up talking all night or having pillow fights and at times drinking booze which we had smuggled in. There was very seldom any homosexuality at these times as it was too open and this was usually reserved for stolen moments in dark corners. One of the worst insults to another boy in this place was to call him a poof, because if the name was given often enough it would stick and guys would be up trying to prove it. There were the few kids who were that way but on the whole most of them were forced into it.

The ordinary staff in the school were very much like those that I had met in schools outside and there was always this feeling of distance between us. During my whole period in St John's I never got close to any of them even to talk to on a superficial basis as all of us kept our distance. There were barriers there and the only one ever to penetrate these barriers was the head man, Brother Paul. He was an admirable person, one who was interested and who cared. He was the one man who made any impression on me, who wasn't afraid to get to know the kids or to give a part of himself to us. He did strange things to all of us with the relationships he tried to build with everyone. He made us all feel very guilty about doing things that were wrong. It's not that he had the chance to get to know any of us really well as he seemed always to be swamped in administrative duties but when he was about and when he spoke, his actions made every one of us pay attention. He cut through all the phoneyness and we were able to see that he was the genuine article. His presence was a luxury, but the unfortunate thing was that he was the only one with this attitude and sensing this he would take progressive steps to include us by discussing things, such as the money that was allocated to him each year. He would inform us as to how it would be spent and ask for opinions. The fact that he brought us into it even though we didn't always understand, gave us some sense of responsibility, so that if we ran out of table tennis balls, for instance, at least we knew what it meant so we tried to ensure that they lasted. Apart from the Brothers who would be prone to using violence there was one other who had a predilection for pornography, and kids would make themselves a good day with him by getting porny photos.

The staff in the school would always use Borstal as the big threat so in many ways it was a challenge and it seemed that I would go there automatically. The Approved School surely played a vital part in my criminal development. It gave me connections that I was to find useful in my adult days. It gave me an introduction to guys from towns and cities throughout Scotland and from many areas in Glasgow, many of whom grew up to be the top thieves or fighters in their areas. There is no doubt at all that most of them gained, in a criminal sense, from their approved school experience. Two names worth mentioning in this context are Ben Conroy and Larry Winters, but there were very many more who were to be quite close to me in my adult years. The fact that we had the same experience by being in the same place was a binding factor and put us on a par with the old boy network that is so effective in other circles. The work within the school was non-existent and I would spend my day in the joiners' shop with some pals, sitting at a stove-type fire, getting warm and skipping out the door to try to steal potatoes from the kitchen so that we could stick them in the fire and cook them. Things were usually monotonous, though there was plenty of football but, as I said, I wasn't a keen footballer.

A few months later I was given leave to go home. It was great to be with my pals again having parties and drinking so when the time came to return to the approved school I decided that I wasn't going to. I had been looking over a new shop that had just been opened in the district which was loaded with electric sewing machines. These were in great demand with lots of women wanting them, so I went with some pals early one morning to break into it. With the shop just opened it was still not fitted with an alarm system so it was lying there very vulnerable. We hit it when the beat cops were changing shifts at 6 a.m. or so. We made off with a load of them and got away successfully. The demand for these machines was something so we had no trouble selling them. We had been talking about the idea of going to London for some time now and I and this other guy finally decided to go on the day that I was due back at the school. The guy with me played the guitar and was really good with it so the idea was that he would get work with a band and I would be his manager — that's how crazy it all was. I had all the cash, so off we went.

I can remember the feeling of going there and how everyone at home had said that the streets of London were paved with gold. Somehow I had taken this literally because I was surprised when I was actually in London to see ordinary streets and buildings. Both of us had some clothes in a soldier's kit bag and we took turns carrying it, although it pretty soon ended up back in the left luggage at the station. From there we wandered all over the place finally getting to the West End and hunted out the "Two Eyes Cafe" where Tommy Steele and other singers were "discovered". But it was empty so we wandered around buying junk from stalls and shops. We slept the first night in a "Model" that was full of old men and passed ourselves off as being of age. We had heard that everyone robs everyone else in these pitches, so we sat and looked at some of them as they stripped, putting their shoes under the bed legs and sitting the bed on top of the shoes so that no one stole them during the night. They put the rest of their clothing into the pillowcases so we followed suit.

Within a few days our money was all spent so we wandered around trying to get dish washing jobs. We were hungry and had nowhere to sleep until we found a back close where we huddled together with our jackets over our heads. During the day we went to the train station and slept on the benches. If we had tried to sleep there at night, the cops would have picked us up and discovered that I had blown from the approved school. One night we were wandering about when the cops came and arrested us and took us into the police station. They questioned us but we already had stories and false names prearranged so, when they separated us and found our stories corresponding, they let us go. A few nights later when we were very hungry we heard two guys speaking with Scottish accents so we asked them for some cash. They had just come back from a night at the dog racing and had done very well so they took us for a big meal and gave us a couple of pounds. This really made our day. It is a great feeling to find people like that when you have nothing.

A few nights later, in a state of hunger, we were walking along this road looking for a place to sleep when lo and behold there in front of us was a shop window lying broken and inside were transistor radios. We looked about and the place was very dark and quiet so I reached in and grabbed a transistor and as we turned to go the lights and engine of a car across the street came to life and made for us and we were pounced upon. It was the cops. Apparently this was an old trick. If a window was smashed and the stuff stolen before the cops arrived, then they would lie in wait for the first unsuspecting victim. In many ways it was the most unexpected thing that could have happened to us. Even though the musician's job was becoming a dream in the distance, then the dishwashing, the last thing we expected was to be arrested because we had been keeping out of bother. But something had to give, as we couldn't carry on in this way with no real sleep or meals. After a brief court appearance we were taken to Shepherd's Bush Remand Home which we found to be much easier than Larchgrove. On the way there, we were being driven in a police van along a busy street when, by sheer coincidence, I saw my brother Tommy who was in London working. I shouted out of the window to him and he came along to the Remand Home to visit me. My pal and I were always hungry and we were a joke in the place for when they shouted that extra food was available, no matter what it was, we would make a mad rush for it. After another court appearance, I was ordered back to the approved school under the supervision of one of the Brothers who had been sent down for me. My pal was remanded for probation reports.

On the train journey, the Brother brought two pack lunches and I consumed mine immediately while he fussed and pecked over his, much to my annoyance. Eventually he fell asleep leaving a sandwich and an apple on the table in front of him with me sitting there looking at it. So while he slept I ate his apple saying to myself that I could tell him that it rolled off the table while he slept but as he didn't waken for some time I ate his sandwich too. I knew he had to waken up and I knew he would be raging at me so I started thinking up elaborate excuses about where the food had gone to. Instead, when he woke up, I closed my eyes, pretending to sleep and I could hear him searching about for his food. I kept my eyes closed for a long time and when I did open them he sat reading a book looking bloody furious. When the trolley came round for coffee he bought only one for himself and said nothing to me.

As a punishment for running away I was to be kept in and not allowed home for a long time. I also had to wear short khaki trousers for a period. The standard punishment for kids running away from the Approved School was the "pants" (a leather belt battered over the bare arse) but for me this was the easiest part. I had a great deal of respect for Brother Paul so that being brought back and having to face him was the hardest part of it all as I felt that I had let him down, and in many ways I had.

When I returned from absconding to London, I painted a lovely picture and exaggerated it saying that the streets really were paved with gold. Within a few days, lots of kids were absconding and heading for London, some being caught on the Edinburgh Road trying to hitch a lift. Now some of them had run away before and knew full well they would go to Borstal if they did so again. But it made no difference. There was this glamour part to it all that as kids we could never see past. Around this time there was an outbreak of gang fighting in Barlinnie prison when the "Scurvy" gang were making headlines and lots of stabbings were taking place. We in St John's loved this and would all talk about it, saying that we would prefer to be doing our time in Barlinnie rather than here, as that was where the real tough guys were.

Brother Paul had a scheme going by which kids in the latter part of their sentence could get an outside job in preparation for going out. I was given a chance on this and it meant going out in the morning to a job and returning afterwards to the school each night. At the end of the week we would hand in our wages and get ten shillings spending money. I got a job in the Gorbals Sawmills that was known locally as a "slave camp". The hard labour of it didn't really matter to me because it allowed me to go home for lunch. I lost the job but didn't tell the Brothers this as it would have been a set-back in terms of my being released for good. At the same time I had to make up the wages so I went out stealing and would go in on the Friday to the room where the Brother took the wages of the workers and marked them in a big book and when asked for my wage slip I pretended I'd lost it. It was a struggle for me getting the wages each week but this carried on for about three weeks. One Saturday night I arrived back in the Approved School after my day out and quite by chance bumped into Brother Paul in the main entrance and spontaneously asked him when I could be liberated. He simply turned round and told me to go home. I too turned round and ran into the night where it was dark and the rain was cascading down beautifully. I jumped on the first bus afraid that he would come after me saying it was all a joke. I sat on the top floor next to the window watching the rain cleanse the city streets and in a strange way wash away with it the strain that I had been under. My entry to St John's had been very strange but then so had my exit.

In a way I left it a much harder person as it tore me from my family for a period, giving me confidence amongst kids my own age who were unknown to me, letting me see that I could more than hold my own.

On leaving the Approved School I was able to get a job with my brother Tommy, who by this time was working in the shipyards in Govan, but I only stayed there for a short period. Although free from the school, I was still on Licence for a year which meant a form of probation under the condition that I could be recalled at any time. The person doing the supervising was the school Welfare Officer and I didn't see much of him though he was quite a nice helpful guy.

I left the job in the shipyards to return to London. Once there, I got a flat in Elephant and Castle. One night I wandered over to Kings Cross where most Scottish guys hang around and there I met plenty from the Gorbals and in particular Frank Wilson and Artie Austin. I was very glad to see them and they me. These were the guys that I used to idolise as did all the kids in the district, so I had a feeling of awe being with them. Frank is small with fairish hair and broad shoulders. He has a strong good-looking face with white even teeth. His eyes are blue and penetrating and seem to mirror his mind which is quick and very smart in a business-like fashion. His fighting abilities were something to be admired as he was very tough and had a reputation for being able to knock out men taller than himself with one punch. When he was a kid he was keen on amateur boxing and dabbled in it for a spell, but he was more interested in street fighting and became entangled in the "Cumbie" gang. He was the leader and was well respected and feared in the gang circles. Frank stayed in a room and kitchen in the Gorbals with his mother, brother and sisters. He was always a serious sort of guy who gave the picture of being straight out of

Chicago in the twenties. He could name all the gangsters from that era and go into detail on the set-up of organised crime in the States. To date he had been in Remand Homes, Approved School and had served one or two small petty prison sentences. From an early age Frank had also been running around the streets and learning all the tricks of the trade which one could pick up.

Artie Austin is over six feet tall, with broad shoulders and going prematurely bald. He had a fantastic personality, good looks and was full of life and would start singing at the first sight of a stage or a party. I started going around with them and we kept very much to ourselves, though through stealing we had to mix occasionally with London guys to fence our goods. But we kept away from the known thieves. If I had plenty of nerve before, I had double the amount now as I was intent on impressing Frank and Artie, though I would never admit this to them. London was a dream as it was so big that one could hit different parts of it each day and so remain anonymous. I stole anything, specialising in nothing. I would take things from lorries, shops and anywhere else that was vulnerable. Life was a merry-go-round of wastage with me stealing to socialise. I would take pills (purple hearts) and wander around the West End in a daze. These pills as well as keeping one awake gave one a strong urge to talk, and I would look for an empty ear and bore it to tears. I would go into a shop to buy something as simple as a newspaper with the eyes popping out of my head and fall into a long drawn-out discussion with the shop assistant almost striking him catatonic with boredom. In the local pubs there were lots of prostitutes and I would hang around with them. They were trouble as they would start fights knowing someone was there to do their fighting but they were good hearted. It was fun for me and one of them from the Glasgow area, Irene, used to take me to this club where marijuana was sold and we would get stoned. It was great listening to all the kinky stories that they told, and being with them broadened my sexual experience.

Sometimes we would get fed up with London and return to Glasgow for a spell and this was when I would bask in the glory as Frank and Artie were looked up to by the local kids of my age and those older than me. I was climbing the local social ladder and quite frankly it was going to my head. But mixing and going around with these older guys I felt that I had to continually prove myself. Neither Frank nor Artie put this pressure on me but it was just something that was happening, the pressures of my situation.

I still got on with the guys of my own age and drank with them and there was no need for me to boast as it was the talk of the district anyway. I would do crazy things very much to test myself and although they were crazy, they seemed sane enough under the cloud of booze and pills, and I thought nothing of them.

On leaving a party one night, in a house full of my pals, I went round to a rival gang corner where the "Bee Hive" loiter and started shouting "Cumbie" slogans and attacking the leader of their gang with a brick. No sooner had I done this when they pounced on me, throwing me face down in the street and pinning me there while someone smashed beer bottles over my head (screw tops) and started cutting me on the back of the neck and head with the jagged glass top. The group made off. I got to my feet feeling the liquid running down my neck and back, thinking I was badly cut and that it was blood but I continued to shout the slogans. I was still standing there, soaking wet, full of pills and booze, shouting "Cumbie", when the Black Maria arrived and I was thrown into the back of it. In the van I started to argue with the cops and they didn't take too kindly to that. Arriving at the cop shop, even more bloodied, I was charged at the police bar and spat a mouthful of blood on the desk sergeant. This infuriated them which they made plain to me physically. I woke the following morning in a white tiled cell with a sore face and head, my clothes sticking to me with blood. I was charged with breach of the peace and making a nuisance of myself. When asked what had happened to my face I told the magistrate that I had fallen so was given a fine and let loose.

There is no doubt that when I was sober, alone and faced with reality I hated myself, almost as though I was aware of the self-destructive course I was on but unable to do anything about it. I was lost. The only way out was to get involved in more devilment and booze. It wasn't as though I was getting into all of this and had no feeling about it, for I did but there was just this completely lost feeling, as I felt myself getting deeper and deeper into it. Yet on the other side, when I was with my pals, there was the feeling that it was okay and that having attacked a gang single handed the previous night, I had in some way proved myself and gained enough confidence to fight alongside them. I had this hunger to be recognised, to establish a reputation for myself and it acted as an incentive being with the top guys in the district at sixteen. There was this inner compulsion for me to win recognition amongst them. There were times when I could see that the others were feeling the same but none of us would put it to each other in words.

Things in my home were going smoothly enough and though I was getting into a lot of trouble, my Ma hadn't a clue about it. Other wives and mothers in the district would hear of it but wouldn't tell my Ma, as there would be this protective thing going on. This wasn't for my Ma only; it was a common thing and basically due to the fact that neighbours didn't want to give the mother any more worries than she already had. There was also the fact that people minded their own business. Occasionally I would return to Ma's and stay for a bit as in many ways it was like re-entering the womb where I could recuperate from the pressures and tensions of the wild side of life. I'm sure Ma heard the occasional rumour; I can't believe they escaped her completely. If she did she seldom said and maybe she thought that I was as much a man as I'd ever be and, with not staying in the house, was leading my own life. This is not to say that she was objective about it. There is no doubt that anything she did hear would have torn a piece from her heart as she loved me and all of us very much. If Ma did mention anything then I would deny it, even though it was probably true, as I could never have admitted my way of life to her.

My two older brothers were working and Harry was still at school. I was the occasional lodger. All of us got on fantastically well together and there was this very strong family feeling amongst us which extended to my aunts and uncles. We were very close and loyal to each other. Ma still held her three part-time jobs and seemed to think that she couldn't do without them. I was stealing materials that would have made her household work easier but there was no way that I could even attempt to bring this up as I knew she wouldn't have any of it. I had one aunt that I could talk to about this and I asked her to persuade Ma to take some of the goods but she wouldn't try either. I thought this was crazy as some of my pals would give their parents stolen goods and I would have liked to have done the same. There would be times when I entered the house after being absent for weeks and I would be accepted as though I had never been away. Of course there were times when I would tell Ma that I was working in London but this wasn't a lie for lying's sake but because I knew it would ease her mind. I'm not sure that she believed me at these times but I felt it would give her an alternative version to the other rumours she might hear. I guess I worked on the principle that most mothers listen only to the good about their own brood.

Artie Austin and I started working as a team while Frank and the others went their way to do their own thing for a spell. We worked out of Glasgow taking a plane to Birmingham, Manchester, or London and stealing whatever came our way. Artie was a guy for the good times and we swept along together on this. Sometimes we would go to these places and not touch a drink while we were working but, returning home, life would be a haze created by booze which cleared long enough for us to take another trip to make more cash to spend on more booze. In many ways it was great as Artie could sing very well and we would always be at parties having a good time. He was Americanised and wore clothes from the States and had a yankee way about him. With his balding hair and me looking like a kid, we were an odd looking couple of pals. One day he disappeared to the States and the next I heard he was in New York.

Part Two

6

Meanwhile I was busy thieving and fighting, still trying to gain a position for myself, which I already had but couldn't recognise. Even if I had, I doubt if I'd have stopped. The law of averages meant that I had to "fall" again as I was exposing myself to the law too much, and before very long it came. I was arrested for shopbreaking, only this time I was taken to Barlinnie Prison.

Although quite new to me, going to Barlinnie didn't hold the same fear as the Remand Home had. There was apprehension and excitement on facing the unknown but there was also this feeling of having "arrived". I was just coming on for seventeen when I went to Barlinnie. I was taken in the prison van with lots of others, mostly old men who had been there many times before. Each of us were taken into the reception area and locked into very small boxes, two to a box. There was a piece of wood nailed to the wall meant for us to sit on but there was only room enough for one. The box was about three feet by three feet in size and about eight feet in height. These are what are known as the "dog boxes" as that's just what they're like. The old guy locked in with me tried to kid me that this was where we slept but I was familiar with the prison routine as I had heard others describe it time after time. There was barely room to stand in it never mind eat together, but they gave us lunch in a small bowl with a spoon so that we had to stand and eat out of the bowl and rest the cup of soup on the small wooden strip that was meant to be the chair. A bolt on the outside locked us in and the doors would be opened by "trusty" prisoners who had cushy reception jobs. Usually these were posts filled by the white-collar criminal.

I was called out and taken in front of a desk where a screw told me to undress in front of all these other screws and "trusties". I did so while he marked all my personal belongings and property onto a card. I was then asked a series of questions: Have you ever been in a mental institution? Ever had venereal diseases? Any insanity in your family? A long list of questions while I stood there with a towel wrapped around my middle. I was then given a bath — we were only allowed three inches of water which a "trusty" measured out with a key that he had for the taps. After a couple of minutes a screw came along telling everyone to soap off. At first I thought he was joking — I hadn't had any time to put soap on. From there, the group of prisoners were taken to the prison hospital and made to drop our trousers while a screw came along to inspect us for crabs. Anyone who had them was whisked away, shaved and put in isolation. The rest of us were taken to the untried hall. It was a massive place and the sound of men's voices, feet on metal stairways, keys jangling, and the loud bang of slamming cell doors was what hit me at first. Those prisoners out doing working tasks would all look over the galleries to see who was amongst the newcomers. The head screw at the desk gave each of us a cell to go to. I was on the third flat, but on going upstairs I was shouted at by a number of familiar faces, coming from either the district or the Remand Home or the Approved School. It was a comforting feeling to see so many people I knew and I felt better now that I had met them. On reaching the third flat I was put into a cell with two other guys, who had been there for some time.

When the door was closed there was the expected questioning about what I was in for and where I came from and vice versa. There was one single bed which was a board nailed to the floor, and a bunk which swayed at the slightest movement and I got the bottom bed there. The blankets were filthy with lots of burn holes from guys smoking. The cell was filthy and there was an overwhelming stench of urine that came from the three stained chamber pots in the far corner. There was no escaping from this stench. There was a table that we were to use for eating on but it was covered with dog ends. There were three old mugs and these were for our water to last us through the night and for our tea when it came round. Men in the untried hall could stay there for nigh on four months waiting on trial and this could be extended by the court. The prisoners were locked up twenty three hours a day and allowed out for half an hour in the morning and afternoon to walk around the prison yard. There were fifty cells on each flat and four flats. Sometimes there were over one hundred men in the fifty cells. The stench in the halls was appalling as there were only two toilets for each flat and men would have to "slop out" their chamber pots in these toilets. Each man wore a suit of prison clothes, ill fitting, with either or both of the sleeves or trouser bottoms rolled up.

This was where I was, locked in a cell with two strangers and determined that I wasn't going to use the chamber pot, come what may. I would lie there bursting for the toilet and refuse to do it, hoping the door would open soon so I could go to the one outside. The other two guys in the cell were used to it all and used it without any hang ups and when they did I would turn to the wall as I felt very embarrassed sitting there watching them sitting on the chamber pot. The meals were piled onto a small wheel barrow and pushed round the gallery. A screw would come in advance and open the cell door as the barrow reached it. "Trusties" would give us the food in a metal bowl and a screw would be behind the barrow to close the door. All this took a long time which meant that the food was always cold. A hot meal was never to be seen. The screws opened and shut doors and ordered us about but nothing more than that. They never seemed to ask for anything in a normal voice, everything was said in very loud shouts and this struck me forcibly when coming into prison for the first time.

The daily routine was for the doors to open at 6 a.m. and all the prisoners would rush out and form long lines to empty their chamber pots and get water for shaving and washing. Then it was lock up and breakfast was brought round the doors after which we would sit about the cell either lying with our eyes closed or speaking to each other; but there were often long periods of silence. At mid-morning we would be opened up for half an hour's exercise and if it was raining then we would be marched round the gallery on the second flat which meant a crowd of men would be crammed in together walking round in circles.

Exercise gave me a chance to see all the guys that I knew and there were plenty of familiar faces. All the guys from the district greeted me warmly and we talked about things, getting the latest news from the guy last in. We would talk about what each of us were in for and what our chances were. Some would be in for serious offences, and others would be in for minor ones. I was tipped for a Borstal Report and Borstal. The guys from my district in the prison were well connected and saw that I got books, papers and other small extras. All these things were the wee perks that made it seem better. After the morning exercise, it was lock up for a period, then lunch would come round then we'd be locked up again till mid-afternoon when the second half hour exercise period would be allowed. After that we would be locked up till after the evening meal then a few minutes to slop out and then that was it till the following morning.

I didn't smoke and I would watch the guys in my cell roll up their dog ends into cigarettes then roll up the dog ends from that.

It was horrible watching this, as being a non-smoker, I hated touching dog ends let alone finding them floating in a tea cup; but these were things that happened in a cell with two strangers. At night, guys locked in cells would shit on a piece of paper and throw it out of the window rather than have it lying in the cell all night. This was called "bomb throwing" and we would lie in our cells at night hearing the bombs hit the concrete yard outside. The screws would go round with a prisoner in the morning with a barrow and he was nicknamed the "bomb disposal man". It was either an old meths drinker or a first offender who got this job. Sometimes the screws patrolling the yards at night would catch a guy for it and he would be put on a disciplinary charge and be labelled "the mad bomber" and he would keep the name till the next one was caught.

Each of us in the cell would have a small metal basin to wash and brush our teeth in. Frequently guys would crack up and everyone would lie very quiet while someone smashed up his cell by breaking the small windows and the table and anything else that he could. If there were two others in the cell they would stand by and let him go ahead knowing that the guy would have to get it out. Afterwards he would be taken to the punishment cell on the bottom flat where at least he had privacy. There were three cells there including a padded one. I had a visit from my Ma and she was able to put some sweets in for me as this was a privilege reserved for untried prisoners who had not yet been found guilty. The visit was fifteen minutes and I had to speak through a glass and wire grill. It was difficult to hear each other as it meant bending way over to do so.

I was taken to court and given a Borstal Report by the judge and remanded for twenty-one days in Barlinnie while the report was being compiled. On the last week I was sent for and an Assistant Governor took me into a cell. As he went in the light conked out, so he sent for a bulb and got me to climb up onto the table to fix it in. I spoke to him for a few minutes and he said that by the way I had climbed the chair to put the bulb in I evidently needed more experience in burglary, so he was recommending me to go to Borstal. It was all said in a jocular fashion. When I went back to court I was sentenced to a Borstal Training. During the three weeks of my reports this was the only official I'd seen. It seemed a crazy system, not one to be taken too seriously. There was a great deal of overcrowding in Borstal at that time so the boys had to remain in one of the halls for convicted prisoners for about six or eight weeks till there was a vacancy for them. The system was the same as in the untried hall, apart from the fact that we were taken to work for a few hours each day, but as there was practically nothing for us to do we would be made to sit around or clean out our cells and polish them. We all had Borstal uniforms and not prison ones. The time went very slowly, though it did give us a chance to get to know the others who would be going to Borstal with us.

The atmosphere was very much like approved school only this time we were in prison. The majority of us would have preferred to have done our time in Barlinnie rather than go to Borstal where it was all bull and kids' treatment. We all classed ourselves as men. The talk was all women and crime, but crime was the main topic and we all boasted about what good crooks we were and exaggerated the size of our hauls. I would love it when the guys in my district smuggled over tobacco and sweets to me. This was a good prestige thing as tobacco was the prison currency and I could give it to one of the guys who smoked and he would buy me toothpaste and soap from his wages. Not all of the kids waiting for their place in Borstal had been in approved school, so it was very much a time to weigh everyone up and make new friends while at the same time trying to establish a position so as to know where we stood in the pecking order. Amongst us were a few kids who had previously done their Borstal training but had fallen into trouble again while out on licence. This licence thing was the same procedure as in approved school where hardly anyone did the full three years but for the remainder of that time they would be kept under supervision. These guys had been out, fallen into trouble and were now back in, but rather than return them to Borstal they were put into Barlinnie and called "Borstal Recalls". Those of us who hadn't done our Borstal were always quizzing them to find out what it was like but they would only tell of the good laughs they had had and would reminisce in a pleasant nostalgic way. They told us a bit about the strict and petty bullshit that went on but they seemed to gloss over this.

At last my time came to go there and I was taken in a van along with five other kids, one of whom had been in Approved School with me. We said we were sick of being treated like kids. We also felt very apprehensive as we'd heard a lot of bad things about the screws in the Borstal. So in a way we were reluctant participants before we even arrived. We were taken into a reception area and given Borstal suits, which were coloured black and called Battle

Dress, and a red striped shirt with heavy black shoes. The first small rebellion from me was with the screw giving out laces for the shoes and demanding a "thank you, sir" from each of us. When he came to me I refused to answer him. It was very interesting as he had been full of confidence up till that moment and he now became unsure of himself as I was an unknown quantity. He glossed over the affair and put it down as nothing, but to me it was a moral victory.

Borstal was made up of what they term Houses, and newcomers or "Rookies" as we were called, went into Douglas House for the initial two months of bullshit, and from there we would be put through to either Bruce, Rothesay or Wallace Houses. Wallace House was reserved for the baddies as they had cells for the occupants, whereas the other Houses had dormitories. Douglas House, where I was as a rookie, had single cells the same as Wallace House and each cell had a bed, a small table, and a rough wardrobe for hanging up the battle dress suit. Everything was made of wood except for the bed and every one of these had to be scrubbed, thoroughly scrubbed, each and every day.

The daily routine was that a pail of water had to be taken into each cell the previous night (a bucket, cloth and scrubber were in every cell) so that immediately on rising everyone would box their bedding in military fashion and then proceed to scrub every wooden article in the cell while a screw came round inspecting to see that we were doing it properly. If he had cause to enter the cell he would shout for the borstal boy to stand to attention while he went round looking in corners for dirt and even if none was found we could be told to do it again. Hundreds of kids must have scrubbed the cell I was in before I came, for it was spotless and I reasoned that it couldn't get any cleaner than it was so I would never put too much effort into scrubbing except when I heard the approaching screw. I could never make a bed military style and this was my weak spot as it would be torn apart by the inspecting screw every other day. I really hated this. Everything in the place had to be done "on the double", so that after scrubbing the cell we had to dress immaculately with shining shoes and best dress and stand to attention, just like all the other places I had been in, and then march single file for breakfast. This was in the main area on the bottom floor of Douglas House. After breakfast we were lined up and stood to attention then split into groups, some of whom would go to a classroom for school lessons while the others would scrub the hall area and other parts of the Borstal.

My rebellious actions took the form of never standing to attention and I would do this when the screws shouted during the line-ups, so that they could never see me. In many ways it was me retaining a part of myself. The minute the screw's back was turned, I would do nothing, so if we were scrubbing and the screw went to look at someone else or do something else then I would wipe the floor with a wet cloth to give it a wet look or I would just rest my knees which would be sore from kneeling down. I was caught at this once by two screws and they came across very heavy, shouting at me but I told them I had been doing it properly. They kept shouting, as they stood over me, telling me to scrub but I got up and threw the bucket of water over the floor and was locked up for it. This was being "put on report" and an offence against good discipline. The following morning I was taken in front of the Headmaster, who was called the Housemaster, and he punished me by giving me a fine. The group who scrubbed in the morning went to school in the afternoon and vice versa. We were given physical training every day and taken into a gym for this. There were rumours that the gym teacher was a black belt at Karate, although it was just as likely to be judo. I'm sure these gymnasium teachers used to spread these rumours themselves as almost every institution that I had been in had one. The P.T. class was very hard going and we would be pushed to the limits.

It was amazing the number of kids that I knew in the Borstal from elsewhere. Due to be liberated was Ben Conroy, and coming in just behind me was Larry Winters. Many guys from my district were in other Houses and sending me over toothpaste, soap and tobacco. The wages for Rookies were very small so receiving these extras from my friends was very helpful. It meant that I didn't have to rely on the wages made from scrubbing, as the favourite punishment was to take money off someone's wages for the slightest thing. There was a great deal of discontent amongst the kids in the Rookies and with this there was always talk of rioting which would raise itself to a very intense level. I would like to have led one but it was all talk and never seemed to come off.

One night, while lying in my cell, I was particularly dreading the thought of getting up in the morning and going through all the scrubbing. I had had enough of it and wanted to get away from it all, so I put all the furniture from my cell in front of the door barricading myself in. I lay there and listened to the nightshift patrol making his way along the gallery looking through judas holes on the way. When he came to mine he shouted for me to clear the judas hole and I told him to take a fuck at himself and just lay there. He went away and I listened to every noise. It was great to lie there feeling that for the first time in months, I was able to decide something for myself. I heard reinforcements coming and they tried to put the door in but I had it well and truly barricaded. Eventually the Governor was called in and they tried to talk me out. It was a big thing for the Governor to be called in at night. It was near morning when I came out but while I was locked in I felt really good and very much my own man with these people speaking to me as a human being for the first time, even if it was only to get something out of me. It didn't really matter what happened from there as I felt I had nothing more to gain by staying in. When I came out one of the people responsible for running the place was there along with the patrol screws and I was taken to the punishment cells, known as the "Digger". We went through a series of corridors to parts of the Borstal that I had never been to before. All the time that I walked I was expecting to be attacked by the screws as I heard there were lots of beatings going on in the place. However, no one touched me, and I was taken into this hall area that was full of cells. At the end of the hall a section of the bottom flat was partitioned off and I was taken through a door there and downstairs to a sort of dungeon place and this was my introduction to the "Digger".

I was put into one of the cells and fell asleep, but was soon wakened by a loud bell ringing which meant that I had to get up and box my bedding. My door opened, I was told to put my bed outside the door, then it was closed again. I was given a pail and scrubber to do the floor and there was no dodging it as someone stood over me all the time. I was given breakfast and then taken out for P.T. into a small yard. Half way through the morning I was dressed up and taken to the Governor's office. I was marched in and told to give my name and number which I did and was given seven days in the punishment cells. There were only a couple of kids in the Digger with me and three times a day we were taken to the P.T. class and put through a very gruelling circuit. Between trips to the gym we were taken to a small yard and made to scrape rusty beds with wire brushes and at any moment while cleaning them we would be ordered to stop and start running round the small yard in circles with our big heavy boots on. The whole day was made up of going from one of these tasks to another so that within a short period there was that super fit feeling, but no healthy mind with it as I hated the bastards. I was always aware of the helpless position I was in down in the Digger so I didn't provoke anyone.

Being under the ground and well out of the way, there was this constant feeling of isolation. They got at me twice while I was in there. The first time a screw came in and shouted at me to stand to attention which I did, but apparently I had clenched fists and that's not the proper way, but a boxer's way, so he asked if I could fight and I said yes, so he slapped me on the face while I just stood there not daring to hit him back. The other time was when I was caught dodging the scrubbing. The screw came in with another, punching me on the back of the head and kicking me on the side as I pretended to be scrubbing my floor. They had crept up to the judas hole and had been looking through for some time, furious at seeing me sitting there resting. On both occasions they left locking the door leaving me inside with my anger and my impotence. There were times when I could hear other kids getting it but all this harsh treatment was to make sure that we didn't come back again. After my seven days, I was taken up to Douglas House and back into my old cell. Barricading my cell door was considered a game thing by the kids and it had the same effect on them as my Larchgrove experiences had had on the kids in Bonny's. They began to put me on a pedestal and in this way I was asserting my position.

Visits from home would be every three or four weeks and the "Rookies" had their visits from their families together. My Ma and Auntie would come up with good butter on bread rolls and hot pies from the local bakery and I would gorge myself on these luxuries. Both Ma and Aunt Peggy would cross-examine me as to how I was doing and I would tell them I was doing great. They brought me up to date with all the news of the district, which I was eager to hear. Things went smoothly enough for me because the screws left me alone not wanting to stir things up too much. I got into a fight with another boy one day and scratched him with a dart. I saw an elderly man dressed in an old coat and hat standing in front of me watching. I thought he was the janitor but in fact he was the Governor, John Oliver. I was to find this out next morning when I went in front of him and was given ten days in the Digger. No doubt they thought I was a nut for going back twice but there I was. The routine was the same but it didn't seem so hard this time as I was familiar with it all.

Eventually I was allocated a place in Wallace House and put in the next cell to a boy from my district in the Gorbals. The routine here was the same as the "Rookies" for a newcomer. There were lots of guys I knew and it was like a meeting of old friends from old places. One hot summer's night the guy next door and I were lying on the floor speaking through the side of the cell wall to each other. This was made possible by way of the heating system which was a metal pipe running from cell to cell. We could hear the night patrol going round as we complained to each other about all the scrubbing. I suggested to him that we should go through the actions of scrubbing the cell as though we were sleep-walking and he agreed. My neighbour set to it but I didn't and I could hear him scrubbing and moving furniture while I lay under the bed covers and laughed like hell. The night patrol man lifted the cover of the judas hole and probably could not believe his eyes. He called the guy's name softly but he continued scrubbing so the night man left to get another screw and they both took turns to look through, till eventually my neighbour returned everything to its rightful place, pulled back the bed-covers and went to bed. When the patrol left we got up to the pipe and laughed together at it. The following morning while scrubbing the floor my neighbour was called down and he vanished for the rest of the day. Late that afternoon he returned and told me he had been taken to the doctor's and given a thorough going over and was taken outside for some tests with wires to his head. We had a right laugh at this and all the more so when he was excused scrubbing for a spell. I met another guy in there from Glasgow, Willie Smith, who came from Govan. Willie had done Borstal Training before and this was his second helping. He had a bad scar on his face from a knife fight. Both of us were to become very close pals.

While in Borstal I was taken to hospital and put through an operation for glandular Tuberculosis. This was a shock to me as my health had always been very good. In many ways being in hospital was fun and I enjoyed the good food which the rest of the patients seemed to dislike. An old man in the next bed told me to watch out for the Borstal boy who was up the ward somewhere but when I told him that I was the Borstal boy, we started speaking about it and got on very well. I met a nurse there and fell in love, but it only lasted till my second operation. She was a very nice person although she lived in a different world from me. I was eventually returned to Borstal and given a period in the hospital there which seldom had a patient in it as it was more a show place than anything else. I was to be given injections every day by the hospital screw. During this period in hospital I should have been given my liberation date having been in for the appropriate time, but with me in the hospital, the Board, who decide such things, seemed to forget all about me. So when the screw came in to give me my injection I told him to stick it up his own arse and I refused treatment till my case was reconsidered. So they gave me my liberation date, which was two months away. I was given light tasks till that day came.

During this time there was a tremendous rebellion by a lot of the kids. The Digger, which had once struck fear into the hearts of the majority, lost its reputation, which was upsetting for the screws. There was a crowd lying down there who were refusing to do anything and smashing everything that they could get their hands on. I would constantly be engaged in smuggling them down tobacco and other small luxuries while it lasted. Most of the kids involved in this were boys from St John's or my district though there were one or two from other approved schools and this breakdown of obedience resulted in the kids being split up and one or two being sent to Barlinnie to complete their terms. By the time I was released I had been in nearly fifteen months and during that time I had made lots of new friends and consolidated many old friendships from earlier places. When the guys and the screws asked what I was going to do when I got out I pretended that everything was all set up for me and that I would go out to plenty of good things. I had nothing, and was going out to nothing, and felt terribly insecure. Although I would never have admitted it, there was a feeling within me that I was being torn away from a lot of good friends and relationships that I had built up. All I had to wear was the Borstal clothes, although they gave each guy a jacket and trousers when being released, but these were such crappy clothes that no one would be seen dead in them and this only added to my insecurity. I was put on the train with the other liberated guys. We were all feeling great and played cards on the journey home with me winning all the money. That eased my feeling somewhat as it gave me a couple of pounds. As loyal as ever, my Ma and the other parents met us at the station in Glasgow. The Welfare Man was there too to organise our licence arrangements and fix us up with a man to visit every so often to report on how we were doing.

It was great to be back in the Gorbals as fourteen months was a long time to be away, certainly my longest. The streets were the same, with the kids running all over the place, horses and carts carrying coal and all the same guys loitering on the street corners, some drinking out of bottles. Some of them shouted for me to stop and they asked how I was. Neighbours were stopping Ma too, speaking to us and giving me a couple of bob. I loved the place and felt very warm and happy to be back. As I neared my street I could see a few buildings had been knocked down and the contractors were in putting foundations in for sky-scrapers. People were being taken out of the houses around us and put into new housing schemes. These skyscrapers were about the first to be built in the Gorbals, but there was Ma saying that she refused to leave as she was happy in her own wee house with neighbours that she had known all her life. She made it plain that if they wanted to get her into a new housing scheme they would have to drag her there bodily. There was a lot of fear about this in the district and there were people staying in buildings that had been vacated, refusing to move till they were rehoused in the Gorbals. There were numerous cases of people being moved to new housing schemes only to come back to houses in their old district.

Ma made a big breakfast for me when we arrived home. It was great to be in the house and see all the small everyday things that I had missed. I remember the surprise when I lifted a cup to drink my tea. In Borstal all cups are pint sized mugs so the small household cup felt like a feather. I ate all my food then made for the house of a girlfriend. I had been going with this girl off and on as she went about with our gang for a time. She was at home as she had heard I was coming out. It was great having sex again. I screwed this girl silly and it was beautiful.

The Borstal doctor had made arrangements for me to see my own doctor, which I did the next day. He said that I would have to go into hospital for more treatment and made arrangements for the following day. I was sick at this news as I was just out and I wanted time to see everything; but I went anyway. The treatment in the hospital meant daily injections. Everyone in the place had T.B. of varying degrees, but I got on very well with the people there. I was the luckiest guy there as my illness was only minor in comparison to some of them who must have known they wouldn't live very long. What hit me forceably in that hospital was the dedication of the nursing staff and the lengths to which they went to help the patients. Some of us were allowed out into the grounds for a few hours and it was very nice. One day I was lying there in bed when a group of my pals came up. Amongst them was John McCue who had just been released from his four year period at Peterhead. I had known of John and had seen him lots of times but I was only a kid then and he wouldn't have remembered me so I was very chuffed when he came up with the others. John was known as a bit of a crazy guy. When fighting he had a fantastic sense of honour about him and there was a lot of respect for him. I had pangs of longing to return to the district and one night while walking the grounds of the hospital a taxi pulled up with two of my pals inside. They had just come into some money and wanted to see me and give me a few pounds. The temptation was too much; I found it just too easy; so I jumped in with them and we headed for the Gorbals.

We went into one of the bars that we used and Frank was sitting there so it was a night for celebration. After closing time, we went to look for a girl that we knew. On reaching the house we went upstairs to fetch her. I lifted a coal hammer from a bunker that was standing on the stairway. I did this because I knew that this girl had brothers who were pretty tough and who didn't like the liaison between their sister and us, and we were expecting them to be there too. We had to enter a very dark lobby to get to the door and sure as hell the brothers came out with a giant of a friend. Words were exchanged and I could *feel* the trouble about to start. A glass struck my hand so I brought the hammer down on them and that ended the whole matter then and there. We got the hell out of there. I split from the others and went to another girl I knew. The following morning I woke up to find a policeman at the door wanting to see me. I had immediate feelings of dread, but these passed when he explained that the hospital had reported me missing, so I told him I'd be returning. When I got back I was taken in by the nurse and given a bawling out as I had placed many of them in trouble. Apparently the other patients, noticing my absence had pulled back the covers making it look as though I was in the toilet. This worked for some time till a Matron doing her rounds during the night suspected. I really felt terrible, especially when they saw my cut hand which was pretty bad and the bother they went to, to stitch it up and take care of it. I felt the proper heel. Of course while I was lying there, friends of the guys I had hit the previous night were going around searching for me with the intention of doing me serious injury. During the rest of my period in hospital I was a saint, all I wanted was release. When I got out a few weeks later things had settled down somewhat and the trouble had ceased to be prominent.

John, Artie and I were going around together and it was one long party. Most of the time we were hanging around the

Gorbals. By this time the gang thing had ceased to exist for us and it was just pals. We would never shout Cumbie or anything like that as we had grown out of it and as a matter of fact all the other gangs that had existed and fought with us had all dispersed too, or had joined with some of their rivals on a friendly basis. For instance, Tam Comerford and Willie McPherson from the "Dixy Gang" were now hanging around with us. But although this had happened we were replaced by younger guys who became the Cumbie and such like so the gang system was being perpetuated.

We were using two pubs as a base in the Gorbals: "The Moy Bar" and "The Wheatsheaf Bar". The chargehands of these pubs were good to us and gave us more or less what we wanted for the sake of a quiet life. When I say a quiet life I mean just that as there had always been fights in their bars, either from the young gangs or others with too much booze in them. If young kids were out trying to make reputations and saw that the barman was a good friend of ours then they would cause no trouble, so it was in his interests to be good to us. There were other bars where we would go at the "demand" for booze and money, but not in these two. About this time the big breweries were taking over lots of the pubs and the guys in charge would be skimming off for themselves so they would end up in debt or with their books in a mess. So they asked us to see that they were robbed and this would be done and the robbery would usually clear their deficiency, and bring their stock situation back to square one.

Guys whom I met in Approved Schools and Borstal and Prison would frequently look me up to sell things for them that they had stolen or ask me to take part in jobs with them. We were all making the best of our institutional experience. We had come through the humiliations and degradations of these places together. We might never see each other from one year to the next but when we did there was that special bond that may not have had a great deal of strength, but was immediately recognisable. If any one of our friends in the prison wanted booze or pills and sent someone over to us for a contribution, then it would be given. This was called "putting a parcel in". So it wasn't a case of the guys on the outside forgetting those on the inside when they left prison. I can say without question that it is ex-prisoners who do more for ex-prisoners than any official organisation such as the After Care. It's just the done thing and something that the guy outside takes for granted which the guy inside really appreciates. Of course there is the odd guy who will leave one of these places and pull some stroke that is against the "code", but this doesn't happen often as he usually has to return to prison at some stage and that's when he will pay the penalty.

The "criminal code" isn't a thing that has been written up by top gangsters. It is an unwritten code of ethics. There are done things and things that are not done. It isn't the done thing to "grass" or inform on anyone. It isn't the done thing to "bump" or cheat someone from a robbery that you have all taken part in. There are lots of these unwritten rules that could fill another book but these are just two examples that exist between guys in crime and on the whole they abide by them.

In Glasgow three guys were causing quite a stir in the criminal world around this time and were becoming pretty big. They were Willie Smith and Malky and Willie Bennett, all from the Govan area. Willie Smith and I were firm friends and we would go down to Govan to see them all the while building a stronger friendship. All of us were young and not really established yet.

Meanwhile back in the Gorbals, Artie and I were moving around and picking up money here and there. We were in "The Wheatsheaf Bar" one night when two brothers, part of a large family of brothers who were very much a mob on their own, came in and tried to hassle the chargehand for booze or cash, so he called to us. We spoke to the brothers in a nice way because we didn't really want trouble with them. We walked outside the pub and along Ruthergien Road. I had a knife in my coat pocket, the brothers had bottles of beer and one had a tumbler. But while we walked the atmosphere began to get very hot and it ended up in a fight with the older brother jumping on my back. I pulled the knife and stuck it into his face while Artie grappled with the other then they ran off. We knew they were going for the rest of the family so we made for a street corner in Cumberland Street where we got together a group of friends and we all went looking for them, but they were not to be seen. However, on the way back we came across another group that we had had trouble with, and a running fight took place in Crown Street. There was quite a bit of stabbing and cutting going on and with the pubs just coming out the streets were crowded. To make matters worse there was a large crowd round a car accident blocking a part of Crown Street so there was panic when the fighting took place amongst them. When the police finally came the whole thing broke up but as a result lots of innocent people were injured.

I found Artie in a close covered in blood, he had a slash wound running the length of his face but when the blood was wiped off it was only a superficial cut and though it would leave a fine mark it wouldn't leave a bad scar. We were walking along Cumberland Street and I threw away my knife as police cars were all over the place. When they saw us they grabbed us into the squad car and took us to the police station. By now the political criminal code was very much ingrained in me and I said nothing to them. Any questions they had to put were met by a wall of silence. We were charged with seven serious assaults and locked up. Other guys had been injured in the fight but they wouldn't dare come forward for fear of being charged. Later we were taken to the Police Headquarters, charged again then locked up in the cells. While we were lying there the brothers we fought with had been to Artie's house, kicked the door off its hinges and raided the place, hoping to get him as he lay in bed. But only his old mother was there.

While lying in the cells awaiting these charges, I wasn't too upset as there had been a good fight and I wasn't thinking of it in terms of society but simply from the gang-fight point of view. At no time did I express concern for any of the people who were injured or give them any thought at all. The only feeling of any kind was my own misfortune at being caught. All through the night, a long line of detectives from the junior ranks to the most senior came in to see us, looking through the square judas hole and shouting names to me as they did to most prisoners. It didn't really affect us and I would laugh at them when they said it in the hope of showing them that it didn't matter what they said as they were the enemy and all bastards anyway. Both of us were given a series of Identification Parades the following day which was a Sunday and we were allowed to see our lawyers. On the Monday morning we were taken for fingerprinting and photographing, but by now I was familiar with the whole procedure. There was no more fear of the unknown.

Both of us were remanded to Barlinnie Prison and taken there. By this time all the guys in the place had heard we were coming and had the usual odds and ends like toothpaste, soap or sweets and reading material ready for us. There had been a lot of publicity about the assaults describing innocent people being injured and though the Press made a big thing out of it, the guys in the prison saw it in another way and they were immediately sympathetic to our getting caught. They asked what our chances were of getting off and how the I.D. parades went, and there they were assessing and judging the whole thing, as we did with each other's cases.

From any point of view the situation was bad but there was this unfeeling thing about it. Both of us were held till after the Christmas and New Year periods and I was given bail in January 1963. As I walked out of the prison gate I was met by Frank and we went home. We went back up to visit Artie and took him the things that he was allowed while waiting trial and we brought him up to date with the news.

About this time the gang of brothers were looking out for me and rumour had it that they were intent on crippling me. I was walking the streets with a revolver and a knife, ready for anything. Not long after being released on bail, I was buying the morning papers which come out the night before and I had a knife wrapped up in the newspaper, folding it very neatly and in my waistband was a Walther automatic pistol. I was approached by two beat cops who asked what I was doing out, and I told them that I was on bail awaiting trial. They followed me part way along the road little knowing what I was carrying. I had decided to leave for London as that was where Frank had been for a good few months and I felt I would be better off down there for the moment. But needing some cash, I managed to do a job stealing a load of whisky and was in a pub one night waiting to see a guy about selling it. The pub was near the Clyde waterfront and there were two exits, one into the main road and the other into a dark side street and I chose the latter. It was extremely dark and the snow was lying pretty thick on the ground when I walked out. Without any warning I was hit on the side of the head, a mighty blow, and my immediate reflex was to go for the weapon I had on me, but I was hit from the other side and dragged towards a small van. I began to struggle as the blows were systematically landed on my head and spreadeagled body. There was quite a group around hitting me with hammers and hatchets on the head, but paying particular attention to my kneecaps and my hands. I lay there feeling every blow land but shock seemed to wash away pain and all I could think of was would I live and all the while sickening blows were landing all over my body for what seemed an eternity. I was left lying unconscious in the snow in the middle of the street.

When I came to I saw people passing by in the main street and cars and buses flashing past. It all seemed very normal and I crawled over to a nearby dark close that had a faint gas light glowing and lay there trying to feel the extent of my damage. I knew that I was pretty bad and the pain was crippling whenever I moved. When I finally managed to get onto my feet I saw that gut was hanging out of my trouser bottom, and the blood was running down my face from head wounds. Every move was an effort as I crawled to get a taxi but I found it hard as they took me for a drunk man. I finally managed to get home to my Ma's and it was just like a "B" movie as I crawled into the house in a terrible state seeing the horror reflected on her face at my condition. I lost consciousness as I sat into the chair. Ma had two aunts in the house and they all came to the decision to call an ambulance which was a mistake because calling an ambulance meant the police would automatically arrive. I kept coming and going and remember the cops trying to get out of me what had happened and me saying that I had fallen.

I woke up in hospital. While the doctors were patching me up they told me that I would be in for some time, but I had other ideas. My problem was being unable to move, but this was resolved by the presence of Frank who had heard that I was in hospital and had come up. I signed myself out and he got transport and we left. No sooner had we arrived in my Ma's house when the cops were at the door — detectives. They were told that I was still in hospital but they went downstairs and waited in the car probably thinking that I hadn't arrived home yet. I was helped down to a neighbour's house to stay the night, every movement an agony. My legs at the knees had stiffened up and my back was a mass of bruises from the hammer blows. A large, deep wound was below my left knee-cap and my head was cut in several places all of which had stitches in them. What was worrying me was that the cops, knowing what was happening, were intent on arresting me on a holding charge as they anticipated all sorts of gang wars breaking out. Sleep was slow in coming that night as the pain was excruciating but I had time to think over the night's events. There was no fear now, unlike before when I had been grabbed by the mob; that was real fear. All my thoughts were on means of revenge, as a "come back" was important. This was a sign of strength in any group, as it would make others think twice about coming after me, if they knew I would come back for revenge. The following morning I was taken to a safe house to lie and rest.

The brothers who had done the damage were dropping it around the district that I was lying in the hospital crippled and that anyone else looking for trouble would know to expect the same. Within a few hours the rumour was going round that I was in a bad way and would never walk again. I discussed this with two friends and we decided that there was no way for an immediate retaliation but that we should blow these myths going round. I was half carried to a car and driven to a pub in the Gorbals. All my injuries were hidden by my hair and clothes, only the hand ones showed. The point was to blow the cripple thing and just to be there would discredit the rumours and the other mob. We managed to get some of the big mouths into the pub and when they saw me they immediately started talking about the rumour going round. We had a good laugh at them, though it was hurting me, but it was important for us to show a good front. We knew that when this reached the other mob they would be puzzled as they knew only too well that they had given me a thorough going over. The fact that I was sitting in a pub was the last thing they would be expecting. It was a small consolation but it was all worth it.

7

By this time the cops were getting really hot in their search for me and putting the pressure on, so I left for London. When I got there I started moneylending with another pal, using a pub that we frequented as a base. Moneylending at this time was a very flourishing business in Glasgow and though illegal was very much an acceptable thing in the districts. It worked by us lending money to people in the area, or who we knew were regulars in the pub. For every £1 that was loaned out, the borrower paid 20p. interest (4 shillings in the £). If the borrower didn't pay or missed a week then he payed a further 20p. and it went up 20p. each week till he paid. We had to do something with the money we had otherwise it would be squandered so we decided to make it earn more for us. The guys who were borrowing it were usually thieves and crooks of various sorts. They would ask for what they needed and it was given. It also meant that we didn't have to expose ourselves to taking risks daily as that was something I couldn't afford with this forthcoming trial. So while in London we kept mainly to ourselves apart from the guys we met in the moneylending. There was the usual existence of girls and clubs. Life was easy and things were very good for the short period I was there, but it came to an abrupt end.

One night in the West End I was stopped by an ordinary beat cop. He was being very nosey and persistent, wanting to know things and I could see that he was set on taking me along with him, so I punched him and put him on the ground. We ran with him in pursuit so we stopped and beat him up and tried to put him out, as my injuries meant that I couldn't get off on a good run. Finally we got him down, but while we were running police cars came and they caught me. I was taken to a cop station and put into a cell. In the cell I could hear a lot of cops outside and knew that they were coming in to have a go at me because no one has a go at the cops without getting their just beating. True to form, they all came in, kicking and punching me to the floor, and left me lying there. To be honest it wasn't very bad, my head had some bumps and my nose and mouth were cut, but on the whole it was next to nothing as they seemed to get in each other's way more than anything else.

Their pound of flesh taken, they took me and charged me with police assault and the following morning I appeared in front of the Magistrate Court where I pleaded not guilty, thinking I would get bail but they remanded me till the afternoon for trial and I thought I'd defend myself. The trial lasted only half an hour or so and the Magistrate found me guilty. After a short talk with the Prosecutor, who told him that I was awaiting seven charges of serious assault, he gave me six weeks imprisonment in Wormwood Scrubs. I was taken to the prison where I did my time then was allowed to go free but as I walked out of the prison gate, two detectives were waiting for me to take me back to Scotland for trial the next week.

The trial was at the High Court Buildings in Glasgow, but it was a sheriff and jury trial. This meant that the maximum sentence the sheriff could impose was two years but if he felt that a higher sentence was appropriate then he could remit us to the High Court for sentence and they could give us whatever they wanted. The trial lasted two days and we were both found guilty of two charges and, as expected, remitted to the High Court in Edinburgh for sentence. The following week both Artie and I faced a High Court Judge and were sentenced, Artie to three years and me to two years imprisonment. We were taken to Edinburgh prison. The Press made a big deal of the reporting of the case and, true to form, Artie was described as the leader of the Cumbie and I as his second-in-command. Edinburgh prison was usually reserved for first offenders so Artie and I were taken back to Glasgow and Barlinnie as soon as possible, but that was fine with us as we preferred Barlinnie.

This was my first time in Barlinnie as a tried prisoner and with the publicity from the trial I was immediately assured of having an "identity". I was only 18 years old so was split from Artie and put into a hall with the under-twenty-ones. I was beside lots of kids that had been in other places with me, amongst them was Ben Conroy. We went around together along with a lot of Gorbals guys, but Ben went out quite soon after that. In this hall there were young men doing sentences from 10 days to four years. The bulk of these were the very short sentences, most of them petty offences committed through drink. The prison garb was brown moleskin suits and they were usually ill-fitting so most of us would get our trousers taken in as was the style in those days. Prisoners doing a relatively long period would split into cliques and I mean cliques as distinct from gangs. These were formed out of companionship as guys would share their tobacco and exchange reading material and any other odds and ends that came their way. Although the under-twenty-ones were separated in the hall they were celled in, the working arrangements were such that we joined up with the rest of the prisoners.

I was taken the following morning and put into the mailbag party beside Artie and there I was introduced to lots of guys that Artie knew, most of whom were from Peterhead but down in Barlinnie for local visits. These were all guys who had big reputations in Glasgow so in many ways there was lots of excitement in this for me. All of us would sit on the long hard wooden bench with mailbags over our knees to keep us warm and a needle and thread in our hands as though we were working. The truth is that there was no need to work if one was sitting in such company. These were the real fighters and the screws would try to keep well out of their way. Due to his age and sentence, Artie was to be sent to Peterhead, which is the long term prison in Scotland. The bus transferred prisoners there every month. All prisoners serving six months and over were allowed nine hours of visits per year and these were spread out to allow three twenty-minute visits every two months with a bonus for the long termers in that they get three thirty-minute visits after the first ten months. The visits take place in very small cubicles and the prisoner is put into it with the visitor on the other side of the glass and wire partition with no privacy to speak to his family. Kids of the prisoner would come in and try to get to their father, but the glass and wire would prevent them. Screws would walk up and down each side of the partition listening to what was being said.

I was in a single cell which had a chamber pot, table, chair, and bed. There was a heavy steel frame with glasspanes in it at the window and a set of thick steel bars. The routine in prisons is very rigidly structured and almost the same in every prison in Scotland. In the morning there is slop out and wash up then breakfast, either in the cell or in a dining hall. Work at 8 a.m. then lunch at noon; after lunch there is an hour's exercise either in the prison yards or round the gallery of the halls if it is raining. Back to work till 4.30 p.m. then evening meal. Lock up at 5 p.m. till the screws go for their tea then slop out at about 6.30 p.m. Those prisoners eligible for recreation are allowed out to the dining halls which act as the recreation halls for an hour or so, then it is lock up and the screws go away at 9 p.m. The only variation is on Saturdays and Sundays when the screws go away at 5 p.m. till the following morning, and on both these days it is lock up most of the time.

The sentence that I was doing was quite big for a guy of my age with no prison sentence before but I wasn't really horrified at it. There was a sort of pride in it as I felt really good to be in beside lots of hard men as I was on the way to being one myself. When we were in our cliques it would be all "façades" and tough talk, but that wasn't what prison was to me. To me at that time prison was just a hazard of the life I was leading. It was all part of the sub-culture for everyone to go about trying to impress everyone else.

The fact is that prison eats your insides out, and ties your stomach in knots, leaving your heart very heavy. All of this takes place when you are alone, but it wouldn't be the done thing to let this be seen by other people. At nights I would get up to my window and look out from the top flat and could see the cars and buses and people walking in the streets and, though this hurt me, I never said that I wouldn't be back because by this time I was fully involved in being a criminal, and I only knew that I wanted to be out and be big in crime. I felt all the feelings but could never get it all together to see what I was doing to myself. Instead I took these feelings as signs of personal weakness and would never dare let anyone see them. What the fuck is it all about? What kind of thing made me pretend that prison had no effect on me? All the frustrations that I had in Approved School and Borstal about being treated like a child, all the bullshit that I always imagined would be resolved when I got to prison didn't turn out that way because they were here but in a different form.

I was allowed to write one letter a week to my family and all in-going and out-going mail was censored. The screws were very petty and would concentrate on small things just like the prisoners. They would come in and search your cell and person. You could be put on report for hanging pin-ups on the walls. Some of us serving lengthy sentences would bribe one of the painters (prisoners working in the painters) to steal some paint for us and we would paint our cells as they were only painted every seven years by the prison and they were filthy. For this the prisoner would lose remission. I lost remission for very petty offences. One day I was walking along in single file with over a hundred others when this screw started shouting at me like I was dirt. Maybe I was, but as far as I was concerned so was he; so I thumped him on the jaw and was dragged off him by some other screws and taken to the bottom flat of the hall and thrown in the punishment cell, after having my clothes and shoes taken from me. While sitting there in this totally defenceless position a group of screws came in and attacked me. I knew that I if did anything back there would be more charges so I more or less took what they gave giving token resistance and they left. Much later I was taken to the hospital in the prison and gave the reason for my injuries as having fallen. The following morning I was taken in front of the Governor and the screw described what had happened and I agreed with it and was sentenced to fourteen days. The fact that I had heavy bruising on one side of my face didn't raise the Governor's curiosity.

I returned to the punishment cell and decided that I hated all bastard screws. What I couldn't accept was their rendering me absolutely helpless before coming in and attacking me. I spent all the fourteen days trying to get my anger out on them, but I never could. The solitary period was spent lying on the floor of the dark and very cold cell and this was interrupted for my one hour's exercise each day. There were days when I didn't take this as I couldn't stand the company of the screws who would walk along with me. I recognised the importance of this sentence as it was establishing a reputation, and what better place to do this than a prison that held a conglomeration of criminals from all over Scotland? This was the place to make important contacts and signs of weakness would do nothing to strengthen these so all emotions had to lie underneath. When I was allowed out after my fourteen days punishment in solitary the guys in the hall greeted me well and gave me one or two luxuries that I hadn't been able to get — a mars bar, and a girlie magazine. I continued to get into trouble and the days were spent with me looking for the screws to slip up and vice versa. They had all the advantages as there is a rule forbidding almost everything in prison, even those allowed in the rule book, as it's all a matter of interpretation.

One day I was pulled out of line for having tight trousers and locked up in the punishment cell. They took the trousers off me to act as evidence, giving me an ill-fitting pair to take their place but I refused to wear them. When the time came for me to go in front of the Governor for a breach of discipline I went in my shirt tail, refusing to dress. He sent me to solitary for seven days but I still refused to wear them. While in solitary confinement I was opened up three times each day to slop out my chamber pot and I would walk to the toilet naked. After doing this for some time the door opened and my old trousers were thrown in. When my punishment was completed I was taken in front of the Governor and told that I was being put on Rule 36, for subversive activities. I was informed that Rule 36 is not a punishment but that I was just being segregated from the other prisoners as I was a bad influence on them. I was taken to a cell at the far end of the hall above which was the Hanging Cell, and outside the window were the unmarked graves where the condemned men were buried.

Rule 36 meant that my routine was exactly that of punishment only they put it under another title and told me that it wasn't punishment. During the day they would give me a load of mail bags to sew and at the same time take out my bedding so I couldn't lie in bed. But I would spread out the mail bags and make a bed out of them, not doing any work as there was nothing they could do to me. I had reached rock bottom and they were playing on my being too bored to sit doing nothing, but even if I had been, there was no way I would do their fucking bags. The days were spent lying thinking and there would be times when I would walk up and down on exercise beside the unmarked graves and think of those lying there. I knew the brother of one and the relative of another. There were stories of them that went round the prison. One of them had attacked the screw before being hung and had broken another one's nose. Screws would tell prisoners the tales of their time on the Deathwatch and how the guys always thanked them for being decent. It was all so eerie sleeping there between executioner and graves. I remember seeing letters that someone had stolen from the files of condemned men and these were crank letters that struck real terror into my heart.

After two months of this solitary I was told that I was being allowed to circulate with the other prisoners but that special arrangements had been made and I was being transferred to the adult hall where all the older prisoners were as that would keep me in line. So without much ado I was transferred to "A" Hall. I found the atmosphere there totally different with prisoners roaming the place loose and free within the hall area. I was only eighteen and the age for this hall was twenty-one and over. I was met with a barrage of greetings as most of the Gorbals guys were there and others that I had met from other districts and they were running the place. So I was given lots of freedom and lots of luxuries as they had fingers in different pies and this was beautiful. There was no bullshit or regimentation here, it was all wild and woolly. Most of the guys that I knew were the tobacco barons and were getting parcels in and there would be the occasional smuggled booze and small parties.

Stabbings amongst prisoners were common occurrences and there was never any great hassle or upheaval over them; the prisoners took them for granted. Prison stabbings are usually well set up events and those carrying them out would take pride in doing a neat job. I did one of these and it was against a guy from my district who had been causing some trouble amongst our group. In things like this the done thing is to make a hit and make it quick because everyone weighs these things up and if they see people getting off with things then they think you soft. So I set this deal up while walking through the corridor, the main "hit" place, as the prisoners walk single file through dark corridors. It usually takes about four to do it, with the guy who is making the hit carrying the knife, with two in front of the victim and two behind. The guy walks up, makes the hit, then passes the knife to the guy in front of the victim and this was what I did. Before the screw can notice that someone has been hit the guy is well away, and only the victim is left, the weapon concealed by this time in a pre-arranged place. When getting to work there is a discussion as to whether it was a good hit or not. In this context, you have the art of violence in which the manner of its execution is very much appreciated just as works of art are appreciated in another culture. People in the art world understand what art is all about whereas in my world we think it's a load of balls, a big con; just as people in most sections of society view our cutting and maiming each other as hideous. The fact is that this is how we lived and if someone were to cut my face I wouldn't like it but I would accept it knowing that it was a hazard of the life I was leading. I would be intent on getting back at whoever had done it, but on the whole slashing, stabbing, shooting and death are to be expected amongst those of us who live like this.

So, ten days after being transferred to the men's hall to be "kept in place" I was being interviewed by the cops for a stabbing. The cops had been through this so many times that they knew it was a waste of time as no one ever talked. The victim would usually say he fell. The following morning I was taken in front of the Governor with three others and we were all placed on Rule 36. I was put in a cell on the bottom flat of the hall. One can only be put on Rule 36 for a month at a time and each month it usually gets reviewed by the Governor who can extend it. It was the same routine as last time and I lay on the mail bags like most of the others.

Around this time there were a lot of "brew ups" taking place in the prison: this means guys making their own alcohol from stills set up in the worksheds or anywhere else. It was a paint extract that they were using and lots of them were being treated for burnt stomachs. Meanwhile those of us on solitary had received a "parcel" of drugs and were lying stoned out of our minds. The parcel consisted of purple hearts and sleepers and during the day the purple hearts would pep me up so that I would be lying in my cell singing, as they had the effect of making me want to talk to someone. When night approached I would take sleepers to get me to sleep. It was during this period, as I lay in this drugged state, that news came over the radio that President Kennedy had been assassinated. This was shouted out of a cell door by a long term prisoner who was allowed a personal radio, but through the haze of the drugs I thought it was some unreal dream that could never be true. Later, when the drugs had worn off, it hit me and I was strangely sad.

Each month I was taken in front of the Governor and told that I was being kept in solitary confinement. As the months went on I hardened myself to expecting this, but deep within I thought I might be allowed off as the rule is that if a prisoner behaves, then he is supposed to be let back into circulation. The wording of the rules are different by far from the humanitarian interpretation that is given when the authorities are questioned about them. As far as I was concerned I was putting all my concentration into showing no emotion at all and to appear as though it didn't bother me. For six months, one after the other, I was taken up and told that I was being kept on solitary, but I always knew that they could not keep me forever. It was a case of giving nothing and getting nothing, the result being that pure hatred was allowed to grow.

The incident with the brothers that I had had was still continuing on the outside with lots of skirmishes and one particularly big battle in which several of my friends ended up in hospital, and one or two of the other side in later clashes. In fights like this guys who get cut quite badly don't always go to doctors; they prefer to see to the injuries themselves rather than have it made official. There were a number of shootings in which charges were made, but when this happened all efforts were made to keep the matter out of the hands of the police. There were also other fights taking place in other areas of the Gorbals and in these some of my pals were badly cut and scarred. If you give it out then you must be prepared to take it and that was the dominant attitude amongst us. There was one guy who was shot in his home and he "grassed" on his attackers. They had certainly taken a liberty in going into this man's home with his wife and family there, but it was still seen as no excuse for his grassing on them. In such cases as this the guy will usually blame it on his wife for putting the guys in jail. Fortunately all was seen to and the guys charged were let off. I was lying in prison during all of this and was very frustrated as I felt that I could solve it all by plunging straight in and defeating the enemy but these were only fantasies brought about by the frustrations of incarceration. My life was crime and all I wanted to do was make a reputation for myself and get money. I was lying in solitary confinement and when my thoughts were not on the events taking place on the outside then it was projecting all my hatred onto the screws who continued to make my life in there a misery with their petty rules and regulations. I would dream of being at the gate when they all came off duty and shooting them all, but I soon found that this was almost every prisoner's fantasy.

Eventually I was let out of solitary after six months. This was the longest time in my life that I had been locked up alone like that and I felt very strange. I felt the tension of living under solitary conditions; my head felt funny and it was very strange being with other prisoners. I couldn't speak for very long as my vocal chords would hurt and the back of my throat would dry up. I always needed a glass of water nearby till I got used to it. The others on it with me were the same. The Authorities gave me a nice cushy job for the remaining few months of my sentence which was now not far away.

8

I was let out one September morning and met at the prison gate by Willie Smith and John McCue and we went straight home to my Ma's house. By now she was staying in the Oatlands as our old house in Sandyfaulds Street had been demolished. My Ma and other neighbours were retreating into the other tenements in the district rather than leave the Gorbals. The Oatlands had once been a sort of toffy district but now we were in it, and it had changed since those days. When the Sandyfaulds Street house was being demolished my Ma and some of the neighbours wept as they all went to see it go. It sounds all sentimental and guffy but they had lived in these old houses all their lives and hated to see this happening. Instead of driving home I would have preferred to have walked, in order to see the ordinary things that prison deprives one of. It's not the expensive or luxurious things that one misses but the basic every day things everyone takes for granted — people walking in a street, sitting on a bus, buying something in a shop; the sound of children and of feminine conversation, away from the coarse male environment that one is subjected to day in, day out.

It was nice to see my Ma and all the family and as it was 7 a.m. they were all in. We had very hearty greetings but, for some strange reason or other, actual physical contact in families that I knew was very limited. I would never think of coming into the house after this long absence and cuddling my Ma or giving her a kiss or for that matter shaking my brothers by the hand or embracing them; these things just weren't done. That was all sissy stuff, therefore not for us. After a drink and a good breakfast, Ma and I went into the room — the new house was the same as the old one — a room and kitchen. Ma pleaded with me to keep out of trouble. She was very old then and very worried and I loved her, but though I was well aware that I could be in trouble the minute I left her house I gave her the answer she wanted to hear. She knew I didn't mean it and I'm sure she knew that I was not wanting to hurt her, but what could she do?

From here, Willie, John and I went to other districts in Glasgow to see old friends and, as is customary, have a drink. At the same time money is given to the guy just out, which is usually the done thing. From there all three of us went to the city centre to get some girls. We went with them to a pub party and a house party afterwards. Life was so good at these times. Without delay I was bedded with a girl and giving her all the hatred stored up over the last eighteen months. I stayed there till I was satiated and that took most of the day, after which it was into another celebration period, making a glut of myself and making up for time lost.

By this time we were looked upon as the top mob in the city and our strength lay in the fact that we were a conglomeration of fighters from surrounding areas. People looked upon us as a group of young guys with plenty of "bottle" who were best avoided. There were other individual guys who were in very strong positions within their own district but all of us were on friendly terms and these guys were very shrewd cookies who had things pretty well sewn up, whereas we hadn't established that kind of stability yet. Because we were a force to be reckoned with this didn't mean that we could rule as a group without opposition, let's say the opposition was limited. Glasgow is a pretty violent jungle and one is never without opposition there, no matter how strong one may be.

At this period I was living between the districts of Govan, the city centre, and the Gorbals. Govan was where the moneylending and shebeen rackets were, and I along with some others were pretty loosely involved there by keeping an eye on things in the capacity of "heavies". At nights we would go up to the city centre and collect girls who were prostitutes, take them to the Gorbals for a booze up and back to the Govan area for a party and bed. Govan was an ideal district for rackets as it took in all the shift workers coming in for booze to the Shebeen. We used a two apartment house run by a friend. One room would be filled with crates of booze, and some women would sit in there throughout the night and sell it while we lay in the other with birds. One room filled with booze and the other with mattresses. This way we were always handy for any trouble that arose, but this was very seldom as it was a well known fact that we were associated with it so that the trouble was kept to a minimum. Both of these rackets were borderline "illegals" and not recognised as potentially dangerous by the cops. People who were short of money would come to the illegal moneylenders as they knew cash would be given then and there without having to put up a guarantor or household goods.

They did not have to sign official documents or wait any length of time for the cash.

The Shebeening was a different matter as all sorts of strokes would be pulled by strangers in the night gasping for a drink, willing to resort to anything for a taste of the stuff. There always seemed to be more desperation for the booze than for money. Therefore stricter rules had to be laid down regarding it and the principal one was that no credit would be given to strangers or doubtful characters.

After prison I was feeling sexually deprived so I would buy enough provisions for three days and head for a house with a girl, locking myself in. I concentrated on foods that were recommended energy restorers; steak, cheese and fruit. These were beautiful times. There was the time when Willie, John and I were in the city centre and we picked up two girls with the intention of taking them back to Govan. We were walking along Sauchiehall Street looking for a taxi, when we saw, parked by the kerb, a white Jaguar with the driver trying to start the engine. We gave him a push to get it started and he gave us a lift to Govan, dropping John off at the Gorbals.

In Glasgow at this time hardly any of the guys in the criminal scene took money from the Labour Exchange but in court this was used against them when the Jury were told that they had no visible means of support, especially when they were seen to be spending a lot of money. So for the first time everyone started taking their dole money. The morning after the lift in the white Jaguar I went to the Labour Exchange in a taxi. As I went in confronting the man behind the desk, I sensed something wrong as he was acting very strange. It all fell into place when cops came jumping out from the doors round about, pounced on me and whisked me away in a car. I was taken to the local Police station where I was stripped naked by the cops and had my clothing searched piece by piece. The only thing that worried me was that I had a dose of the clap and the card for the Clinic was in my pocket so when I heard them sniggering behind me I knew what it was. I could see from the glass reflection in front of me that they were passing it around. The arrest was to do with a four figure robbery that had been committed in the city a few days earlier and our crowd were the chief suspects. I told them I was just out of prison recently and had done nothing but they knew all of that and referred to the expensive clothes I was wearing. They then went on to relate how we had been seen driving in a white Jaguar the night before with classy birds in it. It got a bit ludicrous when they suggested that I was the brains behind it, Willie the heavy and John the driver. I was kept there for hours then released and told to attend an identification parade at a later date.

When I returned to Govan to tell the others how the cops had reconstructed the crime, with us being the arch-villains, we had a good laugh, but this didn't last long as they raided our families' and relatives' homes, searching and tearing them apart. It was as if a campaign against us was on as the cops were on our tails every move we made. There was nothing we could do as all of us had records, so they could pull us up and search us whenever it pleased them. There was no danger of us making any official complaint about it. Life got so bad that we had to make rules to combat it. I was getting my experience first hand and I was now saying the things that I had heard the older guys say years before. If the cops approached us in the street to search us then we made a rule that on seeing them coming we would immediately stop the first passer-by and ask him to search us first in case the cops planted anything on us. The funny thing was that this was a quiet period for us and we weren't really causing any trouble. Although we were hanging around the moneylenders ready to deal with any trouble that might arise, up till this time all had been quiet. Life now became very serious and we began to live cautiously.

I took up going with this girl, Margaret, but the scene was really crazy and should never have been. I don't think I was ready for any involvement. Like the others, it should have been a one night affair, but for some reason it didn't happen like that, even though I knew deep down that it was all wrong. Even at our closest there was always a distance between us. I was weakened by the fact that I allowed it to go on when it would have been better for everyone concerned to bring it to an end. But then how many people say the same thing in retrospect? The point is that I knew within myself that I wasn't ready for a binding or steady relationship and my behaviour went a long way to substantiate that. Never at any time could I imagine myself getting married or settling down. This made me different from other people of my own age who would be wanting to get married soon after leaving school. But I allowed the relationship with Margaret to continue, knowing that it was on a course for disaster, very much like my own life.

It was around this time in December, 1964, when the cops burst into my house in the early hours of the morning as I lay in bed with Margaret. They told us to get up. There were about eight of them, all detectives. The atmosphere was really tense, and it was obvious they were going to give the house and me a thorough search. I was very angry and was asking what they were wanting and what this was all about. No one answered but I could feel the hostility very strongly. Margaret was allowed to dress and I was given a blanket to throw over myself. All the time I was watching their every move, so between waking up and trying to find out what was going on and watching them I was finding it difficult to think clearly. I stood in the centre of the floor with the gold coloured blanket draped over me and watched as they tore open furniture in their search.

I couldn't, for the life of me, think what it was all about as I had been doing nothing actively criminal lately. Certainly the cops had been having a go at us by using harassing tactics but this wasn't the usual thing; the atmosphere was especially tense and serious. They piled up lots of household objects that they were intending to take away and most of my clothing. One or two of them made snide remarks at me but this was just part of the usual behaviour and it didn't really bother me as I knew they wouldn't dare make them when they were alone with me. Initially I thought they were just "noising me up" and I could see that they were intent on frightening me, but just as I was thinking this they told me that I was being charged with murder. This word and all that it means is very frightening, even in the criminal world, and the impact of it on me was tremendous. I really felt weak at the knees and a terrifying chill ran through my body. Their attitudes and actions now fell into perspective, but within me there was this inner defence mechanism telling me that the cops were at it and that their tactics were always to make things worse than they really were in order to frighten the person into giving information or getting him to admit to a lesser charge. I was caught between the seriousness of their behaviour and my past knowledge of how they work and it was this basic uncertainty that prevented me from at once facing up to the reality of a Murder charge.

Wearing the blanket and a pair of shoes I was taken off to the Central Police Headquarters and it was then that the reality hit me. Standing behind the bar of the station was a line of top cops, the head of whom was Goodall, who stood there, pipe in mouth, staring at me. All the cash taken from me and from Margaret's purse was placed on the bar top in front of me and Goodall remarked that I knew what the charge would be. The uniformed

Inspector with them then began to read out the name of the dead man and the charge being Capital Murder, which I could be hanged for. I was asked if I would like to say anything about the charges against me and I told them I had nothing to say. I was now functioning in the way that I would with any other charge, and the old rule of "saying nothing till I saw my lawyer" prevailed, even though I was wanting to burst out screaming my innocence at them and telling them that they had made a terrible mistake. But I couldn't and wouldn't. The cops all stared at me and I at them, none of us saying anything, but the enmity between us was very obvious.

I was taken in front of a Doctor Imrie, a pathologist, and gave him permission to examine me for injuries to my body and allowed him to take material from underneath my fingernails. I was then taken upstairs to a cell with a cage front door on it that was specifically built for observation. Many times when I was a kid along with others I had found myself in this cell while waiting to go to the Remand Home, but now the significance of it hit me. I was given some blankets and sat on the floor with them around me. A uniformed cop was sitting on the other side of the cage door watching me. My mind was in a turmoil. I was charged with murdering and stealing money from a man called Lynch, whom I had neither heard of nor set eyes on. I was also charged with seriously assaulting another man with a knife. I had no knowledge of this man either by sight or name. I was very frightened because although I knew I was innocent, the inescapable fact was that I was lying in this cell charged with murder. By now I was well versed on police tactics of planting evidence and other underhand methods to incriminate known criminals with previous convictions. At this stage, however, I had very little knowledge of what it was all about apart from the charges read out by the cops, so it was difficult for me to try to work out where I was when the damage was done. All I could think of was that I was being framed by the cops. I knew that Margaret had immediately gone for a lawyer but that didn't help me, lying there wondering what was going on.

Meanwhile cops appeared at the cage door looking through at me, calling me all the bastards and other names of the day. Some of them referred to me as a murderer and all of them were inferring this by the manner in which they spoke, but rather than blow my cool I sat there pretending that I didn't hear them. I sat there staring straight out at them putting on a front that belied my true feelings and anxieties. As far as the cops were concerned I had done it, but I didn't expect anything else from them as they very rarely admit to making mistakes, and usually presume that everyone arrested is guilty. I was relieved in the morning when my lawyer came to see me. His first question was to ask if I had done it. I emphatically denied it so he then took down the few details I could give and he advised me to sit down and think over all my movements of the previous evening.

On the night in question, from approximately 7 p.m. I had been in the "Wheatsheaf Pub" in the Gorbals with two girls, one of whom was Artie's sister, Bertha. I had sat drinking with them till time up and we'd left the pub together. It was Saturday night and I had walked part of the way up Crown Street with the two girls. The street had been very busy with pubs and cinemas emptying. I'd had a silly argument with a guy as we walked up the street and it had ended up with me chasing him and falling flat on my face in a muddy puddle which made me very angry. My clothes had been saturated with mud and water and the two girls looking at me had burst out laughing and so had I, as it really was quite funny. I'd left the girls and had asked two kids to call me a taxi. One of the kids had been on the "run" from Borstal and I had offered to let him sleep in my house but he'd declined. When I had got home, Margaret helped me strip off my filthy clothes, then I'd cleaned up and we'd gone to bed.

These had been my movements the previous night but I sat in this cell going over and over them trying to remember who had seen me or who I had spoken to, any little thing that might assist me or my lawyer to clear this whole matter up. I spent the whole of Sunday going over it all and giving it to Bill Dunlop, my lawyer, when he came to see me. He had managed to get some more information to tell me and we compared notes and tried to build a full picture. It was great speaking to him as he had complete faith in my innocence even at that early stage. I needed that sort of reassurance otherwise I'd have cracked up, as the enormity of the charge was tremendously worrying for me. Later that afternoon I was put on an Identification Parade and witnesses were brought in. Amongst them was Artie's sister, Bertha, and she was in tears as she pointed to me saying she was sorry for doing it. All the other witnesses walked past. I was taken in front of a Magistrate the following morning and was remanded in Barlinnie Prison for further inquiry. Once the fingerprinting and photographing procedures were over, I was taken to the prison.

I was put through the usual reception procedure, but after being issued with a prison uniform I was taken to the hospital block and placed on observation in a cell with armoured plate glass on the door and kept there under "strict observation". My day was spent thinking over every little detail concerning my situation and I would jot down on a piece of paper all that I felt was relevant to it and discuss it with my lawyer. After a few days I was allowed into an open ward beside the other untried prisoners. The hospital wing is reserved for psychiatric and murder charge prisoners. There were three of us awaiting trial for murder and the rest of them, ten others, were in for various charges. In the bed next to me was an undertaker in for rape. There was another guy who would lie on the floor and refuse to move except to wrap his body around the legs of the washbasins in the toilet and he would have to be pulled out. There was another who walked about with an imaginary dog, and he would pause to let it do the toilet. All of us slept in the same ward and it was under such circumstances that I had to concentrate on my case.

A couple of days after entering the prison the Police were advertising on television for witnesses in connection with the case against me. After discussing this with my lawyer we asked the television company for the same facility to try to contact the taxi driver who had driven me home that night but they denied us this, even though the same people were doing it for the cops and the requests were identical. The kids who had called the taxi for me would be unreliable as witnesses, as they had previous convictions and the one who had actually called the cab was on the run from Borstal. With the taxi driver no other witnesses would be necessary and it seemed unlikely that the taxi driver could forget picking up a customer in the condition I was in after falling in the puddle. While awaiting trial there were times when I was very hopeful and others when I was thoroughly depressed and thought it all looked hopeless. But overall the fighting spirit was dominant and the support from my family and friends was very strong indeed. I lived with a pen and paper at my side, as my whole life depended on memorising everything that took place that night.

All of my family came up regularly and though worried they were fantastic in the help they offered and the loyalty they showed. Visiting conditions in this sort of situation are ludicrous. Here was I awaiting trial for a charge of which I was completely innocent and the prison regulations stopped me from discussing it with any of my visitors. A screw would sit beside me throughout the visit, and before it began he would warn me not to speak about my charge and that if I did so then the visit would be terminated. How does one sit on a visit with one's mother and not talk about something that has had such an impact on the family? I would have very heated arguments with the screws on this matter but there was no deviating from this rule. There was one occasion when the visit was ending and we rose to walk out and my Ma asked me if I had done it? It was a great relief to be able to say that I hadn't as we had never been able to during my spell on remand. For years my Ma had been asking me if I'd done things that she had heard about and I had always denied it, even when I had done them. This time it was different as it was very, very serious and there was no room for any games. Both of us knew this.

The person that was able to give me a real boost was my lawyer as he had done a tremendous amount of work on the case and I was always eager to see him. Artie, who had just completed his three year sentence, came to see me and told me that his sister said she had been threatened by the cops, which is why she had to witness against me in the identity parade. All this sort of thing had been done before to other guys in the criminal element. Similar tactics, similar threats, the same methods employed. In a case such as this it becomes an extreme "Them and Us" situation between the police and the accused. As far as the police were concerned, I was guilty. There was also the fact that they looked on me and my friends as a constant source of trouble.

It was early in 1965 and although the debate on the abolition of capital punishment was on, it was still in force at the time. As my trial date approached they went through the formality of cleaning out the Death Cell because legally I could be sentenced to death. However, days before the trial Abolition became a reality. It was strange this debate going on in Parliament while I was waiting on trial for Capital Murder. This was a warning to me on how easily a mistake could be made.

On the day of the trial I felt edgy but there was a silent confidence within because I felt that I knew I was making this appearance for nothing. I was cleared of the Capital Murder charge and the following day I walked clear out of the court into the street. It was beautiful walking from that dock as the front benches were crammed full of cops, and they were looking very sick indeed. All of my friends cheered and we embraced and this was what it was all about, Us beating Them. The feeling of enmity and hatred flowed between us and the cops. Although I had done nothing to merit being in court, all of us looked on my walking free as being a victory. The pressure was lifted from me completely with the acquittal. Lord Cameron was the presiding judge who told me I could leave the dock. I had had to work like hell during those past three months to get acquitted as had my lawyer and family and friends. The feeling throughout was that the official side couldn't give a damn if I went down for life or not — innocent or guilty.

The Press mobbed me on leaving court and to avoid them we jumped into the first car available which turned out to be the Daily Express car. It took us away from the crowds to the house of the reporter in the shadows of Barlinnie prison where he set about getting a story and photographs of me and Margaret. There was lots of noise in the reporter's house and this brought his mother into the room to ask us to be quiet as his father was in bed ill and she had had to call in a doctor to attend him. I had heard that reporters would do anything for a story and this sort of thing verified it. I told everyone we should leave, but in the car journey home the reporter was slapped in the face and messed about and years later this was being exaggerated as it is now said that I put a knife at his throat. The Express certainly showed their dislike for me in later years.

It was great to be back in the house again, and to be in the streets of the Gorbals. The celebrations lasted a long time as drink was plentiful and parties were constant. People within the district were telling me to go away to London as the police would wait for their first chance to get me and would make sure the next time. This was said time and time again, but I didn't pay any attention as I felt that I shouldn't be made to leave my district or leave Glasgow and one thing for sure — I wasn't going to run from cops. But there was this feeling that I would be set up by the cops. I was now number one on the police list and there was an open hatred even among cops not involved with the case.

While I had been awaiting trial, John McCue had been arrested for firing a shotgun and was charged with attempted murder and he lay on remand in Barlinnie. This left Willie Smith, another guy Willie Bennett and Frank who had come up from London with a broken leg, although he soon went back down again. I was still celebrating and there is no doubt that the whole thing went to my head. After my release I was the main talking point in the criminal world and lots of guys were looking up to me as it's not everyone who walks out of a murder trial.

There were a number of people in the district who still believed I was guilty and as there was a certain adulation attached to this I didn't go out of my way to deny it. Just like the other times, it enhanced my reputation, which is what I was after. It was just like all the other fears I had experienced while in Larchgrove, that once I was out of it the fear left, and I began to cash in on it. Within myself there was a conflict as I felt a bit of a cheat; I felt I had to prove myself to myself. So ten days after being acquitted, while travelling home from the pub with my younger cousin, both of us the worse for drink, I provoked two guys. I recognised one of them as having been in the old "Bee Hive Gang", and I ended up attacking them which resulted in a fight with me hitting one of them with a bottle and taking one of his eyes out, and cutting the other on the hand. I felt much better after this as though I had somehow "proved" myself, and in doing so created a more terrifying picture of myself. The following morning the cops were looking for me so this meant that I had to go into hiding, but only as far as the city centre where Margaret and I had a house. I stayed in a lot as the cops were raiding houses looking for me. We would go out occasionally and one of these times, while in a big store buying fruit for the movies, I was grabbed by the arm and told to come to the police station; it was a detective who knew me. I was surprised and I thought he was with others as the place was crowded; but as we were going outside the store door and I was giving Margaret all the money in my pocket and instructions to contact my lawyer I noticed that he was on his own. At this, I grabbed him and beat him up and made off while Margaret blocked his way. I managed to get over to Govan and was told some hours later that Margaret had been arrested for police assault, and obstructing justice. For this she was put into prison, but we were able to get her bail at the soonest possible moment.

Things were hot and I went back into hiding, but it's terribly difficult to lock oneself in a house as it becomes very much a prison. Being on the "run" is a tense situation; one is always on the look-out for cops and every waking minute has to be taken up with watching for them. There is no doubt that this wears one down and becomes very frustrating.

During this spell Tony Smith (no relation to Willie Smith) was released from Peterhead Prison after serving a four year sentence. Tony, like the rest of us, had a reputation for being a fighter and he came from the Blackhill district. He was met at the train by Willie and some others, and parties were the result. Also at this time Frank came up from London, with his broken leg healed. So there was Willie Smith, Tony Smith, Frank, and Willie Bennett (who came from the Partick district of Glasgow) and myself all hanging around together.

This was quite a bunch by any standards and one particular night we had arranged to meet in Govan. From there we headed for the city centre for further fun and Willie Smith's girlfriend came to meet him as it was her birthday and they were going for a meal. They left us and we went about our own business, drinking. Eventually at pub closing time we made our way to a party that we knew was taking place in the city centre. Going up the dark, winding stairway we could hear music coming from the house where the party was. To get to the house, one had to enter a long and very dark lobby. The place was full of people, some on a bed to our left inside the doorway. Willie Bennett was standing immediately inside the door and on seeing us the party went quiet. I had scarcely entered the house when a voice from inside shouted my name and it turned out to be Irene, the prostitute from London many years ago, so she came out and we went into the dark lobby to renew our acquaintance. We were surprised to see each other, and while we were talking a fight broke out with bottles flying out the doorway and thuds and crashes. I went towards the door but it closed, locking me, Tony and Frank in the lobby with Irene, which meant that Willie Bennett was inside so we began kicking the door down and we finally got in pulling Willie out. Bottles came flying and fighting took place on the doorstep. Frank was almost scalped by a guy with a big knife, but we got out and made our way downstairs. I grabbed Irene, intending to take her with me but decided against it. We all made off to a house in Blackhill and saw to Frank's head wound which was pretty bad. Some home-made butterfly stitches were put on the wound which seemed to stem the blood. The wound was a long thin line along his hairline and his skin could be lifted up. There were other cut faces and bruising, but nothing else serious.

Blackhill is a crazy place. It was now almost three in the morning and we went into the street where some guys were sitting round a bonfire singing Celtic songs and drinking wine almost in the middle of the street. The atmosphere was very similar to that of the old Gorbals that was now being destroyed by demolition squads. We sat around drinking and it was as though it was the middle of the day rather than the middle of the night. Eventually a van came to pick us up. The driver was a big strong guy who was drunk. He ushered us into the van and then took off. Our conversation was trying to find out what bastards were at that party earlier on as they hadn't half given us a beating. We knew that things would be different in the morning when we pursued the matter. Our attention was taken from this by the high speed of the drunken driver as the van travelled towards the city centre. On the way, he told us that the van had no brakes which had all of us on the verge of shitting ourselves as he pelted on. We were going to my house in the city centre so I had to be up front guiding him. I pointed out the folly of his speeding as the cops were looking for me for assaults. At this he put his hand under the van seat, pulled out a sawn off shot-gun and reassured me that I'd be okay. All of this was very matter of fact with us casting glances at the guy as it was apparent to us that we were in the van with a madman. Be that as it may, he did prove to be true to his word in getting us there, but I'll never forget that nightmare journey. He made miraculous swerves to avoid hitting oncoming vehicles and it was with a sigh of relief that he pulled up though I'm not sure how he stopped the van.

When we arrived at my house, we were informed by Margaret that the cops were looking for all of us for murder, as a young guy had been stabbed to death in that house. Immediately we got onto the phone and found out how true this was as cops were flying round, entering houses in search of us. Within minutes people were visiting the house and one of the first to come was Willie Smith, who had left us to take his girl out, earlier that night. All of us sat very tense, waiting for news to trickle in to bring us up to date. The room went from complete silence to nervous noisiness. Different people reacted in different ways. Willie Bennett was guzzling large amounts of booze in an obvious attempt to knock himself out. Tony was quite calm on the face of it. Frank was pretty shaken but very much in control. I was much the same, the only difference being that I had been on this road before. All of us were finding it very hard to take.

The situation was that now all of us were on the run. I had been on the run for some time with the cops looking for me so in a way I felt disassociated from the murder thing. I was already used to the hunted feeling but all of us would have to live with it for the moment. There was no way that we would go to the cops, give ourselves up and ask what this was all about. People have to understand the intense feeling of suspicion and distrust that both criminals and cops have for each other and that the best policy for the criminal is to keep out of the way until the heat dies down. With the cops already looking for me I couldn't carry a knife as they could use it as evidence. So I was now unarmed and feeling pretty naked.

News came back to us that two brothers had been stabbed at the party, one of them fatally. The house had been full of people but most of the respectable ones had taken off as they didn't want to be involved, or have their names associated with the house or what was going on that night. There were others very much like ourselves who had left for obvious reasons. This left those who were too drunk or too frightened to get away for the police coming. As soon as our names were mentioned the police went on a raiding spree. What a golden opportunity for them, with all of us involved in the one case. They raided house after house looking for us. Arrangements were made for us to go into hiding, Frank went back to London to carry on his normal life there. Willie Bennett and Tony Smith went to New York, and I stayed where I was.

Two days later the cops were still raiding houses. They went into Willie Smith's house in Govan and arrested him for the murder and the serious assault. I went to meet his girlfriend and she told me that she had been to the Procurator Fiscal to explain that Willie and she had left us earlier that night to go for a meal and celebrate her birthday. She gave the time, place and details of their movements. The cops have their grasses and their ears to the ground. All their criminal contacts had informed them that Willie Smith wasn't even near the house that night. So he was now in prison for something he had nothing whatsoever to do with, even in the remotest sense, but they weren't going to do anything about it. He would await trial and no one on the official side would lift a finger to assist him. This is what we in the criminal world call "being slung to the wolves" and this is the very reason why most guys with a criminal record avoid the cops when they are looking for them, not out of a sense of guilt but out of common bloody sense.

A few days later while in my Ma's house — I had barely crossed the threshold — there was a knock on the door and I answered it. I was confronted by the cops who were astonished to see me, although they recovered quickly enough to pounce on me. I was hustled down to Police Headquarters and charged by detectives for taking a guy's eye out and cutting another on the hand. From there I was taken to the Northern police station where

I was charged with murder and serious assault. Detectives made the charge and cautioned me, asking if I had anything to say, to which I replied no. I was then taken in front of a uniformed police inspector where I had the charge repeated and I made the same reply. The murder charge worried me a lot as I knew the cops would be very reluctant to let me walk out of this one a free man. Their attitude towards Willie Smith made my speculation even wilder. So it was a total surprise when I was confronted by a cop and told that I could walk free if I gave them a statement. This told me that they were groping in the dark and it made me feel somewhat easier, but not much, as I knew they were going to make a determined effort to put us all in. Anyway, it was nice to be able to tell the cop to stick his offer up his arse.

One of the fears one has when being charged by detectives is that they are prone to writing down what they think you should be saying rather than what you actually are saying. This is called "verballing". When an accused person is charged by the cops he is usually told of the charge and asked if he has anything to say. This is called "cautioning and charging" a prisoner. The accused person is then taken in front of a police inspector at the station bar and here he is formally cautioned and charged. The police inspector isn't present in court, but the detective is, and it is he who is asked whether the accused replied when cautioned and charged. It is here that he reads out what they say the accused said, which is usually not what the accused actually said. This, of course, can seriously damage the defence of the accused. The inspector at the bar hasn't a stake in the case so if comparisons were made in cases where verballing was suspected, then I'm sure there would be a vast difference in what the detective's notebook said to that of the ledger that the inspector puts in his book. Of course this would be explained by saying that the accused said a different thing on each occasion. At the end of the day it's a difficult thing to prove for eventually it boils down to either the jury believing the police or the accused. There is also the point that most lawyers don't like to directly challenge the police by calling them liars, as it will put their clients at a disadvantage. Most juries take the side of the cops and as "verballing" is usually done with accused people who have previous convictions, then it means that by attacking the Crown witness's character, the defence leaves their characters open to attack. As the accused with previous convictions stands to lose, he has to pray that the other evidence will be so weak as to render the "verballing" useless.

Both Willie and I were remanded in custody but kept in separate parts of the prison. He was in the hospital and I was kept under strict supervision on the bottom flat in the untried hall. Now I was awaiting two trials and the charges against me amounted to three serious assaults and murder. This was heavy by any standards. When I was first accused of murder, it was fairly generally accepted that I was innocent, now they were saying otherwise, even though they hadn't heard the full story. They were making flash judgements and condemning us without any qualms. I didn't give two fucks what they said. Screws would make remarks behind my back which would come back to me; they were thinking just like the cops as they all had the same sort of minds.

After I had been in custody for some weeks, I received a letter from the Procurator Fiscal informing me that the charges of murder and serious assault against me had, for the moment, been held in abeyance. Willie was released but I was held in on these other charges and refused bail. The Press made a big deal of it. This was the first time such a thing had happened in a murder trial. Meanwhile the cops were continuing the search for Willie Bennett and Tony Smith who were languishing in New York.

I received an Indictment for the other two serious assaults and was taken to trial in front of a Sheriff and Jury. My younger cousin had been charged with me although he had played a very minor part and was let out on bail after his arrest. The two guys identified me for attacking them and the Jury eventually found me guilty and I was sentenced to two years imprisonment. I started these two years with an advantage in that I was a known personality on my own merits in the criminal sense. So from the start things were pretty cushy and I was given a nice easy job and allowed the usual perks. The prison routine was still the same and old guys told me that it had been pretty much the same since they first came in. Doing time in this prison system does nothing to penetrate or give a person any better understanding of what it's all about. But every time I went into prison I broadened my criminal horizons by making more and more connections in different areas. These were people who knew what the nick was all about, would go into prison, do their time and go out again to take up where they left off.

I met many of the old guys who had been sentenced by Lord Carmont. There was a time when he had made an example of guys charged with serious assaults and had given them sentences that were meant to shock and put an effective end to razor slashings. In practice it was not an effective deterrent, though certain reactionary sections of the Scottish society still shout for more Carmont sentences. They say how well Carmont cleared up the situation but one only had to look at the guys like me who were doing these sentences at that moment.

A few weeks after Willie Smith was released from our murder charge I got news that he was lying in a Glasgow hospital with his throat cut and waiting to be charged with murder. He had been badly wounded in a fight in which the guy he was fighting had died. This was a shattering blow as we were very close, but it also carried other implications. He was now in great danger through these further disastrous circumstances, of being recharged with the murder charge that was being held in abeyance. When we first got those letters of abeyance we saw them as the Authorities' clever way of getting out of a situation that could have become embarrassing for them as they had no real evidence to support the charge. However Willie Smith's latest incident changed everything. I was lying in my cell trying to weigh it all up and I became very apprehensive and went to the prison Governor, Duncan MacKenzie. I told him that due to the change of events, I wanted some sort of guarantee from the prison officials that, if the police came up to recharge me for this murder charge that was in abeyance, I could have independent witnesses standing beside me as I was afraid of "verballing". This was agreed to. Willie Smith recovered from the cut throat and was charged with murdering a guy in Govan and was transferred to the prison hospital for treatment while awaiting trial.

Within a short period of time, the other two, Willie Bennett and Tony Smith, returned from New York and were also arrested. That meant that all four of us were in custody, so the preparations went ahead for the trial. Willie Smith was now facing a harrowing situation as he had two murder charges to face and hadn't even been near the first one. By now, the cops in the Glasgow force were all very much aware that Willie had not been with us that night, but that Frank had been. But they weren't interested in Frank as he was in London and no bother to them, whereas Willie was a tremendous source of trouble.

During this period some funny things began happening to the witnesses who were under police supervision. Word was seeping through to us that they were now saying that Willie Smith had committed the murder in the house that night. This was very frightening because if this is what they were saying about Willie, who had not been there, then what the hell were they saying about those of us who had been present. All our lawyers were finding it extremely difficult to get hold of the witnesses for statements. This was all very strange indeed and had our minds working overtime. At the pleading diet, which is the preliminary hearing to fix pleas and dates for trial, our lawyers, mine in particular, complained to the Sheriff about his difficulty in seeing the witnesses for the Crown. There was a debate on this, which all seemed very sinister to me sitting in the dock. Newspaper headlines blazoned "Missing Witnesses", so that on returning to prison from court everyone was gossiping, assuming that we had done something with the witnesses when in fact we couldn't even get hold of them.

Fears were expressed by some friends from the outside that we were destined to go down, come what may, and some of them decided that enough was enough and blew up the house of the main witnesses against us with a gelignite bomb. No one was hurt, but by the time we went for trial it was open confrontation with the police. When the trial commenced it became pretty clear that in spite of the fears of those outside, there just wasn't a decent case against us. Halfway through the case there was a recess, during which we were taken downstairs to the cells and locked up. Our lawyers came down and spoke to us asking us to accept a plea of guilty to a simple charge of "Pushing and Jostling". I wasn't too keen on accepting this deal and neither were the others as we knew that we had nothing to do with this. Eventually we did agree to it and were taken upstairs where Lord Strachan accepted the change of pleas and we were given a further three months imprisonment. We put on a happy face, but that was only for the cops who were sitting in the benches behind us, as we did beat them and prevented them from putting us away for good.

In the cells below it was a different matter. Willie Smith and I were put in the same cell in the High Court Buildings and were taken in the same van to Barlinnie prison. In the back of the van on the journey a uniformed cop in the back with us remarked how lucky we were only getting three months. Simultaneously Willie and I remarked that we weren't lucky as we had had nothing to do with it. The cop then said that if that was the case then why didn't we turn Queen's Evidence. We didn't answer simply because the last thing one does is sit in a Black Maria and chat to the cops. But the answer to it was that Willie wasn't even there at the scene of the crime yet he had come closest to being found guilty. I was there but had been with the girl Irene at the time so there was no way that either of us could have attempted to clear ourselves with turning Queen's Evidence even if we had wanted to.

Everyone was now saying that we were really lucky and some bunch of "fixers". No one wanted to see that we may have been innocent. That would have gone against the grain as we were gangsters and no one wanted to believe otherwise. Who actually killed the guy? For me to say I could pin it on anyone definitely would be a downright lie though I had my suspicions. There were a lot of people in the house who made off and really it could have been any one of them. People in Glasgow identified our names with trouble so that if we were near it then they automatically assumed that we had done it. Most of the times we had, but other times — very few — we hadn't. But even then we didn't discourage the wrong assumptions as they all added to the myth which continued to grow around us. Because we all came from different districts and within these districts each of us had reputations, there had never been this sort of gathering by guys in the criminal element in Glasgow ever before. Although we were inside this was still the great motivating force — our reputation.

Back to prison we went and on entering the hall I had been celled in I saw that the place was being turned upside down with police all over the place and prisoners' cells being emptied of possessions. It so happened that someone had made a "hit" on a guy and he had died. This was the first murder to take place in a Scottish prison. All I could say was thank God I had the perfect alibi — I was in court.

But Willie Smith had another murder charge to appear on. Within three weeks he was sent to trial in the same court for the murder. All of us were rooting for him. The two brothers had attacked him in the Govan area, cutting his throat in the middle of the street but Willie managed to get the knife from one of them and in self defence struck back, killing the guy. He had plenty of evidence to support his case but the whole thing was very uncertain, especially with his name still fresh in the minds of people after the trial three weeks previously. But all went well for him and he was cleared. He walked out of the dock to complete his three months sentence along with the rest of us. The overall feeling amongst us was that of victory. All these incidents had been very dramatic not only for us but for the legal profession and the police. Nothing like this had ever happened in Scotland before. In fact it was unusual by any standards.

Within a few months, that would be January 1966, I was to

become a father and when the time came I received a telegram saying that Margaret had given birth to a boy. I really was very happy. It was something I could never have imagined myself being — a father. I never felt I was that type but I was very pleased. But the happiness of this was brought to an abrupt halt one Sunday morning when I was informed by word of mouth through the prison grapevine that my younger brother Harry had been arrested and charged with murder. I was shattered and couldn't really believe it. The thought of him facing a life sentence was too awful to think about. It was one thing for me to be in that position but not my younger brother. I really felt this more than I did of any of the charges that I had been on. My mother was absolutely heart-broken and must have been wondering where it was all going to end. All of my family were deeply shocked. Harry was the baby of the family and held the affection of us all. At this moment, the prison authorities took it upon themselves to transfer me to Peterhead prison to complete my sentence. This was the long term prison in Scotland and I was being put out of the way so that I couldn't help Harry in any way or give him advice. I was sick and disgusted with this as there had been this feeling that so long as I was near at hand he would be okay.

Peterhead is in the far north of Scotland, far away from Glasgow and in an isolated spot. On reaching there I was taken into the reception area which also happens to be the Punishment Block holding sixteen cells, eight on one floor and eight on the second floor. The procedure from there is the very same as that of any prison. I was put in a cell that was a third the size of a normal one where I could barely spread my arms. Every second cell was this size for some reason and though the authorities maintain that a prisoner was never kept in them very long, overcrowding soon blew that one and guys were doing very long sentences in them. There wasn't very much space for moving so that when he was locked in the prisoner would have no option but to lie on his bed. I got on very well and I knew everyone that mattered, as there were lots of familiar faces from the early days. Most of them were doing very long-term sentences. There was an atmosphere between the screws and the prisoners that hadn't existed in any other place I'd been in. It was extremely hostile, with the feeling of constant tension. The two factions didn't speak to each other unless it was absolutely necessary. In other prisons one would frequently see the odd prisoner talking to the screws. It seemed that the Peterhead screws had a particular dislike for the Glasgow guys and though it was put down to the city-slicker and hayseed thing, it was sometimes very personal.

For some obscure reason I was put on Rule 36. I was called in front of the Governor and told by him that I was being placed on Rule 36 for subversive activities. I asked him what the reason was and he said again that it was for subversive activities and would say no more than that. I was locked up in the punishment block which was in an isolated part of the prison with all its own facilities. There were sixteen cells in the small two-storey block and outside the back door block was an area with three small concrete boxes with a catwalk running above them. The boxes were meant to be solitary exercise yards and the catwalk for the screw to walk along and observe. Beside these yards was a large concrete sort of shelter called the "silent cell". This is a cell within a cell which means that you walk in one heavy door then into another smaller cell and the place is completely bare.

I was pretty mad at them locking me up, so when I was inside the cell in the punishment block I decided on a course of action. The cells are bare just like the punishment cells in any prison, but there was a ventilating system in the far corner of the wall to let air in. I heard voices coming from it and discovered that this was how the guys communicated with each other, by speaking through the vents. I spoke through and found I was speaking to Ben Conroy, who was doing a five year sentence and was now in solitary. Within a few minutes I was to find that out of all the guys in the solitary block, three were old St John's Approved School kids and one was from the Gorbals.

At night time, when all the screws had gone home, leaving the night patrol, I went up to the cell door, took my chamber pot by the handle and started banging on the door continuously. The screws came and asked me what was wrong but I refused to answer and kept banging. The continuous noise became unbearable to those about as they couldn't sleep, so they automatically got up and started banging which meant that all the guys in the punishment block started up and the noise went to the outside halls and all the prisoners in those cells started banging which meant that the screws' families, who lived outside the wall, would also hear it and have to bear with it. The Prison Chief was called in and they opened my cell asking me what I was causing all this bother for and I told them that I was in solitary and wanted them to take me off. They left and from there started putting old mattresses up in front of my door to muffle the sounds but it was no good. The reinforcements then came in banging their sticks but I continued as I was being bloody minded and wanted to get out of there.

This went on for some time and eventually they opened the door and took me through the back into this "silent cell". On the way I was waiting for the boots and batons to start flying but I was pulled along and as I entered the second door of the cell a figure was standing against the wall to the side of it and both of us stared at each other. It was Ben Conroy who was waiting for the screws to come in, only to find me entering. They locked us up together, going back to quell the rest as they felt we were the persistent ones. We had an idea that they would be back, so we thought about preparing for this although there was nothing much we could do. It was surprising for the two of us to be thrown into the one cell; unheard of as far as I knew. We were concerned about what to do when the screws came back, and we felt pretty helpless. I did a shit in the middle of the floor and started rubbing it all over my arms and body and face. I thought that if they were going to come in then I was going to jump on them and grab them so that they would get shit all over them. They did come back and saw what I had done and backed out as I positioned myself to throw my whole body amongst them. At first Ben was reluctant to do this but he did so after vomiting. When the screws left we sat looking at each other throughout the night and every so often would break out in fits of laughter.

The screws obviously thought I was insane but I wasn't going to lie there naked and helpless while they beat me up and I was only doing a two year sentence and didn't want to get involved in any violence with them and get extra time onto my two years. There was too much going for me on the outside and I wanted out, but at the same time I didn't want the authorities to start doing what they wanted with me. I was prepared to go to certain lengths to combat this and what we had just done was an extremity that was on the borderline of violence. It was strange sitting there in this very silent atmosphere, hearing nothing on the outside; so silent that there was a slight whistle in the ears. The shit that was clinging to me was beginning to harden and flake off and fall on the floor. In the morning the screws came in wearing overalls over their uniforms and took Ben away leaving me alone and I knew they would be coming back to attack me. I did another crap and spread it over me and wrote "screw bastards" on the whitewashed walls with the crap that was remaining. I also tore up the two blankets that I had and made leggings and a flap to cover my penis, in the style of the Apache Indian. I refused to do anything and when food was put in the door I threw it all over the floor, and urinated there. By this time I knew that my punishment would be severe so I wasn't giving a damn. Later the screws carried me out into the small exercise yard adjoining and left me as I had refused to move from the foul looking and foul smelling cell. While in the yard they paid an old cleaner guy to go in and hose it out then they lifted me back in.

I lay there for days in complete silence putting more shit all over the walls, and lying on the floor covered in slops and urine. I was remanded by the Governor for the Visiting Committee — a body of civilians who visit prisons to inspect and take complaints, or punish cases that are too severe for the Governor to deal with. I just didn't care about anything at this stage, nothing mattered. One morning The Governor came round and beckoned me out into the fresh air and told me that it might be to my benefit to appear before him the following morning. I thought this over and the following morning I went into Governor's Orderly room where he holds his "court" and many charges were read out against me. I was fined in money from my prison earnings so in many ways this was a let-off and I did appreciate it.

I resumed normal solitary in the ordinary strong cell and I looked on it now with the attitude that at least I had caused bloody hell. But they weren't going to budge and let me out of solitary completely so although I felt that I had been able to even the score somewhat I still felt very resentful. It was while lying in these conditions that I was called to the vent by an unknown voice and told that my brother Harry had been found "Not Guilty" of the murder charge against him. The charge had arisen out of a fight that had taken place when some gang of kids attacked him while he was out with his girl friend. Harry had taken the weapon off the boy and the unfortunate incident resulted in the kid's death. It was only when the verdict came through that I realised how much this had been weighing me down. I felt so light and easy and although I wasn't aware of it consciously, it took his acquittal to show what an effect it had had on me.

Solitary in Peterhead was different from that in Barlinnie as the solitary block was on its own — purpose built. I would lie throughout the days and nights listening to the sounds being made and identifying people by the way they jangled their keys, the sound of their footsteps, or other noises they made. The thing about Peterhead is that it's very seldom that one gets to know the screws' names but I did get to know their sounds. Some would whistle, others would hum, there was always some idiosyncrasy by which I could identify them. It was the same for the time of day, as certain sounds heard at certain times gave me a rough idea of what time it was. I was a very ignorant sort of person in the sense that, although very much alone, I could never think of looking at myself and trying to understand what I was all about. Instead I blamed everything on the screws and the authorities. I really hated the bastards for what they were doing and thought the screws the lowest of the low. Even to the most inveterate prisoner there is something incomprehensible, even slightly unreal, about being locked in a concrete box listening to the sounds around the place. Often it was the screws talking outside the cell door about what they were going to do that night or had done the night before. They talked about going to the Screws' Social Club and boozing or a party or something like that. After three months on solitary I was put back into the main stream of things to get on with my time.

It was while in Peterhead that the importance of letters to prisoners struck me. Guys would look on letters as the only unrestricted means of keeping contact with the outside. Prisoners are only allowed to write home once a week but the incoming mail was unrestricted though it was heavily censored. To send out an extra letter meant fabricating all sorts of excuses such as a member of the family dying or something equally dramatic. Most times guys were denied an extra letter. It was a good feeling to come in from work and see the screws standing handing out the mail to prisoners but it wasn't too good if there wasn't one for the guy who was expecting one. Having or not having a letter can be what puts a guy into a bad depression.

Visits also put a strain on guys as they looked forward to them and all of us expecting a visit would get all cleaned up, exaggerating the cleaning up process and the clean shirt bit. The strain shows most as the visit time approaches. Sometimes the visit doesn't materialise for some reason or other and the prisoners dread this sort of thing as preparations have usually been taking place all week, whereas the people on the outside have other things to do and don't attach the same importance to it. Most of the long-termers in Peterhead accumulate their year's visits so that they can go down to the local prison nearest their homes to see their families once a year. This means that he is allowed to save the three visits every two months that he is due, amounting to one and a half hours. This gives him nine hours per year but for some reason he is only allowed four and a half during his spell in the local prison. Lots of guys do this as it means saving their families money making the journey; also it gives them a sort of break from the one prison. The atmosphere in Peterhead is always verging on the explosive so this break is needed. There are other guys who don't go down for visits and just stay in the long-term prison as they feel that there is too much pain in going down to a local prison and seeing their families. Then there are those guys who have no-one at all to visit them. One of the unpleasant things in prison is the "Dear John" letter that guys get from their girls, or guys hearing that their wives are messing around with another guy. When this happens they don't go to the official side to get assistance, though there is the odd guy who will go to the Welfare Officer, but most guys have no confidence in him and see him as a screw without a uniform. Bad news from outside is a painful experience and torturing in some ways as it brings home to the prisoner just what prison is all about — loss of freedom. There is no substitute for freedom. So when faced with problems from the outside guys have to keep them to themselves though they will usually talk them over with a close friend.

During the period that I was completing my sentence, there were lots of other things happening. John McCue was appearing for trial for stabbing a guy in a fight and was charged with attempted murder. The fight took place in Peterhead and he appeared at the High Court in Aberdeen and was acquitted. Willie Smith and Frank Wilson, on the outside, were appearing in Glasgow High Court for charges of attempted murder by stabbing and shooting in the Govan district. Willie Smith was given three years, and Frank was acquitted. This meant that myself, Willie Smith and John McCue were now all together in Peterhead. There were also lots of guys from our district and other places that we had been in before. All the old familiar faces with lots of new kids coming in, and I was still only twenty two years old.

On the outside things were pretty hectic as friends were getting involved in some trouble in London with the top "firms" down there. But in Scotland — Glasgow — things were building up with my friends getting a measure of control in the money-lending. Things were beginning to grow and the basis for more organised crime was entering into our ways. There was a loose but growing connection with the Kray twins in London. Some of my pals had been down to see them, at the twins' invitation, and thought very highly of them. At the same time, on the Glasgow scene, there was some trouble between my friends in the Gorbals and another couple of guys, who had walked up to a friend of mine firing a shot, intending to hit him in the arse, but some loose silver in his back pocket stopped the bullet from penetrating. There had been yet another clash resulting in one of the other guys being given sixty stitches in a face wound, so things were looking difficult but interesting as I waited for my release.

9

I was released from Barlinnie prison on 13th January 1967, and was met at the the gate by Frank Wilson and some others. We all went to my house where breakfast and drinks were organised, and for the first time I was able to hold my child who would shortly be having his first birthday. After breakfast they all left and I was alone with my son and his mother. This was crazy and very unfair to her as I knew then definitely that this should never have been, but I felt that the child was a commitment. However, that aside, it was good to be with a woman again.

I wanted to see what was happening in the district so as to get the feel of the events now taking place. That same afternoon the guys picked me up and we went round looking at everyone and seeing things. It was a time of elation as it's great to have one of your own out from prison. We had all been brought up together so we were very close. Certainly we fell out now and again but usually this amounted to nothing and even when it was serious the opinion of the group would dictate the way it went. There was one particular incident when two of my pals fell out around this time and had a quarrel, resulting in one of them coming to my door covered in bloodstains and the other guy — Tam Comerford — coming very near to death. I helped him into fresh clothes getting rid of the bloodstained ones. After that I went to the house where the fight had taken place and found it covered in blood. I told the two girls who were there to say nothing to the police. Tam was unconscious at the bottom of the stairs with blood pouring out of him. An ambulance was called for him and we left him to be found alone when it came. The following day I was up to the intensive care unit to visit Tam. The whole thing had been over girls and he was in the wrong, so Frank and I acted as mediators and advised Tam and the other guy to leave it there and forget it and this was done. These things went on but they were our way of life and the actions and the part that I played were normal to us. I wasn't showing any disloyalty to Tam by helping the other guy get rid of his bloody gear, nor by telling the two girls to say nothing, nor for that matter by visiting Tam in hospital. These were just done things and the fact that one of them nearly died was the way things go.

Anyway, with me just out of prison, I was given a piece of the action to get me on my feet. With this came some money to start my own money lending book and I wanted to start my own Shebeen. The money and assistance to start this was crime working at its best from my point of view. There was a feeling of strength within our group and we were sailing high.

Things with my Ma weren't so good as she was in hospital suffering from cancer of the breast. When I went to see her, she looked so tired and worn and seemed to be shrinking into herself. The pain that she had suffered through having me as a son must have been tremendous, never mind the physical pain of her illness. She sat in hospital looking very frail. We talked and Ma warned me, as though I were ten years old, telling me not to get into trouble and I responded as though I were ten years old by telling her that I was finished with crime. I knew I couldn't tear myself away from the life I was leading and really I didn't want to. At the same time, I wasn't lying to Ma for lying's sake. She was such a good, kind, gentle person that it would have been very difficult to even begin to tell her the truth. In fact the thought didn't bear thinking about. The nearest I got was to tell her that I wouldn't be taking a job. The reason for this was that she would see me at different times of the day, so it was best to admit that much. Anyway, she wasn't stupid and knew the score by now and we both tried to avoid the subject. Things in the house were very quiet with Pat working, my brother Tommy married with a baby daughter and Harry working away from home.

We were now the top mob so with a little luck we would expand and develop things and make plenty of money. The only other strong opposition was one other guy who at this time had been put away for four years so this left a completely open field. We were going from strength to strength and the financial side was blooming. Moneylending was a lucrative business and the policy was to give it to anyone who asked, because experience had told us that most people would pay back what they borrowed. There was a bad debt list but that was inevitable, and it was small in comparison to the number of people who paid. It wasn't a case of those who borrowed the money being assaulted or having money extorted from them every week of the year. Certainly this was the picture presented by the imaginative minds of the press, and they presented this picture because it was illegal. Why then did the moneylender need heavies? Usually it was because the moneylenders themselves needed some form of protection, otherwise the money would be taken from them; but in our case it was different, with the heavies doing the business side for themselves. I suppose that it was the first hint of organised crime in Scotland.

Moneylending was traditional in most areas of Glasgow, but the majority of moneylenders were illegal, as they were usually ordinary working guys or housewives who had money to lend. They did this at work or in their homes, giving the cash to their neighbours or workmates. The interest was now five shillings in the pound (25p) and if the borrower couldn't pay it back the following week then another five shillings went on top. This was pretty widespread and lots of people used this method for cash rather than go to a legal moneylender where some sort of security had to be given and time had to elapse before the borrower could get the cash. At the end of the day if they couldn't pay, the legal moneylender would impound goods in the borrower's house and take them to court. Also people didn't want to go through all the formalities, just to get a few pounds. The illegal moneylender however, had no such formality, as a known borrower could just vouch for someone else and cash would change hands. They also knew they could never be taken to court. There was very little problem with people refusing to pay back, as it meant that if they didn't, they couldn't go back again. Moneylending was very much supplying a public demand. It was a good way to earn money for nothing and so some guys on release from prison began to get involved and, though it was run on the same lines, it did attract other criminals who wanted to borrow, and it was usually them who would give the problems in refusing to pay back and so the Heavies were brought in to act as "minders". Eventually it became a mixed bag with lots of straight people still doing it and also lots of guys who had criminal records. But on the whole it was accepted as a semi-legitimate game by everyone, and it was very difficult for the cops ever to get convictions for it.

Within our group of friends there were many of us with our own "Books", (moneylending businesses) and as far as finance, profit and losses went these were separate. If any heavy trouble came along then we shared it and everybody came to the assistance of the book having the trouble.

After a few weeks I set up a Shebeen selling booze after hours, and the one rule was that no credit be given unless the client was known. This also meant that guys could borrow money from some of the others and buy the booze from me. As I got into the swing of things, life became pretty comfortable and all of us were doing well, some much better than others but it was growing. Slowly but surely we started spreading our tentacles into the docks and other districts where we began leaning on other moneylenders, taking a share in their profits.

The strange thing about the criminal scene is that it attracts lots of weirdos, and this includes people who lived decent lives and had no reason for hanging around us. There was an antique dealer, who had no connections with the criminal world whatsoever, who paid me money just for being around him. There was another character who paid me an incredible amount of money for sitting in a car outside his house waiting for some guy who he thought was intending to do him an injury. All of us knew that the story was fictitious and that no one wanted to harm a hair on his head. This was the whole crazy set-up but unfortunately life wasn't all that sweet. There was the odd guy who would refuse to pay money and would be thumped on the jaw, but this would only happen occasionally as no business run on fear could survive. If people were frightened about what would happen to them for missing a few weeks then they wouldn't have come in the first place. When given cash, the punters were told that if for some reason they couldn't pay, then they were always to show face and tell us that the money wasn't there and we would come to some agreement or even forget it altogether, so this is what usually happened. The guys who did get thumped were those who had deliberately gone out of their way to get money with no intention of repaying it. If they were to get away with it then the wolves who were all about would be in trying to take it off me. Lots of thieves would come to borrow and they were safe bets as we knew that as soon as they got a hoist then they would pay back.

I got a new house in Rutherglen Road a few closes from my Ma's new house there. As the Gorbals redevelopment scheme expanded, with the old tenements being torn down and replaced with new ones, all of us wanting to stay in the district would move into the next set of tenements. These would usually have a two year reprieve before being pulled down. My new house was on the top flat with a room and kitchen, but I had the place changed a bit and had the ceiling lowered and a bar put in. I also got myself a very large and powerful dog, a Dobermann Pinscher, to guard the house and look after my son. They were both about the same age. It was a very frightening animal. I would take my son into the park opposite the house and some days I'd sit there for hours in the sun. These were the peaceful moments that interrupted the tumultuous life that I was leading. Even during these very happy times I could never question my criminal way of life. I seemed to forget about all the bad things that had happened to me. The beatings, the humiliations of prison, the degradation of instances like the shit over me, I just didn't think of them, and maybe that's because I was still living in it. I had accepted this life and in many ways knew no better, nor wanted to. I didn't look on this life as being horrific, nor did the other guys. The cops pretended that they did, but then I knew so much about their way of life that it didn't matter what they thought. Some of the things that they did were evil and if that was what the "good" side meant they could keep it.

The time I came nearest to thinking a bit more deeply was after having a fight with two guys in the middle of the street one day. A car pulled up and the driver told me to get in. It was an old school pal with his brother, and he had been a member of the Skull gang way back. It was good to see him but he started saying that he couldn't understand why I led this sort of life and talked in great depth, with me just laughing him off and getting out at home. Once out of the car I felt very uncomfortable about what he had been saying. I don't know if it was because I recognised the truth in what he said, or that I knew he had done some very crazy things while in my gang and here he was talking to me like this. I do know that what he was saying stayed with me and gave me food for thought, but this was washed away as the memory of him faded.

Running a Shebeen was quite a funny experience with never a dull moment. It was amazing to see the desperate measures some people would go to for a drink. Old men and women would spin the most fantastic tales to get it and the hard luck stories would be plentiful. There was this old lady who was a Hawker and she would come up with anything and everything to barter for booze. There were others who would come up with handfuls of single shillings or sixpences from the Meters on their gas, T.V. or electrical appliances. There were the few that one couldn't resist — you'd have to be superhuman to be able to refuse them.

I was going away one particular day and I left this guy in charge, going through the whole scene so as to let him know what to expect. But since he had seen it all, having been around quite a bit, I left feeling confident and thinking that he would be able to handle it. The punters of course, hearing that I was away, came flooding to the door and made the most of it. On my return, when we tallied everything up, there was a bit of booze short but I was assured by this guy that it was okay as my Aunt had had it. I really blew a fuse as I knew that it must have been a punter trying her hand — successfully. He told me that there had been lots of them up trying to con him and he had rejected them, but this homely woman had come up with no coat demanding to see me and had walked straight into the house, taking over, and he had fallen for it and given her what she wanted. The point is that lots of these people didn't give a shit how tough you were. If they needed drink and you happened to have it and there was some way it could be taken from you, then they would do so.

By now we had a strong friendship with the Kray twins in London, and we would go down there to big fights or to get a few days away from the Glasgow scene. Whenever we went to London we were made most welcome by the friends that we had there. I have always noticed an innate disdain by lots of Scottish guys for the English criminals — most of them thought they were a bit soft. This is certainly far from the truth, as the majority lived very tough lives but concentrated on cash, whereas we in Scotland were more inclined to weigh things up from the physical side. The English guys realise this of course and recognise that Scotland produces good heavies and that is why they have so many in their firms.

In the summer of '67 we were having a pretty heavy time, as this other gang from the opposite end of the Gorbals had caught one of our mob in Gorbals Cross and had shot him through the chest at point-blank range. This was a declaration of war and meant that we would have to take full precautions. When a person is shot like this the cops swarm all over the place for a few days. We spent those first few days hanging around the hospital waiting to hear how he was making out, and speaking to him when he was capable of it, to get the whole picture. Of course the police had spoken to him and had got nothing out of him, but we soon had the full score though most of it we knew already. This meant that guns had to be always near at hand, but with the cops hanging around and liable to search us we would arrange for someone who wasn't known, and had an inoffensive appearance, to carry the guns and walk well behind us. He would be positioned close enough for us to reach him quickly but far enough away so as not to be associated with us. Any cops giving us a pull and searching us would find nothing.

The strange thing was that at times like this, after the initial blow-up the cops would keep out of the way. I don't know if this was coincidence or whether they wanted us to do their jobs for them, by shooting it out and killing each other. There was plenty of action during this period as once or twice this mob came round taking shots at us which led to daylight shoot-outs. On one occasion we recognised their car coming at high speed up a particular street. In front of the car was a beer delivery lorry about to stop at a pub. The driver and his mate didn't see the car behind them — only us running towards the lorry with guns pointing in their direction. The two guys in the beer lorry stared in disbelief and stopped dead as we used the lorry for a shield while those in the speeding car and us behind the lorry let off shots at each other. The car stopped and tried to run as we poured shots into it, but they finally made off. Guys standing at the corner loitering all panicked and ran like hell. By this time everyone was leaning out of their windows watching and we made off. I know that the cops heard about this and in fact pulled one guy in and he was warned that if it wasn't so serious it would be funny. It was very much like a wild west show.

The cops were now putting pressure on us and it showed in the form of raids on the pubs where we were collecting in our money. Due to the business side of our activities this meant that we were tied down to certain places at specific times, usually bars. This was why we were an easy target for the other gangs as they always knew where we were. They didn't have the same commitments, which made it difficult for us to get them. It was the same for the cops, they knew where we were so they could make raids, but we had various safeguards. Around this time, I was getting notes pushed through my door by the cops telling me to attend the Police Headquarters, which I had no intention of doing. I would hear them knocking at the door but I wouldn't answer. However, curiosity was getting the better of me so I consulted Jimmy Latta, who was a lawyer and asked him to make some inquiries for me. Apparently some cop was identifying me for passing a rubber cheque that had been given to a nearby cafe owner. It seems that some guy went into the cafe, saying he had just returned from London and was short of cash and with the banks closed he couldn't cash a cheque and asked the cafe owner to do so. The owner was very wary so the guy told him that he knew me, and at that moment in walked one of the uniformed beat cops. The owner turned to him and explained everything, including the fact that the guy was a pal of mine. For some unknown reason, the cop told the owner that it was safe enough and to go ahead, the result being that the cheque bounced back in the owner's face. This left the cop in an embarrassing situation and he had to justify himself, so the next thing we know, I was Chief Suspect. Without wasting any time, I went round to the cafe owner and spoke to him. He talked quite openly about it and was surprised to hear that I was being involved. I told him to get in touch with the cops and straighten them out otherwise they would be hauling me in. I spoke to the Fraud Squad by phone and they retracted the whole thing.

As I have said the internal politics of our mob were very smooth on the whole and we got on well together, but occasionally nasty things would crop up. Willie Bennett was on the fringe of our group. He had been very close but due to a series of dirty strokes he was by now the outcast, though not completely rejected. No one told him that he was finished as it didn't work that way, but there would be a cold front presented to him and he knew the score. However, Willie Bennett and this other guy, Babs Rooney, another fringe man who floated around the various districts but mostly in the city centre, had teamed up on an extended drinking spree. When they ran out of cash for booze they would go to the moneylenders and replenish their purses. Now this particular moneylender they were going to was one from whom I was taking a weekly wage, so, if they got away with this then every Tom, Dick or Harry would do the same. The politics of the situation were that Willie Bennett wasn't likely to be hit, simply because his brother Malky, who was doing a ten year sentence, was very much one of us and a person we all thought the world of. If anything happened to Willie, it would be like going against Malky.

One night in July '67 I was drinking with my friends while they collected their money. Along with me was Frank's brother William Wilson who was the same age as me; we left and went to a quiet pub that I liked, for a drink on our own. At time up I asked him to come to Kinning Park with me. The rain was pelting down and we ran through the backs in Crown Street to to go to William's house for his coat, but on the way we bumped into two guys. I was carrying a bag of beer, but in the darkness of the night a fight started between us. I had a knife but it was in the instep of my boot and so was William's. I tried to get it out but by this time the guys got a couple of hits in with beer cans, William receiving the bulk of these. Eventually I got my knife out and cut one of the guys and another kid who happened to be passing through the back at the time, who was only sixteen years old. They all made off and we carried on to get William's coat. He had a small cut from the beer can blows and a few bumps.

On reaching Kinning Park we went to the house of Babs Rooney and the door was opened by an attractive girl who lived with Babs. I also knew her from the city centre where the prostitutes hung around. Babs was in bed, but he got up, putting on his trousers, remaining bare chested. We were on amiable terms as he had returned the money that both Willie Bennett and he had taken from the moneylender guy and so all of us sat around drinking. Babs had been in prison with me a few times and I had known him on the outside but I had only been with him a couple of times. He was known for being around the prostitutes a lot of the time, he was not a bad looking guy with greying hair. We discussed the money situation, about him going at the demand, and he agreed that what they had done was out of order, so we decided to forget it.

After a while he brought up an old score about a pal of mine who went to his house, or his sister's house, with a revolver, intending to shoot him, and we argued about this very heatedly. His girl, Sadie, was in the other room attending to the child that she had, so I took my knife out and ran it down his chest and cut him with a slashing motion. Both of us were standing and Babs just stood there and said nothing. I went into the next room and assured Sadie that Babs wasn't very badly hurt and she should say nothing to anyone and she went along with this. She had been around and knew the score. William stood there in the kitchen with Babs while I did this. I walked outside the house with Sadie, calming her and speaking to her. I stood at the close front with her, waiting on William coming, but after some time when he hadn't appeared, I left Sadie and went back up to the house to get him. The door was locked and when I looked through the letter box the lights were out and no one answered. I took it that Babs had closed the door so as not to get any more. With no sign of William, I could only guess that he had come down behind me and left through the back way, so I rejoined Sadie and spoke to her again until a taxi drew up and a couple that I knew got out and I replaced them. I told the driver to take me home, then I went to bed.

The following morning the noise from the dog barking and

someone banging at the door awakened me. It was two friends and they told me that Babs Rooney was dead and that William Wilson had been charged with his murder. I was completely stunned as I had been so casual about the whole thing, knowing that I had only slashed him. What could have gone wrong? No one knew. I knew it would only be a matter of time till the cops came, so I gave all my clothes and the knife that I had to my friends and one of them took them away. They were burned. I was taken to a house out of town and kept there to await further news. William was charged on his own as it seems he had been caught in the house with the dead body of Babs. I couldn't believe this. To add to it he was charged with theft and found with money of Sadie's from her purse. He was also covered in bloodstains, so things looked very bad for him. However, as is practice in such cases, the cops went over the place with fingerprint experts and my fingerprints were found on a beer can. This did it, they were going crazy to get me when I was labelled as having been there. The search was unprecedented and the cops were pulling everyone in to find me. The information started coming in thick and fast with word that William had been offered a deal and was told that he would be given means to start somewhere afresh if he would sign a statement against me. William, of course, declined the offer. Bandit Rooney, no relation of Babs, was offered money to reveal my whereabouts, he too declined. Because such offers are general practice in an important case, we kept my hiding place a secret among the very few, thus cutting the risk of betrayal. Police were following guys who were known associates of mine, offering deals to others in the criminal world if they would try to find out where I was. All of this came back to me. The Glasgow police were showing boundless enthusiasm. Their resources were vast and they were moving in on me.

My house in the Gorbals was occupied by a friend and his girl, so that while I was in hiding the cops moved in, taking crates of booze and tearing the house apart in their search for evidence. They questioned the people in the house and were taking photographs of things but they never took the photos in the presence of my friends and would move them from one room to the next as they did so. My Dobermann Pinscher was taken into custody. Eventually all the people in my house were taken into custody and held for some hours and questioned. Lots of articles were taken from the house; they were giving it the works. My mind was racing all over the place. What were they up to?

The house where I was in hiding was very nice. It was in a small town with all the comforts of a home. What were my thoughts at that moment? Utter confusion. I was so sick at the whole turn of events that I became physically ill. I lay there knowing that things looked very dark indeed. The house was now very much my prison. I lay inside it for three solid weeks. Occasionally I would peep out of the window to get some fresh air. I lay in bed and stared at the ceiling, trying to forget, and then trying to remember what it was all about. The media broadcast that William was charged with murder, four assaults and theft, and this made me even sicker. The rumours going round were that William was bang in trouble but that the cops were determined to get me in. I was already aware of this and needed no confirmation from anyone. William felt that with me staying away he would be in with a chance. I didn't need to be told this either as I had no intention of going to the cops. Meanwhile the police were sitting in my house in the Gorbals and the uniformed cop detailed to do this was P.C. Howard Wilson, a name to bear in mind. From time to time, I would get visitors who kept me up to date on events. Rumour had it that the heat had cooled somewhat as they thought that I was in a hundred different places. Arrangements were made for me to go to London and within a few days I was down there. The Kray brothers looked after me for some of the time but I preferred to be very much on my own as I was always wary of bringing too much trouble to others. They looked after me very well while I was with them. They have plenty of respect in Scotland from the guys who knew them, and I thought highly of them.

10

I stayed in a nice flat in London and kept very much to myself, with the occasional visitor coming to see me. The Glasgow police were making trips down and raiding houses in London looking for me. Of course they hadn't a clue that I was getting word of their every move as the London scene was incredible for bent cops. One day I was with a friend in a London district and a police inspector offered to put me up in his house. There was no way that I would have taken him up on it, but this was how the scene there was. I walked about London freely as the place is so big and if you aren't known then it's as safe as you'll get anywhere.

I had been away over two months and it was now September with me moving from the gangster scene to that of the Flower Power one in Hyde Park simply by changing into jeans and a sweater. I loved the London scene at this time and for the first time was finding a sort of peace even though I was on the run. It was probably the mood of the times, the general atmosphere, that was responsible. Being amongst strange people in a strange place made me forget the past and its troubles. It was almost as though the real me was emerging and I've often thought that if this trouble hadn't been hanging over my head I might have made a new life. But it has to be remembered that the dominating factor for me now was loyalty. It would have been unthinkable if I just had vanished and left the others with the trouble in hand. Anyway, it was nice for a time to go with girls who hadn't a clue who I was and who were shouting for everyone to make love not war.

All of this came to a halt when one day some guys came down to London to meet me and talk over the situation. Careful arrangements had been made for them to take precautions. They met me in the British Lion pub in the East End. Amongst them were Frank Wilson, Bandit Rooney, and Pat Gilgunn who had just completed a sentence for culpable homicide, along with another guy. We were discussing things in the bar and around lunch time the place began to fill with workers from the factories nearby, most of them dressed in overalls. We were sitting at the bar, and lots of small movements made by the barman seemed rather odd and began to attract my attention. He went over and loosened the bolts of the door leading to the bar from the side street. From the reflection in the bar mirror I could see an enormous furniture van backing up to the pub door. I remember wondering how such a big van was going to manage in that small street, when the door burst open and lots of workers jumped up from their tables, some with revolvers. This was very frightening as I thought they were a gang but they shouted that they were police. I was overwhelmed by them and so were the others, the bar was packed full with cops. It was so bad that we couldn't move, either the cops or us. I was pinned by the arms and crushed, so on seeing this I took advantage and caught the eye of the bar manager and asked him in very clear tones to bear witness that I had nothing to say to these men till I saw my solicitor. He said that he would witness what I had said which enraged the cops who pulled me by the hair and finally extracted me from the pub. In the car were two Scottish cops along with the London ones. I was asked if I had dyed my hair as it seemed lighter due to the sun, but I kept still, saying nothing.

Frank and the others were taken into custody expecting charges to be placed against them. Their car had been impounded and was in the cop-shop being searched. Eventually they let them go but they refused to take the car as they were afraid that something may have been planted in it. Later I heard one of the cops remark that they, Frank and the others, were a suspicious shower of bastards. At no time was I cautioned or charged. I had no idea how they had got onto us and caught me, but the obvious answer is that they had followed the others in spite of the full precautions that had been taken. I was flown home with the two cops who asked if I could be trusted without handcuffs. I said yes and that was the only exchange we had. An escort of cops was waiting at Glasgow airport for us. They were glad to have me and congratulated each other when they met, but they knew that only half the battle was over.

Once in Glasgow I was taken to the Govan district police station and there I was charged with murder and four assaults. The book was being slung at me and this time there was a feeling of doom within me. I was put into an observation cell on the bottom flat which had one wall made out of steel bars with a young cop sitting there on the opposite side watching me. It resembled a zoo with cops coming in all the time to have a look at me, comparing me with the photos that they each had. The young cop was giving a commentary on me to the others, although two hours before he had sat with his mouth wide open in awe at being given the job. Some of the cops coming in and out were at the old game of calling me names. I lay in a corner pretending to sleep just so as I could blot them out. This enraged them and they said I was a callous animal and such like. I must confess that I hated every one of those bastards as they talked. At one point I rose from my bed and told those standing there to take a good fuck at themselves. The small commotion brought in an inspector; he was one of the cops who had escorted me from school all those years ago, and he put them out. Others would come in and I lay in that cell, thinking that these bastards matched everything they called me, but they just couldn't see it. It was as though they were making the most of my being in their custody before handing me over to the prison authorities. I was given an Identification Parade and was identified by a few people for the assault charges but the girl Sadie didn't identify me, and this had the cops on edge. A police guard was kept on all witnesses connected to the case.

Things weren't looking too good for me when I was put into Barlinnie prison where I was kept under strict observation. I had visits from my lawyer, friends and family and was being kept closely in touch with what was going on. Some interesting things were coming back to me. Sadie had gone down to Manchester with a new boyfriend and another guy. They had all been arrested as her boyfriend was wanted on some charges and while in the Police Station she told the third person that I didn't murder Babs and by coincidence he came into Barlinnie which was how I found out. I cited him as a witness. Sadie was eventually arrested again in Scotland and put into Greenock woman's prison under "protective custody".

As the trial period approached, I was able to get an idea of the evidence against me. The most damaging of this was the blood-stained knife that was found, under the linoleum at the entrance inside the doorway of my room in the Gorbals house owned by me. The second piece of evidence was that when cautioned and charged I replied, "I was nowhere near the fucking house". The sixteen year old kid who had been assaulted came from a family that I had had a dispute with in the past. I hadn't known who he was but did very much regret cutting him. Shortly before the trial, a bomb exploded outside the window of his house and the cops threw even tighter security round the witnesses.

I went for trial on the 2nd of November 1967, and sat in the same dock and court as on two previous occasions for murder charges. I knew that I wouldn't walk out this third time. The trial judge was Lord Cameron, the same judge who had presided over my first murder trial. During the trial my Q.C. contested the question of the knife being found in my house, asking why it should be hidden in a place where the first flat-footed policeman entering the house would stand on it. He also questioned the reply to the caution and charge but not too severely. For some reason unknown to me, the police took a photograph of Willie Smith from my house and this too was an exhibit. When asked by the prosecuting Q.C. about it, the policeman giving evidence said that they'd had an interest in Smith at the time. This was puzzling as Willie Smith was in fact serving three years imprisonment. I wondered why they should mention this to the jury? William Wilson was sitting in the dock with me but as far as everyone was concerned he didn't exist.

The big moment came when Sadie entered the dock and exonerated William and me from the murder of Babs. The silence from the benches seating the police behind me was deafening. She had been in prison under "protective custody" but came into court saying that two other men had come into the house and killed Babs. The court was adjourned when Sadie left the dock. William and I were taken downstairs to the cell area below, where I heard a woman crying and voices shouting.

Later, after the recess, the prosecution asked the court to allow Sadie to go back into the witness box, but both our Q.C.s objected and the judge refused as this was unheard of. I noticed Sadie sitting crying between two policewomen in the benches behind me. Lord Cameron directed the jury to find William not guilty of the murder but that it should stand against me. One of William's Q.C.s remarked to him later that he should think himself lucky to have been in the dock with Jimmy Boyle. During the trial it was brought out that the house of one of the witnesses had been blown up with a gelignite bomb, so it was all pretty horrifying.

I was sitting there and I knew that I was doomed, that under no circumstances would I walk out of that court, it would have to collapse first. I knew from the first minute I entered the dock that the only thing I could take out of it was my person, not my freedom. I felt that was gone. The lawyers and judge gave the jury eloquent speeches before they left to decide their verdict. They stayed out for barely two hours then returned to a court packed with cops and civil dignitaries. The benches immediately behind me were crammed with police. I was found guilty of murder — unanimously, also of some of the other charges. William was found not guilty of everything except the theft charges which were against him alone and he was given twenty one months imprisonment.

The reality of doom hit me there in the dock. All was lost but the battle would continue so it was vital for me to show no emotion. This seemed to be the last form of defence left to me in that very lonely, exposed place. When the verdict was given, the small court usher turned round to the cops filling the front benches and the cops were laughing and grinning. I stood for some time while the verdict was recorded, seeing only the civil dignitaries to my left grinning like wolves, leering at me. The sounds of glee surrounding me were bad enough but the gesture by the small court usher tore my guts out. I looked straight ahead. All the time I wanted to scream out to them all sitting in there that they were a dirty stinking shower of shit. How I ever managed to suppress the violence within me while in that dock I shall never know, but it was vital to me to make sure that I remained erect, very much in control. I know that they wanted me to collapse and cower, but there was no way. Lord Cameron went on to tell me that I was a menace to society and would go to prison for Life and he recommended that I serve no less than fifteen years. As I stood there waiting to be let out of the dock, I watched the cops leaving, looking straight at me with big grins and all shaking each others' hands in congratulations. I took a long look at what was going on. I was escorted downstairs to the cells below and was confronted by more cops in uniform, one of whom was actually doing a sort of dance saying to me that I was convicted, I was guilty. He pulled the tie off my neck and took the sheaf of defence papers from my hands and I was put into a cell. All of these people were happy at my being put away and seeing it shook me as nothing ever had in my life before, to the very core. They didn't know me, they didn't even know.*

I lay in the cell at the High Court Building and was stunned by

* I haven't been as forthcoming with the circumstances of Babs Rooney's death as I have been on earlier incidents in the book. The reason for this is that though I maintain I never killed him, I did slash him, therefore, by law I am technically guilty of murder. The point is that while I am writing this I am into the tenth year of a life sentence for it and that is that. I am now familiar with all the facts leading to his death and what happened but I don't feel that they have anything to do with this story. So rather than create problems for someone else I have just given the details as I knew them then and my own part in it.

it all. However, I was soon taken under heavy guard to Barlinnie prison. The journey was spent with me continuing to look straight ahead and with the cops all very silent. I was put into the punishment cell which was meant to be the observation cell in case I cracked up during the night due to the effects of the sentence. I said nothing throughout, knowing that if I did then the violence would pour forth. I was thrown into this cell with the mattress on the floor and dark shadows dominating the place, as the small light bulb was plastered into the side of the wall. I lay on the mattress not moving, just staring into nothingness. My thoughts at that time were ones of tremendous violence and rage: rage at myself for not killing every bastard that they had accused me of killing, rage for not walking into a police station with a gun and blasting every cop in the place. My inner self was broken, torn into small pieces, shattered. The pain was and still is tremendous, penetrating as it does to a depth that no physical pain ever reaches. My whole being was dead, my life was no longer. I was state-owned — forever. I was very much aware of my situation, and how my past history, guilty or not, would be instrumental in keeping me away for the rest of my life. Never would I experience freedom again; it was something that was gone forever, never to be re-tasted. The shock of losing my life is something that I can't express in words as they are so inadequate. My life was now to be lived on memories of home, of my family, of friends, of the Gorbals, and of every other small detail that had made it up — things that everyone on the outside takes for granted.

I lay on the dark floor in a terrible state. I cried that first night, my heart and my eyes cried. I was so angry at myself and the world that I just couldn't think straight. Internally I was a raging storm, but to anyone peering through the Judas hole of the cell door I would look calm, as though I was just dozing. Without that façade I would have broken into a million little pieces. For some reason it was very important that I cling to this and make it see me through till I recovered from this inner blitz. I was a walking time-bomb, primed and ready for exploding, all it needed was one wrong word and there would have been such a holocaust that they wouldn't have believed it. That inner something that seemed to take over the minute the verdict was given stayed with me. By some miraculous means or other I managed to get through the first night and the next few days, though they were very hazy and I can only remember pieces of them. The press were giving it big licks and I covered the pages with the same old crap of being the super baddie. It seemed to keep up for the first week or so and guys showed me what they were saying but by now I was sick of it. For the first time in my life I became revolted at the sight of my name in the papers whereas all the other times it had been a prestigious thing and I had enjoyed it. The press were keeping on about the moneylending rackets and saying that they would have to be clamped down on, so the cops reacted and went round the pubs in the Gorbals lecturing to the customers and telling them to come forward and give evidence and they would be guarded. There were stories printed saying that some of us had "crucified" a non-paying customer to the wooden floor of a house. This was a statement reported to have been issued by the police. Most of what they printed was nonsense.

My hopes during the first few days automatically lay with the Appeal Court and I applied to the prison authorities, saying I wanted to Appeal against the conviction. I began to think it out very carefully as this was my last chance in life and I had no intention of putting it into the hands of anyone else. This time when I went to court I wanted to speak for myself. If I failed then I would be the one to blame, no one else. I had made my mind up on this and set about gathering the necessary evidence and data to help me at the Appeal court.

Prison being what it is, one has to go to the Governor for permission to obtain what are known as Appellant visits. These are special visits over and above the normal quota for an appellant to gather material for his case. I went to my hall Governor to get a special visit from a Mr Davidson. I told him the circumstances about wanting to speak on my own behalf and the need for a visit to get certain information. He began to hum and haw and stretch the whole thing out telling me he would give me an answer later in the day. That was it. I could take no more. Didn't he realise what this meant to me? The anger came up from my toes and I swung a blow that knocked him from his chair and put him on the floor. I lifted a wooden inkwell but was pounced on from behind and put into the cell next door. I tore a piece of wood from the book shelving and stood with it in my hand, as they carried the Governor out. They waited some time allowing me to cool off and then cautiously opened the door, there was a mob of them. The screws said that everything was all right and I would be okay, that there would be no brutality handed out. I told them to remember that if there was brutality it wouldn't end here, as I was now in for the rest of my life and would remember anyone who laid a finger on me. I was put into a solitary confinement cell and left alone without any harm done to me.

A short time later I heard the sound of heavy boots and the cell door opened. There stood the heavy mob all wearing coloured overalls and they told me to take off my clothes. I refused, saying that if they wanted to fight why didn't they get on with it. I was told that there would be no brutality, all they wanted was my clothes for the cops. I thought this over and accepted that they were telling the truth as there were enough of them to beat me up with my clothes on. No sooner had I stripped off than some of them moved in punching and kicking me. I tried to hit back, calling them cowardly lumps of shit. These were shouts of anger, but they beat me to the floor, leaving me in a pool of blood. There is something totally humiliating about being brutalised when naked. Nakedness leaves a feeling of helplessness, and even though I was returning blows it felt as though they couldn't hurt the person they landed on. There was this feeling of impotence. I lay on the floor in an absolute rage, hating myself for being such a bloody fool as to trust them.

Being a Life prisoner meant looking at prison in a totally different perspective. This experience resulting from my assault on the Governor meant that I had to rethink everything. It was obvious to me that my life style would have to change in order to survive in this jungle. Certainly I had lost my life, but not my will to live, to fight. The whole of my thought processes were undergoing a dramatic change. It dawned on me for the first time that my life sentence had actually started the day I left my Mother's womb. Strangely enough I now found a new sense of freedom, which I had never experienced before; it was important to me. I decided that I would now live by my laws, not giving one fuck for society or the laws of society. Their very representatives, the media, were labelling me "Animal", "Maniac" and lots of other names. From now on I would totally reject everything and everyone and label them the "Dangerous Majority" and the "Perpetuators of Fascism". Who was society? I described them as being like every para-military organisation on the government payroll, and all those silly ignorant bastards who would be brainwashed by the media, accepting their every word as being gospel. From now on the world could go to fuck. I hated everyone and distrusted everyone. They made it plain that they felt the same about me, so we all knew where we stood.

I lay with my thoughts on the cell floor in the early hours of the morning, thoroughly frustrated and angry at all that had gone on and I cracked. I ran at the metal door and banged it all that I could, which brought the night patrol in. The noises wakened the rest of the prisoners and they too joined in calling the screws all the names under the sun. The night screws called for reinforcements and opened my cell door. They had a strait-jacket with them and after a struggle I was locked into it, getting some bruises in the process. I was thrown into a padded cell, which was an ordinary cell covered in rough canvas pads. I lay on the cushioned floor struggling with the strait-jacket. It's a very strange experience being locked into one of these as the upper part of the body is completely helpless, even to the extent that one has to do the toilet in it. The rest of the prisoners had ceased their noise but I continued to struggle and by some miraculous means or other managed to break free of the jacket.

This was victory and it restored some power to my much damaged morale; I was elated at freeing myself from this degrading contraption. But it wasn't enough for me to be free, I had to prove it to everyone, so I systematically set about destroying the padded cell. I tore the padding, which was very difficult, and pulled the red coloured coir matting from it. I worked all through the night destroying as much as I could so that by the morning I was able to stand gleefully in the centre of the one-time padded cell floor amidst piles of canvas and woolly coir waiting for the door to open. I was covered in blood and filthy as I stood amid the wreckage, but I felt so proud. They might beat me by sheer force of numbers, but by fuck they would never beat my spirit into submission. I was fully rewarded when the screws finally opened the door seeing me with a big smile on my face amid the one-time pads. The door was quickly shut and in a short time I was taken from the padded cell by a team of screws with my hands cuffed behind my back.

They took me to the prison reception area, bundled me into my civilian clothes and hand-cuffed me to two detectives. There were two others with revolvers showing plainly under their arms. I was put into one of two squad cars and whisked off through the main streets of Glasgow to the Sheriff Court in the city centre. The sirens were blaring as we reached the old fruit market which was so busy that it stopped the police cars. For fleeting minutes we were held up with the congestion. I savoured these moments in the knowledge that I would never see them again. I had walked along these streets many times in my life and felt very close to them. My heart ached as I sat wedged between two cops in this mobile prison. The things that moved me were the workers walking about their business, just ordinary guys craning their necks to look into the police cars and me on the inside craning my neck to look out and drink in with my eyes their every move. I was so envious of these guys that I would have given anything to be one of them carrying a heavy load of fruit and putting it onto the lorries or barrows. They looked in at me, but never could they see my thoughts. I, the monster, the hard man, sat there in chains between two cops, and was pining my heart out for everything which surrounded the police car. The message came home to me, the penny dropped — too late, because now I could see what it was all about, this freedom. In the past I had experienced being transported from place to place while handcuffed but always with the knowledge that I would get out. This time it was different as I felt I would never walk these streets again, ever. There was no substitute for this.

Once the congested area had been cleared, we made quick time to the court with me feeling in a desperately emotional state, my heart very heavy with pain. I was locked in a cell and when it was opened again, in walked two cops followed by the Sheriff in robes then more cops. What was this all about? It was very odd. They held the court appearance in the cell; I couldn't believe that this melodramatic scene was taking place here. This game was becoming ludicrous, what with armed cops and a court hearing in a cell. The ironic part was that the Sheriff had been the prosecuting Q.C. at the first two murder trials and here I was in front of him again at this preliminary hearing. It was the first time that this had ever happened, the bringing of a court to a cell. Later the press said that it was due to a plot by friends to get me out of prison.

After the court appearance, I was taken back to prison and to the cell that I came from, next door to the padded cell which they were busily repairing. However, they decided that something had to be done about me as I was becoming too much, so the next morning the door crashed open first thing, and a mob of screws handcuffed my hands behind my back and pulled me along the long dark corridors across a yard and locked me into a cell in what was once the Women's Wing of the prison. There was a specially selected group of screws to look after me and they were with me night and day. They sat outside my door and would talk in whispers so I couldn't hear them. I lay on the cell floor looking up to the ceiling as there was no window that I could look out of. I would lie there and think, think, think. I was on strict solitary and wasn't allowed to see anyone. I didn't speak to the screws nor they to me so it was utter silence except for the essentials. I would be taken out for exercise for an hour to walk at the side of the building with my hands cuffed behind my back between the two screws. We would pace up and down in complete silence with them not speaking to each other and the sound of our footsteps ringing in the cold morning. It was eerie as here were three human beings all touching each other with the closeness of a sandwich and not a word, only hate flowing between us with me waiting, watching for the first chance to have a go at them. The Deputy Governor and the Chief made their rounds and when he came into sight I would try to run at him and attack him with my hands behind my back but they would just hold me and I could do nothing. I would try to spit at him as I hated every single bastard. In the cell I became enmeshed in my Appeal and fantasised about getting released. The Appeal took me over completely and I would spend my day walking up and down the cell floor teaching myself how to speak fluently and clearly to make sure my points were getting across. This was it; I would put up a fight for them to remember. There were times when I would have doubts and think that I'd make an arse of myself, but there were others when I thought I'd get free and walk out.

Meanwhile outside the walls, the press were making a big deal of the case and still calling for police action. They were looking for witnesses but, as the "Crucifixion" statement was doing them no good at all and was frightening the witnesses off, they retracted it. The press were told that no one had been crucified. Arrests were made for suborning witnesses at my trial and the cops arrested Frank Wilson, Bandit Rooney, and Jimmy Latta, who was William's lawyer during the trial. A lawyer being arrested was big news. I lay in my solitary cell oblivious to all of this. All my concentration was on the forthcoming appeal. I pretended to have a passive period in the hope that the Deputy Governor would come nearer because I wanted to butt him right on the face as he was the one I identified with the order to handcuff me. I was so full of hatred and bitterness and would shout curses and obscenities. I always felt much better after I did something like that. It was my way of letting them know that they could chain me forever and I'd still fight them. Although the screws and I said the minimum of words there was a non-verbal communication of hatred. By this time they did as little as possible to annoy me and had me labelled as a complete nut-case. The same ones were looking after me all the time so they weren't going to create a situation where they would be terrified that I was going to pounce on them each time they opened the door. This happened at the beginning, with them trying me out now that I was in a place all alone, but then I walked out with a chamber pot full of shit and told them that if they treated me like shit I would throw it over them every time I was out. These were the tense moments that marked the thin line between violence and words. The threat was effective, and there is no doubt about it that I owed a lot to shit.

One night as I lay in the far corner of the cell with my eyes shut, thinking, the door opened quickly and a small paper bag was thrown towards me, then the door shut immediately. I was startled and opened the bag to find two small chocolate biscuits. This almost broke my heart. It seemed that two of the screws had left to go and do something and the third when seeing this had opened the door and thrown in the biscuits, even though the strict ruling is that no less than three screws must be present when the door is opened. Although it was obviously the human in him *why* did he do this? It confused the picture, as it brought something human back into me and I would have preferred to think of us all as animals in the one jungle. This guy had no idea what he had done, he would never imagine how this small action caused me so much inner conflict. I didn't ever say anything to him nor him to me, but he had got to me.

Another night I was lying on the cell floor when I heard the judas hole slide back and instead of closing again as is usual, I was told very briefly that my girl friend had had a baby girl. It was in this way that I found out that my daughter Patricia had been born. Margaret had been pregnant before I was arrested so now I was father to a boy and a girl. I felt very sad and very happy, so with this mixture I took great hope, as this birth took place a few days before I was due to appear before my appeal, on 19th December 1967, and I took it as an omen that by some fluke I would win.

On the morning of the 19th there was a great hustle and bustle and sounds of activity outside my door. It opened and I was given my suit of civilian clothing to wear and was made ready for court. Leaving my cell, I was confronted with a large number of Glasgow detectives in the bottom flat of the prison hall. They were to be my escort and some of them were wearing guns. There were no words between us, all we did was stare. Some of them I knew from the past, some I didn't. I was handcuffed between two screws using special handcuffs, and put into a squad car. There were four cars on the escort in all and I was bang in the centre but every so often they would change positions like the pea under the nutshells. The journey passed in silence with us overtaking the commuters travelling along the Edinburgh Road oblivious to what was happening. On entering Edinburgh the cops there met us and escorted us to the High Court.

I had never been in an appeal court before, though I know that three judges sat instead of one. I do know that the general feeling of prisoners who had been to one was that it was an exercise in futility, but try telling that to someone like me who saw it as his last chance for freedom. I had to believe in it. On entering the court I caught sight of the small white-haired macer who had been there when I was found guilty. I told myself that given the chance I would lay one on him. The three judges, all very old men, entered the court, sat down and told me to proceed. I reminded them that I was only a lay man, and might bring out points that had no legal substance in their eyes but that they ought to bear with me. From there I went on to give my points, of which I had many, but as quickly as I put them they threw them out, without so much as an explanation. This procedure really stunned me as I thought they would go over each point that I put to them and discuss it, but I was wrong. It was as though I was the only man in that room who was alive, who had enthusiasm. I stood there for over fifty minutes speaking and putting point after point. To make matters worse I dropped some papers and the court macer picked them up for me, a kind gesture which got through to me. After I had finished speaking the three judges rose from their chairs, put their heads together for the briefest of moments and sat down telling me how they had listened to my case and had given it their full consideration but could find no grounds for altering the conviction.

I was dragged from the court feeling hate, hate, hate. I was carved up, set out and finally doomed to live out my days in a tomb. I found myself back in the cop car manacled, not really seeing anything, just hating everyone and everything. My life was gone, as that had been my last chance, no more would I have a sense of hope. Who could ever measure the total despair that I felt at that moment? Was this dreadful pain never going to cease? All this while the fleet of cars were making a swift exit from Edinburgh and it was some miles on before I was to realise that we weren't heading in the direction of Barlinnie. We were going through beautiful countryside. I would never have asked the bastards where I was going. I was too shattered and wasn't really caring, but I kept wishing that the car would crash or something and kill us all. I had never experienced the countryside before and here I was passing through picturesque scenery in my mobile prison seeing things that I had never seen before. It was nigh on Christmas and there was snow on the ground. As we passed small cottages I could see the warmth emanating from the lights in the houses and the Christmas trees in the windows. There were occasions when we passed a house and would catch sight of families sitting at a table eating. Fleeting glances that showed me the beauty of home life. Seeing these things really twisted my guts causing me terrible nostalgia. The countryside showed me total freedom with deer running in the distance, and here was I travelling in this prison, manacled, squashed between two screws and three other cars. From the roadway signposts I could see that we were heading in the direction of Inverness.

Part Three

11

The prison in Inverness holds about seventy prisoners serving local sentences but there is a block reserved for the troublemakers, so that Inverness is the Siberia for prisoners in the Scottish penal system. There are special rules laid down for treatment in this prison. No prisoner is to stay for a period less than two months or more than six months. Each prisoner's case is reviewed every two months by a Board of Governors to decide if he should return to the prison that he came from. If a prisoner gets into trouble while there, he automatically gets held for another two months. The conditions are spartan with a minimum of recreation, and the whole programme is structured to encourage boredom so that the prisoner will behave accordingly and be glad to get back to his normal prison. I was put through the usual procedure of being stripped of my clothing and having everything taken from me. I was taken into a hall by a large group of screws and it was so silent that the ring of our footsteps echoed. There were perhaps sixty cells in the hall but there were only three prisoners. The cell was the standard size, eight feet by twelve. There was a bed, a chamber pot, and on the inside of the window there was heavy wire mesh to prevent access to the glass, with the usual heavy bars on the outside. In the morning, the cells were opened one at a time for the prisoners to slop out and after each one had finished another was let out, with guards by his side at all times. After the six o'clock slop out and breakfast, they allowed the prisoners out to a workshed at ten o'clock.

Soon I was able to see who was here. There was John McCue, my pal from the district, and Ben Conroy, who had been in various institutions with me. The worktask was making fishing nets which hung over a steel bar attached to the wall. These were a distance apart to discourage conversation. It was very nice to see people I knew. They had obviously known what I had been through, or were able to identify with a part of it, so that was something. Ben was serving his five year sentence and was taken away almost immediately to another prison for release. John had been in the block for six months and reckoned they would be putting him away soon. Another guy was brought up to replace Ben. John was worn away by the boredom of the place so was glad to see me and get some home news. Being in Inverness like this was almost worse than solitary as we tended to get everything out of perspective and would speculate on what was for lunch, even though we knew what it would be. In order to change the subject someone would talk about a letter he received so that before long we were discussing intimate things about each other and our family lives, saying things that we would never normally say. I always hated this when I returned to my cell, thinking that I shouldn't have said this or that, but I would always say similar things again. I was fortunate in that John and I knew each other's families very well, but the personalities changed every few months in the block, and this was a problem.

I had been in the block only a week when I was issued with an Indictment for the charge of assaulting the Barlinnie Governor which stated that I would return to Glasgow High Court on the first week of January. This brought fresh life into our conversation, dominating it for a spell. The other two were looking forward to the latest news I would get while back in Barlinnie. The same escort that had brought me up came to take me down to Barlinnie and it was the same procedure of armed guards and squad cars. I was returned to the same solitary cell and waited there till the trial date. On the day of the trial two cops came into my cell and were handcuffed to me. From there I was taken to the High Court and the three of us were locked into a cell in the courthouse. Here I was back in the same court, going into the same dock where I had been sentenced to Life Imprisonment nine weeks previously.

There were the same old faces, the small court macer, the cops, and then of course the civil dignitaries. In a way I felt good because every bastard in the place had thought they had seen the last of me, but here I was as large as life only this time I had nothing to lose. I pleaded guilty to the charge of punching the Governor on the face and breaking his cheekbone, and was given eighteen months. Afterwards I was to hear that certain people present in the court had been inquiring whether the eighteen months was concurrent or consecutive. This was the ultimate in getting or trying to get blood from a stone as it was surely obvious to everyone that having already lost my life there was nothing more that could be taken from me. I was hurriedly taken back to Inverness and could only relate my own experiences to the guys there, as I had been kept on solitary. I'd had no way of obtaining news that would be a point for discussion. While I was away, John McCue had been transferred to his old prison.

I had only been back a few days when I realised that this place and its regime were bent on turning me into a vegetable, so I went on request to see the Governor. As I entered his office, I picked up a chair lying nearby and threw it through the windows and set about trying to ransack the place. Due to my last assault on the Governor at Barlinnie, they had been taking precautions and had screws waiting in readiness. They came rushing in the door and we all fell about the floor in a fierce struggle. I was dragged along the corridor with some blows and kicks landing on me. I was then thrown into the "Silent Cell" and the door was closed.

This silent cell was the same as the one in Peterhead, and being in one was very much like being in the other. The silence was all the same no matter where one was. I urinated all over the floor and threw my food all over the walls and floor and just lay there. I just wasn't giving a damn. The following morning I was taken to the Governor's room to be punished for smashing his office up, and I went there naked with my hands cuffed behind my back, and a heavy escort. Entering the room I shouted repeatedly "Bastard, bastard, bastard, bastard . . .", which meant that they couldn't read out the charge, so they dragged me out and back to the hole.

We did small things to annoy each other, or punish each other. The screws would give me my food when it was stone cold or with spit in it. In return, cold or not cold, spit or no spit, I would eat it up and put the plates at the far end of the cell. The screws needed them for the next meal so would have to enter the cell stinking of shit and slops to get the plates. I felt that they were humiliating and degrading me, so in my way I was doing it to them. As the filth mounted up to outrageous proportions they would send in a screw who was recognised as being not a bad fellow and he would speak in a low confidential voice, showing every sympathy with me. He agreed that the Governor and most of his fellow screws were fucking idiots, and how I was usually a very hygienic sort of guy and that this was not my usual way of behaving. I knew that this was all part of the game and that this was how the "tough screws" use the screw least interested in brutality but I didn't want to compromise in any way. Certainly I didn't hate him like the rest but there was no way I would let him know that, for then he would be used by the others to sweep up their dirty work when it got too hot for them to handle. I realised that this guy would repeat everything that I said to the Governor so I told him that I intended attacking the Governor and every other Governor that I could lay my hands on. They were causing the trouble so it would be brought directly to them. The stench was foul but I lay there and after a time got used to it and it didn't bother me at all. The place was absolutely freezing so I would leave a patch of floor free of contamination so that I could run on the spot without slipping. There was very little air getting into the place but I ceased to think too much about that. I really hated the screws so much that I wished they would put a small hatch on the cell door to pass my food through so that I didn't have to see them. They would all take part in the brutality as "one of the Boys" but it was this constant and protracted continuance of the trouble that they didn't like. For over a week they had to come in and feed me, and take in the stench as they did so, and afterwards go home to their families and be with them.

Eventually I went back to the segregation block to find that the guys who had been there when I left were now gone and replaced by others. This was the way it went — new faces would come and go, yet I would remain. There were times in Inverness when I would go into terrible depressions and be in the depths of despair. The sheer enormity of having to live with the fact that I was in my tomb was weighing heavily upon me. I lay in my cell one night realising that I just couldn't go on. I had managed to conceal a small piece of razor blade and lay with it in my hand pressed to my wrist willing myself to end it all now. There was nothing ahead for me except moments of relief during periods in solitary My heart was terribly heavy and my insides were tearing me to pieces, emotionally I was in an awful state. I could feel the sharp edge of the razor against my veins and knew that all of it could be over in seconds — I being the decider. This was the first time in my life that suicide had entered my head. In the past I would have looked on it as something only a weakling would do. I would never have admitted that I couldn't face up to anything but now that part of me was crumbling as I lay with the razor against my wrist, my eyes tightly closed.

I didn't do it, and the deciding factor was the images and thoughts that flashed in my mind's eye. All the people with their shark-like grins in the court that day, the court macer, the dignitaries and the cops in the past who had planted evidence on me and verballed me, they were what prevented me from doing it. They were the ones who kept me alive that night. I knew that to do away with myself was the easy way out and would give much pleasure to those who stood in the court that day. The pure hate that I had for them was what kept me from doing away with myself.

I learnt a lot from this and emerged all the stronger. It also brought home to me that it takes a very brave man to commit suicide. I knew that come what may I would carry on and let those on the outside know that I was very much alive and let those on the inside know that they had had their day. I had no intention of sitting back and letting them do what they wanted with me. I was myself and would remain that way, all it could cost me was my life and that was already gone.

During this very introspective period when I was in a state of emotional distress I was given a book that reflected what was going on within me: *Crime and Punishment* by J. Dostoievsky. It somehow matched what I was experiencing internally. I had never heard of the book or the author before and in fact it was the first serious book I'd ever read. The torment of Raskolnikoff was so revealing, so accurate in my own terms that I marvelled at the author's grasp of pain. I identified so strongly with the book that it put me off reading it for a while. It opened up a new dimension in reading and thinking for me, but I had so little knowledge of literary classics that I had to rely on luck more than anything else. Books became a very important aspect of my survival in solitary and I would always try to get ones that would be emotionally fulfilling, books that would become a partner, that I could read time and again. They were mostly by authors like Dostoievsky, Victor Hugo, Tolstoy, Charles Dickens, Solzhenitsyn and Steinbeck. I concentrated on the works of these men and whenever I got one of their books, I felt I'd discovered a new treasure, as the mere possession of it delighted me.

While I was in Inverness a big trial had taken place with Frank Wilson, Bandit Rooney, and Jimmy Latta for suborning witnesses at my trial. They had been sentenced to long terms of imprisonment with Frank getting twleve years, Bandit four years and Jimmy Latta, the lawyer, getting eight years. The fact that a respected member of the legal profession had been found guilty aroused all sorts of suspicions and was felt in all sections of their world. None of us felt that he had done anything wrong and I believed that he had simply fought the case, using the same tactics as the cops, but evidently the jury thought differently. The cops were riding high on the crest of the wave of convictions.

I had been in Inverness four months when a riot erupted in Peterhead prison resulting in a number of the screws there being stabbed. With my feeling of hatred I loved hearing these things as it pleased me to know that other people were now having a go. I knew the guys involved, all of whom were serving heavy sentences. One of them was Larry Winters who had been in approved school and Borstal with me. After a few months of awaiting trial they were taken to court. Larry was given 15 years on top of his Life sentence, the other three were cleared of all charges. They were all sent to Inverness as a further punishment, and the escort that brought them up was the one to take me back. After being there almost eight months, this was me going back into full circulation.

Going back to Peterhead after the trial verdict was a problem, as feelings were running high. The screws were sick, as they looked on the verdict as being a victory for the prisoners, three of whom had been cleared. The atmosphere in Peterhead was explosive at the best of times but this meant that the slightest spark would blow the place sky high. I had been there some hours and was being placed amongst the top security prisoners. The first screw escorting me upstairs was jabbing me in the back and pushing me. I waited till we got to a place at the top of the stairs shadowed by the landing above where I would nip him quietly. The screw continued to jab me as though I were a lump of meat so, at the appropriate moment, I turned round and thumped him on the jaw putting him on the floor where he clung to my feet curled in a ball. This was seen by another screw who shouted a warning and others came running and dragged me off. Prisoners who had seen all of this came on the scene and dragged the screws from me. Two of them took the batons from the hands of the screws so that in the space of a few seconds we had a situation bordering on the explosive. Everything froze as the screws found themselves outnumbered and trying to cool everyone. The cons had taken enough shit from them and were ready to run amok at a given signal. The atmosphere at this point was intense. The ball was at my feet as I had to decide whether I wanted to involve these guys who were mostly doing determinate sentences, some with only a short while to go. The truth was that I didn't and I began to cool the situation. The guys told the screws that there would be no trouble so long as I wasn't brutalised and the screws promised this. Two of them escorted me to the solitary confinement block and there I was searched and had my shoes taken from me then the door closed. The two screws that escorted me to the cells left after I was locked in, but they came back.

That night, an hour or so later, the prison doctor was called to attend to some injuries that I had sustained. There were several scalp wounds, numerous bruises and two suspected broken arms. I refused to let the doctor treat me. The police were called and I was charged with assaulting two officers in the main prison hall, and biting one prison officer in the punishment block cell. After they had made the charges against me I told the cops that I wished to prefer charges against some prison staff for giving me the injuries that I now had. I couldn't write a statement due to the arm injuries so they had to do it for me. The cops had to strip my clothes from me in order to take them as evidence for the forthcoming trial. I didn't know the names of any of the screws that I was charging so they set up an Identification Parade for me to pick them out.

There are two versions given at the subsequent trial of how I got these injuries. The screws, about six or seven of them, testified that they had locked me up in the Punishment block, then came in to search me and at that moment I had pounced on them and started biting one of them on the neck for no reason whatsoever. The senior screw said that he ordered batons to be used on me — to restrain me. He said all the batons were used on my arms and shoulders and the numerous cuts on the top of my head were the result of my falling on the floor when hit by the batons on the arms.

My defence in court was that after having been searched, and the shoes taken from me, I was then locked in. I had been in the cell just a minute when the door flew open and a mob of screws came in the door with batons in their hands. They were being led by the screw that I had punched in the main hall. This was what we call the "Batter Squad", out to extract their own pound of flesh. I backed to the corner of the cell as they came towards me, forming a semi-circle. My only means of protection were my arms. The batons in their hands once again gave me that impotent feeling of helplessness, but experience of similar situations was with me. They started lashing at me but my concentration was on getting hold of one of them which I finally managed to do. I grasped him, wrapping myself around him and sinking my teeth into his neck while the others continued to hit me with their batons. I clung there as long as I could but was stunned by one heavy blow that finally prised me loose. I don't remember falling, only waking and they were still hitting me as I lay there. I got to my feet again and one of them panicked and started shouting while hitting me with his baton, "Get down you bastard, get down". Eventually I passed out, waking to find myself alone. They sent for the doctor and when he came I stood in the corner like a wounded, frightened animal, refusing to trust anyone, but very dangerous. I refused to let him treat me telling him that he was one of them, part of them. The blood was splashed over the walls and running down my face and body.

By the time the police came I was thinking rationally and thought that I should charge the screws and reverse the whole thing. They got an Identification Parade and I went on it and tapped everyone of them on the shoulder whom I was accusing. The following morning I saw the doctor, who treated me and got me out to the hospital for X-rays to my arms. They weren't broken. The horrible part was that due to the arm injuries a screw had to write the letters to my lawyer as I couldn't do anything with them and I desperately needed photographs of my injuries for the trial. It was a terrible shame having to rely on a screw to write for me, so I limited the words to the bare essentials.

I lay in solitary for four months awaiting trial and experienced moments of downright despair listening to the screws beating up guys who were being brought into the solitary block. I would have preferred to be involved in the trouble rather than being in a concrete box hearing the sound of the thuds. At times like this the other prisoners would get up to their doors and bang them constantly, shouting for the dirty bastards to leave the guy alone. This is all one can do as one is in a completely helpless position having to listen to the blows thumping into him, his moans and occasional screams. The whole process is deeply humiliating to everyone. Most prisoners, when they are beaten up, just curl into a ball and accept what is given out as they know that to retaliate will lead to them being charged by the cops which would only lead to an additional sentence. I felt that my position was totally different from most of the others. I was in prison for what seemed to me to be the rest of my life, and the only way I was going to be able to live with myself was not to succumb, not to allow the screws to do what they wanted with me. No, by far the best way was to fight them, even if I lost, and suffered the pain that went with it. One important thing I noticed was that I was getting stronger after each incident. If it can't kill you it can only strengthen you. If I continued to gather strength then the system would be the eventual loser.

When the guys came into the solitary block and were brutalised

I would shout through a ventilator and tell them to make an official complaint. Some guys would but others wouldn't. The official channel for complaining is to request to see the Governor and ask for a Petition to write to the Secretary of State. When this is completed it goes to the Prisons department in Edinburgh where a civil servant looks at it, then returns it to the prison Governor for his comments. The usual reply in those days was "No cause for complaint". I wrote petitions after each guy was brutalised and made formal complaints. It was important for this to be placed on record as by now I was thinking ahead and felt that all this information might come in handy at my trial. After a few such peititions, I was warned that I would be punished for making false allegations. One of the guys, who had been brutalised and had complained by petition, was charged for making false allegations and was put in front of the Visiting Committee and they took a month's remission from him. This was enough to frighten others from petitioning or complaining and I was angry at this, but fully understood their positions. These guys all had liberation dates but I didn't, so it was easy for me. In fact we were in such a futile position that it would have been nigh on impossible for us to substantiate our allegations in any court of law. Most people have preconceived ideas about prisoners so when it comes to a direct confrontation of believing the screws or the prisoner then the latter is usually the loser.

I used to give a lot of thought as to why this sudden spurt of brutality was going on and seemed to be getting worse in the long-term prisons. I know that screws felt they had a form of protection when Capital Punishment was in force, therefore brutality didn't seem to me to be as prevalent then. Most screws are pro-hanging and at this present date are active for its re-introduction. Whenever a screw was assaulted by a prisoner, a bunch of them would get together and go down to get their own back. In the past they would hit the prisoner with their fists and boots but now they were using their batons more frequently. In many ways the baton replaced the birch. They felt that by doing this it would deter others and in some cases it did. Those that didn't lash out at screws felt that to do so was a mug's game as it meant losing both ways: getting a beating and additional time to their sentences. I've seen many instances where guys were openly humiliated by the screws in front of everyone but would refuse to retaliate. This meant that prisoners witnessing or being on the receiving end of such frequent humiliations would withdraw into themselves and make sure that no such incident came their way again. As a result, the screws became a law unto themselves and given the inch they took the mile. I have seen prisoners accept things that made me squirm with embarrassment over petty rules that had been long forgotten in the rule book but could be applied at any time by the zealous screw. The point is that these prisoners were veritable walking time-bombs by the time they got out. No sooner were they released than they were back in again after blowing up when free of the strict regime. By making this point I am not advocating a case for the screw to stop brutalising and let the prisoner thump him on the jaw every time he feels depressed: I am arguing for a system that is going to help the guy while he is in rather than make him worse, as is the case in the prison system today.

Here I was lying in solitary in Peterhead, with quite a few brutal beatings under my belt. I was preparing for another High Court trial, my second in nine months, for assaulting prison officials. As far as I was concerned, it was war and I would use all these past incidents as learning experience so that the next one would be more difficult for them. There was no doubt in my mind that there would be a next one, as by now I was fully committed to having a go at the dirty rotten system. I was still doing daily exercises while in solitary to make sure I was fit for what I was getting into. My hair which had been long and curly was now cut close to my scalp so that it couldn't be grabbed. I knew what the future would be but the screws hadn't got the message yet.

In October 1968 I was taken to Aberdeen High Court. I pleaded not guilty to the three charges, but included Special Pleas: on the first charge that I acted under provocation, and on the other two that they were self-defence. The screws came in and the Crown evidence led, saying that I had attacked them for no reason. The prison doctor came in and said that my wounds were consistent with being hit by batons. Other prisoners came in and said what they had heard. I went into the witness box and offered all I could, the photos of the bloodstained walls, my own injuries, my bloodstained clothing. All of this I gave to them. Lord Johnston, the presiding judge, summed up and here are some extracts from his speech to the jury; ". . . Now I come to the third charge, ladies and gentlemen, and that is the charge of assault in the prison while in the solitary confinement block. Let me remind you of what may have been forgotten or, rather, hidden in parts of the evidence, and that is that it is not the Prison Service of Peterhead which is under accusation here. The person accused is the prisoner in the dock. He stated what he did, and freely admitted that he jumped upon the officer as the officer described, and that he bit him. The question is, whether that was done in self-defence or not.

"Now, a man who is attacked as the accused says he was attacked, is entitled to defend himself, to use reasonable force, and if you accept the evidence of the Accused and the other evidence that he was attacked in the way he says he was attacked, there can be little doubt — though it is a matter for you — that what the Accused says he did was no more than necessary and, indeed, he says it was sufficient to repel the attack on him. But, ladies and gentlemen, the burden of proving that an assault is done in self-defence is on the Accused and he must show you, he must satisfy you, that on the balance of probability his story that he was attacked and was doing no more than defend himself is true. Well, ladies and gentlemen, you heard the Accused in the witness box; you heard all the other evidence and what the Defence described as the real evidence. I don't intend to go over that evidence again, but there are certain questions I have no doubt you wish to ask yourselves, such questions are these — why was it necessary to search this man immediately after he was put into the cell? You ask yourselves, was it necessary for four officers to come in? It is true that the Accused had, if one accepts the evidence, shown some violence earlier, a few minutes earlier, but it seems to be accepted by all the evidence that he walked quietly from the second, or near the second flat to the solitary confinement Block, and you may ask yourselves why, in these circumstances, it was necessary for four men to go into the cell? Now there is the evidence of those in the neighbouring cells and you must consider that evidence along with that of the Accused himself. And against that evidence you must consider the evidence of the Prison Officers and their account of what happened, and it is on that evidence, ladies and gentlemen, that you must make up your minds what occurred, and you must make up your minds whether the charge is proved or not proved...."

The jury was allowed to go and decide their verdict and I waited, locked in one of the cells. I had cited lots of prisoners as witnesses to the trial and for us there was a holiday atmosphere with everyone glad of the day out and the change of food. The Jury returned one hour and twenty minutes later; on the first charge I was found guilty under provocation. Not Proven on the second charge. Guilty on the third charge.

The Advocate Depute moved for sentence and read out my previous convictions dating from 1957: "The initial convictions are offences of dishonesty and, in particular, in 1963 he was sentenced to two years imprisonment for assault to severe injury and assault by stabbing; in February 1963, he was sentenced to imprisonment for assaulting the police and with attempting to resist arrest. He was sentenced to two years imprisonment in 1965 for assault; and in October 1965 there was another sentence of imprisonment with regard to an assault; on 3rd November 1967, he was sentenced to life imprisonment for murder; and on 8th January 1968, he was sentenced to eighteen months imprisonment for an assault — that assault was on a Prison Officer."

Defending Q.C. said: "Your lordship has heard the evidence, and I think that the only thing I would say is that the injury in the third Charge was a very minor one in the nature of assault."

Lord Johnston: "James Boyle, you have been convicted of two Charges of Assault — the first under provocation. You have a deplorable record and you are now serving a sentence of life imprisonment for murder. I cannot emphasise too much that if you are to serve your sentence of imprisonment in such a way as to obtain some remission from the sentence of life imprisonment, you must behave yourself. The sentence which I am about to pronounce will have some effect in that it will be taken into consideration if and when the time comes for consideration of your release. I now sentence you to four years imprisonment."

Throughout all of this trial I had become very hopeful as the evidence came across well in my favour, or so I had thought; but now I was thoroughly deflated. Had I won then I felt it may in some way have helped my behaviour and that of the screws. It now meant that I would go back to take up where I had left off. There was no way out. I felt that I had to kill a part of me in order to go on without thinking too deeply about it. When one is in a concrete box and has bad injuries then one is constantly thinking about the next time the door opens. The further four years added to my sentence was purely an academic exercise. It didn't matter whether it had been four days or forty years, what mattered was the actual conviction. I had committed myself to having a go at the screws and the system in order to expose them for the things that they did, and with this sense of commitment I had hoped that victory would be just around the corner, but it's never that easy. I was led back down the stairs after sentence to the cells where I was locked in. The voices outside the cell door were jubilant at their victory, but what I minded most was a reference to the injured screws being able to get new car engines with the money they would get from the Criminal Compensation Board. At this point I was on the brink of a form of insanity with emotional pain that was burning with a fierce intensity. My god, I've never hated as I did at that moment. I was not returned to Peterhead but sent to Inverness Punishment Block. I had received physical injuries, been given further imprisonment, and now they were giving me yet another punishment. As far as I could see, the whole deal was structured to make sure that my spirit was broken.

The Punishment Block at Inverness had changed its location. Previously it was a few of us in a large hall but now there had been a swap over, with the local prisoners being put into the large hall and the few on Punishment situated in the smaller of the prison's two halls which held sixteen cells. It was a two-tier system with eight cells on the bottom flat and eight above. Next to this hall they were adding another hall that would contain the new Punishment Block and a work shed. The work for this was going on while we were there. When I arrived three guys were already there. Amongst them was Larry Winters. It was getting back to the grind and the boredom that was destroying our souls. Guys would crack up in their cells at night and smash whatever they could. Most of them were getting drugs from the doctor. Some would shout and scream and smash the small pieces of furniture which they had. Sometimes it was due to depression, other times it was to break the monotony of our daily routine. The following day they would be taken in front of the governor and punished.

The remark about the Criminal Injuries Compensation Board was eating into me, so I made an application to claim for the injuries that I had received during the incident in Peterhead. I was refused compensation but I wrote to the Board appealing against their decision, and informing them that I wasn't really after compensation but that I wanted to inform them that prison staff were creating assaults and claiming Compensation. I heard nothing from them and don't know to this day if they received my letter.

I was now doing physical exercises in my cell with an intensity that I hadn't shown before. I came to the conclusion that from now on the confrontations would be fierce and bloody, and therefore I should be prepared both at a physical and mental level. The only way to pass time was to do exercises and reading, and thinking thoughts of hatred. My former life was far in the distance and I would try not to think of my family as it hurt too much.

My Ma would come up with my son to see me on occasions but I tried to restrict these visits as much as possible. When I did send them a pass I would be very excited and looking forward to seeing them, but when the moment arrived there would be glass and wire barriers between us. My son would shout Da-Da and try to get in. We would sit looking at each other, Ma and I, trying to pretend that the barrier didn't exist, nor the screws standing behind me. We would force conversation, deep down realising that things had changed, but clinging to the childhood and growing-up memories. I would have preferred to have just sat looking in silence as the words Ma spoke as she recounted the past and the present opened up the parts that I was trying to kill; the cherished parts of me that made me feel human in an inhuman situation. These were the parts that I felt had to be submerged in order to survive but Ma could penetrate the strong barriers of hatred that had been built up and she could do it with ease. After the visit was over I would feel very depressed because the visits from my family always confronted me with almost everything that had been beautiful in my life, and the part that would never be again. I would get letters during the week from my Ma and brothers and other relatives but I knew that I was becoming alien to all of them and I could sense that it was all taking place within me.

I hadn't completed a full year of my sentence and had been twice in Inverness. How many more times would I experience this? Would I spend the rest of my life being shuttled to and fro after court appearances? This period in Inverness was destined to be a long one; this was made clear from the start. The maximum length of stay was supposed to be six months, the rules were explicit in stating this. However, my first period here had gone beyond that.

I built up a daily routine of exercises and writing my thoughts on paper and this got me through the first six months of my second stay here. The only other guy to be here that length of time was Larry Winters. We put in for the Inspector of Prisons and asked to see him on his next rounds. He made a quarterly visit to each prison to take complaints. I put it to him that I had been here for six months and wanted to be moved out. He told me that they were having difficulty in finding a place to put me into. Meanwhile the daily grind was continuing and by this time there were four of us being kept for an excessively long period. We had kept out of trouble and given them no excuse to keep us there for such an extended period. We thought that things were going beyond the tolerable.

Those of us in the Block were a pretty solid bunch, so one day in the shed, while we were working on the numbing job of fishnet making, one of the guys, the youngest, who had been in institutions since he was eleven years old, walked up to one of the screws and attacked him. The alarm bell was rung and that started it, with all of us getting into a big stand up fight. Reinforcements came running, but somehow we managed to negotiate, with me being spokesman and telling them that all of us were fucking sick of this place, and the sight of their faces, and that it had reached the stage where attacking them was one way of breaking the monotony of our daily torment. The screws said that they were sick of us in their prison, which was meant to be a quiet local one and that they wanted us out of it. We came to a compromise as all of us seemed to have that same hard-done-to feeling. The compromise was that we would be allowed out for an extra two hours recreation that night. With this, all of us, screws and cons, crossed the yard, but some steps on another fight broke out.

All the short term prisoners were up at their windows and shouting out at us. They would enjoy it, as rumour had it that after a spell in our place, the screws would go back to the ordinary part of the prison so tense that they would become very authoritarian with the short termers. We were giving them a sort of grim satisfaction, as they couldn't endanger their short sentences by indulging in our sort of behaviour.

Meanwhile we were all rolling about the yard fighting, but sheer weight of numbers defeated us and we were dragged into the cell area. I was kept for special treatment and was dragged through to the silent cell and brutally attacked. This was the worst beating I had experienced to date and I knew it at the time as the screws were pounding me in their rage. I could only retaliate by punching, kicking and biting but due to the number of screws I wasn't doing much of that. I would have given anything for a weapon at that moment. They pounded me severely and though still conscious I realised I was badly injured. I had been kicked all along the corridor into the silent cell and left there, but my hatred was so strong that I rose to the judas hole screaming at them and calling them all the cowards of the day. I was challenging them to come back and fight but they had me where they wanted. I kept feeling the injuries to my face and tried to gauge the extent of the damage as it was bleeding badly and felt very swollen. Being in this bare cell with the roughcast walls was almost like seeing an old friend. There was nothing that I could use to look through to see my injuries, but I was able to see my body and legs and they were badly bruised. The nearest anyone came to seeing me was through the judas hole but whenever I heard them I was up and shouting and banging the door telling them to come in. No one did. Although I had been angry originally, there was a coolness within me and I occasionally laughed when I thought back to the stupidity of us all rolling about the yard. There was this feeling of having changed the day, of having made it different. It's very difficult to explain this, but the nearest I can come to it is that I felt I was becoming used to all of this, even the brutality. Yes, I had lost the fear of pain. It was a day later that the prison doctor came in and his reaction to my condition was pretty strong though he tried not to show it.

He was not a hardened prison doctor. I knew, as did the others, that what was going on in Inverness was against his own principles and he made it clear that he wanted out of it. The only thing he felt he could do to help was to give us decent medical attention and this he did. Certainly we would have liked someone to stand up and shout out loud and cause a scene about these things, but we knew that this was expecting too much. But certainly the doctor was the nearest thing to a neutral in the camp. There was no doubt in my mind that a riot charge would be made against us all so I was glad that this man had treated my wounds. I was looking forward to another court trial as I would use it as a platform to let people know what was going on in there.

Two days later I was allowed to slop out. By this time I had again thrown all my filth over the floor and was preparing for a long stay in this cell. I went to slop out as curiosity was getting the better of me and I wanted to see the extent of the damage to my face. I could see some of it from my reflection on the chrome tap of the sink. There was a lot of discoloration and swelling but decorating all of this was the imprint of a foot covering my face. The print was clearly made from the tacks that were on the guy's boot. If one was in the business of handing out sore faces then there is little doubt in my mind that here was one to be proud of. I was standing there trying to see it in the sink tap without a stitch of clothing on, surrounded by screws who were waiting for a reaction. I turned to look into their faces and told them that as long as I was alive I'd remember every bastard who had laid a finger on me. They said nothing to me, in fact they were very apprehensive as judging by all previous incidents I should have been grovelling at their feet. They were no longer angry or full of emotion as they had been at the time, but I was letting them see that nothing short of killing me would stop me continuing on my merry way. The only other way they could rationalise my behaviour was to assume that I was mad. To think this and to be left with me was frightening for them. I would never let them know any different.

Later that morning I was taken to the Governor's room to be charged and went there naked. Using all my old tactics when entering I shouted repeatedly, "Bastard, bastard, bastard . . ." till they took me out again. I had decided to myself that I was never going to speak to them again, never to any of the bastards even though this meant not being able to ask for a toothbrush or any essential. I hated them so much that I found it revolting to even see them, never mind speak to them. Moments of succour were when I was locked in the silent cell alone with the silence. Later that day someone shouted through the judas hole that I was remanded pending a decision from the Prisons Department. This was because my continual chanting had stopped them from being able to speak. To me this meant that the cops were coming in, but as far as I was concerned it didn't matter a shit.

I began to dabble in yoga as I had read about it some months previously and had looked at some of the exercises. So I began to try them. I found them very difficult and avoided doing them at the beginning, but finally I felt that if I didn't I was left with only one alternative, staring into space, and one can have too much of that in the kind of situation I was in. The mind dictates the mood and I knew that if I was to sit or lie about all day then black periods would be the inevitable result. I was oblivious to the filth and smell that permeated the place, but I had my clean strip where I could lie, and sleep and do my exercises without slipping. I knew that the shit and the slops were necessary weapons, the only weapons at my disposal and an important part of my survival. It was strange to notice how screws who had seen blood pouring down my face could be quite insensitive to it, yet they would be very upset at having to feed me and face the smell. I was in the silent cell for over a month before being taken in front of the Visiting Committee and charged with attempting to assault a Prison Officer. There was a very middle-class, but quite beautiful woman taking notes on the proceedings and the Committee sentenced me to 28 days solitary and 28 days remission; someone should have told them a lifer has no remission. But with this I was back in the silent cell. The prison authorities had about-turned on this issue that was pretty serious and kept it an internal matter. Little did I know that the other guys had been sentenced to fourteen days solitary by the Governor. I heard later that due to the injuries received by the prisoners there had been a lot of hushing up of the police charges. By any standards, it was a riot, but due to the cloak of secrecy that hangs over prisons the authorities managed to keep it all quiet. It was the first serious charge that I had been involved in that was smothered up.

It was around this time when I was slopping out one day, that two of the screws standing watching me were talking, and one of them mentioned his sister, who worked in a store in town. This matter-of-fact conversation stopped me dead as I had become so alienated from society that I somehow couldn't imagine this guy having a sister, or even being human. My whole way of thinking had become so introspective and introverted that I was practically cut off from all that had gone on in my past life. I was becoming animalised. This simple conversation between two people has stayed with me; it was the only means for me to measure the change that was taking place. But I wasn't too worried about it as I felt it was necessary in order to survive. This world that I was living in was so empty of human feeling that it was difficult to be aware of the inner transformation taking place.

By this time, the screws were saying that I must be transferred to another prison, but the hard fact was that no other prison would take me. I had seen the Inspector of Prisons a number of times about my lengthy period here and he told me this, time and again. The Governor of Inverness prison who was due to retire was in a dilemma, as he was faced with a hostile staff who wanted me removed, and a hostile prisoner who wanted to be transferred. So for the first time the screws and I wanted the same thing. A compromise was reached by which the Governor, having made it clear that no one would take me, offered me a painting job. This meant painting the cells on my own so I was agreeable. It was to isolate me from the rest of the guys, and we knew it, so all of us were let out of solitary to go back to the few hours work that the prison could provide. There had been some movement among the prisoners as a few had gone. Larry Winters and I remained and Ben Conroy had returned. Ben had been out only days after the end of his five year sentence when he was arrested and given a further seven years. He had lost most of his remission for offences during his five years sentence and it looked as though the pattern would be repeating itself in this recent seven year sentence. In his place two other guys had come on the scene. One of them was being given electric shock treatment after which he would come wandering into the hall area looking like a lost soul. The other was an elderly guy who was getting large doses of drugs to quieten him down.

It was around this time while I was busy working on the cell-painting job, that I returned after lunch one day and noticed that someone had been into my cell. A brand new hacksaw was lying on the floor and I immediately sensed that I was being "fitted up". Someone had planted it there. Hacksaws were like gold in the jail, but I didn't know what to do as I sensed that it was a trap. I would love to have hidden it, so that I could have a laugh at the screws when they came in search of it. But there was nowhere to hide it, and even if there had been it would probably have been pointless. So I barged into the shed where the other guys were working and told them. The screws knew something was in the air and we walked out en masse along to the cell with the screws following us asking what the matter was. There was a direct confrontation with me asking them about the plant. The scene was explosive and tension mounting as the screws made denials all round. We were told that an investigation would be made into this, but like all things we heard no more about it.

I was in the Inverness Punishment block for nineteen months and was always on the verge of exploding. The place had been structured to encourage boredom. Most of us here had been labelled as anti-authority which meant that the only thing left to do was to clash with each other, which didn't bother the screws. Tempers would become frayed and we would bite at each other in verbal exchanges that came close to violence but the cardinal rule that we made from the early days and always passed on to newcomers was that there would be no fighting amongst ourselves. There were exceptions to this rule and guys did have their physical fights but they were few and far between. I felt as though I was one of the living dead as I had been there three times longer than the maximum period stated in the rules. It looked as though they would keep me here forever.

In November 1969 at approximately 12.30 a.m. I pretended to feel sick. I rang the cell bell bringing the night screws and asked them for treatment. They went for the nurse screw and one other. They returned some time later. When called in at this time of night the screws usually noise the place up to make sure everyone is disturbed. My door was opened and I was given two aspirins but

I threw them back telling the screws to stick them up their arses. A fight broke out between us and we were outside in the hall area. But there were too many of them and I was held down. The rest of the prisoners were shouting for them to leave me alone. Some of the other screws went round the other cells once they saw that I was being subdued but when they went into Ben Conroy's cell he came barging out of the door and flew into the thick of us and it was a battle once more. Both of us got to our feet and attacked the screws, but finding ourselves next to Ben's cell door we jumped inside and banged the door shut, locking ourselves in.

We barricaded the door with his bed and an old wooden chair, then smashed the windows by putting a metal spar torn from the bed through the metal grill covering the window frame. Ben and I were both stark naked as our clothes had been taken from us before going into the cell that afternoon but we were drunk with pride. The screws were in a right fix now as they would have to explain how it was possible for two prisoners to get into the same cell during the early hours of the morning. The rules stated that two doors weren't to be opened at the one time, particularly at that time. Here we were, locked away from them and sharing a cell when minutes before we thought we were going to be beaten up, so it showed that nothing could be forecast. For a while the tide had turned in our favour. This was a winter's night in November and it was extremely cold. An hour or so after we had locked ourselves in, there were noises and movements outside and they began breaking the windows. They put the nozzle of a hose in the window and turned it on soaking everything and leaving us wet and cold. They kept telling us to come out but we shouted back slagging them. As the night wore on we got colder and colder, so that within a very short time Ben and I lay on a metal bed frame and embraced each other for body warmth, wrapping our limbs around each other. The new Governor who had taken over the prison a few weeks earlier came to the judas hole in the late morning and beckoned us to come out, but we gave him mouthfuls of abuse. Later we found out that there had been an application to the Prisons Department to use tear gas but this had been rejected. Eventually Ben and I were dragged from the cell and I was thrown into the silent cell so that once again I was in total isolation.

While Ben and I had been in the same cell, the rest of the prisoners had become involved in fights as the screws, in a state of rage and frustration due to our barricades, had gone to search them.

John, the youngest guy got involved in a fight and was dragged downstairs and was the first to experience the new solitary block that was being built nearby. Tam, the elderly guy, went to the toilet and burst all the toilet facilities, and he was the next to experience the new block. Larry Winters hadn't been involved but they put him there just in case. When Ben and I were extracted from his cell after the falling of the barricades, he too was taken to the new solitary block. I was taken to the old silent cell. I lay there ten days and then the cops came in and charged me with attempted assault with a knife. They charged Ben with assault using a hammer and we were accused of barricading ourselves in Ben's cell and destroying prison property.

On the 25th November the Governor "brought me up" in front of him and told me that £10 had been sent in to me from outside. I informed him that it was to enable me to buy some Christmas presents for my children. He said the money couldn't be used for this, but I told him I'd done it the year before as one of the office clerks had arranged for the buying of the gift. He denied me the request and I gathered the biggest spit I could and spat it at him then tried to hit him with the desk in front of him. There was a violent struggle and I was thrown back into the cell. All the other guys heard about it and when the Governor did his rounds they shouted abuse and one of them fired piss at him. The following day I was taken to his orderly room and repeated the previous day's actions and was dragged away again.

Later that day a mob of screws came to my door and took me from the silent cell to the new solitary block. There were eight cells in this new block, all in a row on the one floor. I was thrown into the first one, then John, blank, blank, Tam, blank, blank, Ben Conroy. Larry Winters had been moved to another prison so someone had scored out of it. The inside of the cell was bare and painted a clinical blue. Even so there was a novel feeling about it. There was a window that had armour plated glass on it, double glazed, and a heavy metal grill over that. The only space for air was a small ventilator that was made of metal screwed to the wall. The windows were frosted glass so that we couldn't see out. I lay in the cell raging about the two previous encounters with the Governor and trying to think up other schemes to get back at him. For some reason or other I went to the small ventilator and messed around with it. The building was brand spanking new and the cement was still very soft so I managed to get the ventilator off, after plenty of perseverance. I scraped away at the brick work leading to the cell next door and managed to tell John about it and the two of us hacked silently away at the brick work from each end as he had his ventilator. Before very long we had a small hole in the wall but we were constantly listening for the night patrol coming through. We were able to look at each other through the hole in the wall and speak, so it was exciting. However, we kept at it, increasing the size till at long last we had a hole big enough for me to slip into his cell and this was great: it was beyond all possible dreams and we embraced each other and laughed silently, not believing our luck that we had managed to do it. The joy of being together and knowing that we had done it was a fantastic morale booster and what a victory. The new solitary block, the pride of their system, and it was seriously flawed.

We decided to try to get to the elderly Tam and so moved quickly to tear the next wall down. One of us listened for the night patrol while the other went to work. With dust parching our throats and hands cut from working, we finally got to the vacant cell next door to Tam. Each wall was getting harder as our energy was being expended. The sheer success of the operation was all that we needed to get started on the next wall. Who would have believed it? On reaching the wall of Tam's cell we managed to get a brick out. Tam, who was banged full of heavy drugs each night was lying on his floor as there was no bed in the cell. He was next to the part where we were coming through and he was snoring. He was only serving a two year sentence and had been sent to Inverness for repeatedly smashing his cells up due to severe depressions. The drugs that he got were the knockout type and as we worked to widen the hole Tam continued to snore. We worked like beavers to get through and the fact that we were doing what we were and Tam was doing his snoring was such a direct contrast that we would stop and laugh like hell trying not to waken him or cause the screws to come. It was so totally unreal. Here we were covered in dirt from head to toe, having destroyed the walls of four cells only to find the guy in the fifth sound asleep.

We did it and had one helluva job waking this guy from his sweet dreams. He looked at us from the floor where all of us lay, through a haze of drugs and continued staring. This massive man looked at us as though we weren't there. He looked from us to the hole at the side of his head a few times then burst out laughing after it sank in. None of us had said a word, but he laughed and laughed so hard and loud that we had to put blankets over his head to drown out the noise. He cuddled us and laughed some more and then we talked. Inevitably we then decided to reach Ben to make the victory complete. The laugh was that while we were working on the walls to Ben's cell, Tam told us that he had once been a tunneller when he was outside. So with equal enthusiasm we managed to break through to Ben. He greeted us with wild joy and all of us hugged and embraced each other over and over. We laughed at this beautiful victory and knew that this was the ultimate dream. It was agreed that we should knock down all the walls and use the bricks to build a fortress for us to hold off the screws in the morning. We did this and built what we thought was a reasonable fort, then lay down to rest our weary selves. The rest was beautiful as we lay curled up near each other and glad of the company. It was the first time in years that I had been able to be with people without screws prying down our necks and listening to our every word. Although still very much in prison, there was this glorious sense of freedom about us sitting there together, talking quietly and able to say what we wanted. There were good humoured remarks about what we would plead when we went to court for it, as inevitably we would: "We'll do anything for a game of Bridge, your honour" or "The Devil finds work for idle hands" etc, etc. We would have a good laugh at ourselves and make guesses at the media headlines "Hole in the Wall gang strikes again" or form a business on release "Boyle and Company, Demolitions", See Inverness Governor for references. On a serious note we found that each of us had already been charged for the incidents earlier and speculated on going to the next High Court at Inverness. This would be hard luck for Tam who only had two months to go on his two years sentence. We would just have to wait and see.

It was still dark at six in the morning when we heard the screws coming to give us breakfast and my cell door was opened first. They had a torch with them and they shouted to me to come to the door for my breakfast, but when they shone the torch in they found an empty cell. They soon realised that there were no longer any single cells and that a dormitory now stood in their place. The cell door was slammed and the sounds of running feet and shouts filled the air. We laughed, but realised that another battle was near at hand. The cold dark morning was long in clearing and it would be almost ten o'clock before full daylight came to this part of the country. We decided to do an Alamo and fight to the last. Making sure that our fortress was strong, we prepared for them coming back which of course they did. We could see out of the slits in the brickwork and they had heavy metal crowbars and extra long riot batons. There were plenty of them, all in brown overalls; one had a large 14lb hammer. At first they called to me asking if we were coming out and I told them to go fuck themselves, that the fight was for real. High powered hoses were turned on us, causing us to duck below the brick wall. We, of course, were under the impression that our little fortress was impregnable, however, to our amazement we saw the high powered jet from the hoses partly destroy the wall, and with the other mob attacking it with crowbars and 14lb hammers, we were standing exposed in next to no time. Without wasting any time the large riot sticks were used and we were dragged along the corridors into the cells in the old hall that we had originally been brought from. The doctor came to see me and give me treatment.

I now began a six month period of solitary never leaving the cell once during this period. It began quite well with me very proud of our achievement in knocking down the walls of the solitary confinement block. The cops came and charged me with attacking the prison Governor and destroying the solitary block along with the others. All of us now had a long list of charges against us and knew that it would be another High Court appearance.

I took up yoga again during this period and became very involved in it, to the extent that it took over my whole existence. At first I dabbled in it and then went into the meditative side and became quite confident in my involvement in it. I restricted my diet and tried to eat as little as possible. Food was the only thing that I had to look forward to so I would test my will power and self discipline by eating less. This was a period in my life when I reflected on my whole being. Self analysis became a daily habit as I was trying to find out more about myself and to come to some understanding of where I had come from and where I was going. I looked at myself critically and thoroughly till the pain was at times unbearable, and shook my very soul. What was I doing in this place? Was this my life? What was my life all about? The pain from the realisation of my position and its futility was so powerful that I would just curl up in a corner and try to endure it. I went through a period of deep shame about the life I had led. All of this I was finding very difficult to cope with and I sat in this cell suffering as I had never done before. I would think of the kids who were doing the same things as I had done and who would follow my pattern to eventually reach this point of torment only to realise the futility of it, and these thoughts would make me feel sick. Is this what it was all about? I had suffered every year since I was a child but hadn't a clue about anything as I was so dumb and inarticulate and here I was, now an adult feeling pain like I had never done before.

But now I was beginning to put it all together, probably for the first time in my life. Day after day I lay in this cell thinking, thinking, thinking. I didn't speak to the screws and never saw anyone else. At night I could see the moon when it was out and I would long to see it without having to look through bars and heavy metal frames. I could hear the occasional noises outside my window as the short term prisoners walked past with the screws and I would have given anything to be in their shoes. During this period of self-analysis, I heard the sound of civilian workers erecting a new security system on the wire fence that was inside the wall and the sounds of their voices travelled across to me and I would listen to them in great pain. I would hear them checking the alarm system and would latch onto their every word. I would look at the differences in our ways of life and feel the futility of mine. At night they would pack up their tools and I would feel envy running through my whole body as they left, chatting together, oblivious to the fact that a guy was lying on a floor, sick at their parting sounds. If only they knew what misery was going on around them. It was very difficult for me to cope with the fact that I had this big blank in my life with nothing to look forward to. The only alternative was to be an arse-licker to the screws, losing my own personality and individuality, and being their pet lion. The one they had tamed. The rewards being the occasional pat on the head.

The only change would be a modification in my behaviour, but the future outlook for me could never change. The one thing that I could hold onto was the fact that I was me. I felt that I mustn't give this up or all would be lost. I tried to look at myself and see what was happening to me at that moment. Was I cracking? Was my spirit breaking? Was this me just in a pathetic state and feeling sorry for myself? No, for the first time in my life I was looking at myself and seeing clearly what was happening to me. Seeing just what I was doing to myself. The important thing was that I had journeyed inside myself, got right under the skin and into the soul. The pain of finding out more about myself was terrible for I had been living a life of self delusion ever since I was a kid. I now realised that some of the things I had done were very bad and was probably paying for it now, not by being sentenced, but by the real payment which comes with the realisation of what it's all about. Now that I had all this awareness, what could I do with it? As I said, by this time I was fully into yoga — in fact it had dominated me and purified me, having a calming effect. With all this clarity of thought came a realistic appraisal of the present and the future. I had come through this painful period and was now aware of all that had gone wrong in the past, but having reached that point I also realised that I would have to live in the jungle-like existences that reigned supreme within the walls of prison. In other words I had to pull myself together and prepare myself for the future. I had come out of this experience stronger and felt the power surging through my body.

It was around this time that I heard scuffling outside my door and later I heard that Ben Conroy was in the local hospital with his jaw broken in three places. Shortly after this, with barely a few weeks to go of his two year sentence, Tam, the elderly guy, was certified insane and put into the State Mental Hospital. I had not been alone in coming through a terrible journey. I was living in a jungle and there seemed to me to be no alternative but to live like an animal in order to survive in that jungle.

In the middle of May 1970, I was handed a charge sheet informing me of my trial date and preliminary hearing. We had all been charged with maliciously damaging seven ventilators, fifteen panes of glass, seven light fittings, and six brick dividing walls. I was further charged with attempting to strike the Governor by overturning a desk against him. In all, there were about eight or nine charges including the attempted assaults with weapons. The puzzling feature for me was that all of us had charges that would normally have taken us to the High Court yet we had been summoned to appear before the Sheriff court. This didn't smell right to me. It was also on the summons that Tam had been certified insane and was now in the State Hospital and this was how I found that out.

Around this time I had a visit from my Ma, the first in a long, long time and it was beautiful to see her and the two children. She was looking terribly old and I knew that bringing the kids all this way was too much for her on her own as they were full of life and running all over the place. We had a very emotional and heartbreaking discussion. I loved her as I'd always done and she was my world; her loyalty to me never faltered, never wavered. She wrote to me each week and kept me in touch with all of the family and the growth of my children. In order to keep me firmly in the minds of the children she would conjure up little tricks for them, like opening an envelope saying that I had sent their wages — pocket money, and would extract the money from the envelope and give it to them. If the kids were in her house when she was posting a letter she would lift them up to the post box and they could say they had sent a letter to their Daddy. After this visit I went back to my cell and thought, and thought, and thought.

John, Ben and myself were taken to court on a beautiful summer's morning and it was magnificent to see them even though we were all in handcuffs and surrounded with cops and screws. The fresh air and the clear day were a joy to breathe and see. To smell the grass and most important of all, to see the people as we passed in the prison van. The three of us had a brief chance to discuss the situation. We were facing a great many charges and it was a puzzler for us all to be at this court, very much a disappointment in fact, as there would be no publicity and this was important as we wanted everyone to know what was going on and there is nothing like the High Court for giving a platform. This chance had been thwarted and I felt that I should take the blame for most of the charges as I was the one who started most of it off anyway. By the time we got to court it was decided that I would plead guilty. In the court I was given a further six months imprisonment. Ben and John had pleaded not guilty so they were further remanded. Eventually Ben was given six months and John four months. Tam was named in the charge sheet, but wasn't allowed to appear.

12

Ben and I were sent to Peterhead; John to Perth prison. Once in Peterhead I made it clear to both prisoners and screws that I wanted no trouble. I had personal reasons for saying this and was wanting a quiet period. I told all the guys that if there was something on, to leave me out and this was understood. At first, the screws refused to believe this, and the fact that I had such a bad reputation kept them away from me for a while. I was kept amongst the top security prisoners and we worked in the Tailors shop.

Before I arrived at Peterhead there had been three cops shot in Glasgow, two of them were killed. The accused had been to court and the one who shot them was sentenced to Life Imprisonment with a recommendation that he serve no less than twenty five years. This guy was himself a one-time cop, his name was Howard Wilson. He was one of the cops who had sat in my house while the police were searching for me for the murder charge. I thought it very funny that the cop guarding my house should now be locked up a few doors away. Most of the guys sent him to Coventry and were sniping at him for being an ex-cop. I didn't like this because I knew why he had been put in this prison: so that the prisoners would do the dirty work. When any white collar workers are arrested and convicted and finally sent to prison the last place the authorities put them to is a prison like Peterhead, which is very hostile. It's the land of the lost and is known as this throughout the system. Cops found guilty and even screws, are sent to the soft option prisons automatically as they are looked upon as being different from the ordinary scruff like us from the working class districts. This is blatant discrimination. So placing Howard Wilson in beside us was something extraordinary and unprecedented.

There was a lot of bad feeling about Howard amongst the prisoners as they felt that once a cop that was it. I would never have argued with them because some guys have suffered greatly through dealings with the police, such as fabrication of evidence and "planted" evidence and I felt they were entitled to keep their hatred. I went out of my way to speak to Howard. He had done the unthinkable by killing his own kind. His nerves were shattered by everything that was going on around him. Being thrown into a jungle like Peterhead for the first time must have been a terrible experience. His problem wasn't only the prisoners, the screws were messing him around constantly. They would be more arrogant with him than anyone else because they recognised that he was an outcast so was open game as far as they were concerned. This is the worst part of it, because prisoners will go to a certain point then stop, as they can identify with how the guy is feeling, but the screws were oblivious to this and wouldn't know when to stop. As a result, Howard was confronted with some humiliating experiences, that went beyond those of the others. He was always walking about like a guy who was waiting for something to be stuck into his back.

Being in the top security group with him meant that he was part of about twelve prisoners who had a line of cells on the second flat of the main hall. We were kept together and taken in a group to work with extra screws assigned to watch us at all times. We were "A" category prisoners and this included those prisoners with exceptionally long sentences who were liable to escape, or guys who had previously tried to escape, which meant they had to be kept under special supervision. At night, our clothing had to be put outside the door of the cell. Our lights were left on all night and the screws would scrutinise us when we were in our cells. We were being watched all the time at night. For two hours during the recreation period under the constant scrutiny of the screws, the "A" category men were allowed to mix with the guys in the main hall. Other prisoners could go to night classes and for football in the yard outside, but such activities were denied us.

After a few months of me keeping out of trouble, the screws began to put subtle pressures on me. There were a lot of them who hated me and others who feared me. There was this constant feeling of them wanting me to crawl. It was obvious that as far as they were concerned I was a symbol of something — the enmity lay barely beneath the surface. At night they would come into my cell and take the cell searches to the extreme by stripping me naked and telling me to bend over and pull my cheeks apart, so that they could look up my arse to see if I was hiding anything. In many ways I felt that the more pressure they put on me and got away with then the more they would try on the other prisoners who had caused them no bother. It reached the stage where I was so determined to keep out of trouble that I was searching my own cell for as much as a sewing needle as this was punishable. I was overreacting to them and in a sense retreating. The reason for this was that it was vital for me to keep out of trouble. The screws were making it blatantly obvious that they were very much in control. Amongst the prisoners there was lots of talk, petty meaningless talk, directed against the screws. There was an underlying current of total hostility against them. There was also the brutality, which seemed to be reaching a peak, some of which had taken place in full view of a large number of prisoners in the hall next to the one I was in. There was gossip about it during the work period and there would be lots of big talk with guys trying to retain some sort of self-respect even though they had stood there and seen a prisoner being slapped about by screws.

On the prisoners' side there was a group of guys who were part of a clique; they were the prison bullies. They were led by a guy nicknamed "The Poof". He was doing 15 years for offences concerning rape and prostitution, but while serving this sentence he was found guilty of murdering another prisoner and received a life sentence, so on top of his fifteen years this left him very much a hopeless case. The way he coped with his sentence was to prey on weaker guys and there were instances where some younger prisoners, or young-looking ones, were raped by this group. It became widely known and he had quite a reputation for it, so much so that screws in their uncouth way would pass remarks to the young guys on the transfer bus telling them that "The Poof" would get them when they arrived in the prison. As a result they would be terrified when they arrived, and some of them would ask for "Protection". The screws of course thought this all very funny, but personally I felt deeply humiliated that another prisoner could allow himself to be "used" in this way by them. In his own way he was policing the prison for them and the fact that he was causing conflict amongst the prisoners meant that pressure was taken off the screws. He didn't get away with it completely as some individual prisoners would have a go at him, including some of his group. But he had a frightening effect on prisoners in the main and this gave him some measure of control.

The interesting thing here is that before getting his life sentence, the Poof was a non-entity in the prison, although he was recognised as a guy always in trouble with other prisoners. But since receiving his life sentence he was quick to exploit the situation and use the power it gave him over others. He had no future, very much like me, therefore he had nothing to lose. He worked on the same principle as most screws did, which was that the majority of prisoners don't want to lose any of the remission from their sentences and this fact can be used as a weapon against them. I have seen frequent cases of guys that could fight exceptionally well in the streets outside, backing down to guys in prison that they knew they could knock the shit out of. The Poof was an ideal example of an ordinary guy with no exceptional fighting abilities, although he had been beaten up and stabbed a number of times. For me the sad fact was that this guy and his group of sycophants were unaware of what they were doing to those alongside them. They didn't like the screws either, though they didn't have much trouble with them. They had experienced some of the treatment the screws had been giving to all of us, but for some unknown reason they just couldn't begin to see that what they were doing was an awful lot worse due to the fact that they were prisoners. They continued on their way with the raping of young guys, putting knives to their throats and doing so with impunity.

In most prisons there is a place reserved for prisoners on "protection". This takes the form of isolated cells for guys who for their own reasons don't want to mix with the main body of prisoners. Some of them are police informers. Some have debts that they owe to the Barons. Some of them have committed sex offences against children, and others just give the name of a prisoner with a bad reputation, saying he is going to attack them. This may not always be true, but whatever the reason, the guy just doesn't want to mix as he is frightened of prison and the jungle life. The Protection wing is a hall of its own with sometimes forty to fifty prisoners in it. Guys going on protection don't tell the Governor that they are doing so because they are afraid of being raped. They give some other reason, or name someone, so as to save face. While there, they are kept in semi-solitary conditions and even within the prison it is a place where they are looked on as the lowest of the low. The guys there look and feel that way, and they are treated like shit by all of us, screws and prisoners alike.

In October 1971, The Poof had some trouble with a quiet guy who kicked him around a cell causing him to have his eye treated for a cut. The following week, after the movie, when all the prisoners were leaving, The Poof was walking down the prison corridor with a group of his sycophants when he was stabbed three times. It was obvious that something like this would happen and there was rejoicing amongst the prisoners. The strange thing was that the screws didn't take it too well, even causing one prisoner to remark, "You'd think he was one of their own". But these stabbings and the intrigues were all part of the prison jungle that we lived with.

Two days later I was eating lunch in my cell when the door opened and a gang of screws stood there. I was taken to the Solitary Confinement Block. Later that day I found out through the ventilating system that Ben Conroy had also been locked up on solitary. The following morning I was taken in front of the Governor and told that I was being put on Rule 36 for a month. When I asked the reason I was told it was for subversive activities, but unofficially I was told it was for stabbing The Poof. Ben had been put in for the same thing. When The Poof returned from hospital and was put into the prison hospital, the rumours were that I was locked up for it. A guy like him who had trodden over lots of prisoners can never afford to show weakness as there were too many people waiting to trample him into the ground. He was in a sticky situation, for though he knew who had actually stabbed him, there was still this rumour that I had done it. Some knew that this wasn't true but others wanted to believe that it was. He had no option other than to say that he was going to get me. Apparently he was lying in hospital making this pretty clear, saying that he intended killing me the first chance he got. There is no doubt that he was saying this so as to get out of the situation he felt he was now in. The next thing I knew he had been transferred to Inverness prison.

Meanwhile I was lying in solitary thinking that my trying to keep out of trouble had been a waste of time. I really hadn't wanted trouble for personal reasons but it was obvious that there was no way this would be allowed. Whether I liked it or I not felt I would be put on solitary at the slightest whim of my keepers. I was now thinking along the lines of how when prisoners enter prison they experience a loss of their rights as a citizen and how from there everyone assumes you have no feelings — that these automatically turn off. The authorities are quick to tell you that you have no rights the minute you question anything that is being done to you and through this process you are made to feel less than human. You shouldn't question or complain. Of course this was nothing new to me as I had felt very much like this on the outside when staying in the Gorbals and so what was happening in prison was only an extension of that. The difference now was that I was beginning to waken up to the fact that this was wrong. It may be that under the circumstances that I was now living in I would have to accept the forfeiture of my rights as a citizen but definitely not my rights as a human being and this is really what it was all about. This was the whole area of conflict throughout my life and when I thought about it, my past behaviour was that of an inarticulate rebel against what was being done to us in places like the Gorbals, and now in prison. Even at this stage I was very uncertain about this and felt that I may have been making excuses for myself and my past. This was an area of confusion within, one that was to become very clear and strong as time went on.

After two months I was allowed out of solitary and back into the prison mainstream. It was approaching Christmas, a time of great tension in prison. The message was by now coming on pretty clear that the screws would prefer me to be out of their prison. By this time, with The Poof out of the way, I was advising guys to form a group called P.S.M. (Prisoners Solidarity Movement). We got some pamphlets printed, stating that anyone willing to join the group would face the possibility of losing all his remission or facing court action as there would, no doubt, be fights with the screws. It went on to state that anyone of the group who was assaulted by the screws would concentrate on his attackers, passing the names of the brutalisers to those of us in circulation and we would attack them, and this would go on and on until such times as the subsequent court trials brought the whole thing out. While we were getting this off the ground and the pamphlet was circulating, I was given a cell search and taken to the Punishment wing for having an extra mirror. I had been given permission to have it, but no one would admit to this. I gave the screws a mouthful of abuse as I was escorted away, with the realisation that things were moving and that by the time I came out of the solitary block the pamphlet would have been distributed and the guys would have had time to think it over. I knew that the authorities were very much afraid of this Solidarity Movement and its possible consequences.

I was taken in front of the Governor for abusing his staff over the mirror and was sentenced to ten days solitary. I did this ten days doing exercises and keeping very fit. One night the Deputy Governor entered the gloomily lit cell saying he had bad news for me. My immediate thoughts were, ah, they are going to pile on the solitary confinement. I lay back on the floor and he continued "Your Mother died tonight at 6.10 p.m." — it was the 10th

December 1971. The force of this statement caused me to stand, sit, stand then sit on the floor. It was almost as though I was being lifted and pushed down by some giant invisible hand. I just didn't know what had hit me. Anything but this. All that I had recognised as good in the world was gone. . . . I sat alone in that cell crying my eyes out. I felt vulnerable, exposed, and very much alone. I loved her so very very much. It shook me to the core, it was the last thing I had expected. She had written to me her usual letter that very week. What the hell was going on? I paced the floor all night thinking of her and how she was an angel to me, to all of us. The most beautiful person in the world, and now she was gone . . . I felt a terrible guilt at having given her such a terrible life. Even these past months when I had tried to avoid trouble, I had failed. Being told of her death while serving punishment made it all seem so futile. There is no use me trying to put in print what I felt that night and even ever since, as nothing could possibly describe it.

The following morning I was whisked away to Barlinnie prison where arrangements were made for me to attend the funeral. Because I had been in solitary in Peterhead the Governor continued to keep me in solitary while in Barlinnie. I was allowed to see my brothers through the glass and wire partition and we wanted to hold each other as all of us were badly broken. Ma had died of cancer.

Two days later I was taken to the prison reception area to change into my civilian clothes. I was going to try and tell the escort to trust me not to do anything at my Mother's funeral and ask them to leave the handcuffs off. While changing in the dog box I heard the escort being instructed by what sounded like a superior; saying that he was in charge of the escort security and that they were taking every precaution, that though my Mother had died I was still a very dangerous man and should be treated as such. They made it clear that they had weapons. Any idea that I had of asking them to trust me on this occasion was thrown from my head. I was heavily escorted in handcuffs with patrol cars lining the route and elaborate precautions taking place. I was taken to the graveyard. Sitting in the middle of the cemetery was a van filled with cops and police dogs. All around the graveyard were cops with walkie-talkies. I was filled with rage. I was left to feel that by coming to the graveside I had desecrated it. I was deeply hurt by the fact that no one considered me human enough to attend Ma's funeral and be able to give her the respect she deserved. Instead I was taken there hand-cuffed to the screws. My brother approached asking if I could be allowed to help carry the coffin. After a lengthy discussion they decided to go ahead so with one handcuff being released I was allowed to carry it with my other hand chained to the screw. Amongst the mourners were relatives and friends who I hadn't seen since I was sentenced. My son was amongst them and I was touched when he came over and stood beside me, taking my hand as we said prayers over the grave. Afterwards I was taken swiftly back to Barlinnie.

There was no delay in taking me back to Peterhead under armed escort and before very long I was back into the thick of things. It was very near to Christmas with the atmosphere hostile and tense. There was the feeling that things were going to happen very soon. The hall that I was in was full of screws that were the recognised hardliners. This meant that we were sitting on a time bomb. Within myself I felt as though death would be welcome. I didn't give a fuck about my life and somehow felt this more now than at any time during my sentence. I kept thinking that I would be dead within a year as though I had set myself a time limit. Christmas passed and it was just like any other day, though the press rubbed it in by stating how beautifully we were being fed and how the pensioners weren't half so lucky. I thought that the fucking pensioners would be welcome to the shit that I was eating. They seemed to scrimp and scrape all the year round to give us a meal that was really nothing. What does a meal matter in circumstances such as this? I dare say press garbage does something to salve the nation's conscience as to how well even the bad prisoners are treated. New Year's day, the highlight of the festive period for the Scottish people, was the same, with us being built up for this meal. Like Christmas, it too passed.

The bomb exploded on the 4th January 1972, when a prisoner convicted for something he didn't do went into the recreation part of the hall and destroyed the two television sets and smashed everything he could get his hands on. He did all of this on his own and told the screws the reason why he had done it. He was taken to the solitary block. Everyone else was locked up and the following day there was no work, so we knew that a full cell search was on. The screws came round and searched every prisoner and every cell. The prison was very tense. Around lunch time when the search was over, there were sounds of shouts and scuffles coming from the far end of the hall and it was obvious that something violent was happening. Within minutes of hearing this my cell door flew open and there stood a mob of screws who took me with them. At moments such as this I know what is going to happen. As I walked along, surrounded by them, I was planning what I would do when the violence did come. I was as ready for it as I would ever be. As I entered the solitary block there were loud noises as prisoners banged their doors. Ben Conroy was spread-eagled on the floor, covered in blood and seemed to be unconscious. He was in the process of being dragged into a cell.

Before I could begin to do anything I was clubbed on the head from behind and a fight started. There was a furious struggle and I distinctly remember someone trying to pull my hair but it was so short they couldn't grip it and I remember feeling pleased about this while I fought. I heard them shouting for a straitjacket and saw it in the hands of one of them. I strongly resisted this knowing full well that if they got it on I was finished as these bastards would kill me. I struggled with all I had, but realised that it would be in vain. The blood was pouring down my face as the batons battered down on top of my head. They were holding me at waist level, some with my upper body and others with my legs and yet others battering into me. The jacket was being put onto me and tightened up "BASTARDS, BASTARDS, BASTARDS, BASTARDS", I screamed in utter frustration. During this fierce struggle we ended up next to a sink full of dirty water and by this time I was well strapped into the straitjacket but still struggling and cursing them. They lifted me and my head was pushed into the sink full of water to the sounds of someone calling out to drown the bastard. I was aware of a struggle between the screws, some of whom were frightened, trying to pull me out, while others were for drowning me. During all this time I was coughing and swallowing water for what seemed an eternity. I was pulled out, though some, having lost control of themselves, were still trying to push me under. I vividly remember mental flashes saying that it was all over, that I was dead. I was still coughing and spluttering when I was pulled out, all the while being kicked. When I was able to, I used the only weapon that I had, my tongue: "I'm going to kill you bastards the first chance I get". I repeated this over and over and over again making sure that it sank in. I was being carried with my head near the ground and my legs up in the air, all the while being hit with sticks and boots. I could see the trail of blood I was leaving on the ground. My last memory of the affair was seeing a shiny boot bounce onto my face and strike me. I lost consciousness.

I came to lying on a stone floor surrounded by hazy figures, notably a man in a white coat. As my vision cleared I could see that the walls were painted an asylum blue and that I was inside a cage, the likes of which I had never seen before. My heart sank as I knew I was in an asylum. I had always dreaded this sort of thing, always suspicious that it would happen, and now it had. The straitjacket was saturated in blood. I drifted off again and when I came to I was cleaned and smelling of disinfectant. The place I was in looked weird from where I lay. It was an ordinary cell with a large cage front which cut the cell to half its normal size. I was locked in the cage. Outside the cage front was the ordinary metal and wooden door. This meant that to reach me the screws would have to enter the one door then the cage door. On the wall at the other side of the cell there was a notice and I crawled over to it. In large writing it said "Rules and Regulations for Prisoners in Inverness Special Unit". It dawned on me then that I was in Inverness prison and not in an asylum.

Relieved beyond belief, I then looked over the place and noticed how the windows were familiar. I should have recognised them before. A doctor had been called into the prison to attend my injuries, not the regular prison doctor but another one. I heard two screws discussing me and one said that I had arrived like a parcel of butcher's meat. I tried to make out to the doctor that I was all right but my face and body were cut and badly bruised. My head was full of very large lumps. My face was in one helluva mess and I wasn't allowed to send for a visit because of the injuries that were showing.

I didn't make any official complaint about my condition and played it down until I was allowed a visit from my brother Harry and he went to our local M.P. who in turn wrote to the Prisons Department in Edinburgh complaining that I had been assaulted. He was told that I had tried to attack a Prison Officer with a metal tray and any injuries I had received were while I was being restrained. They gave my M.P. a description of the incidents and violence that I had previously been involved in. This list was formidable and my M.P. shrugged his shoulders saying that there was nothing he could do. Had he investigated this supposed "assault", he would have found that I had never been charged for it by the police or through the prison disciplinary system. Had their statement been true, why was I not charged for it? Harry by this time knew that the situation was desperate and took it to the *Daily Express* in the hope that they would bring some attention to bear on the brutality. They printed it but it did no good, except to let the Prisons Department see that I was continuing to fight them. I was now in a position where the people in charge could literally do what they wanted with me. They could justify it by stating that I was "Scotland's Most Violent Man".

Inverness was in many ways a different prison as there had been a change of staff. We were given one book per week and the food was thrown under the bars, just like an animal in a cage. The screws hated me back here as I had been the source of so much trouble in the past. This time they had a feeling of control as the new set-up was to their specification with me in the cage. This was the building where I had helped destroy the cells. They had renovated it and strengthened it by halving the number of cells and putting in four with very strong cages inside them. They had also built in another silent cell. While I was there two other guys were brought up and placed in the cages next to me. One was John, who had been involved in the cell wrecking here in Inverness. He was now awaiting charges of serious assault on screws in Perth prison. He was sporting a bad scar on his forehead which had resulted from his fight with them. The other guy was serving a six month sentence with only weeks to go. Unfortunately he had got involved in a clash with the screws in Edinburgh prison so was sent here. He was brutally assaulted while in Inverness and complained to the Governor and the doctor. The Governor took him aside that afternoon and asked him I if had put him up to this. I told the guy to go to the press when he was released as I could see things coming to a head here and wanted as much evidence as possible about what was going on in these places. He sent me a postcard on his release saying that he had done this.

Governors from various prisons met every two months to decide if those of us in the cages were eligible to be returned to our original prisons. Around March 1972, I was told that the Deputy Governor of Peterhead was coming to see me the following day. I was intrigued by this as it was a very unusual thing to happen. He came and I was put into an office with him. He told me that The Poof was back in Peterhead and he asked me about any trouble I may have had with him. I told him that as far as I was concerned there was no trouble, but that I had the feeling that certain people in responsible positions were trying to create a problem where there was none. He then told me that after I was taken from Peterhead, the screws had searched my cell and found two keys. One of these fitted the cell door and the other the main door leading to the cell block. We argued over this and I told him that this was rubbish. Finally he broached the threats that I had made concerning his staff. He was referring to the threats that I had made while being brutalised in the strait-jacket. Apparently the staff were apprehensive. He then went on to tell me how staff were only ordinary working chaps with families who really didn't want trouble. I was really raging at this sort of shit. This was the same old story of screws attacking someone unmercifully in the heat of the moment and now that it was time to pay the penalty, they were squirming. I pointed out that the same people that he was talking about had nearly killed me. There was a sinister aspect to this meeting that I didn't like and quite frankly it had me worried. He told me to think it over, then he said that he would be coming back to Inverness prison in two weeks to discuss with the Board of Governors the possibilities of my returning to Peterhead.

That night I lay thinking about what he had said. What were they up to? He told me as I entered the room that he had been given official approval to come and see me. He had mentioned The Poof trouble, keys that had been found and the impending clash that seemed most likely with the screws. He had said a number of times that I was a continual embarrassment to the Prisons Department. I saw the prime motive for his visit being that the screws were putting pressure on him because they were worried about my returning to Peterhead. I had very grave suspicions about what game was being played here and I wanted to make sure that I had everything recorded, because there was only one thing I was certain of and that was that I would soon either be attending another court trial or be dead. I wrote a full account of what had been said at that meeting and gave it to John, who was in the cage next door. He was due to return to Perth prison for a trial involving the serious assaults on screws. I told him to keep it with him at all times and to give it to my lawyer if I went for trial but to make sure it got into the right hands at all costs.

Two weeks later the Board of Governors met to decide which of us would return to our normal prisons. They met on their own to talk it over then came into the prison hall where they set up office in a prison cell and the prisoners marched in one at a time. I was taken in to be faced with two Governors and the Inspector of Prisons, who was there as the representative of the Prisons Department. He told me that it had been agreed that I should be returned to Peterhead prison, and I thought to myself that this was the first time that I had ever been sent back at the correct time. Why were the rules functioning properly for the first time? It left me feeling more suspicious than ever. I spoke to the Deputy Governor and he was a sort of deathly pale colour and seemed rather nervous as distinct from his usual casual self. The Inspector of Prisons introduced himself saying that we hadn't met but that he had heard plenty about me and that I was an embarrassment to the Department. This was a phrase that was coming up far too often for my liking. I knew I had been and I certainly hoped to continue to be, but the repetitiveness of the phrase was banging home some message to me. I was well aware of the fact that on returning to Peterhead I was going into a very hot fire. This was very well-known throughout the prison system and was the main topic of conversation on the grapevine.

For starters I knew that The Poof and his gang were broadcasting the fact loud and clear that they were going to kill me. But as far as I was concerned, the main problem was the screws as they had given me a rough going over the last time so now I was in the position where I would have to back up my threats otherwise they would make a thorough job of me next time. The other fact was that Ben Conroy was in the solitary block awaiting trial for the assaults that had taken place on the 4th January when I was put into the strait-jacket; so getting witnesses for this was also a priority. There was much to be done but the odds against me were overwhelming.

I was taken under heavy escort to Peterhead Prison. As the van stopped outside the reception area I could see all the prisoners waiting outside the Governor's room to be "brought up" in front of him. Handcuffed to two screws I was taken through them and into the reception area. It didn't surprise me to find The Poof amongst them. What a coincidence! I put a calm face on it as I moved through the crowd with both hands cuffed to the screws, but I was watching everything. I passed within inches of The Poof but he didn't take his chance, only passing a snide remark for all to hear. As the reception area was part of the solitary block it meant that I could take a look at the list giving the names of the guys on solitary. There was Ben Conroy, and another kid just up from the Young Offenders Institution awaiting trial for stabbing The Poof though the injuries were only scratches. I was changed into prison uniform and taken to the top security hall and was only there some minutes when a guy came up to tell me to watch out as the Poof was going about shouting that I was getting "done in" as soon as I entered the jail. Within half an hour of entering the prison at least six people had told me the same thing and I reckoned that even the seagulls must have known. Shortly after I arrived I was handed a lump of iron that had the point sharpened and this was to be my knife, but as knives go it was a poor substitute. The Poof was allowing himself to be the prime mover, diverting me from the fundamental issue, the clash between me and the screws. The sad fact is that I entered into it because of this silly prestige thing and loss of face aspect. But I vividly remembered what they had done that day. They themselves knew it and I could see the fear in their eyes. They were only too glad of the diversion being created by The Poof. I was aware of all this but became drawn into it just the same.

On Saturdays and Sundays the whole prison population is allowed to mix together. One particular Sunday it was beautiful with the sun shining brightly. On reaching the yard, I noticed The Poof and his questionable crew in deep discussion looking rather sinister. My tactics were going to be that I'd allow him to come to me and thrust, so that any move made after would be in self-defence. I felt enough confidence in my own reflexes to allow him that first thrust. I knew a court case would come out of it and I had my defence for the trial prepared in advance. The ironic thing was that for years now I had been trying to expose the authorities, and now I saw that a fight between two prisoners could possibly be the way to do this. We were in the yard, in full view of everyone, as there were lots of screws on the scene and most prisoners out to see the big fight. It was a carnival atmosphere for some. The Poof made a run towards me and thrust with his knife giving me two slight cuts. I took a swipe at him missing, but he quickly ran back to his gang urging them to join him. They refused to do so. The screws were coming over to split it up and they pounced on me first. I knew that I could have stuck the knife I had right into them but I didn't. It was one thing punching a screw or a cop in the heat of the moment but it was another stabbing them. And really when one is conditioned, as most criminals are, not to stab or shoot cops or screws, then it is very hard to overcome this. So there I was, in the middle of the crowded yard being held by screws when a fight broke out with two guys attacking some of the other screws and this caused a very heavy scene and lots of us were dragged into the solitary block. The funny thing was that there were cops in the solitary block taking photographs of a cell with a tripod camera. One of the guys being dragged in before me managed to get his foot free and kicked it so that the tripod went into the air and fell, smashing the camera in pieces. Later when we were all locked up I lay and roared with laughter at the camera and the face on the cop when he saw it.

The cops came in the following day and made charges against all of us — four in all: The Poof, myself and two other guys. The charges were that The Poof had been cut on the chest and that we took part in a riot in the prison yard where screws were assaulted. This of course, meant me back on solitary awaiting trial. I spent my time doing physical exercises every day and followed a routine that would keep me fit and active. I thought a lot about defence tactics for the trial. Every morning, either the Governor or his Deputy with the prison chief would do their rounds and pass my door and I would be there with a big smile to greet them. They would ask if I was all right and I would tell them I was, often inquiring if they were. Mentally and physically I felt in tip top condition as at long last the struggle was getting somewhere. I had grand illusions of an "expose" of the penal system. I intended citing every top prison official that I could think of, also the Governors and Chiefs of Peterhead and Inverness. The Deputy Governor of Peterhead who made the fateful trip to interview me, and the note that I had given John in Inverness, were also cited so I felt that I had enough evidence to put up a case.

I was able to speak to my next door neighbour by getting down on my hands and knees and shouting through the archaic ventilation system. He was Paddy Meehan, who was on voluntary confinement to protest against his conviction and sentence of Life imprisonment. There was a very large movement by eminent people to get him free as they supported his protest. I became very familiar with his case as it was all he would ever talk about. I already knew he was innocent as did the whole of the underworld. Paddy was never a popular guy with the other prisoners but, that aside, there was total unanimity about his innocence. It was interesting for me to note how he survived; he did this by always assuming that he would be released the following month, and in this way he would live from month to month. Although everyone in the prison system had some sort of belief that he was innocent, for years there was no budging and so Paddy had to lie there and rot. The only hope that he really had was what his own family and the other interested people were doing to help him. There is no doubt that it was a torturing experience for him, and now he is finally cleared, who can assess or give him back what he has already lost? The rest of the solitary cells were filled with guys awaiting trial for various offences and others doing short solitary periods for disciplinary offences.

One beautiful August morning I was allowed out to the small exercise yard. There are three of these attached to the solitary block and the prisoners are taken outside one at a time and put into them for fresh air. They are about fifteen feet square and when in here I would run round in circles to keep my lungs exercised. On this particular morning when my time was up I was taken back into my cell as usual by two screws with a third one walking on a catwalk above the exercise boxes. I was locked in my cell and shortly afterwards I asked if I could get out to use the toilet. The toilet was in a recess next to the top of the stairs on the second flat where my cell was. The screw escorted me and stood opposite the door. Now the doors of the toilets are cut in half so that the screws standing outside can see up to the knees and from the chest upwards if any one was standing inside. The middle part is what the door covers to give the guy sitting on the seat some privacy. After I had been to the toilet I went to wash my hands at the sink and noticed that there were no screws there, which was very unusual, very unusual indeed. I walked out to the top of the stairs and was confronted by The Poof coming up the stairs. On seeing me he pulled out a very long shiny knife from his waistband underneath his shirt. There was a screw a good six paces behind him but he ran downstairs as though going for reinforcements. The Poof came for me with the knife and I backed into the recess. There was no escape, but by a piece of luck I kicked him in the balls and we got into a clinch and I knew that I was fighting for my life as I had never done before. While in this clinch I managed to get the knife from him. Getting it firmly in my grasp I stuck it into him time and again causing him to fall to the ground. Screws came running upstairs and separated us by pulling me off of him, but I managed to give him a kick which caused him to roll downstairs onto the bottom flat. I gave the screws the knife and was locked into my cell, pretty shaken as it had been a total surprise.

The Poof was taken to the prison hospital then rushed to the hospital in Aberdeen thirty miles away with a collapsed lung and other injuries. Voices were coming from the ventilator with guys asking what had happened as they had heard screams from The Poof. I was now absolutely delighted that I had managed to take the knife off him and reverse the situation. Minutes after coming close to killing this guy I was delighted with what I had done. I had had no alternative as one minute I was facing death and the next it was the opposite, but that is how close one comes to being either the murderer or the murdered in this jungle that I was living in. My mind was running in circles trying to fathom what had happened. After the latest charge of the riot in the yard the prison authorities had been given explicit instructions to keep The Poof and me separated. What I couldn't understand was that here I was in the Solitary Confinement Block and he just happens to meet me and just happens to have a knife with him. This was very sinister to me, especially as I was an "A" category prisoner. With all of this racing through my head I went to the ventilator to tell the guys in the other cells what had happened. It was difficult for them to believe it, but when they heard they cheered with delight as we all knew that this was a victory against the establishment. Later that afternoon the cops came in and they charged me with attempting to murder The Poof. I made no reply.

The following morning I was taken in front of the prison Governor who was looking very stern and worried. He told me that the matter was in the hands of the police and that was all. The position I was in meant that nothing more could be done with me. By the laws of this land I had reached the ultimate; I had become that being who had no life or anything at all to lose. Once a person has reached this stage then he can never lose. There is no doubt that it was a state of mind because there were other guys doing very long sentences and they were plodding along getting internally ill. I had come through too much and by this time was committed to fighting back with all that I had. Death was all that would stop me. I knew that and so did everyone else. The Prison Authorities had this feeling of impotence with me simply because I had endured all that they could throw at me and come out all the stronger for it. I had always been told by the prison officials that I was banging my head against a brick wall. From where I stood the wall was beginning to move. As far as I was concerned I honestly would have preferred no trouble with The Poof because I knew that this would give ammunition to the prison authorities who could then say we were always fighting with each other. I had tried as much as I could during the five years before this to avoid clashing with prisoners though at times this was very hard as being so close together one was always liable to bite the one nearest. The Poof was also doing a long sentence and had to endure the same humiliations as I, therefore it maddened me to think that he hadn't been able to see what he was doing to himself never mind to me. In the end, he became a symbol of all that the screws stood for, so that when I took the knife from him it was symbolic of a victory over the screws. It had a profound effect on them in relation to me as all of us could see the day of reckoning being not too far away. This meant that I was now facing two court trials as I had the riot charge in the prison yard and the latest attempted murder charge.

I wasn't worried at all as I had long since given up caring, but I still kept up my yoga exercises and did a lot of reading. Although my Mother had gone I still remembered her and though I am not a religious person I showed loyalty by saying a few prayers each week on the day and time of her death. This was the least I could do. My Aunt Peggy replaced my Ma by writing to me often, as well as my Brother Harry who kept in constant touch; so through these two I had contact with my family and news of the latest happenings.

There was a lot of unrest in prisons throughout Britain in the summer of 1972 and it was at this period that a group of ex-prisoners in England started a movement called Preservation of the Rights of Prisoners (P.R.O.P.). They were calling for better treatment for all those inside Britain's prisons. This was needed and long overdue. This small group gave hope to lots of guys serving sentences, but the important thing was that it was coming from the outside, from people who had experienced what it means to serve a prison sentence. Lots of guys talk about what they are going to do when they get released, I mean in terms of writing to people or similar things to get the conditions improved, but they very rarely ever do it. The fact that these guys had organised PROP was great. It came into being in a blaze of publicity by asking prisoners to protest against conditions. Throughout Britain large groups of prisoners were taking part in sit-down strikes and climbing onto rooftops in massive demonstrations to show support for PROP. The time was right and it had to be seized and they did so in Peterhead. Even as I lay in solitary I could feel the excitement of what was going to happen, it seemed to penetrate the thick walls of the solitary block.

One beautiful afternoon, as the main body of prisoners were being assembled in the prison yard for work after lunch, there was a loud cheer. One hundred and sixty eight prisoners had climbed onto the prison hospital roof and were standing up there shouting and cheering. I lay in the solitary cell very jealous of them and thinking I would give my eye teeth to be with them. The adrenalin was pumping through my body as I jumped up to the small window to shout encouragement. Some prisoners were caught in the act while trying to get up there and were brought into the solitary block, being beaten up on the way in. I was at the small cell window trying to shout to those on the roof that guys were being brutalised but their cheers drowned out my voice. It was a pity they couldn't hear for what an ideal opportunity they had for making it public as they were on top of a roof in full view of the world. They were all up there singing and cheering for all they were worth. The screws were all called in to stay overnight and were issued with riot batons. The mood of the prisoners was one of solidarity. Light aircraft and helicopters were circling overhead, carrying newsmen and others from the media. The prisoners stayed up there all night and into the following afternoon. Before they finally came down, a spokesman for the prisoners spoke to the Chief Officer of the jail saying that it had been a peaceful demo and that they wanted assurances that if and when they got off the roof there would be no brutality. The Chief gave his word to all the prisoners who were listening to this exchange and so they all descended. All of this was done in a lighthearted fashion, the atmosphere was reasonable. During these negotiations the Deputy Governor was doing his rounds of the solitary block. He asked me if I was okay and went on to say that there was one thing to be grateful for which was that I was locked in the solitary block. I told him that had I been out there the demo would have been far from peaceful, and that was very true.

A couple of hours after they descended, the solitary block doors were thrown open, which was an indication of new admissions and things to come. One can always tell when something is on as the sounds outside one's cell go very quiet and the screws talk in whispers and a sort of electricity permeates the air. The fact that both doors to the entrance of the block were opened meant that a large number of admissions would be UNWILLINGLY admitted. The sounds outside the cell become a sort of language. The preparations were being made for the forthcoming brutalisation and the doors opened so that no one could grab onto them when being dragged in. The passageway leading to the block was cleared so that nothing would stand in the way of the ritual. I lay waiting for the first sounds with butterflies in my stomach. Instead of the usual blows which I was expecting I heard footsteps coming up the flight of stairs as though under a weight and the sounds of heavy laboured breathing and occasional groans as though someone was unconscious. The sounds led to a cell then a door was closed. This sort of thing was repeated four times and then three others were brought in accompanied by the usual sounds of pain as blows banged off them. Those of us on solitary responded with the only means available to us, which was banging on the steel-backed doors and shouting for the dirty bastards to leave them alone.

Later that night, I shouted through the ventilation system and asked for details of what had happened and who had joined us. The few who were not unconscious answered, identified themselves and told me what had happened. Some had been walking down the corridor, had a blanket thrown over their heads and were beaten up all the way into the cells. Others had been on their way to the solitary block and had been set upon while coming through. Out of the one hundred and sixty eight prisoners who had rioted, these had been selected by the screws for the treatment for reasons that they alone knew. When they had all regained consciousness and identified themselves, I found that one of the guys brutally attacked was Howard Wilson. Another was Willie McPherson, who was serving twenty six years for bank robbery and political offences. Willie was from the Gorbals and had gone around with me when we were young. He left our gang in order to do more for his political beliefs. His robberies were to boost the funds of an extremist group. These two and the five others were identified by the screws as being the leaders of the demo. Once again I was left with the impotent feeling of having to listen to stories of guys being brutalised. It constantly reminded me of my true position of being totally helpless and completely at the mercy of those in charge of me. I have had to endure many times the humiliation of having to listen to these sounds thus causing me to relive them, and it was a form of torture. During such periods one was faced with the fact that this was all that the future held. All through the night most of us sat at the ventilators and tried to think ways of destroying every one of the bastards. There had to be some way.

By an amazing coincidence, on the morning following the brutalisations, the screws entered my cell with my civilian clothes and told me to get dressed. I did so, wondering where I was going and thinking that it would be Inverness. When I got into the police car the cops told me I was going for a preliminary hearing for the attempted murder of The Poof. I was delighted at this stroke of luck and began formulating a plan in my head as we drove there. I was handcuffed to a screw and when we reached the court I was taken upstairs to the Sheriff's Private Chambers. On the way we passed a group of people sitting on a bench outside the Chambers, they were all civilians waiting for appearances or just to watch.

The brief charge was read out and the Sheriff went about putting the necessary signatures to the charge papers. I interrupted him saying that I would like to bring something to his notice. He looked at me and asked what it was. I told him about the recent peaceful demonstration at Peterhead prison the day before and told him that I wanted to report a crime to him. I said that at least seven prisoners were lying in the solitary confinement block with bad injuries due to being brutally assaulted and as the law's representative I would like to ask him to do something about it. I told him that I could give him the names and injuries of those victims. The Sheriff leaned back in his chair fiddling with his pen, and thought for a minute. He asked me if I had brought this to the attention of the prison Governor. I told him that I hadn't as I had no confidence in the internal investigative procedure. I went on to tell him that by bringing it to him I was seeing that everything was being done fairly. Again he thought for a short time then leaned forward in his chair in a decisive manner and told me that his duty was to the law of Scotland and with this in mind he suggested that I report the matter to the Prison Governor when I returned to the prison. I pointed to the Procurator Fiscal and implored the Sheriff to instruct the Fiscal to look into the matter. The Sheriff looked at me sternly saying that he had said all he had to say on the matter and would hear no more from me. The screws and cops began to usher me out but I tried to jump on the Sheriff's desk screaming at him, calling him a whitewashing old bastard. There was pure panic in the court and I was dragged out.

As I was led by the bench full of civilians I held onto the banister at the top of the stairs and shouted to them to go to the press and tell them that prisoners were lying in the solitary confinement block after being attacked by screws for peacefully demonstrating. If anyone ever spoke to a stone wall it was me that day. The people on that bench just sat like lumps of wood staring at me as though I was off my head. It was so bloody pathetic and I was so angry at myself for failing to get through to anyone. The cops and the screws were in pure panic and I was taken downstairs and locked into a room along with the screw who was still handcuffed to me. I turned on the screw asking if he was one of the bastards who attacked the guys the previous night but he kept his head to the floor and wouldn't look up. I challenged him now that we were alone and reminded him that I could kick him up and down this room and would never be found guilty as we were on our own. I told him that I'd probably regret not having done so as he would most likely be into my cell with the rest to batter my head in. All the time I spoke, he sat with his free hand holding his head as he looked at the floor, not daring to look at me in case I did give him a going over. Eventually when the cops did return, he sprang up on his feet and told the cops to get us back to the prison. I then learned that I would be brought back for contempt of court.

This really lit up my heart; it had not all been in vain. These were the words I was wanting to hear. The cops drove us back to the prison and the screw didn't mention a word to anyone but I knew he was raging, not so much at me but at the cops for leaving him alone with a madman like me. When locked back into my solitary cell I went straight to the ventilator and shouted to the guys telling them what had happened. My plan, which I had formulated on the way to court, was that I would speak to the Sheriff in the nicest way possible asking for him to investigate my allegations, and if he didn't accept this then I would attack him so that the subsequent trial would be in the open court where I would be able to state my reasons for doing this. However, I wasn't able to actually hit the judge but had done enough to warrant a contempt appearance. All of us again sat at the ventilator and speculated on how the appearance would go. The fact that it was to be a form of punishment for me didn't alter it at all as I was looking upon it as a place where I could bring out what was happening in these tombs of secrecy called Prisons.

The following morning, the Governor and the Chief Officer entered my cell, half closing the door behind them leaving the accompanying screws outside. The Governor said he wanted to thank me for not taking advantage of the officer with me at court the previous day while he was locked into the room with me. He went on to say that I could have taken advantage of the situation with impunity but hadn't. I told him that it was his mob who were the liberty takers. I said he had given his word that none of these guys would be punished but here they were lying in these very cells with bad injuries from have been brutalised. Pointing to the chief officer, I told him he had given his word to the demonstrating prisoners on the roof that there would be no physical reprisals if they came down in an orderly fashion. What happened after that was without his knowledge. The Governor went on to tell me that what he suspected had happened the previous night would not happen again. He then went on to explain that when a prisoner received injuries, the staff put in written reports to him as to how these injuries come about, and if all the reports that injuries were received while being "restrained" or because the prisoner "fell" then he, the Governor, was not in a position to dispute this. When he sees the prisoner, he may accuse the staff of brutalising him, but the Governor has to weigh up the evidence of the one prisoner and his accusation against the reports and verbal evidence of his staff. He said that although he may sometimes doubt it, he has to go by the evidence in front of him. Having had first hand experience of what actually happens in situations like this, emotionally I was totally rejecting what he was saying but intellectually I knew he was correct. In spite of all the anger within me, I did feel the Governor was concerned and intent on doing something. The following day I was also told that the Sheriff had been in touch with the prison and that the Contempt appearance would not be going on. I was very sick indeed at this and explained that I wanted to be taken to court. They left and I sank to the floor utterly deflated and miserable. It was the first time in my life I had been sick at *not* being taken to court and charged. There is no doubt about it 'that justice moves in mysterious ways.

For the next week we concentrated on getting the story out to the press. We had this obsessive belief that getting it into the papers would be the panacea although earlier experience had shown us differently. The feeling amongst us was that the screws could kill us and no one would turn a hair. There was this desperate feeling within me that there was only one person I could depend on and that was myself. The other guys were taking the matter through official channels and had requested Petitions to write to the Secretary of State complaining of brutality. I had been through all of that scene before and recognised its uselessness. The solitary confinement block was full of brutalised prisoners and the place was yet again a very tense and fragile time-bomb just waiting to explode. All of the guys who took part in the demo were taken in front of the Visiting Committee and given from six months to a full year's loss of remission and a spell on solitary. I was lying in my cell early one morning when the door burst open and a mob of screws came in and told me to change into my civilian clothing. Once again I started on the long road to Inverness.

13

This was my fourth spell in Inverness so I was getting very familiar with the roads. I was put through the normal reception procedure and taken by another group of Inverness screws to a cage and locked in. I had spent most of my five years in solitary conditions and by now was used to it and looking on it as my way of life. In the cages next to me were two other guys, Ben Conroy and Larry Winters. Ben sounded as fit as ever but Larry didn't. He shouted to me that he had wounds in his head from a beating in his previous prison. Both of them were allowed out to make fish-nets in a small, newly-built workshed, though only for a couple of hours each day. The screws were sick at the thought of having us three in together again as it meant that they could expect anything in the way of trouble. Just the fact that we were under the one roof was enough to send the shit running down their legs. Therefore, it came as no surprise when the Governor of the prison told me that I wasn't to be let out with the others as I was awaiting two court trials and the Prisons Department had instructed him to keep me locked up. We argued all the way on this but they wouldn't budge and the reasons were obvious to us all.

I would lie in my cell cage all day doing exercises and reading the one book I was allowed each week. I came to know the cage well during this period. It had a large cage front which cut the cell in half and it had the effect of making one feel very small. This was a comment made by most guys who had experienced the cages. The only way the cage door could be opened was by someone who was outside the cell altogether. There was a locking system there that had special keys to open it then a bolt locking device that ran through the centre of the cage door which had to be drawn before anyone could open the door. This ensured that no one person could open the door on his own. I was pretty angry at not being allowed out to see the others as I should have been and was frustrated at being so totally helpless under the circumstances.

A week after my arrival in Inverness, I heard noises of others being admitted into the two vacant cages. They were Howard Wilson and Willie McPherson, both of whom had been sent here the day before their punishment ended in Peterhead. This was a form of further punishment. Both said that their introduction to Inverness had been a bit hectic but neither would elaborate on this as they thought the place was bugged with listening devices. They told me that a few days after I had left Peterhead, two young guys, just into the prison, had climbed onto the Tailor's workshed roof as a protest and had been pulled off and brutalised by the screws. Both Howard and Willie were kept on solitary in Inverness along with me though after a couple of weeks both of them were allowed into the workshed for a few hours each day. Two nights a week all four of them were given recreation in a very small room above the cages.

After four or five weeks, I was allowed out to work beside the others. The building was self-contained and the workshed was purpose built with red brick walls and no windows. We were made to work on fish-nets about ten feet apart. I was taken into the shed while the others were working and for the first time I saw them in the flesh. Although we had spoken to each other regularly it had been over a year since I had set eyes on Ben, three since I had seen Larry, a year since I had seen Howard and fourteen years since I had seen Willie. All of them had changed but none more than Larry who had long black hair and a big beard. He had sores on his face and around his eyes and he was heavily drugged. The other three were reasonably fit looking. Out of the five of us, four were serving the longest sentences in Scotland. The screws at Inverness were angry at us being put together under the one roof. The atmosphere in the place was very hostile. We badgered the Governor each day to get us out of these cages and into the routine the same as the rest.

On the 19th December I was given an Indictment that said I was to appear at Aberdeen Court to face charges for the prison yard riot. There was a feeling of excitement amongst us, I had cited all the prison officials as witnesses. The trial was to be a Sheriff and Jury, and though I would have preferred a High Court, I decided that I would make the best of this one. There was panic in the ranks as prisoners would be quizzed and asked why I was citing so many top prison officials. I also cited lots of prisoners so that on the morning of the 19th, all of us were locked into cells at Aberdeen Courthouse. There was bedlam with the prisoners making the most of their day out. Elaborate security precautions had been taken in getting us there and these were maintained during the actual hearing. The Poof was put to one side of the courtroom and I to the other with the two other guys charged beside me. The normal dock was dispensed with and we were put on the front bench surrounded by cops and screws. I had both hands cuffed. Legal arguments were made on the actual charges and they lasted for a period of two hours after which the Sheriff stated that he was dismissing the charges as the Indictment was irrelevant. A screw sitting next to me on the journey back said to one of his colleagues that he felt it was a fix. I was ambivalent about the acquittal as I would have preferred to have seen the officials in the witness box. The two guys next to me were delighted about getting off as they could see themselves getting out at a future date. No time was lost in getting us back to Inverness.

I had to appear at one more trial for the Attempted Murder in the Solitary Confinement Block and I was looking forward to this as I would definitely be going to the High Court for it. In Inverness, rumours were circulating about a new prison being opened in Barlinnie Prison, Glasgow, for potentially violent prisoners and I was left in no doubt that this was where I was going. Speculation was rife and wild as to what it would be like. It was to be psychiatrically orientated and supposedly a half-way house to the State Mental Hospital for those prisoners that were not certifiable. Rumour had it that prisoners would be injected with drugs and kept down, that there would be television monitors throughout the place and that everything in it would be electronically worked. The impression I had of it was the same as that of the State Mental Hospital. I was scared of being certified insane and looked on this new place as being the means for the authorities to do this. I had never had anything to do with the rare psychiatrist that came into the prisons as I just didn't trust them. The screws in Inverness and in the whole of the Scottish penal system were looking forward to this new establishment opening in Barlinnie, purely as a means to get us out of their way. The Prison Officers Association had been calling for such a place for years now and it couldn't come soon enough, particularly for the screws in Inverness at that moment who made it plain that they just didn't want any one of us in their prison, never mind all of us together.

Inverness was the prison that I felt most helpless in. It was structured to be that way and built for boredom. Being inside a cage, inside a cell in the solitary block which was only a part of the prison as a whole, made me feel that I was at the very core of isolation. I realised just how alienated I had become. Every day a screw would come round the Segregation unit and check everything, such as toilets, workshops, and cells to see if anything could be used as a weapon. The only thing that we were allowed was plastic, such as cutlery and a mug. I was constantly on the look out for anything that could be used as a weapon. I saw one or two things that could be used in an extreme emergency and would watch this screw doing his rounds each day. He would walk by the objects that I had already decided could be used, but how could he see such things as he wasn't in the desperate situation that I was in. How was it possible for someone to render a place "safe"? There was a feeling of confidence amongst the screws as they felt that they had it all under control. Even the safety razors they supplied in the morning had locking devices on them. Each night we were given a cell search. My whole life was tuned into making the most of any flaw in the system.

Two nights each week we were taken to the small room above the cages for an hour or so and we would sit there and listen to an old battered radio. On the day of the 27th we were into our usual routine, though Ben Conroy was locked in his cage as he was sick. Although we all appeared to be working on our nets, I was in fact constantly keeping an eye on the screws and listening to every move. There seemed to be a change in their behaviour pattern. These changes would be hard to explain but one comes to know or sense things, and being very perceptive I knew that something was going on as there was plenty of coming and going. I thought maybe they were transferring Ben, as a guy is usually ghosted out without warning. The screws were supposed to stand at each corner of the shed observing us but for some reason this day they seemed to be speaking more together. There was a jittery feeling running throughout the place.

It was two days after Christmas but it was like any other day as far as I was concerned as I had forgotten what the Christmas feeling was like. This particular night of the 27th December 1972 the four of us were taken to the recreation room and by the end of the evening six screws had been taken to hospital and three of us prisoners with them. A fortnight later, four of us were charged with attempting to murder six prison officers and attempting to escape. At the court trial the screws said that when we went to the recreation room we attacked them, pulling out knives and stabbing them and a fight erupted with the alarm bell going off bringing more screws, all of whom denied using their batons on the prisoners. One of the prison officers lost his eye during the fight and others were stabbed a number of times on the body.

My defence was that while working that afternoon I noticed a lot of activity amongst the screws and there seemed to be a lot of coming and going in the cell area where Ben was. On going in after the work hour I looked into Ben's cage through the judas hole and he was bending over a plastic basin with blood running from his nose and baton bruises on his back. Ben gestured that he had been beaten up. I told the others about it as we were getting water to wash ourselves and we came to a quick decision to make a protest that night in the recreation room. We were then locked into our cages. I weighed all the pros and cons up and at first came to the decision that we should cool the whole thing till the next morning and get the Governor and Chief Officer on their rounds. I was of the opinion that to take it to the top might have the desired effect. I wasn't interested in taking part in a peaceful demo as I could vividly remember the last one, and this was even more dangerous as being in Inverness we were that much more vulnerable and remote. I knew that it would only end in violence but if we were to go ahead then the emphasis should be on us doing as much damage to the enemy as possible. Earlier that month I had managed to pick up the heel plate of a boot that I had sharpened up and when my cage was searched that night I hid it in my mouth as I did whenever searches were given. There was little chance of this being discovered as the talk was minimal between screws and prisoners.

We were taken to the small recreation room and I made my views plain to the others and tried to push my past experiences onto them by telling them that violence was necessary. Both Howard and Willie weren't interested in getting in too heavy and so were pushing for a peaceful demo. Larry was for going along with me so that we were evenly split but this is where the unwritten code enters into it. In this case it would have been out of order for me to go in heavy with the violence when in fact two of them didn't want to know. It would have been okay had I been able to do my own thing but that wasn't the case here as we were all in on it. I compromised by telling them that I would go along with the "Peaceful Demo" but that if any violence was used I would be cutting as many screws as possible. They knew what I had been through in the past and agreed that they had no intention of letting others have a go at them. Feeling like a bloody fool, I took part in the demo and linked arms with the other three and sat down on the floor.

I told the court that the screws rang the bell for reinforcements and when they came Howard started by saying that this was a peaceful demo and then a baton was battered down on my head. I grabbed the old radio and crashed it into the face of one of the screws. I got my piece of metal and started sticking it into as many as possible. The whole place was like a battle field. The first baton that landed on me had splintered and as I fought I could feel the blood running down my head and the blows still landing. Finally we were subdued but I was thinking of the next move and that would be their coming into the cages afterwards so I managed to hide the small piece of metal in the vague hope that I would get away with it. At the top of the stairs I was made to run a gauntlet of screws with batons and someone repeating over and over again to kill that bastard Boyle. I fell onto the landing below on top of Larry and Willie. I rose to my feet and another baton was broken over my head. Finally they managed to get me into my cage, and there was so much of a panic that they didn't search me so I still had my piece of metal. Once locked in I knew that I was badly injured. I felt no pain, only a numbness. I heard them going from cage to cage and beating the others systematically. This time I was listening to it not feeling too bad as I knew they were coming back to me and I was prepared for them.

Eventually it was my turn, and the cage door was opened. They came in and I pulled my metal and struck out as much as I could. I lost the metal in the process as the batons came banging down on me. It felt no different from many gang fights that I've been through in my life. As the batons continued to crash down on my head I remember thinking that this was it. I didn't feel fear or anything — just that this seemed to be it. I remember coming to and I was lying naked on the floor and a screw took a rush towards me and kicked me but I don't remember feeling it. This was the night of the 27th December.

My next recollection of anything was coming to on the 2nd January 1973. I was in a cage, and I couldn't move as the pain was racking my whole head and body. Later I was told that I had been in hospital though I can't remember a thing about it. All I do know is that I was badly hurt. I couldn't stand up. My food was thrown under the cage door, the first few meals having to lie there till I could crawl over and reach the plate with my face lying beside it while my hand scooped it into my mouth. I felt terrible during this period as I knew that they could do what they wanted as I was helpless. It was essential that I get back to health. The doctor told the court that I was in such a bad way he didn't expect me to last the night.

I was lucky to be alive. Although I realised I wasn't well I had this obsession to get back to being fit and on my feet. I was naked in my cell with four blankets, but once they saw me on my feet they gave me pyjama trousers and took the blankets. There had been lots of damage on both sides but to what extent I just didn't know. One night I heard a voice calling and it was Ben. The ventilator system was useful in the cages too. We knew that the screws were sitting outside listening to everything we were saying so we had to talk generalities. He told me that three of us had been taken to hospital with injuries and that Howard was the only one who hadn't gone though he had had bad injuries too. He told me that I was supposed to be at death's door, that out of everyone injured I was probably the worst.

A week later the cops came in and charged me with attempting to murder six screws and attempting to escape. I honestly couldn't have given a shit about the injuries to the screws. It was the first time I'd been involved in a clash with them where I had been able to do some real damage. I looked on this as a consolation. I was now awaiting two High Court trials and from where I sat I began to think that this was how life would go on with me getting into one piece of trouble before another had been cleared up. I wasn't worried as I felt that this is how it goes and that death was all that lay ahead. I was handed an Indictment to appear at Aberdeen High Court for the attempted murder of The Poof on the 30th January 1973.

I consulted my solicitor and decided to let the evidence unfold as it was. I called about thirty witnesses. Ben and Howard were amongst them. I was taken from my cage to the High Court in Aberdeen. On previous occasions when travelling I envied the people that I saw walking the streets but this time I didn't. Something had died within me. I was now animalised and felt nothing, only a complete numbness. During the trial, the screws gave evidence saying that I had not asked to go out to the toilet but had, by some means, escaped from my cell and into The Poof's cell. The screws gave their account of how this could be done and there is no doubt that it was unacceptable. The Poof came in and reluctantly gave evidence saying that he couldn't remember much about anything. I had lodged a special plea of self-defence. Other prisoners gave evidence to the fact that The Poof was a bully-boy and how the screws hated me. Evidence had come out that a young guy had committed suicide because of The Poof's interest in him. I was acquitted and immediately sent back to Inverness and my cage. This was a great morale boost to me.

On returning to the cage, I was able to distinguish by the noises that Willie was no longer with us. Within a few days, Larry and Ben vanished and the only possible place they could have gone to was the new place in Barlinnie Prison. A couple of weeks later, Howard was moved so this left me alone. There had been lots of hostility from the screws with the four of us there so it became more intense now that I was alone. There were open confrontations between us. I began to lose sleep due to noises being made in the corridor. Loud banging would resound through the block and these noises would go on throughout the night. I knew that my best defence was to take the offensive. I started calling them all the names I could whenever we came in contact to show them I wasn't worried, although I was.

The result of not getting any sleep was having a tremendous effect on me. The screws would come in mob handed and search me. I would be told to pull the cheeks of my arse apart and bend over while they inspected it, and open my mouth while they looked in. All I had was a pair of pyjama trousers and I had cast them off as it felt humiliating to be told to take them off before the searches. These searches took place three times each day even though I hadn't stepped out of the cage for one minute. This was all part of the psychological campaign that was taking place. I thought that just by knowing that it was all against me it wouldn't affect me. How wrong I was. As things were, I was very suspicious of being left alone in this place so I was constantly on guard in case the screws came into my cage. The noises continued unabated and I would jump awake whenever they happened so that before very long I was under tremendous strain and very much aware of it. While the noises went on I used to walk up and down my cage singing at the top of my voice. This was to let them think that it wasn't bothering me. After three weeks of this I was cracking up. I knew I was on the verge of insanity. It got so that I challenged the screws to fight and would ask them where all the mice were that were making the noise.

After a month of this I was taken from my cage one day to an upstairs room where I met a psychiatrist, Peter Whatmore. He told me that he was a representative from The Special Unit, Barlinnie Prison. He interviewed me with the purpose of my going there, but I can't remember too much about it as I felt quite far gone and my insides were in a turmoil, though I managed to put up some sort of façade.

Part Four

14

My torture continued till ten days later my cage was opened and I was taken to another cell along a corridor. This was a brand new silent cell that must have been newly built. I was put in here and they brought in my civilian clothing for me to change into. Not a word was spoken between any of us. I was then told that I was being transferred to the Special Unit. I didn't believe them as I felt this was still part of the campaign. I was heavily cuffed then taken to a prison van with police car escorts but even then I thought they would go round the prison and back in. I didn't dare let myself believe that they were telling the truth because I knew that to accept this and find myself back in the cage would be the last straw. Even when we were well on the road I refused to believe it as the distrust was ingrained in me.

I was too numbed to feel anything about the Special Unit, after all I didn't know what to expect. All I could compare it with was the places I had been in during the past. I was totally alienated from many things. I knew that I was a stranger even to myself, so many things had changed within me that utter chaos and confusion dominated by very primitive survival instincts were what I lived on. On my entrance to the Special Unit I was greeted by Ben Conroy and Larry Winters who came over to meet me. They immediately saw the very strange look on my face and felt the alienation within me and were visibly shocked. All of us recognised this but nothing could be done about it. These were inner barriers that I had built to help me survive the last weeks alone and they would not come down easily. I felt extremely weird and thought that I was quite mad.

The screws were very friendly towards me, calling me Jimmy, but I wasn't being taken in by that. I did find it very hard to accept but through keeping up my façade I managed to pull through this first stage without causing any bad feelings. I felt like someone lost in a wilderness. Ben made me a coffee and took me aside to whisper in my ear that the place might be bugged. He explained to me how the screws were very friendly but they had to be watched — he didn't have to tell me. He also told me that there were a couple of screws who had reputations for brutalising prisoners in the place but that there were one or two others who seemed okay. I was then *asked* by the screw if I would come round and sort out my personal property with him. I went, and while we opened the parcels containing old clothing he did something that to him was so natural but to me was something that had never been done before. He turned to me and handed me a pair of scissors and asked me to cut open some of them. He then went about his business. I was absolutely stunned. That was the first thing that made me begin to feel human again. It was the completely natural way that it was done. This simple gesture made me think. In my other world, the penal system in general, such a thing would never happen.

With the abolition of capital punishment, the Scottish Prison Officers' Association expressed concern about the vulnerability of its members particularly with regard to those of us serving life sentences who were being violent. A Working Party was set up and they took oral evidence from officials in the Prison Service and senior medical officers throughout Britain. The recommendations of the Working Party were accepted by the Secretary of State and it was decided to provide a Unit as quickly as possible, and after looking into one or two locations it was decided that the former woman's wing of Barlinnie Prison should be adapted for this purpose. It was obvious to everyone within the system that Inverness, even with its cages and strong disciplinarian regime, was an absolute failure and as the level of trouble there was much higher than in other prisons, there seemed there was nothing else they could do for virtually everything had been tried.

But here I was now in this other extreme — the Special Unit, and my first afternoon and evening in the place were confusing and utterly bewildering. In order to survive the cages I had had to use "craziness" as a defence mechanism and it had become so much a part of me that I now felt very much like a crazy animal in this new atmosphere. The one thing that struck me immediately was that I was able to walk more than ten paces without screws standing at my side, but although I knew I could do this I felt too uncomfortable. I kept waiting for the hands to come down on my shoulder and push me into a cage. I was conscious of the fact that I wasn't acting or feeling normal and at times felt that the people moving around me were very frightened as they too recognised this crazy animal part that was dominant in me. I felt so much alone. I didn't feel at ease with people moving around and occasionally speaking to me, or with having so much space to move in and I couldn't understand it when two of the prisoners who had come from relaxed prisons showed anger at the claustrophobic atmosphere of the place.

I try to recall standing there that day watching the movements of everyone and one screw coming to me with a cup of coffee and asking how I was feeling and me so bound up and watchful not answering him just asking myself, what the fuck is this place? That evening a screw came in wearing civvies and took me into a small room and gave me the usual line of patter. Instead of stopping there he went on to talk about the philosophy of the Unit as he would like to see it. His name was Ken Murray. I sat listening to what he had to say but remained silent. What he was saying was fine and along the right lines but as far as I was concerned he was just another lying bastard who was looking for a quiet time while he tightened the screw on me. There was no danger of me falling for the load of crap that he was spouting.

That night I was locked in my cell at 9 p.m. along with all the others. The cells had prison furniture: a locker, a chair, a mirror nailed to the wall, and a chamber pot with a lid on it. The bed had a mattress and a pillow and these were all very novel to me. The first thing I did was to throw the mattress off the bed and lie on the hard board with a blanket, staring at the ceiling. I had my transistor but couldn't play it. My inner self was in a turmoil and though I was terribly weary through lack of sleep my mind was so active I couldn't sleep. I kept waiting for loud banging on the cell door. I lay there hating myself for taking the cup of coffee from the screw, and reprimanding myself for being so weak in even acknowledging them. I thought I was an idiot for letting their tactics get me into such a state. Some of what Ken Murray had said was going round in my head but even if every word of it had been true, it was no good. "Its too late, far too late. My life is finished. Don't give in Jimmy, don't give in. . . ." I didn't sleep one wink all that night.

The following morning I was on my feet when I heard them coming to open the doors at six o'clock. One thing that I noticed about myself both in the extremity of the cages and on this first day or so in the unit, was that my senses were "heightened". I could actually smell people, especially the leather from their boots or shoes, from a good distance away. When I ran my fingers over the rough walls of the cell or over the skin on my face it felt different somehow. I could also hear sounds from a great distance, but I am digressing. Like other "A" category prisoners in normal prisons, I had to strip off my clothes and leave them outside the door the night before, so when the door opened I pulled them in, dressed (this was a luxury as clothes hadn't been allowed in Inverness) and went along to the toilet archway to wash and shave with a razor. I was allowed to open it and change the blade myself. After that sleepless night and endless thinking, I found myself mentally much more settled and more able to face the day.

The unit is an "L" shaped building with a small hall area where the cells are. There are two floors in this part with five cells on the second floor and five on the first. There is a small kitchen, with a cooker for making tea and coffee, and some sinks. There is an area just large enough to accommodate a small billiard table, and a small television room, then a governor's room and staff room and the psychiatrist's room. We were free to move about these areas when they were opened up. We could make tea or coffee whenever we wanted, or go into a small workshop on the second floor where the cells were. This was a joinery store but as yet it was empty. One of the ten cells had a double door and was to be used as a punishment cell if necessary.

There were five of us in the place. Ben, Larry and I kept very much to ourselves. The other two guys, Rab and Ian I didn't know. They had come from more relaxed prisons than Inverness and they were the ones who found the place very small and claustrophobic, whereas the three of us felt it to be very big. That first morning I felt better able to speak with Ben and Larry, but we were terrified of bugging devices and so would lean into the other's ear to speak or would get into a huddle with all our heads touching and whisper. Whenever a screw came we would jump up straight and be silent till he passed us by. I put them in the picture about my spell in the cages alone but it had been so long since I had held any conversation with anyone that my vocal chords became painful when I spoke for any length of time. Ben and Larry told me that the screws would come round and try to talk to us. They said the only time we would get any peace was at meal times, as they always left us alone to eat. We told each other to watch the bastards; this was just a move to get information out of us.

As there was no work I just stood about all day. I felt very guilty about this and it also bothered me that if I used the toilet no one would follow me. Larry and I had the Inverness trial to attend, so we spoke in whispers to each other about it. We had someone to watch out for the screws while we searched our cells for listening devices. We would come up with endless permutations as to what the game was. A screw would mention something completely innocent and we would pounce on it later when alone, dissect it and interpret it in all sorts of different ways. Each morning, after a hard night's thinking, Larry, Ben and I would meet and discuss our latest theories fantasised the night before. The whole day was ours to spend as we pleased. I could if I wanted go up to my cell and sit there away from everything and everyone. Having this time on my hands in solitary was one thing, but having it to walk freely about the place was another, and I felt utterly lost.

But being able to speak freely to one another, to see and to touch one another, was tremendous. Just being with other guys was so good for me that this alone eventually reduced the overpowering feeling of helplessness that had existed in Inverness. I hated the screws, police and the whole system so much; basically these were the topics that dominated our conversations. The Unit had no electronic devices either in the locking-up system or elsewhere. In fact it was just another small prison — structurally. The screws wore white coats to distinguish them from the screws on the outside. Apparently before the unit started they had discussed civilian clothing but had decided against it, opting for the white medical coats that gave them a hospital look and went a long way to confirming my thoughts that the Unit was a half-way house to the State Hospital. All the staff had volunteered for the unit and had gone on a six week course to places like Broadmoor, Grendon Prison in England and Carstairs State Hospital in Scotland. I had no doubt that the unit was psychiatrically orientated — I sussed this out the minute I walked in the door. Also some of the staff had been involved in attacking prisoners in other prisons. We knew this, so to us at this stage it was the same old game of "conning" us. One screw took me aside and said in a sympathetic manner that he realised that I had had a lot of "stick" in my day but that was all finished now. They didn't use the stick here but an injection instead, to drug us if we caused any scenes. I'm sure he thought he was being very considerate and understanding but inside I was using what he had said to reinforce all my fears that they were intent on drugging us at the first chance.

I was told that there would be a staff/inmate meeting every Tuesday and at these meetings I could raise any subject I wanted to. If I had any complaints about the place or staff then I could voice it here. I could also express myself strongly in a verbal way during these meetings so long as I didn't carry the aggression out of the room and keep it up afterwards. A complete load of balls thought I, and when speaking to the others about it we would laugh our heads off, knowing that the screws thought we were nut-cases. The day following the meeting, the staff would have a meeting of their own. This confirmed all my suspicions. Any meeting that they had as a group was to talk about us, and it was obvious to me that they would put a false face on during the meeting with us on the Tuesday and express their real feeling at their own meeting the following day. The general idea of the place, I was told, was to create better relationships between staff and prisoners, therefore it was a unit geared towards experimentation that would be used to improve the general penal system.

That first day the screws came over and tried to talk away as normally as possible but the whole atmosphere was extremely difficult as we were two factions — enemies — and the hostility was stark between us. I felt very strange just standing there. We were told that the day was our own to structure, so Larry went into the T.V. room and turned on the television. One of the screws came in and made a scene so this caused the first confrontation, ending with the screw admitting he was wrong as he was acting as he would in the main prison. The Governor was someone whom all of us had known. He had the nickname in other prisons of Dr No, as he always said no to anything that anyone ever asked for, even if it was only a pencil. Here in the unit he was quite different and said we could call him and the staff by their first names.

On the prisoners' side there was Rab, who had come in as a boy of fifteen to serve the sentence of Her Majesty's Pleasure. He had come from Scotland's model prison in Edinburgh, Saughton. He had been in 13 years and was sent to the unit for causing slight management problems there. Then there was Ian, a guy with deep personal problems who was in for Life for the murder of his girlfriend after a suicide pact that had gone wrong. He had done five years of his sentence and had been sent here as being potentially violent while at Perth, which was a training prison. These guys had only heard of Ben, Larry and I, so they felt thrown into the deep end as they knew us by reputation, as did the screws, and realised that any trouble that we were involved in was likely to be very heavy.

Larry and I were considered the hopeless cases as we had these very long sentences on top of our Lifers and were now awaiting a

High Court trial for six attempted murders of the Inverness screws in the riot. I had no future, so what the fuck did I want to get to know screws for? Ben was doing a seven year sentence and had lost all his remission but at least he had a date, and was our "star" witness for the Inverness trial. This forthcoming trial was on all our minds and made any talk of building anything in the unit very difficult. Although Larry and I would discuss it in depth, we realised that there was nothing ahead anyway so it didn't really matter. The great thing about being in this sort of situation is that nothing really matters. I felt that most likely I would get anything up to twenty years on top, but it seemed irrelevant. I knew that the screws in the Special Unit had this fear in their minds that Larry and I would react violently to the sentences if they were very long. They didn't realise that once you have reached a certain depth you can go no lower.

Two days after my arrival in the unit my brother Harry, his wife and my two children came to visit me. The visiting room was the one we used for the weekly meetings and so they were able to sit down at a small table in comfortable chairs; but most important of all, we were able to touch. One of the staff sat in the background making a genuine effort to keep well away. It was a terribly moving experience for me. How can I express what it felt like to touch my kids after a six year absence? To sit beside my family without a physical barrier between us? To realise that all I had to do was reach out a hand and touch one of my own? In the other prisons the visiting conditions had been nine hours a year, with wire and glass barriers dividing us from the visitor and screws standing behind listening to every word. I wasn't at ease during the visit, in fact I was terribly apprehensive for numerous reasons most of all because I knew that I had become something of a stranger to my family due to what had gone on within me and because of the physical restrictions imposed on us as a family by my imprisonment.

The visit was to last two hours and I didn't think that I could sit with them that long. When I saw my son and daughter I was scared to attempt to give them a cuddle and kiss as I was afraid of being rejected by them, yet I wanted so much to grab them in my arms. I just didn't know what to do and both of the kids were very shy indeed. Those past few years I had tried to blank them from my mind in order to survive. I had lived too long as an animal trying to bury this part of my life and here I was confronted with it in the flesh; confronted by people that I deeply loved, yet whom

I had tried to cast out of my thoughts because the thought of never being with them again was too painful to think about. I could see in my brother's and his wife's eyes concern for me as I was thin and a deathly grey colour. The air of detachment that I felt must have been frightening to them. I said earlier that people in Glasgow, or Scotland for that matter, very seldom express themselves to their nearest and dearest by physical embrace, but it was something that I longed for now and felt was very important after what I had come through. At the end of the visit I did embrace them all after drinking them in with my eyes like a thirsty man.

That night I lay in torment thinking about the visit. I was in a quandary. I was in a terrible state of mind as I had a tremendous amount of suspicions about the unit and everything in it, but in conflict with these thoughts was something that meant so much to me — my family. That day's visit had hit me so powerfully that I was now in a state of total confusion. My whole way of thinking was so dominated with the past experiences that it was impossible for me to think rationally about anything, but I knew what I wanted, and that was to be near my family. I felt a certain amount of comfort and ease being back in the Glasgow district. I was home. This night of tormented thinking didn't bring me any answers but I did see my family and even if that was all the unit had to offer, it was what I wanted most of all.

In the days following I had visits from other members of my family that I had not seen for over six years and it was very moving. My aunt Peggy would organise and bring up other aunts and we would have emotional hours together. They would cry over the loss of my Ma as it was the first time they had a chance to tell me about it, though it was now eighteen months ago. My cousin Margaret, who is almost a sister, would come regularly. These were the people on the outside who were bringing me alive again. They were piercing the barriers that I had put up to protect myself. I had tried to eradicate them from my mind but it was impossible and being with them proved this, as the emotion pouring from me on these visits was something special. I needed to touch them, as though to assure myself of their presence. They brought the children as well, as if knowing they were the key to bringing me back to being the Jimmy they knew.

Work was thought up for us and it took the form of painting the unit walls as they were the usual institutional battle-ship grey and so some fancy colours were made available to us. This was revolutionary, as was the fact that some of the staff joined in by helping us, or making the tea and coffee while we worked. It was our first collective effort and though it started and ended in a strained manner, we did it together. Tools were supposed to be coming for a small joiner's shop but we were told they were held up in the "pipeline" due to administrative reasons. Naturally I thought this was just an excuse, but I was proved wrong. A few days after my arrival, one of the staff, who was a joiner by trade, brought in a box of tools for us to use. While I was working with him I wanted to use the chisel to work on a piece of wood. I remember being very self-conscious about the way I lifted it so as not to raise his suspicions in case he thought I was going to harm him with it. This was the state of mind I was now in after living in the plastic world of Inverness. It was as though I had to relearn how to be at ease and to live again alongside other people. I had been so used to living in a world of deceit and enmity that it was difficult to have an innocent conversation with a member of staff without trying to find hidden meanings.

It was strange during this period because there was a great amount of hatred in me for all screws, yet some of the unit staff would approach me in a way that was so natural and innocent it made it difficult to tell them to fuck off. Something inside me, in spite of all the pent-up hatred, would tell me that there was something genuine within them. I knew I didn't really want to recognise this part of the screws. I preferred to see them all as bastards, this would have been so much easier for me. There were one or two of them even at that very early stage, coming across as very genuine: in particular, Ken Murray. He is a political animal and was on the Executive Committee of the SPOA and had a part to play in the setting up of the unit. He was committed to improving the role of the Prison Service, and in doing so wanted to improve conditions for prisoners in a very realistic way. As full of hatred as I was it was very difficult to reject any conversation with a person like this. It was the staff like him in the unit who gave me the moments of conflict and inner turmoil, as they were so unlike the screws that I had known in the past. At nights I would lie in my bed tearing my guts out thinking intensely about this place and what it was all about, and often wishing I were back in solitary.

At that first Tuesday staff/inmate meeting I sat and weighed the whole thing up. I could see that Larry totally rejected the staff, calling them a load of codswallop. Ben, like me, would sit and watch the faces of the screws, seeing those who were uncomfortable in the meeting and those who were natural and at ease.

The three of us would occasionally look at each other and burst out laughing at this silly game of men all sitting around feeling self-conscious and stupid. But it is true to say that even at that first meeting, I realised the potential and did make a statement to that effect. Minutes were taken at every meeting and a Chairman was elected. The process was a democratic one with each person given an equal vote, from the Governor down.

It was at these meetings that we were to put forward any ideas we had to improve the unit and help to make the rules for running the place. Any proposals we put could be adopted there and then. If it was a tricky one the staff would use the stalling technique by saying they would discuss it at their staff meeting the following day. This sort of crap we just didn't go for and we made this clear to them; however, it seemed it would have to be. The meetings would be the testing ground between us and the staff and so we would ask for more materialistic things, such as tools to work with, and weightlifting equipment etc. etc. The other two prisoners, Ian and Rab, would sit and say nothing as the whole experience seemed to be overwhelming for them. If one of us had a go at one of the staff then the rest of us would support him all the way, conversely most of the staff would back each other all the way so the "them and us" situation continued. These early meetings consisted mainly of petty bickering and sniping at each other. Some times they would be flat with nothing said, but such meetings were rare.

The Prisons Department officials played a prominent role in the place and the Controller of Scottish Prisons, Mr Alex Stephens would come in frequently to see how the place was going. His position was pretty powerful within the Prison Service and he was probably the man most responsible for getting the place off the ground. Everyone looked on the unit as being his "baby". He was quite different from anyone I had met on the prison side; he was a creative and intelligent person. The fact that he came down and showed interest was very important as others in the Department also came down following their boss's example. For the first time in their lives these officials who were responsible for the whole Scottish prison system, were coming inside and speaking to the inmates. All the time I was weighing this up: it was the first small but positive sign that let me see the Special Unit could be different from any other prison. Although I was able to see it, the difficulty lay in accepting it as my instincts were so opposed to integrating with the screws.

Apart from the unit and my personal difficulties within it, there were the wider issues to be taken into account. I dearly wanted to see much improved prison conditions and hated the thought of anyone else experiencing what I had been through. But even as I sit here typing this I know that there are still guys lying in these terrible conditions, being subjected to daily humiliations. I had the foresight to see the potential of the unit for introducing change into the penal system but I knew that it would take a long time and herein lay the problem: I hadn't got enough sense of security to make me believe that I would be here for any length of time. My previous six years had been spent mostly on the move from punishment cell to punishment cell in prison after prison which is why I could never believe that I would be in the one place for very long. I had truly felt that the only way this could be achieved was by violent means: using violence and being on the receiving end of it; this had been the only way I could see myself working.

There was another problem that had been with me for a few years now, even while I was in my cage in Inverness. I'm sure those people who had seen me in my cage thought me a right bad bastard with no good thought in my mind. The unfortunate thing is that we mostly weigh others up and pass judgement on them from what we see physically, not by what we are told. The fact is that I often thought of the vicious circle of staying in places in the Gorbals and how I had always looked up to all the hard men in my street and district. Then the kids looked up to me and saw me as the game guy who would do anything and had done things which they saw as heroic, but never did any of us see or want to see the other side of it. And yet if only they could have seen me in that cage with no future nor even a cotton vest to cover me. There is nothing more painful than becoming "aware" of it all when it is too late. I could see all the traps that I had fallen into during my life and I felt passionately for those younger kids about to step into them. I would have given anything to stop them doing so.

I would hate this to sound as though I'm on the evangelistic trail for that is not my purpose and I don't give a shit for that side of it. I have simply been on a journey and experienced terrible pain of a physical, spiritual and emotional nature and I want to stop those of my ilk from doing the same. My feelings in this direction were heightened even more as I had children of my own and was fearful for their future. They are still in the Gorbals and in very much the same environment as I grew up in. It was bad enough thinking of kids in general but because of my own kids the issue became a personal one. I feel the situation is even more critical now than ever before as the kids are getting involved at an earlier age. It was all of these thoughts that were racing through my mind and I hasten to add they were not all of an altruistic nature, but the complexity and intensity of them were giving me a hard time. For the first time in my life I was having to think very deeply about violence and other methods of gaining status.

During this period I was full of indecision, it was a turning point in my life — I would have to decide one way or the other. At nights I would lie in my cell thinking of my family who were playing an increasingly important role in my life. I owed them something, and that could be staying and accepting the unit. They re-opened all the old wounds that had been almost closed and I seemed to have no control over this as I lay trying to come to terms with it. The strange thing was that during this period I sometimes yearned for solitary confinement and the simplicity of it. On the other hand during the day to day running of the unit the staff were getting closer to us, especially Ken Murray, to whom I was getting quite close and beginning to respect.

Finally I decided that I had to get the fuck out of the place and so I went to the Governor and told him. I got a Petition to send to the Secretary of State and wrote to him saying I wanted to go away. I gave no reason why, as I was afraid to admit the problem: some of the screws were genuine. This would have been seen as a weakness not only to the others but to myself. I certainly had good vibes about the unit but felt it wasn't for me. The only way for me to get any peace of mind was to get out of it and return to the solitary situation as that was the method I could handle best. I knew where I stood there. This wasn't a complete denial of the unit, as part of me was screaming out for it, to accept it. Another part of me was saying that it had come too late, and regretted that it hadn't come along sooner. On hearing that I had put in for a transfer Ben and Larry did the same as they too were going through similar experiences. But at the next staff/inmate meeting, Ken Murray informed us that there was no way we would be allowed to leave the unit as the place was for us. He expressed this as a personal opinion as did some other staff, and at no time did I, or the two others, get an answer to our Petitions.

15

On top of the normal difficulties, there was the question of the Inverness trial which seemed to be always looming in the background. By this time we knew that the other two involved with us, Howard Wilson and Willie McPherson, were in solitary in Peterhead. Eventually, we were all served with our Indictments that charged us with attempting to escape by overpowering the prison officers and attempting to murder six of them. My lawyer had been visiting me regularly since I arrived in the unit and he now brought my Q.C.s and we discussed the defence. I knew that I was in a hopeless situation, so as far as I was concerned the emphasis of my defence shouldn't be on getting a Not Guilty but should be on bringing light to the conditions of Inverness Prison; the brutality, the cages and the treatment in general. I couldn't see any future at all for myself so I didn't see why I should bother one way or the other about acquittal when, win or lose, I would be going back to stay in conditions that would probably bring about another riot, if not for me then for someone else. If a client is concentrating on a not guilty verdict, then he is putting a harness on his lawyer or Q.C. as caution becomes the tactics rather than exposure. I wanted the facts brought out, so the latter was the order of the day.

As the trial date approached, tension began to build up in the unit as we anticipated returning to the cages for the duration of the trial. We were very suspicious as I thought that once the trial was over we would be kept on there. Alex Stephen made the arrangement that half of the unit staff should travel with us to Inverness, which meant that they would look after us and do the escorting to the court. Some of the Inverness screws were cited for court as witnesses so they were all emotionally involved.

The day for transfer to the cages came and we all travelled in a large prison bus. On reaching the prison the hostility between us and the Inverness staff standing nearby was raw but we were quickly taken to the Segregation Unit. On entering the building a remarkable change took place, with Larry, Ben and I, all bunching together, the unit staff doing the same. Everything that had gone before in the previous months completely vanished. They became screws and we became prisoners in the traditional roles. It was as though a barrier had suddenly fallen between us. On entering the small dark corridor where the cages were, it all returned with Ben going into his cage and slamming the barred door behind him and screaming out obscenities, and Larry curling up on the cage floor. I walked into my cage and looked around feeling as though I had never been away. The interesting thing was the reaction of the unit screws, who stood staring in disbelief as they hadn't believed that such conditions existed in Scottish Prisons. One or two of them had heard about them but hearing was one thing and seeing another. On the whole the cages were kept very quiet. The prison grapevine is usually fast and reliable but at no time did I hear about the cages till I actually woke up in one in a strait-jacket.

At the short preliminary hearing the security precautions included massive police escorts with arms, and a helicopter flying overhead. I informed the judge on the bench that I didn't understand the Indictment and when questioned about this I stated that the screws had attempted to murder me and no Indictment had been given to them for that. I was told I would have to bring this up at the trial when it opened.

The trial started and the screws gave their version that we had attacked them without any provocation and tried to escape. All but one of them denied using their batons on us, and the one that admitted it said he hit one of us on the arms with it. During the cross-examination of the staff it was brought out that the Segregation Unit was to give a "short", sharp lesson to prisoners; describing the "sharp" as "Just strict supervision and a minimum of luxuries", and that we had to eat our food on the cage floor or on our knees and that we prisoners were searched daily. Included in the evidence were some very revealing exhibits: a long rope of knotted sheets, two knives about a foot long, a dry-cell battery and a radio.

At the conclusion of the Crown evidence, that of the Defence started and each of us went in. We told our side: that we had been fitted up by the staff after a peaceful demo. The Jury were then spoken to by Counsel. The verdict was returned and the attempted murder charges were all dropped, but we were found guilty of assaults and attempting to escape. Each of us were sentenced to a further six years and that was the end of the trial. The sentence didn't bother me nor the others as most of us didn't feel we had a future anyway. Willie McPherson, doing twenty six years, was the only one with a liberation date but it was so far away that he didn't think about it. We had satisfaction in that we managed to bring out the conditions of the place and highlight the brutality in the system. All of us had spoken of this while in the dock. We felt that we had achieved something.

Larry, Ben and I returned to the Special Unit in Barlinnie; Howard and Willie back to the jungle of Peterhead to face further hassles. For the first time in eighteen months I was without criminal proceedings hanging over me. With this weight off me and the idea of leaving the cages behind, combined with the satisfaction of having exposed the system a little, I felt better about the new experience of the Special Unit. I thought over my present position and figuratively speaking I had the Life sentence with the fifteen years recommended minimum, eighteen months, four years, six months, and six years, so it was very difficult to think of anything for my own future with this on my plate.

But I felt very much at ease and ready to give it a try. I could see that bit more clearly now, realising that the unit could have the potential to show that change was needed and could be made within the system. We were now speaking openly with the staff, and usually the discussions would focus on the penal system and they admitted that there was a tremendous need for change; so that just by talking at this level we were able to see that something could be done. I began to accept Ken Murray, I was now able to see that he was genuine in a practical sense and not the usual "fanny" man who smiles to your face and sticks the boot in it the minute you're down. Before very long there was a small nucleus of staff and inmates interested in proving that we could do something. This was the purpose of the unit.

I realised that to talk about "commitment" to something is one thing, but to practise it day in and day out is another. I had lived the previous six years in a life style that made me accountable to myself, but this was something new, it meant all of us had to be accountable to others as well as ourselves — Responsibility. Whenever I was in solitary I realised that a routine was essential in that spartan existence but though the unit was new I did realise that the struggle for survival was still very much the name of the game and so I would have to get myself a routine. This meant a great deal of self-discipline, but as I needed it there was no problem.

Within the first few months we had managed to break down many of the barriers that were between us. This was a vital period as it could make or break us and the unit. Larry was still rejecting the unit and had been involved in two scenes that were on the verge of violence. He was also still getting his official dose of barbiturates. Ben's problem area was different. He had lost all of his remission and was full of hatred. He said he was going out in eighteen months and there was nothing the authorities could do about it. He didn't want to owe them anything as he had been brutalised and totally degraded in every way. At the same time he had tremendous loyalty and knew that the unit was something I was beginning to believe in, so although he was sceptical and dubious he kept going at a superficial level for my sake. There were times when he would get terribly angry and bitter about his past experiences and we would go away and talk about it. Ian was always locking himself up away from everyone. Rab was so much a victim of the system that he was a living indictment on them. But in spite of all these problem areas we were still making progress. A girl was allowed in to show us soft-toy making and this was quite revolutionary. Soon after this another woman was allowed in; she was an art therapist called Joyce Laing. Having women in was great for us and a big deal as it made us smarten ourselves up and watch our tongues, as one tends to use swear words every second word due to being in the coarse male environment.

The most important development taking place at this time was through the staff/inmate meetings. I suggested that we should do away with the punishment cell with the double door. There was a mixed reception to this as lots of the staff were very apprehensive and felt that it would leave them without a means to punish whenever something went really wrong. I was continually testing these meetings and this was why I threw it in. However, this was one issue the staff wanted to discuss at their own meeting. I pointed out to them that all of the inmates had been on solitary for different lengths of time, but the majority of us had been for a number of years. I said that this had done nothing for us or the prison we happened to be in. The presence of the punishment cell meant that sooner or later one of us were going to be taken in front of the Governor and given solitary and that would be the beginning of it. By doing this the real problem wasn't being faced. Whenever I had gone in front of the Governor of any other place he just gave me solitary and we parted, neither of us any the wiser as to how the thing happened in the first place. The unit was different as it had a group meeting situation, therefore a means to get to the source of any problem that arose. The staff listened and took the matter to their own meeting, but it had to be carried over for a number of weeks.

Eventually they conceded and allowed the extra door to be taken from the cell. It was a tremendously symbolic gesture taking the door from the hinges, and a big cheer went up. By doing this it gave potence to the meetings and let us all see that change could be made through the group. It also meant that any problems we did have would have to be absorbed by the group meetings. Up until then we had had some minor problems to resolve when an inmate or a staff member had been particularly abusive to someone or something like that. They had to face what we now called the "hot-seat". This meant that anyone doing anything anti-social would have to explain it in the staff/inmate meetings and he might well receive some very harsh words from everyone. If it was the opposite and someone needed support due to some problem, then everyone would reach out and touch him, and by that I mean help him over the bad patch. Either way the group meeting was a very powerful force. There was less closing of the ranks amongst us now though it still went on to an extent. There was less petty bickering and complaining and more straight talk which in itself could be quite an experience. The "hot-seat" is extremely effective as it is a system that gives everyone a say on the matter in hand. There is nothing magical about it as there are times when the guy will return the following day and be in the "hot-seat" for the same reason as the day before. But when the pressure is put on by all present and the breakthrough is finally made then it's most rewarding.

The screws in the rest of the prison system had sighed with relief when the unit opened and took us out of their way. They could now get on with the job of doing things with the prisoners who presumably caused them less bother than we had. To get into the Special Unit the staff had to come through the gate and pass the other screws in the main prison. When they did so, remarks would be passed and hostility expressed so that coming in became an ordeal for the Unit Staff. The screws in the main prisons were saying that it would only last three months till we got fed up with it and then we'd have a riot. When this didn't happen they started justifying this by saying that the Unit staff were giving us all we wanted and were afraid to say no to anything. The hostility from the Barlinnie staff started having an effect on the families of the unit staff as nearly all of them stayed in the prison quarters. In a way this helped to bring us closer as a group.

The unit as a whole became US and the rest of the Barlinnie staff became THEM. However it wasn't as easy as that, because it began to affect us in a practical sense. The staff who were more vulnerable to the criticism from their Barlinnie colleagues, or who had close friends amongst them, began to show signs of cracking. These signs usually took the form of them wanting a more disciplinary regime within the unit, but they were told by the group that this was not the reason for its existence. If the person couldn't come to terms with the unit he would move out back to the main prison but this happened on very few occasions.

The predictions from the main prison staff now were that come the festive season the place would erupt, that is the time we would feel the tension. It was almost as though they were willing it to happen in order for them to say "we told you so". They wanted us to be animals and nothing more, to prove that the cages in Inverness were the only way. One of the other problems the unit staff had was that they were now working in a regime that had no Rule Book to shield them, which meant that they were more exposed. In the old system the prison officer is always right, but in the unit this isn't the case. They had to find things to do as their time was loose, very much in the same way as ours. Before the Special Unit opened, in the pre-planning stages, the department people and the professionals involved had sat on the working party and tried to predict the problem areas when the place did open. In doing so they missed out on the one side that now seemed to pose most of the problems — staff. They never predicted the hostility from the rest of the service and the pressures this would put on the staff working in the unit. Inertia was also a problem as a good number of the staff couldn't cope with having to structure their own day but there was a great denial of this because in most institutions the staff would do anything but admit that some of their problems were the same as that of the inmates. Just like us, the staff would show, on occasions, a tendency to revert to the traditional whenever they came up against an issue where they would be seen to be wrong.

Although I had decided to have a go in helping to get the unit off the ground, it didn't mean that all my problems were solved — far from it. Accepting responsibility was the crucial one as that entailed making decisions, having to consider others, and looking at my own life in relation to others. These were things that I had to learn as I had come from a world where decision making was taken out of my hands. If I had wanted a cup of water, the toilet, soap, etc. etc. then I had had to ask for it. Now I was having to cope with not only these decisions but to think in terms of other people and it was pretty frightening. In order to be able to do this and to understand others I had to find out more about myself. This is what made the Special Unit such a tough place to live in — the fact that every single one of us had to look at himself, warts and all, probably for the first time in his life. In the general penal system one could be next door to a person for years and think that one knew him, but all one really knows is the superficial "front" that that person wanted one to know. I had known Ben and Larry off and on for fifteen years in Approved School, Borstal, and prisons but I was to find that they were comparative strangers to me till the point where we entered the Unit. Only then was I able to get to know them in depth; and they me, I suppose. I had been in solitary in Inverness with them and it was smaller than the Special Unit, but it was the general penal system structure that existed there and this was the difference, as the Unit allowed the individual to be himself. There lay the problem, as many of us, staff and inmates, began to realise we really didn't know who we were. I personally felt that the best way for me to adjust to this new way was to look on it as a rebirth; it is true to say that I was experiencing lots of things for the first time in my life.

Meanwhile the materialistic side of the Unit was progressing as the mysterious "pipeline" was beginning to open up. At the meetings it was agreed that the inmates should be allowed to use metal cutlery. Until now we had been using plastic and when we were eating we would take our food in a bowl and a spoon and stand around talking to each other as we ate. One day about six months after the unit had been going, one of the staff approached us and asked why we didn't set a table out and eat at it. My thoughts were that this was rather silly as I always ate standing up or sitting on the floor. However, he persisted and the truth was that I felt embarrassed as it had been so long since I had sat at a table and eaten a meal with others. I can remember when the first table was set I sat there feeling very self-conscious and I lifted the plate off the table onto my lap and ate it there. I had never been consciously aware of losing the ability to sit at a table to eat and it was only when confronted with it again that I was able to think about it and the very subtle way that we do become institutionalised.

It was at this time that we asked for our rations to be sent down from the main prison uncooked, so that we could prepare them for ourselves and present the food in a more tasteful way. It was a struggle, but they came round to the idea. We were still wearing the old prison uniform and so we asked for the use of our own clothing. This too was finally accepted after lots of talk and fears that it may present a security problem. When we were allowed to wear them it seemed very strange but it was nice to wear denims and casual gear. Our visitors were now allowed to bring food up so that we could eat during the visit and it was good to eat things like well-fired bread rolls, "burnt rolls" and other things that we hadn't eaten for years. It was only having experienced things like this that people on the outside see as insignificant, that I was able to see that these are among the things that make one feel alienated.

By now I was making my own daily routine and playing a principal part in the day to day running of the unit. I was still doing my physical exercises, still sleeping on my hard board, and I was also doing educational courses for mental stimulation. The courses were General and Social Psychology, so that between all of this I was keeping myself very busy. Some of the staff were still resisting progress within the Unit and I kept looking at this in a very subjective way, little realising the pressures they were under from their colleagues on the outside. I did know about some of the hostility from outside but was uncompromising and felt that they should have had the strength to resist it.

On the other end of the scale Ben was having serious problems and wanted out of the Unit back to the old penal system. He felt he would be safer as he recognised the enemy there. Lots of us tried to work on him to get him away from this way of thinking but eventually we had to accept his wish and so after eleven months he was transferred to Saughton Prison in Edinburgh. He found the fact of being confronted by himself and having to accept the staff in the unit too much. Although he recognised it wasn't for him, he had respect for what it was doing and would never have done anything in a physical sense to damage it. He was in the prison system only weeks when he was sent back to solitary and into the way that he knew best. I was allowed to write to him, but once he got into trouble they refused to let him get in touch with me.

There is a great deal of honesty in the unit, as people are encouraged to say what they think and express themselves freely, which meant I was able to debate and criticise the penal system in a rational way with staff. There was something good about being able to discuss the earlier incidents and frustrations with the people whom I felt in many ways had been responsible. These discussions took place sometimes in the presence of the Home and Health Department officials and the mere fact that such a group could sit and discuss it was revolutionary. This direct link with the Department and the fact that the Controller, Alex Stephen, was coming down and playing an active part in meeting us and getting to know how we were developing, was very important to our survival. The then Under Secretary of State, Alick Buchanan-Smith came to see us and it must be said that he felt the Special Unit was the model for the penal system of the future. He left us in no doubt that we had his support and he stood by this after he had gone as he was keeping a watchful eye on our progress. This sort of encouragement from the "top" was what we needed. It gave us the impetus to carry on as a group and acted as a balance to the hostility from the Prison Service staff.

In the first few months on recognising the close proximity and claustrophobic atmosphere the majority were experiencing, we felt that outside visitors should be invited in. There was also the fact that initially this was thought to be a safeguard as all of us, staff and inmates, were very suspicious of each other and so to make sure that all of us had to be straight, we thought that inviting outsiders in would act as a sort of balance. I was delighted at this as it helped all of us who were insecure about the future of the place. In the beginning it started with the two women and from there other people came to give us lectures on various subjects. Whenever one of these people came in, we would show them round the unit. We wanted this to be unlike other institutions, so an inmate was usually the one to take them round and that would usually be my task as the others were still very suspicious of it all. By now our individual cells were wallpapered, unlike those in other prisons. Whenever I took the visitors around I'd always remind them that other prisoners were staying three to this space that I had to myself and I would let them know about the conditions in long term prisons. I wasn't being sneaky about it or anything, this was the consensus of opinion within the unit anyway. I felt duty-bound to remind people not to get carried away or complacent because the unit was a good thing. Certainly it was, but conditions elsewhere had to be remembered. I reminded them that if shown around the main penal system, they wouldn't be allowed to speak to prisoners and would get the "guided tour" treatment. It was important for me to explain these things to the people coming in as I couldn't forget what I had gone through and what others were now going through at the moment. I elected myself spokesman for everyone living under these conditions.

Being confronted with this sort of honesty certainly affected visitors and before long we found many of them coming back to see us. As time went on they grew in number and variety. We were pleased with this as all of us were proud of what we were building and felt we had nothing to hide. We believed that people should come into the penal system and get to know what it was all about and play a part in helping to improve it. By doing so they were better able to understand an ever increasing problem in society. There was so much to gain for us all that we went out of our way to encourage them to come in.

Joyce Laing, the art therapist, was coming in from time to time and though we were very wary of art and the therapy bit, we liked her coming as she was a pretty good looking bird. So we had to compromise and pretend to have an interest in art in order to keep her coming back. One day she brought in a 7lb bag of clay for us to mess around with and the five of us sat there humouring her and having a good laugh till such time as she had to leave. Although I had been joking along with the others I felt as though I had an affinity with the clay, almost as though I had known it before. That may sound like a cliché but it's what I felt and I did mention it to one of the others. When Joyce left, the clay was abandoned by the others but I kept on with it. The day was hot and we sat in the prison yard and I sat messing around with the material doing a portrait of one of the guys. I liked it and that was what mattered. Then I did another straight off, without a model and this pleased me. I felt excited as did some of the others when they saw them. I made arrangements to get hold of more clay and I did some more pieces, so that when Joyce returned a couple of weeks later she was surprised to see the results. I felt great pleasure in creating the sculptures and knew that I had stumbled onto something within myself.

It was tremendously exciting to discover this latent talent, especially in art as this had been poofy stuff to me in the past. The nearest I had ever been to an art gallery was when we found a way of stealing empty bomb shells from the museum part of Kelvingrove art gallery. I soon got one or two books on sculpting techniques and read them while I worked, learning how to cast pieces of sculpture and the basic tools that were needed. I knew nothing whatsoever about it and Joyce herself knew very little, but this suited me fine as I personally felt it was all to do with this rebirth thing. I began to pour all my energies into this new means of expression and was knocked out by the depth of feeling when I completed a piece of sculpture. The only thing I could compare it to was when I won a victory when fighting in the past or beating the system in some way. The difference was that I was using the energy, knowing I was just as aggressive, but creating an object that was a physical symbol, yet perfectly acceptable to society. I worked at a prolific rate with most of the work based on the expressions of my soul with pain/anger/hate/love/despair/and fears embodied in it. This was very important for me as a person because it allowed me to retain all these very deep emotional feelings but to channel them in another way — sculpture.

Meanwhile I was still giving thought to the past and the life I had lived. All the older guys that I had looked up to when I was a kid were either dead, alcoholics, or serving long prison sentences. The Gorbals had changed physically with all the new buildings and different people moving in and out but the problems were still very much the same and possibly worse. Parts of me had changed and for the first time in my life I was thinking not as a victim but as a person who had been responsible for doing things that I shouldn't have. I qualify this by pointing out that whenever I was sentenced in the past for something and came into prison, the humiliation and degradation I met with there made me think of myself as the victim. I hadn't given a shit for the person or deed I was in for, or had any sympathy, as I had been too concerned with my own miseries and misfortunes .The reason for this was that the unit was allowing me to function responsibly and in order to achieve this one had to think responsibly. As a person I was growing and developing, seeing things through new eyes, and a clear mind. The visitors coming into the unit played a big part in my becoming more socially aware, and my relationships with the Unit Staff were still strengthening.

By now the staff/inmate Meetings were becoming something special and we dropped the old institutional tag and replaced it with Community Meetings. We had by now decided to stop censoring incoming and outgoing mail and our family visits were unsupervised. I was helping to make decisions that I would have to live by. If anyone abused the rules of the Community then they would have to be answerable to the Community. Punishment wasn't a physical thing i.e. locked in solitary, or being beaten up. The hot seat became the ultimate weapon and this was very effective. The key to the whole thing lies in the relationships of the people within the group, and the understanding that no one person is bigger than the Community, that the commitment is to the Community and not the individual. Before experiencing this I could never have believed it, but it's true and it works. I've experienced all sorts of punishments in my life and all have been very easy in comparison with the Community hot seat. The idea of having done something that will have an effect on your friends and then having to face those friends and explain your behaviour is very heavy, especially when you have to work and live alongside them immediately afterwards still feeling as guilty as hell within yourself. There are some people that I will never get on with in my life but will still have to live with in a fashion that is tolerable to both of us. Violence is no longer my means of communication. I was becoming articulate and learning how to use it effectively. It was a whole new ball game. Small parts within me were blossoming and I was experiencing the glory of being alive. Things looked and felt differently and in a way I was gaining a form of freedom. This was freedom of the mind, a sense of awareness and the pain that goes with it. The sculpture took on a vital importance, not only in the sense that it was a medium to channel all my aggressions but a medium in which to build up and repair the damage to my inner self. I was developing with each piece and the work that I was creating was a very strong symbolic statement relevant to my past. I was purging myself of the past. I was interested in trying things with the sculpture that I would never have attempted before. I was fully aware that the barriers I was breaking through were significant. Through all these experiences I was able to see that prison staff whom I once hated were very similar to the prisoners they look after in that they too are very much victims of the system.

Rab, one of the inmates who had an alcoholic problem at fifteen years of age and had killed a kid in a drunken stupor, had been sentenced to Her Majesty's pleasure and had spent the first thirteen years of his sentence in the rigid structure of the main penal system. As he had missed all his adolescent years and his experience of a kid at that age, he came to the unit very immature and faced tremendous problems as he developed. In the early days he would run into his cell and slam his door shut in a petulant manner. He made many mistakes along the way. The unit system was flexible in that it allowed for these inevitable mistakes. They would be discussed, sometimes at a rational level, other times not, as we too were learning and therefore could at times be very intolerant. Despite that, the problems were discussed as well as the successes.

Three years later, Rab, still in the unit, was in the position of a lodger. He matured to an extent that if the unit is to be measured as a success, then it has to be through the development of Rab. He had a full time job and went every day to work outside. The people that he worked for have offered him full time employment on release. He is now a very stable character who has been shown to be responsible during the year that he worked. He has built up relationships and made friends with people on the outside. Rab has been given his liberation date and told that a year from now he will be released. This is a tremendous boost to the Community within the unit. The unfortunate side to it is that Rab has had to go to an ordinary prison to finish his sentence. His visiting situation is that of an ordinary prisoner where the glass and wire barrier separates him from them. After nine months to a year he will be allowed to get a job under the normal Training for Freedom scheme. He will be put through all of this to get to the stage which he has already reached. The Special Unit still has a lot of new ground to break.

When Ben left for another prison he was replaced by someone else, and by this time some new staff had come in. The ones prone to the authoritarian line had moved on into what they felt were safer settings for them. Up to this point all of us had entered the unit more or less at the same time, so with the new inmates and staff we could gauge our progress. It was quite an experience for the new inmate to see me talking away and drinking coffee with staff. Afterwards one of them told me he thought they were drugging me. We had made tremendous progress and all of us knew this. I was often asked what other prisoners thought of us in the unit, and of the unit. I kept my ear to the ground and had a good idea of the feelings on the subject. It seemed to me that most of them liked the idea and felt it offered some hope for the future. Most of them knew that those of us in the unit weren't building castles for ourselves but were aiming at changing the whole decadent system. This is the only place that I know of that is offering any realistic hope for guys serving long sentences, or short ones for that matter.

Just over a year after it opened the Prisons Department asked the Community what they thought of an open day for the Press. We thought this a good idea and so members of the Scottish

Information Office (SIO) came along to speak to us and told us that the National press would be invited in and a date was fixed. They came in very much like other visitors and we took them round with an SIO man trailing behind with his ear practically placed in my mouth but after a while he left us alone. For the first time in British history the press had been allowed to sit down in a prison with staff, Prisons Department people and prisoners and have a straight talk. The SIO were in a state of near hysteria at some of the things we were saying and I was to see that there was tremendous paranoia on the official side about the press. But the Prisons Department had achieved a tremendous breakthrough in penology at a time when Attica, Parkhurst, Inverness, and the Italian riots were fresh in everyone's minds. It was a bold step indeed to open and allow such a place to develop immediately after a riot, as the usual step is higher walls, more guards, more locks, and other expensive security gadgets. The fact that the Special Unit was happening in the West of Scotland where more people are being imprisoned than anywhere else in Europe, was in many ways a miracle as it is so paradoxical to the Scottish way of thinking. Scotland, with all its provincial attitudes, was for the first time leading the world by taking a bold and imaginative step in the field of penology. A friend of mine described the unit thus; "A lily in a turnip field". The Press came in to see us, except for *The Scotsman*, who refused to come in under the terms that they submit their article to the SIO before publication. The others, after submitting their articles, published them and supported us tremendously. During this period I was sure that from here on we could make tremendous progress by expanding the unit's philosophy into the penal system, as all the encouragement for the Prisons Department seemed to be there.

I followed my strict routine every single day. It meant rising at 6 a.m. and going out to the small yard and running round in circles, like the mouse in the wheel, then going into the small weightlifting room to do some heavy training with weights, boxing and yoga which would take me up to 8 a.m. I did exercises that kept me strong, full of stamina, and supple. This part was like a religion to me and I couldn't do without it. From here on my routine had to be flexible as my position within the Community was demanding.

I generally split my day between sculpting, doing a psychology course with the Open University, which by now I had entered, and writing. Prison is all about freedom or lack of it and the definition of this as far as I'm concerned isn't purely physical, it is also a state of mind. Being in prison usually means that one is left with the enormous problem of having to cope with time and keep out the boredom, so in many ways I was reversing the process which meant that instead of too much time on my hands I found too few hours in a day to allow me to get all the work done that I wanted. There were times when I was getting three or four hours sleep a night. The fight for survival is just the same and I am determined not to vegetate or succumb to the pressures of being imprisoned. Living in this environment where one determines one's own daily routine it is simple to opt for the soft and easy like so many on the outside, but the stark reality of the past is so vivid that apathy has no place in my life.

The sculpture was playing the most prominent part in my life and was gathering interest from art circles. I had by this time thirty pieces and so Joyce Laing introduced a Mr Richard Demarco to me. He is the Director of the Richard Demarco Gallery and on seeing my work he offered me a place in his gallery to exhibit during the Edinburgh Festival. Naturally I was delighted as this was the first outside agency to have had any contact with me. Richard Demarco and I discussed the philosophy of the unit and his gallery and we found that we were working along similar lines as he was trying to open the art world to society and take it away from its elitist position. I was drawn to this idealistic principle as I was aware through my own experience of how taboo art is to those in my environment, and how barely a year ago I thought it was for "others" and not for me. I felt that I had something to offer in this direction as I realised the significance of my being labelled "Scotland's Most Violent Man" in the negative sense and turning this into the positive sense of my being a creative person. I do not remember this ever happening with any of the older criminals.

There was no dramatic change in me as basically I am still the same guy who was locked up in a cage. It's just that I am now capable of channelling all the energy and aggressions. Having said that, I am realistic enough to know that if I were thrown back into the jungle of the ordinary prison system, although I would go to great lengths to avoid violence, it's the law of the jungle there and the survival instinct is strong in me; it's not like being outside where one can walk away from it. Thinking of my past experience, the Community talked about my going to Borstal to get something going with the kids there to try to help in that area.

During these discussions it was suggested that I could also speak to prison staff at their Training College and I agreed to do this but only if I could have complete freedom to talk in a constructively critical way if necessary. The Prisons Department people who were present agreed to this and left the matter up to the Unit Governor and the person in charge of the Borstal and Training College to arrange the details. I had made it clear to all concerned that I wasn't doing this in an evangelistic sense but in a realistic one as I felt the only way to get anywhere was to cut the crap and hypocrisy. I feel that if one can get to the level of basic honesty and straight talk with groups like prison staff, or cops for that matter, then things can grow in a positive way from there. Not like the police liaison, or community officer, or priest, or minister, who churn out complete rubbish, saying for example that the police don't do this or that, or that good and evil are anything from masturbation to always showing respect to your elders.

Around this time the Prisons Department made it clear that they would look favourably upon my being allowed out on a day parole with two escorting officers from the unit staff to visit Edinburgh and see my sculpture on exhibition. The Community discussed this and recommended it, so it was formally put to the Prisons Department who approved. I just couldn't believe it. I had been given a date for a week hence and I lay at nights not sleeping for thinking about it. I kept thinking that they would change their minds at the last possible moment and so the days dragged on. The atmosphere within the unit was tremendous as all of us felt that we had made the first major breakthrough. Not one person in the place had any doubts or fears about my going out. When the day came I was driven by two of the staff in one of their cars to Edinburgh and the mere fact of sitting in the back of the car alone was wonderful. The day was beautiful with a clear blue sky and the sun shining down and all the early morning commuters making their way into Glasgow or going to Edinburgh. When we parked the car in Edinburgh, I stepped on to the street for the first time in seven years. It's not so much the seven years, but what had gone on during them. I couldn't believe it, as barely two years before I was lying in a cage with nothing, no future, nothing, yet here I was standing in a busy Edinburgh street. The whole thing was so overpowering and emotional. To feel people brush against me as they passed me by. To look at their faces. I remember stopping to look into a shop window and as I felt the glass I could see my mirrored reflection and though my face glowed it only showed a fraction of what I felt within.

The two members of staff who were with me gave me plenty of room and didn't breathe down my neck all the time. By that I mean I could have run off at any time but the thought never entered my head. I was fascinated at the way people were taking their freedom of movement so much for granted. Out of all the things that I wanted to do, my greatest longing was to go into a shop and buy something. I went into a book shop and bought a book for Larry. Just putting my hand out to buy the book was tremendous though I was slightly edgy about the decimalisation. I went to the Demarco Gallery getting a tremendous welcome from the people there and spent the day drinking in all the things that you on the outside accept without a thought. I was very much alive and walking on a cloud. The last time I had been out in Edinburgh was in a police car taking me to the appeal court when I was surrounded with a massive security guard, some of them armed, yet here I was acting responsibly a short period later. My day on parole went far beyond that of the ordinary prisoner as my whole history was against anything like this happening. All of us knew that I could have made off and nothing could have stopped me, but none of us believed this would happen. The simple basis for this belief was that we knew each other, and had built up a firm relationship over the eighteen months we had been in the unit. There was talk from our critics that we had moved "too fast too soon", but this day out was proving that we hadn't, we were sure of what we were doing.

It was obvious to me while in Edinburgh that I now had a life ahead of me. There was no way I could act irresponsibly as I was too well aware of the past and interested in investing for the future. There was this tremendous amount of responsibility placed firmly on my shoulders in that I was now in a situation where I was putting eighteen months hard work by all of us in the unit to the ultimate test. I was concerned with helping myself and building for my own future but there was the wider issue in that I was now committed to helping the general situation on the penal and social fields. It was now that I was tasting a short spell on the outside that I realised just how committed I was to proving that people in hopeless situations like myself, who are serving very long sentences, can act responsibly and through their own experience, give something back into society. I felt that by being out I was an ambassador for the Special Unit; that I was acting on behalf of every long-term prisoner to show that change can be made; that people serving unbelievably long sentences could, if the parole system was allowed to function properly, take part in a proper re-socialising programme that would give them a realistic chance to make a future for themselves that would be acceptable to society.

I spent the day mixing with the general public. When introduced to people I wouldn't hide where I came from, as I felt it important to stress what was being done and how conditions could be improved for prisoners. I found tremendous support for the unit and what it was doing. The only near problem I had was when I entered the gallery where my sculpture was being exhibited to find a crew of BBC film men recording a show of the work and as the announcer knew me I had to hide in the toilet till they left. The reason for this was that I knew the Prisons Department abhorred publicity. Had I allowed myself to be seen by the BBC it would have been misinterpreted to look as though I was seeking publicity, and therefore it could have looked as though I was acting irresponsibly. I was also aware that if the press got hold of it then it could cause a backlash against me. It seems to be one of those paradoxical situations where in theory it is accepted that something must be done to improve the conditions of prisoners and help rehabilitate them so they become better citizens. When this is eventually tried in the only logical way possible some sections of society scream out in horror at the thought of murderers walking the streets.

One of the highlights of the day was meeting Joseph Beuys, the German sculptor, who was lecturing at the Demarco Gallery on his piece, Documentation with a Coyote. Beuys had locked himself in a cage for some time with a Coyote, one of America's most rejected animals and after some days with the creature he learned to live with it and vice versa, though in the beginning it showed hostility towards him in a very threatening way. By doing this he proved that if we make the effort we can communicate with each other no matter how polarised. We talked and I explained to him how on many occasions I had felt very much the Coyote of the human race, yet here I was by a strange coincidence standing here and speaking to him.

The glorious day came to an end and it was time for us to return to the Special Unit. All of us were filled with the success of the day as the impossible had happened. On entering the unit the others met us and questioned us about it. All of us in the Community had worked terribly hard since the beginning and realised the tremendous breakthrough that had been made this day. The place was alive. This was a positive concrete mark in its history. I had a sleepless night going over the day's events. I never thought I'd ever experience this but more to the point I had proved to myself that my thoughts of being positive were now my deeds. I was more alive then I had ever been in my life. I was allowed out two more times in the next three weeks to visit the Festival and these two days were comparable to the first.

One morning in September, a few days after my last visit, one of the Scottish dailies reported the fact that I had been to the Edinburgh Festival on one occasion. Someone had leaked that I had been out. This shattered me as it was something I had gone to great lengths to prevent. It didn't matter who had leaked it, the fact was that it had happened. I knew that the Department dread publicity and would go on the defensive. I asked them bluntly if my paroles would now be stopped and was told they wouldn't but they said a short "cooling off" period would be better till things cooled down. The Community were against this, pointing out that the Department should be standing up and using this as an example of what they were doing not only in the Special Unit but in the penal system as a whole. We took the view that by feeding regular information and allowing more access to prisons by the media and the public, then the reactions which were now occurring would be reduced. The Department took the view that all the media wanted was what sold papers or raised viewing rates. We challenged the Department on their decision but at this period certain changes took place that involved the transfer of Alex Stephen, the Controller of Scottish Prisons.

The unit was now the direct responsibility of a man who was very traditional in his outlook, who had started his career as a prison officer many years ago and had worked his way through the ranks to his present position. He had come a long way and was a pioneer in his own right career-wise. There had been a change of Government some months before and the Labour Party was now in power and though we were sad to see Alick Buchanan Smith go, all of us or most of us had more faith in the Labour Party as all our parents and friends were supporters. We finally ended up with Harry Ewing as Under Secretary, which included Prisons.

There was a complete change of thinking from the top. The first blow came in the form of refusing me permission to speak to the Borstal boys. The Scottish Prison Officers Association at the

Annual Conference voted that prisoners should not be allowed to lecture to them. Understandable perhaps, but I hope that both these things will materialise in the future. The SPOA issued a statement saying that prisoners in other prisons were causing trouble to get into the Special Unit. Ken Murray, who was on the Executive Committee, dis-associated himself from the statement saying it was untrue and made statements to this effect showing convincingly that what he said was true. He was removed from the SPOA executive. Shortly after this the nucleus of staff who were solidly behind the unit concept found themselves being transferred for one reason or another. Ken Murray was put on the transfer list, and all of us, outside visitors to the unit included, came together and fought this all the way. Ken appealed and won. We were fighting for our very existence and we knew it. It now became clear that I wasn't going to be allowed out on parole again. This was never said in words, but the Department were preparing us for tightening the place up, as they were saying it had got out of control, that prisoners had too much say in the running of the place.

During this very difficult period, we all went through personal crises. One morning by sheer chance I happened to look into Larry's cell: he was lying on the floor unconscious from an overdose. He was hovering between life and death. I had found him and raised the alarm and what he had done had a tremendous impact on me. I spent the day sculpting in my makeshift studio, expecting to hear any minute that he had died. We had known each other for 15 years or so and had been through similar experiences. Larry was born in Glasgow's Townhead district, then his parents moved out into the country and he was brought up there. I met him in St John's Approved School and Borstal, from where he had joined the army. While on leave in London he shot a barman, was convicted of manslaughter and sentenced to Life Imprisonment. He was transferred to Scotland and in Peterhead and Perth was involved in riots and convicted of stabbing prison staff, which resulted in him getting fifteen years, five years, six years and six months on top of his lifer. Larry is tall and good looking with shoulder length black hair. He is extremely intelligent and over the years in the unit has become a very good poet. By now he was getting massive doses of drugs to overcome very deep depressions. He could never see himself getting released and so the drugs were an alternative way out. Over the years his tolerance level increased and with it the amount of drugs, which were seconal and nembutal barbiturates. Both of us were in similar positions but our outlooks radically differed at this point and although each of us knew this we managed to live tolerably together within this small space.

This is where one of the real problems of the penal system lies, as guys like us are being sentenced to very long terms and being kept in conditions that the general public seem to find acceptable for "criminals", although such conditions would be abhorrent to most people even for their dogs. There was also the fact that the Parole Board and the whole parole system had become a joke to prisoners from working-class districts as they tended to select prisoners from the first offender type prisons. A few guys were released from the long-term prisons but just as token gestures: they would have been going out in a few weeks anyway, and it was seen as the Parole Board trying to dispel the rumours that they were discriminating, rather than as a genuine attempt to let guys see that if they wanted to change, then this facility would be there to help them. All it seemed to do was to further polarise the situation between prisoners and authorities rather than improve things. All of this was very much a part of Larry's present condition and I kept thinking of the "masked violence" of executive decision-making power that played a major part in perpetuating most of our problems. It was while working in the studio that day with all of this in my mind that I created my first sculpture through the feeling of love. Until this period it had been motivated by feelings of anger and hatred. Later that day I was told that Larry was out of danger.

Most people when in discussion with us, always refer to the high cost of the unit and this is an area that must be looked at. Because there is a higher ratio of staff, the cost of running the unit is higher as the wages are what makes up the bigger portion of the sum. Initially the higher ratio was justified due to our past histories and the fears that the staff had at that stage. Three out of the five of us were labelled as violent towards prison staff and there had been a Standing Order that no less than three prison officers must be present at all times when our doors were opened. With this in mind one can see that the "high cost of the Unit" didn't hold much water. "A" category prisoners have a higher ratio of staff with them at all times and staff doing this duty spend their time watching prisoners. This is a far cry from the unit situation which is giving society a great deal in return for the cash being spent. The unit was by now in the centre of an internal political struggle and we felt it was largely because of its success and the fact that it was raising some fundamental questions about the penal system.

With this traditional authoritarian attitude coming from the people now in control of the unit at Prisons Department level a lot of the creative thought died within the place. Larry had been producing poetry and had been encouraged to write a book for publication, everything was very much in the open. Staff had been putting lots of very positive and creative ideas forward, but with this new regime many of these things were killed off. I made sculptural statements symbolising "Censorship" and "Injustice", but the main thing for me was to continue to work creatively by writing and sculpting and playing an active part in the place. By now I was writing a comprehensive daily journal of the unit and what was happening in it, the way in which it was growing and developing, the crises and the changes taking place in all of us, so this was a very sad part of what had to be documented as all of us felt that at this stage the Prisons Department were looking on us with disapproval.

We were under the microscope and had the impression that the first excuse would see our demise. Whenever we could we would put this to the officials who would tell us that the unit wouldn't close, but this wasn't our biggest fear. The biggest fear was that they would make life so difficult by slowly introducing more authoritarian measures, that they would effectively kill off the reason for the Unit having been set up in the first place, and by putting this sort of pressure on us something would crack within. It was all very subtle but one thing was clear, the goodwill was gone from the Department and it was being turned into a "humane containment" unit. The Department people were saying one thing publicly and another internally. In spite of this we had fantastic support from the very thing that we had introduced to act as the initial balance between staff and inmates — outside visitors; people who by now had become part of the Community and who recognised the potential of the place. All of us knew that what was happening in the Special Unit had consequences wider than that of the penal system, and that some of the lessons learned here could be applicable to society in general. We had greatly expanded our policy of inviting members from the general public in, also people working in the socially deprived areas of Glasgow and the West of Scotland. We felt it was our duty to show what could be done, and is being done.

Another piece of news was giving us a considerable amount of encouragement. Ben had been released from the traditional prison and had been out for almost a year. He returned to see us and sat in at a Community Meeting and told us that a part of the unit had rubbed off on him and that he had been out of prison for the longest period of his life. He could now see its importance. Ben was particularly close to me as we had been very friendly from approved school onwards. He had come through all the institutions with me and was now a very bitter man about the treatment he had received, particularly during the last years of imprisonment. Now that he had been let out the door after seven years he felt that he owed them nothing but his difficulties in adjusting to life on the outside were tremendous. I could feel the pressure he was under and we discussed it. The thing was that Ben had no one else to discuss them with, so it was great that he found he could come back to the unit and find some succour.

We are fortunate in that we have not had any serious problems in the first few years, although this has come as no surprise to those of us in the place. If you treat people like human beings they will act like human beings. There is no doubt that being in this line of business, crisis will eventually occur, it's almost inevitable. No doubt it will give our critics a field day but by any standards we can hold our heads up. Everything has been tried from the downright brutal to the inhuman, but this is the only thing that has worked and even our critics must accept this.

During these past years I have worked tremendously hard, and am now in my third year of an Open University course. My sculpture is now in some private collections and I have had it in galleries throughout Britain. I feel I have built a strong foundation for my future in that world. I have come a long way since the days when I hated all screws and now find that I look on some of them as friends. I say this openly without fear of contradiction from guys suffering at this moment in the main penal system. The reason I say this is because the desire to change the conditions lies very deep within me. I know that to the guy lying in prison it's not so much the actual physical conditions that count but the treatment he receives from the prison staff, because within that world he is completely at the mercy of the man in control of him. Out of everything that makes up this Unit, the thing that costs nothing in terms of money is staff and prisoners getting together and talking; it is the one thing that has brought about results. The emphasis is placed on seeing the individual as a person in his own right without relying on labelling or categorisation in order to identify. It is unique in the sense that two opposing factions have come together and worked towards building a Community with a remarkable degree of success. An important lesson is that no professional psychiatric or psychological experience was needed to make it so. Our basic ingredients have been some people, goodwill from all sides and with those we became the architects of a model that could be used anywhere.

As far as my past goes, I don't think that it should be forgotten about or swept under the carpet as though it doesn't exist. It does exist and is very much a part of me. My own personal experiences have taught me that mistakes made are very much a part of living. Certainly we must try to learn from them, as in this instance, and use this knowledge to let others see what can happen. I dread the thought of other kids going through my experience in order to gain the insight that I now have. Perhaps this could be used as a short cut. What worries me in the field of human contact is that there are too many professional status seekers and not enough patients. By that I mean not enough people wanting to look at their own personal problems but quite content to diagnose the problems of others. What I have written here is not intended to be an apologetic account about what happened in my life. Certainly I have caused much suffering and have suffered, but the disease is much larger and older than me. An environment has been created that has encouraged change and that is what must be looked at.

The Pain of Confinement

Prison Diaries

*This book is
dedicated to my wife Sarah
who in giving so much of herself helped me
make it, and to my editor at Canongate
for her faith in me
and my work.*

First published in Great Britain 1984 by Canongate Publishing Ltd
This edition published 1985 by Pan Books Ltd,
Cavaye Place, London, SW10 9PG
9 8 7 6
Text and illustrations © Jimmy Boyle 1984
ISBN 0 330 28687 0
Printed and bound in Great Britain by
Hazell Watson & Viney Limited,
Member of the BPCC Group,
Aylesbury, Bucks

This book is sold subject to the condition that it
shall not, by way of trade or otherwise, be lent, re-sold,
hired out, or otherwise circulated without the publisher's prior
consent in any form of binding or cover other than that in which
it is published and without a similar condition including this
condition being imposed on the subsequent purchaser

1

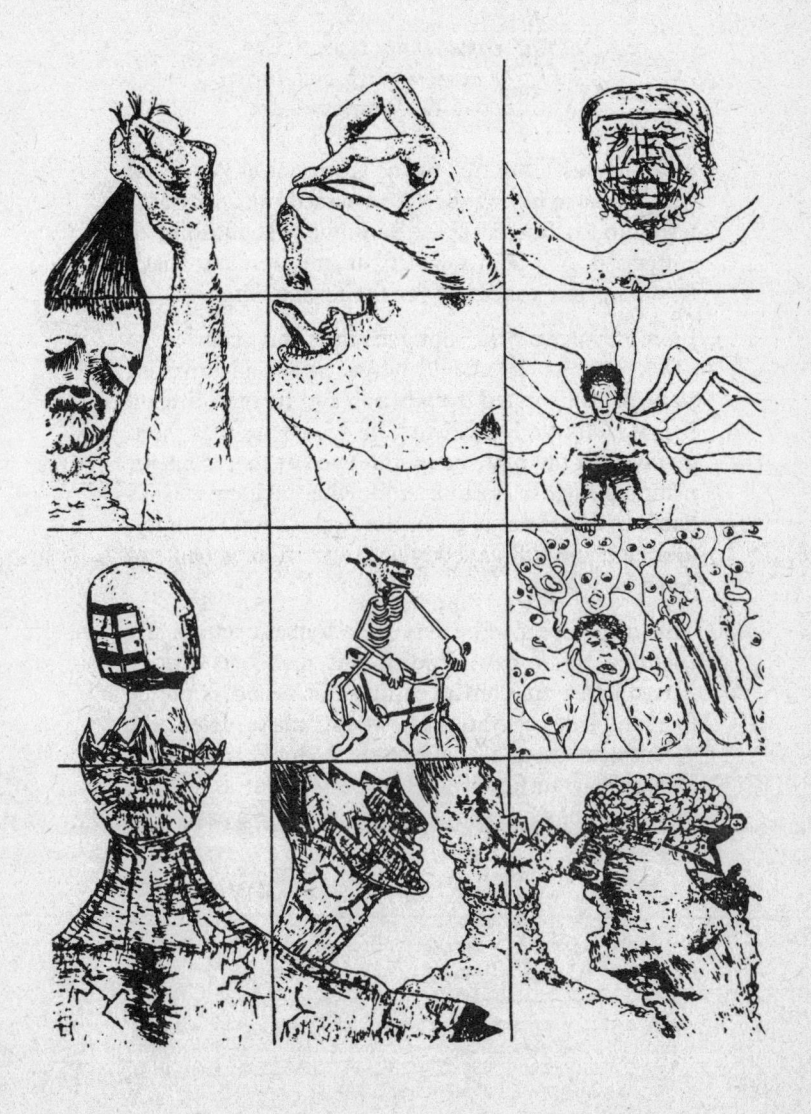

FEBRUARY 1973

275/68 James Boyle Born 9.5.44
3.11.67 Glasgow High and Jury
Murder – Life Imprisonment

A report was submitted by the Governor of Peterhead with a view to having the above named prisoner transferred to the Special Unit, Barlinnie. I should like to emphasise two points which, in my opinion, make Boyle a prime candidate for the Special Unit.

I am firmly of the opinion that this man is so dangerous that he should never, under any circumstances, be liberated from prison and further, despite the assaults and incidents in which he has been involved in the past, he is still, even at this moment, planning further assaults and further incidents. He is liable at any time, if given the slightest opportunity, to attack and kill anybody with whom he is liable to come in contact.

This may appear to be very melodramatic and highly coloured but I have studied this man over a long period and I am convinced that this report is purely factual. One alteration I would make from the recommendation of Peterhead, I think that Boyle should be transferred to the Special Unit as soon as possible, not when the charges at Inverness have been disposed of.

GOVERNOR.

Unknown to me the preceding report had set into motion a series of decisions that were to have a profound effect on me. My last book, *A Sense of Freedom*, gave some insight into this but ended leaving many of its readers – if my mailbag is anything to go by – feeling angry at the state of our prison system; relief that I had survived the physical brutality of it; and wanting to know why the revolutionary concept of the Special Unit was being systematically undermined by politicians and prison authorities. *The Pain of Confinement* is meant to give a better understanding of this and is a personal account of the day-to-day struggle involved.

It would be presumptious to assume that people buying this book will have read the previous one and so for this reason I want to give a precis of the situation that led to the introduction of the Special Unit.

In 1967 I was one of a group of young men sentenced to long prison sentences in the wake of the abolition of Capital Punishment. I was sentenced to Life Imprisonment with a fifteen years recommended minimum. The media labelled me 'Scotland's Most Violent Man'. Like others I considered myself a young man with no hope or future. I was part of a group known as the living dead.

When such a devastating sentence is pronounced on a person it dramatically changes him or her. On the one hand I knew I didn't murder the man I was convicted of killing but on the other I was sensitive to cynical prison governors and policemen mimicking 'Every prisoner in prison proclaims his innocence'. This is their way of reinforcing – and perhaps living with – the system they represent. I was determined not to be seen to be bleating, complaining or showing weakness in the face of such people. If they wanted tough and ruthless opposition then they would get it. I had nothing to lose.

I found myself connecting with other prisoners who were in the same boat. We had a lot in common and built up personal relationships when in solitary through an archaic ventilator system that was linked to each cell. In this way we began to plan and co-ordinate our actions. We soon learned that the system which copes very well with individual troublemakers doesn't when these same individuals begin to organise and co-operate with each other.

In response to this the authorities became more reactionary and oppressive in their measures to contain us. After a succession of fights, riots and demonstrations five of us found ourselves held in the Cages in Inverness prison.

These were iron-barred cage fronts that sub-divided a prison cell; reminiscent of those used to hold animals in a travelling circus. We were, at times, kept naked and given one book per week to read. The decor and structure of the whole block was built for sensory deprivation. The rules – blatantly plastered on the wall – stated that no prisoner would be kept in the Cages for less than two months or more than six. This was flagrantly abused.

Having taken us to the ultimate in official punishment the authorities had in fact played their last card. They were now helpless in the face of our rebellion. In a strange sort of way we had been set free. I was aware of having an unpretentious naked truth and dignity in that cage. The authorities would publicly portray us as monsters and animals, but privately we knew that the degree of brutal violence exerted on us by gangs of prison officers was no different to that for which we were convicted. It was condoned by people turning a blind eye to it and the public not wanting to know. In essence, it was an unconscious, unspoken collusion that was rooted in revenge. The underlying belief being that acts of physical violence have an instant 'cure' in the exercise of a more powerful physical violence. In fact, it made all of us worse.

The climax of this downward spiral took the form of a bloody riot in the Cages. Many prison officers and prisoners were injured. The doctors announced that I wasn't expected to last the night. Four of us were eventually charged with the attempted murder of six prison officers. It made no difference to any of us. I simply worked my body back to physical fitness in preparation for the next bloody occasion. I thought there was no alternative.

Behind the scenes, outside our sphere of knowledge, the authorities were stretched to the limit. A number of prison officers in Inverness resigned from the service in the aftermath of the riot. Prison staff in other prisons were saying they wouldn't have the hard core of us back. The pressure was on to get the Special Unit opened.

It was a February morning in 1973, that two of my caged fellow prisoners were whisked off to an unknown destination. I arrived six weeks later. We found ourselves resident in the newly-opened Special Unit. It was a strangely disorientating experience. In earthly terms, it was as though we had landed in an unknown foreign country. Our suspicion, hostility and aggression clashed with the attitudes of the staff setting out to be warm and friendly. It was easier for us to cope with prison staff who were unhelpful, authoritarian and potentially violent.

My two fellow prisoners were as bewildered as me. Ben and I had come through so much together, starting with approved school then Borstal and continuing here in prison. Although from different cities (Ben was from Edinburgh) we had forged a strong, binding relationship in these institutions. Both of us had attempted to organise the Prisoners' Solidarity Movement and paid the consequences for doing so. Although he was the fifth prisoner in the Cages he was not directly involved in the riot. His being the smallest sentence – seven years with small additional sentences for assaulting prison officers – we thought it best he refrain from participating.

Unlike the rest of us, Ben had a determinate sentence so knew when he would be released. His perspective of the Unit was different from that of all the others. Having been brutalised and given these additional sentences throughout the previous years he was not impressed by the fact that the authorities wanted to be considerate when he only had eighteen months of his sentence to serve. His anger and hostility towards them was at times uncontainable. The real dilemma for Ben was that his loyalty to me meant that he had to restrain himself in the Unit. He knew, the way things were going, that it was life or death for me. He hoped for my sake that this place was for real.

Along with Ben and I, the other prisoner, Larry, had come through approved school, Borstal and prison. He was serving a life sentence for manslaughter. In addition he had incurred twenty years for riots and fights. In order to cope with this Larry demanded, and was given, drugs. Over the years this increased till eventually he was on a massive dosage. It was sad to see the transformation that took place in him as the daily dose began to take effect. He was extremely intelligent and witty but as the drugs took over he would become a rather pathetic, incomprehensible shadow of himself. He had been involved in the riot and was a co-accused, charged with six attempted murders.

Individually and collectively our reputations went before us. Ben and Larry informed me that the Prisons Department had resisted my transfer to the Unit. They considered that I would be a disruptive influence. Knowing that I had been kept in the Cages alone – the two other co-accused rioters having been dispersed to

Peterhead prison – and fearing what might happen to me there, these two had put pressure on the Unit staff to get me here. Both of them had been told that the Special Unit was a whole new ball game. They suggested that it should prove itself so by bringing me down.

There were two other prisoners in the Unit who had been transferred from other prisons. Rab was a very thin, shy young man with thick, greasy black hair. He wore heavily-framed spectacles which made his face seem thinner than it was. Sentenced to Her Majesty's Pleasure he had been inside since he was a boy of sixteen and was now twenty-nine. He had been transferred from Saughton Prison, Edinburgh, more because he was an embarrassment to the system than because he was a troublemaker. The fact that he had been confined throughout some of the most formative years of his youth meant that he had been denied experiences and difficulties other youngsters have been through by the time they reach their late twenties. He found it very difficult to converse or communicate with anyone. He simply sat in front of the television all day. Emotionally he was still sixteen years old.

The remaining prisoner was a man called Ian. He was serving a life sentence for killing his girlfriend in a suicide pact that went wrong. He had served five years of his sentence. An obese man with very complex, personal problems, I marked him as someone not to be trusted. He was big, heavy and going bald and wore wire-rimmed spectacles with thick glass. He was thirty years old.

Out of all the staff in the Unit the one who stood out at this very early crucial period was Ken Murray. He was a principal nursing officer and also a member of the Executive Committee of the Scottish Prison Officers Association. A tall, striking man, he emanated an aura of sincerity and integrity, qualities that I seldom associated with a prison officer. He stood out above the others because he spoke his mind, often to the acute discomfort of his colleagues. He was also a very sensitive man and articulate with a keen interest in politics. He was a member of the working party that set up the Unit, playing a prominent part in its inception. Ken was the one person amongst the staff who was idealistic in viewing the true potential of the Special Unit as a meaningful alternative to the old penal system. Never at any time did I doubt his sincerity, but I had a lot of problems dealing with it.

In those first few days I took the opportunity to look around the Unit. Over the years I had been conditioned to think that I was only allowed to go where I was told. Here in the Unit there was access to all the nooks and crannies. It took some getting used to. Having come from solitary confinement I had the distorted perspective that the Unit was huge. In actual fact it was small and claustrophobic. It was originally used to hold female prisoners but had recently been made secure to hold us. Although a part of the main prison of Barlinnie, the Unit was completely segregated by a wall and barbed wire.

There was a small courtyard where we could exercise. Inside there was the reception/meeting room adjacent to which stood an open space where we envisaged putting a small pool table. Nearby was a hotplate and kitchen, the food being brought from the main prison. All of this was on the ground floor. Through a double-door entrance was the cell area. This was a slim double-tiered block with a wide corridor-type hall and five cells which looked over the hall. The cells had heavy oak panelled doors with steel linings. Each had a judas spyhole. One cell, No. 5, on the ground floor had an ominous double door, the one place to which we had no access. This was a punishment cell. There was an enclosed stair leading to the upper-level cells. This was where I was housed. The interior of this part of the building had four long windows that never seemed to let in any light. At the far end of each tier was a toilet area with some sinks for washing up. On the top floor there were two showers.

It was clear from the start that this prison was different from all others we had been in. We were told that we had the freedom to fill our days in whatever way we wanted. There were tools to use and this in itself was remarkable. We were given access to metal cutlery and other utensils that could be used as weapons. The attitude of the authorities was in giving trust instead of withholding it. This was established as soon as I entered the Unit with my personal possessions in a tied parcel. The prison officer, Ken Murray, gave me a pair of scissors to cut the string. Here I was, still awaiting trial for six attempted murders of prison staff and being given a weapon by one of their colleagues. It was mind-blowing.

What made the Unit unlike any other place was the way staff and prisoners were allowed and encouraged to sit down and talk together. This was the single most important factor of the Unit. It allowed us to break down all the barriers of hostility between us. This was by no means easy. In conjunction with this there were built-in weekly meetings where we all sat down as a group and discussed the week's events and decided on domestic issues. There are a number of examples of how effective these groups were. In the preliminary discussions which the staff had before the Unit opened they initiated some daft rules; being allowed one shower a week, and locking up the access to the shower taps. These were issues which we eventually tackled through these meetings. Another silly rule was that staff would make up our weekly wage on the basis of our daily attitude or dress tidiness, etc. The wages in total were sixty pence. If our attitude was wrong one particular day they would recommend that two pence should be deducted. When we heard this we honestly thought the staff were a bunch of loonies. The origins of these rules could clearly be traced to the old prison tradition of 'good order and discipline'. This clearly clashed with our history of chaos and lack of discipline. The reality for Larry and I, because of the pending High Court trial, was the prospect of a further twenty years each. How anyone could expect a two pence deduction to modify our behaviour was beyond me.

It was sheer coincidence that the Special Unit was conceived at a time when I was struggling with my own identity. In having a vague notion of where we were both going and what needed to be done I had to handle these realities even at this early stage. Ben and Larry were so full of hate and mistrust for the authorities that their behaviour constantly bordered on physical violence both to each other and to the staff. Being the recognised leader, I soon found my position was to support, and prevent them.

An example of this took place within a month of my arrival. I happened to be in one part of the Unit with Ben and some staff when Rab came running in, excited, saying that Larry was in trouble. We all ran through to the cell area to find Larry standing with a pair of scissors at the throat of a member of staff. I walked in and across to Larry and told him to give me the scissors. The atmosphere was very tense. The staff who had been following Ben and me stood there and let me do the talking. Larry reluctantly gave me the scissors and Ben moved in to separate Larry from the staff member. There was a whole series of on-the-spot decisions taken here that resolved the matter without physical injury. On seeing Larry threatening a colleague, the staff didn't go for their batons and rush in, but stopped, and allowed Ben and me to handle it. Had they drawn their batons then we would have turned on them as a group. By doing what they did, they brought out the best in us.

Having defused the incident, we were left with how to deal with the aftermath, as there were a lot of high feelings buzzing around. In another prison Larry would have been locked up. It was decided that a staff/prisoner meeting should be held immediately, so everyone assembled in the meeting room. The Governor wasn't in but that seemed to be an advantage as it meant we could deal with the matter without the traditional 'official'. Feelings were still running high and though we didn't realise it at the time, this was the most crucial experience in deciding which way the Unit should go.

Larry was confronted by everyone asking him to explain his behaviour. The atmosphere was very heated. I was most vocal in taking him to task but Ben also spoke up leaving no doubt that he was angry at Larry. Rab and Ian said very little as they were out of their depth and possibly frightened. I could use hard words with Larry and get through to him. We were given the story as to why it had all started. Larry had been about to snip off his beard with the scissors when a member of staff intervened. Larry, like me, was awaiting trial for charges placed against us at Inverness and the rule is that accused persons are not allowed to alter their appearance before the trial. This rule applies mainly to people coming into prison on charges from the outside where identification is vital but once in prison it is unnecessary as the staff can identify prisoners with or without beards. When the staff member intervened, Larry thought he was trying to provoke him so he reacted violently. It was clear that Larry had been in the wrong and so in my view had to be taken to task, as should a member of staff had he been wrong. He admitted that he shouldn't have gone for the staff member and apologised. There followed from this a general discussion on staff/prisoner relationships and it was agreed by everyone that there should be no restrictions placed on disagreements being aired verbally but that physical violence must be forbidden in this Unit. The tension within the room was so thick, it could have been cut with a knife.

After the meeting, both Larry and the staff member went to his cell and sat there for almost two hours discussing the whole thing. They came to an amicable understanding, shook hands and left the matter like that.

We had redefined 'punishment' as we knew it. Had Larry been

locked up in a punishment cell, he would have lain there and reinforced his anger, and his belief that all staff were bastards. Had he been beaten up, it would, to him, have justified what he had done and made him determined to do it again to show that he wasn't afraid of them. It came to me then that the issue of punishment as practised in the normal penal system is counter-productive and can only make matters worse. However, having experienced this meeting, I could understand why people want to lock the offender up – it is easier. The very fact that we had to sit with Larry, expressing our views on what he did, meant that we were committing ourselves to the Unit and, beyond this, accepting responsibility for our own and other people's behaviour. But it wasn't easy, as some of those people present saw Larry as a very frightening character, and the fact that they were openly reprimanding him was in itself scarey as we were still not sure of these meetings or their possible repercussions. It let us see, however, that there is a lot to be learned from incidents such as this one and that through confrontation we could come to understand why people behave in an anti-social manner. In fact, all of us were being taken to higher levels of sensitivity. We were learning to learn from experience.

Although this may sound as though the matter was concluded to everyone's satisfaction and that we were all happy, this was far from the truth. It affected all of us in different ways. Some of the staff felt vulnerable with Larry still walking around amongst them. They were worried that they might be attacked. The fact that I had disarmed Larry, and that Ben had also played a positive part, receded into the background. Ben, Larry and I were too closely associated with violence and with each other, and when one of us did something, the other two were seen to be his allies. It was difficult for the staff to see any of us as individuals. I distinctly remember, while blasting Larry at the meeting, thinking that my whole world had been turned upside-down. The thought of my having a go at another prisoner in this way for going at a prison officer would previously have been unthinkable. I felt quite treacherous. That night, locked in my cell, I went through intense periods of torment at the thought of 'selling out'.

No sooner had this incident cooled when all hell erupted between Ben and another staff member. It started with a heated exchange but Ben left and stewed it over and the whole thing started to build up inside him. He was intent on beating up the staff member and I had virtually to hold him down in his cell till his rage and anger had subsided. These things happened outside the knowledge of the staff. Ben had been good in dealing with Larry's anger, but in dealing with his own he wasn't so adept. These incidents confronted us with parts of ourselves that we just didn't know about and couldn't handle. In these tense moments both Ben and Larry would ask me why I stopped them going ahead, reminding me what bastards staff were. I would agree but my thoughts were on the potential of the Unit not the hatred I felt for staff and this was the difference. They were both going round constantly watching staff, taking their every word as being against them. Sometimes they were right and other times they were wrong. The damaging part was the obsessive nature of their attitudes. In spite of the fact that my sympathies lay with my friends I could also see the good things staff were doing and I did not want to ignore them or see them as part of a 'con game'. Ben and Larry were making me question myself. Maybe I was falling for a 'con game'? There were moments when I would look with penetrating clarity at my life sentence, my treatment in prison, the brutality, the further prison sentences and now another High Court trial overshadowing me. Maybe I was being too naive.

Ironically, it was a group of prison officers who helped dispel my doubts about the place. It was impressive to see them push forward radical steps for the development of a more humanitarian regime. An example of this was when we debated the abolition of the punishment cell. This was a lengthy discussion on an emotive issue. When winning the vote by an overwhelming majority, a group of us – prisoners and prison staff – armed with hammers and chisels went through to dismantle it. We immediately transformed it into a weight-lifting room. 'Punishment of another kind', remarked the obese Ian. It was a powerfully symbolic moment for all of us. Having no punishment cell meant that if things went wrong and a prisoner became violent there would be nowhere to punish him or keep him out of harm's way. Trust would become paramount.

Three months after the Special Unit opened we were taken to trial and, as expected, there was elaborate security with armed police and a helicopter buzzing overhead. I didn't know why this was, for no one was going to attempt to get me or the others out as we had no money and didn't know any people who would be willing to help. It was like a circus and though we were the main performers it was stage-managed beyond our control. In my view this whole procedure tends to be nothing more than a deliberate propaganda exercise initiated by the police. It is effective in prejudicing a jury. Knowing this I set out to counter the propaganda by replying to the judge when asked to plead to the charges that I didn't understand them. On being asked what I didn't understand, I replied that on the night in question I had almost died and yet no one had been charged with attempting to murder me. This captured the headlines the following day.

At this point Larry and I didn't really care what we received as we both felt that our lives were finished anyway, so whether it was two or twenty years hardly mattered. I was more interested in exposing the conditions of the Cages and the whole penal system and so arranged my defence around this. The evidence unfolded with prison staff saying that the prisoners had made an unprovoked attack on them while attempting to escape. Despite the seriousness of the occasion there were moments when we were all dumbfounded or doubled-up with laughter during the telling of the tale. One prison officer told of finding a transistor radio in a chamber pot. Another told of finding a twenty-foot makeshift rope in a cage. Almost all the prison officers denied using their batons although there was extensive medical evidence that our injuries bore traces of their use. The medical evidence also showed that I wasn't expected to last the night as a result of my injuries.

The four of us, aided by Ben, had our turn in the witness box. Even amidst this massive security the court refused to take the handcuffs off us. Our defence was that we held a peaceful demonstration but when the prison officers attacked us with the batons, violence erupted. We made it clear that our protest was about the brutality and the conditions we were kept in. We highlighted the fact that our human rights were being seriously abused. The attempted murder charges were reduced to assault, of which we were found guilty and given six years. The attempted escape charge was dropped. Larry and I were returned to the Special Unit and the other two accused, to Peterhead Prison.

There was considerable publicity surrounding the trial and the conditions we had been kept in. The point was made that if human beings are kept in such conditions, it is little wonder they react like animals. What interested me was that the Cages had been implemented without public knowledge. It was clear that most politicians were unaware of their existence. Even more intriguing, many prison officers didn't know about them. The Departmental Working Party set up to look into the treatment of long-term prisoners (whose findings recommended the setting up of the Special Unit) noted in their report that the Cages, in fact, made some prisoners more violent. It was good news that they weren't to be used again. We took the opportunity to suggest that the solitary block be converted to a Special Unit type block. The fact that we had been given an additional six years meant little to us in our no-hope situation.

Having it all out of the way was also of considerable relief to our families who were another crucial aspect of the Unit. They were initially allowed to visit us on Saturday and Sunday afternoons in the meeting room. We would sit around tables in a relaxed atmosphere, one prison officer sitting nearby. In the normal prison system, the visiting arrangements were that long-term prisoners would be granted nine hours per year, and usually that was in a small cubicle with glass and wire barriers separating visitor from prisoner. We could now sit around an open table with coffee, chat and even touch if we wanted to.

Although I could never openly admit it at the time, there were a number of problems attached to this new visiting situation. Over the years in prison I had almost become a stranger to my family and was very apprehensive about their coming to see me. I didn't know what I would be able to talk about for this length of time. I was dreading those moments of long, drawn-out silences when we were all lost for words. Although the prison system had done nothing to help matters over the years the blame could not be laid entirely at its feet. I was suddenly faced with the fact that never in my life had I really sat down and had an interesting conversation with my family. We were all inarticulate, and didn't know about such things as politics, or other matters that dominated our lives. I would simply have to get to know my family all over again. However, the overwhelming advantage of the visits was the humanising effect it had on us. Larry was a different man with his mother and family. I would glow when my old relatives visited me bringing my two children with them. We embraced each other with tremendous warmth and comfort. Sadly, some of the others had few visitors. The good thing about the Unit was that these guys got to know our families so in this way they also felt connected to outsiders. In recognising the value of allowing families to become closely associated with the Unit the visiting situation was allowed to develop so that visitors could have free access to the place during its opening hours. Prisoners were soon allowed to have their visits in their cells without supervision.

Another development of the visiting was to encourage interested members of the public to come in and see how the place worked, to discuss crime and punishment, law and order or any other topic of interest. One early visitor was Joyce Laing, an art therapist, and she started coming in every week. One day she brought in a small bag of clay for us to fool around with. I know it sounds corny but I did feel something magical happening to me while fingering this clay. I did a portrait of Ben. This was the first time I had ever done anything creative. I could feel the adrenalin pumping; I could feel my insides soaring with pleasure; I could feel the elation of seeing the finished object. Within a short space of time I was involved in sculpture to a serious degree. I was soon working with hammer and chisel on large blocks of stone.

As the months progressed, some of us were beginning to get deeply involved in what we were doing; others were drawing back and beginning to feel threatened by it all. It became apparent that some of the staff didn't want to continue in the Unit as they felt they were losing their authority. On one occasion when Joyce Laing was sitting with us, a senior member of staff stood up and made a startling outburst. He wanted to get out as he didn't like calling prisoners by their first names, and that as a result of working here, he and his family were on tranquillisers. Most of us were surprised at this as he had been making positive suggestions. The truth of the matter was that he, like one or two others, was under considerable pressure from colleagues in the main prison with whom they socialised who were opposed to the Unit.

You see at first, when Ben, Larry and I were brought into the Unit, there was a sigh of relief throughout the prison service that we had been taken out of their hair. But the rumour amongst staff was that the place would only last a few weeks before we got fed up with it and rioted and stabbed staff willy-nilly. However, as time wore on and they saw that this wasn't happening, they then accused the staff of being afraid to say no to anything we asked for. Rumour followed counter-rumour and soon it was being said by outside staff that we were getting breakfast in bed and that the staff were serving us. This resulted in tremendous hostility from prison staff throughout Scotland. The pressures on Unit staff were considerable. They would, for instance, be openly heckled by their colleagues coming through the main gate on their way in. Most stayed in prison quarters within the shadow of the prison walls and the hostility became so intense that as well as the men being given the 'silent treatment', their families were also. On the one hand, this brought the staff and prisoners closer together within the Unit, but on the other hand meant that those who were undecided would say little at our meetings if a progressive suggestion was made.

Despite all of this, progress was being made. Rab was now allowed out on escorted paroles. Ian and Ben were also allowed out under the same conditions. Ben was very much ill-at-ease taking prison officers to his home. After his second visit he refused to take any more. Ian and Rab developed theirs so that they were soon going out on a daily basis. These outings were invaluable to all of us. In giving the prisoners contact with the changing world outside it would eventually assist their readjustment when finally released.

One problem we had was with the Governor, who up until now had remained in the background. He was a man that most of us knew from the old system. He was a Governor Class 4, the most junior rank, working in a place where the Community meeting – staff and prisoners – discussed the day-to-day events and made decisions on them, a situation far different from that in any other prison. As a result he found himself in a sort of no-man's land. He seemed to find it difficult to become a part of the group, so kept himself distant from all of us. He was certainly uneasy in his present position and made no secret of this. He was putting pressure on his superiors to define his role more clearly. But then most of us at times longed for a more black and white situation when we found the going tough in this new place. We all tended to long for the world we knew rather than grasp this new concept and make something of it. The Governor's hesitancy to become a part of what was happening contributed to the split in the staff. Those who were career-minded and who could see the Governor as being influential in this respect, tended to play the game according to him when he was present, and to the rest of us when he wasn't. This was something that we, a nucleus of staff and prisoners, couldn't tolerate. It was my view that in accepting the Unit, one had to be loyal to the concept and the philosophy of it, and not to any one individual. If the staff were being loyal to the

Governor, who appeared to be opposed to the Community decision-making process, then it would be damaging. Equally, if the loyalty of any of the prisoners had been to Larry during the scissors incident, it would have killed off the Unit then and there.

Out of all the people who visited the Unit in those early months it is well worth mentioning Alick Buchanan-Smith, Under Secretary of State for Scotland for the Tory Government. His arrival was a big occasion. It was important that this guy, the first politician to come and see us, should know that what was happening here was unique and indeed was showing the way forward for the entire penal system. He came in surrounded by civil servants and other officials. We made it clear to him that he would get an honest account and not a whitewash, and he said he appreciated this, acknowledging that this sort of thing goes on with people in his position. We made what we thought was a solid case for expanding the concept of the Unit. He agreed but said that he had to play his cards right due to the public attitude over these issues. He felt sure that it would expand. He made it clear that he was hanging his political hat on this place and had great hopes for it and that if we were experiencing any problems we should not hesitate to get in touch with him direct. I was impressed with him. When a minister makes a visit such as this to a prison, he has to inform the local MP and this was Hugh Brown who expressed a willingness to come too. He was a Labour MP and also a man who made a good impression on us. He became a strong and loyal defender of the Special Unit.

Peter Whatmore was the Consultant Psychiatrist to the Unit. A tall, handsome man with a benign manner, he moved around almost like a shadow without real presence. Knowing our hostility towards his profession this low profile was wise. After the initial settling-in period he had a chat with me saying that after a while he would like to do a sort of case history on me. He had approached the others with the same proposition. I told him I didn't want to know and he accepted this. However, we did have interesting discussions about the Unit and he said he would be quite happy to be made redundant from the place if people had no need of him. He visited us on a three sessions a week basis. I found that his views were similar to those of Ken Murray and myself. So in Peter I found an ally. It was important for me to be able to connect to people who were like-minded as they would help me to keep my thoughts clear on what we were doing.

While we were having these discussions, Peter Whatmore frequently suggested that I should keep a personal diary of what was going on within me and the Unit. This struck a chord in me.

Within the Unit hierarchy itself, the official second-in-command was Chief Nursing Officer Walter Davidson. He had twenty odd years' service behind him and had missed the beginning of the Unit because of a serious car accident. He had joined us almost four months after the place opened and was a real asset. Most of us had known him for years in Peterhead Prison where he was looked on as an old traditionalist. It was interesting to watch a man of his service and rigidity try to break into the way of the Unit. Some mornings, he would come on duty looking bedraggled after a long night tossing and turning. All of us could identify with it but in him it was most noticeable and touching.

I was beginning to recognise that the Unit could be a golden opportunity to create a new model for the penal system and would be an important springboard for radical changes throughout. In order for this to happen we had to formulate a realistic and practical concept that could prove its worth. This meant for me, having to make a superhuman effort not to succumb to either group but to remain loyal to myself and what I felt to be right. There was much to learn from the past experiences that all of us had had and this could be used to gain knowledge and understanding of the whole law and order issue. I got tremendous support from Ken and Peter Whatmore at this point, but they were going home each night and having time off whereas I was constantly in it, there was no break for me or the other prisoners. I could not allow my problems of adjustment to effect others. Sometimes I was successful, other times I wasn't. In short, it was bloody hell.

In contrast to me, Ben was more at a disadvantage as he would fluctuate from the relaxed to the tense. We would occasionally sit in his cell where he would lie on his bed all day, full of anger. We tried to talk through what it was that was bothering him but he was so mixed up that he didn't know himself. I was very close to him, but always wondered why he had so much anger bottled up inside him. He felt that he had lost most of his remission, had been given further sentences, had been brutalised by staff and that in putting him in this place they were trying to palm him off, and the truth was that he just didn't want to know. He simply said that he wanted to go back to the world he knew best, the old penal system.

During the process of my coming to grips with the Unit, I began to structure my own day with a series of activities that would help me to survive a very long period of incarceration. Rather than lie passively and wish my life away, I decided that I would continue the fight to stay alive; this time, my tools would be used in a creative and constructive manner.

I got up every morning at 6 am and did some jogging round the small outside yard, then inside to do my weightlifting, yoga and other exercises. I had a punishing routine that gave me strength, stamina and suppleness. I would spend the latter part of the morning on my studies – sociology and psychology. In the afternoon I would do some sculpting and reserve the evening for writing or visitors. When the doors were locked I would do creative writing into the early hours. I was reversing the prison routine by not having enough time on my hands to get the day's activities done. I became a workaholic – this was my drug. Although I tried to keep to my set routine, life in the Unit was such that unforeseen incidents would arise and get priority. Added to this was the fact that we were getting many visitors and as I played a prominent role in the place I would take them around or be deeply involved in the discussions with them.

n March 1974, thirteen months after the Unit had opened, there was a change of government, with Edward Heath being replaced by Harold Wilson. There was jubilation amongst us as we were all sympathetic to the recent miners' cause, and against the three-day working week. But there were also mixed feelings about Alick Buchanan-Smith leaving as he was a genuine person and in regard to the Unit we were sad to see him go. But overall we felt that we were on to a winner with Labour taking over. Normally, it doesn't make much difference who is in power as far as prisons go, simply because politicians tend to shy off them as they are low priority in any government's policy. It was our naive view that the Labour Government would recognise the value and importance of the Unit and use it as a wedge to make inroads for change in the penal system as a whole. At a junior ministerial level within the Scottish Office we had Hugh Brown MP in charge of the prisons, along with agriculture and fisheries. God knows what they had in common but there you are. We were glad to see that it was someone we knew who had the post and who had been in the Unit. I'm sure it was important for Alex Stephen to have as his boss an under-secretary who was sympathetic to what we were doing.

There was no doubt that Alex Stephen was doing all he could to promote the Special Unit. As one of the Unit's founders, his most encouraging innovation was to take one of the large halls in Peterhead Prison and model it along lines similar to the Unit. Clearly he had support of the Governor there. What made this particular experiment so bold was that Peterhead Prison was believed, by both prisoners and staff, to be a place of no hope. A young, energetic Governor was put in charge. It was meeting lots of opposition, just as the Unit was, but was moving along in the right direction.

In addition to this he was planning the new semi-open prison, Dungavel, in a similar way. This meant that there would be a larger model of the Special Unit standing on its own. When it did open, he placed in charge the young energetic Governor from Peterhead Prison. It was very exciting as it meant that others were benefitting from the work we had been doing. The Unit concept was given a further shot in the arm when Alex Stephen informed us that his opposite number in the Home Office was flying up from London to see what we were doing. It seems they were looking for ways to resolve the quite complex problems they were having. They were contemplating an isolation system similar to the Cages in Inverness. Alex advised against it, recommending that they visit the Special Unit. We were told to expect them as their flight was booked. It was cancelled at the last minute. Apparently this was because of inter-departmental wrangles. The Home Office went ahead to implement Control Units which were based on sensory deprivation.

In the midst of all this Alex Stephen put it to us that he was thinking of bringing members of the media into the Unit to see what we were doing and he asked our opinion. We felt that it would be a good idea and an ideal opportunity to put our case to the general public. There was a great deal of discussion on this with varying opinions being expressed. The Department suggested that we should speak to some representatives of the Scottish Information Office. This was the first I had heard of this group but it was explained to us that they are the official government body who deal with the media for all governmental departments. They asked if we could help them write up an official press hand-out which we did.

Concrete moves were made to prepare the way for a press open-day and we were trying to ease them in by doing some P.R. first. There were lots of discussion on this matter. We were protective of the Unit and would have hated to see it torn apart by journalists who had no idea what we were trying to do. We invited the editors of the Scottish press in and although only two came, we made the most of this.

The relationship between the Department and ourselves was good and things were moving along smoothly. We still had regular visits from the various departments within the Prisons Division and even the Parole Secretary had asked me to help him work out a new booklet that they were intending to circulate round the prison system. This sort of thing was indicative of the relationships we were establishing. Knowing that these were the people who really made the recommendations and decisions I missed no opportunity in bringing home to them the plight and conditions in the main system.

This was an important reason for inviting more and more outside visitors to the place. We were actively working to break down the myths that ordinary people tend to believe concerning prisons and the people incarcerated in them. Hugh Brown MP, now Under Secretary of State in charge of prisons was exceptionally good on this as he wrote saying that although he had now become a minister, he would like to keep in touch and come in on an informal basis to visit us. He was a very earthy speaker who liked a good argument and we enjoyed his company. He was a man of the people who was concerned about social issues. Another MP who was less sympathetic to us was Teddy Taylor, also from Glasgow, who was loud in his hardline views on the issue of law and order. Many people said he believed in what he preached though I was never convinced of this. I see him as no more than a 'political illusionist', pretending that there are simple answers to this very complex issue. A wily politician, he seems to cover his underlying thirst for revenge behind a façade of crusading zeal for the public safety.

Another person I was introduced to at this point who would be important to my life was Richard Demarco, the Gallery Director from Edinburgh. He was a small man with a strong personality and a tremendous amount of energy, a one-man tornado. Coming in he moved around, never standing still, always talking. Joyce Laing, Alex Stephen and another departmental official Tom Melville brought him in. Ricky then took over. He walked around my sculptures that were on display, examined and discussed them using words that I was ignorant of. He said, there and then, that he would like to put my work on show at his gallery during the Edinburgh Festival. I was quite happy about this and it was arranged that Larry, who was doing poetry, should have his work displayed alongside it. An exhibition of my works was something that I hadn't thought about, though I was excited by it. I had been doing these sculptures and putting them on shelves in the Unit and now had a good collection. The next logical step was an exhibition but as it was all new to me there hadn't seemed to be a next step, until now.

On the day of the Press Open Day, we all made the necessary arrangements, including the making of tea and sandwiches. We were told that there were so many they would have to be split into two groups, one in the morning, the other in the afternoon. Some of the younger representatives of the Scottish Information Office were present and they seemed very nervous, more than we were. In the morning group, we split them up and everyone helped to take them round, while the SIO stayed hot on our tails, listening to every word and in a constant state of agitation. We then sat down to have a question and answer session. We had agreed to be as open and honest as we could and try not to hide anything, even the warts. We felt proud of what we were achieving here and were quite prepared to talk about it and stand up for it. During the discussion one journalist asked what was the most serious issue we had had to face to date and I began to tell him about the scissors incident and how we had handled it. I happened, at this point, to catch sight of one of the SIO representatives and he looked as though he was going to have a fit. He was shaking his head from side to side so blatantly that all of us were sure that the journalists must see it. The fact was that the SIO wanted us to play a nice safe game and not give the media anything they could get their teeth into. I believe that they wanted the media to get as little information as possible and that they disapproved of this type of session.

On this occasion I think that the journalists, on the whole, reciprocated our honesty. One of them made the point, in reference to my sculpture and the brief chat we had, that he found it hard to accept that I possessed anything other than violence. Another, who had attended most of my trials, thought that nothing could be done with guys like me. One of them said that he had just completed a pre-recorded TV programme in which he had put across the view that no murderer could be rehabilitated, but during our discussion he had come to realise how wrong he was and he now retracted all he had said. The one newspaper that didn't come in was *The Scotsman* and an SIO guy told us that they had refused on principle because they would not submit their articles to the SIO for vetting prior to publication. This certainly endeared me to this newspaper as in my view the interference of the SIO is an infringement of the freedom of the press. It was through examples such as this that I was gaining more and more insight into the subtle controls that exist in our so-called 'free society'. After the question and answer scene, I was interviewed by journalists, as were Larry and the other prisoners.

In the afternoon, we had a similar situation to the morning. One journalist remarked that he was totally against gangsters and the like but since speaking to me, if he could, he would take me to his home that night. It was all good stuff and somehow we felt we had made a breakthrough. That night, exhausted, I lay in bed. The reports wouldn't be out till the following week as they had to be given a going over by the SIO who said they would keep us in touch with what the articles were like, as they received them. Throughout the next week, the SIO guys called in giving us the latest. By now all their nervousness was gone as they were over the moon at the quality of the reports even from the 'gutter press'.

The newspaper reports came out and were unanimous in applauding the Unit, saying what a good experiment it was. The SIO phoned, with a big sigh of relief, to say how pleased they were. In conversation we were told by them that they had had to advise the newspapers to drop one or two things from their copy, on the grounds of security. The same representative remarked that on the whole the press were self-regulatory, knowing what the SIO expected of them. It seems that this subtle censorship on prisons is adopted because the media as a whole are dependent on them for a mass of government information. On this occasion it worked to our benefit but I was made aware that this was a case of the tail wagging the dog.

With all this going on, I was told in confidence that the present Governor would be getting transferred shortly and that we would be getting a new one. I think this was welcome news to both him and us as it just wasn't working out. Although it was becoming quite an emotional issue amongst us all, we felt that a parting of the ways was best for all concerned. It was soon after this that our new Governor arrived.

Just before the Festival exhibition, the BBC and ITV television companies were given permission to come in and do documentaries on the Unit. The directors came to see us and explained exactly what their thoughts were, and asked us for ours. Because of the recent publicity, the Department was being inundated with requests from overseas, from journalists and television people, to come in and see the Unit. Within the next four weeks, three different television programmes were made. But the climax to this whole period came when I was told that I would be allowed to visit the Edinburgh Festival to see my work on show. I just couldn't believe it. The psychological jump that was needed to leap from being a no-hope person to someone walking the streets for a day was too much to accept.

On the morning of the 15th August '74, I labelled all my sculpture, crated it, and with the help of two members of staff, put it in the van and we drove it through to Edinburgh prison where the final selection was to be made. We off-loaded it and then went into the city. The elation I felt at my feet touching the first street pavement in many years was a shock. Here I was walking along the street, almost as though I was in a dream. I had lain awake all night expecting someone to shout through my cell door that it had been cancelled, but no. Just simply seeing people and being with them outside the walls of the prison was wonderful. I watched cars passing by, people going about their everyday things, unaware that I was looking at them enviously. We walked along to the Demarco Gallery where we met all the artists I had been introduced to from there. The reception was fantastic. All of us went to the well-known Henderson's Restaurant for a meal and then to a pub for a beer but I went outside and stood there alone at the doorway as I wanted to watch all these everyday things. I stood there, alone with my thoughts, letting my mind think over the past eight years and what I had been through in prison, and yet here I was, standing in a busy street, alone, but knowing I was returning to prison in the evening. It was a strange experience but much as I abhorred prison, there was no way that I would have done anything impetuous or silly to harm the Unit or the future which I now felt I had. If anything, my standing there in the street with these thoughts was proving the success of the Special Unit.

Later in the day, I went with a girl to the private view of the Paul Klee exhibition in Edinburgh's Botanical Gardens. While there, I was introduced to many other artists. We then walked through the gardens to see the Henry Moore sculpture, *Reclining Figure*. This was the first sculpture that I had really seen and I let my hands run over it, caress it, putting the upper part of my body inside it. We returned to meet the two staff members and drove back through the busy streets of Edinburgh on our way to Glasgow and prison.

That night, I lay in bed afraid to go to sleep and blot out the events of the day. I was so alive within myself that every fibre of my whole body seemed to be tingling. All that had happened was now a kaleidoscope of images in my head. On two occasions during this Edinburgh Festival period I was allowed out on the same basis. It was a fantastic morale boost for me. There was now real hope injected into my life again.

Alex Stephen told us that Larry's poems were being favourably commented on at the Festival and that a publishing company had approached him about the possibility of publishing them. Larry was asked what he felt and he said he was interested so it was arranged that the publishers be brought in. This was a tremendous boost for Larry. He was making an effort to come off his drugs and the fact that he was gaining recognition as a writer came at the right time. All of this was bringing him to the point of trusting the people around him.

On the subject of publishing material, I spoke to Alex saying that I would like to write about my life, thinking along the lines of an autobiography. He informed me that the Department were looking into this and encouraged me to continue in the hope that something might come of it.

Within the Unit, generally speaking, there was a sense of achievement amongst everyone. The morale of the staff was very high as they felt the work they were doing had some purpose, they were seeing an end product. This was very rare within the penal system. Their recommendations were very progressive. They put forward a proposal which was accepted, that prisoners could have access to the phone. They took the view that as visiting conditions were open and most of the prisoners were going out on daily paroles the natural extension of this should be the availability of the telephone. Each of these freedoms that we were given had to be used responsibly. If we abused any of them then the matter would be reviewed and curtailed. In doing this they were throwing the responsibility on to us.

One day the Governor told me that the SIO were on to him as the local press were making enquiries asking if I had been out at the Edinburgh Festival two weeks before. I spoke to Tom Melville, the Department official, on the phone and he told me not to worry or lose sleep over it as it would be okay. There were small factual pieces on the front page of two daily newspapers. A few days later it was followed up in another paper with Teddy Taylor quoted as saying he was writing to the Secretary of State for Scotland about this. I shouldn't have been shocked but I was. What did they want? Here I was, still in prison, but behaving responsibly. Is this not what people should be looking for from people like me? No one had thought to say how well behaved I was when out. I was left feeling that all people like Teddy Taylor wanted to do was to crush me into some sort of merciless submission. In addition to this Joyce Laing told us that two people from the press had approached her, offered her money, and tried to get her to say that sexual orgies and drinking parties took place in the Unit. One of them asked if it was true that I had given a social worker a child. Teddy Taylor had written a letter to the Secretary of State alleging that he was receiving alarming rumours from a source saying that girls were coming in and out of here as well as the allegation that a social worker was pregnant. In the letter he only made a brief reference to my being allowed out on parole.

It was at this point that a major row broke out among the Executive Committee of the Scottish Prison Officers' Association of which Ken was a member. The Committee issued a statement to the media saying that prisoners in other prisons were assaulting staff to precipitate their transfer to the Special Unit. Ken told them that this just wasn't true and asked if they had been to the Department for the official figures of assaults since the Unit opened. The General Secretary of the Scottish Prison Officers' Association hadn't been but he insisted on publishing the statement just the same. Ken said he was disassociating himself from it and said that he would like to make a public statement to this effect and they agreed to this. The result was that both Ken and John Renton appeared on television to be interviewed on the matter. Ken had the official figures which showed that the amount of assaults on staff had greatly decreased since the opening of the Unit. There was tremendous anger against Ken from some of his colleagues for showing disloyalty to his Executive Committee colleagues and as a result of this, he was expelled from the Committee. Ken is a born negotiator and thinker and it was crystal clear that in expelling him, the prison staff had cut off their noses to spite their faces. No one amongst them could equal him. Ken himself was deeply hurt by this and very bitter at having been treated in this manner. He wanted the Committee to be a leading force in advancing public thinking away from the usual sterile arguments surrounding crime and punishment. From our own selfish point of view, we knew we were now without a voice in this important policy-making body.

Added to this, Tom Melville appeared in the Unit and announced that Alex Stephen was to be transferred to another department in the Civil Service to take over the Scottish Devolution issue at Dover House in Whitehall. His successor was to be Mr John Keely who was coming from Planning – Roads Division, with no experience of prisons whatsoever. This was quite a stunning blow to us but at this point we didn't realise just how much it would affect us. Tom offered some reassurances by saying that he was to be promoted to Senior Executive Officer and that he would have the ear of the Director, but this wasn't much of a consolation to any of us. The only touch of humour at this point was my receiving a letter from a crank, addressed to Babyface Boyle, and she offered to come and sing for us.

We were informed that the man taking over Alex Stephen's position, John Keely would not be directly responsible for the Unit but that this would be handed over to Mr John Oliver. Now Oliver was a man who had come from the prison service as a basic grade officer, and worked himself up to Governor and now found himself in a very powerful position. For obvious reasons the post Alex Stephen held was to be divided in two, with John Keely as Controller of Administration, and John Oliver as Controller of Operations. The fact that someone who was steeped in prison tradition was now responsible for us left us in a state of more than a little trepidation for the future operating of the Unit. I had come to know Oliver over the years in prison. He was Inspector of Prisons when I had been kept inordinately long periods in the Inverness punishment wing.

We arranged a farewell lunch party for Alex Stephen, inviting some guests in. It was a moment of false gaiety for us as we felt as though some giant force was manipulating the wind of change against us from behind the scenes. After lunch Alex spoke to the prisoners individually and he came to my cell to have a talk. He said that a lot of responsibility would weigh heavily upon me. I asked him what was on hand for me. He went on to say that my escorted paroles would continue. He mentioned that there had been some controversy over them and that David McNee, Chief Constable of Glasgow and later Commissioner of the Metropolitan Police in London, had been on to the Department about it but had been told, diplomatically, to stick to his job and let the Department get on with theirs. He then revealed to me that he had seen me in Inverness, looked at me through the spy-hole into the Cage lying there unconscious, shortly after the riot. He felt ashamed of what they had turned me into. It was an emotional scene between us. In each of us was the unspoken question – what was going on? The Community was seeing first hand the very civilised way in which the System disposes of its radicals.

Alex pointed out things that I should bear in mind. I took them seriously. He said that the Unit and its future were pretty secure as we had a number of influential visitors who supported the place and we had had very wide, successful press coverage. He said, wisely, that only the prisoners could blow it, or provide the ammunition. I took this very much to heart. In telling me this Alex Stephen was warning me of the opposition we would meet when he moved on. I made sure his words and advice were taken seriously.

Most of the prisoners were having plenty of personal visitors as well as outsiders coming to see the Unit. I had my family, and most of my other visitors were from the art world. I had more or less lost contact with the people I used to go around with on the outside. I was moving into new spheres of understanding and so was rapidly changing. On the other hand, both Larry and J.C. had friends up to visit them that they had made in prison which meant that some of the local criminals from Glasgow started coming in and I was apprehensive about this. During my spell in the Unit I could have had a great number of guys like these in to see me and in fact had refused quite a lot who had asked. It's not that I didn't like them but simply that the emphasis of my life had changed. There was also the fact that I knew the Glasgow scene and how if the police got to know, and no doubt they would, then they would automatically assume that they were bringing other things with them. These guys could have made problems had this been the case, but it would have been more from sympathy and misguided loyalty than badness.

Larry and J.C. found themselves getting into this scene but felt they were out of their depth as they didn't know how to talk to the guys on this level and so they approached me to speak to them. I had to explain that the Unit was a different scene and that it wasn't on to abuse the trust we'd been shown. The amazing thing is that the guys respected it and this to me was heartening. It would be silly to say that none of us ever had a drink in the Unit as that would be a lie, but it had to be discreet and not too often. It had to be done in such a way that the staff didn't know. My own view was that if I was asking prisoners, who were in prison and had been for many years, to exert self-discipline and try to accept responsibility, then I shouldn't expect them to be superhuman.

On writing this I feel trepidation knowing that those hypocritical sections of our society interested in sensationalism will make meat of this revelation to justify their allegations of drinking parties and orgies in the Unit. But such was not the case. Comparatively speaking, the Unit was a model of restraint and good sense when put beside the abuses that exist in the main penal system. There, drugs, drink and sexual exploitation play a considerable part in day-to-day activities.

Rab, by now, was going out every day to do 'community work' in the Citizens' Theatre. Ian was breeding budgies and still going out on paroles but on the whole he was a loner. He would go into deep depressions and lie in his cell for days on end. He should have been getting help in a psychiatrically orientated hospital setting. J.C. was still going out daily and had been home to his mother's house in the Shetlands. Both he and Rab were awaiting decisions from the Parole Board. The strain of this was apparent in them.

I was heavily involved in my sculpture and had a boost on hearing that the Director of the ICA in London had seen my work and was keen to exhibit it. I hadn't really thought of other exhibitions so this was a pleasant surprise. There was also a request for me to speak to a group from the Howard League for Penal Reform and the Governor said he would support this.

When my case for getting out was put to the Department on 1st October '74, they were hesitant, saying that I wouldn't get a day out until the following summer as the Chief Constable (David McNee) had sent them a letter and they had to be careful. They accepted totally that there was no problem in terms of security and knew I wouldn't do anything silly, but they would like to have a 'cooling off' period. I found it difficult to comprehend that the Chief Constable could influence the Prisons Department to this extent. It was something that Alex Stephen had told me had been sorted out.

Whatever happened at that fateful meeting between Wattie, the Governor and the Department people, it certainly wasn't to our good. There was a distinct feeling within the Community that our activities were being looked on as subversive in some way. There was a wind of change in the air, and no mistake about it. Information started to seep through the grapevine that Alex Stephen had been doing things without informing the Department. We found this very hard to accept. In certain circles of the hierarchy, the new trend seemed to be that anything that Alex Stephen touched stank. The flow of visitors from the Department swiftly dried up and communication with them became somewhat restricted.

As though to reflect the changes at the top, things began to fragment within. There was a bad scene between the Governor and those members of staff committed to the Unit. The Governor was having difficulty accepting that Ken was their recognised leader. He said he was too involved with the prisoners and that staff couldn't trust him. It was clear that Ken had become a target. Word was shifting through to us from the Department that we had moved too fast too soon, that prisoners had too much say in the running of the place, and too much freedom. The Governor was in the unfortunate position of being the man in the middle, which wasn't a problem when Alex Stephen had been keeping regular contact with the Community, but now this was gone, a more cautious regime was there and the emphasis had clearly shifted.

Until the point that I entered the Special Unit I was considered a product of a failed social and penal system. From the age of twelve I had been in and out of institutions, some of which were considered the harshest and toughest in the country. Since that age I had spent twelve and a half months on the outside, never sustaining freedom for more than three months at any one time. On looking around me I could see many others with similar backgrounds. Institutions as they exist at the moment are a danger to the community. They simply harden attitudes and make prisoners more dependent by taking away all responsibility. When locked behind the walls prisoners are forced to depend on each other. They will band together to beat the system, sometimes for the most commendable reasons: to help someone smuggle out a personal letter to a wife, for instance, when their marriage is under considerable pressure. They share books, magazines and tobacco. By the same token they will share techniques in crime and make new contacts. When feeling the pain of their confinement at its deepest level they have to listen to politicians, the media, and public, calling for tougher sentences and prison regimes. However, when being critical of this traditional system one must be able to offer a constructive alternative and in this I will nail my colours to the mast at the outset of this book.

Penal reform does not mean an easier time for prisoners and I hope the following pages make this point quite clear. There can be no punishment more severe than the loss of one's freedom. If we work from this premise then we should be gearing our system to making offenders more responsible people so that on release they will be capable of playing a useful role in society. How do we do this? First, we have to accept that some individuals, because of their irresponsible behaviour and danger to others, have to be taken out of society for a period of time. Once they are inside we must try to understand why they resorted to, say, violent behaviour; from the understandable though unacceptable domestic murder to the more complex sadistic killing. Our learning from such incidents will be invaluable in building up knowledge and perhaps preventing similar ones. At this and other levels the prison system would be making a valuable contribution towards crime prevention.

We should make our prisons more accessible so that members of the public could go inside and discuss crime with prisoners. It may be that they would want to confront them directly as a result of offences in which they have been the victim. Prisoners who never really see the effects of their offences would be made to think more deeply about it. They should have more access to their families: a wife having to cope with a family and household responsibilities would allow the prisoner to share the emotional trauma that his irresponsible behaviour had left her with. The full burden of the offence would be brought home to the offender. In doing so it would introduce an outside perspective into the heart of the institution.

We should ensure that the day-to-day running of the system is geared to making people more socially responsible. How do we go about it? We should be building up people's confidence in small things: cooking, how to budget and manage the small finances they will have to live on, how to articulate and discuss their needs and problems without resorting to violence. We should be teaching people how to drink in moderation which would mean having supervised access to alcohol. They should be allowed to have sex, and to share their feelings with a partner at an intimate level. The prison authorities should be making every effort to link the prisoner to a group of people making a positive contribution in the area he is returning to. This would mean the prison system running along lines parallel to society, the dividing line being the wall that surrounds the institution.

As for the more complex cases, and it should be remembered that these make up a very small percentage, there should be Special Units for them. They need a highly skilled and specialised regime; one that can help unravel their deep needs and problems. In saying that their crimes are bizarre and often outrageous, I am quick to add that they are human beings, and much as we are revolted by their misdeeds we still – for the sake of humanity – must learn from them. What made them do what they did? Only they can tell us, or can they? At least we should be attempting to find out. In removing people from our society we should bear in mind that we are exercising a powerful punishment. The least we can do is ensure that all of us learn from it.

I began to keep a detailed diary of what was going on in the Unit. In the process I took copious notes of daily events. Publishing the diary seemed the best way of telling the story, since it is a record of my thoughts and reactions to each day, not judged with hindsight and distorted through time. All of this has shaped my past and present experience into a vision of what the penal system should be.

2

Speak not so loudly
For I am in pain
your voice's sharpened edges
Are cutting my brain

Larry Winters

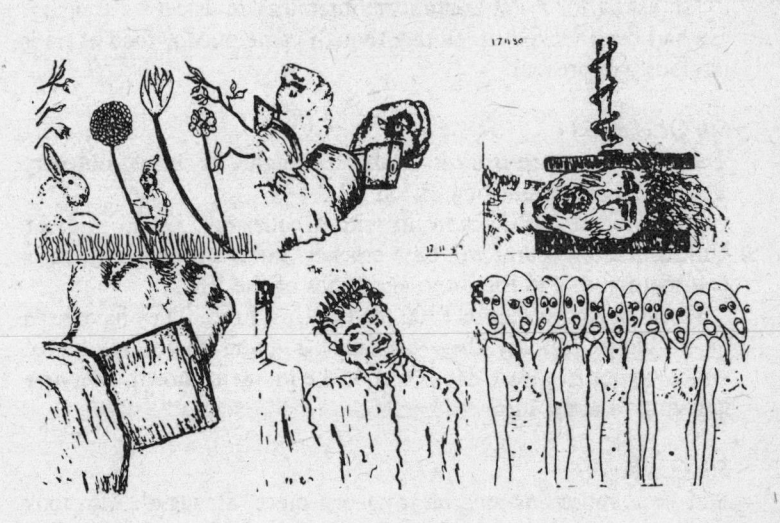

28th September '74
Rab went out with a staff member today and had a good day. Larry isn't sleeping too good and had to get his drugs increased. He is on a lot of drugs and I'd like to see him reduce them...

3rd October '74
This morning I went straight into my studio/cell and cast the two pieces I was working on. I was in there till 4pm.
  Rab went out to work at the Cits [Citizens' Theatre] today and J.C. went out for groceries.
  Ian asked for a Petition and is intending to ask for a transfer. He had been locked up all day though came out for food as he is obviously depressed.

5th October '74
Took my sculpture from its cast – 'Struggle'. It turned out very well. I did some finishing off on it.
  David Scott (BBC) came in with a colleague. David said the Unit film is okay and will be a cracker. He is putting it off for a few months due to the internal politics of the BBC.
  World in Action sent us £100 for the Unit fund. They have been okay. James Lindsay (new prisoner) is going about bewildered and is trying to adjust. He is lost at the moment though everyone is trying to assist him.

6th October '74
Did some more finishing on my latest piece 'Struggle'. Also took 'Mantrap' from its cast and it looks good. Spoke to James Lindsay quite a bit today. He is still very much at a loss and will take a bit to settle. He stands about not knowing what to do.
  Larry is doing fine but is in a bit of a drugged state. I told him he should reduce them and he says he will. He had a visitor today and I sat in with him.

7th October '74
Did my usual exercise routine this morning. 7.45am – something made me go over to close Larry's cell door as I was about to punch the heavy bag, but peeping in, I found him lying naked and unconscious on the floor behind the door. There was hardened mucus around his nose and mouth. I pulled and slapped him but he wouldn't move and was very cold. I lifted him on to the bed

and ran for the medical staff. The doctor came in and examined him, taking blood pressure, etc. He was rushed out to hospital.

I felt terrible at seeing Larry in this condition. He is now in the Intensive Care Unit and is still unconscious. Everyone is very depressed and feeling lousy. At 4.30 the Governor returned from the hospital saying that Larry may not recover.

Ken came in later in the evening saying that Larry had recovered consciousness and that the doctors said that he had taken a massive overdose. It is thought that he was keeping drugs back from his official dosage and took them all at once.

8pm: Larry reacted violently and started a fight with those around him and pulled the tube from his nose. Another member of staff was detailed to go to hospital, making three in all.

I went into my studio/cell and did some sculpting until 6.30, working in a frenzy, under a cloud of total depression, thinking, after the Governor's statement at 4.30, that Larry would die. I created my first tender piece of sculpture. It was a weight lifted from my shoulders when Larry regained consciousness.

For some reason, Ian seems to be jealous of the attention being given to Larry as he told me he is going to do the same. I gave him a telling off and he got embarrassed.

8th October '74
It was a case of waiting all morning to hear any latest developments concerning Larry. He had a peaceful night and was to be brought back at 2.30 pm. His mother came with him in the ambulance.

The Governor called me from the Community meeting to say that everyone was relying on me to help Larry as I was closest to him. Mrs Winters, her husband, and one of her sons came in, with Larry on a stretcher. Mrs Winters fainted, obviously she had been through a harrowing experience.

Larry, still a bit dozy, embraced me. . .

9th October '74
Did some casting this morning and sat speaking to Larry. He said, 'Trying to die isn't easy.' We discussed suicide and he admitted doing it and said he wrote a note of some sort.

I discussed this with the Governor and Ken, as Larry may try it again. Ken was saying that Mrs Winters told him that Larry was very depressed because I was allowed out to the Festival and he wasn't.

Today Larry said that the screws beat him up in the hospital. It's clear to me that Larry's mind is very disturbed and that he is crying out for help. He is also acting strange in the presence of J.C. I think he is playing out the brain damage bit. I could be wrong as he may be bad but he is always okay in my presence. One of the staff on his way into the Unit was told by one of the main prison staff that Larry had been to hospital. The Unit staff member asked 'Is he bad?' He was told, 'He can't be as he's still breathing.'

James Lindsay is helping to prepare the lunch today though is still a bit lost but settling in okay.

2nd November '74

Larry and I discussed the 'silent scream' – that moment when one is alone in the locked cell facing the full horror of confinement. Those of us who have experienced long periods of confinement immediately recognise the torturous 'silent scream', but rarely talk about it. Larry said that in finding himself in one of these moments, the futility of his position crept up on him and he felt that continuing was a waste of time. Prior to Alex Stephen leaving, Larry was reduced from 'A' to 'B' category. He was so suspicious of the system that he looked on the reduction to 'B' category as just another ploy, part of the whole psychological game of the Unit. He still hadn't come to accept that we could work positively to change the system. My relationship with Larry was still linked to our old prison life but always I was trying to use our new life in the Unit to get him to see the potential. He often made it clear that what he didn't like about it was that it took away the only weapon he had had in the old system, the power that he could wield through the use of fear. He would, on occasions, revert to this in the Unit, using words and almost theatrical gestures, but this was acceptable as it was a big improvement and a step forward from actual physical violence. Time would be the only thing that would completely eliminate this. Obviously, the important ingredient was his being in a place that wouldn't give credence to his suspicions. The difficulty was in getting Larry to have some belief in his own talents as he was an exceptionally intelligent man and a gifted poet and musician.

2nd December '74

This morning I went into the joinery room and built a cage and doll's house. I was in there nearly all day.

Ken came back from holiday. Peter Whatmore also returned from a month in Broadmoor. Arthur Dooley, the sculptor, called me to say he will visit me this Sunday.

Larry and J.C. were in a fight in Larry's cell. I was sitting in my cell with Ken and Bob Riddell (staff member) discussing the next issue of our magazine *The Key*. There was a rumpus and a staff member ran past my door downstairs. He got to Larry's door, saw the fight and was about to go for assistance when I went in and broke it up. A meeting was called. Larry said it was his fault. After a discussion the Community accepted their explanation and let it end there.

It's very good to notice that the Community is maturing and keeping such incidents in perspective.

Tom Melville phoned through and is perturbed about two articles in the forthcoming issue of the magazine. One is Gerry Ryan's (staff member) poetry. He feels if Gerry is identified it could ruin or affect his career. Gerry wrote a poem about prison life in the main system and it was very good. The other article is by Prof. Shelly Killen, a visiting art historian, who has been equally blunt.

4th December '74

I went into my studio/cell early this morning and cast two pieces. David's head and a two-figure form. I was in there till 4pm and am dead beat tonight.

The Governor said that he has been asked for a Parole dossier on me. This is normal procedure after seven years of a life sentence. There is a lot of narkiness amongst the prisoners, me included, and this seems to come in cycles. I think it happens as we get fed up looking at each other. Jim Gillespie (staff member) approached me today saying he would give the prisoners £1 every week to eat lunch with us! We agreed to this.

9th December '74

Ken, Larry and I put up the Christmas decorations today. Larry stripped the wallpaper from his cell and Rab is papering it.

The Governor gave me my Parole representation for my 1st Review. He remarked that he didn't think I would want to fill it in. I told him I would. My representations are:

That this paper is an exercise in futility as will be the ones following it, for a good number of years. Being in the Special Unit has given me the proper atmosphere to reflect on the past and I realise the futility of it equals that of this paper. The inner change of an individual may be seen on a superficial level but can never be measured in depth. Therein lies your problem, one that will be with you for many years.

This representation has some value in that it allows me to record that on three occasions this year I have been permitted to make, with an escort, visits to Edinburgh on an educational basis. It should be noted that on these occasions I mingled freely with members of the public and acted responsibly at all times.

I was, and am, aware that parole by your board is a long way off but must emphasise that I found tremendous value in the educational/social aspects of these days out and at no time did they delude me into thinking I would get an early release. I fully understand my situation and am aware of the position. However, I re-emphasise these trips did much for me as a human being. Having reciprocated the trust shown in me by the Unit Community and the Prisons Department I certainly hope this practice will continue.

19th December '74

This morning I lost my cool with Walter and gave him a blasting. It was my fault and completely uncalled for. It was over the daily papers that hadn't come in but I was fed up anyway when I got out of bed. After falling out with Walter I went to my studio to work on the casts. Later I went round to apologise and both of us aired our points of view. Dr Neil Smith was in touch with the consultant who can't take me into hospital (for my cartilage operation) till 6th January. The police have to be informed and two staff have to be with me at all times. John Oliver says he can appreciate the Unit's feeling in only wanting one staff at the hospital with me but they have to watch in case of political repercussions if this got out.

25th December '74

Sat up till twelve listening to carols last night. The first time I have done this as I usually get to sleep as soon as possible. Felt very emotional.

This morning Larry brought me breakfast in bed. J.C. went to Aberdeen for the day.

Ian stayed in his cell all day as he was feeling bad about Christmas. Rab was the same, though he came out, but took no part in activities. I put a face on today but was emotionally disturbed, so much so that I was surprised at the strength of it. Wanted away on my own to think things out but couldn't as everyone was hanging around.

4th January '75

Larry came in with a magazine, *Bananas*, published by Emma Tennant. One of his poems is published in it. He is delighted.

A senior policeman phoned Ken about my going to hospital. Ken told him they don't want an escort but was merely informing them. The policeman asked what was wrong with me and when told replied, 'It should have been his fucking neck'. Larry didn't get his visit today.

6th January '75

Larry was on his pills heavy last night and is really down at the moment. I spoke to him about it but he slung me a deafy. He had a mild clash with Wattie prior to my leaving the Unit.

I am writing this in hospital, left the Unit at 9.40am with Bob Riddell and Bob Malcolm who will do a twelve-hour shift throughout the day being relieved by two other staff at night.

We stopped at my cousin's shop and I collected some fruit and then went for a coffee at the restaurant across from the hospital. I sat there amongst all those people like any one of them and yet not so long ago I was, and still am sometimes, labelled by the media 'Scotland's Most Violent Man'. It somehow makes nonsense of the whole thing.

I sit here speaking to other patients around me and though they see the two Bobs with me they don't fully comprehend yet, and as we are so friendly to each other they wouldn't imagine we were jailer and jailed. My leg was shaved and I was told to go to the bathroom and have a bath. During my absence a nurse approached Bob to tell him to keep an eye on me as I may not go for a bath (meaning that I may go out of the window). Bob told her it was okay and just sat where he was.

After lunch I was given a change of bed and screens were put around me. This isolated the three of us from the rest of the ward.

MERRY CHRISTMAS
BATTERED BODIES BROKEN BONES
BURIED FEARS FLEE THEIR OWN;
CHASING HOUNDS BAYING SOUNDS
PARTING FLESH ESCAPE THE MESS;
GNASHING TEETH BRITTLE BITE
RUNNING FEET ESCAPE TO FIGHT;
AS WE FORAGE THROUGH THE
JUNGLE OF LIFE
8
THE CUSHIONED LANDING...
SITTING ALONE AMID BROKEN DREAMS
I SEE YOU IN THE DISTANCE
A GROPING HAND WITH STRETCHING
FINGERS
SEARCH THE LANDSCAPE WHILE
YEARNING LINGERS
HEARTFELT PAIN CRUEL
DISMAY
HANG HEAVY THIS XMAS
DAY

I asked Bob R. to speak to the Sister about this but he took fright saying they usually run their wards with an iron hand. I jumped out of bed and approached the tall, formidable lady and asked her if it was necessary as it made me feel like a black guy in the Deep South. She gave the okay for it to come down, much to my relief. Lying in this bed I feel very much the prisoner with two staff at my side. Patients around me are casting furtive glances when they think I'm not looking. I don't like this sort of treatment but I intend facing up to it.

Invisible chains are holding me.

7th January '75
Didn't sleep last night as the ward was very noisy and the mattress too soft.

J.C. and Bill Allen came down to visit and said Larry is acting up in the Unit and is on the verge of ruining the place. Wattie, Ken, the Governor and changes in the shifts also confirmed fears about Larry. It was agreed between the two Bobs, Ken and myself that I sign myself out of hospital if Larry doesn't improve.

I had had my operation by this time and was in great pain but it went okay.

It seems to me that everyone is terrified. Apparently a meeting was called and Larry asked to be sent away. Davy (staff member) and some others agreed to it. Larry tore out a page in the Minute Book and took a sort of brainstorm, apparently grabbing the Governor by the tie.

Ken said that Larry should stay and Davy cracked up, shouting at Ken, swearing at him and calling him a lot of names, insisting that Larry be put to Carstairs or Peterhead. A decision was made – staff and prisoners agreed that Larry be put away. There was complete panic in the place.

Wattie came down telling me that I mustn't sign myself out of hospital as things were okay.

8th January '75
Spent a restless night which resulted in the nurse giving me an injection to kill the pain. The Governor came in to see me today and we discussed Larry saying that he might need to lock him up (solitary). I told him that I thought this would make matters worse and he agreed. I still feel that he would have carried it out though.

I am getting physiotherapy treatment and my leg is much better for it.

10th January '75
Had a good few hours' sleep last night and felt better for it. Did exercises this morning and managed to lift my leg off the bed. David Scott (BBC) came up and we had a good chat. We discussed the Unit and the latest crisis so he will go up this morning and talk to Larry.

The Governor came down but was quite evasive. Later Bob told me that apparently a kitchen knife in the Unit is missing and there is a lot of suspicion going around. It seems a staff member has taken it but no one knows his motives.

The police called the hospital to ask if I was still in, then asked the nurse to keep them informed.

11th January '75
The Sister came round this morning and told Bob M. that there was a piece in the *Daily Record* about me. I was dreading this. The newspaper article was front page and says that a patient's family is concerned about my being in the same ward as him. I feel terrible lying here having to face these people, almost as though I am some alien from another planet.

Once the newspapers circulated the ward, there was a strong reaction from the patients who were angry at the *Record*. 'Cheap journalism' is what they called it. The reports were taken up by television and radio and our 'dial-a-quote' MP, Teddy Taylor, was reported as saying that I should be locked away in a room, separated from ordinary patients. This had the patients fuming and they all signed a petition which was sent to the newspapers. They spoke to Radio Clyde stating how they are being used and going on to say that I had a first-class relationship with everyone in the ward. I am so glad of this as it once again shows me how papers like this have no hesitation in exploiting situations like this.

David Scott came in saying that he had been to see Larry and told him I was disappointed in him. David heard most of the story from Wattie as he drove him home, about Larry grabbing the Governor by the tie and spitting in a staff member's face. David is going to try to get to know Larry better as he recognises that he is lonely.

13th January '75
There was a radio comment on my being in hospital and the controversy. It mentioned the patients writing a petition and all of them signing it stating that the *Daily Record* article was untrue. The comment was accurate which is all I ask for. The *Glasgow Herald* printed the content of the patients' petition and also presented the article factually. It lets people see that there is another side to the story. The doctor came round this morning and saw me. I told him I was feeling fine and he said I could go.

There was relief at my entering the Unit, from everyone present, and as I didn't show much warmth to Larry, he went off to his cell. I went in after him.

We had a tense confrontation, with me pointing out that he had gone a long way to damaging the Unit and I asked him why? He said that he didn't know why and at one point he thought he was mental as he couldn't control himself. I told him that the position is that he is the one big question mark in this place and that no one can trust him, that the days of frightening people are over. He sat there accepting it, offering no excuses. I think he is really disgusted with himself.

I called a Community meeting concerning Larry's transfer and how it was a waste of time as no other prison would take him and that in fact he had now thought about it and didn't want to leave the Unit. The staff and prisoners pointed out that in agreeing with his transfer, they had simply responded to the position Larry had put them in.

14th January '75
Larry burst in on Wattie asking for his pills because there were no letters for him. He was expecting one from his girlfriend. I met him coming out of his cell. He was chalk-white and so we went back into his cell where he stood shaking like a leaf. 'Jimmy, I'm cracking up, I feel it, they'll [staff] see me and put me away,' he said, breaking down and crying. I comforted him. He told me he can't cope with this new experience. He has no confidence or drive and thinks he is mentally abnormal.

We sat there till 6.30pm when the pills took effect and he was drugged and began speaking about himself. Ken came up afterwards and sat speaking to Larry for a long time and then came in to my cell and we talked. Ken looked worn and drawn. He is taking too much on himself.

27th January '75
Slithering, sliding through the darkness in search of shadows that flit in and out of my life like seconds in the minute. Creeping, crawling along the passage in search of that which is non-existent as though I am certain of finding it. Feeling, groping, trying to assess what really is. All in the vague hope of surviving. There is a touch of reality about this fantasy so that if one tries hard enough the dream will exist. . .

11th February '75
John Oliver and Tom Melville came this afternoon. We had a discussion on the transfer issue. John Oliver said that the transfers were for the good of both prisoners. Everyone disagreed with this except the Governor. It became clearer as the discussion went on that the Department were acting on the Governor's recommendation. After a prolonged, and at times heated, discussion they agreed to let both remain.

Ken brought up the issue of civilian clothing for staff saying they were still keen to wear it. Previously they had been refused permission because it might stir up trouble amongst the main prison staff. Mr Oliver said he would reconsider this.

Bob Riddell asked him to consider my paroles being continued on an educational basis. Other staff joined in to support this. John Oliver eventually agreed that I could go out for a constructive reason. The Governor surprised us all by stating that I was aware that I could go out on an important sculptural event.

We debated the whole penal system, trying to persuade him to implement what had been learned from the Unit into other prisons. He asked how it could be done and we explained that it could start with the 'A' category men in Peterhead prison, a group that are already segregated to an extent and who are all doing long sentences. He voiced the opinion that if this were done then it would make the other prisoners jealous. We pointed out to him that in most prisons, 'A' category men were already deprived of football, night classes and many other things and that the authorities always seemed to be sensitive to jealousies when it was a case of being more humane, but when responding in a less humane manner there didn't seem to be any problem. We suggested that it should only start with this small group and then most certainly expand it to other prisoners with less trepidation when they didn't need such careful watching.

J.C. had to leave hurriedly to attend his father's funeral in Aberdeen. We, at least, have some good news for him on return.

12th February '75

On the day of our second anniversary we held a lunch, inviting the Director of Prisons and other Department officials. Only Tom Melville appeared besides some outside visitors. The first overt sign of the Department's thinking came when the meal ended. Tom Melville informed the Governor that J.C. and Rab were to be transferred to Saughton Prison in Edinburgh in two weeks time. This was a bombshell and against everything that we were supposed to be doing in the Unit. All of us within the Community believed that if we were to be meaningful at all, in terms of preparing prisoners for release, then we should be able to release them direct from the Unit. J.C. and Rab were visibly shaken at this decision and the remainder of us were astounded at the stupidity of it.

It meant that they would be stopped from going outside on day paroles and that any visitors going to see them in Edinburgh prison would revert to speaking through a glass and wire barrier. It meant that they would be restricted to censored mail and entitled to one letter a week, nine hours visiting time per year, prison uniforms and all the other degrading and humiliating aspects that are a part of that system. They wouldn't be able to speak to the majority of staff in anything other than a subservient way and they'd be constantly ordered about. All responsibility would be taken away from them. If all of this would be an ordeal for J.C. it would be even worse for Rab who had progressed so well in the Unit and we had doubts about his ability to cope with this sort of regime after having been encouraged to adapt to living and working in the outside community. Anyone from the Unit going to a normal prison would find himself subjected to a great deal of hostility because of the attitudes of staff to the place. We felt that it was grossly unfair to subject both these men to this. In addition to this, they were both under 'review' by the Parole Board, hopefully, for a provisional release date which was usually two years in advance. We assumed that when the time came the Community would be consulted on this issue at which point we would ask that they both be released from here. But the Department had taken the bull by the horns and recommended that they be transferred. The Community in turn demanded to see Mr Oliver.

24th March '75
I was with Ken when he phoned Alex Stephen (Dover House, London) about my manuscript *A Sense of Freedom*. Alex said that we should give it straight to the Director and that the Director would get on to a Mr Ford who is a specialist on these matters. He said he feels strongly that prisoners should be able to publish their own material. Alex feels that we should by-pass Mr Oliver and everyone in between and go straight to the Director.

6th April '75
I am in good form, keeping the moments of despondency away by keeping busy.

There are times when I get the urge to move along to the empty cell a few doors away. A big part of me doesn't want to get too dependent on the materialism of this place. I am thinking constantly of this and try never to forget the past. I have to keep re-opening old wounds in order to stabilise myself here. If temptation comes my way, yesterday's memories keep me from succumbing. In many ways my revenge against the system will be in making this place a success. I know this will hurt every pig who took a liberty with me. There are times when I feel my existence seems to be motivated by hatred. I keep having flashbacks of sitting on the bare floor of my previous cells in other prisons where the stench of urine was mixed with everything. There are times when I would like to rest from my physical exercises but I can't. They are a part of my survival kit.

8th April '75
The Governor said that the Unit came in for heavy criticism at the recent Governors' Conference. He said that his colleagues objected to the recent *World in Action* film, and the Unit magazine *The Key*. The editorial in the latter was described as 'Jimmy's editorial'. It was pointed out that the editorial isn't mine but that of the editorial committee. The Governor stated that the message coming across was that the magazine was undoing a lot of the other Governors' work, taking the feet away from the training they are doing. Everyone laughed at this.

He went on to say he was dreading the forthcoming BBC film,

and that in his opinion the press publicity and TV programmes were the worst thing to happen to the Unit...

9th April '75
A social worker and the Assistant Governor from Polmont Borstal came in and we sat speaking to them. I enjoyed the talk as they asked some penetrating questions. They asked the old question that most visitors do: 'Do you ever get fed up talking to people like us about prisons or the Unit?' I replied that we never weary simply because we realise that there are guys living in abominable conditions in the main prison system and we must talk for them. Tonight the Governor came in and asked to see me. On going into his office he had a piece of paper in front of him. He told me that Mr Oliver had a copy of a manuscript purported to have been written by me and the Department had a copy of it. How many copies were there? I conceded that there were two, one that I sent to Alex Stephen and another that my family had. He asked how Alex Stephen got hold of one. I told him I posted it through a friend. The Governor said he had no objection to it being printed but he would like to see it before going to the Department on Friday. I told him I couldn't get it for him tonight but would tomorrow. He replied that it would be his day off but to give it to Wattie and he would deliver it.

I intend making sure that I photocopy the manuscript before giving it to the Governor.

24th April '75
Moods that come and go, fluctuating from bad to good. Going off people without really knowing why. Getting irritated with small things that are really of no consequence. Feeling smothered by the surrounding walls that stand so firm and menacing, feeling so powerful at times that one mighty blow could destroy the walls, and then so weak that I cringe with fear as they overpower me. There is no escape, only confrontation. It is here and now, this very second that is now the past. Why am I locked in? Venus and Mars are at work tonight, each has moments of domination, each taking its toll.

It's 10.30pm and I've spent the whole evening trying to rid myself of something. It seems as though I've wasted a lot of time sitting here, doing nothing, but the truth is I couldn't concentrate on anything else as I must try to understand what is going on inside me. There is something in there pushing like fuck as I remain trapped in this concrete cube, restlessly trying to console the bubbling energy. My thoughts aren't concentrating on the one thing; they move from one subject to the next. I'm sure I could pull the locked door off its hinges if I really tried. I really should do some meditation to rid myself of this restlessness but there is a perverse side of me that wants to examine it, to find out more about it, that wants to sit here and type it out. I am really speaking to myself at this moment, putting it down on paper, all the time realising it's a load of crap. Be that as it may, I still have to face it. I cast an eye to the window and notice the sky is darkening. Saturday night in prison is this: sitting locked up with one's thoughts – reason enough for going stark crazy.

The thin veneer of the outward appearance means nothing – it's what goes on within that counts. Take for instance the screw that goes round every now and again to peep into the judas hole to see if I'm all right. He does this and sees me sitting here typing and says to himself that all is well. He cannot see inside my head, that my thoughts are 'the next time he comes round I'm going to pull out my cock and flash it at him'. It's all so superficial. 'Last night I had a dream, you were in it, I was in it with you...' so goes the song. Reawakens some beautiful memories that song, takes me to a time when I was out of here for a few hours – hours so beautiful that I cherish them. It's now 11.05pm and the night is dark so I may as well go to bed, put the light out and lie thinking what this has been all about...

Thoughts brought to life.

25th April '75
My mind is working overtime on the problem of the book. I asked the Governor this morning for a petition and sent it off to the Secretary of State. In reality it goes to someone in the Prisons Department.

Dear Sir,
The Prisons Department have two copies of an autobiographical manuscript written by me and I would like to know if I could have permission to have it published?

I would like you to know that the prime motivation for my writing the book is to illustrate – using my own life experience – how a child can go from a normal life to become enmeshed in a life of crime. It will be apparent to you that the main theme of the document is the waste of human life and how there is nothing glamorous about the criminal way of life. I don't think I've excused myself in it, nor anyone else, but I feel that this is important in order to help the worsening crime situation.

I do hope you appreciate that the copies the Prisons Department have are rough and untouched for libel, etc. I did feel it only right that you see it in this condition. I would, if you agree to publication, be pleased to accept your advice and assistance on this matter.

Yours sincerely

26th April '75

This morning Ken and I were sitting outside in the yard when Peter Whatmore came in. I asked him about this Crime Council he is on as they are recommending Stop and Search powers, etc. to the police. He tried to give excuses then bolted into his office.

The Governor came in at 10.15am. Ken and he went into his office. Some minutes later Ken came out fuming and told me he is being transferred. I was as stunned as he was. He was given a letter from the Department saying that he is to be transferred to Saughton Prison, Edinburgh. I sat with some of the staff when the Governor came in and joined us. One of them expressed his fears that his prediction made some weeks ago that the Department are intent on 'changing the place' is coming true. The Governor denied this. I told him my opinion is that Ken's transfer is part of a calculated attempt to control the place and that he, along with the Department, are intent on wiping out all that Alex Stephen has achieved. The Governor stood there saying nothing. I feel so utterly sick being near the man as he is so subversive. He hung about all morning trying to ensure that no one started blaming him. It was all in vain for he is being blamed.

My heart went out to Ken as he has done so much for the Unit and lots of us in here. Who could ever imagine that I would be thinking like this about a screw. They seem bent on destroying him. What chance have we of improving the penal system when people resort to strokes such as this?

The Governor came in this afternoon for an hour and stood about not saying a word and looking very much like Judas.

Over lunch I spoke to James Lindsay, Larry and J.C. saying that we must stand by Ken right to the end. They all felt this anyway. Larry wanted to give the Governor an ultimatum but I felt we must wait till Ken says all is ended as we don't want to jeopardise his case at this stage. Whatmore, in speaking to Larry, told him that he is relying on him and me to pull the Unit through this period. There is a lot of suspicion that Whatmore knew about it but that is a matter for debate.

What do we do from here? It is obvious that the Unit is going to be staffed by what the Department call 'more reliable staff'. I must come to a decision as to whether I want to continue in the Unit the way things are going. It seems to me that the Governor and the Department will continue catering for Larry and me. There are indications that the other prisoners will be transferred shortly. At the moment Larry and I are still fresh in the minds of the prison staff in the main system so the pressure on the Department will be bad if there is any talk of moving us back. At the same time I don't want to continue here in a watered-down version of the real thing.

Rumours unofficially circulating say that Jim Gillespie and Bob Riddell are being persuaded to move on to the Nursing Course. They are two decent staff. If this is true then we are in even more trouble.

27th April '75
This morning Ken came in to my cell. He described how his wife woke him up in the early hours crying about his transfer and the diabolical way he is being treated. There is no doubt that everyone is livid at the way Ken is being stabbed in the back. It is not a move to help his career in any way but one to sweep him under the carpet because of his outspoken views. The Governor had a personality clash with him and rather than work it out he made the necessary moves to get rid of him.

Larry had a good visit from his brother. James Lindsay had a visit from his mother. I had my aunt Peggy, aunt Maggie and the kids in. J.C. was in at my visit, playing with the kids. I thoroughly enjoyed it and haven't laughed so much in a long time. Peggy is a real funny person.

Rab had a visit from a couple he met.

Ian sat with the Governor (spew!!!).

The staff are peculiar people. Not long after expressing their disgust about Ken's transfer they were all sitting together discussing who would get promotion and who would take over his duties. They are insensitive people with little loyalty to anyone. I've no doubt that some of them will support Ken a hundred per cent but most of them couldn't care less as they all look to see how it will improve their position.

The Governor came in this afternoon for two hours as Ken had to go off and give a talk to the Penal Reform meeting. He came upstairs with mail for me. I was so involved with my visitors that he took me by surprise. I began to introduce him to my aunties but stopped dead and left him standing there.

29th April '75
This morning I tried to do my Open University but could feel things building up about the forthcoming meeting. Larry was the same as he was in and out of my cell all morning.

At the meeting Kay Carmichael and Dr Keith Wardrop came in. It opened with me saying that the issue with Ken is the only thing I want to discuss. There then developed a lengthy and heated discussion about the whole affair. I blew up telling the Governor that he had been instrumental in putting this into action and that he is a filthy rotten bastard and one of the most dangerous men I know. He has been set on destroying the Unit because he has this personality clash with Ken and that any staff who build up a relationship with prisoners are given the heave. Larry was also heated in his remarks. Ken also expressed the view that the Governor has played a dirty trick.

The Governor gave the impression that he was sorry that Ken was going but that he was subject to transfer just as he himself was. This is absolute rot. Ken asked the Governor to resist his transfer. He said no. The Governor said he felt that a gun was being held at his head. In other words he was saying that Larry and I were threatening to be violent if Ken's transfer wasn't stopped and he wasn't going to act under duress. I told him that I had not threatened violence under these circumstances as I wouldn't be violent in the Unit. Larry rose and walked towards the Governor in a gesture of sheer frustration. Lots of others had their say, unanimously opposing the transfer. The Community stated that they wanted a meeting with John Oliver to discuss the issue with us. I don't want to give an opinion on what effect the meeting or its intensity had on the Governor. I will be watching him like hell.

After the meeting he came up to me and said I am doing him

wrong in judging him on this and was about to tell me how he has fought hard for all of us. Bill Allen (staff member) standing next to me called him a dictator getting rid of him and Ken as he thought they were opposition. Bill told him he was fooling no one. The Governor then went to Larry to speak to him but Larry isn't wearing it.

30th April '75
I went downstairs and saw the Governor making coffee. I challenged him about ruining the whole Community. He said I must believe him, that he wants the Unit to go on and that if he thought the Department were going to close it he would put his resignation in tomorrow. I told him I thought they weren't going to close it but they were going to make life in here so intolerable that trouble would break out and it would inevitably close – that is how they work. I told him that the staff getting transferred were not intimidated by rank but were working in the best way for the Unit and that was why they were 'moving' on or being shanghied. I said that he is the one holding the gun at our heads by threatening to remove staff who oppose him. I walked out and left him sitting there.

Murray Stewart (staff member) caught hold of me and asked if I had words with the Governor. I told him I did. He told me that the Governor will be underestimating the rest of the staff if he thinks that Larry and I are the only ones who will react to the transfer. He candidly expressed that some of them aren't go-getters or for that matter very vocal but they want the Unit to go on the way it has been.

I understand that Kay Carmichael has heard a whisper that I am to be transferred. I am not putting too much on this. Anyway, I am inwardly prepared for it and have been since talk of Ken's transfer. In many respects moving me would be tantamount to murdering me as I know what prison staff in other prisons feel about me.

The fact is, I have never been so fulfilled since I became caught up in the work I have been doing here. I have been using my past experience to help the situation but I have always kept myself aware of the possibility of the whole thing falling through. I knew that if it did then it would be the fault of the authorities.

2nd May '75
The Governor came into my studio with a signed letter from Tom Melville saying that the request by the Community to get permission for me to go out to the Demarco Gallery exhibition has been refused. He told me the Department are concerned that my being allowed out could attract publicity and that this would put pressure on to the Ministers.

5th May '75
This morning I was loathe to get up as it was back to the grind of the bad atmosphere and being faced with false people. I sat outside with Larry trying to do my Open University but couldn't concentrate on it. We sat in the sun as it was a beautiful day. The feelings were very tense inside both of us.

I am being extremely watchful of everything and already see small signs of deterioration creeping in. Larry and I are staying close to each other. The staff are keeping very close to each other too and already they are starting to prepare, a noticeable feature being their going back to carrying their batons. This is the start and from here on in, unless something dramatic happens, it will go from bad to worse.

Malky (staff member) put his resignation in but let me see it before doing so. He explained his reasons, saying that it is due to the Prisons Department and the Governor. He told me he has too much respect for me and would never work under circumstances that would mean screwing me down. Both of us discussed this later and Malky said that only the staff can do it by putting in a block resignation paper to the Department. He says someone approached him to say he is next on the Department list for shanghai. All our outside support is making moves to Harry Ewing, the Labour minister with responsibility for the Unit.

Larry's mother came in this afternoon and told us both not to resort to violence as this is what we are being provoked to do. She says she can't understand why for two and a half years they've allowed this to go on and are now turning back.

6th May '75
I had a long talk with Wattie about the situation and asked him to be more forward on this issue as he only has two years to go till he retires on pension. He replied that after twenty-seven years in the Prison Service he is finding it difficult to question the

Governor and the Department due to conditioned loyalties.

We had our meeting in the yard as the weather was so good. Wattie told the Community that the Governor is off sick for two weeks. This confirms a staff member's comments on some Governors having the ability to Houdini in order to get themselves out of a tight situation. Wattie then told us that John Oliver will come down next week.

I pointed out to the Community that things were reaching a dangerous level and that the two groups, staff and prisoners, have stopped talking to each other and that staff are now carrying their batons. There was a general reluctance at first, by staff, to discuss this. They made excuses, one saying that it is part of the dress. Other staff denounced this. Gerry said he was carrying his because he has been feeling very insecure. Bob admitted that the present situation has made him start carrying his. This was reiterated by others. It was good that we aired all of this.

7th May '75
This morning while eating my breakfast in the T.V. room Ian came in and told me that when he and a staff member were out buying groceries yesterday they bumped into the Governor...

9th May '75
I am thirty-one today and received some nice cards. It may be taken as a sign of old age but I did feel mellow this morning. It has felt like a birthday and that sure is saying something in the light of our present problems.

Everyone is very talkative and open in discussing the Governor. It seems that Wattie was on the phone to him and they had a blow-out. Wattie was questioning the fact that the Governor had the staff in the main prison standing by with riot batons and hadn't informed him or any of the Unit staff. The Governor replied that he had told a Unit staff member. Wattie asked for the name. The Governor said he couldn't remember as he has had them on stand-by a number of times.

10th May '75
I sat speaking to Ken for some time this morning. Wattie phoned saying that he now knows where he stands for the first time in two years. He said that for the first time in weeks he had a good night's sleep, saying he took some tranquillisers. Wattie now

seems to be on the trail of the righteous.

Ian had his parents up today. This is the first time he has seen them since being in here. It went very well and he seemed pretty relaxed with them. The atmosphere in the place is really quite good. I hope this continues for Oliver coming.

11th May '75
This morning Wattie came in at 7.30 looking terrible. This is his weekend off and it shocked the staff to see him in this condition. They felt he was on the verge of a breakdown. Ken took him out of the prison and they walked arm in arm round nearby Hogganfield Loch. Wattie told Ken that he isn't sleeping. He said he has been rotten to the Community and to Ken in particular as he had supported the Governor in doing things that were pretty devious. He said that he had discussed Ken's transfer with the Governor six weeks ago. The Governor made it plain that Ken would have to go and changes would have to be made. Wattie said he told the Governor that he would have to watch what he was doing and at this point quickly left the office – this, he says, is where he lost out and withdrew from the Community.

I had a visit from Harry, Margaret and my kids. They are looking great. We had a good visit.

12th May '75
This morning, after advice that he should take the day/week off, Wattie came in. He looked euphoric and this remained throughout the day. He caught hold of me in front of staff saying that he is going to tell 'everyone' in the Community the truth. This is the day he will start being truthful. Ken was worried and phoned for some medical assistance.

Wattie called a Community meeting and told everyone what he had told us. Most people gave him support and sympathy. The bad feelings towards the Governor intensified. Wattie explained that it all started when he went with the Governor to the Prisons Department last year. The intention was to discuss Unit policy and the external programmes for individual prisoners. Wattie said that the Governor opened up the meeting by telling Oliver that the place is out of control and it would take him six months to get it into line. Wattie told us there was next to no policy discussed.

I can't help tninking of the past and present staff problems and saying to myself, 'These are the people responsible for controlling my life'. What is despairing is that I have to rely on them to assess, and put in reports on me. Thank fuck I'm against arse-licking otherwise I'd have succumbed to being controlled by them and found myself completely fucked up. No wonder injustices are perpetrated with this calibre of person being in complete control over another.

14th May '75

This morning I phoned Anne, Ricky Demarco's assistant, and discussed the ICA exhibition. Also had a letter from Denis Rice who is organising the Leicester exhibition. Wattie has been pretty bad today and I sat with him for five hours. He didn't want to leave me all day. He told me his life story, how he was a staunch Boys' Brigade fanatic, how he met his wife, married and settled down. He sees the meeting with Oliver as being the panacea for the problem. The meeting tomorrow will in fact be an anti-climax for us all but I'm sure that it will be good for Wattie as it's to them that he supported the Governor, therefore, it's to them that the biggest trial of honesty will have to be.

Wattie was saying that while on the phone to Tom Melville the other day talking about my manuscript, Tom said there is no chance of me getting it published. It will be interesting to see how they respond to my petition. Wattie said that when I gave the Governor my copy of the manuscript to read he went to the Department taking the copy with him. They compared them to see if they matched. He returned to tell Wattie that there are more copies as the two didn't match. It seems that if they had I would have been told that the two copies would have to be confiscated. Now they suspect that there are other copies, they will play me along. Wattie said they are frightened of it getting published as it is too near the mark for comfort.

I have been keeping check on the number of hours the Governor has been in the Unit. Between 8th April and 5th May he has been here a total of sixty-six hours. He has been off ill since then.

15th May '75

At the big meeting John Oliver started by saying that the Unit was not going to shut and that the Department were learning from it. The staff then came in asking why the Department changed in attitude, giving my parole outings as one example. Melville answered this by saying that the Department had information that the *Daily Record* and *Evening News* were waiting for me at the exhibition and that was why I was knocked back. We rejected this. We referred to the transfer of staff and asked why they were being pulled out and they replied that all of them, Oliver included, were subject to transfer at any time. Staff came in heavy on this saying they would be contesting the moves via the SPOA. We referred to the prisoners' individual external programmes that they shelved when the Governor gave them last November. They expressed surprise saying they had never received them. Oliver was asked if he thought the prisoners had too much say in the running of the Unit and he replied that he didn't. Dr Keith Wardrop, Ian, Wattie and the prisoners had lunch together. Wattie dominated the scene telling Keith to fucking shut up. It was all taken in good spirits.

This afternoon Dr Neil Smith from the main prison came in and stood about very suspiciously, speaking to me as I chiselled my sculpture. It was as though he was examining me and the others he spoke to. I never felt like this before with him.

16th May '75

This morning I slept in till 7.30am, then got up to do my exercises. It's been a very quiet morning with Wattie off for the day.

Dr Smith came in again and spoke to me as I chiselled. Again, I felt he was examining Larry and me when we spoke to him. I found out later that Oliver was so concerned that he called a top doctor in the Department and got him to speak to Dr Smith in the main prison to have a look at Wattie in particular but also everyone else. This will continue for a week.

17th May '75

This morning I lay in quite late before getting up to go outside and work in the sun as the day was beautiful.

I really got into the carving of this latest piece enjoying it immensely. I lost myself completely with the feeling, for the first time, of knowing the tools. I spent the whole day at it working patiently and very relaxed. When I parted from it at five o'clock I placed it so that, when in my cell that night, I could look out my window at it. This seemed very important to do and so far I've looked at it several times.

I've been thinking over the publication of my book and have

decided to give permission to publish. There is no doubt that when I look at the possible backlash to the Unit I hesitate, but yesterday I was told a pal of mine in Peterhead prison is lying in the solitary block – brutalised. Jim is doing four years for trying to help me in the Inverness trial – he sent a bomb to one of the staff there – and as a result is paying for it. When I hear things like this it brings me back to earth, to the realities of the situation. It is okay for the Department to say that the Unit is changing the penal system and point to the new wing in Peterhead but there is the real side of it which continues unabated – brutality, and how does one fucking change that! I feel all the old hatred welling up in me for the bastards. Ian was speaking to me this afternoon. He is getting worried about going to Edinburgh prison. It is clear that he is having second thoughts. He is going to ask for a date for his transfer next Tuesday so he can get away as soon as possible. . .

19th May '75
This morning after my exercises I went out to the yard and worked on my piece of stone, making good progress. I sat there for a part of the morning but Wattie came in wearing civvy clothes and dark glasses. He seemed okay at first but then started pulling me into the kitchen to make him coffee and toast which I did. He had some phone calls to make and wanted me present. The short time he was in the Unit was spent beside me.

There is a lot of activity over Ken's transfer as it seems that someone at the Department doesn't want him to get his interview with the Director. He had a letter asking his reasons for an interview with him. Ken said he was noncommital in his reply.

14th June '75
This morning I spoke to Barry Barker from the ICA in London. He was saying that my exhibition and the work is being complimented by people visiting. There have been a few offers to buy pieces but he hasn't had time to sort this out yet. He is taking photographs of the exhibition for me and will send them on. He said that there is a strong need in viewers to touch the work. I thought that was fine.

Ken came in this morning to see if there was any mail about his transfer situation. He is very concerned and looks under tremendous pressure but is keeping his cool. Both of us sat in the

Governor's office and he described a weird dream he had last night.

He was in the Unit with lots of new staff, all had tanned faces as though they had been lying in the sun. They were telling him they were behind him in what he was trying to do. He couldn't identify who they were. He left the Unit with two of them and when he returned he noticed a change in the place. Prisoners he didn't know were on their knees scraping the floor and on a nearby table sat all our belongings. The staff were sitting on the floor in a drunken manner celebrating their victory over the Unit. Ken then recognised that we were lying in our cells manacled and naked. Ken tried to get the drunken, victorious staff out by the scruff of the neck. He made no impression. They told him they were a new tactical squad sent in to change the Unit. Ken said that at this point the door opened and I came in with a big knife and they all started screaming and running away. Ken shouted after them, 'Go on you bastards, let's see how victorious and hard you are now'. End of dream. I know little about dream interpretation but it certainly shows the depth of Ken's anxiety about what is happening to us.

15th June '75

This afternoon I had a visit from aunt Peggy and Maggie, Pat and my kids. It was a good visit though Pat is looking bad with the booze. Patricia wasn't too well and fell asleep on my bed holding on to me. Larry, J.C. and James Lindsay had visits today.

Ian is back on sleeping tablets – Seconal – as he is all tensed up with his pending transfer. He is now saying that his visit yesterday – to his aunts – has made him think a bit more as they want him to stay here rather than go to Edinburgh on the terms offered.

16th June '75

I didn't get to sleep till after 3am. Thoughts were flashing through my mind about my position here. There is no doubt that I am going through a crisis point with myself. Freedom is a balanced diet of the mental and physical, and though mentally I feel I'm as free as I'll ever be, the fact is that I am physically restricted. This is a telling factor in my present problems. I went out a few times last year and some this year for physiotherapy after my operation. I thought that because I had played my part in acting responsibly it would be an on-going thing. I was wrong.

I spent the whole day from early morning till late afternoon working on the piece of stone in the yard. Every hit of the hammer on the chisel was full of violence; so much so that I lost count of all time. I was so absorbed in my thoughts and the piece before me. Tired and worn I went to my bed at 4pm and lay till this evening.

17th June '75
This morning I awoke fresh and feeling much better.

Received a letter from Paul Overy, *The Times* art critic, saying he stumbled over my exhibition by accident and what a find he said. He has put a short piece in *The Times* and it is a good review. I was pleased.

Wattie came back to work this morning looking very well but still not far from breaking point. We sat in my cell speaking. He feels that his conscience is his problem now due to the fact that he connived with the Governor. We spoke on this for some time and I'm sure he is the better for it.

Tom Melville came in this morning and we both chatted. It was a superficial discussion as Tom doesn't want to know about profound talk on the Unit and this is why I hate speaking to him.

At the meeting today there was a general discussion on three Peterhead prisoners nominated for the Unit. Peter Whatmore, Ken and Bob gave their views on the interviews they had with the three. After discussing each case it was decided that Mathers and Bathgate should come but that there was no place for the third. It was decided that Mathers was an emergency case and should be brought first, then Bathgate.

A group of social workers came up today. During our discussion with them they described a lecture they had with a senior prison official on the platform. After his talk he was asked about the Special Unit. Without naming names he stated that Larry and I are getting on okay here simply because it's an easy time. He said that if either of us were released we would cut the first person's throat we met. He went on to describe how evil we were and put the Unit down. I was bloody mad at this but not really surprised. This official comes in here and makes out he is one hundred per cent behind the place but I can tell he hates the idea.

18th June '75
This morning after my exercises I went outside and started

sculpting, getting lost in the piece and making great progress with it. I truly love carving as it really gets into the soul. For the first time I felt as though the hammer and chisel were extensions of my arms. The rain came down but it was nice to stand there in the middle of it and get soaked. This is what sculpting is all about. The piece is taking on a masculine form but underneath and inside there is something feminine about it. I would like to carve something large, a full-sized figure.

Ian went out for the weekly groceries and got on okay. He is still upset about going to Edinburgh and I feel that if he is kept hanging on much longer he will crack in some way.

There is a lot of sick leave by staff and really the tension with the limbo situation between Ken, the Governor and the Department is out of order. I discussed the matter with Wattie and Peter Whatmore who agree that the Department are treating us harshly on this matter.

24th June '75
Ian went to Edinburgh prison this morning. He shook hands with everyone before leaving. Murray (staff member) returned saying, as they got nearer and nearer to Edinburgh Ian got higher and higher. Murray took him for a meal and a walk round Edinburgh before going into the prison. Murray said, as they entered the prison a screw said, 'Oh, another one from the Special Unit.' Ian was thrust into a 'dog box' – a small cubicle where the depersonalisation process begins. God knows how Ian will get on.

27th June '75
I heard information that the Cages in Inverness have been repainted and it looks as though they may be re-opened. At our last meeting Tom Melville declared to us that when the last riot was over the Department gave an assurance to the staff there that certain classifications of prisoners would be kept out of Inverness and the Department were now regretting this.

Tom McGrath, director of the Third Eye Centre came in with another guy. Shelly brought them in and so I took them round. Tom is wanting to do a show of my work and is away back to the Third Eye to look at dates and will send me an official request.

Davy Mathers, the new prisoner, seems to be quite settled and getting on all right. He is getting through the overpowering parts of the Unit though he is full of the old prison culture.

29th June '75
While speaking to Davy Mathers this afternoon all he talked about was the quality of the programmes on the TV. It's clear that on just coming straight from solitary to here he sees everything as great. He is completely bewildered by this whole place. He whispered to me that we should watch these bastards – the screws – but there is no sense me plunging in and telling him about the situation here as it will have to come with time and experience.

3rd July '75
Wattie was telling me that Brian Coyle (a social worker) received a reply from Harry Ewing, Under Secretary of State, saying that due to sickness Ken won't be transferred at this stage. However, he could be transferred some time. It looks as though the Department have taken this way out and are feeling the effects brought to bear on them by outside parties. It looks as though we have reversed the decision but Ken won't be satisfied with this reply. We should now talk very seriously about plugging this gap by getting serious negotiations going about staff transfers. The emphasis should be on staff who do want to be moved but can't.

4th July '75
Mr Aithie, from the Department phoned to say Ken's transfer was cancelled. Ken was standing beside me as Wattie talked on the phone. It was terrific as the weight literally lifted from his shoulders there and then. The news was sweeping through the Unit and the prisoners had glowing faces.

10th July '75
I had words with J.C. and James Lindsay at the table during lunch as I notice that the new prisoner Davy is doing both of their cleaning tasks in the morning – they having sunk into retirement. I told them that they had better not be taking liberties with him and they denied this. Both of them know that Davy is a big easy-going guy who will do anything anyone asks. All this week I have seen him either scrubbing out the kitchen or the hall area. I really was pissed off at this as both James L. and J.C. said they would do their bit when this was raised two weeks ago. Even Larry who is heavily drugged every night gets up to do his bit along with me. James L. has taken the huff due to my giving him a pull.

J.C. and I are having bad vibes too. He puts on a face that is near to tears and really does mean what he says at such times but his resolutions fall away within a short period of time. We will wait and see what happens but really I can see that J.L. and J.C. both dislike me but that's the way it goes. There is no doubt that at such times I feel rotten and very much like a screw which isn't very nice. I often wonder if I am being too forceful.

There was a meeting today to discuss the case of the new prisoner Bathgate coming to the Unit. There are rumours that Ian is in some trouble in Edinburgh prison so with this in mind we decided to postpone bringing Bathgate down till we had more knowledge of Ian's situation.

14th July '75

I had a very strange night late on, a powerful one, and I thought about something that has been coming to my mind on and off for some time. I lay listening to music – classical – till the early hours, full of emotion. I wasn't sure whether it was a mood or something that is very deep within me. Doing away with myself raises its head in moments of solitary despair. This is the 'silent scream'. I wonder if I made a decision some years ago and am living it out. I don't know. No one seems to be taking an active part in consolidating the Unit's position now that we are welding together again. I put this to Ken, Wattie and some of the other staff.

I intend to hold a sculpture exhibition in the Unit courtyard over a period of five days/evenings from 6.30pm–8.30pm. I would like to select a group of people to visit each night to view the work and the Unit. It will mean using the exhibition to get people here to see the Unit and what we are doing. I have been talking to others about it and they seem to think it is a good idea. I will bring it up at tomorrow's meeting.

Wattie was looking very drained when I saw him talking on the phone and I sat speaking to him for some time. He said he badly needed someone to talk to. He said he felt like getting up and walking out earlier this afternoon but felt much better after sitting speaking to me.

17th July '75

The Governor had a day off today. We were surprised when Wattie returned from the main prison, very angry, to tell us that the Chief Officer there told him that our Governor has taken an office in the main prison. I had to calm Wattie down as he was concerned at the Governor making this move without telling him. The whole scene is getting more bizarre every day. David Scott and Bill Hook who made the film for the BBC brought it in on video for us to have a preview. David did very well and I think it was okay. The only sticky bit, as I see it, is when Alex Stephen, summing up on each of our futures, states that Larry, as he says himself, has no hope of release.

22nd July '75
This morning I went into my studio after doing my exercises. I worked on 'Censorship' and made good progress.

While some visitors were in, J.C. approached Larry who has been feeling very depressed these past few days. As he was going out he asked Larry if he needed anything. Larry told him to fuck off. He did this in front of the visitors. J.C. told me he is afraid of Larry as he is injecting himself with Codeine and this is why he is down. Ken says that Larry has approached him saying he wants away from the Unit. He told Ken that he is going to die in prison and wants to do so in the old system. We came to an agreement that we should work together to pull Larry out of his depression. Peter told me to warn Larry of the dangers of injecting but I told him Larry was well aware of this.

I spoke to Larry after lock up and he was saying that he thinks he has hepatitis and they are going to take tests. He said that Dr Smith was in and looked for puncture marks on his arm. He had fooled him and he showed me his ankle and four puncture marks on it. Larry told me that he had given up injecting but feels he needs this danger element as he knows that every time he injects himself he could kill himself with an overdose or air bubble. He said when lying in pain the other night he wanted to die.

23rd July '75
The Governor came in this morning but kept to his office. At the Community meeting the Governor attended with Tom Melville and a Tom Donoghue, also from the Department.

Ken brought out and read the paper he was asked to write for the Community concerning the Negotiating Board which will represent the Community when dealing with the Department, so as not to be at the mercy of one person's opinions of the place. The Governor asked if he could have more time to think it over.

Ken replied yes but went on to ask the views of everyone else. It was approved unanimously.

1st August '75
This morning during the early hours I was awakened by Larry getting more pills from the night-shift – the sound of his door opening wakened me. It really disturbs me as Larry isn't seeing that this is killing him. This morning at 6am I found him in the toilet area with his chamber pot over him as he lay on the ground; urine covered the floor. He had fallen as he was heavily drugged. He came down to help me with the daily cleaning task but I told him to leave it to me.

I pulled Ken aside this morning and told him that unless he and Peter Whatmore were prepared to sort out Larry's drug situation I was going to bring it up at the meeting as I was seeing that they were helping Larry to kill himself. Larry told me that he had nineteen seconal since eight o'clock last night which is incredible. I pulled Peter Whatmore and told him to do something. We spoke in the hall area and he kept looking up towards Larry's cell in case he was listening.

4th August '75
Last night Larry went on his bell and was given two extra tablets to put him to sleep. I had a very bad night as things seemed to build up in me. Eventually I went to sleep but it was restless and I awoke in the early hours. When I wakened this morning it was as though I hadn't slept a wink. Every inch of my exercises was torture but afterwards it was good as I relaxed through Yoga.

The Governor came in and walked past Larry who spat at his feet. He repeated this some time later as he passed again. I wasn't there but heard about it much later.

Sometime this morning the Governor sent for Wattie. He told him that I am running the Unit and what are they going to do about it. He came on very strong against me but Wattie said he refused to be drawn into this. He told the Governor to take it up with the Community.

Peter Whatmore came in this afternoon and I cornered him about the Governor having a go at me via Wattie, about me running the place. I reminded Peter of the deal he made with me when the Unit was fragmented, about his defining my role to the Department. He explained that if someone tells him I am running the Unit, he admits this, saying I'm making a good job of it. Afterwards Peter had a session with Larry. Larry came to me saying that Peter wanted him to have shock treatment. I don't know whether the truth is that Larry has asked for this.

By this time I had heard about the spitting incident. I told him that this was bloody stupid and that he is giving the Governor ammunition to use against us. Larry said he knew it but couldn't restrain himself. We then talked about the bad time he is going through at the moment and I told him I am finding things difficult also. I told him about last night but Larry doesn't want to know this. I switched topics and told him he is frightening staff by pushing things too far. I think he is glad of straight talk as he seemed much better afterwards.

Staff are getting frightened of my going back into hospital soon and some are suggesting this is the reason for Larry's present behaviour. I don't agree with this.

12th August '75
This morning I felt terrible and went to get my chisels and begin a new piece. I started work before nine o'clock and worked straight through till four. The anger in me is really bad and I kept thinking of sculptors from the past wondering if they worked with such torment. I took an untouched piece of stone and nearly completed the sculpture by the time I stopped. I didn't have the remotest idea what I was going to do when I started and it's turned out great. There is no way that the feeling of working while angry can be measured but I am very tired and weary and have to get out of this fucking place or I will go crazy. Prison is killing me.

Arthur Dooley the sculptor said in a letter today that a friend of his who runs a gallery wants to put an exhibition of my work on. There was also a nice letter from Mike Meyers, the artist from Kansas City with a photo-slide of one of his works titled 'The Egyptian Sideways Blues for Jimmy Boyle'. It is hanging in his Chicago exhibition.

21st August '75
At lunch today Davy made a nice meal for us. I was kidding him on that his cooking was terrible and we were laughing at this. Larry was joining in. The whole thing was very funny and Davy was laughing heartily. However, for a few brief seconds Larry and him were joking then out of the blue Larry stood up and

threw a cup of hot tea in Davy's face before any of us knew what was happening. I flew up and shoved Larry away and Davy just stood there. Absolute rage came right up in me and I turned to Larry calling him a dirty fucking coward and that he had taken a liberty. I called him every name under the sun and he sat rigid in his seat. By this time I was over him and have never come so close to punching him on the jaw. I was totally disgusted with Larry. He sat for a few moments then got up and left and we haven't said a word to each other since. I am not giving a fuck as I can't stomach the bastard at the moment. Both J.C. and Davy were very frightened at what happened, and by any standards it was out of order. Davy wasn't burned though his face was red.

Alex Skade brought Laurence Demarco who runs Panmure House in Edinburgh, a place for kids in trouble. We had a good talk. He seems okay and is intending to do good things.

J.C. and I walked up and down the yard tonight talking. He was saying that he thinks Larry is crazy, also that it's a case of him either being at your feet or your throat.

23rd August '75
I have just emerged from a period of sitting in the darkness with earphones playing Vivaldi's *Four Seasons* to blot out the prison sounds around me. I have to think. I have to go inside myself and find out what it is that is bothering me. While sitting I look at the closed/bolted/locked door and recognise it is this, the fact that I am in here and in torment. What am I to do? An assortment of solutions come to the fore, each as silly as the next. There is this feeling of absolute aliveness in me and it's hard to control because the physical reality is that of a cripple within this tomb. My whole heart and soul aches with the pain of being here. I know that I've reached the stage where freedom must be given to me. I feel they may take me beyond the brink and in a way that even I can't tell, destroy a great deal of what's within.

It mostly comes on a Saturday night simply because that is the night I am locked up from 5pm till the following morning and the diversions for the mind are severely restricted. Self-confrontation does no good as I've gone over it all before; it's the freedom thing and nothing can solve it. Minute by minute I am faced with it. The will to live again is tremendously strong within me. I want to see life and in many ways for the first time as I have never lived. . .

The curtains are closed to shut out the light from the dying day, to blot out of sight that there is an outside. Earphones and darkness keep away the reality, and are measures taken to help me through the night as tomorrow the day will bring new hope.

It's at moments like this that I love classical music, it somehow seems to match my mood and go to the core of my pain and caress it. The key to everything is patience and that is a very painful process, as I am experiencing. Thousands of us are locked up in similar boxes thinking/dreaming of the same thing. Beyond the wall lies our dream and beyond that lies another dream. . .

Tomorrow the Edinburgh Festival opens and I have some sculptures on exhibition at Ricky's. In a way part of me is outside as I put tremendous feeling into the pieces on show.

It seems to help when I write out my thoughts like this, as though I am ridding myself of them.

It's 8.45pm and the night has a long way ahead. I want to get up and pace the floor and not think about anything. I want to run away from what's inside me. The walls stand firm and the locked door becomes an intimidating enemy. I am locked in with myself. I see me – too much. I hate to be confronted with the fact that others have this terrible amount of control over me. I am not bad. I AM NOT BAD! The fantasy of taking them inside my soul to show them all is well will remain a dream.

Someone said to me – again – that if I had given the Governor his position and crawled to him then I would be out on paroles today. Is this what they really want? Is this what they want me to become? Deep within I know that the person who said this is speaking the truth. I cannot have freedom at that price. I don't want to know.

26th August '75
Ken and I talked about the Unit and the advantages it has for the whole of society in its success. I really love getting into this sort of dialogue with Ken as it brings me to life. . .

29th August '75
Apparently the Governor came in and asked Gus (staff member) to show me a letter from the Department:

Dear
I refer to a note sent to the Department some time ago about a proposed external programme for J. Boyle.

The requests that he be allowed to visit the Kandinsky Exhibition at the Scottish National Gallery on 3rd Sept. and attend a tutorial at Langside College for Open University students in November are not approved.

Yours sincerely
T. Melville

31st August '75
Larry, James L. and I are still not speaking to each other. Otherwise things are going smoothly enough. I am quite content with things as they are, simply because I feel that by not speaking it's the lesser of the two evils as Larry and J.L. have never contributed more than they presently are and by this I mean in their relationships with others in the Unit. Both are being considerate to others.

Ken has to write up a log every day and was trying to find out if the Governor had been in this morning and no one could say. What a crazy situation.

1st September '75
This morning I went about getting things prepared for the Unit exhibition tonight.

It was a bad start with Mr Scrimgeour, Director of Prisons, sending a brief letter saying he wasn't coming. It was word for word what Mr Keely the Controller's letter said. It's disappointing as the whole thing was meant to encourage these people to come in.

I started getting everything together and sorted out in the yard and it looked really good. The work gave the area a different feel. I thought it was looking great.

Around thirty people came in, staff and their wives, Governors and their wives, and others. The atmosphere was good and everyone tucked into the food we had prepared. Gus took photos of the whole thing. All in all the night went very well and I'm sure the show did wonders for the Unit. I think the four other nights will be even better. Afterwards all of us remarked on how well it went. We were full of enthusiasm for it.

6th September '75
Murray Stewart (staff member) was telling me that three young teenagers who stole a car and crashed against three screws' cars

from Barlinnie in the staff housing quarters were given a terrible beating by the screws. A senior cop came on the scene as they were attacking the kids. He turned a blind eye to what was happening. The kids were given bail straight from the Royal Infirmary. This really upset me.

2nd October '75
Tonight I spoke to Gerry (staff member) and he was telling me that three weeks past Monday he went to the Shooting Club that another staff member attends and while there the Governor, who is a member, 'happened' to drop in. He told him that he will be leaving the Unit by the end of October. He expressed his dislike for certain members of staff, particularly Ken. He said he is being transferred to the Department but not on promotion. He advised the staff member to get out in six months' time but he said he was staying. Gerry then asked him why he isn't coming into the Unit. The Governor said he wasn't going to allow himself to be 'broken'.

Rab and J.C. were given their liberation dates. Rab was told he will go to Edinburgh prison, the Peninghame Open Prison and then Training For Freedom (TFF) and will be released in February 1977.

Rab came in from his work in the Citizens' Theatre tonight and was informed. He was sick as he thought he would have been given better than this. It's terrible as Rab has to wait another two years for freedom and more to the point, give up a good job and go back into a prison situation. It is an indictment on the Home and Health Department.

4th October '75
The Governor was in the prison this afternoon. He told the staff that he wants J.C. transferred to Edinburgh prison on Wednesday. He stated that the Governor of that prison wanted J.C. transferred in the way of other prisoners as Ian's going through with a member of staff from here made it more difficult for him to settle and adjust to Saughton.

I am really sick at the way J.C. and Rab are being put back as it is cruel.

10th October '75
Ma is dead forty-six months tonight and I said prayers for her and miss her terribly – she is well remembered.

I went up to read my mail when Ken called me saying there was a meeting. When I came in he was sitting in a furious mood. He read out a letter from Tom Melville saying that Davy (the new prisoner) had sent a letter to a Mrs Morrison at St Andrew's House, asking her to send another enclosed letter to the head man, Mr Fraser. In the second letter he said the Unit is doing nothing for him and that he wanted transferred, asking him to contact Oliver and Melville on his behalf. In it Davy referred to the falseness of the Unit in pretending to do something for him.

Ken then threw the subject open to the community. There was pure anger directed at Davy by me and everyone else. He was visibly shaken by it. This is his first experience of the hot seat and the first I've seen in some time. It was pointed out to Davy that at this stage we are beginning to make up some ground that we lost due to the Governor's setting us back and here he is doing something blatantly stupid. Melville said in his letter that it may be that Davy's mail will have to be censored by one of the senior staff. Davy tried to squirm out of it but eventually admitted it was stupid and he apologised. We discussed the situation and Ken proposed that Davy have his mail censored from here on in – incoming and out-going. Staff – Gus and Bob – proposed that his use of the phone be terminated but this wasn't accepted as his mother phones him and as she is in bad health this restriction would affect her.

24th October '75
J.C. is gone. I will miss him as he was okay and had many loveable qualities. I am sure that one bloomer has been made, that he's been prematurely transferred from here. He had a lot to learn from this place and was taken away at a time when he was ripe for it. He says he will go to Edinburgh and put on a front and build barriers to keep them at a distance in order to get through the anticipated provocation. I think of him as I write this knowing he will be in a cell with two others. In the morning he will wake to the sounds of the old system, scraping keys in locks, chamber pots being emptied. . .

25th October '75
This afternoon we all had visits. . . I had a lovely time with my daughter Patricia. We both went off to sit in the weightlifting

room. We sat for a good while speaking. She seems to be getting on very well.

30th October (am) '75
It's the early hours of the morning and I have been lying listening to Larry, in a drugged state, fall all over his cell making tremendous crashing noises. I went to my cell door and shouted through asking him to go to bed. I asked again. In the end I shouted, 'You fucking idiot, get to your fucking bed'. This had no effect whatsoever – he is too drugged. I ended up shouting to him as I type this, 'I hope you break your fucking neck'. The pain of having to listen to this is unbearable. It takes me back to Inverness and the Cages when they were loading him up with drugs. The bangs of him falling could be heard all through the night as he crashed against the Cage front. I know all of this scene off by heart and want to fuck away from it. He is doing this by choice in here but it shouldn't be, it just shouldn't be. . .

31st October '75
This morning I went through my usual routine then got into my OU studies and made good progress.

There was some talk about Duncy (new prisoner) coming and it was relayed to us that he had destroyed his transistor radio as some screw in Peterhead told him that he wouldn't be allowed his radio in the Unit. Also that he had been given a dose of drugs on leaving prison.

I greeted him when he came in, a small oily-skinned man with shifty eyes, and Larry welcomed him with a cooked meal. The staff escorting him said he sat silent throughout the journey. This guy is really steeped in prison culture, probably more than any other in here apart from Davy. Duncy began by trying to impress me, saying that he was going to attack a screw, that he did make an attempt but failed to connect, almost as though I wanted to hear this. Probably in the past I would have and that's the way it goes in that culture but it's alien to me now. He came straight from solitary where he had been kept for a few weeks though he says four months which isn't true. This isn't to say he didn't have a hard time.

Larry was incapable of walking at lock-up time tonight so I had to help him to his cell with Murray Stewart. The drugs had really worked. He had his emergency dosage this afternoon and a full whack tonight. What a state he was in. He seemed apprehensive about Duncy coming down and has been on about his religious bigotry. This showed when Duncy was speaking to us. Larry sat there very quiet before getting up and walking away.

10th November '75
A social worker from Saughton prison phoned the Unit. In conversation she mentioned to Ken that J.C. is having a hard time. He is in a pretty depressive state because staff there are picking on him. It seems that even the two prisoners sharing his cell are getting a bad time since J.C. joined them. . .

10th December '75
Tom Melville was on the phone saying that the Governor looks as though he is going to put a sick line in every week till he is transferred. He was saying that a Departmental circular of Governors' moves will probably be issued at the end of this week or the beginning of next. We know our new Governor – unofficially.

Wattie quizzed Tom about J.C. who is lying in solitary and refusing to shave or anything. He suggested that J.C. be returned to the Unit but Melville replied no. Apparently they are thinking if he has to go anywhere then it will be Peterhead. It really is rough. The Department don't seem to have learned anything.

25th December '75
This morning we all had breakfast together, except for Rab. The meal was good. A short time later Ken called me aside to say that Rab had been violently sick in his cell, that last night he had taken an overdose of pills. This came as a great shock to me. Ken called a Community meeting and told everyone. One of the staff had spoken to Rab who told him that he had left farewell letters in the homes of his family. On going back to speak to Rab in his cell Ken found the door barricaded. He wouldn't let anyone in. I went to his door telling him that I didn't want him to open the door but to let me know he was okay. He said he was but wanted to be left alone. I reckon he has made an attempt on his life and having failed is now ashamed to face anyone. The Community agreed to call Dr Whatmore and the Governor. Bill Allen (staff member) went to Rab's family and retrieved the letters. They were worried and at a loss what to do.

The whole day had a gloom cast over it. The fact is we can't pick and choose when to have crises and this is what the Unit is all about. Bill Allen did a wonderful job with Rab's family, he is an exceptional person. He went off duty to take his family out for Christmas lunch but afterwards returned to see how Rab was. These are the things that matter, not the superficial tinsel of Xmas. Later I sat speaking to Rab. He apologised for causing us trouble and ruining the day but I told him not to worry, that our priorities were about people and not the day. He said that he was sick with his girlfriend falling out with him and not being allowed home for five days.

Moira (Unit visitor) went to Davy's mother's house last night in time to save her taking an overdose. She was in the house, cold, lonely and with nothing to eat. Moira detected something in her voice over the phone and went to find her in a terrible condition. The doctor had to be called and the old woman taken to hospital with pain from a heart condition. She told Moira that she wants to die and would only for Davy who needed her. Ken has kept this from Davy till tomorrow. There is no doubt that we will get a reaction from this. Tomorrow is the Governor's last day, Hoooorraaaaaayyy!

26th December '75
I spoke to Rab and he was up walking about but not very talkative. He says he is feeling much better.

The staff aren't paying too much attention to anything that is going on except for Ken and Gus. This is the second day we have only had two staff on duty and the place seems to run more smoothly. I am going to make a note of the times we are working with one or two staff on duty for lengthy periods. Although they won't say officially that they work best with less staff they all agree that they do. The Governor was in and made farewells to one or two staff. He didn't come near any of the prisoners. I'm glad he didn't come near me. Thank fuck he has left.

27th December '75
Duncy seemed upset this morning due to his pills being reduced. Wattie was on to Peter Whatmore and it looks as though Duncy will be put back on his pills. He tried to stop his wife visiting today but she came anyway. They had a good visit.

29th December '75

This morning I was very tired and wakened full of pressure and tension. I found it very difficult to get up and on finally doing so it was hard to do anything. I dragged myself through my exercise routine knowing that I had to complete it.

The place is getting to me; the pressure from the Governor experience was all coming down on me. My whole body is listless and aching with tiredness. My right eye had a sort of tick to it. I completed my exercises then came to my cell and lay in solitude. Ken and Wattie came up and I told them I was tense. Wattie said he felt the same.

Tonight I had a long talk with Rab. He said the visit from his girl yesterday brought a lot of things home to him. He now realises she had nothing to do with it but that he brought it all on himself. There is no doubt that Rab has grown out of this and is already seeing things he hadn't seen before. This doesn't mean it will be smooth for him as it won't. He said the fact that he has to leave here is getting to him. I feel proud when I speak to Rab at times like this as he has matured a lot since coming to the Unit. Thank Christ this latest lapse happened here and not the conventional prison, otherwise they would have put him on Strict Observation. He is looking forward to returning to work tomorrow.

30th December '75

'Masked Violence' is what I am experiencing at the moment. There is no physical bruising for the eye to see. Who can measure the scars on a person's soul? Who can measure the pain? Do I really want to become a part of this? What am I striving for?

I am sick of tiny minded bureaucrats who violate my person with impunity. I realise they have me in a position where they can and are doing what they want. I have to live with myself. Am I going to sit in this cold storage and let them rub my face in the shit? Jimmy, what the fuck are you allowing to happen? When the ultimate coyote rejection was taking place and you lay animalised in your cage you were able to see life in society for what it was. Why pretend it is different now? Why climb the mountain to fall down the other side? Between the past and the future lies the pain of today. The height of impotence – being violent with a typewriter.

Who soothes the heart that beats in agony? Who kisses the soul that writhes in torment? Who mends the shattered self?

2nd January '76
It's an exciting time for me at the age of thirty-one as I am finding out a great deal about myself. I am making new relationships and living in a world totally unknown to me. I love it yet there are times when I hate it. I am torn between two worlds – alienated from the old one and a stranger in this new one.

I love it as I feel the inside of my head blossoming like a flower and realise I am changing into something else, but with this come many insecurities. I have to work on a level that is different in style. Who could possibly begin to understand what I am experiencing? With this change comes the fear that in adapting to their way, those 'respectable' enemies will do as they want. As I am now accepting their ways they will expect me to retaliate similarly but they will be in a position to manipulate the scene. I do feel they have the upper hand and what I find difficult is the thought of continually losing to people who hate me.

Even though I am in prison, these are the finest years I've ever known. There are times when I am not in prison, when I have transcended this and feel free. There is one thing that I am sure of, that I have been in a personal prison all my life until these past few years.

There are times when I think I do too much thinking.

There are also times when I am really in a prison and I think this is due to the fact that I am freer in the mind and realise that mental freedom is not enough, it's at these moments I feel the walls smothering me. I feel more a machine, getting up at the same time each day, doing exercises, working, being locked up. Although all of this comes and goes I have come to terms with it and realise that I am going through a phase that will last a short spell. I'd love to see my children more and get even closer to them but I can't surmount the fact that we only see each other a few hours a month.

Sporadic thoughts made in the night for reasons I don't know. I do feel pretty good and have all through this writing. Some day I'll look back and wonder why I sat typing this.

3rd January '76
At lunch time I spoke to J.L., Davy and Duncy as we ate. I told them that this is a crucial year for us and that we should help the Unit as much as possible. I told them to treat people in the Unit with the respect they are due. If Larry abuses a member of staff

they don't have to side with him. Davy told me Moira is going to see his mother in hospital. He was saying his mother is getting out. I was pleased to hear this.

Duncy had a visit from his wife this afternoon. She told me that she couldn't manage to bring the kids as her social security money didn't arrive on time. Duncy has saved £2 and he gave it to his wife for her birthday and their anniversary.

4th January '76
Davy came down with another letter and told John (staff member) that Moira had better not see his mother as she has been sneaking behind his back to tell Ken and Wattie things, that she had ransacked his mother's house and told tales about his mother not having any food in the house. He threatened to stab Moira if she visited the Unit. He said he was suing her and getting a court order to stop her seeing his mother. . . Ken reminded Davy that Moira had virtually saved his mother's life. Larry came in strong against Davy as did everyone in the Community. He was verbally abused for threatening visitors to the Unit who had done us a lot of good. Davy is definitely sick and I told him so. He asked to be put back to Peterhead prison. He has gone on long enough within the prison system without help; he needs treatment. It may be that the Unit has served the useful function in Davy's problems being seen whereas elsewhere they were ignored. I don't think there is anything more we can do for him.

8th January '76
Wattie and I had a chat with Moira when she came in this morning. We informed her of the meeting with Davy. We suggested that a Community meeting be called and she agreed.

The meeting opened with all the same old things being regurgitated and Davy jumping from excuse to excuse. Moira grew in stature as the meeting went on. She handled it magnificently. The meeting was one of the best I have attended and of a high standard. Lots of earthy facts were put to Davy, as well as compassion. He sat agreeing with everything. It always seems to me as though what is being said shoots over his head. A decision had to be made as to whether Moira should continue to involve herself with his mother by bringing her to visit Davy. Moira said she initially got involved at the request of Davy. She did so hoping it would help him get more involved with the Community but this didn't seem to be working so she thought she should leave it for a spell. Davy thought this right but was clearly shaken.

After lunch Joyce came in. She had a newspaper clipping from *The Scotsman*, it quoted Nicholas Fairbairn Q.C. (now on a Tory platform). 'The treatment of prisoners on life sentences should be known to be different from other prisoners. It should be more rigorous more like a detention centre than like the Special Unit at Barlinnie, which is an art shop.'

9th January '76
Tom McGrath came up and we had a long talk over the exhibition. He has taken it to the Arts Council and told them that he is putting it on and that it may arouse controversy. He went into detail and they backed him. Tom and I discussed the whole thing and he took my material away to use at his discretion. He is doing another exhibition in the Third Eye early next year about various forms of violence and has asked me to contribute. He is holding an open night on the second week of the exhibition inviting members of the Establishment along as well as other people. He is intending to do a good catalogue. My knee collapsed this morning.

12th January '76
Peter Whatmore has received a letter saying that Anthony Lester Q.C. (Roy Jenkins' advisor at the Home Office) was wanting to meet him on 11th February. Peter showed Ken the letter he received from Keely and Meikle (Dept.) saying that they want to meet him on Monday. They are doing an in-depth study of the Unit (I imagine for the Home Office) as they want to see Alex Stephen. Things are beginning to move. The hypocrisy of the Department people is diabolical as they know they are going to be asked questions so are now scurrying like rats to get all the information they can at the last minute. It will be interesting to see if they come into the Unit. They have arranged to meet Ken and Wattie separately – outside the Unit.

Between 5 and 6.30pm lock-up Davy came to speak to me and went into the whole situation about his carry on. We had a good discussion about everything and I would like to believe that we have come out of it with something, but time will tell.

Larry came and told me he feels Duncy is being snide to him and is now introducing his Orange Order talk into discussions. I advised him to speak to Duncy now rather than wait till it gets worse. He did. James L. is growing one of those funny beards but seems much better than he has been lately.

14th January '76

This morning I did my exercises and then helped get things prepared for the Department reps coming in. Ken brought in the mail and with it a copy of the Department Whitley Council Minutes held in the Conference room at Government Buildings, Broomhouse Drive, Edinburgh.

The Official representatives were: Scrimgeour (Chairman) Oliver, Keely, Aithie, Collinson, Burnett, Frisby, Hendry, Peerless, Beveridge.

The Staff were: Adams (Chairman), Donaldson, Lawrie.

6. *Barlinnie Special Unit*

The Staff Side referred to recent correspondence regarding the shortfall of volunteers for the Special Unit, and since they were anxious that the experiment should continue they would welcome a discussion of that matter.

The Staff Side expressed concern about the regime in the Unit. It had been suggested that because of the extra pressure on staff the incidence of sick leave is higher in the Special Unit than elsewhere, although this has been refuted by Personnel Branch. The Staff Side felt that a fresh look should be taken at the Unit and that a limit should be set on the length of time officers serve there. It was further suggested that Barlinnie was the wrong place for the Unit.

The Official Side reported that recently Mr Oliver had met with the staff of the Unit in two groups at the College. The discussions had proved useful and informative for all concerned and it was generally agreed that the Unit had moved too fast too soon and prisoners given too much latitude. The situation now is that the staff have been asked to draw up guidelines for the running of the Unit. It is hoped in future it will be possible to meet annually with the staff.

While the Official Side agreed that Barlinnie might not be the ideal site for the Unit, it was the only place available. Whether or not a time limit could be set for service in the Unit would depend on there being a constant flow of volunteers to replace officers due to move.

> The Staff Side were glad to hear that things are changing and asked how this could be conveyed to the staff.
>
> The Official Side said that this might be done during courses, etc., and of course the minutes of this meeting would give some indication.

Ken was very angry at this as were other staff who feel that the two-day conference has been completely distorted by Oliver. Ken and Wattie who were waiting to meet Keely and Meikle intended bringing this up with them. I am very suspicious of what is being said here as I am being told the exact opposite by staff and Department whenever we see them.

After their respective meetings they came into the Unit. I took them both round. I explained that the weightlifting room used to be our punishment cell. Keely joked that it still was a punishment cell (meaning the weights). I took them to the cells and into mine explaining to them how we have our visits here. Meikle enquired about my children. He asked how I was and I said okay except for my knee. He asked how hard it was for prisoners to settle into the Unit. I replied that it was very difficult for staff and prisoners. I was as enthusiastic about the Unit as I could be without going overboard. Meikle asked how long I had been in and I replied that I was into my ninth year. I told them that we hadn't seen them recently and they said they didn't want to be seen breathing down our necks.

We then went into the meeting room for a coffee and general chat. All the staff were there. The discussion went into how the Unit should expand. Meikle replied that there was a financial crisis but we hit him with how it costs nothing to encourage staff and prisoners to make relationships. Bill Allen (staff member) said that the feeling in the Unit is that the Department are not doing much to encourage staff to take up working here. This was supported by the rest of us. Meikle went on about how the Department have a lot more than the Unit to contend with. He said that if the Department wanted they could have halted the experiment any time during the last three years just as this could happen any time during the next three years. Keely sat not saying much, just listening. I think it is clear that the Department presence within the Unit in future will be very limited. I explained to them that the cost of the staff training was going to waste as the staff were being put back into ordinary working places where their experience could not be put to good use. He said the staff would be rubbing it off on other less experienced staff.

16th January '76
Larry was making a terrible noise last night. He didn't sleep a wink and when I saw him first thing he was still heavily drugged. He was falling about. Ken had a word with him about it but Larry is saying that he feels hostility directed towards him from everyone in the Unit at the moment.

He came in and spoke to me later saying he is depressed but won't say why, that is if he knows.

28th January '76
This morning I wakened very early but wasn't feeling right so did a part of my exercise routine that included running round the yard, rowing, sit-ups and yoga. I did the right thing as I am weary and needing a rest and felt better for the light exercise period. Some people who work in Panmure House came in from Edinburgh. I showed them around and they put some pertinent questions and we had a good session going. In the meeting room we had a lively debate on corporal punishment.

I had to leave them as Tom McGrath phoned asking me to write another paragraph for the catalogue, along the lines of what I'd do if I suddenly found myself released tomorrow. Tom said he has a small play going at the Traverse Theatre just now but would like to do one on violence and asked me to write it with him. He said that he would split the profits right down the middle with me. He went on to say if I did want to write it myself then he would have no objections. I told him the phone isn't the best of places to discuss the matter so we should do so when we meet. He will be up shortly.

29th January '76
Ben was pouring his heart out as he is having serious problems adjusting to life outside. He said that after a full year out he should really be well, whereas he is finding that this isn't the case and is only now encountering the problems and there is no one to talk to about it. He said it was when under this black cloud that he left a pub under the influence when a young cop approached him, gave him a push and told him to get on. Ben realised that if he punched him it would make matters worse but

the pressure was on him and he did. He said that he can best describe it as the alcoholic who takes a drink knowing he isn't going to stop.

10th February '76

Anthony Lester Q.C. (Home Office) and Tony Pearson (Governor grade) came here at 11.20. Before they arrived, a message was sent by Lester saying he didn't want a staff meeting but just to enter and speak to people informally. When they came in the new Governor was highly excited – all of us were remarking on it. On taking them round we were trained by Meikle and the new Governor. What was pleasing to me was Anthony Lester saying that the place wasn't as luxurious or expensive as had been made out. Afterwards they left for the Garfield Hotel for lunch.

They returned to take part in a Community meeting. Ken chaired it and after the Minutes had been read we concentrated on general business. After the normal meeting we broke for coffee then re-assembled. Anthony Lester told us that he was here at the request of Roy Jenkins to look the place over as the Home Secretary had heard so much about it. We then had an extremely long and interesting discussion on the Unit. Anthony asked us about privileges and we told him about the use of the phone, uncensored mail, unsupervised visits, community meetings and being allowed to express ourselves freely. We did say that though these weren't looked on as privileges they were what made the Unit conditions better. The meeting went on till after 6pm.

There were lots of things said that I haven't mentioned here as I can't remember them all. Anthony will return tomorrow morning. The day was very rewarding and most informative.

I spoke to Tom McGrath and he said that over a thousand people had visited my exhibition on the first day and a half.

12th February '76

The Barlinnie Governor Bob Hendry, Dr Neil Smith, Giles Havergill and Joyce Laing came in for our third anniversary lunch and we had a very enjoyable meal. The new Governor gave a good speech thanking the guests for coming. Kay replied with a speech that hit us all.

Wattie mentioned to me that Tom Melville phoned him saying Harry Ewing (Labour Minister) wanted to know who was paying for the Unit anniversary meal. Wattie told him the prisoners and

Thoughts of an Alien

Just dropped into this planet today. What a strange place it is. I am glad to be an alien — there is no way I want to become a part of them. They are what I would call nit-pickers, plucking away with their microscopic eyes, delving into each nook and cranny. The drone of their drivelly voice-box, like a sophisticated piece of reflexing technology geared for sending one into a deep cataclysmic state. They have graced me in this small cell with its speckled walls. The window looks out to lush green hills, past the wire fence and walls that is. This, they say, is progress. They are having me through what they call "the system". There are a number of myths and rumours about this. The officials state — and this is a lie — that I am merely following the well trodden route of "the system". Others, individual staff and some of the inmates suggest that it is to justify the system as a whole and not only that of the social unit. They are engineering the situation to produce comparisons between the special unit and the traditional system. Bitter as I have they lack up into a catch 22 situation. So, it is here dressed in their uniform which feels, looks, smells however this experience is felt much more deeper than ~~I have~~ just as remindful of the clothes, it's what it does to one far beyond this. The appalling act of stripping one of his own clothing and coercing him to wear an ill-fitting uniform that has been worn many times before, to pull on socks that smell of another person, to shove the slimy feet of another in the shoes that are wrinkled with use. In the corner of this very cell trying to put mine in a lie a pair of smelly slippers. I still can't bring myself to lift them and less will not never bend near them. Last night previous to coming here — only two years and all the doors were open for me — I was staying in the normal practice that auts can use hot water from a tap to make coffee or tea as this is better the tenant allowed. Some were told bluntly to "fuck off" they guys work to become a part of this, to 'toughen themselves up'. So just as I can be looked up to as "hidros". It's this world I want to stay away from. I want to remain an alien. Really, it is a house of heartbreak, of human tragedy. Persons are no human as human misery, being in there amongst these guys, I don't see them as the sick people section of the and public portray them as, why is it the responsible section-sick our society can mislead as easy as why? Am I not allowing myself in here myself sickfold, to avoid our own personal responsibility out in the same breath I want to point out that this so-called responsible section of society don't appreciate or understand that other sections of society — from which groups of the prison population come from have values which for some deviate somewhat. Research has shown that a large percentage of kids in these areas are born to fail. No caution to one who lives in a scientific age, a world scientific age, one that is going to increase and expand our economy or else. No artistic passions and comforts and there equally valued evidenced in human misery without building our long torn peninsula for ourselves. I doubt if we are creating an imbalance going at the present rate this is going to a large amount of the population which have perished. A large amount who will be very much less active in their attitudes.

Thoughts continue to race through my head as I sit here in early evening I can see the city lights from my confinement, cars and buses filled with people pass by my window. Householders have arrived in their houses unaware that I look down upon them. The world in which now I hate it. I sit out here on the outside. I sit here trying to instill patience in myself, telling myself that it will come. It is hard, it is very hard but it must be done. Less than two years to go out. I tell myself there are many others around me who have a long time to go. I do not have much solace in this as I am in the very same time. I am sick of locked and closed doors, sick of the both of them, of living in a world where others dominate my every action. I need so much to be free. I want my freedom! I have fought for 13 years to resist becoming a part of this world. I have become very frightened of its clinging disease of being institutionalised and yet the very fact of living in such a place means I am contaminated by it. I take solace from the fact that most people are also contaminated by the institutionalised rut of their daily lives. I suppose part of me was unreceptive and you've been assisting. This is the outside also and continue to walk I am out. At this moment it has been the struggle of this institution's life that has dominated me. I have been resisting this in all its forms and diffusing levels refusing to bring its willing prisoner. There are moments when I nearly cut ultimately I know I want submit or let it have its way. Deep in me I know that i will. I leave this the sun will struggle, continue my struggle of whatever price we may be facing. This is my way of giving meaning to my life. I know that I feel that it's right is what I'm doing. I know that my life must be to upgrade human standards. I often talk hard that I am merely the vehicle which this lesson is travelling. The surely humanity must learn from it. Saying I think of this world I live in and ask if these were learned from I can't answer this. I just believe that I must let people see and learn from what I have come through and trouble that largely can be a long, slow process.

staff had paid for it. Most of us don't believe that Harry Ewing wants to know, we think it is the Director.

They are probably on about the expense but we question the public money being spent to take Anthony Lester and the gang of them to the Garfield Hotel when we could have fed him.

10th March '76
This morning I did my exercises then started cleaning the floor as usual. While putting the polish down I heard a bang coming from the hall area and looked to Davy who was preparing the vegetables. He looked then went back to work.

I thought of a precariously balanced sculpture in my studio. Going to look I found it okay but James Lindsay's door was locked. I looked through the spyhole and he was sitting on the edge of the bed naked covered in blood. I could only think that he had tried to commit suicide and shouted through to ask if he was all right. I went to the staff and told them. J.L. was badly shaken. The cuts were pretty bad on the leg, hand, arm and chest. I then realised he had been attacked. I went upstairs to look at Larry. He was all right. Duncy was standing in the toilet area covered in blood. He was talking his head off as he took off his clothes and began to wash them in the sink. I called him all the fucking idiots of the day and was extremely angry. I did everything I could to stop myself punching him. He kept saying that he asked J.L. to call a meeting and he wouldn't but this was lies. He then told me he was insane and came out with lots of irrational statements. All the while he looked away from me.

I went back downstairs and caught hold of Ken coming on duty and put him in the picture. I then told Wattie. Everyone worked on helping J.L., getting him fixed up. A doctor was sent for. Everyone was shattered.

At this point most people didn't know who had done it. All eyes were fixed on Larry. I made it clear that it wasn't Larry.

Ken called a Community meeting. Duncy sat there calm and composed. It was a remarkable performance. Ken asked the person who had done it to speak up. The Governor was told and he responded by telling Ken and Wattie to lock everyone up and search them. I could see all the old traditional methods being introduced. I refused to be locked up as did Larry.

The staff went through a very loose motion of searching me. Mostly they congregated in my cell to talk. Larry started vomiting with tension and I felt sorry for him. He was afraid that he might be blamed. Duncy's cell was searched and bloodstained clothing was found. They also found a knife. He then started asking staff if he had cut Lindsay's prick. Ken went in and spoke to Duncy and he broke down crying, telling him he had done it.

I sat in my cell thinking. I was shattered as I feel this is the sort of incident that could do us terrible damage. Staff and the Governor sat around my cell chatting. There were many questions as to why. Although there was a lot of understanding towards Duncy it was felt that he had done something inexcusable. There was wild speculation trying to guess the motive but no one was any wiser. Everyone wants to protect the Unit.

The police were called and they interviewed us one at a time. The 'code' came in. J.L. was in a position where he would have to say something and he wanted to do what was best for the Unit but was caught in the 'code' conflict. It was a terrible position to be in. To inform on Duncy would result in him getting more time and nothing would be done for the guy. Also, what would happen if he was transferred to another prison? He saw the police and told them it was Duncy. I saw the cops and told them my part.

There is no doubt that the police were impressed with the co-operation they received. Duncy was charged and taken through to the main prison hospital where he would be kept.

11th March '76 (7.45pm)
The morning after the night before. . .

Duncy is lying in a bare cell under constant observation. J.L. is below me licking his wounds. This whole incident had raised many questions within me. Yesterday the emphasis was on finding out who did it and this didn't take long with Duncy being caught with the goods. The focus then went on getting J.L. to identify him as the assailant. The Unit was used as the lever to get him to make this identification and it was successful. He was told that to come clean would help as it was a tricky situation and this mess could close the place. He was put in a terrible position.

The one question I have is, what is the purpose of hounding Duncy? What good will it do? It doesn't seem likely that he will get any treatment as he will simply be sent back to Peterhead. I know this will only make the guy worse. The prisoners are being asked to show how good the Unit is by sending Duncy away.

When he was being taken through to the main prison by Ken

he was like a docile little kid. The strange thing is that this is possibly the period when we could do Duncy the most good but the legal machinery has moved in and taken its course.

Wattie was saying the Department have been asking if a 'cover up' is going to take place and he proudly says it isn't. They are delighted. Talk is that the Unit has broken the usual prison culture that reigns supreme. I believe this is so but there is no sense breaking it if the answer is just to slap the guy back into jail.

14th March '76
Ken and I have been talking about the possibility of bringing Duncy back. I feel that if he has to go to prison then it should be back here. If he is recommended for hospital treatment then there is nothing we can do. If we can absorb Duncy then we are giving a lesson to society as a whole. They seem to throw people into prisons and forget them. We would be doing the same thing. There is the problem of how J.L. will react. There is the problem of his mother who visits him.

Ken is worried about Duncy in the main prison and feels he is about to blow up.

25th March '76
I spoke to Larry for a spell tonight and he is okay. We discussed freedom and I was saying how there is no substitute for it. Larry remarked that if he was offered the choice between a girl for the night and a gram of heroin, he would take the heroin. I said that my problem was in coping with the walls and how they restrict me.

The Prisons Department was given an historical document by us to distribute in the Prison Officers' College and throughout the penal service, and elsewhere for that matter. The document gives a rough idea of the development of the Unit since its inception. The beginning of the document states it is for information only.

At the meeting yesterday the Governor pointed out that Mr Meikle in the Department wasn't too happy about the part relating to Communications that states the prisoners can use the phone. The big fear of this is that the press could phone in. He contradicted this by saying Meikle says this doesn't happen in other prisons and that they – the Department – didn't know that the phone was being used by prisoners.

9th April '76
Tom McGrath came in and spoke to the Governor about putting his play on here. It was accepted. Tom and I discussed the play that we are writing and I gave him the material I had done. He is very enthusiastic about it and feels I should write the whole play and he will put it together. I don't want to. I need his expertise and knowledge at the moment and told him so. I would like to do other things at a later stage by myself. We went through everything and he stayed for lunch.

14th April '76
Meikle caught hold of me to ask about the latest work I am doing. He asked how things were with the prisoners and I told him all was well but the Duncy thing had been a blow to us all. We talked about this for a period and he said he had played it down as much as he could, that they were treating it as an incident like in any other prison. I told him how proud we were of the Unit so took it as a personal blow. He said he realised this but it was bound to happen at some time. I then asked him what he would feel about Duncy returning to the Unit. This was unexpected and he said off-hand he could see that there would be wider issues to take into account and that the matter would have to be viewed with the greatest of care. He said he doesn't want to prejudge anything but one would have to consider what would happen if it occurred again. . .

Ken and Meikle had a session on the Whitley Council Minutes. Meikle tried to spin it off that these were before he came (in Oliver's time). He said that Ken may be over-reacting to them and Ken replied he hoped he was but time would tell. Ken told him that Department behaviour recently had caused lots of fragmentation in the Unit amongst staff. He told Ken that the Unit is under no pressure to change and that it is still experimental and that the experiment will continue.

16th April '76
This morning I did my exercises then got ready for Tom McGrath coming. While waiting I did some more writing for the play. Tom brought in his wife but she had to leave soon after. He has already spoken to some actors about it and they are very eager to take part. He will type out the first part this week. He is saying that it could be off the ground for September.

17th April '76
When I got locked up at 5pm I was feeling great having just come from a new piece of sculpture.

I wrote up my diary then read up on my OU course but eventually the mood began to change with my mind wandering into the future and wondering what is there.

I thought of the beautiful cool evening, how I long to be walking in it outside this cell. All of this took place while I sat in the semi-dark reading a book. The thoughts on freedom were only momentary but so powerful that they seem to tear my soul apart. There is something about being alone in a cell, about the inability to rise from a chair, open the door and speak to someone. I would like to get up this minute and discuss this subject with someone. I would like to put these feelings into a piece of sculpture and although sitting typing out the feelings is important there is a tremendous amount of strain and frustration attached to it. During these periods I find it hard to read a book or watch TV, which I hardly do anyway. The only solution at such times is to tackle the mood and try to do something with it.

Others lie in neighbouring cells either in drugged hazes or dreamy sleep. Each in his cell bound in himself as I am. Walls separate us from each other.

26th April '76
As I type this the TV is showing Frank McElhone (Gorbals MP) and the Under Secretary, opening a new security wing at St Mary's List 'D' School. He said his heart ached opening this new wing as he hoped that fewer such places would open as he doubted their need. I was very impressed with this.

My children visited me with my niece and her boyfriend. . . I made a point of getting the children on their own so we could speak. We sat in the sun in the prison yard. Patricia was curious:

'When are you leaving this place?' she asked.

'I don't know but I hope it isn't too long,' I replied.

'This place is worse than Colditz,' said James looking round the walls and to the TV monitor focussing on us.

'How long have you been here?' asked Patricia.

'Nine years.'

'I thought it was six,' she said.

'I was only a wee baby, wasn't I?' asked James.

'Yes, and Patricia was just born,' I informed them.

'Why can't you come home now?' asked Patricia.

'Hmm, eh, it's just that I can't,' I stumbled.

'Because the court gave him a set time and he has to do that,' said James with protective exasperation.

'Were you in a court and found guilty?' asked Patricia.

'Yes, I was in court and found guilty,' I admitted.

'I've seen that in Crown Court on tele,' she said smiling.

I fumbled and shuffled around trying to hide the inner confusion the dialogue presented me with. I was feeling terribly protective towards them.

27th April '76
The Great Escape – Larry

He holds his palm out to take the multi-coloured barbiturates, lets them sit there on the surface while he counts to check the numbers are correct; four reds, four yellows and three pale blues. He counts them again then looks, savouring the sight. Quickly he scoops them into his mouth then swallows, washing them down, knowing the hot coffee will melt the capsules and rush on the tingle. Having taken no meal he knows the effect will be heavy on an empty stomach. Shortly afterwards his hands spring open and shut convulsively with the fingers and thumbs rubbing against each other like antennae searching for the first sign of the oncoming buzz.

An hour passes and the facial expression begins to change, his movements become stilted. His spirits rise and he becomes 'high' though in a moderate manner. He speaks with confidence as though he is master of himself. His company is excellent.

Before very long his mouth begins to hang open, his eyes start to close and his speech becomes slurred. The movement of his limbs becomes totally un-coordinated and the figure pathetic. The drug controls. He has to walk thirty yards to his bed and each step is that of a baby child learning to walk, only this is a grown man. His manner is peaceful. There are times on this short journey when he falls against things and those around him pretend that they don't see this sight – the degradation of man.

He is now at the top of his escape ladder, reality no longer exists for him. Life is a gold-coloured haze that blots out the feeling of doom that smothers him in the cold light of day. Deep within he recognises his own weakness – no amount of drugs will blot it out. He can't see a future for himself. There is none because he will not recognise it. The will to fight has left him.

Tomorrow he will waken with signs of the night-before haze still evident as the movements are stilted, the eyes glassy. He looks to the nights ahead and wonders how to fill the time in-between.

The techniques have been acquired so that effort is minimal. He sits and sits, and talks and talks, and talks. The hours are few but long to the waiting man. The cycle of self-destruction has been perfected. He regurgitates the past and throws it in the face of those around him but cannot look at the future, except to the night ahead when the magic rainbow is placed in his palm. Is there a tomorrow?

29th April '76
While speaking to the Scottish Arts Council Committee and telling them that he would like to involve a few artists in his project and named Jimmy Boyle as one, a prominent member of that committee told the applying community artist that this wouldn't be a good idea. He went on to say Jimmy Boyle had been getting too much attention as an artist and anyway the publicity would hurt the feelings of other prisoners who aren't getting any attention. During this speech the Committee member stated that I had been exploited by Richard Demarco. Personally, I do not and never have asked the Arts Council for any assistance.

The Prisons Department have been approached by a number of responsible journalists from the media to gain permission to interview me about my sculpture in order to show how change can take place in a person. They were told that this would not be permitted as they don't want to turn Jimmy Boyle into a star or cult figure. They say that there are lots of other prisoners and one can't pick out individuals.

The sort of problem facing an individual like me in trying to improve the situation is in handling the statements above. Both these groups must have some idea how younger kids in some of the poorer areas of Glasgow look up to me already for my violence and see me as a tough guy. To most of them I am already a cult figure only in a negative context as they want to see the violent part of me. If no information is being presented on the area of change then the authorities are actively suppressing an important issue. I really detest the way they put their argument in humane clothing – that other prisoners will be hurt by all the attention being put on Jimmy Boyle. Shit, pure and unadulterated. These people are hypocrites who will use any means to prevent change as they have built ivory towers and don't want to be toppled from them by allowing more freedom of expression or they will cease to exist. They feel so strongly about using other prisoners as an excuse that they don't for one minute give any further thought to the conditions that these men are being kept in this very minute. They are aware of the situation concerning other prisoners and know that to allow me to be successful in a real sense, either artistically, academically or socially, is to allow me a platform to put a case for the other prisoners.

Somewhere along the line the original good intentions of these official bodies has been corrupted by individuals who have bent and distorted their responsibility in order to have a sense of power. Now their main purpose is to retain the status quo.

28th April '76
This morning I did my exercises then took my radio to the studio where I worked on a small piece of sculpture. Ken Wolverton (community artist) was coming in as he wanted me to show him the casting technique. It was a relief-type piece so by the time he arrived it was almost complete. We worked on it together with me showing him the short cuts, etc. He was delighted with the simplicity.

30th April '76
Today I had a discussion with a psychiatrist on delinquency. He told me that in most cases when he asks kids what they want to be when they are thirty they stare at him then eventually tell him they haven't a clue. As he told me this my thoughts flashed back to when I was a kid – my response would have been similar. I was puzzled that he should find this appalling, the fact that their lives are so empty. I then asked him what answer he would give if the same question had been put to him at that young age. He replied that he wanted to be a doctor. Now I find this truly amazing and alien to anything I have known. I would have found it impossible to predict such a thing at that age, it would have been beyond me. When I say that I mean that I knew my place. No one ever told me but somehow I felt my place was labouring at something or other and no more. There was a feeling of inferiority that permeated all our lives. I could hardly speak, and was

conscious of this, never mind being something like a doctor. The fact is, that by the age of twelve the education system has one 'placed'. Once slotted into this place it is very difficult to break out of. Out of all the guys I was brought up with I don't know one who has a professional position in any field. Being a tradesman is the nearest to being anything in the world. The thought of anyone becoming a doctor is a dream.

26th June '76
I am a human being. You must understand that imprisoned terrorists are also human beings. There is no sense doing away with what you call the barbaric capital punishment if you are going to replace it with a slower form of death. At this very moment I am in a state of total isolation, caught in a trap that is imprisoning my soul. I hate every one of you pretentious bastards who purr up against the leg of the system while telling those trapped within that you are for reform.

Blood is pumping through my whole body. It's passing through my heart to the soles of my feet. I live. I hate; oh God, how I hate. . . What keeps me from ending it, why have I put off the inevitable for so long? Perhaps it's those that I see as the enemy – the cops and the screws of the past who keep me alive. It's hard to believe but it's true. . . It's hard as I have found more enemies when making a positive contribution than when acting irresponsibly.

You who sit out there, what the fuck do you know? How can I expect you to understand what it means to be in the control of people who look on me as an animal?

I've had a bellyful of pussyfooting with you stinking shits and your cowardly ways. I want to destroy your system. I want to live. I want to walk for a spell without having some great fucking wall stopping me taking another step. I just want to be free. I want to see the stars without seeing bars. I want to be caught in a busy shopping crowd. I want to see children playing nonsense games. I want to see a dog pissing against a lamp post. I want to take my girlfriend for a walk. I want to sleep a whole night beside her. I want to see all of you suffer less. I want away from institutions.

27th June '76
At the meeting today Ken said that he would like it recorded that

Rab is leaving and during his spell here has made tremendous progress in every possible way. . . Rab was out at the Citizens' Theatre working (for the last day). The Governor said he had a letter from the Department refusing Duncy coming to the Unit.

28th June '76
This morning I did my exercises then walked up and down the yard speaking to Ken . . . all was ready for my going to hospital.

At 9.45 while standing in the yard speaking to Ken, two cops came in – detectives. The Governor obviously knew them. Malky (one of my staff escorts) said there was no need for them as I'd been out before. . . The cop in charge said he hoped I'd changed as he knew me in the Gorbals.

I was SICK. So absolutely and totally sick. I was told the cops would be with me at all times, even sitting with me in the ward. I just felt bloody angry. I went into the small room and lost the grip on myself. I broke (cried). All these past three years gone for nothing. Here I was, in prison terms 'B' category and with lots of cops. Ken held on to me. My insides were falling apart. This is the essence of power and its corruption, the whole twist of torture through the decision-making process. The Governor came in saying I must forget the politics of it and think of myself. He kept saying that it had nothing to do with him or the Department. He said the decision has been made and the cops were there to protect the Public. This is pure crap. On discussing it in detail he said that if I don't go it will prove that I had something on for escape. I couldn't/didn't argue with this as it is so stupid it's unbelievable. I told him I don't need to prove anything.

On reaching the hospital the cops were very pushy and energetic – ultra cautious. On speaking to me one said that he personally sees no need for their presence but that their boss put the high-powered show on when hearing it was me. He told his superior that it would only be for a day or so as I would be crippled after the operation but they were told they would remain throughout. Two of the cops mentioned to Malky that they were embarrassed.

The nurses and sister were upset at all the cops. They remarked that there wasn't any of this last time. Malky and the other staff member see no need for their own presence as the cops have taken over. The whole scene is pathetic but more than anything it has torn lumps out of me. I really broke this morning. I know I did. I am not a hard-man any more.

29th June '76

I managed to pull myself out of this state of anger and withdrawal to try to find out more about this. I didn't sleep at all during the night as my mind was active... Gerry (staff member) told me his partner is lapping up the cops with their guns, etc...

The cops sitting next to me are wearing shoulder holsters and revolvers. They sit staring at me all the time. One of them seems to be friendly but the other sits leaning on an empty bed staring straight at me. I wonder how long he can keep this up. I cannot sleep, in fact I find it difficult to do anything but opt for pretending to read or sleep. Gerry says that even he feels under scrutiny.

I was taken to the pre-operative room where I was greeted by the anaesthetist who asked me how I was. The young guy taking me there enquired who the two following me were. They identified themselves as police, though one was a staff member. The guy then turned to me saying, 'I feel sorry for you'. The two following were being put into green gowns and the cop asked if he needed to take off his cardigan. The nurse replied no. He remarked that it was just as well as it may cause panic; obviously referring to his gun. It hit me then that they were loving this.

Coming out of the anaesthetic certainly amazes me, to think someone has been working on me when dead to the world. I lay there looking around me. Two cops, a man and woman, came in to relieve the two already there. She took one cop's gun and put it into her handbag – without the shoulder holster. She sat a few feet from the bed putting her handbag on the floor. After a few moments she got up from her chair, went over to the window to look out, leaving her bag near me. Groggy as I was, I beckoned Malky across to tell him there was a gun in the bag which was near me. I told him to stay close.

Mr White, the specialist, came in to inspect my leg, asking me to lift it. I take it he wants me out of here as soon as possible. The four cops and two Unit staff were present as he did this.

Later the two staff came across to tell me that when I was unconscious the cops had got hold of one of them to say that someone had seen me go into my locker, take something out and go under the blankets with it. They wanted to search me and my locker. Both the staff told them I was unconscious, that they were satisfied and to leave it at that. It was then that Bob (staff member) referred to them (the police) wanting to handcuff me to the bed when I entered hospital.

I feel as though I stick out like a sore thumb in here. Terribly self-conscious. I must get away from here. I am trapped and no good can come of this venture. I must extricate myself from this situation causing as few bad feelings as possible. I must conduct the withdrawal using the highest level of diplomacy. The point is that these cops are brutes. In the past I was very much at home with this sort of thing but my reaction now lets me measure how far I've developed as a person. These guys are actually trained to distrust everyone and everything. They would be the first to deny this but their whole training is geared towards suspicion and hostility. There is no sense me projecting everything on to them as they are only the tools of those above issuing the orders.

The pain of my leg has become secondary. The hard part is seeing into the faces of everyone around me – nurses, police, staff and patients – that I am not wanted. I feel an alien. I see the patients pointing me out to their visitors. When speaking to everyone as individuals they all state the scenario is unnecessary but none of them do anything about it. Everyone looks to the police before they smile, talk or make any gesture towards me. Meanwhile I am regulating my trips to the toilet so as not to be constantly followed by a gang of watchers.

30th June '76
This morning at 4.30am Gerry told me that a story has appeared in the *Glasgow Herald* saying that I am in hospital. This comes as no surprise the way the cops handled it. David Scott and Scott Devlin (BBC) came in to see me. I have been given crutches and allowed to sit up. This is the fastest anyone's been allowed up. David passed the head of the CID who had just been in. Apparently the cops showed David a photo of Ben Conroy saying that he was the guy coming to do me. I told them this was utter nonsense. A cop was sitting next to us with his shoulder holster and we could all see it.

A matron came across and I explained to her that this was embarrassing for me and I'd like to get out without hurting anyone's feelings. She said she understood and went for the consultant. She brought him down while Scott and David were present and he told me he would have to have four clear post-operation days before letting me out. This was to keep himself in the clear. I agreed with him. David told me that the Nurses' Union and the SPOA were having meetings this afternoon. The latter with the Department in Edinburgh. The issue is over guns being carried in an open ward. There certainly is a lot of activity.

My brother Harry and his friend came in. The cops came in and pulled his friend out and went to pull Harry. He refused. The cop said he was CID. Harry pushed his hands off telling him he doesn't care who he is that he is here to see me. I shouted to the cop that Harry is my brother. Jim (Unit staff member) said so too. I was so mad at any scene being made and felt really bad. The whole thing was sickening. All the other patients and visitors were looking at us.

After the visit one of the nurses came across saying to me, 'You are in a bit of a cage here, aren't you?' The tension was tightening in my head and she gave me headache pills. She remarked that the whole action of the police pulling Harry was unnecessary; she had watched it all.

On BBC television David Scott gave the matter good coverage. The piece was pretty long and went into detail about there being no communication between the police and the prison authorities. The police boss said they had a tip-off someone was going to harm me – shoot me. A young cop came in tonight saying this was a load of crap and that the escort came from the top. The press have been on to the ward but have been referred to the hospital superintendant.

1st July '76

Wakened at 4.30am and had to get headache tablets.

Gerry told me that the front page of the *Daily Record* has a full story about me. With the head of CID making it clear that this is a security operation because of my past; that I am a dangerous prisoner and a high risk one, that the police make the decisions where security is involved.

Visitors have been turned away all day. My son James came up to visit me this afternoon and got in okay. He didn't say much but we sat together eating strawberries. He said he had brought his two pals but left them at the main gate saying he was going to visit his aunt. James is a very quiet but very deep boy. I feel he is very close to me.

Bob (staff member) came up to Malky to ask the Governor's home number. Malky asked why. Bob said it was for secret reasons. Malky reminded him that he was on escort with him. One of the cops was present. Bob reminded Malky that he was in charge, that he was the senior officer. Malky replied he doesn't mind him thinking he is in charge but in reality he isn't. They got involved in an argument. I spoke to Bob reminding him that we are living under strenuous circumstances and he should bear this in mind. I told him that solidarity would bring us through this. He turned to me saying that only two people will be able to visit me during visiting hours. I asked him who said this. He replied that CID Chief MacKenzie and Medical Superintendent Anderson had told him. I asked one of the policemen sitting nearby about this. He said it was the first he had heard of it. At this Bob returned, his face almost purple saying he had made a mistake. He said he is under tremendous pressure and feeling it.

2nd July '76
This morning I wakened at 6am after having my best sleep since entering hospital. I went to the toilet myself. The two armed cops on duty I haven't seen before but they were tall. Gerry was sleeping in the lecture room, the other staff member, John, was elsewhere. Later he told me he had been under the passages of the hospital. I had particularly asked the staff not to leave me alone with the cops but they don't seem to take it seriously.

There was nothing in the press today but I sent a letter to *The Scotsman* on the hospital/police issue.

Mr White came in and found my pulse and temperature were all right. I sat around reading and speaking to Malky and one of the cops. The cop said if ever he was involved with policy making he will make sure I get an even break. He thought what was happening was a liberty, that it was unnecessary. He remarked that the week with me was an experience for him. He shook my hand. . . Some of the patients came down to say goodbye. I went to see the others, bidding them all goodbye. Malky, Bob and I bought the nurses a box of chocolates. I wrote a small note to them all apologising for any trouble my presence may have caused, thanking them for their support.

I felt the tension ease from me as I left the hospital, felt so tired. It was very confusing for me. I wasn't feeling glad to be leaving the hospital for prison – the Unit. I felt sad at the fact that I wanted to leave hospital but in a way I was numb at going back to prison. Back in the Unit I went to see the Governor. I told him I would like a Petition and that I was writing to my MP. He asked what I was intending to do. I gave him small but loose pieces of information telling him the rest is for my MP. He remarked that if I wanted a future I should move to England. He said this showed that the police were out to get me. I told him the solution to this wouldn't be running away from it.

3rd July '76
This morning I got up and went into the yard. I sat in the sun with the staff, leaving my crutches in the cell as I don't like them. Last night I didn't sleep. I was weary but had an active mind, also my leg was giving me pain. It seems that a detective sergeant phoned the local branch of the SPOA to ask if it was true that a string of prostitutes were coming from Edinburgh to visit me. Ken got the local branch to take this to their Governor. When he spoke to the Department they said that police have been reporting seeing me in pubs and all other such nonsense. The Governor of the main prison said that whenever he is invited to speak to the Police College they always go on about the Special Unit but particularly about Jimmy Boyle and their hostility towards me.

The Governor spoke to me saying that someone from *The Scotsman* called saying they had a letter from me, asking if it really was from me. The journalist read it out. The Governor said it sounded very much like my feelings and unofficially confirmed it. He said he wasn't to be quoted then asked him to give the Unit a break and leave us for a spell. He told the guy to go to the SIO as he wasn't supposed to speak to him. I told him that I did send the letter.   He was in a nervous state saying he will get a call from the Department.

4th July '76
The Governor took Malky and Gerry into his office and asked what they were going to say about the letter I had sent to the press. They said there is nothing they can say as it will all fall back on me. The Governor told them this wasn't good enough as they were in charge of the escort. Malky told him this wasn't the case, the police were in charge of the escort – they took over. The Governor said the press had taken up the letter.

I went into the Governor's office. I asked him how he was. He said okay then went right into the article in the *Sunday Mail* which says, 'A row broke out over a letter from a convicted killer'. He said it looks as though the Department and SIO have been brought in. I told him we discussed this yesterday and I admitted doing it. He then got very angry and replied that the press report today was making him angry. I reminded him that all this week I had been lying in hospital being subjected to all sorts of humiliating and degrading treatment and that he wasn't interested in this, but this letter seemed to upset him more than anything else. He then went on about the prison regulations being breached. I told him yes that was right, just as they had by the police, the Prisons Department and everyone else but it's only when a prisoner does so that punishment is called for. I was shouting at him by this time saying that he is only interested in building his own empire and making sure he isn't hurt. I left the office.

The Governor kept saying the whole thing is political now, that it has been taken out of our hands. He shouted at me saying there are more people in the Unit than me. I told him he's fucking right there are more people in the Unit than me, that's what's worrying me as precedents are being set that will affect others.

5th July '76
There is no doubt about it, these bastards are trying to destroy me mentally. Blows come in psychological form, ripping through my defences, tearing me apart internally. In the face of this new, but very effective game of destruction I cry like a child. Shattered! No injuries are apparent. What is going on, why?

Retaliation is called for. This violent typewriter shouts bloody anger. Punching holes in the fucking enemy with each tap of the key. Fingers filled with fire and vengeance as they press each lettered key – hatehatehatehatehate. Fuckers causing mental anguish, I HATE YOU.

They would like to see it. Oh God, they would like to see it. If I were to strike out and hit one of them. 'See!' they would shout. 'Look, the bastard is an animal.' All would turn to me and point. 'Animal, Animal,' they would cry.

What the fucking hell am I doing sitting here suppressing all this natural anger and keeping it under the surface? Does this make me any more civilised? I'm supposed to sit here like some vegetable with a mandarin smile accepting it all.

6th July '76
At the meeting today Bill Allan brought up that Davy's mother was sick after making a long journey here. He asked the Community to let Davy go home on occasional visits to see her

whenever she can't come here. There was lots of discussion on this and it was agreed it should be left for a week or so.

The Governor brought up the letter from the Department on staff follow-up when a Unit prisoner had been transferred. It said the Governors in other prisons are against this and the Department concur with their views. Malky brought up that my mail should be censored for a month as I had broken the Unit rules, that I was accountable to the Community. I answered this by pointing out that I had been taken outside the Community into a situation where they could not protect me therefore I had to protect myself. A discussion followed with Bill Allan wanting to know the reason why I was being punished. He said he had no fears of me doing this again, that he didn't condone what I did but couldn't agree to punish me in this way. The Governor stated if they didn't do something then it would seem that there are two sets of values in the Unit, one for Davy and another for me. Staff pointed out to the Governor that Davy had breached the mail issue a number of times before his mail was censored. It was put to a vote. The Governor and Malky voted for, the rest against.

8th July '76
Tomorrow John, a new prisoner, comes to the Unit from Perth Prison. He is serving an eighteen-year prison sentence for bank robbery. Nicknamed 'The Bat' because of his bad eyesight and thick glasses, he is an ex-Gorbals guy and we get on very well.

9th July '76
John and I had a long talk with him telling me things are much the same if not worse than when I left. He is very bitter about the Parole Board, saying he wouldn't take it if they offered it to him. He is also extremely bitter about his experiences in Perth and Edinburgh prisons. I didn't want to overload him with this place so I gave him a small bit and on the whole just listened to him pour out his experiences.

10th July '76
This morning I wakened, did my exercises then asked Davy to give me a hand to unpack the sculptures from their cases as they had returned from the York Festival exhibition.

Beth (American artist) came in this afternoon bringing a note from Tom McGrath. Tom is always apologising for not coming to the Unit. He is going through a confusing time because of the Unit, or maybe himself. He had a chat with Maurice (lawyer) about me and is afraid the Unit is getting to him. This happens to people when they come here. It makes them look more closely at themselves. Beth said she was sitting with a girl the other day when Tom came in remarking 'The Jimmy Boyle fan club'. Beth feels she has to keep arguing with people that there are more people in the Unit than Jimmy Boyle. I am going to write to Tom.

21st July '76
Tom McGrath came up today saying the reason he has been keeping away is that while attending a weekend conference at the Prison Officers Training College, three of the Governor grade caught hold of him during the evening social events and had a go at him about me. They said I was an evil manipulator, that I had certain people under my control and he is one. Tom said they went on at length tearing me for shit paper. There is no doubt that he got a fright. He said if these allegations are going to be levelled at him then he is going to stay away. He said it was very nasty.

Tom went on to tell me that Lord Balfour of the Scottish Arts Council phoned him a few weeks ago to say the Arts Minister would be meeting him and Sandy Dunbar, also of the Arts Council, in an hour's time in the Third Eye Centre. He asked Tom to put something simple on show as the Minister would like to be shown round the Centre after the meeting. The reason he said put something simple was, when taking office, the Minister had thrown an abstract painting out saying they are a waste of money. The Minister in question is Under Secretary of State for Scotland (Education) Frank McElhone MP (Gorbals).

After the meeting McElhone went down to the gallery with Balfour and Dunbar. Tom said on approaching him McElhone said, 'This is the man giving me all the problems'. Tom, Balfour and Dunbar looked at each other puzzled. McElhone went on to say 'He gives a man called Boyle exhibitions and glamorises him'. He went on to tell them what I was really like and came out with a stream of filth that shocked all three. He not only verbally assassinated me but stamped me into the ground. He made references that he knew of 'six people I had murdered'. He said kids in the Gorbals are all looking up to the sculpture that I was doing before the sort I was doing now. He went on for ten minutes about me without interruption.

Afterwards Tom said he pointed out that he had my work on show for three weeks and never had he heard any man in the street say anything bad about it and he was shocked that a Minister could talk like that. Tom stated that a relative of someone I had fought at one time remarked that he liked the sculpture and was glad to see how I was doing. McElhone wouldn't listen. Both Balfour and Dunbar were trying to get cash out of McElhone for the Arts, so were cringing at the ferocity of his attack. It ended with Tom arguing the case for more cash and on the way out McElhone turned to Tom telling him to stop being radical, come into the centre away from the left and you'll get the help you need. These were his parting words.

I have never met McElhone but the ironic thing is that I've always been glad to see him get in during an election. His attack seems very personal and the strange thing is I've just had Department permission to write to my MP to complain about the police treatment while in hospital. I must get him up here and confront him but I am in a situation where I don't want to fuck things up for Tom. If he is saying this to Tom he is obviously saying it elsewhere so I won't name the source as his mind will do the rest. I want to nail this fucker on this 'six murders' rubbish as this must be the shit being put round about me. They are bastards with their innuendo and psychological warfare. These bastards really know how to kick someone in the balls. It's no wonder Tom had been giving me a body swerve recently. The poor bastard must have been in a turmoil; still, he should know the game these people play but should he? I never expected shit like this. At this point I feel tiny and helpless as the State machinery prepares to crush me.

22nd July '76

Dear Mr McElhone,
I have a very pressing and important issue that I wanted to raise with you but while gaining the necessary permission from the Prisons Dept. I was informed that you had expressed some very hostile opinions of me, and this has put me in a dilemma.

It is understandable that people will have very emotional opinions about me and my past. No one is more aware of this than me as I have to live with my past. I am now in prison nine years, and the past three and a half years the Special Unit have given me an opportunity to make a genuine effort to change. All of this with the intention of contributing something back into society. In making this change I've had tremendous support from my family, relatives and friends, who are ordinary decent people living in our district. There have been others but the locals have been particularly encouraging.

I realise that there are younger kids in the district who may want to emulate my 'violent ways', just as I wanted to emulate Dan Cronin or Paddy Slowey's 'violent ways', and this is a factor that weighs heavily upon me. My son and daughter are still staying in the Gorbals and like any other parent I am frightened of what's going to become of them, that they could possibly get caught in a situation resembling mine and this I would dread. But for the first time someone with my violent experience is realising that crime and all that it entails is completely wrong and futile. My attitudes have changed from those of a negative outlook to a positive outlook. I want to try and improve the situation in whatever way I can.

The problem is that in making these efforts to change I have received hostility, not so much from the ordinary people, but from the Teddy Taylors and Nicholas Fairbairns of this world. Each rejection of my efforts is a blow to me. By refusing to accept that a person like me can change it leaves the situation rather bleak for 'the man from the Gorbals' people now in prison serving sentences.

I fully appreciate the heavy schedule that you now must have as Minister and understand the Parliamentary situation at the moment but I would like to ask if you could possibly come and see me here in order to discuss the important issue I have and the contents of this letter?

Yours most sincerely

26th July '76
Ken caught hold of me to say Davy has written a letter to his mother upsetting her to an extent where the doctor took all the tablets out of her house in case she took them. Ken feels his mother is every bit to blame as he is.

Another meeting was called. We were told Davy had gone into the Governor's room where Wattie, Gerry and Mike sat. He pulled out a long, sharp needle and put it at Wattie's throat saying he will take his eyes out and flush them down the toilet pan and cut Ken's throat if restrictions are placed on his mail or use of the telephone. Everyone froze and he put the needle away. They tried to get it off him but he refused to give it till he got to phone his mother. Ken said he could and he gave him the needle. Mike stayed while he used the phone. Davy sat in the meeting very tense saying everyone is interfering in his life. It was pointed out to him that his mother had got on to Ken and Wattie and they had to heed her fears. The argument became heated and Davy threatened violence. He refused to see anyone's point of view saying we must get him out of the Unit. He threatened to do a Duncy. He left the meeting but returned to say he is locking himself up and going on a hunger strike till he is moved from here. We decided that things had reached a serious stage and that Davy needed some sort of treatment. Peter Whatmore was present and said this was a matter for the Community. He was asked if Davy needed hospital treatment and replied there is no place he could be put as he isn't ill. Davy's behaviour is more than odd. I think he should be put in an open hospital for help. Peter said this couldn't be so. Everyone agreed if he is going to use violence then he will have to go.

27th July '76
Davy is gone. The Governor called a meeting and informed us that he had phoned the Department to put them in the picture about Davy's latest incident. Tom Melville told him they had just received a Petition from Davy saying if he isn't moved from the Unit he will do a Duncy. With the information given by the Governor, the Director of Prisons authorised Davy's transfer. There was a part in me hating this. I said nothing. I couldn't.

> The womb that consumed
> The penis inserted
> Made it possible
> for me to be
> Here.

28th July '76
This morning I wakened with Davy on my mind. He is on solitary and anywhere he goes two staff go with him – exercise and slopping out, etc. I did my exercises then went outside. I did some sculpting with the sandstone and felt really great. I thoroughly enjoy being back at work again. I had a letter from Duncy's wife.

He goes to court for his pleading diet on 6th August and the 16th August for trial. He has been charged with serious assault causing permanent disfigurement. There is a Welsh nut who labels himself criminologist who is making a scene about the hospital. It seems the Chairman of the Police Federation in commenting on my letter to *The Scotsman* said that I was illiterate and the letter had been written by an educated hand and not by me. This Welshman wrote saying he wants heads to roll. The Governor brought it to me himself long after the mail had been distributed so he is a bit panicky. I thought it very funny.

1st August '76

Frank McElhone, J.P.M.P.
House of Commons
London SW1A 0AA

Dear Mr Boyle,
With regard to your letter of 22nd July, I find the contents most surprising. Could I point out to you that I am delighted that you are attempting to make the effort to change, as it is something I have tried to encourage in all people, who end up in prison.

I should also point out however that many people have complained to me. Prisoners, the families of prisoners and people in my constituency area that there are many people, who are serving very long sentences, who don't get the use of the Special Unit, or the encouragement to pursue an interest in Sculpture. I am not against these things, but feel that you have been a victim of too much publicity, regarding your Sculpture, and this has brought more criticism than it has praise.

Unfortunately, I have been off from Parliament for several weeks, with a slipped disc and therefore a lot of engagements had to be postponed and will have to be fitted in to an overburdened diary, in the next few months, therefore, it will be impossible for me to fit in a visit to you, in the near future.

I would suggest therefore, that you should write to me, on the important issue you wish to raise with me and I will deal with it as sympathetically as possible.

Yours sincerely

11th August '76
I was up till 4.20am working on the letter to Frank McElhone

and trying to get things off the ground on this whole matter. My mind was alive and there was no way I could go to sleep. I managed two hours then got up to do my exercises:

Dear Mr McElhone,
I am encouraged that you are delighted that I am making the effort to change and was heartened to hear that many prisoners and families of prisoners within the constituency area have complained to you that they don't get the use of the Special Unit or the encouragement to pursue Sculpture. Like you, I feel that they should be given the chance and it is great to see that so many people feel so strongly about it as it does show a desire to change their ways. It is high time that what is happening here in the Special Unit should be expanded and I hope that you as Minister will add your weight to this. Certainly there is a financial crisis but the specific areas I am talking about cost nothing financially and it would be a feather in the cap of Scotland to be showing this remarkable progress at a time when the crime rate is increasing and the financial situation is very bad.

I am rather puzzled by your statement that I am a victim of too much publicity regarding my sculpture and that it brought more criticism than praise. I have heard this statement before from the civil servants at the Prisons Dept., but I can assure you that it is a total contradiction to the reality of the situation. I have piles of documentation here to prove this and you can see it anytime. I know that there are certain people in 'responsible positions' who are saying that I am being turned into star material, etc., etc., but I feel that I should give you a breakdown of the situation. I started sculpting in 1974 and was encouraged in this by the Prisons Dept. It was they who first introduced the media to the Special Unit and in the press handouts declared my remarkable talents as a sculptor. I was encouraged to have exhibitions like any other artist and initially there was a great deal of publicity about it but afterwards both press and the galleries where my work was being shown throughout Britain handled it in a very mature way. In fact I was delighted that the press handled it so maturely while my work was shown in Glasgow. I was very apprehensive beforehand about the man in the street's opinion but let me tell you the response was something that delighted me. You see, what is worrying me is that certain people are too quick off the mark to quote in public when the fact is that it just isn't the case. Let me tell you that last year while in hospital Teddy Taylor was making media statements due to the public having supposedly complained about me being in an open ward with them. It was the very same public who were incensed by this lie that answered him by making a collective statement to the media refuting this. I am very much aware of this tactic and that is why I now keep all the documentation to substantiate what I am saying. I must say that I am bitterly disappointed that there is no way you can manage to see me in the near future concerning this very important issue. It is a very complex matter and will be very difficult for me to put on paper but I suppose I must if I am to get it seen to. I was very sorry to hear about your slipped disc and hope that it is much better.

Sincerely

20th August '76
The Governor . . . went straight to the court to watch the proceedings. . . Duncy was given six years consecutive to his present sentence. The Judge told him had he not received the letters from me, James L., Larry, and the letter he wrote to his wife then he would have been given ten years. The Judge said there were no mitigating circumstances as he had gone into J.L.'s cell and attacked a fellow prisoner while he lay in bed. The radio said Duncy went berserk because his wife was suing him for divorce. The TV had similar reports. Duncy now has an extra six years to serve and what does this prove? What happens to the guy now?

21st August '76
The press had reports about Duncy's trial and the *Scottish Daily Express* was vile to say the least. The headline screamed BARLINNIE KNIFE ROW and quoted Teddy Taylor as coming up to see what we were doing, that he doesn't agree with the Unit philosophy. It is a complete distortion of what went on in court. The rest of the press, *The Glasgow Herald*, *The Scotsman* and *Daily Record* are fair. . .

Ken phoned to say he is getting Hugh Brown MP to ask him to fix it to get Teddy Taylor to come in. Ken was very angry at this bastard Taylor jumping on the bandwagon.

31st August '76
Teddy Taylor MP came in. . . He is a small, balding man who was quite apprehensive though trying not to show it. He offered us all a cigarette and then I took him round.

His main theme was vandalism and how this problem could be solved. I showed him the kitchen and he could see the knives lying in the cutlery box but made no comment. . . I showed him inside every cell and we had a brief chat with J.L. as we entered his cell. He asked him about vandalism. He asked what I would do when I got out and I told him I'd probably have to get a job. He said that I am now pretty well established as a sculptor and asked pointedly if I would become a celebrity when I got out. I told him as far as I was concerned I'd try to help the situation in the Gorbals and other districts.

We all sat in the meeting room and had a long debate on the Unit and he was all for what we were doing but should do it without publicity. We discussed this and he was so full of contradictions that it was difficult to accept. He mentioned all his mates and friends who have just come out of prison, some of whom are working for him in the Conservative Party – locally. Then he would say prison nowadays is a soft option and on the other hand state that it must be terrible to be locked up with no privacy. During our discussion he had a phone call from the BBC and came back and told us the press were waiting on him. He came on very heavy against the Department saying they are a bunch of intellectual civil servants then came in heavy against social workers, psychiatrists, and sociologists. He stayed for three hours then left but first asked if he could come back. . .

Teddy Taylor held an impromptu Press Conference at the prison gate. We understand he said that it is too soon to say whether it (Unit) is a success or not. He thinks the experiment is going very well and thinks it should continue. This will be on radio tomorrow morning. We understand Harry Ewing is quoted as saying he is glad to see Teddy T. has come into the Unit after three and a half years.

18th September '76
Today was really good for me as I worked hard and thoroughly enjoyed it. This carving really has a hold on me at the moment. I like the pieces I am turning out as they are very strong and much to do with what is going on in me personally. Prison ceases to exist and more to the point I become a whole person. I reasoned that what I was doing during this, what we are all seeking, is to become a whole person. All the petty niggles that the mind uses to occupy itself in the fragmented person disappear. I get the most

fantastic feeling of being alive. This experience is exactly what I need and want. It seems to put everything into proper perspective and has left me typing this feeling both exhilarated and thoroughly exhausted.

30th September '76
Roy Rogers had a big influence on me when I was a child, so too did Jesse James and his gang. It depended what mood I was in but they were both good at shooting and getting what they wanted. It was amazing how I would gallop through the dirty backcourts, skirting muddy puddles as though they were deep, dangerous chasms in the Rocky Mountains, letting my clever horse Trigger guide me safely home. Then I would be Jesse, with the neck of my pullover hiding the lower part of my face as I went to rob the stage or the train. No matter who I was, there was constant vigilance in case those dirty Indians ambushed me, but to be fair there were times when I would be one of them too. I loved Geronimo and always believed I was a true Apache.

Then there was Rocky Marciano; he was the number one hero of the district. Boy, he could really put them away. One punch and they lost their senses. I can remember when he fought Don Cockell, we all sat around the wireless listening, men, women and children. I went to the window that dark night and looked out to the wet street that was empty, hearing all the wirelesses going. The fight game had us all captivated that night. One of the local legends was Benny Lynch who came from our district in the Gorbals so we were brought up on a diet of tales about him. I remember how I used to shadow box on a sunny day or have 'dummy fights' with my pals and we would roll over the streets as though being pounded by the opponent but always I managed to make the last minute recovery to put him away and leave him sprawled on the street.

Tarzan was also important to me as he would come swinging down from the trees and fight off a million darkies who were about to boil Jane in a pot. But then who could beat Flash Gordon who would be trapped in a room with the walls closing in . . . with me suddenly finding myself thrown into the street to await the next chapter the following week. I would run out of the movies either swinging on an imaginary vine as Tarzan, or driving a spaceship into Mars as Flash. My pal's father, who was big and strong, used to really impress me and others by clenching his fist and letting the muscles on his biceps juggle about while we stared wide-eyed in awe. After a session of this we would all be lying on the ground doing press-ups. One of the real favourites was that man at the Barrows who would let himself be tied with chains and put in a strait-jacket only to escape. I would then get my pals to tie me up tight with a rope and squirm about for ten minutes to get out, and would end up cursing them for tying me up too tight as I couldn't get out.

The real favourite though was the gang-fighter in our district as he could really fight. His gang was so tough that no one in the district would challenge them. Whenever we heard they were going to fight we would run to the meeting place and watch the enemy disperse with a flash of blade. Who could beat them? Afterwards we would pretend to be them and have dummy fights among ourselves.

I tried very hard to be as good as Roy and as bad as Jesse, a winner like Rocky and a loser like Don but very much a fighter like Benny, to have the guts of Tarzan and the speed of Flash with muscles of my pal's father and be as tricky as the escapologist in the Barrows. I then used them all to become the leader of a gang. I was now all my heroes wrapped up in one.

2nd October '76
Wattie came round asking if anything had come up during his day off and I told him no. We discussed Larry going into hospital to get his tattooes removed and Wattie felt it may make Larry think about his future. He went on to say Larry and him had a long talk recently, the first in a while. I know that Larry has reduced his barbiturates by one. There is no doubt that he is responding to the hospital outing and I firmly believe if the penal system were to give guys more hope then this response would be common.

John has been in bed a good part of the day. I had to waken him at 4.50 to get up and go for his food before the 5pm lock-up. He was dead to the world. Prior to coming here, John was very much into drugs officially, and any illegal drugs that came into prison you could be sure he was into them. It's not that he likes them but more that he sees them as an escape from the reality of the time he is doing. There is no doubt that the Unit is getting through to him. He is going through a particularly bad period and I will have to make a point of spending more time with him. When he is not sleeping, he is deep in thought and brooding. It's the same with Larry, and the thought has just struck me that he knows more about drugs and the drug scene than most guys on the outside yet when he was outside he didn't know what drugs were. Someone remarked to me that Larry must have been heavily into drugs before coming to prison but the truth was that he wasn't. All the newly acquired friends he has who are part of the drug scene are from prison.

12th October '76
Larry came back with heavy bandaging round his leg and hand because of skin grafts, etc. The trip went well and there were no police in sight at all. One of the staff who escorted Larry was saying there was bad hostility from some of the hospital staff who were saying that lots of people with serious defects are being turned away because of the waiting list (which Larry had been on for ten years) and yet here is Larry getting this done. After a spell they softened somewhat but this is the sort of attitude we have to break down. The fact that Larry comes from prison makes his treatment seem less deserving to them and this is wrong. They said that if Larry wanted this he should have paid for it. Instead of playing one off against the other they should be saying that the facilities should be expanded to cater for everyone. Anyway, Larry seems well enough.

26th October '76
Joyce Laing said she had bad news for me. She explained that the press had been on to her, two journalists from the *Sunday People*, one from the Manchester office and the other from Scotland. Joyce had been working in hospitals all over the north of Scotland and apparently they had been following her but kept missing her. After four days searching they finally caught up with her in her house. They asked if it was true that she was pregnant to me. Joyce was taken aback by this and went on to ask why they were doing this. The guy said it was a very big story and was hinting at large sums of money if she would substantiate it. They also told her she would be helped with her art work, publicity, etc. Joyce tried to find out where they were getting their information. They refused to disclose their sources saying it didn't come from a prisoner or staff in the Unit but hinted at the police. They strongly emphasised Joyce's name being linked with mine in pubs throughout Glasgow. Joyce tried to tell them what the Unit was

about but all they were interested in was the story. She was badly shaken and asked what sort of money is being spent on this sort of thing when a newspaper can send a man up from Manchester for four days and two of them can travel all over Scotland on expenses – all in the name of sensationalism. We talked it over and I told Joyce that this rumour has been going around for some time and pops up continuously in different forms, though this is the first time her name has been linked with it. She said she has spoken to Peter Whatmore about it and asked what I thought. I told her I'd speak to Peter also but it should be left to die a natural death. When I did speak to Peter he agreed with this but told me he had advised Joyce to have an off-the-cuff talk with Meikle at the Department. He thought I should mention it to the Governor some time and I agreed to do this.

10th December '76
This morning I wakened and thought of my Ma. She is dead five years to the day. I rang my bell to get the door opened then went into the yard to do my run. Snow had fallen overnight. I ran round the yard though taking it easy. The hard crispy snow crunched under my feet as I ran. After my exercises I knelt before the bed and said a decade of the rosary for my Ma. It's strange, I'm not in the least religious but Ma was so I feel this is the best way to remember her. Only I could possibly know what she gave me throughout my life. I knelt thinking of her and how beautiful she was in standing by me. Also how much she did for my brothers. Doing this is very important for me as I feel as though I'm giving her something in return.

21st December '76
A delegation consisting of members of my family and friends approached Frank McElhone. They visited him in his surgery in Gorbals Street and had a long session with him about me and my future. It was put to him that he had been saying derogatory things about me. McElhone denied this saying he knew me well. My brother Harry replied angrily that he didn't know me. They put his back to the wall and extracted a promise from him to come and see me. He said he would visit before the end of the year.

30th December '76
At 2.15pm Ken came across with Frank McElhone. He told him

his wife and daughter were in the car so Ken said he would collect them. I came upstairs with Frank and we sat down with coffee. He talked about the good work he is doing in List 'D' Schools and in football hooliganism. He went to great pains to describe how he is all for reform in prison and that being an abolitionist of capital punishment he must believe in redemption. He went on to say he had words with Lord Balfour and others about their making me into a star through my sculpture after having seen the catalogue for the Third Eye exhibition. He then said the more they put me to the fore the harder it will be for me to get ultimate freedom.

I explained to him that over the past four years I had worked constructively but that some months ago I was hit with a very damaging problem in that he as Under-Secretary of State had made public statements to the effect that I had – that he personally knew of – murdered six people. This knocked him quite a bit as it was the last thing he was expecting. I went on to say this is a very cruel statement as it has no foundation and if I had the money I would sue to clear my name publicly. He was in a bit of a state at this as I was unemotional, rational and low key. He didn't even deny it. Instead he rambled on about the good work he does. He was waffling. I pointed out to him the damage this could do me and my future, reminding him that if anyone said to me that a person convicted of one murder had murdered six others I would tend to believe it, particularly if the person telling me was an Under-Secretary of State. People like to think that a person in such a position is responsible. He then went on to say he had never made a public statement about this as it wasn't his Department, therefore he couldn't. I told him that by public statement I mean in an informal social context. He said he appreciated the damage this could do me. . . I expressed concern as to what was on my file as a result. He promised he would look into this and that he would speak to Harry Ewing about it and tell me in writing that this was not in my file.

He went on to talk about my future and asked what I thought of it and the situation. I pointed out that I was realistic and that I made up my own long-term programme but must have an external programme as an integral part of my development as it's the only logical direction for my future. He wholeheartedly agreed saying that Harry Ewing was being told that I am manipulating everything to get out immediately. I told him I knew where this was coming from. . . He said he has told Harry Ewing that anything he sends to him he intends sending me a copy whether it's good or bad as he doesn't want me to think he is doing the dirty on me. . .

There is no doubt that he was impressed, but what came home to me is that this guy is extremely limited. I think that he is doing some pretty good work but I am appalled at the calibre of people in these jobs; it must be a contributory factor to the present state of things. Despite the damage McElhone has done to me there is something lively about him but I don't think this balances out the deficiencies.

The only reason he came here was due to heavy pressure. He mentioned his alarm at my brother Harry coming on so heavy and that this will only do me harm. He said the rest of my family were very good. He is gone now and we will have to wait to see what develops from here.

8th January '77 (12.21am)
There is a real anger in me. Oh my God, it's almost as though everyone is abandoning their brains. The position is so delicate, so absolutely fragile yet, within this, I am holding on by a very thin thread. Larry seems set on a course of self-destruction. If a person is set on this course then there are times when very little can be done about it and I reluctantly admit this. Even so he cannot be allowed to continue on his course as it not only destroys him but all of us.

On the other side of the coin there are others quite prepared to sit and not take part in any of this. Martin Ritt, the McCarthyite blacklisted film-maker said of that era: 'You know my mother said to me at that time, "Marty, what have you done? This is a fair country." That's what the pressure was like. Millions of ordinary people couldn't contemplate what was happening.'

I am so burnt up that I want to sleep yet can't. There are times when I feel it is all too much for me, that it is all about to fall in but from the depths comes this tenacity that refuses to let go. I was speaking to Dr Curran of the Local Review Committee the other day. He started to tell me I'm an exception, that there is no one here like me. I pointed out to him that this was the wrong way to look at it and went on to say the others are improving and showing progress in different ways. Inwardly I was saddened. The Unit can't afford this to be the case. I certainly don't want it to be. I want my ideal to be correct, that every prisoner given the chance can respond in the way I have, can make the most of the opportunities given them. I feel so frustrated tonight, so locked in, so alone, so tired and weary with life.

Tonight I stare at the veins as they protrude from the skin on my arms and hands. Frequently I put my hand to my hair and run it through. Then backwards to feel my neck and round towards the throat, all the while touching skin. Touching, trying to share the feel of myself with myself.

14th January '77
The Problem Escalates
I am very worried about Larry's involvement with heavy drugs. He is hitting heroin and cocaine at the moment and is looking wasted. I have discussed this with one of the staff at an unofficial level and feel that it should be handled quietly. The reason for this decision is that if revealed that heavy drugs are being used in the Unit the Governor and some staff would panic and it would almost certainly result in the problem being handled in a traditional way. Larry had been getting drugs smuggled in when he was in the main prison system and it was never brought to the surface. The good thing about here is that some of us are discussing and trying to tackle the problem. To be honest, I have seen heavy drugs used frequently in the main system and simply shrugged my shoulders, often wishing the guys the best of luck as anything that beats the system was great to me, but now that my attitudes have changed, I cannot condone this at any level. I also think that to take this to Peter Whatmore would be more than useless as Larry would say nothing and neither would he to anyone connected to the establishment.

Ken told a group of us that last night he was in the Officers' Social Club with two others. He went to buy a drink for them. A member of staff from the main prison was sitting cursing and swearing. Ken told him to watch his language as there were women sitting at the next table. The staff member turned on Ken calling him a Special Unit bastard and getting up he kicked Ken on the thigh. Ken said he was livid and grabbed the man but refrained from hitting him. –

A discussion took place on this particular member of staff covering a whole range of offences from initiating a group of staff going in to beat up a prisoner (causing one member of staff to leave and join the Unit) to pulling a knife out in the local pub and getting banned. This is the sort of person in charge of us and as my diary has indicated throughout he is by no means an exception.

24th January '77
... Ken gave me his letter to Harry Ewing, asking if I would type it for him. It is very good as he is telling him that he is going to put a resolution at the Scottish Labour Party Conference in March asking them to back a penal policy on the lines of the Unit. I feel it will frighten Ewing.

25th Feburary '77
Tom McGrath came up and we had a good discussion. It was nice to see him again. He told me he's had comeback to the McElhone saga. Seemingly Sandy Dunbar of the Scottish Arts Council had phoned him a week or so after he had received a copy of all the material from me. Dunbar phoned at the unearthly hour of 9am (Tom's words) asking what he had told me as McElhone has been raising holy hell saying that I have been sending him threatening letters. Tom didn't know what to say as he had to be diplomatic – these are the people who give funding to the Third Eye Centre. He stumbled through by saying I already had knowledge of what McElhone was saying and so he discussed this when I mentioned it. Dunbar went on to say that McElhone had made it clear that he was going to veto a decision that was pending for another administrator of the Arts Council. It seems McElhone does have the power of veto. Tom said he brought this up at a meeting of his Board, one of whom was in the Labour Party. The guy's face fell. It seems Tom had to get Sir William Grey to write to McElhone and smooth it out. They have heard nothing about it since. The meeting to veto the Arts Council administrator was to have taken place the day all the MPs coming from the Commons got stranded in a train due to bad weather. Tom said that had he not been in possession of a copy of the documentation I sent him then he would have been wondering about the threatening letter part.

I went into the matter saying I would not have left him open to this sort of thing. At no time did I mention his or anyone's name but relied on McElhone's guilty mind to do it all – it did. Tom said he wasn't concerned if I had mentioned his name as he knows what was said.

We discussed the play that we have been working on and though I thought he had been too busy to start on it, he has. We went over what has been done and it's shaping up well. It will be ready for showing in *The Traverse* on May of this year. Peter Kelly will play the part of me. Peter Lichtenfels will direct it. We will have a long working session on it. We went over the whole thing and he wants to get our lawyers to write up a contract on a 50/50 split so that everything is official. I brought him up to date on my book and the Trust Fund I intend setting up.

3rd March '77

This morning was spent waiting on the Parkhurst Prison people coming. Bob (staff member) went to pick them up at the Central Hotel. Dr Cooper is the psychiatrist and Mr Bryant is the Governor. I took them round and the Governor followed all the way – it was annoying. I was trying to spell every point out to them, concentrating on the areas I thought important. I gave them all the information I could. On seeing the oxy-acetylene equipment the Governor (Bryant) said that red lights are ringing in his ears. I showed him the hacksaw and other materials I use for working. I spelled out to them that these things were built up through 'trust' and through staff working with prisoners to build up relationships. I showed them the weight room which was a former punishment cell and how we no longer use it to lock people up. I went into detail on the process of this. In the joiners room they turned to me and said I was unique and a special sort of person as I had talent, and was articulate. I came in very strong here saying this wasn't the case and if other guys were given the same opportunities they would be equally successful. After this they went for lunch. While they were away I told the others we were going to have a difficult job with these two as they reminded me of myself when I entered the Unit. The Governor was very tense and extremely 'closed'. The doctor was less so but still closed.

Dr Cooper introduced what they were doing in Parkhurst and the kind of guys they had. He gave examples: one guy an arsonist who has to light fires in order to masturbate and how they have got him over this; the Kray twins both of whom have their personal problems. The discussion opened and it was clear they were here to justify rather than find out. I personally felt they were giving a whitewash of what they were doing.

They said their unit in 'C' wing had effectively cut violence in the penal system. I said we only have to look at the media to see this isn't true. There was silence on this. Denis (Jewish prisoner) told Cooper that with his attitude there is little wonder there is so much trouble in the system. The meeting was very heated at times with Governor Bryant saying little. Everything we told them we were doing they replied saying similar things and it ended up with me wondering why they were here if this was so. The doctor said this place is unreal and that we should be sent back to the main system to be tested. We came in strong on this and pointed out that the one priority of the Unit is not to make them fit for a prison but to return to society. They were confused at this and felt we had adopted a technique to handle such questions. They were so full of prison culture and felt that by repeating prison priorities to them we were somehow cheating. Nearer the end Larry got up and left.

I wound the meeting up by saying it was nice having them but I felt we were working in different ways, the one thing that makes or breaks a situation is the staff/prisoner relationship. The doctor said we had exchanged views and they are leaving with some ideas from here in their heads. The Governor, Bryant, who was sitting quiet throughout, was asked by Meikle if he had anything to say. He said he was here to observe and take in what was happening.

I will be surprised if they implement any of our ideas.

4th March '77

This morning I had Neil Cameron and Paul Nolan across from the Craigmillar Festival Society. We discussed the children's play sculpture, Gulliver, that I am designing for them. We discussed the technical side and other areas such as safety and construction. I will do a small-scale model of Gulliver for them to submit to their Executive Committee. The project will need £500 for the actual piece of sculpture – it is hoped that kids can run through the body and head. They will get a team of workers from Jobs Creation and they will be local people. They will get finance to go to London to get some experience of concrete techniques.

18th March '77

There is a part of me that dreads wakening to face the wall again. I get out of bed and run round the yard, sit in my cell, talk to the same faces, get screwed up by the same people, stimulated by the same people. Always its the sameness that is killing me. I need external stimulation. I need to live, I need to expand and broaden.

Having entered at a disadvantage and got myself into the rut of the disadvantaged I wonder if it is possible to extract myself from it. I only have one life but am living in a society that wants me to pay with that life for things that are also their responsibility. I didn't set the standards for having to live this way. I am not trying to exonerate myself, all I am saying is that much of it was inevitable.

25th March '77

I went upstairs to read the proofs of my book, *A Sense of Freedom*, and after an hour or so I went back downstairs as I felt something was in the air. . .

I met Ken and we sat chatting. . . The Governor came in and dropped a bombshell by saying he has word about a job on the management side of the oil industry. He got word today that he has it. He said he is wondering how to drop it to the lads. He is also wondering how he will drop it to Meikle as he starts on 12th April. He feels that the job has been getting on him as it is a dead-end job for anyone interested in trying out new ideas. He said no matter how bright a person is he cannot get on as promotion is based on seniority. This means that any young man with potential has to suppress his personality and initiative as he is always under a boss who assesses and reports on him. This means the status quo remains as they are resistant to new ideas.

13th April '77

Hugh Brown and Harry Ewing came in today (an unofficial visit). We talked in generalities, mainly in a lighthearted way about various things. The Governor and staff were present. I get more and more impressed with Hugh Brown every time I see him. We talked about the penal system and I stated that any fundamental change in the system must come from the politicians. Harry Ewing agreed. He said it's the inflexibility of the system that gets to him. He gave an example. Jim Sillars MP phoned him on a Sunday night about a constituent/prisoner serving twelve months for a driving offence. His father was dying and he wanted to know if Harry could get the guy out to spend the last few hours with his father. Harry said he got on to the Prisons Division and a day or so later they said they had checked it out and phoned him saying there was no truth in the father being in a serious condition and that it was all a ruse. Harry had to inform them that the guy's father had died that morning. He was furious but it was a moving example of what the Department are doing.

Hugh went to speak to Denis (new prisoner). He then popped his head in the door and asked me to explain about my book. In full hearing of everyone I reminded Harry that my family had written to him about its publication. He said he had a letter from my sister-in-law and had heard about the book from many other people. He hadn't read it but certainly would like to. I then explained to him that I felt it would be important for it to be published and gave reasons why. I asked if he knew about the Trust Fund and he did. I outlined it to him for the benefit of those present. Harry Ewing then said he would read it, not to censor it but to see if it should be approved. If it is along the lines he has heard, then he will authorise its being published.

I then took Harry round the Unit. We stood in the hall area talking. He told me he is as hated as I am by the division (Department) as he has a go at them continuously. . . He told me he knows I won't get into trouble again as I have a future for myself. I said I was aware of this just as I was aware that a section of society demanded I remained in prison till the price had been paid. . . He went back to the book and said he won't be reading it as a censor but as to its merits on it being published.

24th April '77
Last night I did a very unusual thing by going to bed at 7.40pm and sleeping till 8am this morning. I wakened feeling I had wasted a lot of hours and felt guilty about sleeping all this time. Later while sitting in my cell Malky (staff member) came in dressed in civilian clothes. He had been at the Training College for the past three days on the Assistant Governor's interview course. Meikle and some of the Governors were there. He felt he skated through it and did very well but the last ten minutes let him see the way it was going:

An outside assessor – an old army man – took him into a room saying, 'between us and the four walls the consensus of opinion is that you are your own worst enemy'. Malky asked what he meant and was told that from his reports he is down as anti-authority and seems always to be looking for the bad points in his superiors. He told Malky his reports say that he is wanting to change society and that his antagonistic attitude isn't doing his career any good. He told him to remember what Tennyson said about looking for the good points in our superiors.

It makes me wonder if we are ever going to make any progress.

28th April '77
Had better make a note of the letter from Joe Black of the Police Federation whom we invited in:

Jimmy,

Just a note on behalf of Tom and myself to say thank you for taking the time to show us round the 'Special Unit'. We found it very interesting and enjoyed the dialogue with the boys. We are aware that this is a new dimension in the penal system and we thought that it had merit. At least it provides for a frank exchange of views which is necessary if we are ever to understand each other's difficulties and problems.

We would esteem it a favour if you could pass on our sincere thanks.

Yours sincerely
Joe Black
General Secretary

I will read this out tomorrow at the meeting. I think it is an indication of the new and important ground we are breaking here.

30th April '77

Dear M/s Murray,

Thank you for the draft copy of the book written by Jimmy Boyle and also for the further page you sent to me on Monday morning (25th April).

I will certainly read the book with great interest and from an earlier reading of it, I must admit that I am inclined at this stage to give my blessing to publication. I have no objection to Jimmy Boyle's reference to me in the book but if you feel at this stage you should now remove it, I will be most content with that as well.

I will write to you again when I have considered the matter fully and assure you that in this respect I will not keep you waiting too long.

My grateful thanks for all your kindness and all my good wishes.

Yours sincerely
Harry Ewing M.P.

I must admit this was a great relief to me as it overcomes a lot of the fears I previously had in terms of the Unit copping the backlash.

5th May '77

Tom McGrath phoned to say he would like to speak to me and asked if he could come up. He did and we had a short talk as he had a taxi waiting outside. Tom said that it is out that I am co-author of the play. A photographer called Liddell and a journalist from the *Sunday Times*, George Rosie, had come to see him. They asked him about my part in the play but Tom said he was extremely heavy with them saying he doesn't want to know the press as they are too irresponsible, even the so-called responsible Sunday ones. They talked and Rosie said he understood what Tom was saying but that he would be most responsible in anything he did. Tom asked me to think it over and if I felt they should come in then he will make the arrangements. I told Tom if I did they would have to slant their articles along the lines that they hadn't been in. . .

I spoke to Wattie this afternoon telling him the book looks as though it will be out very soon as Harry Ewing is about to give his consent. He said this may have something to do with the fact that the Department put it to their libel lawyers some time ago. . .

16th May '77

This morning I did my run in the beauty of the sun. After my exercises and cleaning work had been completed I sat outside. Ken brought in the newspapers and there was a piece about me in the *Daily Record*. It was about my book saying it would be published . . . that the proceeds are going to a Trust Fund.

All the tickets for the first night of our play *The Hardman* have been sold.

23rd May '77
The Living Dead – Larry

'The buzz was supreme. On Saturday night I had four diconal (a morphine substitute) which left me with a major decision. Two can give a pleasant glow, but four can take me to the heights. Should I have two nice evenings or one beauty? I decided on the latter. Taking the four, I lay on my bed smoking some hash and felt myself disappearing into the mattress. Occasionally, I had to shake myself as I felt I would disappear into death, yet there was this reckless part of me that said so what? But the other part kept saying Hey man, it's death we're talking about. And the other would pop up and say so what? Life and death. My heart had slowed. It felt so good! The sexual muscle twitched with pleasure – a sure sign of life.'

We talked. Going into great detail, he explained the fantasy as he lay there. A tunnel, worm-like but magnified, was directly ahead. It was a black tunnel with a great death-like attraction that enticed the wanton suicide to dance on its lip. He was aware of the danger yet sought it out.

The other day, his friend had been in to see him. Crippled, he rolled in on a wheelchair. A healthy being who, because of mainlining with a dirty needle, got an abcess which resulted in him losing the use of his lower limbs. A lesson for any man? No. Carrying the cripple up the stairs, they settled into the nest where they broke out the stash and punctured their veins. Music heightened the tone as they disappeared into their own individual worlds. The cripple told the story of his doctor who is a drug pension but who has suddenly taken fright and signed him on to the local Clinic where he can get his drugs regularly. They laughed at the doctor's impotence. They emerged, each on his own cloud, the wheelchair and its occupant symbolising their present and future.

Tonight as we talked he had seconal in him. He talks of Saturday night with deep nostalgia. People tend to complicate his life therefore he isolates himself with drugs. Certainly there is an element of danger and death but these are a part of everyday life. He much prefers to choose his own way of life and death. Recently, he had a massive swelling on his foot, the result of a dirty needle shooting drugs into his vein. Though it was a source of great pain he remarked, 'It was worth it'.

The real pleasure of his life is the Dream Maker. He has eagerly jumped from the lip into the abyss. Dancing through the tunnel of torment on a suffocating cloud, his sexual muscle lies limp as the body shell twitches in pain. Death and beyond. The reincarnation, the new rut: the bowler hat, the pinstriped suit and the brolly. Ahh, the new tomorrow. The Great Dream is out there. Over the hill, somewhere else, but never NEVER here and now.

25th May '77
I am going through a very bad period of internal conflict. On the

surface, I am very plausible to people and am doing my everyday things but underneath there are faint stirrings that have a frightening insight to NOTHING.

I am feeling the pain of confinement acutely at the moment. Whenever people come to mind I feel a wave of desire to be out. Ken mentioned going to Stornoway for his holidays this year and I am longing to be out of here and into the countryside. Although I try not to look too far ahead I seem to be doing so frequently. I can't see myself getting out of here. I know I have reached the optimum period for release. I can see real difficulties ahead.

On the whole I live day to day with a vague sort of long-term ideal of my own future. It would be too painful for me to sit down and consciously plan my every step for the next two or three years. The way to get through this sentence is to keep to the foreseeable future. In spite of this there are times when I get glimpses ahead and still see myself sitting here. They are momentary flashes into the future and somehow they obliterate everything else. They are so painful that I wilt. It could be because of the good weather; the sun is shining and I deeply yearn to walk in the countryside. I want to do the simple things of life but can't.

Being confronted with this brutal reality, the timelessness of which shakes me to the core, I feel utter despair. How do I handle it? These inner defence mechanisms come into action and bury the momentary flashes, but although buried I am constantly aware of their presence. In having a better understanding of my inner machinations, the burial of this painful reality becomes more difficult as I am able to penetrate it, to seek it out and become consciously aware of it. The dichotomy of wanting to know and wanting to hide.

For instance, this very date and time next year, I will be sitting in this exact same spot and doing the same thing. Intellectually I am growing and the only way I can live with this expansion and development is in a world large enough to accommodate it. I am growing beyond the Unit and this is dangerous as the restrictions containing me are now becoming effective weapons. I fear that it is all building up to something that could eventually destroy me. With the inner growth there must be a balanced physical growth and in this I mean getting released.

In many ways all of this is very much in my private thoughts but the time is coming when I will have to discuss it with someone who is very close to me. Occasionally I will meet it head on for a fleeting glimpse then run. As time goes on, the encounters with myself get more and more frequent but not lengthier. I sense it all building up to something. These past couple of years there has been a strong sense of freedom in me that is slowly vanishing. As time goes by, any talk of freedom seems to recede into the distance. I am afraid of the past and the nothingness of that existence. I could never dream of living in that world of nothingness again. I thought over a passage from Jung that I read today:

'Understanding is a fearful binding power. At times it can be a veritable murder of the soul as soon as it flattens out vitally important differences. The core of the individual is a mystery of life which is "snuffed out" when it is grasped. That is why symbols want to remain mysterious. They are not merely because what is at the bottom cannot be clearly apprehended. . . All understanding, in general, which is a conformity with general points of view, has the diabolical element in it that kills. It is a wrenching of another life out of its own course, forcing it into a strange one which it does not understand, yet lives and works. . . We should bless our blindness to the mysteries of others, for it shields us from the devilish deeds of violence. . .'

This seems to express some of what I feel and somehow gives me great consolation. Meanwhile I get tired and weary, and with each day get more tired and wearier. It is almost as though I've reached the roof and yet I continue to grow but the roof remains strongly in position.

27th May '77

I had a visit from Ben and we sat in the sun. He was delighted by *The Hardman* and went into detail about it. I enjoyed hearing it from him as he has experienced most of it.

Ben then went on to tell me how he is coping outside. He said there are times when he lies in his bed for three days at a time, sometimes even a week. He said he isn't depressed or anything but just enjoys being a recluse. He said that his mother is in the house but doesn't come near him, he said he could be lying there dead for all she would ever know. When he does come out she tells him he will sleep his head off. He said that of late he has been getting strong suicidal thoughts. He is questioning his whole way of life and feels he cannot get on the same wavelength with other people on the outside. I was very interested to hear what Ben had to say as I could identify with a lot of it. He feels that his prison experiences have torn something out of him as he has been out three years now and is still trying to adjust to life outside. I could see his tension easing as we spoke. He is obviously needing to speak to someone who understands. We reached a very deep level that surprised even me as he talked frankly about his thoughts on suicide and frustrations, but the heartening thing to me was that he seemed to have a better understanding of what makes him tick. He talks well and with a good deal of knowledge about his violent feelings and aggression. He said that he locks himself up in his room like a prisoner and feels quite happy as he lies reading books and watching TV. It's almost as though he has created his own prison outside.

28th May '77
Looking around me as I sit locked in my cell with the natural light pouring in through the window, I think of how last week I thought of this week and how it would be the same. It is. Now I look and think and see the barbarity of it. The lock shut tight, alone in the early evening – it's not as though I would be a lonely person by choice. I am a private person who likes to retain his own identity but this is an imposed solitude. I think of the image of the past and how it is no longer me, yet it hangs around me, clinging. I look at the barbed wire that hangs outside my window and want to throw myself at it, not to climb over but as a gesture of defiance. It wouldn't be meant as a gesture of self-destruction though that would be the obvious consequence. It would be more a cry to humanity, to the people of the world as to what they are doing. It's all about these very strong passionate and very tender feelings deep within that have been buried for so long, that have been expressed in snide ways. I always knew they existed but didn't know what they were or what they meant. Having gained this knowledge and having learned a lot about my life and society, I feel my earlier life has been stolen from me. I look to Ben and think of how he has been stolen from, of how he is lying in torment – a free man?

It's time to talk openly about returning to the soil.

29th May '77
Last night I went to bed at 8.35pm as I couldn't face looking at the cell walls, doors and windows. I felt exhausted and was soon sound asleep. This morning I wakened and went outside to do

my running exercises. While doing so I thought, in the freshness of the morning, of my thoughts of the night before. I thought of the soil and my returning to it. It's inevitable at some point, and the daily struggle in here has reached a level where I am facing each day in a condition of rawness, where exposure to the actual surroundings is excruciatingly painful. Strangely enough the one moment of respite I got this morning was when I lifted a 400 lb weight. I don't know why but somehow the heavy weight matched what I felt. I showered, shaved and dressed. While doing so I looked at myself in the mirror. I looked very healthy and thought of how the external belies the internal.

John has just come in to tell me that he has been with Wattie trying to sort out an outside programme for himself. He was in a state of confusion about it. John's problem is that he has been too long in prison and doesn't have the basic skills to negotiate this for himself; or for that matter, the ability to sit down and think through what it is that will be beneficial to him and his future.

In every sense I love life and people but I have become caught up in this little world that is suffocating me. The alternative to it is returning to the main penal system and that would be like throwing myself on to the barbed wire. It's now about choice, restricted though it may be, I do have a decision to make. It is all about selecting what is best and in this instance I feel that the only feasible choice I have is to return to the soil simply because I am not prepared to accept any of the others. Out of the others, there is the choice between returning to the nothingness of the past or the very painful continuance of the present and I feel I have reached the limit in this.

If I choose to go a certain way then it will be open to all sorts of interpretations. The strange thing about writing one's thoughts on all of this is that it is so inadequate. Certainly it gives insights but shallow ones as the issues and complexity of them are of a multi-dimensional nature. You see, as much as I want to shout out for everything to STOP! and open my soul for everyone to see to give them a look at what is going on inside, I can't. It's about not wakening up. It's more than last night when I went to bed early and wakened to start facing and rethinking about it again, to sit here where I left off the night before. There is no sense in kidding myself, as some superficial event may rear its head in the morning and tide me over till the next day, only to be confronted with it later. It's about myself coming to terms with this situation which is incompatible with my present growth and development. The development has to be at all levels or one finds oneself caught in this painful situation – one part tugging, the other part pulling.

The reality of life is that as I sat here a member of staff came to my door to say 'The local shop have no rum and raisin ice-cream but they do have vanilla, strawberry and tutti frutti.' I tell him to get a mixture of all three. I really feel as though I could curl up in bed and sleep till the earth crumbles.

This afternoon my aunt Peggy and cousin came to visit me bringing my two children, James and Patricia, with them. I put on a 'mask' and sat with them, but it was flat, and yet I felt so terribly close to them. I managed to get my children away on their own and have a chat with them. Here I am in this situation just as in previous nights. Is it this, or am I using the confinement as an excuse to avoid the deeper issues lying inside me? Why do I feel as though all that is inside me is blocked in my throat? I feel the best thing I can do is to remain away from everyone for a day or two till I work this thing through. Thank God for the music that is playing – a Brandenburg Concerto.

There was a time when the things that now hurt me never would have as I would have been too insensitive to them. Therefore, is sensitivity a bad thing in a situation, or, more to the point, in a world such as this? No, the answer must be no.

Where do I go from here? It's all a matter of choice. Do I realise what I am considering? Yes, and it is no big thing. It is closing the eyes and leaving, entering a deep sleep to the darkness; it is leaving behind the daytime and the night-time and all that goes on during it. It is stopping the heart, the breath, the sight and sound. It is entering the unknown. Why am I thinking of doing so? Because I have entered a world that has dyed and cast me, like so many others, where certain parts of myself have not been allowed to express themselves; a world that didn't allow my mother to kiss and cuddle me; a world where natural affection was seldom shown. To the present day I am labelled 'Killer', when in fact parts of me were done to death and only now am I discovering them. I look at my fellow convicts and see it in them. I look at my family, my very own children, and see it in them. Entry into a so-called civilisation that murders the soul of man. There is now very little appreciation of the fact that I am blood, sweat and tears. Being labelled 'Killer' I am now a thing.

I think of Jap and when we were in the Cages together. He was a big strapping boy serving a six-months sentence and sent to the Cages because he was too difficult for the screws to handle due to his size and build. My heart hung heavy for him. I was a year or so older than him though my life was finished and here he was with it all ahead of him. All he had experienced was orphanages and institutions. I continuously implored him never to get into a situation similar to mine as that was the direction he seemed to be heading in. It was water off a duck's back as no sooner was he released then he was back in again and returned to the Cages. He told of how, when outside and sitting in a pub with a pal nursing the dregs of a beer, a girl, a whore, came in to tell him there was a woman outside asking for him. On going outside he looked at this elderly woman and was puzzled – she was a stranger. They stared at each other till finally she said, 'William, I'm your mother'. He looked at her and then to his pal beside him and they sniggered. He asked if she had any money and she said she had so he invited her in to buy them drinks. They got drunk at her expense. I stood there listening to him telling me this and felt emotionally choked, expecting him to say that he burst out crying at finding his long lost mother, but no, he laughed heartily saying, 'We drunk the silly old cow's dough.' He felt not one thing for her. He arranged, at her insistence, to meet the following day and they did. He took her bag from her and went into a dark entrance. When he returned he gave her the bag to carry for him as they walked along the road. On reaching a cafe, he took the bag from her, opened it, took out a bottle with a rag jammed in the spout, lit it and threw it into the cafe. Both he and his mother were arrested for throwing a petrol bomb. He told me he pleaded guilty to the charge and got her released but he went to great pains to tell me that it wasn't because she was his mother, simply because it's the done thing if a man and woman are arrested on a charge together.

Could I, as I sit here, take the necessary and return to the soil? Yes I could, but I won't. Not because I am afraid to but because this moment isn't right. There has to be meaning to it. I think of Ben and his visit on Friday: 'Jimmy, the working class are their own worst enemy.' He talked about the recent visit of the Queen to commemorate the Jubilee Year and how the old people in the district cried as they watched her. I seethe with rage and tell him about this old woman, who put me in mind of my own mother, who said on TV that her life had been fulfilled as she had seen the Queen in the flesh and shaken her hand on the walkabout. We both sat in this cell and looked at each other with bitter anger when in fact we wanted to fall into each other's arms and weep. We don't need to read Marx, or anyone else for that matter, to tell us, as we are living it; we see, we feel and smell it. It's not so much what we said to each other as we are both still too inarticulate to express what we mean, but we felt it.

I can remember, in the past, time after time, saying to myself 'Why did I do that?' From stealing a bar of soap to slashing someone. Does the woman crying in the street when meeting the Queen say the same thing when she returns to the reality of her street, her house, when she watches the authorities who have put flowers in the area for the Queen's visit come and remove them after she's gone?

God, to think that I am labelled 'Scotland's Most Violent Man'. Is it right that I should think these thoughts or should I do as I have done in the past and fulfil people's expectations of me? Am I doomed to eat raw meat and live in a Cage to satisfy the masses? I come to the present day and watch those very same people who gave me that label say that I am a 'con-man' who is trying to work his ticket out of prison – such versatility I must possess. Could it be that the consequences of someone like me changing would be too much for the establishment to accept? Not so much my changing as my awareness of the games they play and the traps they lay for fodder such as me and those poor souls who cry at seeing the Queen. Ludwig van Beethoven, your sonatas with Kempff on piano are soothing my savage breast. So much so that I want to rest my weary head and let them lull me to sleep as my whole self is so tired and exhausted. So weary of the struggle and the conflict of the pain of my past and present life. Tomorrow, I know what you hold. I will speak to the same people, see the same walls and look for the same escape routes – books, writing and sculpture. There is this feeling within me that I have done all that is necessary, that having made my contribution, the continuance is unimportant.

Having spent a good part of the day sitting here in front of the typewriter, I am no further on in bringing the underlying issues to the surface. These thoughts are only fragments of the whole. We can never say how we know it all. We may gain insight to a past but that is about all.

THOUGHTS ON THE DAY

Have I really changed? Looking through the looking glass I see the eyes that have seen this face since my time break. The flesh, the bones, the hair, it's all the same. They have all grown older. But the inside my head is still the same though new dimensions have been experienced over the years. I am yet I am not the same person of 13 years ago. We are a well lived in body, a well tested mind. I can endure. The flesh and my bones have been stretched. The gut on my emotions pulled taut. The flow of my thoughts stemmed but still I go on. Sitting here today, I can see the sun perched high in the sky through its light through the barred window on this cold new years day and I feel alive. I sit here, my 10th year in prison completely devoid of any self pity or anguish as to my plight. I try to watch carefully what is going on in a place like this so that I may understand it better. There are many things going on here that have to be told, have to be discussed and improved on. I have changed in that I don't take my experiences I have gone and understood much of what is right and wrong in prisons and rather than do something about it negatively, I now seek viable alternatives which are constructive. So, yes, I have changed though there is no man-made technological device that I have developed. Is that it takes the form of articulate change of the kind that I have developed in the present social structure. My logical and constructive change in so far as establishmentally including people which defeats the status quo is so-called responsible people to turn on me. Have I changed... Do I look the same... are concerned. This allows so-called irresponsible behaviour to devalue what I say using my past violence and irresponsible behaviour to devalue what I say. But, this is all part of the process of change.

Although 13 years seems a long time ago it, I do not feel crushed I don't feel old. I feel alive, full of energy with plenty of drive & resistance to all the negative parts of the prison system. I feel young with a passionate belief in the necessity for change and the need I must play in this change. I know that spiritually I'm very strong, that this is an unquenchable quality that will continue to live with me.

My life seems to be lived in perforated sections. When one segment is filled I tear it off and move on. I live out the rest. It's like a cheque book. You fill in the amount, tear it off keeping the roots/stubs of the experience to yourself. Now, who is each one knowing is going to experience ups and downs similar to the last. It's all a great repetitive reality.

Mirror mirror on the wall tell me the truth tell me it all, am I changed, have I really? Why does looking at me seem so lonely why do I feel so isolated, so alienated to my solitude? Sitting here in the blackhole cell, I feel the old is all around and yet there is the excitement of being who knows what is taking me nearer and nearer to physical freedom. I notice in the closed world of my cell the fluctuating pattern of my thoughts, particularly when I focus on specifics. When I look into the mirror I see myself. I see the loneliness of my solitary figure in the physical sense and try to make the leap from this to the richness of my whole world which has material resources full of saturation that I am used to living with over the years. I am used to being with it. I am a very very selective in who I become close with. I now have to move from this into being a socially orientated person. It does have shapes of buck rogers in the 25th century. And yet there is the realisation that not only have I come back an improved model from where I've been let alone survived. I really don't want to dwell too much on the past as I prefer the challenge of what is and can be. I am very much a new man person. It will be a traumatic experience when I am finally out with this. When I am in the wide world and have the freedom to do all the small things that I've been so long deprived. Like at this very minute I'm sitting cramped on my bed bursting for a shit I don't want to do it in the chamber pot as it means I weep a time I open it to piss. The stench fills the cell. Can I hold it in for another hour (7th) when the door is opened for us to wash and finally closed till tomorrow morning. This is July and of thousands of small things that I've had to be deprived of. The prospect of physical freedom is deep in me. I can feel it strong, feel it close. I long for how I long for it.

Before me I believe is the spontaneity of what is, actions, I don't erase, just let it pour out as I was wrong to this book earlier when to read it my thinking, it will be one night and days like this when I sit here in this cold cell walking on this wyp crap through in this way as when one looks back on of ones feels good at having this shot of oneself recorded at this point in time. It's interesting to see how much one has developed since what point will I be, where will I go.

I have changed in that I have opened new faces of me. I have seen the soft and gentle parts of me own themselves to the world. I would cry when for so long I lived my life without doing so. I have Sarah who is my partner in life. She has been like a key to parts of me, the single biggest influence in my life. She has revolutionised my thinking in regard to myself, she has unlocked parts of me that were tightly locked. Since meeting her I've cried alone and with her. This has been important for me. The world I was brought up in was hard and violent, I am far removed from that that I have difficulty trying to understand what kind of person I was then. When I look at this I am in awe at the process of human development. I am fascinated by it all but recognise how frightening it all is for most people. My journey has been and continues to be most difficult but it does have very rewarding results. The real struggle in life is in developing oneself. Each step is filled with pain and joy. Unfortunately the lifestyle of the majority is to run from pain which means that we are conditioned from an early age to see pain as a bad thing. My view when undergoing pain is to tell myself: "This pain is life" and see/experience it as a necessary ingredient to life. In all of this, for myself, to the multi-dimensional reality of life; taking it all in. I am excited by my existence and though I long for freedom from prison I don't avoid the beauty of life as I live it even in prison. As I sit here I am feel it to the full. I am in touch with myself, with my physical and mental processes. I work and fight and struggle with myself to stay alive - the fullest possible sense. I am alive!

I will return to all of this when I waken, and search for the truth of my soul.

30th May '77
Early morning and I find difficulty in sleeping. Getting out of bed, I look out of the window into the blackness beyond. In the far distance, I catch sight of red car-lights as they pass by. TV cameras and searchlights are much nearer but I concentrate on the areas beyond. Ten years, ten long miserable years, and how many more? I hear the sound of a bus as it brakes in the nearby road. I try to imagine the occupants as they pass, sleepy-eyed, drunk and probably returning from parties or visiting friends. How many times have I passed that way and thought of the prison as a place I had experienced and was going back to?
Later
I waken and do my exercises. While running round the small yard there is a lightness within me but soon afterwards the reality of what I feel hits me. While doing my other exercises I feel weary, not a normal weariness but something much deeper.

I sit in my cell and John comes in telling me that he has clashed with a member of staff. I immediately sense he is drugged and ask him. He admits that he is, saying that he was given two seconal last night as he is having trouble sleeping. I personally wanted to scream at John due to this inner crisis I am in but instead told him that it has nothing to do with the member of staff but comes back to himself and the way he is behaving. John sits there furious and I tell him that I am not going to agree with him just for the sake of peace, as the truth is he is wrong. I reminded him that he has no right taking drugs when he knew he was going out this morning, also that he is sitting here trying to justify the clash he had just had. It was clear that he was upset. Eventually he grabbed me in a jocular manner to break away from the seriousness and the truth of what I was telling him. We laughed and he said he felt much better. I was glad to see the back of him as I was heavy with emotional turmoil within myself, but angered, which differed from the feelings I already had, at someone being so stupid as to give John these pills. I caught hold of Larry and he said he had given them to John from his nightly dose. I didn't go into a bad scene with Larry but let him know that it wasn't a nice thing to do. There was a malicious air about him.

Ken came in later and there was no sense trying to hide the crisis I was in. I explained to him in detail what I felt and he was visibly moved. He came in with what I knew he would, supportive statements. He told me that he was speaking to a politician recently and that he mentioned the fact that I could be released tomorrow and never be in trouble again, but I didn't sparkle as this sort of superficial political talk no longer impresses me. Ken noticed this and we discussed it. He tried to communicate with me but decided that it would be best to leave it. I like Ken tremendously but as I explained to him, the situation that I am in can only be resolved by me. He understood.

It's only when I speak to someone else that I get a proper indication of how deep I am into this 'down'. So far down that were you to shout on me from the surface of your normality then it would echo. Music remains my only companion for the present – Beethoven's Ninth. Somehow the music seems to strike chords that release others deep in the unconscious.

I feel battered and bruised. What has happened to the Spirit? That magical spirit that always lifted me out of the depths of despair in the past. I have gone beyond that, or so it seems. I find myself convoluting in a bottomless pit where there is nothing to grasp on to but my soul.

This inner heaviness that I am experiencing is not unique to me. Others have it from time to time and at varying degrees but the question is why do we hide it from each other? Here I sit alone because I feel others here won't understand, or have enough on their plate, and because I have been conditioned not to share these inner feelings with others. To think that we spend our short living experience on this earth in such a way that stops us sharing experiences that would be invaluable to our existence. My God, it's bloody stupid.

Where do I stand on the fourth day of this encounter? I feel lost. Lost because having gone over everything that I possibly could, I am left with the same helplessness. This is a time when I should be pleased with my achievements as a sculptor, playwright, and author, but no. It comes down to freedom. You can keep a person in the most luxurious hotel and give him what he wants but if you restrict his movements to a room of that hotel then it will become his hell. Ultimately the *need* is for freedom.

31st May '77

Still struggling with each moment of the day. Feel lost in the myriad of corridors within myself. The morning sun shines outside my window. It holds no comfort for me. I feel at this moment that I am somewhere beyond. It's almost as though I am in my head. Could it be the hospital?

There is no doubt that it did something to me. It was being confronted by that part of the past that I had erased. Not entirely erased but had somehow left behind. Certainly the memories of the past have always been very much in my consciousness but actually to be in amongst it again was crushing. It would be on a par with my getting involved in violence again – I see it as unthinkable. My reaction to violence now would be far different to that of the past when I accepted it as part of my life. It was exactly the same as the hospital incident where I was confronted by this situation and instead of reacting to it in a way that would have been typical, I was horrified. I wept. What did this do to me? I don't know and haven't really gone into it. The last time I had this operation the post-surgical pain was bad but this time it was nothing. I think it was because of the brutality of the police presence. The subsequent press coverage was also pretty damaging. Again, the image was that I am Scotland's Most Violent Man and as a result they treated me accordingly. It was almost as though I had no feelings. Again, I couldn't scream with rage as I would then be seen as the animal. What do I do? Fortunately, in that hostile situation the parts of me that have grown so strong emerged and pulled me through, or did they? For if my present state is a direct result of that experience then the damage has been much deeper than I first appreciated.

What about my yearning to be free? I visualise walking in the country, seeing green fields, birds singing, the horizons far in the distance – as far as the eye can see. Oh to walk the streets full of people. To look at my hand and see the clasped hand of my girlfriend, to look at her face and eyes. These are the dreams of the incarcerated. I want so much to taste freedom because for the first time in my life I will be able to appreciate it. I desire the world beyond the walls.

And what about the expressions of my soul? The hammer and chisel that sculpt the stone from the tenement buildings of my past into a new form for the future. A transformation that is comparative to my own. The ingrained pollution that covers the stone is shorn. I take it in this filth-covered condition, devote the time to it and give it another life. When it is complete I leave it with a bright future. The part that I envy in this unfeeling, inanimate object is that its transformation is widely accepted, and not questioned.

And the writing. I need it as a testament to my experience. To reflect, in some small measure, what I feel. To help me see, like the sculpture, the natural development of me – the human being. Threads of life brought to the surface. Painful though it may be there has to be an understanding of what we are doing. For example, many people in this place will notice my absence and presume that I am studying hard when in fact I am going through one of the most painful experiences in my life. I am locked into this crisis where I am questioning my continuance as a human being. What do the days ahead hold for me? Can I pick myself up from the floor, scooping up the millions of scattered pieces, and face the nothingness of tomorrow? The writing can only reflect a surface image of what is going on. This does not devalue its importance. Its very existence may be the key to another person's feelings.

Feelings. Those parts that we all try to hide from each other. The shame, the jealousy, the guilt and insecurity. Our inferiority. Who can put up the most convincing mask to hide the inner turmoil? It's all about chasing illusions that don't really exist. It's like hating some bastard yet when he dies we realise he wasn't so bad after all.

1st June '77
I think of the Unit Community while doing my exercises. The once strong foundation of our Community – the meetings – is crumbling. Crumbling in the sense that it will evaporate into the impotent ways of the whole prison system, be smothered by their stringent restrictions, bound up in bureaucracy. And even if this did happen, people would still visit the place from outside and say what a fine place it was because it will always be that bit different from the main penal system. They will see it only as it is, unaware of the destruction that has taken place. The bureaucracy is making a perfect job of strangling the life out of us, slowly but surely we are dying. There was a point this morning when I believed that something had lifted, taking the weight off me. It was a moment of optimism simply because I reached a depth last

night that had me almost touching the soil. But in spite of this, the weight returned this morning. The *weight*, yes, that's what it feels like. A very heavy weight hanging heavily from a thin thread in my chest, almost as though it's about to snap and plunge into my guts. It's the weight of *life* and the price of being alive.

Later
Having spent the morning reading, thinking and resting, I am feeling that bit brighter. The afternoon of the fifth day and I feel a lightness in my head with much of the pain lifted from my body. What remains is reality. You allow yourself to go through this very painful introspective examination but when you emerge the prison walls are still there. They stand there, high and forboding, a monument to the failure of our way of life, mocking the 'civilisation' of man. I don't know if I can live like this. Only time will tell.

I think of the physically handicapped and what they have to live with. But I compare my situation to the recovered cripple who is forced to remain in the wheelchair.

PM
The sun shone down on me. I had entered the world of the living. Sitting on a seat away on my own, I let the heat enter my weary bones. I was absolutely shattered. There was a hesitancy in others as my face was set and I gave out signals to leave me be. There is no doubt that these five secluded days have taken their toll. One cannot experience this sort of thing and emerge unscathed. The fragmentation could be felt and I wondered if it would ever heal. Ken tactfully sat beside me and carried on a low, one-man conversation whilst I soaked up the sun.

I don't know what to make of the past five days but here I am having gone all the way down. I am shocked at the intensity of the experience and am utterly bewildered by it. The only feeling I have at this moment is that I shouldn't keep this to myself, that people must understand or be aware about this sort of human misery. It is a universal experience but having gone to the depths I feel that something must be done to help others who are likely to make the same trip. Other than that I will have to wait and make sense of it. I really feel brutalised at this moment.

3

He's a man without a colour,
Standing in the rain;
Blankly sees the future now,
With all his hopes in ruin.

Larry Winters

5th July '77

After reading my mail I went outside to put some finishing touches to my latest sculpture. While doing so Larry and Denis (prisoner) came across and began discussing it. We had an interesting dialogue on the piece with Denis being quite imaginative. He said it reminds him of a peasant woman who is pregnant. The piece is attractive to me because of its lines. I worked away and finished it.

When staff came on duty after the meal break one of the main prison staff informed them individually (as they entered the gate) that the girl visiting John is a well-known prostitute. Ken told me about it. I replied that I knew her and she wasn't. Ken caught hold of John afterwards to ask him about this. John blasted Ken and the other staff. John said he should have been told about this when his visitor was here. I told him no way as it wouldn't be right for his visitor to walk back through the main gate knowing this. John is now alone in his cell all bottled up. Ken is reporting this to the main prison Governor in the morning. . . I brought my new sculpture up to my cell tonight and it sits with two others. I like it and will let it sit there for now. It is a tremendous feeling when completing a new sculpture.

12th July '77

I was sitting in the yard when Ken called a Staff Meeting. He had just returned from a meeting with the representative of the local branch of the SPOA. Ken had been given a copy of a letter from the Prisons Dept. to the General Secretary of the SPOA. It contained proposals that all of us consider devastating: 'In our view the time has come to make firm plans for the gradual replacement of staff now on duty in the Unit, which may mean that it will not be possible to rely entirely on volunteers to replace them. . . Apart from the Chief Nursing Officer, to whom I have already referred, we have in mind that we should seek to make the necessary changes over approximately the next twelve months. . .'

There is no doubt in my mind that they are going to these lengths to 'get' Ken and Malky (prison officer). In doing this they automatically get me. My strength lies in the relationships I have with staff here and so it vanishes with them being transferred.

On the prisoners' side, we are in a position where we just cannot win. With the introduction of staff being detailed to take duty here the whole concept will be lost. The Department are frightened by what we are doing here so they are resorting to this.

14th July '77
As I ran round the yard this morning I could hear staff deep in heated exchanges about the present situation. There were very strong feelings being expressed and it looks as though the Department could meet a united staff, which is very important.

This afternoon I went outside and did some sculpting. I took a piece of stone and worked, and worked, and worked getting all the aggression into the piece. It was great as I made fantastically good progress and sat on a chair looking at the rough form. . . The other prisoners are feeling the effects of the present crisis.

15th July '77
The Governor came in and Ken went to speak to him. Afterwards he came out saying the Governor was shaking like a leaf. Ken asked him if he had known about this letter. He admitted he had and that three weeks ago Wattie had advised him to say nothing about it. . .

Later this afternoon Ken told me the Department have also censored the Departmental Working Party Report which set up the Unit. Ken found he had mislaid his original copy and asked one of the younger staff for a copy they get when applying and training for the Unit. Half of the material has been taken out. The parts omitted are relevant to what the Unit is doing and the comments made by the Working Party on the Inverness Cages. They're a shower of fuckers. I asked the Governor what his views were on the Department letter. It was bloody pathetic as he waffled saying that he is making observations of the situation and intends making his remarks to the Department. Malky asked what his observations were and again he waffled.

The Hull Riot Report was made public today and it is disgraceful as anyone with any experience of the penal system will recognise. It states, 'The staff had shown considerable tolerance in the past towards demonstrations and free and easy relationships between staff and prisoners had tended to obscure perception of what was actually happening. . .'

27th July '77
Neil and John from Craigmillar came in this morning. I had the

small-scale model of Gulliver ready for them. They are pleased with it. I'm pleased I redesigned the whole thing. We had a very constructive meeting working out detailed plans.

29th July '77
Ben came in today saying he had been to see my play *The Hardman* again last night. He said it was a special showing for Councillors and Judges, etc. Afterwards he started chatting to some of them. The general opinion was that I wouldn't get released. Ben made the pertinent point that even the Judge who sentenced me recommended fifteen years so he thought I should get out. They were stumped at this. One of them remarked that I have murdered eight people, and so once again we meet the McElhone myth. Ben replied that he had heard all Councillors are either homosexual or corrupt and they denied this. Ben told them this is the myth going round about them. If they are prepared to believe the myths about me then it must apply to them also. Ben is so funny and brilliant. I thoroughly enjoyed his visit.

Stephanie (my publisher) came up this evening. She said she would like to do a publication of *The Hardman*. I told her I would get in touch with Tom . . . she heard that Nicky Fairbairn is delighted Pan are doing simultaneous publication of *A Sense of Freedom* as he intends to sue. A big publisher means more money. Stephanie and the Pan people seem slightly worried at this. . . Stephanie said she received an irate phone call from a Glasgow schoolteacher saying she thinks it disgusting that she is publishing my book – me, a criminal. She said she had written a book and couldn't get a publisher. It takes all kinds. . .

30th July '77
Kay came in this morning and was saying she is on BBC radio tomorrow morning with Teddy Taylor MP. It concerns the publication of the book and the Trust Fund I've set up. His opinion is that I am conning everyone to get a parole date. He said that I am not sorry for the things I've done and don't say I'm sorry in the book. He also mentioned Fairbairn remarking that he is going to make a fortune suing the publishers.

6th August '77
Bruce Millan (Secretary of State for Scotland) states in the morning paper that there will be a review of the internal running

of the Unit, and the visits in particular. I can't understand this as Harry Ewing knows everything about the book.

12th August '77
Ken was called over to the main prison to an Investigating Officer and told he was being charged with a breach of discipline and given all the material relating to it. The charge is that he wrote an 'open' letter to the *Glasgow Herald* relating to material and knowledge gained through his job, and did so without authority. Ken phoned John Renton, General Secretary of the SPOA and he agreed to be a witness for him. He also phoned the *Glasgow Herald* and the assistant editor, Tony Findlay, and he too will be a witness.

17th August '77
. . . Stephanie came in and had been to see Tom McGrath to talk about publishing the play. When they came to the point of joint authorship Tom hesitated, saying he would put a note on the inside saying that I had collaborated. In other words he was taking the whole project over. I feel extremely sad at this and my immediate internal reaction was 'Oh no Tom, not you too. . .'

21st August '77
Larry came in tonight and was heavily drugged. He sat down and we talked. He said he is now on six seconal a night. He said he doesn't know how I can work the way I do. I replied that I don't know how he can get drugged the way he does. He shrugged his shoulders and said he would like to work the way I do but can't. We talked about death and I pointed out how we are all dying, everyone, and not just us. I found it very sad as Larry has given up and is accepting his lot. He should fight it every inch of the way. We discussed suicide and Larry said he wouldn't do it as that is what the Department and others want. I sat there looking at him in his drugged state and thinking how this is the way the Department want him.

2nd September '77
6am and the dark tarmac recedes underfoot with every step I take. The clear blue sky belies the coldness of the air that causes beads of sweat to sit frostily on my forehead and face. Each step, as I run, wakens the still sleepy body as the muscles stretch and

contort. Lungs contract and expand as they take in and expel the cold morning air. The red track suit and brightly coloured shoes are in sharp contrast to the ground level surroundings. Like the mouse in the eternal wheel, I run round the small enclosed yard that is 'L' in shape and has high, thick walls topped with specially designed barbed wire. Out of reach but well within sight, a close-circuit camera focuses on the yard. The anonymous, ever-vigilant eye that accompanies my every step. Windows on the nearby buildings have steel bars and then more steel bars.

I look to the beauty of the morning sky not bothering to look ahead. Each morning, hail, rain or snow, I take this jog knowing its every crease and crack. Letting the silence of the morning enfold me, I look to the one symbol of freedom – the sky. The occasional car can be heard in the distance and like its engine my mind is ticking over. I lose myself in the inner world of thought letting the automatic pilot of familiarity guide my way unseen. I watch a wisp of cloud as it mars the unstained blue. Thin and wispy it moves with the slight breeze and we mark time till the wall changes my direction. Being State property one appreciates the privacy and luxury of thought. I fleetingly focus on my colleagues as they lie in their beds in slumber or listening to the padding of my feet as I pass their windows. Pulling the bedcovers tightly around them they think of my insanity at rising and running at this unearthly hour.

My gaze is distracted by the sight of a beautiful blackbird as it sits decorating the cruel barbed wire. Passing underneath where the bird is perched, I hear its tuneful whistle with a clarity that astounds me. So powerful a symbol of freedom that it nullifies the superstructure of modern technology containing electronic eyes, barbed wire, radar equipment, all surrounded by high walls. I wish myself to be the blackbird as it lifts its beak to throw another loud clear tune. The bird flies off in the direction of freedom. It must have landed nearby as its tuneful whistles floated in from beyond the walls. Visually I look to the sky and audibly to the tune of the blackbird. I am so fortunate.

I think of the sky and the bird, symbols of my future. Tomorrow I will run the same run and breathe the same air. This is the period of torment and discovery. It will finally come to an end but meantime I will roam the abyss. I know it is ahead, the visual impact of what's up there tells me that, the sound of the blackbird that floats in to tell me it all. Ah, the future! Now there's a thought to equal the beauty of the morning and the blackbird. Unlike the past, that dark menacing shadow, I take responsibility for creating the future from this moment onwards. I look at the wispy cloud as it fades in the distance – going in my direction. I want to follow it, to run on air and see the height and breadth of the land, to look as far as the eye can see without walls restricting.

My body functions like a well-oiled machine and I press to keep it that way as my survival depends on it. All of me has to be geared to coping with this purgatorial period that is constantly trying to erode the parts that want to stay alive. The faces of those around me, the feelings that I have about the faces are tiring. We cannot avoid each other. Regardless of what may happen between us, we still have to look at each other all day and every day. I may hate the sight of a person but there is nothing that I can do about it. There are sheer joy moments when one is alone, the technicoloured world of fantasia where one can create one's wishes and see them all come true. They are never so grand that one cannot believe them in the light of day. I think of myself sculpting in some remote area next to a log cabin with my girlfriend nearby. I imagine myself in a flat with her, having a meal or making love. The simplistic beauty of these dreams moves me to the core. Poignant moments that have a strengthening quality. I roam the countryside with many friends. There is sun, flowers, long swaying grass and a feel of warm intimacy. Hazy moments of love and tenderness that are both dreamlike and real. Simple things that I want to do.

Reality, however, is this heaving chest, this sweating body, this well trod path within this small eternal wheel. Reality is here and now. Each step I take is another time and a changing space. I am living in a world of constant change and yet the sameness and repetitiveness of each day eats into me. And so the beginning of another day.

11th September '77
Larry is dead.
 Sitting here with my lunch.
 Knock!
 Knock!
 It was a desperate knock, with Murray Stewart (prison officer) asking me to come with him. Getting out of my chair I went with

him trying hard to anticipate what was ahead. He entered Larry's cell where I could hear slapping – a fight I thought, and so pushing myself forward to pull the standing person off the other, but with an ease that turned it from a fight to something else. 'He is cold and having trouble breathing,' said John. Putting my hands on Larry I started thumping his chest. Rigor mortis had set in. 'He's dead. He's fucking dead!' and they all looked at me. 'Get the doctor for Christ's sake,' and Murray left to do so. The prisoners stood looking at me as I pulled at Larry to make sure. He lay there in a crouched position with the plastic chamber pot still askew under his buttocks. Blood was in the pot, a smattering, some trickles had also coagulated on his nose, some at his feet. Very little blood in all. His eyes were tightly closed, veins in his neck protruded and the whole pose looked strained as though some massive pain had overtaken him. He was cold.

Internally I was wanting to vomit, was feeling shattered and asked him, the dead body, why? Larry, why, why, why? Next to the blood at his feet lay some pills, sleeping pills. Taking his cover from his bed I placed it over him. Others kept their distance and left it all to me. There was a part of me that recognised the inevitability of it all. Perhaps the responsibility of having to keep things in control held me together as I desperately wanted to run off. To go outside and run for miles, to cry and express all that I wanted to. I sit here shattered but still with a part of me knowing that Larry had played with fire, had seen some of his close friends die over the past years from the effects of drug taking. Knowing all of this it is still hard to take.

Police, the Governor, doctors including Peter Whatmore arrived and all the other legal procedures attached to death were formalised.

And here I was, faced with what I had contemplated doing in recent months. I don't want to end up like this, but the fact is that we all do – none of us can ever escape it. The great leveller of mankind. This man lying there, stiff and cold – useless. I could still feel the coldness and death of him clinging to my skin.

Going into the yard, I let the wind enter my lungs and cleanse the stench of death from me. Why is it that we all go through the pain of living to end up like that? His lying there brought it all home to me. Why is it that we all fight and squabble together and make life so bloody miserable for the short time that all of us are here? Why do we find it so difficult to let those loving parts of us flow to each other and at least make this short stay something precious?

At the time we found him, a phone call came through saying his mother was at the gate to visit him. She had travelled a great many miles and was now sitting waiting to see her son, sitting there as contented as I was with my lunch, not knowing that we would be hit by a mighty blow. Throughout the next four and a half hours we wandered around, sometimes in the silence of our own little world and at others speaking with a great emptiness. The police questioned us as to his state of mind and all the while Larry lay where we had found him – dead.

The police photographer took some pictures and a few seconds later spoke to one of the guys asking if he had seen the big football game yesterday and the guy expressed to me the harshness of this. We discussed how these guys are living with this every day and seem to have become hardened to it. Yes, and even society has become hardened to it. John sat in his cell crying his eyes out. Peter made a meal of sausages and eggs. J.L. wandered about with his head in his hands. Denis sat silent. The Governor wanted to know if the prisoners should be searched in order to establish that the formal procedures had been adhered to. One of the staff told him that Larry had always been the weak link and that searching was out of the question. Rape my person while I mourn thought I.

There is no doubt that we all think that it will never happen to us. Stripped of all dignity as the rigor mortis is snapped and you are placed in that coffin, reduced to nothingness. I returned to see him time and again as he lay there throughout the four and a half hours. The last time I saw him he seemed slightly more relaxed than when I first set eyes on him, or maybe it was that I got used to it.

There was something about going back to see him lying there a number of times and it was as though I was trying to understand more about life through looking at this dead friend. Is life as sacred as we would like it to be or is it something we should look on as we do a friend emigrating? The inevitability of death is something that we refuse to look at and it seems to me that by accepting its inevitability we will come to learn more about our own lives. But it is taboo. No one wants to look at it or accept it. This morning as I ran round the yard, Larry sat on his chamber pot – dead. And all through the morning I did what I did while he sat there dead. Even in this small claustrophobic place he died alone. We are all alone.

And in the midst of the crumbling façades of us all, one of the staff and I tried to focus on the repercussions from this situation. If it is an overdose, where does that leave us? Is this selfish when a guy is lying dead upstairs? No, it is reality and doesn't detract from what we feel for him. We must salvage what we can.

Larry was carried downstairs locked in a green, heavy-laden coffin. I ran to look out the window and see him pass. They carried the coffin out of the gate and it locked behind him. Larry has left us – physically. His cell door is sealed with brown sticky paper.

I have pieced some of it together. Drugs had been brought in. This morning Peter went into Larry's cell at 9.30am and found him sitting on his chamber pot so quickly closed the door thinking he was doing the toilet but he was sitting there frozen in death. Naked and sitting on the pot it looks as though a massive attack locked him into this position. Murray (prison officer) had something to say to him at lunch time and went in to find Larry still sitting there. He went to speak to him but he didn't reply and so he touched him then came to get me. John and Peter were taking Larry's lunch to him and were there for me coming seconds later.

The last time I saw him was last night before lock-up and we were laughing together and I distinctly remember saying to myself that he looked well. Shortly after this he offered Peter some pills but Peter refused them.

After being locked in this cell tonight I looked into the mirror at my image and saw a clear-eyed, physically fit human being and compared it to the dead body of Larry. Last night he looked so well, and this morning lifeless. I look at myself and wonder, what will yours be like?

Larry didn't mean to die – consciously – of that I am certain.

The impact of the experience is tremendously thought-provoking. The sight of Larry lying there stiff with rigor mortis made me wonder about life after death. How can there possibly be? There was something very brutal about the shell of a man lying there – it is difficult to believe that the spirit of life, as I am experiencing it, would be callous enough to abandon this physical shell as it lay pathetically alone and helpless on the floor. Being so sensitive to life, I didn't want to believe that this is how all of us will end up. It's just like a car engine: switch on, switch off.

There was no dignity in the death that I experienced today, it frightened all of us. No one wanted to accept it. There will never be dignity in death so long as we continue to deny it. Only when we can begin to accept it will we fully understand its meaning. Seeing Larry there today made me petrified of death and only now, locked in this cell very much as he was last night at this time, can I begin to examine my reaction to it.

I sit here feeling slightly afraid. The shadows are cast over the cell as the earphones blast Beethoven's 'Missa Solemnis' into my soul. The depth of the music touches the fear that I feel and soothes it, but the great fear of dying in this cell remains with me.

12th September '77

The night was very long and uncomfortable and full of symbols of Larry. Two cats meowing outside my window; he had a love of cats. Two singers on the TV singing an old Scottish song: 'Dance, dance, wherever you may be, I am the Lord of the dance said he...' a song that I associate with him. The night was troublesome with little sleep and thoughts racing through my head. I was relieved when the door was opened and I went outside to do my exercises. Running round the yard I felt so tense and full of sorrow but determined to live – not wanting to die under these circumstances. I felt so weary running round but persisted just to prove that I was alive – Larry was dead. It was vitally important for me to do my exercises this morning, nothing but death could have persuaded me otherwise.

From a window looking into the main prison was heard the comment from one prison officer to another, 'The only good thing to come out of the Special Unit was Winters in a box'. No matter how much progress we make this is what we are up against. These are the same people who go around asking other prisoners and staff why we hate them so much.

The Governor called us into the TV room and thanked us for our response to the whole situation and the way we handled it yesterday. Peter Whatmore came in the morning and afternoon. We all sat chatting. He said that Dr Harland, a pathologist, will be doing the post mortem on Larry.

My day was very busy. It was difficult to concentrate.

Tom McGrath came in. I told him about Larry and we talked about it for a while. Eventually we got on to the problem of the play, the co-author issue. I sorted it out by reminding Tom of the reality. He could do nothing but agree with me. We discussed touring... He has resigned from the Third Eye Centre and intends to take his writing more seriously... It was nice to speak to him and sort things out amicably. I was finding it hard to concentrate on what we were saying as Larry was uppermost in my mind. The news has broken to the press and was on the radio. This afternoon Rab visited us to say the press has been on to him about Larry. We talked about it and he seemed pretty shaken. Tonight he was interviewed by STV and came across pretty bad.

I went along to John Neeson tonight, calling all the others together. I asked John if he was aware of the implications of what had happened. He looked upset and just stared at me. He then said he had done nothing. Peter said that Larry killed Larry. I said I knew that but had heard John had given him the pills. John was looking and feeling as guilty as hell. John said he didn't know where Larry got them. I know John gave them to Larry and told him so. The others remained quiet. He eventually made it clear the drugs came in via the Douglas Inch Clinic and was saying everything except that he gave them to Larry. I tried to tell him that Larry was destined to die this way and that was that. I reminded him that we had to concern ourselves with living and the future of the Unit; the people in it, and its future... I can't help thinking of Larry and how he had to live up to a role that he didn't quite fit. He was just a country boy serving life for manslaughter who ended up in Peterhead Prison and the system there twisted him beyond all recognition. He is the classic case of the guy getting 'used' and criminally educated while in prison...

The big problem has now to be faced by those of us who knew nothing about the drugs Larry had taken. The Department are almost certain to restrict us and there is little we can do about it – they will crush us with it. Larry has left us but his shadow still remains. He got the release he knew he would and I suppose that's about all one can say. In many ways his death has given me a will to live like nothing I've experienced. The fight to remain intact and survive this has put his death in the distance.

13th September '77
I read my mail and the newspapers which had front page coverage of Larry. The emphasis was on his past violence and his drug taking. On the whole they were pretty sympathetic to him.

I thought over what I was going to do... I called a meeting and outlined to everyone that they were aware of Larry having strange drugs, that there was a lot of suspicion going round about these. I asked the Community if anyone knew anything about it. There was silence and after a lengthy time I pointed out that one of us here was responsible for the drugs and I would like him to speak up. Again there was silence. I said that my loyalty was to the Unit and what it was trying to do. I believed in the Community and not any single individual in it. I named John pointing out that I couldn't prove it but knew John was responsible. There was total silence for a long spell; the meeting was very tense. I was feeling very shaky and explained to John that I abhorred doing what I was, but for the sake of the Unit and everyone else in it I was doing so. He kept letting out deep, loud sighs. Some others in the group asked him to speak up. John stated that Larry is dead and he has nothing more to say...

Although we all knew that Larry's incarceration in the main prison system and the Unit, along with prison officers, psychiatrists, nursing staff and even Larry himself, were all responsible for his untimely death, the unfortunate fact is that John the prisoner, the most innocent of all these people, was nevertheless the person who got Larry those particular drugs that caused his death a few hours later. This puts us into a dilemma. Should we have joined what is bound to become a cover-up? The meeting ended.

The Governor phoned Mr Meikle at the Department. He said John should remain where he was as they don't want to be seen moving him at this point – before the results of the post mortem. It was only later that Gerry (prison officer) told me he was horrified when listening to the Governor on the phone to the Department. Apparently he told Mr Meikle we had a meeting but nothing of what took place. Gerry said he was shaken by this and seriously doubted the Governor's ability to cope with the Unit. We weren't told any of this by Gerry till later in the evening.

During our ordinary meeting this afternoon Wattie remarked that Peter (Whatmore) has always known that he could be slain for giving Larry as many drugs as he was. His dosage was massive but he felt that he had to do it as Larry was a threat to staff and made this clear. In many ways I agree with him as Larry was so into drugs, in a way they were his life and all he seemed to have. Larry had made it clear that he would use violence if not given his drugs, therefore, the system used Peter Whatmore as the magician. Drugs were what he felt secure with – they were the only alternative for him.

This afternoon John called a meeting. He told us in a very moving way that he had brought the drugs into the Unit – he had collected them from the Douglas Inch Clinic. He said Larry had asked him to take them from a guy who would deliver them to the Clinic and this is what happened. . . John was on the verge of tears. It must have taken a great deal for him to do this and he was thanked for it. Immediately he stopped talking the Governor told us he would have to rush off and report the matter to the Department. He returned to say that the Department ordered that John be locked up in the Unit till tomorrow morning. Those of us with visits were advised not to say anything.

As I went upstairs the Governor was telling John – in his cell – that the matter will have to be reported to the police. He instructed the staff to take John's shaving gear and other small items in case he tried to do himself damage. John told the Governor he was expecting a visit from his brother-in-law tonight. He replied it would be better if his visitor was told by a staff member that he can't see John as he isn't too well. John replied that this was foolish. The Governor said John could see his visitor for two minutes. By this time John was crying over the Larry thing.

I came upstairs at this point and met the two staff with shaving gear, etc. When I asked what they were doing they looked sheepish. I let loose at them saying that they are the staff who are supposed to guide this inexperienced Governor rather than jump to his silly commands.

The Governor came in tonight and had a meeting with staff. Malky (member of staff) came up raging like a bull. He said he was calling a meeting. As we sat there the Governor stated that he realises we aren't happy with the situation and the way it is being handled. Murray (member of staff) said he doesn't want to lock John up as he has been very honest. He said preventing his visitor coming in is senseless. He pointed out that we have never done things this way in the Unit before and we shouldn't start now. Davy (member of staff) said they are being asked to look in on John every fifteen minutes and this is no good. The Governor kept falling back on his statement that he is getting directives from the Department.

The Heap

LOCKED IN THIS COMPLEX IT
HEAP IS A MASS OF HUMANITY
EACH HEAVY FOLD FILLED
WITH HUMAN WASTE. IT SITS
IT'S HEAVY WEIGHT HEAD OF THE
THINNEST OF SKINS, ALMOST
BURSTING AT ITS SEAMS. FOLDS
OF FAT PRESS DENSELY DOWNWARD
THE HEAP SITS IN ALL AUTHORITY. YET
UNAWARE OF HIS GROSS VULGAROUS APPEARANCE
OR PERHAPS HE NO LONGER CARES. HE IS
RESPONSIBLE FOR ALL THAT IS AROUND HIM
BUT LIKE A BUDDHA HE SITS
A HULK FULL OF BULK WHILE FLAG CATCHES
LIKE FOLDS IN A FALLING CURTAIN. HE'D
A SYSTEM GONE WRONG, ALLOWING ALL
THE WRONG THINGS A GATHER KINGDOM
TO CHURN AND CLAG, TO CORRUPT AND
DISTORT. WE LIKE HE SITS SPAMO IN
HIS OWN MESS, A PRISONER OF HIS OWN
GREED, LIKE BLURB WAT OBHE CON-
FESS THIS IS THE IMAGE THAT ACCOMPLISHES
PRISON TO IS IT'S THREE QUITE,
CONTINUING THE SAME AND ALL THE SHIT WILL
SPILL OUT AND SMEAR EVERY ONE. I SAT HERE
TODAY LISTENING TO TWO YOUNG GUYS
DESCRIBING LIFE SENTENCED FOR MURDERS WHICH
USED TO BE MORE SERIOUS, YO YOUNG OFFENDER
INSTITUTION YUBAKWAINE PRISON, QUITE A
MATTER OF FACT, THEY DESCRIBED THE
BRUTALITY THAT THEY HAD EXPERIENCED.
THEY TALKED OF Y.O.I.' AS BEING A
KIND OF ELITIST CLUB SURROUND
ING BY GEN FORSHALL. THERE
WAS MUCH OF A SYMPATHY SHOWN
AND FULLY NO OF WHAT THEY
HAD EXPERIENCED. QUITE OF
CONFIDENCE ONE OF THE
MENTIONED A PRISON OFFICER
WHOM LITTLE DOUBT BE
SPECIAL WHO TWO GUYS
DIDN'T KNOW THIS THE
VIOLENCE OR BRUTALITY
THESE GUYS EXPERIENCED
IN THE Y.O.I. HAS ME
FEEL SICK. NOW, I KNOW
AS AN ABUSIVE STAFF THAT
WHAT WAS TOLD TO ME WAS
TRUE — WE ALL KNOW IT
IS HAPPENING AND AS I
SIT HERE IN PRISON.
WRITING THIS. NOW
I'M NOT LOOKING FOR
SCAPEGOATS OR VICTIMS
I'M TRYING IN SOME WAY
TO GET ENOUGH TO
TAKE THESE YOUNG GUYS
WHO ARE HELL
INTO THEIR
SENTENCES (AGE
9, 10, 11) I
WOULD LOVE TO
TRY AND GET
THROUGH TO
THEM BUT
THEY ARE SO
FULL OF
MISTRUST
BITTERNESS
FROM THEIR
EXPERIENCES
THAT IT IS
CLEAR THAT
ONLY A
LONG
TERM
APPROACH
WITH
THEM
COULD
HELP
THEM

② GIVEN WITH THIS SORT OF
BITTERNESS I FEEL OVERWHELMED
AT THE TASK AHEAD TO CHANGE
SUCH ATTITUDES. THERE IS A CLEAR DISTINCTION BETWEEN THE VIOLENCE
I WAS INVOLVED WITH PRISON STAFF IT WAS A TWO-WAY THING IN
MY CASE — IT WAS A CONSCIOUS POLITICAL USE OF VIOLENCE TO CHANGE
PRISON CONDITIONS AND CALCULATED TO FIGHT BRUTALITY SO, IT WAS
BRUTE FORCE AGAINST BRUTE FORCE. IN THESE GUYS CASES IT IS VERY MUCH
DIFFERENT. I HAVE DISCUSSED SIMILAR INCIDENTS WITH OTHER GUYS WHO HAVE
THE SAME YOI. HAD WHO WERE IN THIS UNIT. THE PATTERN IS THE SAME
THE BLATANT ABUSE OF POWER AND RESPONSIBILITY BY PRISON STAFF WHO WANT
TO BY MEANS OF VIOLENCE SQUASH THE HIGH SPIRITED NATURE OF YOUNG GUYS
IN INSTITUTIONS, LOCK — UP HIM SOLIDLY UNABLE BUT STOUT, AN HOURS
IN THEIR HAIR FULL OF CHEEK AND AGGRESSIVE MANNERS. IN ORDER TO
SQUASH THIS GROUP OF STAFF HAVE WHAT IN THEM CELLS AND BEAT THEM
SEVERELY SOMETIMES DOING IT IN FRONT OF OTHERS. THESE YOUNG GUYS ARE
DISTORTED ALL THEIR LIFE AS WHAT HE IS AT A CURTAIN AND SOMETHING THEY
ALL COME TO LAUGH WITH FLYING COLOURS. IT SAYS IN THIS PRISON NOT BIG THAT
MY AUTHORITIES WE WORK HARD TO TRY AND BE SENT TO PETER AND PRISON
IS A HEAD BEING IN OPENED ANARCHY BUNCH, IN CHARGE OF PEOPLE ETC. THESE
AND WHO TELL ME NUMEROUS "FUCKING WITH THE FREE" THE DEFIANCE AND
ANGER VERY MUCH SHINING OUT THEM IS THAT THESE GUYS DON'T WANT TO DO IT'S
SIMPLY A CASE THAT THEY DON'T WANT TO. THE AUTHORITY FIGURES TO THEM LIKE SOME,
MOULD AND THEY CALL THE AUTHORITIES BUFF MERELY HOLD IT ALL UP AND ARE FOLLED
WITH BITTERNESS BUCK OF THE G.P.S TODAY AS THIS LATEST GROUP THAT HAVE
MASS AND POSITIONS OF TRUST IN THE PRISON AND KNOW THIS IS OFF KILTER
ON THEIR CONTINUOUS SUBSERVIENCE. THEY HAVE GAINED A SUFFICIENT LEVEL
OF TRUST WHICH MEANS STAFF TALK OPENLY IN FRONT OF THEM. THIS MEANS
THAT BOTH THESE GUYS. THOSE II, UNKNOWN TO EACH OTHER HAVE
APPROACHED ME TO WARN ME OF PARTICULAR STAFF MEMBERS WHO
HAVE EXPRESSED BAD FEELINGS ABOUT ME. I FELT
REALLY APPALLED LISTENING TO THEM THIS MORNING. THEY
TALKED WITH GREAT HUMOUR ABOUT WHAT HAPPEN IN
THE YOUNG OFFENDERS. I AM MORE CONCERNED ABOUT
THE FUTURE AND HOW OUR EVENTUALLY GETS THROUGH
TO THESE YOUNG GUYS. THEY ARE SO DISTRUSTFUL
AND CYNICAL OF ANYTHING POSITIVE OR GOOD.
THEY ARE ALWAYS LOOKING FOR THE ANGLE, TO
SCREW OR TO GO INTO WITH HOOKS
ON THE RIGHTS OR WRONGS OF IT BUT COME WHAT
MAY WE CAN'T ESCAPE THE LONG TERM PROBLEMS
ALL OF THIS IS BUILDING UP. THE PRISON IS
FILLED WITH YOUNG GUYS LIKE THIS. IT'S THIS
SORT OF THING THAT WAS SITTING AT WITH A
SENSE OF FREEDOM. IF WE ARE TRYING TO RAISE
THE STANDARDS OF YOUNG GUYS LIKE THIS
THEN PRISON STAFF MUST RAISE THEIRS. AS
IT IS GANG WARFARE IS BEING ACTIVELY
ENCOURAGED BY THE AUTHORITIES OR PEOPLE
ABUSING THEIR POSITIONS OR POSITIONS.
IF PRISON STAFF ARE WANTING MEMBERS
OF THE PUBLIC TO SEE THEM IN AN
ENLIGHTENED WAY THEN THEY MUST
STOP BEHAVING IN A BRUTAL MANNER
THE THING IS THAT OFFICIALLY THEY CAN
SAY IT ALL THEY WANT BUT WHEN ONE
GOES UP AGAINST GUYS LIKE THESE
THEY WHO ARE NOT OUT TRYING TO
IMPRESS THE TRUTH OF WHAT THEY
SAY TO ME BUT ARE TELLING IT IN A
MATTER-OF-FACT WAY THEN ONE
IS RELYING ON ONES OWN
RATIONAL JUDGEMENT & INSTINCT
BETWEEN WHAT IS TRUE AND WHAT
IS FALSE. THE BIG ISSUE IS —
IN BROAD HUMAN STANDARDS IN PRISONS
HOUSES. THIS ISN'T A POLICY FOR
OUTSIDERS TO IMPOSE BUT IS ONE
FOR PRISON STAFF TO IMPOSE
ON THEMSELVES AND EACH OTHER
ONCE THEY PRACTICE IT THEN
IT WILL AUTOMATICALLY BE
SEEN AND FOLLOWED BY THE
PRISONERS. MEANWHILE THE
HEAP CONTINUES TO GROW
WHICH MEANS THAT ALL
OF US ARE LOSERS
AND FOR WHAT? THESE
SHORT-TERM SOLUTIONS
ONLY CREATE LONG
TERM PROBLEMS
AND A MORE
DIFFICULT LONGER
FOR ALL OF
US TO
SURVIVE.

Mr Meikle came to the prison tonight. The staff asked that he come to the Unit and see them. Meikle asked to speak to Wattie and it lasted till 10pm so I have no idea how it went.

14th September '77
This morning Malky opened my door and came in. He said the meeting with Meikle and the staff took place and the Governor sat silent throughout. It seems Meikle said that he understands the staff aren't happy at locking John up and went on to explain that he has to be seen to be doing something. He said he is trying to look at things for the good of the Unit. . . He asked that visitors be restricted to family and official, those we know but no ex-prisoners or rag-tags, whatever that may mean. He said it's best if John is kept locked up and not seen to be mixing with other prisoners so that accusations of his being pressured cannot be levelled at us. Staff said they can't have this for too long and Meikle agreed saying it wouldn't be allowed to drag on. Meikle said he isn't going to hammer the Unit or be repressive. He has had to answer eighty odd enquiries since Monday, and these were outwith the official ones. . . Meikle asked the staff how much Larry's being in the shadow of Jimmy Boyle, with the book and other things, brought this on. The staff dispelled this saying it had little bearing on the matter. Meikle asked if Larry could be called a Unit success.

Malky said he got the impression Meikle wanted the whole thing to cool off and that he wasn't interested in repercussions. Malky said he didn't seem to be interested in Larry's death.

14th September '77 (pm)
The days have become so jumbled it's hard to keep track of the time. The police came in this afternoon and went in to speak to John. He made a very honest statement to them. They said they weren't sure there would be any charges, saying it would be up to the Procurator Fiscal.

It is my view that the Department are having to be very careful here as they could be accused of making Larry's end inevitable. They offered him no alternative to the drugs. When speaking to Peter (Whatmore) he asked me what could have been done to prevent this happening to Larry. I told him that as far as I was concerned, a lot could have been done. Larry wasn't given any hope and so he took the drugs. It is my view that Larry could have been offered a realistic future but the Department policy towards guys in our position is so horrific that they leave no alternative.

The newspapers had wide coverage of Larry. His family are asking for an Inquiry into how drugs were smuggled into the prison and the press are having a go at us. . .

15th September '77
My sleep was restless. I had a dream. I found myself in Peterhead after being transferred from the Unit. I was in the main prison yard surrounded by enemies. Standing nearby but seemingly out of the prison stood Ben. I turned to him saying, 'I'm all alone Ben.'

The door was unlocked and I went into the yard and did my exercises. I felt absolutely drained and bone-weary but forced myself to complete my exercises. Having done so I felt much better. The front page of the *Daily Record* had a story and a big photo of Daphne, a prison visitor, standing in his prison cell. It advertised an exposé on the inner secrets of the Special Unit – Drugs and Sex. All of us felt sick at this. We sat chatting about it and there was doom on the faces of all the staff.

On seeing it the Governor turned a whiter shade of pale. Meikle phoned him to say that he would like a breakdown of all the female visitors we have had and our relationship with them.

The Governor called a meeting when he returned from lunch. He said that Meikle had been on the phone to say that the press in England have been on to him and that it looks as though they are out to do a hatchet job on us.

Jenny (Unit visitor) phoned Harry Ewing and had a reassuring talk with him about the Unit. It isn't going to close but there will be changes. He said the *Record* had been on to him about the allegations being made by Larry's brother and he told them it's up to them whether they print it or not. He said Bruce Millan had been on to him earlier and said he would back him all the way whatever he does. No matter what way it goes things are pretty black but I am going to hang on in there as long as I possibly can. There have been times today when I've felt like screaming – even right now.

Tonight BBC television announced the police know how the drugs got in and have interviewed a prisoner. It says the papers are at the Crown Office for a decision. I went to see John and he is looking very drawn. Jim (ex-Unit staff member) came in tonight and was obviously shocked at Larry's death. He told me that some staff in the main prison hospital wing are rubbing their hands with joy and making snide remarks. Another member of staff said some of the remarks they're making are disgusting.

I had some nice letters from people reading my book.

16th September '77
This morning I wakened and immediately wanted to pull the covers over my head and blot out what the day ahead was bringing. Despite this I dragged myself out feeling physically exhausted and started doing my exercises. Later I collected a pile of mail but left it aside to go see the morning papers. The *Daily Record* had it all: Larry's mother and sister talking about our being allowed girlfriends, sex, and how I had given Larry a bottle of whisky for his Christmas. They went on and on about how lax the Unit is. I don't know what they are trying to do but it does nothing for their dead son. They state they don't want others to die the same way Larry did but the truth is Larry loved the drugs.

The staff were all jittery and soon after the Governor came in he received a phone call from Meikle. He called a meeting and announced that he had been given a directive from the Department that no female visitors will be allowed in our cells during visiting time, and that all visits will be supervised from today. This brought another heated debate with all of us arguing that Meikle in taking this action is justifying the allegations.

Malky called a staff meeting and requested that local members of the SPOA be present. Staff want to take legal action against the Winters family and demanded that the Governor get on to Meikle and tell him that by making radical changes in the visiting conditions he is accusing the staff of negligence and prejudicing any legal action they may take. The Governor by this time was shaking and licking a dry mouth. He got on to Meikle in the presence of Malky and Bob and was surprised when Meikle relented and said the visiting should return to what it was but for our own safety we should initiate some supervisory measure and we agreed to this. Malky and Bob will visit the SPOA lawyer. The whole thing has been getting wide coverage on TV, radio and in the press.

The police were in this afternoon and took away most of Larry's correspondence as the Procurator Fiscal has asked for it. I was really sick at this as some of the letters may be incriminating.

Due to the intensity of events during the day all of us seem to have forgotten John. There is also a lot of bitterness against Larry's family as we all feel that they should know better. It is very tense indeed but tonight Denis, Peter, J.L. and I sat speaking and comments such as 'I'm going to ask for Parole on medical grounds' and 'I wish I was a non-smoking, teetotal poof who hated drugs' to 'Do you think we're being victimised?' had us in hysterical laughter – more out of nerves than anything else.

Teddy Taylor has entered the controversy and is calling for an Inquiry. I got masses of mail today containing good responses to the book.

Mosta
Malta

Dear Jimmy Boyle,
I expect you've received quite a few letters from strangers since you wrote your autobiography 'A Sense of Freedom'?

When I first saw it displayed in a Valetta bookshop, my thoughts were far from charitable. Like you, I'm from the West of Scotland and I too have a working class background and I was three quarters way through writing my own autobiography.

But I bought your book, albeit grudgingly, and was on the bus going home when I read the dedication. I was moved to tears.

This isn't the first prison book I've read but the others were 'soft shoe shuffles'. Yours was a vigorous highland fling. It isn't the kind of book one enjoys. But I despaired of you, laughed with you, cried for you and finally cared about you. Most of all I am so very very grateful to you for articulating the frustrations and humiliations of prison life. With me, this is a personal gratitude because two boys whom I love dearly are in prison at the moment.

They are my brothers George and James (Jim), who hailed from a wee place called Hardgate which is near Duncocher which is near Clydebank. (Glasgow boys used to meet me in the dancing and say 'I'd lumber you only I'm frightened I'll miss the last stagecoach!') Our George is serving that most sadistically named sentence 'Her Majesty's Pleasure' in the Butlins of the Bampots known as Carstairs. My other brother, Jim, 'the baby', is serving a life sentence in Peterhead for murder.

Unlike you we weren't brought up in a slum area. We had an estate (a council estate) to play in. So when George and Jim 'went wrong' local people condemned them, as did judges, as animals, etc. Hadn't they lived in a spotless home and didn't they have a mother who was respected by everyone as a hard working church-going woman. Moreover their stepfather had been an NCO during the war and came from a family 'a cut above ours'.

But the inside of our home was a 'socially deprived area'. From the minute we were infiltrated by my stepfather there was no happiness in our home. The boys were aged 11 years and 9 years and they'd come in from school and my stepfather would shout 'Get those hands washed on the double'. They'd march to the bathroom single file giggling and he (my stepfather) would shout louder.

Eventually as the boys got older – Jim got off the hook a little and George became the prime target. It was 'Get those hands out of your pocket when you address my wife' or 'How dare you sit on the sink in my home'. Then he teased 'You know what you are?' and poor George was something different every day. Once my stepfather said 'You're a poof'. None of us knew what the hell a 'poof' was so we at least got a laugh out of that one. But as you can imagine it wasn't really funny. Getting this mental bullying day in day out wasn't all George got. He was also the only one in our home who got physical punishment because we all ran and he was too proud for that. My mother who, like yours, was naturally kind and gentle, would nevertheless explode every so often and I've seen George's arse bleeding when I finally plucked up the courage to take the belt away from her. He was asked about bruises in school once, and said he fell. He began drinking and staying out all night as an adolescent and when he returned home one night my stepfather wouldn't let him in and he said 'Your mother says you are no longer her son'. It wasn't even true but we only found out later.

By then George, who was working as a coal carrier, got fed up walking about covered in dust with nowhere to sleep so he and a mate tried to rob the post office. George went in and asked the assistant for the money but he said 'Away home George or I'll tell your mother', so George went out and told his pal (the lookout). Drawing himself up to his full height (4ft.) the pal said 'Get back in and demand it'. So back he went and she was in the back room. George jumped over the counter intending to grab the money but the girl screamed so he ran out empty handed. He and his pal decided to make their getaway to England – on foot! They'd actually reached Clydebank when they were arrested. Had they been students it would have been looked on as a silly prank but they got Borstal.

Your book is a ray of hope for people like my brothers and a revelation to those who have never been inside. May you go from strength to strength. Actually I could have gone on reading when I reached the end of it. My daughter whose taste in literature is very different to mine, felt the same way. So I feel you have a future as an author.

Kindest regards
Mary

Greenford
Middlesex UB 8QJ

Dear Mr Boyle,
  I have just finished reading your autobiography 'A Sense of Freedom'. To say that I am impressed is indeed an understatement. Perhaps the greatest compliment I can pay is the following request.
  I run a small school for adolescents who have been deemed by the Authority to be in need of special education under the heading of maladjustment. You would recognise many of your school mates amongst my students. I would very much like your permission to tape the book for my kids to hear. We would play it over at our morning Assembly. Needless to say it would not be used anywhere else and please believe me not as an 'awful warning' – rather the reverse – to show how someone with spirit and, as you so generously admit, a little help from his 'friends', can win through in the end.
  May I wish you every success in the future.

Yours sincerely
Headmaster

Ballarat, Vic. 3350
Australia

Dear Jimmie,
  I have just read your book 'A Sense of Freedom' and I have the feeling a word of support from the other end of the world would be the decent thing to offer, seeing I got such a lot from it. It occurred to me you might have suffered a bit from writing your life story. I hope not. May your effort bring about the desired reform you have been working for.

There were many things in the book I very much admired – let me mention a few. First of all it was beautiful to read of your love for your mother and the grand things you had to say about her. She too had great courage and a deep love for you. As you said she was a wonderful person and I have joined with you in offering a little prayer for her.

How correct you are in laying the cause of the problems of many young people at the feet of the society in which we live. Too many of us do little to bring about change, but you certainly never gave up. I was touched by your desire to help others and if possible prevent others from suffering as you did. At times you didn't think much of yourself but all the time the goodness deep down in you came to the surface and it was great to see you were able to accept the goodness in others – even those you regarded as your enemies, before we came to the end of the story. I enjoyed your thoughts on Community (p. 252), some day I hope to write more on that theme. Too often we give in when the going gets tough but you always came back, still seeking an alternative way of living and you found enough courage to change heart and accept, even value humanity, when so many had been opposed to you. How many times did you call yourself an animal and deep down there was a humanity so warm and genuine that surged to great heights whenever you were allowed to be human.

Jimmie there is still much for you to do for yourself and others. No man can help others better than the one that has had a taste of all sides. You are not proposing theories but Truths, derived from personal experience. You could not possibly have a more powerful message.

I write primarily to encourage you to KEEP ON, first for yourself and secondly for others. It is possible your life story will return you material satisfaction – good luck to you if it does, but there is a more valuable satisfaction which I feel you are more interested in, the good you wish to others. I hope you will never lose sight of that.

Jimmie we will probably never meet but that doesn't matter. I salute you and congratulate you with all my heart. You probably made many mistakes in your life but you did one mighty deed for all of us when you wrote 'A Sense of Freedom'.

I would like to be allowed to call myself 'an admiring friend'.

Very sincerely yours,
Catholic Priest

London SW6

Dear Jimmy,

I have just read 'A Sense of Freedom' and am writing to tell you that I found it extremely moving.

As a solicitor I have several times acted for prisoners who have been extremely violent while in prison here in England. While I always sympathised with the fact that they suffer an extremely repressive regime I never fully understood their need to fight back. But what they said to me fits in exactly with the feelings that you write about so clearly in your book, that in some situations you have to fight or you have nothing. As a result of reading your book I feel I can understand their situation much better. No doubt this is the same for all who read your book and that is why it is so important that it was written and published.

Yours sincerely
Solicitor

Saughtonhall Terrace
Edinburgh

Dear Jimmy,

I've just read your book, can I just say how much I enjoyed it, it's left me a bit stunned. I'm a bit like yourself, I've been in and out of homes since I was eleven, I'm now 21, the point is, reading your book made me see what I've done to my parents and friends, it's no good really, going out to try and make a name for yourself as a hard man, or a great crook, the bit is you do get caught in the end, no matter what! Your book really put the shits up me in parts, and in others made me cry, can you imagine if my mates seen me? When reading the book I sat and thought of the grief you must have caused your wife and family, that's that position I'm in now. I've thought very hard about what you have described in your book, how you feel, what you've lost, can I just say I was out last night, got really pissed, had a great chance to be financially better off, but thought about what you said and declined. The book itself has, and will, make me think twice before I do anything stupid again.

Thanks a lot
Ronald

Geneva

Jimmy Boyle
>   FOR YOUR NIGHTS
>   AND DAYS OF FEAR
>   I SEND LOVE.
>   Dougal

Dear Jimmy Boyle,
    I saw you on the news tonight and I could hardly believe it. You see, I've just read your brilliant book 'A Sense of Freedom', and I never imagined you like you are! I thought you'd be really old and horrid! I cried practically the whole way through your book, but as I'm only 15 I can't do anything about penal reform I would if I could. I hope you don't mind me writing to you, but I loved your book so much that I'm going to study it for my 'O' Grades in English. I'm glad you're happier now and can have visitors. I live in Edinburgh and I often pass the Courts in Royal Mile, and it's hard to imagine anything 'real' happening there. I think that the Special Unit is a very good idea, but it was probably better before your two friends left. I pray that you'll be free soon to see your children, and I wish you good luck in everything.
    I hope you don't mind my writing,
                    Good luck
    P.S. Please write another book soon, I loved the last one. Thank you.

                                      51 Stronend Road
                                              Glasgow

Hello Jimmy
    its been a long time since I last saw you I hope you are keeping allright Im sorry about how things went for you at the start as you had it tough well jimmy I read your book it was some book you came through it hard I saw you on the TV news it was good to see you I have seen all the Boys over the South side as I go over to Tuckers Bar sometimes well jimmy about me I have been in and out of hospitals about a dozen times and had shock treatment quite a few times well jimmy its not much of a life at the moment I am staying up in possil with my Ma she is 77 years old and I have to look after her if it wasn't for her I would be away down in England for a job well jimmy you must have quite a lot of pals but I thought I would write to you

as I never write much tell everyone I was asking for them I will close now jimmy hoping you get out in the near future
from wee Tam

Glenburn,
Paisley

Dear Jimmy
I'm writing this letter to you after reading your book A Sense of Freedom *it was very interesting to see how another 'Con' lived his life in jail. I'm only nineteen years old but have already done A-School, Borstal, Detention and YO's in Bar, Glenochil YO's, Saughton YO's. So your book made me some interesting reading and put some ideas clear in my head like it isn't all that glamourours to have a name or reputation as it only falls back on you as you have shown. I would very much like to speak to you so as to see the person you are and come to terms with you in a frank talk as maybe your book has put others down. I don't really see it as a deterrant to my self as you said in the book you picked your way as I pick mine.*

Well Jimmy I hope this letter reaches you if not then maybe I'll meet you some day myself (S/Unit). My Mum worries a lot about me and like yourself I love her very much but give her the same patter as you (I'll never get in trouble again Ma) but always seem to do. Why I do I don't know maybe it is born in me like yourself Jimmy. I'm not sure it may take me the same road as yourself before I find out (Jimmy I do not know only God) Some day you'll go free (I hope) Maybe that day I'll start my lifer who knows but I hope not. Many people say your just biding your time soon you'll be a lifer I hope to God not Jimmy as from your book I seem to have the very same attitude (I'm doing life so what have I got to lose 'nothing' only what I have lost 'my life'). Well Jimmy I have hard times myself nothing to boast about as I've not done my full stretch yet so hoping you can give me a little assurance against a life sentence then I would be most grateful. I don't know if you have many letters like this but reading from your book and of some things you've done it was a certainty I was destined to follow in your foot steps if I hadn't read your book or if you hadn't got it published so thanking you on a little help and God Bless you for giving me something to think about God Bless Jimmy Cheers

Yours sincerely

Ware
Hertfordshire

Dear Mr Boyle,

I have just finished reading your book 'A Sense of Freedom'. I thought your book was good and interesting because it made me feel that I never want to go to prison myself.

A member of staff gave me your book to read and another boy has also read it. I am at a Community Home because I used to steal things. In 1974 this home changed from an Approved School to a Community Home. We get on well with the staff generally and call them by their first names. I also went to Latchmere House which is a Remand Home and has high fences around it. At Latchmere House we were locked up for many hours a day. It was not as bad as the places you describe in your book.

I am writing this letter to see if you can give me any advice at all about keeping out of trouble. Are you writing any more books about your life?

I know you have a lot to do, but hope that you can write back to me.

Yours sincerely

17th September '77
This morning I lay awake with my mind in a turmoil and asking myself why? Why must I be subjected to this intense psychological pressure? I feel threatened as never before. I realise the gravity of the whole thing. It's not so much the Unit closing, it's more to do with my losing access to the things that are keeping me alive. There is a part of me that knows if I come through this then I'll survive anything. The amount of pressure on is almost crushing.

I sat with Wattie in my cell. He is sick at Larry's family for making these kinds of statements. I was telling him that Peter Whatmore looked worried. Wattie said he knows Peter will be under pressure for having Larry on so many drugs and went on to say that none of them want to bring out the dosage Larry was getting in Perth and Inverness as it was illegal and unethical. Wattie said he mentioned this to Meikle when he was through at the Department. Meikle said he was worried about this but didn't think it would be necessary for people to look back that far.

Meikle was the Governor of Perth at the time. I can remember the drugs Larry was getting in Inverness and it was unbelievable when one saw the amount.

Tom McGrath had a piece in the *Glasgow Herald* about sex and drugs in prison, saying that homosexuality and hard drugs are prevalent and people should understand this. It was a good piece.

I walked up and down the yard this morning and thought of Larry. The finality of death is awesome. I thought of him lying there and wondered if the spiritual side of him continued? I thought of McCaig's *Poem For A Goodbye*.

> The elements which
> Made me from our encounter rich
> Cannot be uncreated; there is no
> Chaos whose informality
> Can cancel, so,
> The ritual of your presence, even gone away.

5th October '77

Tom Melville phoned to ask Wattie when our non-censored mail was introduced. He said that Bruce Millan was reading my book and when he came to this part in the book he phoned up to ask the question. Tom was in a panic and suggested to Wattie that Alex Stephen was at that particular meeting. Wattie agreed. This isn't true as the Minutes of the Communiiy meeting show. It's this whole civil service game of throwing it on to someone else instead of fully explaining the truth. I'm sure Bruce Millan would accept it. Tom was saying it has been question after question from the Secretary of State since the whole thing blew up.

Teddy Taylor was on the news a few minutes ago saying he's been sent a letter from an ex-Unit prisoner supporting the fact that drugs, drink and prostitutes go into the place. It is reported to be an anonymous letter.

15th October '77

Devil this life of anguish and pain as I sit here locked in this world of forbidden fruits. Each twist and turn, each breath and sigh, each look and laugh – monitored.

Delicately I move on tiptoes – afraid to arouse the emotions of the masses who browse sombrely in the false security of silent containment. Eyes reversed, I look into the matter of their minds searching for signs of consciousness. God, it's frightening, long dark corridors with doors shuttered and bolted to keep out all areas of understanding and sensitivity. Tears, heavy with sorrow, roll from the eyeballs to wash away the dust of time.

Look at them, spread all over the world, self-opinionated bastards they condemn others from a base of ferociously insensitive ignorance. Shallow minds, all but blind, they beat their breasts in self-righteous hypocrisy. Long bony fingers point in my direction 'Him! Him! Him!' they chant accusingly. He bears the mark of Cain, the wrongdoer, the leopard with the branded spots.

Shit, thick and brown with a high fibre content, masses of body waste rubbed into their faces in the hope of fertilising their brains. Numb, dumb and blunt, they lift one leg and then the other, each limb dim as it stumbles unintelligently on. Blisters on the heel, water on the brain – a mere pinprick could start a flood! Fucking idiots! Pools of pain swim in my soul seeking areas of joy to drown in or that's what it feels like. Leaden lifebelts are thrown my way but sink heavily to the bottom and they call themselves friends, huh! Bastards! Cast off your masks of deception! I scream into the echo-chamber of my soul. Para-fucking-noia is looking over your shoulder and seeing yourself – dogs experience it when they chase their tails. It's like popping air bubbles into your own veins, they soon burst.

17th October '77
Tonight the media have announced the date for the Fatal Accident Inquiry into Larry's death. It will be in Glasgow High Court Building on 28th November. The media are already turning it into a circus by stating there will be the tightest security ever mounted . . . it really is shitty.

18th October '77
The Governor came in. He sent a member of staff to tell us that Meikle and Melville will be visiting the Unit to speak to the staff at 10am. We (the prisoners) were locked up during this meeting. They informed the staff that at 3pm yesterday they had been given authority by the Secretary of State to start an Internal Inquiry. They were seeing ex-staff and ex-prisoners from other prisons. They will return here in three weeks to see the staff and prisoners here. Meikle apparently said that anyone giving evidence would not be liable to disciplinary action if anything is found to be

wrong. This is not a witchhunt. He feels that three weeks should cover interviews and two weeks to write up the report to put to Millan. He said the Unit won't close but if the Inquiry reveals areas that should be tightened or restricted then that will happen.

27th October '77
I've been sitting here thinking that I seem to spend these days of crises with every part of me alert and expectant, apprehensively anticipating the next move or blow to come our way. I stood in front of the mirror, looking at myself in the shadowy light as I pissed in the chamber pot and thought to myself 'Christ, you can't keep this up much longer'. A weariness overtook me with this silent admission but almost as quickly I reinforced it with a surge of inner strength. I can't afford myself the weakness of relaxation. I seem to spend my days searching faces, listening to phrases and feeling all the underlying tensions as they expand and contract inside each individual. I try to strengthen their vulnerable areas and give them support.

30th October '77
Meikle and Melville came in. J.L. was interviewed by them. I was taken in. Meikle informed me that his Inquiry is separate from the public one into the cause of death. He said if during the interview I admit to having a few beers then I won't be put on a disciplinary charge as this is a fact-finding survey.

He said that allegations have been made by people who know the inner running of the Unit and that part is factual but some of them relate to sex, drugs and drink being in the place. He would like to know the truth of this. He asked about sex and I told him I had never had sex with anyone. I didn't know of anyone else who did either. He asked if it was possible to have it. I told him irregular checks were made by staff during the visits and though it was possible it was unlikely. He asked if I knew of any prostitutes who had come in. I told him I didn't. He moved on to drugs and asked if I'd known of any being smuggled in. I told him we had one incident with Larry in the medical office and John on a visit. I reminded him that drugs, particularly where Larry was concerned, were a worry to some of us. He asked me about drink and I told him I had never heard of drink being in the Unit. He pointed out that Rab had admitted this in a recent newspaper interview. I replied that I didn't know of it. . . We left off at lunch, with him saying he would like to finish me off on Monday or Tuesday.

I spoke to John when he came out from his interview. He was pretty open with them on the whole incident and told them the Unit had done a lot for him. When asked by Meikle if there should be any changes he replied no and went on to explain that only fools like him will make mistakes like this but this shouldn't detract from the genuine people in the place. John felt his meeting with them went well.

1st November '77

Denis (prisoner) called a meeting this morning. He pointed out that he is concerned at the way this Internal Inquiry is being handled. He said Meikle is asking questions that have nothing to do with the specific allegations being made. He is aware of the way in which past interviews between staff and Prison Department have been distorted and Denis wanted to know if Meikle would come across to the Community meeting at the end of this Inquiry to discuss the Unit problems with us. He said that all of us want an opportunity to talk to him about the place outside of the allegations and we have shown full co-operation with them over the Internal Inquiry and would like them to do the same. This was immediately seconded and everyone supported it. The Governor was asked to speak to Meikle about it.

The reply to Teddy Taylor from Bruce Millan was flashed on the radio news this morning. It stated that no evidence of sex or drink in the Unit had been found but that visits were such that it could have been possible. Staff are now supervising visits. It went on to say that letters would remain unopened but that parcels would be opened and use of the phone has been stopped. The statement refused to mention drugs saying it will be subject to the Public Inquiry. It pointed out that all ex-prisoners would be stopped from visiting the Unit. The Secretary of State said he believes the Unit is a success and the measures taken are simply to safeguard it and people should see it in that context.

That vile little man Teddy Taylor was interviewed and spat his political venom saying he was happy with the result. Millan said it would be foolish to make a final decision on the Unit at this stage as this is only an interim report due to public concern shown.

The Crown Office people came in to interview us. They asked me about sex and I denied sex taking place. They asked me about drink and I denied this. They asked about drugs and I told them about Larry. . .

The TV news this evening gave wide coverage to Millan's statement. Norman Buchan MP was interviewed. He said he was disturbed that ex-Unit prisoners were barred from going back to visit the Unit. He was worried about the restrictions and searches imposed as they would be harmful to the Unit and the relationship between people there. He was also very concerned about the intention to change the staff.

2nd November '77
The Governor said he would like to speak to me this morning. He said that Meikle wanted my sculpture stored and I looked at him puzzled. I asked what he meant. He was hesitant then said my sculpture work displayed in the hall had to be crated and stored. I really took offence at this and asked what possible reason could he give for this? He said he wasn't sure so I told him that this was not on and is out of order. . . He told me to cool it and he would try to get more information.

6th November '77
This afternoon John had a visit from his mother. I went in for a spell and she seemed worried. I felt sorry for her as she reminded me of my own mother and the pain I had caused her. She said to John, 'I suppose if you live in hell you get used to it.'

John and I sat speaking. We discussed prison and the humiliation of it. John said he would love to murder a screw as he hates them all. He told me of how when he was in the main prison system he used to follow one round the gallery, watch when no one was about and have a dummy run as though he was going to do him in. He said he lies and thinks of doing a screw in and said this with lots of anger. I told him I used to do the same thing but now I no longer blame them for my present position. I asked him if we are going to be losers all our lives? I reminded him how we come into prison and think nothing about it. We went on to discuss his getting out and thinking only of returning to villainy. John replied that this is the only alternative to a lousy job.

8th November '77
There was a piece in *The Guardian* about Russ Kerr MP and his group meeting Harry Ewing. It made some scathing remarks at

Millan taking the Inquiry out of Harry Ewing's hands. It goes on to say that the group want to know about Larry being on an excessive amount of drugs prior to coming to the Unit, while in Inverness he was getting amounts that were unethical. . .

At the Community meeting . . . the Governor said he brought up the sculpture issue with Meikle and said it is really only floor space he is on about and if some of the pieces occupying floor space can be moved that would be fine. He wanted me to know that he isn't discouraging me from sculpting. There was a barrage of questions from different people in the meeting saying the question of arranging furniture is for the Community. The Governor replied that the Controller if he so wishes can over-ride this.

10th November '77
This afternoon I went in to be interviewed by Meikle and Melville. . . Meikle asked the number of times I had been out to Edinburgh. I told him three. . . After he had finished with his questions I told him I'd like to mention one or two things. I had been told that he was asking about my role in the Unit, was I too dominating a personality, was I giving them problems? He said the reason he was asking these questions of people he was interviewing was because whenever the Unit was mentioned it was always my name that was there. He said no matter what journalist is writing about the Unit they mention me. He said he wanted people in the Unit's opinion of this, the fact that I get more attention than anyone else, more mail, etc. The reply he got from everyone was that I have always been constructive and helpful to people in adjusting to the Unit and have alleviated violence on a number of occasions. He said he is clear on this. I said I cannot separate this from the storage of my sculpture and wondered whether this was a practical way of eliminating that 'dominant personality'. He said he sent a letter here with two points in it referring to me: 1) To ask me to keep a list of all sculptures I have done, where they went to, the price they were sold at and the donated ones. 2) The Governor should discuss with me and Wattie the possibility of finding alternative space for the freestanding sculptures on plinths.

24th November '77
. . . I received a copy of a letter that Willie Hamilton MP had from Harry Ewing on the question of the Unit '. . . It would be

difficult, and inappropriate, to attempt to reproduce all aspects of the Unit throughout the prison system. It has been successful in dealing with prisoners who have proved exceptionally difficult to handle elsewhere in the system, but relatively few prisoners come into this category. More so, its methods are very costly, particularly in terms of staff, as we could not hope to reproduce them on a wide scale. The lessons of the Unit have nevertheless been absorbed and similar concepts – especially the establishment of a close staff/inmate relationship – are applied elsewhere in the Scottish prison system to a considerably greater extent than is sometimes recognised. . .'

What sheer hypocrisy!

29th November '77
I worked till early this morning then went to bed feeling extremely tired. It was 2.20am. I expected to fall asleep but no. My mind was active as I kept thinking about the Public Inquiry. There is something frustrating about tossing and turning in bed within a locked room.

The van arrived and we all went into it; John, Peter and I, along with the staff; some of whom were witnesses. Once out of the prison I tried to look through the frosted windows of the van into the foggy streets. There have been many changes in the east end of the city since I was last there. Most of the houses have been knocked down. Here I was seeing cars, buses, shops and buildings – districts that I have known in the past. It was strange not to feel any emotional tugs. It is as though I have decided never to live here when I get out. It wasn't like other times when I was out or my past thoughts when I would long for the streets that I knew. I felt that I was never going back.

We arrived at the High Court after passing through the Gorbals. A TV camera was outside the court. On going into the building and along the white tiled corridors I felt all the old associations of the place hitting me. I'd have given anything not to be here and yet there was value in being exposed to it. The three of us were locked in a cell for fifteen minutes. The police returned to split us into separate cells. He couldn't understand why and I asked him who issued the order. He said our Governor did. I shook my head with disgust at the silly bastard as all he can think of is negative decisions. I walked up and down then across: six paces one way, three the other. Cold white tiles surrounded me.

The steel-lined door was covered with prisoners' pasts. There was a small square opening of six inches. I stood looking out of it thinking how familiar it all was. I felt desperately sick and spiritually weakened just standing there. I felt so helpless. I began a long walk around the cell singing 'The House of the Rising Sun'. Before very long I was singing it in a wailing fashion . . . it was soul singing, it was the pain I was feeling. It was a very powerful experience. How many people have stood here full of fear and all the other feelings that go with a High Court appearance I thought. I wondered how many condemned men had stood on this spot.

In order to get to the court I had to walk up stairs that led into the dock, through this and into the witness box. Once there I looked up to see many of the Unit staff sitting in a row with the Governor sitting alone in the bench in front of them. I wanted to call a meeting and demand why he authorised us being put into separate cells. The Sheriff swore me in. I was asked to give some indication of Larry's state of mind. I said he was in good form the night before. The family lawyer asked if I thought it unlikely that Larry took his own life? 'Absolutely,' I replied. With this I vanished back down the stairs.

The verdict was that Larry died as a result of the ingestion of regurgitated matter while he was subconscious as a result of an overdose of the barbiturate Tuinal. The Tuinal was brought in by John from the Douglas Inch Clinic. He thought that Larry's death might have been avoided by strict searching of prisoners returning from escorted visits. He made no recommendation on this but went on to say that those in charge of the Special Unit should, with a view to preventing further incidents of a like nature in the future, consider how searches of prisoners and visitors are consistent with the aims and methods of the Special Unit. I was left in no doubt that it was one big cover up from start to finish. They really have the system sewn up.

Apart from the publicity, it is all over. There are fears in all of us that Meikle and Co. will institute changes far beyond the ones at present but we will have to wait and see. Meikle, Melville and two other officials were present at the Hearing. . .

My play went on in London last night. . .

30th November '77
Press coverage on the Public Inquiry was pretty factual. . . Russ Kerr MP, challenged Teddy Taylor MP to spend two days in the

Unit (Christ, as if we don't have enough on our plates) with him saying he would change his views over that period. Teddy Taylor, is quoted as saying the Unit has become 'a left-wing cause celèbre'. . .

3rd December '77
. . . This afternoon I had a visit from Sarah Trevelyan. We had lunch together. We discussed many things concerning prisons and her involvement in the Control Unit in English prisons. She works in Inverness at the moment as a doctor in a hospital there. I thoroughly enjoyed speaking with her as we are really into similar things. . . I showed Sarah round the Unit and soon afterwards she left.

5th December '77
. . . Word came through today saying John is to be moved out of the Unit. It was a phone call to the Governor from Meikle saying John was to be transferred to the main prison, that he will be put into circulation there even though they don't as yet know if charges will be preferred against him.

12th December '77
I am sitting here feeling worn and tired. Late this afternoon I felt like coming up to my bed but instead made some brown bread. Tonight as I watched the TV news I thought 'Christ, the same old blurb and here I am still in this torment of a place'.

Spent tonight buried in deep personal pain trying to deal with this confinement. I am getting many thoughts on the subject, in fact, I seem to be getting pummelled by them. Tonight on Panorama I watched a film on human rights. It concerned political prisoners and had the slogan 'Minds in Prison'. I felt pangs of torment and wanted to shout out what I was feeling. Listening to some of these prisoners, men of high intelligence who are deep-thinking with strong beliefs I thought of how unjust the world is. People in my world aren't brought up to think such things, they are merely the donkeys of our society. Only now, after having travelled a road of misery, am I able to think and believe.

I listened to this man from Amnesty International speak of 'subtle psychological torture' and how difficult it is to detect. I know exactly what he means. I want to sit here into the early hours and try to write what I feel, but how can I? How is it possible to write about this pain, this searing stab that slices through my mind, body and soul? It is not a pain that touches one specific part, it permeates every little fibre in every little way.

22nd December '77
Wattie got on to John Renton, General Secretary, SPOA, to ask him about the Internal Inquiry Report. Renton said he hadn't heard anything but can't see much coming out of it. He said if there are any radical changes then they (SPOA) will have to be consulted. He told Wattie that Millan is expected to make a statement about the Internal Inquiry when Parliament re-sits, or during the recess. It will only concern the report and not give details. I had an international telegram from Hollywood:

> Feel passionately your story warrants the greater freedom and integrity of film over ephemeral television both for Glasgow relevance and international significance with which Sean Connery concurs. Best regards, Murray Grigor.

I managed to speak to Stephanie. She has been trying to get hold of me to say that two guys want to visit me on Tuesday to discuss a film. . . She said that Murray Grigor is asking me to stall any decision for as long as I possibly can. The fact is he's had a brief chat with Connery but nothing of any significance so in actual fact the telegram is a piece of bullshit.

29th December '77
This morning I completed my exercises then collected my mail. There was a letter from the OU giving results of my exams. I had passed. . . I was glad to have it done with. James and Patricia came in this morning. We came up to my cell where we made coffee and sat watching TV. It was great being with them. They stayed all the way through to 4pm. Jimmy Mac (staff member) on passing congratulated me on my exam results. James and Patricia asked what this meant so I gave an explanation. Patricia immediately responded, 'Does that mean you get home early?'. . . Both of them worked hard on my typewriter, writing me small letters. . .

Harry brought my three visitors in. We had a good chat about the proposed film. Peter MacDougall was very good, a right earthy guy. Frank Roddam and Ted Childs were also good. We discussed the social and political implications of the whole thing and it was very interesting. They feel they could do a TV film almost immediately but that a feature film may be more profitable and worthwhile. They want to come and see me, get to know me before doing the film. They were sensitive to everything and went out of their way to ensure that they weren't putting pressure on me. I liked them as people. I told them I would have to think things over and though the vibes were good tonight we will have to wait and see. Peter is staying up for the New Year and would like to return next week. . .

2nd January '78
3.14am. I've been wakened for over an hour, am irritable and restless. The Radio Clyde disc jockey is speaking to people in their homes via telephone. I get the atmosphere of home parties from it. Pop music is blasting in my ears and I marvel at radio and how it must comfort lonely people. It's almost as though it's reassuring me I'm not alone. 3.55am. One of these days I won't be 'still here'. It's amazing how difficult I find it to think of myself being anywhere else. I read some Yevtushenko poetry:

> Consider that city – it is your past,
> wherein you scarcely ever managed to laugh,
> now raging through the streets, now sunk in self,
> between your insurrections and your calms.
>
> You wanted life and gave it all your strength,
> but, sullenly spurning everything alive,
> this slum of a city suffocated you
> with the dreary weight of its architecture.

12th January '78
. . . There was a piece in the new SPOA Magazine on the Minutes of the Whitley Council meeting 16th Aug. '77. On the staffing changes proposed it says: 'The staff side could not accept that lack of volunteers was the cause of the proposed changes and that this was not a manoeuvre on the part of the Department to change the regime of the Unit.' It went on to say:
  2) The staff side expressed their concern over the impending publication of a book by an inmate of the Special Unit and pressed for an assurance that should an officer be the subject of any defamation in the book he would be given financial assistance by the Secretary of State to pursue a civil action in court.

The Official Side said that it was not aware of any financial authority that would make such assistance but undertook to make enquiries to see whether it was possible.

They then go on to discuss the Inverness Segregation Unit. They are all pressing for it to be put back into action.

18th January '78
This morning the weather was icy and bitterly cold when I ran round. I mentally worked on the new sculpture and must admit that I'm getting tremendous satisfaction from working once again.

After my exercises I collected my mail and the papers. There were letters from readers of my book saying how it affected them . . . they were really nice. I collected my tools and went outside to work on my ideas of early morning. It was cold and icy but I enjoyed working. It's amazing to watch the piece come alive as I work on it. It all began to click and I thought of the process that creates a piece of sculpture like this. First I start out with a rough block of stone and let my hammer and chisel eat into it. I have a vague idea of what I want to do but it's so distant that there's no real form in mind. As I go on it starts to come together, this is what happened this morning. I went into a sort of 'high' and the whole process happened like magic. I fused with the stone. I tasted freedom as I never have before. I thought of how physical freedom is only one part of it. Many, many people on the outside won't have tasted this sort of freedom. . . David Markham came in this afternoon and we had a good discussion. I was very pleased with his visit. He seems a genuine guy. We had a very open and frank discussion on things. He is the sort of person one can speak to on this level. I am delighted that he is willing to try and get things moving for me as I desperately feel the need for something of this sort to be done. It's strange that as he talked about it I felt guilty of doing something for myself and promoting my case for getting out. I never get into this with visitors who come into the Unit and so talking about it on this very open and subjective level was quite strange and difficult. . .

19th January '78
I went outside in the falling snow to work. I lost myself in the piece and felt very close to it. The sculpture has come together so well. It was constantly getting covered in falling snow as I worked and so I had to get a tin of hot water to throw over it so

that the snow would melt as it landed. I'm sure people walking into the building must have thought me mad. I can understand this but then if they knew what I was experiencing they would see how sane I am. In this extremely cold winter morning I am glowing, the cold and discomfort didn't matter, it didn't exist. I was spiritually connected to the stone I was working on. . .

22nd January '78
All the snow had melted and I could see the ground. It made the yard look naked. I missed the snow. I mentally worked on the piece of stone that stood dressed and ready for sculpting. Peter (prisoner) came out and told me there was something in the *Sunday Post* on the Unit. I thought 'God, don't say all this is going to come up again?' It read SPECIAL UNIT – NEW ROW IS BREWING and went on to say that staff in the main prison are saying procedures haven't been tightened at all and that prisoners there are upset about this. This garbage is such that I suddenly understand why the Scottish people are years behind other countries. . . I had a walk in the yard with Peter this afternoon. He told me he constantly feels the hammer is going to fall on the place and is always waiting for it. I asked him if this is because of the newspaper report and he said it is. I felt sorry for him. He admitted that he knows he is insecure anyway but he is very nervous about the future of the Unit.

28th January '78
Getting up I went down to collect my mail and the newspapers. The headline in *The Scotsman* concerned the Unit. It went on to say how an all-party deputation led by Alick Buchanan-Smith and Norman Buchan, MPs, are intending to approach Bruce Millan on the matter to advise him not to make any severe restrictions on the Unit that would damage the atmosphere of the place. In the *Glasgow Herald* there was a headline on the opening of the Inverness Cages with the Department quoted as saying it would be 'humane containment'. The first article pleased me while the second filled me with anger. . .

There was a letter from Stephanie saying she has sent £2000 (royalties) to the Trust Fund with more to come in April and May. . .

31st January '78

Ken came in and we sat chatting till the Governor came in with Lord Longford. We were introduced. I took him around the Unit. He said he had come as a result of reading my book, that he had enjoyed it and thought he'd like to see the Unit as a result. . . Afterwards we had a meeting with plenty of staff present. We talked about violence and prisoners giving problems in the system and then he asked if we have any questions for him. Denis asked him what he was doing here. Lord Longford explained what he had previously told me and added that he is a peer, that he and MPs can get into places like this. . . Denis said the present situation is that he has to sit and listen to someone like him when he can't listen to friends or make new friends because of the stupid restrictions imposed on us. Lord L. stated that no one need sit and listen or stay in the meeting if they didn't want to. Denis said that wasn't the point he was trying to make. We explained to Lord L. and asked him to use some muscle to get these restrictions taken off.

The Governor sitting there was beginning to get worried and strained-looking, his face beet red, his hands kept going to his face and rubbing it. Throughout the meeting the Governor kept having to leave for phone calls. I went out to make coffee when he came round saying the press are outside in their hoards, hundreds of them and saying he had better get on to the SIO. He was in a bloody panic. On my return Ken was telling Longford that if Millan is restrictive in his final statement the staff will walk out of the Unit as they see this sort of thing being destructive, making conditions intolerable to work in. We discussed the press, first telling him the situation was that we were 'hot press' and he was 'hot press' so it would be to the good if he played it cool on leaving.

He told me that he would have recommended my book as Book of the Year to *The Times* but he did with Wally Probyn's as he knew him. I told him I'd prefer it through merit rather than through the 'Pals Act'.

Overall I found him a much harder person than I expected. He was a shrewd, hard politician and for some reason I didn't expect someone this hard. I felt from what I'd heard, read and seen of him on TV, that he was a naive person. But no. He knows what he is doing when he is dealing with the media and this makes it all the worse as he seems impervious to the destructive way the media use him, particularly the way he has given Myra Hindley the 'kiss of death'. This concerned me and is totally different from what I expected. When he left there was only one reporter and photographer.

3rd February '78
The *Glasgow Herald* has a statement from Bruce Millan saying that there were no plans to bring the Cages back into use. He said he wants to make it clear there is no intention of placing prisoners in the Cages at this time. The article and Millan's statement waffle quite a bit . . . parts stating that the only recent action taken by the Prisons Department has been to identify certain prisoners who would be suitable for transfer should this be judged necessary. No such transfer can be made without Millan's authority and this will be given only if and when it is necessary.

The Scotsman's article about the Cages is pretty detailed and hardhitting. It's obvious that the politicians have been put on the spot with this one – the Department have inadvertently put them on to it.

I find it ludicrous that the Secretary of State can make this sort of statement when the Inverness staff have been told that Brian Hosie and Sinclair will be transferred from Peterhead to Inverness Cages this Tuesday. They have been told this officially. Millan is saying that he will decide who goes there when in fact the Regulation for the Inverness Segregation Unit recently circulated states quite clearly that Governors will select prisoners for the Cages. . .

The Regulations for the Segregation Unit, Inverness, state there is a ratio of:
1 prisoner: 1 Senior Officer plus 3 Officers.
More than 1 prisoner: 1 Senior Officer plus 4 Officers.

The rules for the running of the Cages are pretty horrific with no provision for the standard of behaviour of staff in it. Everything is geared towards controlling the prisoner. No mixing with other prisoners in their Cages. It is quite clear that the Department and prison staff have learned nothing from past experiences there.

13th February '78
After being called to the phone to speak to Tom Melville the Governor returned to say that Millan was making his statement to the press (on the outcome of the Internal Inquiry). I asked him if anything had been said and he replied that Radio Clyde phoned

to ask for a comment on a Grade 3 Governor being put into the Unit. He said he was surprised. This meant that we all had to sit and wait for news. I thought it appalling that here we were not knowing the contents of the statement and Radio Clyde phoning to tell us.

The staff immediately went off to the SPOA to complain. The local branch tried to get hold of their Executive Committee but they were at the Department. Ken got hold of the Governor to ask him to phone the Department and ask them the content of the statement. He did and Tom Melville is supposed to have said that he doesn't know as it's being released from London. The Governor bolted.

Throughout the early evening, news programmes gave their own versions but they still leave it rather vague as I write this. There is reference to ex-Unit inmates being allowed to visit, that the allegation of drink, sex, and drugs was largely unsubstantiated. Millan was interviewed and I didn't like the way he was coming across about the Unit developing away from what was intended. He said we are now getting it back to what it was meant to be in 1973. He said he no longer sees the Unit as experimental as it has a lot to offer the system. He said it is too early to see it expanded. He said there have been irregularities within the Unit but we don't get what he means on the news reports.

The big thing they seem to be hitting on is the change of Governor and how a more senior man is being drafted in as soon as possible. They are at great pains to stress that it is no reflection on the present Governor or past governors. I don't know if the present one has the savvy to appreciate that this puts him in a bad light. . .

14th February '78
Ken caught hold of me saying he went to the Governor telling him that although he didn't particularly admire his performance in here, the way he's been treated in this Report is abominable as he has been made the scapegoat. Ken told him the Department have a lot to answer for as they have put him and other governors into this post without proper training or briefing. He said it was out of order putting this statement out without telling him. The Governor became shaky at this and told Ken he had been told 'in confidence' something about it but nothing about the rest of the statement. Ken was saying that as he spoke to him it was pathetic

as he didn't want to criticise the Department. This is what happens to these guys, they become so 'tied' to the Department through blind loyalty that they cannot offer constructive criticism. The Department seem to call for total obedience. Ken said the Governor remarked that it may be in the new Governor's best interests for him to get out as soon as possible.

11th February '78
A letter put by the staff brought the following reply:

1. As previously indicated this meeting will be attended by staff only and the request that the inmates should be present is refused.
2. The agenda for this meeting is as follows: 'Confirmation and amplification of the Secretary of State's instructions concerning the future operation of the Unit'.
3. As the meeting is being convened to relay the Secretary of State's instructions for the future operation of the Unit the presence of representatives of the local branch of the SPOA or its Executive would not be appropriate. All members of staff should be informed accordingly.

T. Melville.

Ken called a meeting of all the staff about the Department not meeting the measures they had asked for. He got 100% support from the staff saying they shouldn't go into the meeting without SPOA reps.

23rd February '78
I've been asked by Jim Taylor, administrator of the ARC to lend them the Jarrow Heads as they are having a visit from the Duke of Edinburgh on 3rd March. I went down to the new Governor (Grade 3) and asked him about this. He collared me and took me into his office saying he wanted to speak to me.

We sat chatting and at first it was generalities but soon I could see through the façade. He told me that his phone has been ringing all night – his superiors, far above the Prisons Dept. – and they were asking him to brief them on the issue of prisoners not having a say in the running of the Unit. He said that his superiors were saying 'this place' is causing too much trouble and would be as well closed down. He said he mentioned this to the staff this morning saying there are people who want it closed. He said if it becomes too troublesome then it could be closed as he knows that

Millan was thinking this way at one point, and did I know this? I told him on the contrary I know Millan has always wanted it opened. He said he told his superiors this morning that if they closed the Unit and put the other inmates to other prisons where they would be absorbed, where could they put Jimmy Boyle? He asked me where I could be put. I replied saying I could simply be put into any prison and that's all there was to it. He was playing a game here and I was letting him know that I knew his game.

Tonight John Renton was interviewed on radio and television. He said that when he went into the Working Party meeting this afternoon he was confronted with a document by Department officials and he understands that the document was given to Unit staff on Tuesday. He said the first point in the document meant that the points in it could not be negotiated and this wasn't on. He said that the document, contrary to what the Secretary of State said last week, certainly ended the democratic concept of the Unit. He said it was full of intolerable changes. He said they didn't get past the first post as he walked out of the meeting.

25th May '78

Dear Sarah,

Thanks for that lovely card, it touched me deeply. I must tell you about this dream I had last week. It was a sunny day here and I met Max in the yard where he was wearing a light-grey suit and tie. I felt his attitude towards me was condescending and so I confronted him with this. On doing so he swiftly turned his head to the side as though not wanting to discuss it. I moved to face him saying we must speak. He agreed and we walked towards my cell but at the foot of the stairs I turned to say something to him when this force surging from the pit of my stomach pushed up to the top of my mouth. A gush of blood, thick and powerful, came out of the top gum and covered Max, causing him to throw up his hands and shout 'I'm stained' and then quickly, as though to cover up what he said 'My suit is stained'. I fell to the floor with a feeling of death approaching, and from nowhere you appeared and knelt by my side and held my head trying to stop the flow of blood. You looked with anguish at Max, 'Get an ambulance, he's dying'. For some unknown reason I was dragged into a cold cell in the main prison. It was filled with debris and pools of filthy water. You sat with my head on your lap this time imploring a screw, standing at the door clutching a baton, to get me out to hospital. He said he couldn't without orders from his superiors. You kept insisting you were a doctor, but still he wouldn't budge. At points many recognisable faces appeared in front of me and I told you I was going to die. You told me that I wasn't but the eyes said different. I ended up lying on a stretcher in a hospital with people moving around but no one interested in my situation. At this point I wakened...

Yes, it is okay for you to bring Sam... I look forward to meeting him. Till such times as I see you,
                    look after your soul.

17th June '78
This morning I wakened with the sun shining through the bars on the window. 'I'm going out of here,' I thought. Pretended to be numb to it. Getting up I went downstairs, collected my mail and looked at the official paper lying on the Governor's desk.

I went out to the yard. Ken came out and sat beside me. He immediately told me that he sees this being played very close and straight as it is vitally important for the November Parole Review. In many ways it's like starting all over again, building up trust in another area but within me there is a frustration as I look at Ken and part of me resents his 'prison officer' attitude.

My own feelings are a mixture of frustration as I would like to do some simple things like go into a shop and purchase something for each of the prisoners. At the same time I look on this as a new beginning so don't want to screw it up though I hardly see going into a shop as screwing it up. My one desire is to see into the distance, to see for miles without a wall blocking the way. It is 1.15pm and I feel the excitement building up inside me. This morning when lying in the sun I kept getting this vivid image of locking myself into a room in the Arts School and killing myself so that I would never have to return to prison. It's difficult to believe that I will finally walk out of here for good one day. I know that I will. This is just the beginning.

My first impression of sitting between the two doors and watching the one open to let us into the outside world was overwhelming. There is no feeling on earth like this. To suddenly see people, cars and most important of all, wide open spaces is unbelievable. As the car drove down the approach road I felt tears about to come pouring down. I was blitzed by the movement: people, traffic, space, noise, colour and all that one could never imagine unless one had been locked away for all these years. The feelings within me were tremendous. Men stood about while their wives shopped, women stood looking into shop windows, were being served in them, and children were running around. I was being bombarded by a million little things. We met the guy at the Arts School which he unlocked and showed us round. I was thrilled at seeing the Rennie Mackintosh building for the first time. I had known it since I was a child but really, was seeing it for the first time. We looked at the various exhibitions in the place; sculpture, paintings and so on. The building itself was the real work of art – quite outstanding! Later I went into a shop and bought some food. It was an Italian food store. The smell of food was fantastic. I bought pizzas for the guys, some cheese and olive oil for myself.

All too soon we had to return. . .

29th June '78

Dear Sarah,
I find myself sitting here thinking of you, not really having anything to say but simply wishing to communicate with you. Basically, I'm interested to see and hear how things go after those rapid-fire letters with highly inflammable content. It's strange how twists & turns lead to confrontation with areas that one thought oneself immune from.

26th September '78
Ken told me he met David and Vladimir Bukovsky last night for half an hour or so. They got on okay. They both came in at 9.30am and we had a chat in my cell. David left Bukovsky and I to talk and we discussed the dissident issue. It was enlightening and what struck me was that they have a much wider base of appeal than comes across in the media. He described the conditions of prisons there, of the social conditions outside Moscow. He made the interesting observation of how the authorities there tried to beat and torture prisoners into submission but found that this made them more violent. And this meant that the society became more violent. The authorities then had to use a more subtle approach. We later joined the rest of the Community and had a lively discussion.

5th November '78
This morning I wakened early and on going downstairs found

Ken and the other staff reading the *Sunday Mail*. An article by Ruth Wishart on the Cages was using excerpts from Malky's dissertation. I thought it was an excellent piece of journalism. While doing my run I thought of the impact it would have on the Department. They would be furious. I was also interested to see the Governor's reaction. After my exercises I made some brown bread and spoke to the Governor who had just entered. He mentioned going to Springburn last night to buy a *Sunday Mail* at 11pm. He was first in the queue. He was angry at the piece, calling Ruth a silly bitch. He said he had two roles to play: Community member and Governor. He said the former was spitting fucking mad – forgive the French. The second would have to await the official response: a Disciplinary Code for Malky. I played dumb on this and remarked that Malky would be furious about the dissertation being published and asked who did give it to Ruth Wishart? I then reminded the Governor that the Department had a copy of it, as did others. He came out defending the Department saying they would never do such a thing. . . It was interesting to watch the Governor's dilemma here. He kept reassuring me he was against the Cages but thought this article was damaging to the prison staff. He explained that although he had to go along with the democratic decision of his Association he had let his feelings be known that he was against them. He then went on to tell me that it was him who had updated the design of the Cages; a concrete mound for the prisoners to sit on and a small metal sheet on to the wall as a table. It made me want to vomit. . .

6th November '78
I'm just this minute back from outside – what a feeling! Wattie and Gordon came in early. I told them about the possible police presence and we agreed to play it low key. We left the prison – everything hit me, again. . . It was great seeing Gulliver; we stood beside and on him. A sleeping concrete giant; he is well used by the kids who play on him.

10th November '78
This morning I wakened and said a full decade of the rosary to my Ma. When the door opened I went to do my exercises. Afterwards I collected my mail, amongst which was a letter from Craigmillar with some photos of me on Gulliver.

In the morning papers there was news that Millan had okayed the media going in to see the Cages. I think this is a good thing though feel people won't see them as being bad after the portrayal in *The Hardman*. They will try to put them over in a humane way so I have written to Ben and Paddy Meehan asking if they will get in touch with STV and BBC to speak to them when they are shown. A Bruce Millan statement has come through as I write this. He has conceded the issue to the SPOA. The Cages are to be reopened. What a weak shit of a man, what a tragedy. I feel sick and I know that all the prison staff will be congratulating themselves and feeling all-powerful which means they will be exerting this on the prisoners. It really is sad.

11th November '78
Amongst my mail was a signed copy of *To Build A Castle* by V. Bukovsky. . . I sat with Wattie who told me that the material was in for my Parole Review. . .

I am heartsick at Millan giving the okay to the Cages opening. I thought about it deeply for a while. It isn't that I personally want to 'defeat' the authorities on this, it's having had the experience of that situation and knowing that it damages everyone involved. I feel bad when I think of our horrific experience there being pushed aside. . .

15th November '78
Listened to a report on the Cages issue and Ken being interviewed after his Labour Party meeting last night. He was very strong stating that the use of the Cages was unacceptable, they would cause more trouble for SPOA members and further damage prisoners. He was also widely reported in the press. . . I'm hoping he hasn't left himself open to breaking the Official Secrets Act. . .

I had a chat with Wattie and he was telling me that there was a call from the Department yesterday asking for Davy's (ex-Unit prisoner now candidate for the Cages) psychiatric report. It was put into the post by the Governor last night. I am hoping this is as a result of the detailed letter I sent Hugh Brown two weeks ago requesting he do this.

In the papers this morning the Cages feature prominently. Photographs of a Cage (in colour). The *Daily Record* and Gordon Airs (no less) were openly condemning them and the media view seemed to be unanimous on this . . . at least it's something.

The Governor came in this morning as we sat in the kitchen speaking about them and looking at the photographs. He leaned over and looked then remarked without mentioning the rights or wrongs of the Cages, that the table-shelf and bollard designed by him look nice. . .

Wattie was telling me that feelings about Ken in the main prison are running pretty high. The staff there are furious. He said there is talk that they may toss him out of the Union for disloyalty. . .

17th November '78
I sat in my cell typing when a knock came at the door. A voice said the Governor wanted to see me in his office – it was 8.45am, unusually early for him. On going down I found Wattie and Peter (staff member) sitting with him. It all looked very strange indeed. The Governor was pure white. He opened a file and brought out a letter saying that he was hauled up to the Department yesterday and given this, and asked to account for it. The letter was the one I had sent to Ben, containing the Instructions for the Operation of the Inverness Cages and asking him to go to the BBC and STV studios with them. I also urged Ben to give his views on what like it feels to be kept in a Cage. It was returned with the words 'gone away' scribbled on it. The GPO sent it to the Department. I was now plainly in shit street. Nevertheless I pointed out to him that I would have to take the consequences but in my view I felt so strongly about the Cages that I had to do this. The Governor then said he wanted two senior staff to search my cell. I told him that first I'd like to call a Community meeting and tell the others.

I explained to everyone and there was silence amongst them. I tried to cool the situation by saying I had done wrong but I knew what the Cages are like and desperately want to stop them opening. I also respect the Community but it was a decision I made.

While in the Governor's room he asked me if a member of staff had given me a photostat of the Instructions and I told him no. While my cell was being searched he called staff into his office one at a time and asked if they had given me a copy.

Later:
One of the prisoners told me that when my cell was searched he immediately thought I was going to be shanghaied (transferred) so he took a knife up to his cell just in case. It is obvious that they are all feeling insecure and so I tried to tell them, tried like

hell to put it into their heads that they must keep this place going at all costs and make sure it isn't looked on as a one-man show. It was hard to convince them. They felt if I went it would only be a matter of time till it closed. I felt at an utter loss on seeing this attitude. Rather than support what we were doing they were resigning themselves to its inevitable collapse which is something I don't like.

Sarah came in the door this evening and I left her to go to another meeting. . . Afterwards I returned to spend the rest of the visit time with her. I was glad she was here as it allowed me to talk the matter over with someone outside of it.

22nd November '78
Community meeting: the Governor produced his file of all the material relating to the Inverness Cages document I sent to Ben. He said he found a copy of letters I had from *The Sunday Times* and Ruth Wishart. He was sitting like a shaky judge on a three-legged chair. He asked what everyone thought of the situation and demanded that they speak up. They did by telling him they had taken action yesterday (a meeting at which he was not present) by imposing restrictions on my mail. He said he totally agreed with this. Wattie censored my mail this morning and did so with the embarrassment of someone who knows me, and the efficiency of a prison officer. The more I get into it the more this whole process of imprisonment cripples me with humiliation and degradation. Instead of getting used to it I get more and more hurt by it.

25th November '78
Malky came in today and we had a chat. He is looking very well. . . I agree with Malky when he says that I'll get nothing out of the Department in terms of parole. And from what I gather Ewing is saying it looks like the politicians are accepting what the Department people are saying. . . I sat with my kids eating sweets and drinking coca cola. During this James came out jibing at Patricia saying two of her pals were debating a film of a prison with one of them saying it's Barlinnie and the other saying it's some other prison. Patricia suddenly burst into tears. James was scornful of this saying she's stupid. . . I felt this slice deeply into me. . .

4th December '78
The Governor called a Special Meeting. He opened it by saying that we haven't seen much of him for the last two weeks as he's been having continuous talks with the Department. He intimated that a Department person has been trying to impose the Secretary of State's Rules on him, telling him to get down here and implement them. As a result of this a personal clash has developed between them. He was accused of not 'Governing' the Unit and not obeying an order. He said he sought support from his Association and got it. They said the SOS rules were shelved because of the non-negotiable tag. He went on to talk about the fears going round about another Unit Governor being broken but in this instance it wasn't the case, and more to the point had nothing at all to do with the Unit.

13th December '78
Peter came in saying there was an announcement on the radio that the *Daily Express* in Scotland had a piece about me. . . It was an extremely vicious piece. The front page was covered by an article stating that the Parole Board shouldn't let me out. Inside it used pieces of my sculpture to say how terrible I am – clenched fists, etc. The article regurgitates my past and has people like Teddy Taylor and Joe Black, and an un-named prison officer having a go at me. It said things like, the public are dead against me getting out. . . It was ferocious. It was a piece set on destroying the impartiality of the Parole Board. There is no hiding the fact that this article hurt me deeply but I tried to get beyond this to understand why? I know why, and it's to do with people like me trying to gain status as human beings. It's because I've come to symbolise change, and in fact it shows the hysteria of some people in certain positions who are afraid of the implications of my changing and the apparent success of the Unit.

15th December '78
The *Express* had a follow-up article quoting from Joe Black saying that he agreed with the *Express* article and that if my behaviour is exemplary after fifteen years I should be let out. The editorial said I should be kept in to the last second of the last day of my fifteen years. . .

21st December '78
The headlines in the paper blazed that Davy is to be sent to Inverness. I felt sick and terribly sad. There are clear inconsistencies. On the one hand we are being told a Committee will be set up to decide who goes into the Cages, and today it states Millan has decided. Davy will go to the Cages for a short, sharp lesson and then be put to a long-term prison to complete his sentence. What appalls me about all this is the amount of ignorance from Millan down. They have no idea what they are doing and it's all to do with short-term revenge.

26th January '79
This morning after my exercises I read in the morning paper that a staff member in Inverness, a Mr Darling, was sentenced to Life Imprisonment. He had eleven years' service and went to Inverness as a volunteer for duty in the Cages.

The Court of Inquiry into the dead patient in Barlinnie prison hospital has been postponed for a month, what is going on?

I was given a copy of a reply from Harry Ewing on the Cages issue:

> The Secretary of State has decided that the Inverness unit should remain an integral part of the Scottish prison system but that no prisoner will be transferred there without his personal approval. There are no 'cages' in the Unit, which comprises a number of extra large cells each divided internally by a grille which provides a measure of protection to the Unit staff. However on the instruction of the Secretary of State trials will be made to find an alternative method of providing for staff safety.

17th February '79
I sussed Wattie wasn't looking too well and asked him what was wrong. He then pushed aside the papers he was working on to tell me that last Thursday when the Governor had left, a 'Staff in Confidence' envelope came in. Wattie opened it. He said he began to tick off some of the papers and came to the last one which was his own annual report. It was pretty devastating and said he did anything to avoid crisis because he is into his last year. Wattie said he couldn't believe it as it was the Governor's report to the Department about him. Wattie said on the back of the report was

an official question stating, 'If the report is critical of the officer, have you informed him? If not why not?' This was left blank and the Governor hadn't mentioned it to Wattie. He said that later that afternoon he and the Governor worked on the Duty Roster but he couldn't bring himself to mention it. He said he just felt terrible and couldn't mention it to anyone. He said he did so to his wife and she immediately reacted by telling him to go to the Governor as the truth is that the Governors have constantly run from crisis.

20th February '79

This morning after my exercises I sat with Wattie. He seemed nervous about confronting the Governor but determined to do so.

Wattie confronted him with the report and he was at a loss. He mentioned to Wattie that he sent up a supplementary report (something unknown until now) giving an explanation as to what he meant in the report Wattie had seen. Wattie asked him what crisis he had ever dodged in here. The Governor seemingly bumbled and mumbled and stumbled his way through saying he didn't actually mean that. What he meant was that someone of Wattie's rank and service should not be in a crisis situation. Wattie reminded him this isn't what he said. The Governor replied that he would ask the Department for a copy of the supplementary report to show him. Wattie said he wants to see it but this isn't the end of it.

27th February '79

I had a telegram saying that Jeremy Isaacs and Peter MacDougall want to visit me on Friday to discuss the film of *A Sense of Freedom*...

28th February '79

Darling Sarah,

It was lovely to spend that evening with you in celebration of your birth. It is a night I shall cherish for it captured all that is beautiful in life, and the fact that two people coming together can create such feelings in a setting such as this says much for the human spirit.

However, life is an ever-changing role in a series of dramas – and I feel my life has had more than its share. It would be too easy for life to be monotonous and dull. Mine is full of 'aliveness'. In saying this I don't mean that it's full of what is good in life. It means I am open to the pains of existence, and my position is unique in that I seem to be the source of so many people's fantasies. I sit here wondering if you have any idea what I am up against, of what you've put yourself in for in connecting yourself with me. . .

2nd March '79
I made lunch for Jeremy Isaacs and Peter MacDougall. Peter is now working on the script of *SOF*. He is now filming in his home town of Greenock. We had a long talk about the Unit, with Jeremy asking pointed questions. He is a Glasgow man. We discussed the book and Jeremy said he has talked with the people at STV. . . He said he had a handshake on the deal and is now going to sign up the contract. He will bring up John McKenzie, who will direct the film. He also wants to bring a quality cameraman. We discussed the appalling state of Scottish television with Peter saying neither of the companies here will touch his work.

Peter and I arranged to meet on Monday to sit down and talk about the material. We all discussed the sort of pressures that would be put on us getting it off the ground. Jeremy said there will be plenty but has told the STV people that he must be given a free hand to get this thing going. He said he wants to do it his way and will handle any pressure or controversy.

4th March '79
Wakened from the misery of last night into the misery of this morning – shit! It's this gut-sapping part of the situation that gets to me . . . feel like screaming but decide against it. I turn some lively music on and let my body shake the tiredness out of it while I put on my track suit. This works wonders for as I hit the yard I get into the rhythm of running . . . bastards, bastards, bastards . . . just let it all pour out and begin to feel distinctly better. . .

Quite spontaneously I made breakfast as a sort of celebration. Afterwards I walked into Larry's old cell where a pigeon now stays. I was intending to put it out. Behind the door lies Collie (new prisoner) – sudden flashback to Larry lying there. He's depressed to fuck. I sit talking to him about the pigeon and we laugh. All the while I want to tell him, 'Make it on your own kid – don't reach out'. At the end of the day it is down to him. I won't help to create illusions for him. Instead I'll help in practical ways. Perhaps I'll move a mountain for him.

1st April '79
Teddy Taylor (shadow Secretary of State for Scotland) was interviewed by Ruth Wishart in the *Sunday Mail*. He admits that conditions in Peterhead are terrible but goes on to say that he wouldn't change them as people there are convicted criminals. He said he wouldn't close the Special Unit down but would see that there was no publicity about it. He would concentrate on deterrence. . .

9th April '79
Malky, Gerry, Ken and I had a good dialogue going this morning. This afternoon the Governor phoned the Department to tell us that John Maxton, the prospective Labour candidate (opposing Taylor in Cathcart) was coming in later. The Department man said it was okay but would contact the political office to clear it with them. He did and was told that Maxton should contact Bruce Millan or Harry Ewing. He did, getting hold of Bruce Millan who told him the Unit is a very sensitive area and that he should leave it alone but if Taylor mentioned the Unit once then he has complete authority to walk straight in here. We saw this as a cop-out by Millan. By coincidence Ken met an Assistant Governor from Barlinnie who told Ken he was also going to canvass for Maxton in the Cathcart district. He mentioned to Ken that the prospective Tory candidate was being shown round the main prison at this moment. Ken was pretty angry at this and is going to try to get hold of Millan at the Prime Minister's talk in Glasgow tonight.

3rd May '79
This morning I lay awake listening to the results of the General Election. I was delighted to see Teddy Taylor being thrown out but bitterly disappointed to see Margaret Thatcher getting in. It all makes for terrible times ahead for the poor and needy. I stayed up all night and listened, feeling moments of elation to terrible disappointment. . .

Ken came in this morning and he looked tired. We agreed that Teddy Taylor was merely a consolation prize as the general picture is bad. . . A member of staff pulled me into the surgery to ask if I'd heard anything about my parole, had the Governor spoken to me about it? I told him no. He then went on to tell me that Jack Crossley of the Sunday *Observer* had called him to say that he had it from a number of good sources that my Parole Application had

been refused. It stated I would be considered again next year. He
is doing an article on it this Sunday. . . My personal reaction to
this is one of numbness as the way in which I've been told doesn't
make it seem real. I don't know if this is delayed action . . . we'll
see. One thing I do say, it is abominable that I should be told
third or fourth hand.

4th May '79
George Younger has been appointed Secretary of State for Scotland. According to many people he seems to be an okay guy. Let's
hope so.

11th May '79
There was a piece in the *Daily Record* on conditions in Peterhead.
Prisoners there sneaked out a letter stating that conditions in the
prison are worse than the Cages and Renton of the SPOA agreed.
It pointed out that prisoners are kept on solitary for a year at a
time and have to eat their food off the floor.

At 11am Mr Allan came in with the Governor. He is a small
man with black greying hair and a moustache. He has strong
looking hands. On taking him round he listened intently. We all
assembled in the TV room. He was asked by the Governor to give
his views. He said he is just new to the job and to the penal
system. He went on to say how he wanted to know more about
the place. He emphasised to us that the previous Secretary of
State had made it clear that when breaking new ground in the
Unit he should take personal responsibility for it. He said the
judgement as to what should be passed on to the Minister lies in
the hands of the Department. He said that being civil servants
they have political masters to follow and went on to say they have
no idea how the new Administration is going to look on the
Unit, that they are waiting to see. He was using some hardline
phraseology when saying 'Your very congenial surroundings' and
'It's an airy fairy world' . . on confronting him with this he said
he is being devil's advocate or just a bureaucratic mind at work.
He agreed to give us reasons for refusing anything we ask for and
went on to say the communications between us and the Department would improve. He would be down on a regular basis. He
made it clear his hands are tied as far as decision-making is
concerned.

5th June '79
I spoke to Dr John Basson and he was telling me he is on the new Advisory Board for 'difficult prisoners'. This group will recommend what prisoners should go to the Cages in Inverness. He was asked to go on it along with Mr Allan. Peter Whatmore was asked and refused. I didn't get a chance to pursue this as other visitors came in to see me.

7th June '79
The morning papers had articles on the STV press conference stating that they are filming *A Sense of Freedom*. The *Record* continues its attempt to seem fair and grudgingly has to concede certain points about me, but very grudgingly and makes its usual negative noises. It's this whole issue of how these papers feed off crime and yet are quick to moralise. In many respects I no longer see all of this as about me, it's about people in general and the future. I am merely the vehicle in which this lesson is travelling. . .

8th June '79
This morning I was up early and said some prayers for my Ma before the door was unlocked. I had a restless night and dreamt about rats in the Unit biting me on the chest. It was a troubled night and my brother's marriage splitting didn't help.

After my exercises I collected my mail and read the papers. A piece in the *Daily Express* quotes Joe Black, the Police Federation man, appealing to the public to boycott my play. . . Basically, all of this reinforces that it isn't simply about me. It's the struggle between civilisation and barbarism. Guys like him in these influential positions are certainly not trying to understand the social ills that surround us. They want to state that anyone having problems is either inadequate or criminal. . .

> Petition: James Boyle: 5/73
> Life
>
> Please inform the prisoner in reply to his petition of 7 May that the copy letter from the then Governor of Inverness Prison dated 9 February to the Governor of the Special Unit at that time which was sent to him and various members of the staff at the Special Unit, was submitted to the Serious Crime Squad

of Strathclyde in an attempt to establish how this letter came to be sent to them.

Exhaustive enquiries were carried out by the police in Glasgow, Edinburgh and Inverness in an effort to establish the identity of the person(s) who sent the letter. They were unable however on the evidence available to them to establish who sent the letters and their investigations proved inconclusive. The Department is most concerned that a letter from one Governor to another Governor should have found its way into the hands of an unauthorised person, who was able to send copies to James Boyle and to members of the Unit staff; this is clearly in breach of the rules and regulations governing official correspondence and every effort will be made to ensure that there is not a repetition of this breach.

With regard to the rumours which he has heard about the alleged attitude of some members of the Department towards his work, these are completely without foundation and like all rumours should be ignored. His undoubted talent as a sculptor is recognised by the Department and any publicity which has been attributed to him in this respect will in no way harm the concept of the Special Unit.

16th June '79
... This afternoon I had a visit from Peter MacDougall who has just completed the first draft of the script. He described it to me in detail saying he will send a copy when it is typed. We then went on to discuss what direction it will take... We talked about many things related to it and Peter opened to talk about himself. It was a really good talk and I thoroughly enjoyed it. We find ourselves very much on the same level.

17th June '79
The morning was beautiful and so we sat in the sun.

As we sat there the Governor came in the door with Ken. They both looked glum and the Governor veered off into the Unit as Ken approached us. He told us that he was being transferred to Lowmoss Prison. He said that he met the Governor in the car park by chance and he invited Ken to his office in the main prison. Ken said that the Governor then told him about the transfer. He stated to Ken that it is his (the Governor's) doing as they just don't get on. He said he has had this in mind for some months now. He accused Ken of not being loyal to him, saying that he isn't committed to the Unit and that he is here only for his own personal gain. Ken accused the Governor of wanting a staff of arselickers. The Governor told Ken he wants him out as soon as possible.

We are all shocked at this but immediately set about looking for ways to overcome it. . .

This afternoon was shadowed by the news of Ken.

18th June '79
This morning I was up early and out doing my exercises. Ken came in after 8am and we had a talk. He was in to sort out material as he was defending three staff colleagues in the main prison who were on Disciplinary charges. He is very controlled and thinks the whole thing is a set-up. Most of us suspect the same. Wattie came in quite shaky but settled. He informed us that he has known since Tuesday but couldn't tell anyone.

SPECIAL MEETING:
MONDAY 18.6.79
Staff Member: Said that there was news yesterday of Ken being transferred from the Unit. He said that he wants to express his fears about someone being posted out of here, and asks what the reasons behind the posting are. He says that he sees Ken as a figurehead in the Unit and finds it strange that while we still have not resolved our problems with the (new) Working Party, and our future, Ken is being moved out. He said that the other thing that bothers him is where he is left if Ken can be treated like this. He asked if it means that if he confronts or questions the Governor he might be moved. He said that if that is the case then there are serious implications for everyone in the Unit.
Staff Member: Said that he feels exactly the same way.
New Prisoner: Said that he would like to ask where this leaves him. He said that Walter is due to go soon (retire), Jimmy Boyle may go soon too and Ken is to be transferred. He said that we will be having new staff and new prisoners and there will be no experienced people.
New Prisoner: Said that he was going to ask the same question.
Staff Member: Said that the reasons for the transfer are not what worry him. He said that staff in the Unit are all volunteers and should therefore be allowed to continue working here as long as they want to. . .

Staff Member: Said that he has made the point before now that there is no way that he will go back to working in the traditional system so he is out of a job if he is posted like Ken. He said that people like Ken have given a lot to the place and it is wrong to cast them aside.
Staff Member: Asked if it's a case that staff are subject to being posted. . .
Wattie: Said that although there is nothing in the original Working Party Report to cover this it has been the unwritten rule that whilst staff still operate under general staff rules they were allowed to stay in the Unit unless they asked to leave. He said that if it's the case that Ken's activities upset people they should be saying so, both to Ken and the Community so that it can be discussed.
Staff Member: Said that although he is leaving the Unit he believes in it. He said that since Larry died we had had a set of rules, a Working Party on the Unit whose sole function is to ensure the implementation of these rules, a visit from two of the seven Working Party members (a farce) and now the transfer of Ken. He said that he sees a disturbing pattern in all this and he is afraid for the future of the Unit. He said that if he had not already asked to leave the Unit he would have if the rules had been implemented. He said this place will never work if these rules are implemented. . .
Prisoner: Said that he can see the whole concept of the Unit being destroyed if this goes through.
Governor: Said he will not talk about the transfer itself as Ken has the right to appeal and will no doubt exercise that right. He said that the reasons for the transfer are his and his alone. He said that he had made the decision, not the Department, although they had granted his request to transfer Ken. He said that he gets a lot of satisfaction from the fact that the fears expressed today are the same fears he has to take into consideration when he makes such a decision. He said that having gone through them all he still decided that Ken should be transferred. He said that P.C. (prisoner) used the word manipulation and that quite often managerial decisions are seen as manipulative. He said that as far as he was concerned this decision is not a manipulative one. He said that in the Unit's situation such manipulation would be destructive. He said that as far as a personality clash is concerned that any decision based on that would be a bad one. He said that if anything, he and Ken could be considered of similar personality in that they

are both single minded. He said that the fear that Ken's transfer is part of a bigger game involving the implementation of the rules is groundless. He said the rules played no part in the decision he took. He said that his commitment is to the Unit document of standards, not the rules. He said that he had already expressed his fears about the possible implementation of the rules. He said that as far as staff fears about being posted if they fall out with the Governor are concerned, he has the same problem with his bosses. He said that this would not be a reason for him to recommend staff transfers. He said that everyone is aware that the Governor's role in the Unit is a split one with responsibility to both the Community and the Department.

Staff Member: Said that (the Governor) has not really answered the questions he opened the meeting with and is obviously not going to discuss the transfer although one of the fundamental principles of the Unit is that the Community discussed what affects people in it. He said that he thinks there has been some type of managerial decision which could be taken on any member of staff in the Unit, or indeed on any prisoner.

29th June '79
Ken met with the man from the Department. He told Ken it was in his own interests to go back to the mainstream nursing and this is the reason for his transfer. He went on to point out that Ken's annual reports were of the highest calibre and were held in the highest respect. Ken said he really opened up on him saying that Malcolm Rifkind (new Tory Minister) is alleged to have said that Ken is being transferred because he is a 'discipline problem. . .'

There seems to be a spate of problems in other prisons throughout Scotland. Davy (out of the Cages) is charged with two stabbings in Peterhead. Another prisoner there is charged with two stabbings and breaking a prison officer's nose, and two staff in Polmont Borstal have been suspended and one charged with theft.

7th July '79
In *The Scotsman* there was an article and photograph showing some Lords being installed into the Knights of the Thistle Order. It showed Lord Cameron, Lord Douglas-Home and some others who are part of the Scottish Establishment. Although Cameron sentenced me this had little to do with it. My anger is about what

they represent. On another page was an article on Len Murray, General Secretary of the TUC receiving an Honorary Degree at St Andrew's University. I felt the same about this. All these forms of patronage make me sick as I think of all the wonderful ordinary people I know living in Glasgow, people housed in ghettoes who are doing more than any of these people. There was a photograph of the Queen and some lovely children walking in this procession and I thought of all the kids in places like Easterhouse, the Gorbals and other areas who would look just as lovely but never get the opportunities these privileged kids get. Our kids grow up to fill our penal institutions. . .

12th July '79
This morning I had trouble getting to sleep . . . the strain on me was considerable. I kept waiting for someone to come and tell me that my day out was off. . . John and I went on to a bus which took us to Duke Street. We walked to the nearest stone merchant in Gallowgate. Sarah was waiting there and it was fantastic to see her. Being with Sarah was beautiful. . . We walked hand in hand along Sauchiehall Street and it was fantastic. . .

14th July '79
This morning I got up quite early with Ken on my mind. Going downstairs I sat with him and the other staff. We talked about various things concerning the Unit. The newspapers came in and on the front page of the *Scotsman* was a headline about Ken: 'Barlinnie special Unit leader fights transfer'. I hope to hell it does some good.

The Governor came in and Ken sat in his office with him. The Governor wanted to see me. He read out a letter approving my 'C' category and approving my sculpture exhibition at Stirling. He also stated that I could go to the exhibition but not to the official opening. Now, I find this interesting as I didn't ask to be allowed out. It strikes me that what is happening here is that the authorities are giving me this sort of thing but at the same time putting the knife into Ken. They don't want to be seen sabotaging the Unit. . . On speaking to Ken he showed me a letter from the Department which stated he has to get his appeal in if he is going to but meanwhile the Governor is to continue making arrangements for his transfer and it's to be no later than 23rd July. They are going all out to railroad Ken. . .

Ken is really shattered as this virtually means that come what may he has only a week left in the Unit . . . it is brutal.

18th July '79
Tonight the prisoners had all their visitors in for a social evening. I had my aunt Peggy, her son Freddy and Sarah in. The Governor gave a speech assuring the visitors of the continuance of the Unit and how glad he is they are here. On finishing, Sarah said she was sorry that he didn't take the opportunity to mention Ken's situation. Betty and Mrs. L. (two prisoners' mothers) came in and they had a good session with the Governor on this.

A member of the nightshift came to my door tonight. He said the Department are on the phone and want to know if I was in a pub tonight.

19th July '79
Ken said he was exhausted as he has been phoned all day and night by the press. He also had to write out his appeal.

In the papers this morning was a statement that I had written to a newspaper about Ken. It was front page news in the *Glasgow Herald* . . . there was a piece in the *Record* both of which were good. . .

The Governor came in and said that his phone has been going all last night with newspaper enquiries. . . He informed me that he had the press on to him about a letter that I had written and there was talk from the Department about disciplining me. He went on to say that he would not take any formal action as emotions were running high at the moment.

Sarah came in tonight and was very shaken. Two *Record* reporters had been to the hospital to see her and had later come to her house. She spoke to them giving her views of the Unit, told them she wouldn't discuss her personal life or relationship with me.

21st July '79
This morning I wakened feeling slightly relieved. Lying on the floor I looked up at the ceiling for a spell and felt the weight coming on to me. What would today bring.

Sarah's father – John Trevelyan – was in the papers telling them what a charming chap I was! He seems to have handled them with some skill. Wattie came in this morning and we sat chatting. He was of the opinion that Ken's transfer would not have been reversed unless Jesus Christ himself intervened. . . I told Wattie that Ken had a moving letter from Larry's mother expressing sorrow about his transfer and reminding him of the contribution he made to Larry's short and tragic life in the Unit.

Ken came in looking taut and worn. He had a briefcase with him to empty his desk. I was at a loss what to do and sat with him as he did this. Both of us were on the verge of tears and felt literally crushed. Agonised thoughts raced through my head – what are they doing to this wonderful man? We talked in a rambling fashion, both of us finding it extremely difficult to say anything to each other. We held an informal Community meeting and most of us were near to tears. Wattie opened the meeting by saying how despicably he thought Ken had been treated and that he personally wanted Ken to know that it had been great for him (Wattie) to have worked with him over the years. Ken talked but the tears were at surface level and his throat choked. He said we must continue to fight and that we mustn't let them frighten us off because of what was happening to him. I eventually spoke telling Ken that our testament to him will be solidarity of the Community, the continuance of the Unit and the satisfaction that the prison authorities will never regain credibility amongst any of us in the Unit. The meeting became too much for Ken and he abruptly left.

His exit left an emptiness, a hollowness and tremendous feeling of loss. This man has been tremendous in his caring for individuals. The establishment have condoned his downfall in their deceitful and calculated way and yet have left no tangible evidence of having done so. Anyone like Ken who tries to do something effective within the system is soon squeezed out and rendered impotent.

And now as I sit here I can let the loss of Ken enter into me. I want to feel his going to the full. I want to soak up every last bit of it so that I never forget what the small-minded, petty men of this world are capable of. It is a pyrrhic victory for them. I am trying to imagine how someone like Ken will survive in this outpost they have sent him to.

23rd July '79
Wattie was telling me that the Chief Officer in Barlinnie Prison called him over to his office this morning to tell him that his

Governor had instructed that under no circumstances is Ken Murray to step over the gate at Barlinnie Prison. Also, that they are not providing transport to Ken's new post where he was to start this morning...

24th July '79
This morning I wakened feeling pretty beat but got up and went down for my exercises... I met one of the staff who told me that I am on the front page of the morning paper – saying that I am to be transferred to Dungavel Prison. The adrenalin started pumping. There is a feeling of strength and sureness almost as though I'd been expecting them to make some sort of move towards me.

On seeing the article I was quite untouched by it, PRISON MOVE FOR BOYLE and the leader inside was headed GOOD MOVE FOR ALL. The general feeling in the Unit was that a deal had been done and I was being moved. The article stated that their sources had made it clear that the transfer was on and only needed clearance from the Scottish Secretary. It stated 'sooner rather than later'. Immediately I took steps to prepare myself mentally for such an eventuality, giving thought to the sort of pressure I would come under in the main system. I felt calm knowing that I could cope with whatever came my way.

This evening Malcolm Rifkind, Scottish Under Secretary responsible for prisons was interviewed on television by David Scott about the Unit and the continuing allegations. Rifkind was nervous and didn't handle the interview very well.

This evening Sarah came in and was apprehensive about the impending transfer. She was expecting me to be moved at any time. I replayed the interview and the part where it was stated that I wouldn't be moved. It eased her some.

26th July '79
I was shown a copy of last night's *Evening Times* where Harry Ewing is reported as saying the Unit should be moved to Greenock prison, away from Barlinnie. He claimed this would benefit the work of the Unit, curb the threat of a 'personality cult' amongst prisoners, and reduce strains and jealousies affecting prisoners and prison staff in the main prison of Barlinnie. He goes on to state 'It is far too small and one person in an establishment – who I do not propose to name – can impose his or her personality on

that small establishment.' He goes on to say 'If the establishment is bigger that person must learn to live with the establishment.'

3rd August '79

Dear Jimmy,
  I am suffering from severe 'Unit withdrawal symptoms'. Your note was helpful in my battle to face this unreal situation. I am being treated very badly but I am fighting. It is rather ironic to discover that I have to justify the upgrading of the nursing post here. It is clear that no one considered the implications of the move. All the Governors have disappeared and I am left trying to negotiate with an A/G who doesn't know the time of day. . . I am sure that I will eventually win but it is tough going. . .

30th August '79

Darling Sarah,
  The Governor in a confidential exchange with Malky told him that I will be going to Edinburgh prison but prior to going the Governor of that prison will come through to see me. It seems that my present Parole Application will be rejected, possibly next month or October and will begin again the next month – November. It seems the provisional release date will be '82. . .

31st August '79
I was in the yard when the Secretary of State, George Younger, came in followed by his minions. Wattie introduced us and we stood speaking about my sculpture and his love of music. . .

23rd September '79
This morning I went downstairs to be met by the Governor coming in. I told him that I intended raising a personal issue with Mr Allan when he came next but thought the Governor should know about it. I explained that Sarah and I wanted to get married and would like to do so with the co-operation of the Prisons Department. He was most calm and said he was very glad we have come to this decision, it didn't surprise him and he is delighted to assist in any way. I told him Sarah's family and my own were behind us. We then discussed ways in which it could be done as I told him I'd prefer it without any publicity, if possible.

18th October '79
I had Jeremy and Peter in for lunch to discuss the script. The meeting lasted three hours, was wide-ranging and very probing. We discussed specific areas and the fact that STV is doing it and the fears they have – turning me into a star. Jeremy asked questions related to the mythology surrounding me. . .

24th October '79

Darling Sarah,

Well, Mr Allan was here today as expected. It was very much as my own sources had told me. He said that last year's Parole Application has been rejected and the new one will start almost immediately – 3rd Nov. During this period I will remain here. He stated that my paroles out will be opened up considerably next year and then mentioned the recommended minimum saying they have given a date to a guy before the recommended minimum.

I asked him about our getting married and he gave me the same thing he gave you but went on to say that he is sitting in a meeting tomorrow on this question as two more guys in Edinburgh want to get married. He suggested that I leave it for now and let the case be discussed over these two guys and he'll keep the Governor informed. I asked him what time scale he is thinking of and he said weeks. I told him we'd like to get married without any publicity and as quietly as possible and he was in agreement.

22nd November '79
Amazingly Mr Allan phoned the Governor today to ask him to tell me to put up a formal request to get married. . . My Parole Dossier came down and has to be returned to the Department by 4th Feb.

29th November '79

Sarah, the sheer poetry of this morning spent with you is something that all people should experience. I cherish my sensitivity as it makes me 'feel' this to the core. I love the way your presence makes me happy and full of love. I get tremendous satisfaction from the way we discuss things and although I totally dislike my present circumstances I have the ability to see that it is providing an opportunity for us to connect in this way, despite the obvious difficulties. . .

19th December '79
The Governor came out into the yard where I was sculpting and told me I can now go ahead and make arrangements to marry Sarah as word has now come through, giving permission. He also told me that I will be allowed out once a week to purchase groceries between the hours of 10am – 3pm. The Department suggested my going out on different days. I was really bowled over by all this. I immediately phoned Sarah and she was delighted. I cancelled another visitor for tonight to make way for her coming in. It really is good, good news. I am feeling tremendously strong at the moment. . .

4th January '80
Sarah came in this evening shortly before Giles (Director of Citizens' Theatre). She had been to Balfron (village) to lodge the marriage papers and it felt good. Giles came in and we had a good meal and discussion on the Unit, our marriage and other things. It was a lovely evening.

5th January '80
Lay in bed feeling a virus bad in me but eventually got up. I felt shaky and stuffy.

Wattie was in and we wished each other happy new year. He seemed snappy today and we talked about his retirement being just round the corner. He seemed to be feeling this. I asked him if he was conscious of it and he replied that one day he just won't come into work and that will be it. He seemed pretty pessimistic about the future of the Unit and said that it would be good if I was moved before he went or shortly afterwards. He said the place isn't the same.

11th January '80
Davy and I left the prison just before 10am. The weather was dank and muggy but in no way detracted from the sheer joy of being out. It was wonderful going into the flat. Sarah and I kissed and hugged excitedly. We went shopping and I bought various articles of food and clothing. It was fantastic, utterly fantastic walking down the streets. On the one hand I felt normal, it all seemed so natural but on the other I was walking on air. I bought some clothing for the wedding day. . .

THOUGHTS ON BOXING DAY
PEOPLE TURNED INSIDE-OUT REVEAL ALL THE CRACKS AND FLAWS THAT THEY NORMALLY HIDE. THEY'RE ALL THE SAME; RICH OR POOR, GOOD OR BAD. IT'S FUNNY HOW THEY ALL TRY TO PRETEND DIFFERENT... WE'RE ALL JUST TRYING TO KEEP IT TOGETHER AS BEST WE CAN. IT'S REALLY JUST THE STRUGGLE OF LIFE
SO HOW ARE WE GONNA GET OFF THIS PLANET?
?
I AM...
FEELING LOST AND STRANDED...
FUNNY-LOOKING THOSE GUYS! MUST BE A LONG WAY FROM HOME!
AMONGST THE ALIENS...

14th January '80
I was hit with my photograph in a front page splash: 'A taste of freedom soon for murderer Boyle'. It went on to describe informed sources as disclosing that I would be going out shopping with an escorting officer. Inevitably, it regurgitated the past. It was so unnecessary but beyond this I wondered where it came from, who released it? I could only think of someone in the main prison or the Department. I started thinking of the wedding day and how it could mean the press getting on to this. The Governor came in and I showed it to him. He was shocked and got on to Allan, at the Department. His immediate response was that it was the police, saying that the wording of the article was similar to a previous letter.

19th January '80
This afternoon Sarah came in and we spent a really good afternoon together. We discussed the arrangements for tomorrow and our visit to Father Anthony Ross. Afterwards we'll go to Margaret's for lunch (my sister-in-law). We went into the possibility of the press appearing at Balfron the day we're to be married and agreed to be diplomatic. Both of us hope they aren't as it's our day and we would hate them to be there. . . Sarah is being quite realistic about the day saying that in real terms getting married won't dramatically change our lives due to the physical situation of my being here. However, we will try to make it special whilst at the same time realising it won't be perfect.

20th January '80
This morning while running round the yard I thought of the day ahead and felt the freedom seep into me. Thoughts flickered through my head like a movie screen, it felt wonderful knowing that in a few hours I would be outside all of this. . . I thought of when I was in Borstal and one would get out like this though through my adult experience it is different; it is all for real now whereas in those days there was no belief that it was.

The day was pleasant weatherwise. We stopped at a shop down the road and I bought the Sunday papers, an insignificant action that brought me much pleasure. This was the first Sunday I've been out in thirteen years. As I went for the papers the church bells rang and it was beautiful. . .

We then drove to Sarah's flat. . . I felt excited running up the stairs. Taking the flat keys from my pocket I opened the door. Sarah walked round, not hearing me and the look of surprise on her face was funny. We warmly embraced and it was great. I scurried all over the flat like a dog looking for a bone . . . the happiness in both of us could be seen on our faces. We sat having a coffee. Sarah and I called her Dad and he wished us well. We went to Margaret's and had a meal . . . Sarah, Davy and I went to the Gorbals and into St Francis chapel. It had changed though the basic structure was the same. All the old nostalgic thoughts raced through my head; it was here that we came for candles when our electricity was cut off; and where we came for confession and had our sins cleansed away. The sheer power of the catholic church suddenly weighed on me. It was here that we kissed and embraced, almost a consummation of our marriage. I thought of my Ma, and somehow she was more real in this old building full of memories. I thought of how she would have loved to have known Sarah, of how proud she would have been of all this. . . We met Father Anthony Ross in his flat. We talked about various things and then the ceremony. . . He looked tired but there is always a spiritual liveliness about him.

From here we drove to Wilton Street and dropped Sarah off. This is the sad part of the day, the opposite of the beginning. I have to get into the frame of mind that this is only a start and that we are moving in a positive direction. Nevertheless, it is hard, very difficult. This stress is important and should not be cast aside. . .

I could see Sarah was feeling it and leaving her was the hardest part. It is so natural our being in the flat together, a place that holds a lot of comfort and security for us; there is a feeling of 'home'. I feel so happy with her and know it's where I should be – that day will come, it will come soon.

26th January '80
I felt sort of tense this morning but couldn't put my finger on the reason why. . . Sarah came in saying that a journalist, Phil Davies, from the *Sunday Mirror*, called her at midnight last night saying he knew everything about our plans to marry. He said he would do a sympathetic article. Sarah replied she had nothing to say. The journalist then told her he knew about the ceremony taking place on Friday and that Anthony Ross would be doing one privately in the flat afterwards. Obviously this guy knows every-

thing. Sarah asked who his source was but he wouldn't say. . .
Sarah refused to give him anything and put the phone down.
Later a freelance journalist called saying he was a friend of the
previous chap and perhaps he could persuade her. She refused.
Shortly afterwards they appeared at the door. . . This morning
when she got up and went out they took a picture of her, obviously
they'd been sitting there all night. Phil Davies said he isn't black-
mailing her but if she doesn't speak to them they'll give her
address and telephone number to all the newspapers. Sarah told
him this is blackmail. . . All of this hit me like a ton of bricks. . .

It has serious implications as it seriously curtails the arrangements we had for that day. I know that it will screw up the flat
ceremony and means that it will only be a short Registrar
ceremony and back to the prison. . . Sitting here I am realistic
enough to know there is little I can do though I feel terribly hurt
at being betrayed in this way. I feel fragile as I've been caught in
a vulnerable spot in that an issue of this kind heightens my
impotence due to being in here. It leaves Sarah out there on her
own having to deal with it all in a practical sense.

27th January '80
This morning I lay awake, not sleeping a wink. There was a
feeling of total impotence and frustration. I wondered what the
papers would say and kept my ear to the radio in the hope that
something would come across. It came on the news at 8am and
was the first item. I was deeply upset and felt that something most
private and personal had been raped. Getting up I dressed in my
exercise gear and went out to pound the yard. Jesus, it felt much
much better than lying here locked in this cell. I thought of Sarah
and wondered how she was coping.

Malky went down for the papers. The front page of the *Sunday
Mirror* and *Mail* was 'Boyle to Marry', and showed a photo of
Sarah. Going through the articles I could see comments attributed
to Sarah which indicated the pressure she must be under; and I
am in here *protected* from it fucking all! I sat with staff reading
them and they had an appreciation of what Sarah must be having
to deal with. . .

28th January '80
The night was slow in passing. I felt terribly restless, sweat pouring
from me as I tossed and turned while waiting for the door to open

so I could burst out of my cell . . . after a laborious wait I threw myself into the yard with the adrenalin surging through my body.

The morning papers splashed headlines covering the story. The *Record* had a photo of Margaret (the woman I already had two children with) wishing us all the best. On the whole the press coverage was sympathetic though I was feeling the effects in a different way being aware that Sarah was out there on her own and having to do duty at the hospital. I knew how difficult it would be for her. . .

This afternoon I was bound with pent-up anger and frustration so got the gloves on and battered the heavy punchbag. . .

This evening Sarah came in and she was looking tired. We embraced and she just cried. . . It has all been too much for her and this is the first we've been together since.

29th January '80
Wattie came in and soon after I had a call from Sarah. She was angry at a vicious article in the *Express*:

THE CHEEK OF KILLER BOYLE

Scots are staggered yet again by the astonishingly successful effrontery of killer James Boyle, the most notorious and most pampered man in Britain's jails.

This week he caps his unprecedented privileges by getting out of Barlinnie's special unit to marry 29-year-old psychiatrist Dr Sarah Trevelyan, but it is not a romance that captivates the nation. Law-abiding people are deeply disturbed that a dangerous felon, serving life with a 15 year minimum and a further 12 years on top of that for creating mayhem in prison, should be allowed so much scope for intimate, personal activities.

NOT ONLY IS BOYLE GIVEN PERMISSION TO BE MARRIED. HE WAS ALLOWED OUT TO BUY HIS WEDDING CLOTHES, AND APPARENTLY HAD LUNCH WITH HIS FIANCEE AT THE SAME TIME. He has been permitted to visit her home on several occasions. And she visits him twice a week in the Special Unit, where the visiting hours are nine to twelve and two to five daily. Yet the Prisons' Department claim that Boyle is being given no special privileges and assure us that his marriage is not a stepping-stone to freedom. To say the least is it not a strange, unexpected match, between a half-educated thug and killer from the heart of Glasgow's Gorbals and the gently-nurtured, highly-educated daughter of Britain's former film censor.

She does not find it strange. She initiated the courtship by becoming a Special Unit visitor after reading Boyle's book. One may wonder how the romance may have flourished had Boyle's 'control unit' still been the Cages at Porterfield instead of the Special Unit at Barlinnie.

Dr Trevelyan is one of the large group of academics and intellectuals who have been campaigning for Boyle's early release. He has served 13 years of his life sentence.

IT WOULD BE A SOURCE OF SURPRISE, SHOCK AND ANGER TO EVERYONE IN SCOTLAND IF BOYLE WERE TO BE RELEASED BEFORE THE 15 YEARS NOMINALLY DECREED BY LORD CAMERON HAD EXPIRED.

Justice has to be seen to be done – and it has to be seen to be served.

I explained to her how the *Express* was a nothing paper which is desperately trying to get readers in Scotland. Sarah said that someone had been up at the door and torn the nameplate off. I am wound up knowing that Sarah is having to deal with all this.

30th January '80
This evening Sarah came in and she kept herself very strong though I could see the strain on her face. I am deeply moved at the way she is handling this whole thing. We ate some food and talked. She said Phil Davies of the *Sunday Mirror* made an offer of £10,000 for a series of articles, including photographs. Sarah had the presence of mind to ask him to give it in writing. He said that now our address is known the money may help to buy another flat! We both discussed cheque-book journalism and how it seduces people into selling their souls. Sarah will reply in writing saying she is refusing their offer. We intend to keep all this documentation in order to do something about it in future. . . In all that is happening at present the media are writing their own indictment. . . In contrast to this we are both receiving many many greetings from people in letters, cards and telegrams. Some of these from unknown people. . .

31st January '80
God, I feel weary this morning but once in my track suit and out

running I felt much better. My nerves were jangling in my stomach. The press have been outside the prison since 6am. When we left the prison a cavalcade of cars pursued us. There were hoards of press, radio and television journalists waiting for us at Balfron. On getting out of the car I waited for Sarah and we walked through flashing cameras and questioning reports. I kept saying 'no comment' as I had been instructed. In the Registrar Office we were ushered into a small room.

The woman Registrar proceeded with the ceremony and had to stop to mention that she was nervous and I appreciated this admission from her as it added warmth to the ceremony. We slid our rings on and took photographs before leaving to push through the mass of journalists.

Once back in the prison we sat in my cell with Heidi and Margaret (our witnesses). No sooner had we settled in than the Governor wanted to speak to us. The media were crowding the main road and they were harassing people. I got the feeling he wanted Sarah to go and speak to them. She was firm and stated that they should be able to do it. At the end of this debate it was agreed that the Governor and Malky would go and tell the journalists that Sarah would appear at a press conference later.

Sarah was near bursting point and I was angry at the Governor for being so insensitive. On returning to my cell Sarah was in tears and being comforted by Margaret and Heidi. I asked them to sort out some food and we sat alone. Sarah burst into deep sobs. I knew what she was feeling . . . oh I knew. Anthony Ross came in and he sat with us.

Once Sarah had washed and sorted herself out we then sat in a triangle of silence and got into the feel of our being married. This was a strengthening silence which seemed to bind us all together. There was a powerful atmosphere of love. Anthony read out two brief passages on love which were appropriate. He then gave us his blessing and all three of us stood embracing.

Sarah distributed little gifts to the other prisoners as we wanted them to share in it. I was concerned about the press conference and suggested she take Anthony with her. She jumped at this and he graciously accepted.

I sat on edge listening to the news and watching television. It was given prominent coverage on the national news. Sarah gave a fantastic interview and came across as a very warm human being. Some moments she was fragile, the others strong . . . at least we've come through this with dignity and left the others who tried to turn this into a circus looking ridiculous. . . I am now a married man and feel it has been the right decision. Only Sarah and I know the truth of what we share and feel. This is a special moment in our lives.

1st February '80
Lay in bed till 7.30am feeling extremely tired. Getting up I dressed in my track suit and went out for my run. I kept thinking of yesterday and that I am now a married man! I am wondering how Sarah is coping, can't wait to read the newspapers and phone her. The press coverage is massive . . . in all it is pretty fair but on the whole I am aware that this marriage, this happy event has shown the press up as nothing more than vultures who will stoop to anything.

I phoned Sarah and she is full of the joys, and I'm infected by it, am so happy that she is happy. We both know the score, we both understand the fight on our hands but there is now a solid base; we're in it together. We both laugh at our being man and wife knowing that this will take some getting used to but feel good about it. The headline in a paper is a quote from Sarah: WE'LL MAKE THIS MARRIAGE WORK.

I sit with the Governor and Wattie, both of whom are delighted at the way Sarah dealt with the press conference. The Governor tells of many phone calls he had from people in the Department stating they were delighted and moved by Sarah's courage in dealing with the media. This evening Sarah came in bringing some Italian food and both of us were overjoyed to see each other. We sat eating and she remarked how, spontaneously, she has decided to be known as Dr and Mrs Boyle. I laughed at this and felt good. I think it important that she made this decision on her own and am glad she did so. We both share our bumper mails and it is good to know we are getting support from so many people.

Kelvingrove
Glasgow G3

Dear Jimmy,
Just had to write and let you know that I've only now read your book (what a cracker) I mean very good by that. And as we say here in Glasgow, I had an honest to good greet. I came across it by chance one night in my brother's house, but I had to leave it there as he had

just started to read it himself. Well anyway I ordered it myself at my local newsagent and got it within a week. By God Jimmy you've come through the mill. I felt an old hurt wound open up while reading it. And I'm only going back 4 years ago, when my favourite brother who is the youngest in the family got sentenced to 5 years. You see Jimmy we were so close then (and still are). It just about broke my heart when he was sent to prison. People used to think me daft the time it took me to get over it. I think I went through every day of his sentence with him I couldn't eat, couldn't sleep, couldn't face my work. The only thing I was good at was getting (blitz) out of my mind with booze. I remember one night, I was so God damned full of the stuff, hailed a taxi to Barlinnie, and stood outside for about 2 hours singing all the Johnny Cash songs I could think of. Don't know how to this day I never got hailed inside. And this is honest Jimmy, on my way back down the road, the eyes a pure mass of mascara wae the greeting and the snotters tripping me, this voice pipes up and says 'Thank Christ for that, RENT-A-MOUTH is going home'. I would love to have shook the guy's hand, because I had a bloody good laugh to myself the next day thinking about it (Hope it wasn't you Jimmy) Ha Ha.

Well I went to visit Barlinnie to see my wee brother (as I say) he's now 32 and I still call him that, he was then moved to Peterhead and I never saw him till he came back down to Barlinnie for the last 6 weeks. There's a lot of things you write in your book that I identify him with you. He was a bit of a rebel at times, but a good hearted bloke well met. The family used to shout and bawl their heads off at him, but my wee mother Nellie and myself were the only two who really understood him he used to always confide in me and to this day he still does. While he was inside his wife divorced him the only sad thing about that is he hasn't seen his wee daughter since, but the good part of it Jimmy, is that since he's come out of prison he hasn't been back. He's got quite a good job on a building site and he's now met a nice girl and they've set up home together. And may I say this Jimmy and I truthfully mean it, I wish you and your lovely wife Sarah all the happiness to come. You deserve it and I'm praying for you that you'll be granted parole before this year ends. Hope you don't mind me writing I'm just one crazy mixed up sister.

God Bless you Jimmy Boyle
          from Margaret, a friend

Cramond St.
Glasgow G5

Dear Jimmy
I only finished reading your book, which was given to me as an Xmas present by one of my sons. My husband and I are pensioners and retired so we read quite a lot to pass the time. We liked your book so well it touched us to the heart, so we felt it right to write to you even as strangers to tell you in our own way how happy we are for you, and to wish you every happiness in your marriage which we saw on telly.
And to say we hope it will not be long until you are home with your lovely wife and be happy.
Good-bye
God Bless

St. John's College
Oxford

Dear Mr Boyle,
I hope this letter gets through to you as I wanted to tell you my relief and happiness when I read in the paper the other day about both your imminent marriage and release from prison. Having read 'A Sense of Freedom' I found it very depressing to think that you were still in prison and going to remain there for the foreseeable future. I haven't totally sorted out my attitudes to the penal system but your book among others has led me to reject the principle of punishment. Bertrand Russell compared the penal system to a garage which treats cars that don't go by saying 'you are a very wicked car and I won't give you petrol till you go' instead of trying to find out what is wrong. One sees after every violent crime splashed across the headlines 'MONSTER' or 'SAVAGE' or 'ANIMAL'. But how often does one see that all important word 'WHY?'

The only use I can see for prisons is as a way to keep violent and anti-social people away from Society while reminding Society that it is to blame and not any 'moral guilt' of the individual. The whole penal system has been built up and is still justified on the principle of guilt which I see as a direct link with the idea of original sin. If we could only learn to look from the effect to the cause we might prevent the spread of the illness instead of desperately trying to repress the symptoms when they surface. In that respect it is depressing though not altogether surprising that the Tories have just increased spending on 'Law and Order' while cutting nursery-school building projects in half.

Your book has helped to make me think and for that I thank you. Nobody who reads it can afterwards believe in the 'conventional system' and that can only be good (I lend it to people here). I see 'A Sense of Freedom' as a great and necessary donation of sanity to a controversy which seems sadly short of it.

I would like to end this rather muddled but sincere letter by wishing you all the best for your return to civilised (!) society and your plunge into matrimony.

Yours sincerely

*Weybridge
Surrey*

Dear Sarah,

This is to wish you every happiness and success in your marriage. I am writing to you as though you had joined my own family because it feels like that! Two of my friends who have read 'A Sense of Freedom' feel the same. We couldn't be more pleased to hear of the engagement to an attractive intelligent girl of one of our own sons. You must both have needed courage and faith to get married before you are able to live together, but that is what so many did in the wars, and at least your hopes and plans are not likely to be upset by enemy action. It is really something to come through a childhood such as your husband had and overcome the bitterness. The direct style of his writing has made me feel I have known him all his life. I would think you have chosen a man of courage capable of deep affection. It must be good to feel he is like a man born again – a man who will not ultimately let the past make him a prisoner. At the marriage of a young friend of mine, her father, who was the priest conducting the service, spread himself in his address on the difficulties to be encountered in the daily lives of married people, and it is true that none of us escape tensions in close relationships. However you have before you an opportunity to make a contribution no other couple could make to the well-being of children in the poorer areas, and in the direction of prison reform. No one can put the whole troubled world to rights, but it is nice to be able to do a little to help people.

Yours sincerely

Uddingston
Glasgow G71

Dear Mr Boyle,
Let me first of all congratulate you on your marriage, and wish your wife and you a happy and successful future.
I would also like to add a few comments about which I feel deeply. You are, more than anyone, aware of the vile resentment and hostility your situation has caused among that (unfortunately large) section of society which feels that criminals should be boiled in oil, left to rot, etc . . . the 'Hanging's too good for them brigade'.
Despite this benighted viewpoint, there are a great many people, not just sociologists seeking material for their next thesis, or middle class ladies seeking lunch dates with yourself in order to thrill the others at the next coffee morning, but ordinary people who on a simple moral level believe that, as Anthony Ross put it, an individual can be 'reformed' or 'rehabilitated'.
Mr Boyle, these people have argued on behalf of you and the Special Unit in bars, cafés, railway carriages, buses and places of work all over the country. They are called everything from fools to 'trendy liberals' – but their faith in man's ability to reform himself is unshakeable. So much of that faith is invested in you.
Well, I've said it. Maybe I am a crank – I don't know. I don't expect a reply – I just hope that my words might come back to you some lonely night when you might be feeling pretty low, and who knows – maybe they'll help a wee bit.

Good luck – Stay strong

6th February '80
As the day progressed the Governor asked to see me. In his office I was faced with Wattie and two other staff members. The Governor then told me that my day out tomorrow had been reduced to two hours instead of the usual five. Also, I wasn't to meet Sarah. The Governor said that he and his senior staff were furious at this as George Younger had previously stated I would get five hours weekly. I asked him why I was being punished? He replied that he couldn't answer this. One of the staff said that we didn't want to get into conflict with these people again and although I can see the sense in this I am angry.

7th February '80
I lay in bed till 11am. I felt really tired and couldn't face anyone downstairs. One of the staff came up and asked if I was going out for the two hours? I told him yes. I must admit that I had given thought to telling them to stick their two hours. The staff member then told me that a letter had come from the Department, signed by Mr Allan, the Controller of Operations, confirming what he said yesterday. Downstairs the staff member showed me the letter. It stated re our phonecall yesterday and because of the publicity last week there are certain restrictions he wants carried out:
1. I've not to meet Mrs Boyle.
2. I've to state which shops I'm going to and return immediately from there.
3. The outing has to last a maximum of 2 hours.

The staff member and I went out at 2.15pm and drove to Great Western Road. It was beautiful being outside. I thought, if I had been a weaker sort of person how stupid it would be for the Department to exert this sort of pressure as the temptation would be to run off.

The Governor phoned the Unit after we returned. He was at the Department and told Unit staff that Mr Allan told him that the cutting of my outing was an arbitrary decision by the Secretary of State himself till such times as he meets his junior Minister. The Governor said he was happy with this meeting and had an opportunity to make his views known. I had a chat with one of the staff this evening. He said that the position is that his (SOS) decision is making it intolerable for staff as we have it in writing that my hours will be five on outings and that this will be increased after a month or so. He said that he pointed out to the Governor today that if this isn't sorted out there'll be no staff left here.

8th February '80
Two staff members, in the Unit for a week, gave their views to the Community today. The first started by telling us his preconceived ideas of the place, pointing out that his colleagues in the prison he worked told him that Jimmy Boyle ran the place and everything revolved round him, and that the Governor was in my pocket. He said his week here showed him how untrue this was and he was surprised to see how it worked in reality. He said he could work here and would like to. The other staff member gave similar pre-conceived notions saying the same things and

how amazed he was in the changes in people here. He talked of how I had handled the knock-back of my paroles and could never have believed it could have been handled this way. His coming here had shown him the reality though he said that if he did come here he would find it difficult to adjust to this way of working.

11th February '80
The Governor called me in and said my paroles are now back to five hours. He said Younger stated this himself before receiving the Governor's submission. He said that they don't want me meeting Mrs Boyle. He didn't agree with this and was sharp in his comments. I know they are very sensitive to the press taking a photo of Sarah and I together but explained they had and that we're married now. I said that Sarah and I don't want publicity between now and my parole reply and they must give us credit for being circumspect in this. He agreed with me saying I should speak to Allan when he comes down next week. . .

14th February '80
There is a piece in *The Scotsman* on those jokers refusing STV access to some council houses for the film. It is quite witty:

USE OF FLATS FOR BOYLE FILM REFUSED.

> James Boyle, best-known inmate of Barlinnie's Special Unit, was at the centre of a council-house wrangle in Glasgow City Chambers yesterday.
>
> It was not that the recently-wed Boyle had prematurely applied for a council house in his native city – but because Scottish Television had requested the use of council flats to film scenes for a programme based on Boyle's autobiography *A Sense of Freedom*. However, had Boyle applied for apartments in the City Chambers itself, the reception could not have been cooler.
>
> Not one of the seventeen councillors on the tenure and rehabilitation sub-committee was sympathetic to the request. They were outraged at any connection being made between violent conduct and their city.
>
> There was laughter when a council official reported that STV had said the play was not about Boyle, but his autobiography. But the laughter stopped abruptly when Conservative Councillor Dyer moved to reject the request. He thought vacant property should be used to house Glasgow families . . . although

the city has 3,000 untenanted homes.

Councillor N. Stobo, Lab. said he didn't want Drumchapel to get the same image as Easterhouse through adverse publicity.

'It would not be in the interest of the people of Drumchapel to associate Boyle with the area,' he told the meeting. 'I am not anti-Boyle, I am pro-Drumchapel, or any other area in the city this crew want to film.' Councillor Stewart, Conservative, felt it was no part of the council's function to aid the glorification 'of this particular individual'. He added, 'He's had enough glorification. We would only be giving him aid and succour. When one considers the things Boyle has done and how he is held up to public esteem as part of his bid for reinstatement into society, I don't think we should have anything to do with it. He should have been hanged in the first place.'

A spokesman for STV said: 'It appears the emotions running on this issue are unjustified. The idea is to take a book about a criminally-violent man and consider what society can do about him!'

I find the hypocrisy of these politicians, both locally and nationally, difficult to accept; and yet, there is something hysterically funny about them. I should look on all that is going on as one would a continuous stream of clowns which evoke responses ranging from the deadly boring to the absurdly funny. I've got to stop their rantings from hurting me and this is possibly the best way of doing it; in my mind I'll fit them all with bulbous red noses, outrageous costumes and flappy feet.

26th February '80
This afternoon Mr Allan came in and I opened up the meeting on the subject of my paroles explaining to him the unnatural strains placed on me as a result of not being allowed to see Sarah. He referred to a letter he sent to Sarah saying the publicity is the main problem here and that they haven't shut this off by any means and his general attitude was sympathetic. He said that people like Sproat and Fairbairn MPs have been writing letters about me saying I am getting more privileges than other prisoners. He said that I am getting similar privileges to other prisoners. I then asked him if I am getting treated differently and he admitted that I am a victim of my own popularity/notoriety and agreed I am getting less than others. I told him that I am asking supporters

of mine to keep a low profile and as a result they are having to deal with negative ones from Sproat and Fairbairn. He told me that lots of letters received immediately after the wedding were positive and I pointed out to him the amount of support Sarah and I had received from unknown people.

On the subject of violence there were some strong statements made when we were discussing our violent backgrounds. Allan stated that there were moments when he has been filled with tremendous anger but has never resorted to striking anyone. He said he's now fifty-three years old and has never hit anyone in his life. I explained to him that where we come from violence is a part of one's upbringing. I said that within the Unit one learns new skills and techniques as a substitute for violence; that when one develops these areas of oneself then violence becomes less necessary. One of the prisoners stated that there have been times in here when he's been so angry he desperately wanted to attack someone and stab him but what prevents him is that he knows there is no danger of the other person attacking him; whereas, the thing in the main system is that if conflict arises then 'Get in first' is the name of the game.

Throughout this meeting and this particular topic Mr Allan opened himself and so the Community responded to this. It is a lovely process and one that lets us see the human face of a bureaucrat.

14th March '80

BOYLE SHOPPING TRIPS BANNED

Scottish Office Ministers have placed a ban on controversial prisoner James Boyle's weekly shopping trips to buy supplies for his fellow inmates in Barlinnie's Special Unit. Last week, on one of his shopping expeditions Boyle, a convicted killer, had a 'chance' meeting with his new wife and they were seen in a restaurant together.

This latest episode proved the ultimate embarrassment for Scottish Office Ministers who had been unhappy with the publicity surrounding Boyle on trips about Glasgow under escort of prison staff. . .

A Scottish Office spokesman confirmed last night that Boyle's outside visits had been suspended 'for the present'.

Glasgow Herald

16th March '80

FURY AT TV FILM ON KILLER

A television company's attempt to film the life story of rehabilitated Scots murderer Jimmy Boyle in Glasgow's meaner streets is proving almost as bizarre as the man himself. The £350,000 90-minute blockbuster from Scottish Television's studios is derived from Boyle's autobiography *A Sense of Freedom*. Before filming got underway there were outraged squeals from Glasgow district councillors. They felt that Boyle – described by his trial judge as 'a menace to society' – was being 'lionised and glorified'.

Scottish Television defended their actions: 'The film will portray Boyle as he was, a vicious, ruthless thug. In no way will it show him to be a martyr or a hero.'

Observer

And Sarah? In the midst of this whole mess we are both surviving under trying circumstances. Moments that we've had have been stolen, like thieves in the night. She represents that soft underbelly; she is the soft loving part of me. She is my vulnerability. And the tears that I would want to shed at this moment are pouring through my fingers, these fingers type with all the emotion of a man who is crying. . . In the past few weeks I've raised the inner question 'What have I brought this lovely person by marrying her?' Both of us knew it would be hard but never this hard. The brutal harshness of the political and bureaucratic processes have taken their toll.

Those moments when she has come seeking refuge in my arms, crying wracking sobs, her anguish all pouring out, I give her all that I possibly can, that soft vulnerable part of me flows into her, the strong exterior guards her. 'When will all of this end?' I ask myself. And there are those moments when I have cried. . .

The conglomeration of boiling emotions within me at this moment has an intensity that is bordering on bursting point. I am a man filled to the brim. So full that I want to close my blazing eyes to prevent the overspill of anger.

I must push my way through this, must emerge healthy and strong. The weight, the burden, the pressure that is on me must somehow be overcome. It must! And in telling myself this, I extend it to my loving woman. We both must survive this; together we must thrust our way forward, letting no one and nothing stand in our way.

22nd March '80 (Evening)
I tell you dear paper, sweet confidante in my isolation, that I am this good night dancing in my feelings. I am in touch with my joy. Though the snow is thick on the ground I am warm and happy inside. I am at this moment the personification of love. I feel deeply the breadth and depth of my woman. How do I describe it?

If I close my eyes I feel the intense waves of ecstasy race through my entire body, my heart seems to have quickened just as it would had I taken drugs. But there is no chemical could match this. If I close my eyes I find myself anywhere but here, no-place specific but the sun is shining on me, it smiles, it actually laughs. I am alone as I've been for thirteen years. The happiness within me is so intense that I can almost see it bounce off the walls as it shoots from my body. All I can do is share it with the inanimate objects but most importantly, with myself. I feel 'high'. At this moment if I were outside I would go to her and share it.

27th March '80
Four prison staff from Grendon Underwood Prison (England) visited us today. They paid for the trips out of their own pockets and came in their own time. They've been looking at a few places in Scotland so didn't come specifically to see the Unit. It was interesting to listen to their views which were a mixture of good and bad. They complained about not being allowed to get closer to the prisoners in Grendon, and yet were disgruntled at having put prisoners on a disciplinary report only to see him fined a paltry 50 pence! They used this example to indicate the lack of Governor support. Some of the staff were good but from what we gather they are seriously inhibited by professional staff. They have doctors, psychiatrists and psychologists as well as therapists. We explained the Unit concept and how we do the job ourselves. They talked of how staff are put into Grendon and don't want to be there and they tend to cause trouble. One of the guys said he didn't want to be there but had to lump it.

28th April '80
A source told me that the Parole Board are wary of me because

of the pressure to release me. Apparently there is no talk about my being transferred to Perth Prison but that Edinburgh is more likely with my being put into an artistic situation so that I could pursue my work.

Ken came in and it was lovely to see him. He told me that rumour has it that although Malcolm Rifkind is sympathetic, he is wanting to abide by the sentencing Judge's fifteen-year recommendation. Ken said Rifkind is ambitious and that there is no way he is going to move for me, and that the Labour mob are the same.

Sarah came in and it was nice to have her, Ken and I standing in the Unit again. We then had to sit down for lunch (Wattie's retiral lunch) with many other people. Sarah had to leave soon afterwards. I presented a crystal decanter and glasses to Wattie and made a speech which gave some perspective to his role and contribution right from the start. Wattie shook my hand warmly and then stood up and gave a speech. He was torn right from the beginning. It was a moving scene. He is a lovely man with lots of weaknesses that show him to be a sensitive human being. Wattie, retiring after thirty-one years in the Prison Service, made no bones about it, the Unit and his years here were the most difficult.

9th June '80
I had a call from Frankie Miller who has seen the film and says it is very good. He thinks David Hayman, acting as me, has done a great job. Frankie said it is strong stuff and he loves it. He is working on the music for the film and will have it completed for Friday. He wanted my permission to title the song *A Sense of Freedom*, and I agreed. He is getting Rory Gallagher to back him musically.

18th June '80
I went out for the shopping and was widely recognised by people. . . We had lunch in Sauchiehall Street and two girls asked Ron (escort) if I was Jimmy Boyle. . . I sat next to a guy on the new tube and he asked if I was me. I told him yes and he said he had read my book and loved it.

There was a piece in the evening paper saying I had been nominated for Rector of Glasgow University. . . The Governor came in saying he's been on the phone to press all night about this.

1st July '80
After the Community meeting the Governor caught hold of me to say he's been on to the Department and the Director has said that final word of my parole will come sometime in September. This floored me as I was expecting it much sooner. He said that although it's September that doesn't mean there won't be movement between now and then. It will go to the Board in August and at that meeting he expects two of their members to come and interview me. He said he has to be careful what he is saying but there are no negative noises.

3rd July '80
This morning I wakened feeling totally exhausted and drained. Getting up I sat waiting for the door to unlock. I couldn't help but succumb to the negative feelings concerning my parole. By the time the door was opened and I was out doing my run I felt physically drained.

I just can't go on. Despair was so deep in me that I sat for a long spell on the rowing machine in a daze, desiring to have a nervous breakdown or something, anything but having to live with how strong I am. I sat there in that condition, dazed, numbed and near to tears but still telling myself that I've got to do those exercises. This is what I hate about myself at times like this; I keep going and live through this torturous situation.

12th July '80
This evening Sarah came in looking much stronger and brought some food with her. Going out to work this morning she found the nameplate torn off the door again. When she went downstairs to the street her car tyres were let down and the paintwork scraped with the words 'Killer Boyle'. Sarah showed a strong front here but I was shaking with anger. She said she was at first but gave some thought to it and tried to understand it. We both thought the likely perpetrator would be the guy who is writing anonymous letters to us. I am afraid for Sarah. She tried to alleviate this by showing a remarkable strength. We both looked on it as some badly damaged guy who has fed on the media pap. When the Mirror journalist tried to blackmail Sarah into giving her a story or he would publish the address of the flat, this is what he was putting her in for.   All this bureaucratic nonsense about not being able to see her when out for the groceries doesn't help. I

want to comfort her, support her in a practical sense. . . Internationally recognised as husband and wife we must act like secret lovers. . .

Secret Lovers

Perhaps I'll be there waiting in the shadow
out of sight; unnoticed by others passing by.
Try not to be conspicuous when you approach;
I prefer the anonymity and the solitude.
There is something profoundly comforting
about living in the shade; far from the glare.
Should we meet then make it betwixt and between;
if possible in the softness of dusk.
Let your movements be slight and subtle;
a flick of your wrist; a smile on your lips.
It is enough for me to see you; to feel your
presence; to smell your sweet smell.
Make it so the observer sees nothing;
not even the casual brush of our bodies.
We should remain apart yet together in all
but the obvious; our secret shared.
Forgive my discretion it's simply that I hold
precious our love wrapped in intrigue.

14th July '80
This afternoon two of the staff returned with the new prisoner. He immediately went into the Governor's room and then came into a Community meeting. On entering one could see he was under extreme pressure and making nonsensical noises as though he was in control of the situation. This let me see just how much pressure there is on people coming into meetings like this. The Governor opened the meeting by asking if there was anything anyone had to say. One of the prisoners wanted to know the position between the new prisoner and Jimmy Boyle. The new prisoner came in saying we know the score so there will be no trouble. I then explained to him that I would be no threat to him in terms of violence. He said the same. He seemed to relax after a few minutes. He said he wanted out and that was why he was here. There was some discussion on the Unit and then we were left alone.

In many ways I couldn't help feeling sorry for him as he is

under tremendous pressure and so steeped in prison culture that he was at a gross disadvantage. The contrast between guys entering the Unit like this and those who have been here was never more clear than now. We discussed the past and he tried to justify everything saying that he hadn't raped guys, hadn't bullied them and so on. We talked about this and I let him get it off his chest. He said that he was hated by everyone and that people kept putting the mix in for him and that he never did many of the things people accused him of. It was interesting listening to him justify his position telling me that he didn't grass me in the High Court trial all those years ago.

On talking about the Unit he said that he is only intending to pay lip service to it as there is no way that he intends grassing anyone. At the same time he won't do anything in here or get involved with anyone. He said it is okay for me as I'm not going out to live in the world I came from whereas he is. He said he is concerned about his son now who is in the nick and so on. At one point he became so emotional I thought he was going to cry. I tried to be as sensitive as possible with him while at the same time making the boundaries of the Community plain. I tried to point out to him that I can appreciate and understand him saying the things he is at the moment but that it isn't as simple as what he is saying. He said he doesn't want to get involved or take on what I have done. It is quite clear that he is intent on paying lip service to the place.

He mentioned that at one point he had considered coming down here to get me and had spoken like this to the Interview Team. But now all he wants is out. He said that he has to save face now and doesn't want to be seen pulling with me or being too friendly with me. He talked of having lived with hate for me for years and I can understand this.

27th July '80
I sat with a member of staff. He asked me how things are going between the new prisoner and myself. I told him there was an uneasiness between us but that this was to be expected as he is loaded with old prison culture. The staff member nodded at this saying the new prisoner is obsessed with me – his hatred that is. We agreed this is to be expected but that he must be encouraged to look to the future. The staff member said he spent most of yesterday afternoon with him and continuously he returned to the

subject of me. He asked if he should condone this and let him get it out. I said yes but the consistent message to put to him is that the past is the past and he must get on with the future. I explained that if we were to continue to harp on about past conflicts then all we would be doing is wasting time debating the rights and wrongs of that period – which was eight years ago – instead of the present and future.

28th August '80
While sitting talking to some of the others the papers came in. The front page headline in the *Glasgow Herald* says BOYLE TO LEAVE BARLINNIE SPECIAL UNIT. It stated I would be told today that I was being transferred to Edinburgh or Perth and that I would be given a date for a year's time. There were inaccuracies in the article but nevertheless it gave me a feeling of being from an authoritative source. The article quoted a prison source. I was very angry and immediately thought of Sarah.

I phoned her . . . she asked what the news was? I told her there was no truth in it and expressed my anger saying the article was opening up all my expectations of a parole reply. Sarah said someone from the *Herald* called her at 11.30 last night telling her he got the information from an official source. She refused to comment. This morning a reporter from the evening paper was at the door at 8am. Sarah told her to 'Piss off'. I asked Sarah to go to the editor of the *Herald* and complain about this article as it is tearing us apart emotionally. Sarah, rather shrewdly, advised me to see the Governor first.

The Governor came in and I let him see it. While reading it his only response was, so you're being moved next week. I told him Sarah would like to go to the editor of the paper and complain but we need a denial or confirmation from the prison authorities. He replied that he'll speak to me at 10am. He said he's expecting a call at 9.45, giving a reply to my parole. He expressed anger at the press getting this saying he had to leave the prison yesterday to go home and make calls about me and that only three people knew this information: Mr Allan, Mr Hills (the Governor of Saughton) and himself. At 10am he spoke to me saying my release date is Nov. 1982 and that I'll be transferred to Saughton Prison, Edinburgh. Next week Mr Allan, Mr Hills and Mr Ogilvie, Assistant Governor from Saughton, will come to Barlinnie to discuss with us what my programme will be. I replied to this saying whilst I was pleased to have a release date I was disappointed it was so far away. I was also concerned about the conditions under which I would be transferred to Saughton. Sarah came in and I told her the news. As we sat discussing it the Governor came in and Sarah was forthright in telling him how stupid it was to keep me in this length of time. His response was that he would have it otherwise but those above deemed '82 as the time. We said we would challenge this.

This evening the news came over the BBC. There was a lengthy television piece saying the Prisons Department have broken precedent by issuing a statement about an individual prisoner. It stated I would be getting no preferential treatment.

It's been a momentous day. The one clear thing is that I have a date and from my point of view it's tremendous to have a release date. All of it will take some time to sink in and next week will let us see what Saughton has to offer.

29th August '80
I spent the morning writing letters seeking support about the distant parole date and transfer. It won't do any harm.

The press coverage was pretty wide and accurate in issuing the statement that Sarah and I gave. There was speculation about my imminent transfer to Edinburgh. The press took relish in describing the contrasting regimes; my leaving the soft-option of the Unit for the harshness of Saughton. When reading all of this I could understand Sarah's trepidation. I am merely blanking it till I know what the decision is come Wednesday. The Department are stating publicly that I am getting no preferential treatment and yet they are coming through here in a high-powered fashion to sit and discuss things with me. This in itself is preferential treatment — I don't see them doing it for other prisoners.

I can see the effects of my transfer seeping in here. There is concern amongst people about my going. The new prisoner is certainly hit by the decision about me. He said he can't help but see it reflecting on himself (a twenty-year recommended minimum).

3rd September '80
Sitting here I couldn't help feeling trapped. I certainly didn't like the position I was in. J.L. said he wished me well but was fearing the worst. On entering the main prison gate building I found the

door to the Boardroom. Malky and I could see Mr Allan with his briefcase standing outside. We entered the room and all the people standing there sat down. Edinburgh team: Mr Hills, Governor of Saughton, Mr Ogilvie, Assistant Governor and a Principal Officer. Glasgow team: Our Governor, Peter Whatmore, Malky and me.

Mr Hills wasted no time in opening the proceedings by saying that I was coming to his prison and he would now outline what would happen to me. First, I would be going into his prison like any other prisoner.

1) I would be going into 'B' Hall for 4 weeks.
2) To Forth Hall for 3 months.
3) To Pentland Hall for one month.
4) To 'C' hall for the rest.

I was told nothing about what would happen after this, only that at each of the above stages I would be consulted. I was then asked if I had anything to say or to ask them. I told them that what they were telling me was that I now have to learn to adjust to Saughton Prison instead of adjusting to life outside. I asked them to explain the logic of this. Mr Hills replied that this is to be the laid down procedure for any prisoners coming from so-called 'untrainable' prisons. When I challenged them on the points about my conditioning and training here and what they had to offer, they were speechless. I mentioned the things I do here, shopping, art, visits, etc. and comparatively speaking, what had they to offer? None of them could answer this. I was told that I would be put into a prison uniform and given three half-hour visits every two months and that my mail would be censored. . . They were telling me that I wouldn't get any special treatment and yet Ogilvie explained that I would be the focus of attention on visits so could have mine in the overspill room.

On returning to the Unit I immediately called Sarah. I told her briefly and she knew I was holding it all in. God, this is the hard bit, this is the one bit that kills me. I just don't know what the hell I'm going to do. I called a Special Meeting. On explaining what had happened to everyone they voiced that they were sick and made this known. Peter Whatmore said that he had made his feelings known to the Controller and was disappointed. The Governor said that Ian Stephen forcefully opposed it and he did also. They had a go at Mr Allan but apparently he was carrying the message from someone else. Whatever, it is patently clear that there is no support for the move by any of the professional consultants. They, as well as the Governor, will make their views known in writing. The Community will too.

I was barely holding myself together. The new prisoner made an interesting remark saying that his cousin on TFF (Training for Freedom) in Saughton was given immediate parole and he can only imagine it's because I am going to Saughton.

Tonight Sarah came in and we fell into each other's arms. I fell apart and cried deep sobs of pain. Going back there is like a nightmare. That is my past and I feel myself being dragged into that tunnel, far into the muck of that life. Oh, am I never going to get away from it? What, just what am I to do with this heaving knot of emotion inside? I held Sarah with all the pain in my arms. I held on to her for love's sake. Why, why are they doing this? I am naked and vulnerable – that system will creep into me, it will tear my insides apart. I feel deep, deep anger. I feel the full weight of the nightmare on my shoulders. I am caught, trapped and feel that they want to shut me away . . . feel them wrapping a blanket over me, feel so helpless to do anything about it.

At this writing I am like an open sore. . . I worry for Sarah, don't know what I'll do without her and yet know that the love we have will bring us through though this rings rather hollow at this moment. My tears are running and this is the man I am now.

4

In solitude and peace
Think deeply
I am you and
You are me
Only space lies
Between us.

Larry Winters

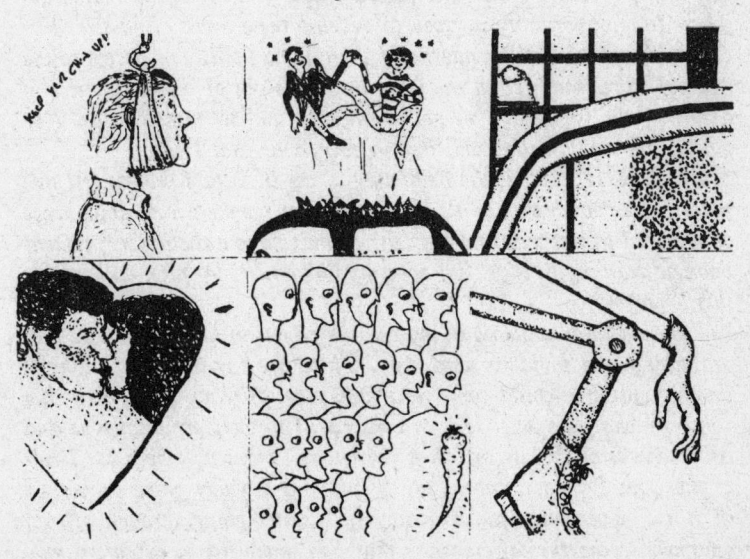

8th September '80

Darling Sarah,

Well, here I am lodged in my new place of residence. The contrast is sharp and startling between here and the Unit. A simple thing like writing to you on prison notepaper is very strange. I'm trying to gauge my reaction to all the things that pre-Unit were things I took to without thought. At the moment I am pretty bewildered by it all, and felt just like a first offender. I feel anonymous wearing this coarse prison uniform . . . although only here a few hours I have pin-pointed what I feel will be the major problem for me; the dull and boring routine. Having been used to a high-pitched, dynamic routine where intellectually and physically I was disciplined I now find myself in a situation where little opportunity is given to develop these areas of oneself. For example, in this hall I understand there is no facility or access to the gym. Also running round the yard would be out of the question. I'm aware of the fact that I've got to improve and set myself tasks. I've got to keep myself alive and free in every way that I can.

Being in 'B' Hall is the beginning of the induction process. At this point I have no idea what it's all about. I can see there is an abundance of material to research and look at. I don't have a dictionary, sketchbook or drawing pens yet but hope my Governor's Request will resolve this tomorrow.

I have a large window in my cell which lets in lots of light. It's an ordinary house window with bars. There are two beds so I take it another customer could come in at any time. Already I am becoming conscious that this letter will be censored. I'm wondering what is and isn't permissible; if it isn't then my letters to you will help us. Prior to the Unit I'd have known all of this and anyway being so steeped in it I'd never have put anything in a letter going through official channels. Now the difference is that I'm interested in exploring new areas and taking note of what is really going on. I'm allowed recreation with other prisoners two nights a week. I'm just too bewildered by it all to comment. . . The cell light is switched off at 10pm so I'll have to find something to while away the other four and a half hours. I have thrown off the foam mattress and one lovely possession is your photograph. . .

9th September '80

Darling Sarah,

I now have my own pens, sketchbook and dictionary but would not *like these to be seen as concessions as it's ridiculous that such things should be taken away in the first place.*

Today was interesting as I spent the best part of the morning in the mailbag party. It was an incredible experience. But, first things first. I went to the doctor for a cursory check-up and on entry was marched in and told to stand side-on, on a small black board sitting on the carpet. I don't know why. One of the things that concerns me, and came more to the fore as the day progressed, is the rigidity of the regime. All the decision-making is taken away from the prisoner and I can now see at first hand how the system makes prisoners dependent on it. As much as I try to detach myself from this, it will be impossible. By being in it one falls prey to it. What I find ironic is that the undoing of all this was very difficult for me in coming to terms with the Unit and latterly in helping other prisoners re-learn social skills. . . I'm still confused by all of this as it really is severe, much more so than I could have imagined. In a strange sort of way I want this to be with me throughout my stay in this place. I'd prefer the continual pain of culture shock to the acceptance of life in here. I can never erase from my mind the problems I've seen guys have in the Unit as a result of this system. I feel the transfer so much because I know that even though individuals here have the best will in the world to do good they haven't my insight or awareness of what just being here does in terms of personal damage. There are some heart-rending stories here. I'll tell you about these when I see you. Basically, I'm feeling severely the loss of my creative outlets. It is difficult to explain to the non-creative person what this means. The procedure in 'B' Hall seems to be that prisoners are given nothing so that when they move on to other halls they will appreciate the petty concessions: the 'carrot' system which in effect works in relation to a smooth running penal system as opposed to gearing prisoners to cope with life outside. The horrifying part is that every single prisoner here will return to society sooner or later. They have to fit into the system which means it does not focus on the needs of the individual.

10th September '80
The hustle and bustle of early morning ablutions permeate the air. Everyone makes for the sinks which sit in two large archways. While shaving one guy tells another, 'It was on the radio that three cons have escaped from Perth.' The other stops his razor half-way down his cheek, 'Did they get away?' The other replies, 'They rammed a lorry filled with concrete and the cops are looking for three hardened criminals'. Humour does play an important

part in people's lives here. I did a few exercises on the floor: press-ups, sit-ups and some yoga. . .

Darling Sarah,

I'm now having to leave for breakfast and won't return to my cell till the evening. . . I won't be able to write any letters till tomorrow which means I can't send any off to you till the following day. . .

11th September '80

My Dearest Sarah,

I'm so at sea in this place that I'm trying hard not to be drawn into it. The whole process is so insidious that it's like a creeping disease. The 'them' and 'us' is quite strong. I'm listening to everyone but trying to remain detached. I'm now working in the engineering shop which is okay in terms of being left alone to get on with it though I have to contend with the boredom. There is nothing remotely related to life on the outside. Yes, my conditions are spartan to say the least but that isn't a complaint. As I said before I can't enthuse about an extra shower or pair of socks a week as part of the upgrading scheme. Guys in here talk about other halls and the 'perks' there as though they are meaningful. This affects me deeply as it has no relevance to their lives outside. . . I'm puzzled by your letter as you keep (twice) mentioning that you'll see me tomorrow. The position is that I have to book a visit and the only vacancy was the 28th, so I'm concerned that you may make the journey here for nothing. . . The visit will be for one hour round a small table under supervision. Alternatively, we could use the 1½ hours at half hour intervals but these would have to be through a glass screen. Let me know your thoughts on this? You won't believe this but every Friday night everyone has to polish their cell floor and a Governor comes round on Saturday morning to inspect it. I needn't tell you that on Friday we got our weekly change of socks, shirt and underpants, all to match the floor I suppose!

27th September '80

Darling Sarah,

Well, I've just this minute returned from getting my extra pair of socks, etc. in this new Hall I'm in. The whole structure of the place is almost identical to the other only this one seems older and more worn. The cell is very much the same only I'm on the bottom flat. Being here again raises the question, what is all this about? I've just been given a sheet outlining the rules of this particular hall. One of them states the four visitors will be allowed on any pass, this includes a babe in arms. What saddens me is the way other prisoners in the previous hall were all hung up about wanting to get to this one. At that point one begins to see the uglier side of it. The Assistant Governor has just come in to do his inspection, and we talked about my being here. He himself appreciated that it was all a waste of time but that I've just got to go through with it. He said he was surprised I was put in here and not on TFF. The one stand-out feature is that no one here seems to have any control over my present circumstance. I get the distinct impression they are all observers watching the train go by. . .

Sunday:

Beautiful morning outside and I know you'll be making your way over here for the visit. . .

You looked great even though I knew you wanted to break down and hold me. I wanted to but what was so important was holding ourselves together. Just to hold and kiss you was wonderful, to look at you and feel you close. Sarah, this they'll never break. This was our first visit and I was truly in need of it though the appalling lack of privacy was most difficult to accept. I'm sure you'll agree with me when I say it had a cattle-market feel to it. At least we can take some comfort from knowing that our experience of it is limited. Some guys I spoke to afterwards were in the first year of a life sentence. It's so depressing. Can you imagine trying to keep a marriage together under such circumstances. . .?

29th September '80
I went on request and spoke to the Hall Assistant Governor, asking to be put on the Special Escorted Leaves Scheme (SEL). She said there is a big waiting list but wasn't very clear about any of this.

11th October '80
My Darling Sarah,
I was told officially that I can go out on SELs. Prisoners, having done a certain length of time can get four of these outings a year; each four hours in length. However, the problem is in getting a member of staff. It's all done on a voluntary basis. Here is what I have to do: approach a member of staff and if he agrees I get a form from the

Hall desk and fill it in. I then have to save up £1 from my weekly wages and put this into my personal property. I can go out two weeks after this. The first SEL has to be in the vicinity of Edinburgh.

18th October '80
I approached another member of staff today and asked him to take me out. He already takes guys out and says it's a lot of pressure on him and the few staff who do. He refused me but said he would ask one or two of the staff on my behalf. It is a crazy system in that it's extremely difficult to get staff to take me out. One guy I know said he has asked thirty odd staff members. Another guy told me he has asked fourteen. He has been trying to get his since April. You can see how frustration builds up in people as a result. The two guys I spoke to are pretty bitter and so as we get into this part of the system one is faced with problems hitherto concealed. . . For lunch I had a baked potato with a scraping of cheese on top, one small roast potato and a scoop of mashed potato – the spud in all forms! This is my veg. diet!

22nd October '80
It's tremendous to see the effect all our outside support is having. Apparently the Department has been swamped with letters condemning my transfer and on top of this the hunger strike and court action by Joseph Beuys and the others has them jumping. . . I had an interview with the Governor, Mr Allan and a Mr Whyte, education man here. They tell me that negotiations with Edinburgh University have fallen through as they have been pushing to get me on a course when it is into term. The University said they will take me full time '81–'82. The problem is that none of this was worked out well in advance. The public pressure has caught them with their pants down. So, it's back to the drawing board. Mr Allan suggested that I do something at Craigmillar or Wester Hailes or at Ricky Demarco's Gallery. They will contact the community groups first as this is my preference. . . I hope to hear from them very soon. I must admit I'm pleasantly surprised at this turn of events – we're winning! As for the SEL, I took the opportunity to mention this to Mr Hills. He said he will raise it on Monday. As you can see they are all aware of the situation but no one is doing anything about it. Yes, the ironic thing is that even with a 'D' category one needs an escort. The crazy system is this – make sense of it if you can – that one guy goes out alone

one day a week to college but when he goes on an SEL he has to go with a prison officer...

3rd November '80

My Darling Sarah,

It's amazing how good I feel since seeing you yesterday. The contrast between 'before and after' showed in your mail. One card showed all the cracks of stress and strain, of how you were letting it bite into you and eat you up. The other showing the magic of us together and what we do for each other... I approached officer No. 10 and yes, he's taking me out on an SEL. I wonder if you could make space on Tues. 24th Nov. between the hours of 2–6pm? I can tell you, knowing you will feel the same on reading this, that it was pure relief when he said yes. I thought it would be nice to have a meal and we can go and look at the new flat...

7th November '80

My Darling Sarah,

It was great to get your letter today and find out all that you've been doing. I'll go into this later but first let me bring you up to date on events here. The Assistant Governor explained to me that the Wester Hailes management team will be coming to see me on Sunday afternoon to interview me for a job in their community. As you know the Governor and Mr Whyte went to see their activities earlier this week. The management team there have put feelers out to the grassroot groups to get their views on it. There is a possibility that I'll be working on their Art Festival programme. Initially it would mean my going out two days a week with this expanding to full time after January. The Wester Hailes group would want to issue a statement to the media on the Monday, if it is agreed I go there, and this way take the initiative.

9th November '80

Darling Sarah,

The Principal Officer came in to give me a hurried look at the parole conditions for my going out. It stated that I'll be allowed out every Tues. and Thurs. between the hours of 9 and 5pm and that I would be under the guidance of Laurence Demarco; that I won't be allowed alcohol, that I won't meet the press, take part in any commercial or private business, make any pre-arranged meetings with anyone *outside the Wester Hailes group; that I have to stay within the Wester Hailes area and if not back in the prison in time I will be arrested.*

Shortly afterwards I was taken to the Governor's room and introduced to the Wester Hailes management group; Mr Allan, Mr Whyte, etc. We discussed what my work would be. . . The atmosphere amongst the whole group was good and we were together in all that was being said. It was agreed that Malcolm Rifkind has been quite courageous in this as it's his constituency, and after all he is the Minister responsible for prisons. Mr Allan stated that Rifkind has been solid in his support in this. So, in all it was a very good meeting and a sigh of relief all round. I am looking forward to starting work on Tuesday.

11th November '80

My Darling Sarah,

By now you'll have read or heard about today. I'm just back and it seems strange sitting in these stark surroundings after spending a day of freedom – from one extreme to another. . . Let me tell you about it. The morning started with two letters from you. I could tell you were down. Here I was reading your letters knowing that you are unaware of what is happening with me – sitting here waiting to go out. I was taken to the reception area and locked in what is nicknamed 'a dog box' – a small cupboard space approx. 3ft square. Once dressed in my own clothes I felt like superman. I seemed to smell and feel different. I was taken to the Governor's office where Laurence and Jack from W/Hailes were waiting. The Governor said no press were at the gate but if they got on to my being out sometime during the day and it became overbearing we should decide when to come back, all of which sounded sensible. What a momentous occasion, the first time I've been out of prison without a prison escort in thirteen years. How can I describe it to you? Can I tell you what it feels like to stand on the surface of Mars? No, I can't because I haven't experienced it. There was a feeling of nervousness and excitement in the Community Workshop but a definite friendliness. I was hungry as I'd given the prisoners at my table my prison breakfast knowing I was going out. They piled a big breakfast on me – lots of beautiful greasy goo. . . Laurence, Jack and I discussed the possibility of the press getting on to it. Laurence was nervous about Mr Hills, saying he may call me back to the prison if the press do turn up. He said Hills had mentioned not having slept last night. No sooner had we finished when a girl from STV was on the phone. The local community cop came in and we had a chat. A local councillor came in saying the Express had been on to him asking 'Is he not outraged at someone like me being near a primary school?' Predictably the Express were the only negative ones. Lots of local people, men, women and children came in and talked to me. They were full of support. The work being done by the people here is impressive, it's thriving. Due to our caution I stayed in the building all day but there was more than enough for me to digest.

24th November '80

I'm taken to Glasgow Sheriff Court on a mistaken identity trip. I told them prior to going (Tues. and again yesterday) that it wasn't me. While waiting a young guy approached and asked for my autograph – I declined trying not to offend him. I'm handcuffed and taken through to Glasgow in a prison van with two prison staff as escort, what a waste of time. I'm apprehensive as I may lose the SEL. I think of Sarah and worry about how this will affect her. I got to court and immediately on seeing me the policeman said it's a mistake. It really is appalling this waste of money; one staff member brought in on overtime, a driver, a van and another staff member all for a mistake. A phone call could have cleared this up and I did protest enough to bring it to their attention beforehand. It was as though it suited them, even if it was a mistake.

PM: On return to Saughton it was early lock-up due to the POA meeting. I didn't take any lunch in anticipation of the SEL, hoping to get some decent food outside. The POA meeting went on past 2pm and I was pacing the cell floor worrying if I'd get out at all. These uncertainties were taking their toll. I was feeling drawn and tired with strain and desperately worried about Sarah, waiting on her own. My chest was tight, my guts knotted. It was almost 3pm when I was escorted to the reception area and locked in a small, claustrophobic 'dog box' to dress. I had a good laugh at this as an all-party penal reform group publicly condemned the dog boxes saying they should be abolished. I sat for some time waiting on the staff member coming for me. He eventually came and I was full of anger but having to fight this in order to get into good feelings so that we could enjoy our four hours. I told him we were over an hour late because of the POA meeting and he said he would speak to the Training Governor which he did, leaving me outside the door. My guess is that he was given a good warning as the last prisoner he took out returned drunk. On coming out of the office he told me that 25 minutes had been knocked off the 4 hour SEL. I was furious, but this regime doesn't allow me access to the Training Governor to question his decision. Here the fucker is, lopping off a precious 25 minutes of my contact with Sarah. By now I was sickened and yet trying desperately hard to keep my cool. The officer told me to call him Jimmy when outside and said normally he allows a guy one lager or two glasses of wine. He prefers telling me now so he doesn't have to do so in front of my visitor.

Outside The Gate: Sarah comes up from behind. She looks fantastic and yet I can see all the waiting and uncertainty has taken it out of her – she looks fragile. I love her so much and hate to see her being upset like this, particularly by a System that I despise. We question what car to take and this distresses Sarah as I feel she just wants to concentrate on being with me. We take our car and this eases me as I feel a sort of 'home ground' security about being in it. Our whole dialogue is inhibited due to this stranger sitting with us. I am aware of a constantly boiling anger in me. All our reactions and feelings are muted and we realise we are miles away from our usual spontaneous loving selves. However, we talk to the escort and bring him into things. We drive to our new flat. The owner is in and greets us. We walk around and I love it. For the first time our natural loving feelings emerge and overcome all the bad ones. Sarah and I examine the house in detail, inspecting every nook and cranny. We talked of ways the front room could be decorated. We stole an embrace in that front room. This is our future, our home. This is our life. We grudgingly left the flat.

Outside we bought some food and wine and went to a friend's house. We thought the escort would give us some privacy, but no. We ate and had a drink. The subject was prisons, prisons and more prisons. Eventually Sarah asked if he would give us some time on our own and he went into the next room. I could see that all Sarah wanted to do was cry. He left the room and she broke down. We embraced clinging to each other, both of us asking when this nightmare would end. When she cried she stifled it, afraid the escort would hear. I held her tight urging her to let it flow, telling her I love her, oh how I love her. I told her just how good it was for me to be able to support her at times like this and yet at the same time was aware that I was the source of all this misery. All I wanted was to make my wife happy, to be with her.

I told her all of this, about the degredation of sitting having to whisper to each other with a strange man sitting behind the door probably listening to every word. I constantly felt intruded upon. It wasn't about sex or anything like that. This doesn't even enter it. Basically, it's about a man and his wife wanting to share some of their deep personal feelings for each other. Sitting there cheek to cheek I could feel her tears roll down my face. I love her, I deeply deeply love her. After a few minutes we got ourselves together and decided to leave these surroundings for a more public place.

In The Streets: It was beautiful walking hand in hand along the dark rainy streets. We discussed plans to move from Glasgow to Edinburgh, ways of decorating the flat, talked about our families and all the while the escort clung to our sides. He tells us how he has to hide his true personality in this job, how he would like to do more but can't. He tells of me being looked on as a 'hot potato', of varying staff views, good and bad. He talked of comments made by colleagues when it became known he was taking me out. Yes, it was courageous of him and we both acknowledged this.

Back At The Prison: It's difficult... Sarah and I have a few seconds on our own, express our love to each other; she reassures me she is together now after her cry. I know she is saying this for my benefit and me going back in wants to believe it. We part with all the poignant melodrama of a B movie.

Inside: The gates clang a desperate doom-laden noise behind me. The prison interior is dark, like some Dickensian scene. Inside, the reception area is well-lit. One prisoner is cleaning his boots; he's just returned from one day a week out to college. He has a wound on the back of his head and tells me that on leaving the prison this morning at 7.45, he was running for a bus when he collapsed after a paralysing pain in his side. His head crashed on the ground cutting it badly. Rather than return to the prison he got on the bus and went to college, then to hospital where he had four stitches put in the wound. He said there was no way he would have returned to the prison before his due time. One of the reception passmen (prisoner) told us the staff were taking industrial action starting tomorrow but didn't know what or how a work-to-rule would affect the prison.

On returning to the Hall the Principal Officer sent for me to say that as a result of industrial action I wouldn't be going out to work tomorrow. He had no idea how long it would last. I felt numb. He asked how my SEL went and I told him it was stressful. He then pulled out a newspaper with a photo of 'Birth', a sculpture of mine and asked what it meant. I told him. He then told me he wrote a poem called Birth. He has two adopted kids and then his wife fell pregnant. He explained in detail the full impact of this event, closed his eyes putting a clenched fist in 'thinker' style to his forehead and recited it. He then explained how he watched some bullies taunt another inoffensive prisoner and was so angered that he wrote a poem about it, which he again recited. I explained to him that he was known as a bastard amongst the prisoners. He said he was a 'book man'.

I think of Sarah and worry, I wonder and ask myself how she is coping. . . I lay in torment through the night, exhausted but not being able to sleep. I do feel empty and flat.

25th November '80
I should be looking forward to going out today but am not. Prisoners see the dispute in different ways. At slop-out time (6am) some are delighted to be off work so as to get some extra sleep. I understand what they mean. At the same time I want out. Others hate the idea of being confined in their cells because of the tension between them and their cell mates. In this early morning period there is a rush for hot water which tends to run out quickly. We are locked in till breakfast time.

In the dining hall prisoners are surprised the work-to-rule is preventing me getting out to work. They seem angry about it. At the table ex-doctor Ghia approaches me to say he went in front of the Visiting Committee yesterday to complain about being kept in the mailbags for eleven months. I sympathise with him and give support. He leaves and this arouses dialogue at the table. My table mates talk about the way some medical staff seem to resent the doc. because he let the side down. There is also a strong racial element in it all. He has been assaulted, harassed and picked on by staff and prisoners. Most prisoners, distrustful of the prison medical doctors and staff, approach the doc. for a second opinion which he invariably gives. This has caused him great difficulties with the medical staff who have warned him about it. There seems to be a euphoric atmosphere in the dining hall due to the dispute but really it's about the change of routine.

I asked the guys at my table about the tension in a shared cell, turning it to masturbation. There is a false bravado by all three saying they don't care about their partners, they just do it. But, as the talk continued and got more serious one admits to waiting till his partner has gone to sleep – he listens for the heavy breathing. Another has arranged the beds so that his partner's bed looks the other way. He can turn the radio up. . . Each admits to experiencing high tension in other areas, the stench of doing the toilet or just wanting to be alone.

Back in my cell I sit dreaming, expressing some of what I feel in the form of sketching. Here I am locked up in a solitary situation again. It all comes flooding back, all the old memories of the past. As the morning goes on staff come in with mail; letters from Sarah from the weekend. I'm wondering how she is, how she will take this industrial dispute. I'm supposed to be at two meetings in Wester Hailes this morning. I asked prison staff to ask Mr Whyte to deliver my written material for these meetings. Staff seem to be trying to lessen the load by having reasonable attitudes.

26th November '80
This morning it was the same old rush for hot water. The strong stench of urine and excrement filled the air as we slopped out. As we stood at the sinks shaving, the medical officer came into the toilet area with a prisoner carrying the medication box. He gave prisoners treatment as we stood there. Owly (one-eyed table mate) told me he approached the nurse officer last night to ask for something for chest pains and was told 'Fuck off'. Those of us at the table have been trying to persuade Owly to report sick as he hasn't been eating his food. At the breakfast table we discussed how each spent the time; studying, playing chess, reading. One said my name was mentioned in relation to the dispute when it came on the radio.

Later a senior officer who is on the local POA committee told me that he wants me to know that this action isn't anything personal, that staff aren't wondering ways that Boyle can be done dirty. I said I appreciated this. He was very critical of the Governor saying he is always away to Round Table meetings or similar ones. He said they are interested in getting the prisoners their recreation and have made this known to a 'mole'. The Governor will have to approach them about it. They will consent. I told him they should refuse to accept prisoners into the prison but he backed off this. I have spent the time writing to Sarah. The W/Hailes people have told her about the dispute. I worry about her as all these knocks are putting her in a vulnerable spot. I find myself being affected by it as the door keeps opening and closing in my face. I'm more vulnerable because of Sarah, as I keep thinking the system is putting us both through so much that she won't be able to take much more. Perhaps I'm underestimating Sarah's strength and endurance. Someone sent me in a Butlins holiday camp brochure. It's obviously someone trying to be snide.

27th November '80
6.20am. . . I realise that rather than waken at my usual 5.30, I am sleeping on till the door is unlocked. This is so unlike me but there is a creeping sense of 'What does it matter?' – I've got to fight this. There is a real air of depression. I can smell the strong stench of urine and excrement . . . prisoners' bodies and cells smell of stale sweat. I go out and wash but don't shave, even though I usually do every morning. Thursday is laundry day. It's great to change my underwear, shirt and socks. One change per week and I really enjoy it. The medic goes into the toilet areas as usual to distribute medicine. A staff member goes to the small wooden mailbox, opens the flap and takes out the mail. He comes to the toilet area where there is a small table, puts the letters down and begins censoring them. I have written one to Sarah. My eyes keep straying towards him as he reads letter after letter. Watching this I feel as though part of me is being raped:

My Darling Sarah,

The long drawn-out hours take their toll in the form of mental depression which affects me physically also. It's like being a helpless pawn in a giant game of chess; there's nothing more demoralising than the feeling of being picked up and slammed down whenever and however it suits the person in control. At moments like this one can only fall back on one's inner resources with a little help from you. At this moment some mail has just come in from you so I'll leave this to read how you are. . . Well, where do I start? I plummet at the way all of this has hit you; stop, start, spurt, torn apart and yes, I know what you mean about the part inside wanting to break down and scream at not being able to take any more. I can't help asking, what the hell am I doing bringing you through all of this? There is this feeling of living a schizophrenic existence; this raw bleeding part in me wants to howl and scream at the pain of it all, and the exterior façade that presents an unruffled face. Oh yes, Jimmy copes with it well. I feel like the Hulk and want to throw the walls aside.

Mid-morning

A letter from Sarah just as I am writing to her. Oh fuck! It tears me apart to the point where I find it difficult to read her letter. This has hit her so hard just as I knew it would. She went to the Third Eye Centre and broke down with Chris; and I am bleeding profusely inside, raging at this impotent and helpless situation. SARAH . . . why did you let them see this? I start writing to her but have to stop. I lie on top of the bedboards feeling painfully contorted. I can't keep still and yet I'm so fucking tired and weary. I just can't take any more of this. It's pushing me to the limits and yet I know there is an iron part of me that is solid and won't be moved – that will push through it. The pain I feel is incredible. Why did I marry Sarah and pull her into all of this? It's bad enough coming through this on my own without her having to endure it. I want to cry at the moment, feel all the tears welling up but they aren't coming. I won't let these bastards see it's getting to me. I won't!

I've just done a good hard work-out and feel so much better. . .

Evening

Prisoners are now openly stating they want the dispute over as soon as possible. Staff are saying they are losing money – overtime, etc. One prisoner told me a member of staff came into his cell and told him he could go under the covers of his bed as long as he didn't take his clothes off. We had a laugh at this.

There is a good letter in *The Guardian* about my being sent here. This also brings me to the heart of the matter. My continuing imprisonment is nothing more than a vengeful act. My stay in here is futile and has nothing to do with my learning to adjust to life outside.

28th November '80

This morning I wakened very early feeling extremely cold. I had a headache. My body is sore with lying down. Last night a guy told me he is getting headaches due to being enclosed in a small space all the time. This is what I feel as I write this. I lay in bed till the light was switched on. There are four giant cockroaches on my floor so I jump naked out of bed, grab a shoe and smash them. I lift a bit of cardboard and scoop them up and toss them into the piss pot. I hate this place! Everything in here gets to me. The door is unlocked for slop-out and I manage to get some hot water, have a nice wash and shave.

There was an article in yesterday's *Guardian* by Jill Tweedie, on the way crime is reported in the press and she has cleverly related this to women in Holloway. I wanted to send this to Sarah. This meant my having to acknowledge the censor who, until now I've tried to wipe from my mind. I felt terrible going to him with my letter and article asking if I could send it out. He is a young guy of no more than twenty-four. He says he has no objection but when it gets to Security they may not allow it. At this point I discover our letters are read twice. I gave him the letter and article and slopped out. On looking down I can see him reading my letter and a senior officer the article. I am not ashamed of the love I express in my letters to Sarah. I am consoled by telling myself they are just a shower of insensitive bastards. On coming into my cell I kiss the photo of Sarah. I whispered loudly so I could hear, 'I love you'. It's dark outside as I sit here feeling very cold. I'm hoping the rumour of the dispute ending today is true but I'm not building up my hopes. I've got to keep some sort of balance. It's depressing to think of another day locked in here.

Last night I curled naked in the sleeping bag made out of blankets and hugged myself. I masturbated to Sarah, imagining her in different poses. It was beautifully erotic and warm, in sharp contrast to the cold outside the blankets. I love the way I am able to fall back on the richness of my inner world for comfort and love. Bed is a very attractive place to be as I can pull the blankets over my head and crawl into the total darkness. I write me a poem:

Horizontal Shuffle

Grind your goddam pelvic rhythm
as your muscles flex their
erotic collusion with your man
in the horizontal shuffle

Feel him snake his flesh with
slippery smoothness deep into your
cavern with its silky walls
and frictionised motion

Cry your guttural sounds as he
utters his moans in that
mutual primitive chorus
of the horizontal shuffle

Toss back your head as you twist
to thrust a wet tongue through lips
into his throat with
passionate hunger

Tense your body in expectation
as he probes your throbbing need
to explode into fragments of glitter
that climax the horizontal shuffle

Sparkle with joyful convulsion as
you jerk uncontrollably into
those soaring skies of infinite
distance and beauty.

Grunt your pleasure as he spurts
his sperm of milky fluid to mix
with your juice while peaking
in your horizontal shuffle.

29th November '80
This morning I lay in bed listening to the footsteps of the night patrol clicking off the stone floor. It rang a metallic sound throughout the hall. I felt so restless and thought of how in the past I would have blown up at this stage or rebelled in some way or other that would have resulted in me being punished. Life has been a series of instances like this, of being unable to express myself and so irrationally exploding and in this way labelling myself the baddie and having got an additional sentence I still would have savoured the immediate short-term gratification. One never thought of the consequences. It was a case of live fast, die young and have a good-looking corpse.

Breakfast:
At the table I told some of the guys about my angry thoughts related to all this frustration and boredom. . . The youngest responded immediately saying he has been fantasising about taking cans of polish up to the roof and setting the place on fire. Another

says he wants to do a bastard screw in. The oldest guy says his thoughts would leave us standing. He said this in an angry manner, full of aggression. He went on to say that he's seen guys in pure torment because they've heard something about their wives and it has nothing whatsoever to do with their wives but the mind in prison distorts it all and the guy goes through sheer hell.

30th November '80
This morning I wakened very early. It was extremely cold as I lay in bed so I rubbed my body with my hands to keep myself warm. I thought of Sarah and imagined her lying in bed. I remembered our flat bedroom well and could vividly imagine her lying there.

At 7.30am the staff come on duty; a mass of footsteps can be heard. While lying here I hear the sound of the judas spyhole open to reveal a naked, probing eye to check that I'm still here.

Spoke to an old guy who said this lock up is making him angry. He has a bad heart condition. He said he put it to staff that if he is feeling this way, what must some of the younger guys feel like? He asked who would be blamed if a young guy grabbed a screw and threw him over the gallery? This old man is certainly feeling it. He had heart tablets in his hands as he spoke.

1st December '80
On waking this morning I lie in the darkness listening to what sounds like an army of cockroaches walking the floor.

Speaking to a guy in the dining hall this morning he said he hasn't gone more than three months this sentence without a smoke of hash – he is in nine years. He said he was glad to be out of 'B' hall as there was too much heroin there and he could feel the temptation. He was into hard drugs before this sentence. On speaking to him and an ex-Peterhead prisoner they remarked that the hard drug scene has changed in recent years in the nick. At one time in prison it was all pills (barbiturates, etc.) but now it's all hash that is on the go. They say that everyone, even the screws, are more tolerant of this. But, if it is pills they go mad searching everyone and everywhere knowing there is violence associated with them. On hash everyone is passive.

This morning it is very cold so I've put a blanket around me while I walk in a small circle on the floor. There have been

moments when even my dreams have deserted me, leaving me to
stare at the blankness of my situation.

2nd December '80
On waking I thought of Sarah, telling her out loud I love her. It
was 5.25am. I got up and did some loosening up exercises before
going into my yoga.

The strike is over! Going out this morning was fantastic. I
stood in the reception area speaking to two brothers serving life
sentences who were going out to their Granny's funeral. I left and
walked out the gate alone to jokes from staff, 'Is this allowed?'
Turning into the main road I could feel the energy soaring in me.
How do I contain this when walking normally along the road? I
find myself wanting to run, to sort of take off. It is magnificent
seeing cars and buses again.

10th December '80

My Darling Sarah,

*I had an interview with the Governor today. We discussed the
possibility of getting transferred to the Training For Freedom Hostel
and his view is that the matter is for the Parole Board and Department
to decide. The view is that I am here like any other prisoner. It seems
that there will be no move to the TFF Hostel till next November.
Twelve months prior to release. When I quoted the part in George
Younger's letter about 'Individual programmes to suit the needs of the
individual' he told me this was only within the established programme
set-up.*

25th December '80

My Darling Sarah,

*Christmas Day rings hollow in here as we are all caught in the
dilemma of wanting to be with our loved ones and yet trying not to be
openly dispirited. I found it amusing to see an Assistant Governor
appear at breakfast time – something unheard of.*

*For one young guy it was a tragic day as his Mum, Dad and brother
were burned to death in a fire earlier this morning. This has made the
rest of us count our blessings. Generally a sadness hangs over the place
and no amount of pretence or acting will eliminate this. I wakened
first thing, thought of you and wished you a Merry Christmas. The
day passed quickly enough and now at 4.50pm we have been locked*

up till tomorrow morning. I've done some images of Christmas in prison in my sketchbook, and lost myself in this for a while...
Boxing Day: *Hope your day has gone well. I'm locked up and shutting out all the emotions of the occasion but keeping myself intact and together. I see everyone here struggling through what is obviously a difficult period for them.*

3rd January '81
Although very tired when I wakened this morning it was a great feeling knowing I'd be going out again. I stepped out of the gate and it was cold but sunny. I felt deliriously happy. I find that I'm unable to walk along the street. I have to run. This personifies what I feel inside. My thought process is like a newsreel out of control with everything going at high speed. I feel my physical freedom to the full; taking in the sky, the road, the horizon, feel the air, take a deep breath of it and run, run, run. . .

At the workshop I had a coffee with Laurence and he brought me up to date on things. We are joined by others from the one-parent family group and Mick, who fills me in on various activities. . .

Tonight I returned to the prison after a full day of community activities. Here the tension lies in me like a dead weight. I feel it tight and taut. It's a far cry from my feelings earlier today. I feel stretched and strained sitting in my bare cell dressed in prison uniform. I feel like Cinderella at the stroke of twelve. Two tangerines sit forlornly on the bed reminding me that I was outside. What am I doing here?

8th January '81

BOYLE WAS THE BOSS

Amazing attack by former Scots prison minister.

A former Government Minister in charge of Scotland's prisons yesterday launched an astonishing attack on Jimmy Boyle and the way he 'ran' Barlinnie's controversial Special Unit.

MP Harry Ewing said: 'Boyle was running the place. He imposed his personality on the Unit'. The MP for Falkirk, Stirling and Grangemouth was speaking to Rotarians in his home town of Leven, Fife.

He also alleged that a bid to put another 'hard man' into the

Special Unit beside Boyle failed . . . because convicted killer Boyle did not like anyone else with a strong personality. And after an incident with Boyle, the other prisoner was taken back to Peterhead Prison after only six weeks.

On conditions in the Unit, Mr Ewing who was junior Minister responsible for prisons in the Labour Government said: 'It has a rarified atmosphere. It is an unreal world where Boyle had made a bust of Nicholas Fairbairn, now Solicitor General, in appreciation of him defending him on a number of occasions.' Mr Ewing told the Rotarians that lifer Boyle, now in Saughton Prison, Edinburgh, and being prepared for freedom, could not stand another prisoner being introduced into the Special Unit.

He went on: 'Boyle was running the place and imposed his personality on the Unit. I wanted to see another prisoner with a similar personality introduced. One man was there for six weeks before he had to be removed.' Mr Ewing said the controversy about Boyle would spring up again next month when STV screen a film about him. 'It is his case that will be put in the film. I want to put the case of those looking after the 4999 other prisoners in the system who are liable to be painted black.'

But a spokesman for the Scottish Office said they had no record of anyone who had been removed because of a personality clash with Boyle.

And last night Dr Sarah Boyle, who married Boyle in 1980, also denied the 'hard man' incident. She said: 'I think I know the Special Unit's history as well as anyone and I don't know what Mr Ewing is talking about.'

An STV spokesman said: 'We must let the Boyle film speak for itself. Mr Ewing has accepted an invitation to discuss it the night after it is screened.'

Later last night Mr Ewing said attempts by the Scottish Office to deny the incident were 'Ridiculous'. He added: 'They know it is true and if they continue to suggest I am a liar I will reveal the name of the prisoner I'm talking about. I feel that too much eulogizing of Boyle can happen and it should be contained.'

Daily Record front page

Darling Sarah,
Harry Ewing splashed all over the front page of the Record. *What*

a pathetic little man he is. Although I was angry at the whole untruthful content there is a funny side to it. The idea of me doing a portrait of Nicky Fairbairn is hilarious. I am sure that even he must recognise there are limits to my artistic talents!

9th January '81

EWING RAPPED OVER BOYLE

Former Prisons Minister Harry Ewing, at the centre of the latest controversy over the Barlinnie Special Unit, came under fire yesterday.

Attack No 1 was launched by the present Home Affairs Minister Malcolm Rifkind. He described as 'extraordinary' Mr Ewing's claims that convicted killer Jimmy Boyle ran the Unit when he was a prisoner there.

Attack No 2 came from one of Mr Ewing's own colleagues when he was a Labour Junior Minister in the Scottish Office. MP Neil Carmichael claimed that during the period Mr Ewing was the Minister responsible for the Special Unit, he only spent 20 minutes there. . .'

My Darling Sarah,
I was pleased at Malcolm Rifkind's reply today as it certainly places it all at the feet of Harry Ewing who is being shown for what he is, a political opportunist of the worst kind. . . I'm delighted that our lawyers are going for him. . .

21st January '81
In the workshop a phone message for me to call Sarah. . . She is feeling ill. I find myself torn apart to an extent that I've never experienced before. My most vulnerable spot has been hit. Sarah is badly upset as her legs have gone numb. She suspects multiple sclerosis. I can't take this fucking situation which keeps us apart. Robert drove me to our house. I cast caution to the wind – fuck them all. Holding Sarah I take her in the car to hospital. Conspicuously, I pull a cap over my eyes and a scarf round the lower part of my face. I know I can get into serious trouble for taking my wife to hospital. I find it difficult to comprehend these rules. All I'm doing is what any normal husband would. If at the end of the day it falls apart and they do me then fuck it. I know Sarah is feeling all the worse for being ill as it exposes us to this sort of danger. Both of us are trying hard to be protective and at

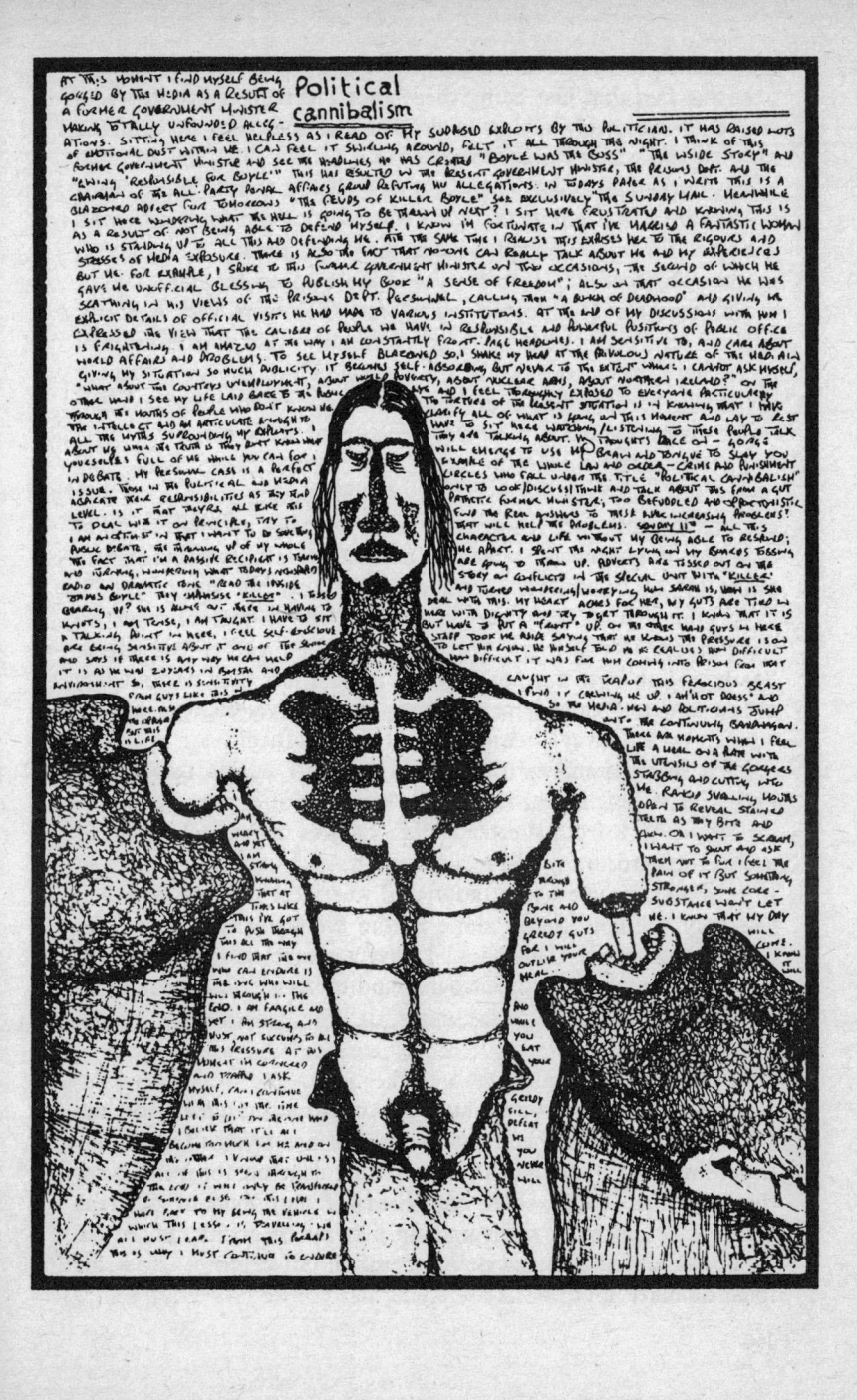

Political cannibalism

At this moment I find myself being gouged by the media as a result of a former Government Minister making totally unfounded allegations. Sitting here I feel helpless as I read of the supposed exploits by this politician. It has raised lots of emotional dust within me. I can feel it swirling around, felt it all through the night. I think of this former Government Minister and see the headlines he has created "Boyle was the Boss," "The inside story" and "Living responsible for Boyle." This has resulted in the present Government Minister, the Prisons Dept. and the Chairman of the All Party Penal Affairs Group refuting his allegations. In today's paper as I write this is a blazoned advert for tomorrow's "The Crimes of Killer Boyle" See exclusively the Sunday Mail. Meanwhile I sit here wondering what the hell is going to be thrown up next? I sit here frustrated and knowing this is as a result of not being able to defend myself. I know I'm fortunate in that I'm marrying a fantastic woman who is standing up to all this and defending me. At the same time I realise this exposes her to the rigours and stresses of media exposure. There is also the fact that no-one can really talk about me and my experiences but me. For example, I spoke to this present Government Minister on two occasions, the second of which he gave me unofficial blessing to publish my book "A Sense of Freedom"; also on that occasion he was scathing in his views of the Prisons Dept. Personnel, calling them "a bunch of deadwood" and giving me explicit details of official visits he had made to various institutions. At the end of my discussions with him I expressed the view that the calibre of people we have in responsible and powerful positions of public office is frightening. I am amazed at the way I am constantly fronted page headlines. I am sensitive to, and care about world affairs and problems. To see myself blackened so, shakes my hold of the unknown, nature of the head, am giving my situation so much publicity what becomes self-absorbing but never to the extent where I cannot ask myself, "What about the countrys unemployment, about world poverty, about nuclear war, about Northern Ireland?" On the other hand I see my life laid bare as I become days and I feel tremendously exposed to everyone, particularly thanks to the actions of people who dont know me to the virtues of the present situation is in knowing that I take the littlest of our articulate enough to clarify all of what is happening at this moment and lay to rest all the myths surrounding my exploits. I have to sit here watching/listening to these people talk about me when the truth is they just know half they are talking about. My thoughts race on — going yourselves full of me while you can for will emerge to use my brain and brave to slay you in debate. My present case is a perfect example of the whale law no check — crime and punishment issue. Those in the Political and Media circles who fall under the title "Political Cannibalism advocate their responsibilities as they had only to look/discuss/think and talk about this from a gut level. Is it that you're all here the patriotic former minister, too befuddled and opportunistic to deal with it on principles. Try to find the real answers to these ever-increasing problems. I am anxious to but I want to do so through that will help these problems. Sunday 11th — all this public debate. The throwing up of my whole character and life without my being able to respond; the fact that I'm a passive recipient is through the apathy. I spent the night lying in my bunk tossing and turning, wondering what today's newspaper are going to have up. Sweats out on the radio and dramatic topic "Read the inside story and conflicted in the special duel with "Killer story Boyle" they harness "killer" and twisted whatever/voyeuring, am Sarah is, how is she quaking up? She is always out there in having to deal with this. My heart aches for her, my guts are tired in knots, I am tense, I am taught. I have sit more with dignity and try get through it. I know that it is a taught artist in here, I feel self-conscious but now I put a "lout-" up. As the other man guys in here are being sensitive about it. One of the senior staff took me aside saying that he knows the pressure I am and says if there is any way he can help to let him know. He himself told me he realises how difficult it is as he now 22 years in Bushel and how difficult it was for him coming into prison from not environment so, there is sensitivity from guys like this. I was

Caught in the trap of this ferocious beast I find it crushing me up. A hot press and so the media, and politicians jump out: the continuing bandwagon. There are moments when I feel like a meal on a plate with the utensils of the gougers stabbing and cutting into me. Ranted snarling mouths open to reveal stained teeth as they bite and chew. Or I want to scream, I want to shout and ask them not to, for I feel the pain of it but something stronger, some core-substance won't let me. I know that my day will come. I know it will

weary and torn up inside knowing that at times like this I've got to push through this all the way I find that the one way you can endure is the one who will allow through in the end. I am fragile and yet I am strong and must, not succumb to the pressure at any moment in contracted and tearing I ask myself, I am convincing in this, is the time I believe that it is all passing through for me and as I do when I know but will I am the is this in through to the crux is and only the foundation on working on this. I am I have rest in my being the vehicle by which this less is traveling. We all must leave I am this puddle this is why I must continue to endure

bite through to the bone and beyond you cannot guts for I will outlive your heal

and while you eat your

greedy sick deceit in you never die

the same time attend to our needs. I can at least take satisfaction from the fact that just being there gave her a great lift. It was a soul destroying job having to drop her at the front door of the hospital and watch Robert help her in. I sat watching her stumble and it burned its image deep into me. I felt a traitor and coward for leaving her. I felt as though I was running out on Sarah, who has stood up and defended me against all and sundry. The anguish in me was terrible. Robert was unable to understand why I couldn't go in. The people in the workshop were very sensitive when I returned. Some of them eventually went to the hospital to see her. I spent the rest of the day ploughing my way through my work. Sarah called four hours later saying that she had had exhaustive tests and it is a viral infection of some sort.

There was pure relief in me. I asked her to take it easy, stay in the flat and I would be across. I did, taking some food and champagne with me. It was great to be with her and in our house together. We drank the wine and had some food. I was constantly aware of the rules I was breaking in all this but was intent on supporting Sarah, but keeping in mind the danger of what we were doing. It was lovely lying on the floor together and letting Sarah cry; oh how this got to me. I guess I just held her but was aware that our time here was very short. Eventually I had to wrench myself away. It was difficult, very difficult.

I felt stunned and exhausted by the time I arrived back at the prison. The jangling of keys, the slamming of doors, the shouts of: 'Boyle back from Wester Hailes' rang in my ears. I stumbled across the yard to my cell feeling numb. . . I now sit here locked in with all the anger, frustration and weariness of my situation. I can only think of Sarah alone in the flat knowing she will be feeling even worse than I am. I have to leave this pen down to curl up on my wooden bed boards and moan at the mental stress I feel. . .

22nd January '81 (6.23am)
I've slept in snatches throughout the night feeling tense and torn. I love Sarah so much and the thought of her being ill and alone is getting to me. There is also a part that nags me for putting her through this. Little shits like Harry Ewing put tremendous pressure on us both when making statements about me. A sad little man trying to make political capital out of me – Christ, he must be hard up!

6.59am. I burst out into the main prison drive and the streets like a high velocity bullet. I ran towards my work, past people and traffic. I passed a 'For Hire' taxi and was tempted to jump on it and head for home to Sarah but again found myself caught in a dilemma, trying not to be irresponsible, trying to strike some sort of balance, trying not to take too much of a chance. I hate this fucking authority and its inhuman rules, and myself for being so subservient to them. I had to run past two telephone booths as they were within sight of the prison and I'm not allowed to use them. Eventually I reached a 'safe' phone booth and spoke to Sarah. She sounded weak and tired. I awakened her; I implored her to stay in bed today. . . I told her I love her, told her again and again. . .

I bulldozed my way through various meetings except one. This young girl wants to see her father who was committed to the State Hospital when she was five months old – she is now seventeen years of age. He was committed for rape and murder. She wants to see him as her life has been a living nightmare. Her mother is an alcoholic but remarried and had two children to a military man. He beat the shit out of them all. . . Speaking to her seemed to help me in relation to my own situation. This place is filled with tragedies. There must be some way of dealing with them.

24th January '81
Somehow it all seems to be caving in. I received a letter from Sarah that seems to mirror my thoughts and feelings:

My Darling Jimmy,

As I write this I realise you'll probably be worried about me knowing that I'm not well at the moment. Tonight I sat here with the core of pain boring through me, feeling just terrible about the whole situation – and more than the sickness itself, just sick inside about it all. It got so bad that I really couldn't do anything else at all but groan in agony, feeling to the full my present futility and helplessness; no, even more, what it must be doing to you if it's affecting me as much as this. But you reach a point where you just have to turn around and find something positive to focus on – pull together, make the effort, start up again and face it, whatever it is. And I must say I'm no clearer about this, just that this numbness continues. . .

A voice calls for Governor's inspection and the sound of footsteps can be heard as each door is unlocked and slammed closed.

Mine opens and I stand casually giving the impression that I'm only going along with this because I have no option thus any participation is reluctant and minimal. 'Good morning?' the female Assistant Governor asks. I say 'Okay,' and there is an embarrassed and awkward pause and at least she has the decency not to pretend to be inspecting my cell and moves on as the door is closed by one of her entourage.

25th January '81
The sun is shining as I sit on top of my bed writing this; the sound of a bird can be heard singing. Someone in the cell block is playing the guitar and singing. Looking out of my prison window I can see over the fence to small plots of land where people grow vegetables and flowers. I wonder if they ever think of the prisoners vegetating in here? This morning after breakfast I can see guys all spick and span, faces shaved, clothes pressed, shoes polished for church and chapel. Clearly, for the majority it is an avenue for increasing their chances of parole, for the few others religion is something they have grasped on to. One can be sceptical and say they are all at it for parole but I have spoken to a few who have really grasped it to satisfy a deep need – remorse?

I noticed two assistant governors sitting in the office used by the officers and drinking tea. They are trying to be seen as 'one of the boys'. These guys have entered the prison service by the 'open competition' and find themselves in a prison setting. I suppose in principle this is seen as healthy but in practice it runs into problems. It's here they come up against case-hardened prison officers who have lots of experience. Most of these assistant governors are young guys who haven't really matured yet and are out of their depth in here. In my experience they tend to spend the first few years ingratiating themselves with staff who are threatened by outsiders coming in. As outsiders they tend to overcompensate and it isn't only the junior governors who are guilty of this – social workers, priests, ministers and teachers, etc. . .

8th February '81

My Darling Sarah,
I didn't send you the usual letter this morning as I've been presented with 'another' problem – wait for it! I was taken in front of the Governor and one of his assistants and told that my Wester Hailes

community project was 'suspended'. This is because I watched a preview of A Sense of Freedom.
I've already told you about the paranoia in the Prisons Department over the film. Well, it exists in the workshop to some extent. The view taken there is that in taking me on they are in the front line for criticism so asked if they could have a preview. I was approached by Laurence to arrange this and did. My view was that the people who had taken me on should have a look at it – this is the least I could do! The film was sent up by John McKenzie in video form and shown to us. Later in conversation with two assistant governors Laurence mentioned it. They took it back to the Governor and now I'm in trouble. . . Further to all this, though it isn't a major factor, there is the insidious process of censorship. Why shouldn't I see the film? This then takes us back to the origins of the book and how it was handled at that stage. They say that no official confirmation was given in writing but there was more than enough oral encouragement away back in the good old days.

10th February '81

BOYLE LOSES FREEDOM

Killer Jimmy Boyle has lost his freedom to work outside prison. Prison bosses imposed the ban after Boyle was caught grabbing a sneak preview of his TV life story.

Until now Boyle, who is in Saughton Prison, has had licence to spend two days a week working as a helper at Wester Hailes community centre. Last night MPs were asking for a full statement by the Prisons Department about events at the centre last Friday.

It appears that film producer Jeremy Isaacs, now boss of ITV's Channel Four, travelled up from London with a copy of the TV documentary *A Sense of Freedom* which tells Boyle's story and is to be shown on Scottish Television. . .

Scottish Daily Express front page

GET BACK INSIDE!
KILLER JIMMY BOYLE. . .

Daily Record

My Darling Sarah,
 Well, it's been a day filled with drama and fiction that will far

outweigh the film itself. It's reached such a level that I'm beginning to believe I shot the projectionist! Who would believe that such headlines could be made from someone seeing a film...

15th February '81
Tonight I was sitting in the TV room when I was called out. The officer told me that Mr Hills wanted to see me. Walking up the passage I was nervous, wondering what he wanted to see me about; in that short walk my fantasies ran wild; it could be something wrong with Sarah, bad news about my future release... Whatever, I prepared myself.

On going into the Assistant Governor's room he – Mr Hills – was taking off his watch and placing it on the desk in front of him. He told me I could walk out if I wanted to. He said he was looking for my help as tomorrow he was going to the preview of this film with a panel of people and would like to talk it over with me. He seemed extremely nervous and edgy. It must have taken a lot for him to see me.

He then told me he was angry at Isaacs stopping the film where he had, why had he done this if he was supposed to be a friend? It would have made his job tomorrow easier if they had shown more of what came after, he said. He thought Jeremy Isaacs was just stirring it up. I told him I doubted this very much and that if he himself wasn't so defensive about it then it wouldn't be so bad. Mr Hills then went on to declare that the penal system does do good. I told him if he wanted to get specific about this then just outside the door all his staff were clustered in a cell-like office and prisoners were in their cells, that they all had one thing in common – boredom. I reminded him that this was the best that Edinburgh as a Training Prison had to offer. He readily agreed to this, accepting it as true.

We then had a discussion on the penal system and I told him that every time someone from officialdom talks about it they rarely make constructive criticism. I said it's the same old repetitive stuff.

All of this was extremely puzzling to me but one thing's for sure, Mr Hills is nervous about tomorrow.

18th February '81

My Darling Sarah,
  Well, I'll give you reactions I've had from the film. Two prison

officers said they thought it was a really good movie, one recommending it to win an award, the other saying he was surprised the time passed so quickly. Another was witty, 'Going through all that when all you wanted was a knife to open your parcel'. Those who spoke openly to me about it suggested mixed reactions amongst the other staff, something that is inevitable.

19th February '81

My Darling Sarah,
 It was tremendous to get your letter today reading your account of things. I've been getting some mixed feedback on the discussion programme last night. It seems to have been a disappointment. The favourable comments reserved for Wattie's contributions. I understand Mr Hills kept a low profile.

20th February '81

This morning Mr Hills sent for me. I went in front of him and his Deputy Governor and was told I'd be resuming my two days at Wester Hailes, starting on Tuesday. He warned that one more slip and it would be taken away from me altogether. He said he would put it straight to the Prisons Department and Secretary of State.

24th February '81

Acclimatising to the outside world is becoming increasingly difficult as time goes on and I enter new areas. I feel very guarded and defensive and at the same time I'm putting up a front. It's difficult to explain this as it's all so complex and multi-layered. I went for a walk with Laurence this morning and explained some of what was going on. I now fully recognise that one can't be locked in a closed institution and not feel to the full what I'm experiencing now.

 When I'm with people on the outside I'm tense, feeling as though my guts are tied in a knot. The people around me are what I believe to be the very ordinary, salt-of-the-earth kind that I come from. They aren't armchair revolutionaries but simply people who have got off their arses and done something about their particular area and are working together to improve it.

17th April '81

Dear Mr Harper, (my lawyer)
   Thank you for your letter of 6th February ref; *JRH/RP* regarding your client Mr James Boyle and comments that I am reported as having made regarding Mr Boyle when he was an inmate in the Barlinnie Special Unit. . .
   Dealing first of all with the reported quotes to the effect that Mr Boyle 'ran' Barlinnie Special Unit and that he attempted to deny the entry to the Unit of another 'hard man'. I have twice since the report of my speech made it quite clear that I said neither of these things.
   What I said was that 'Boyle has a strong personality and in any small group, whether it be a small class at school, a small political group or as in this case a small group of prisoners it was relatively easy for that strong personality to manifest itself'.
   That statement was made in the context of an argument being advanced in my speech that the Unit was too small and ought to be made bigger and it was in the same context that I related the story of the prisoner (who I did not name) who was transferred to the Unit and because of an incident had to be sent back to his original prison.
   Never at any time did I say that Boyle attempted to prevent the man being brought to the Unit in the first place and indeed I was aware that the Unit as a whole had made representations to have the man kept in the Unit even after the incident to which I refer.
   In this part of my address I was arguing that had the Unit been larger with more prisoners, say up to fifteen, the possibility of two men coming into conflict is reduced because of the number of other men with whom the other prisoner may enjoy more in common.
   As I indicated at the beginning of my letter I have dealt with this twice already, once on Radio Clyde in the presence of Mrs Boyle who agreed that Mr Boyle had a strong personality and the other occasion when I clarified this matter on the STV programme the evening after the screening of A Sense of Freedom.
   I do hope that both points are now fully cleared up.
   Turning to the reported statement to the effect that Mr Boyle had made a bust of Nicholas Fairbairn in appreciation of defending him. I have to tell you that the first part of the report is correct, i.e., 'that Mr Boyle made a bust of Nicholas Fairbairn', but the second part is not correct and is again a case of a reporter combining two entirely different parts of my address. When it was pointed out to me by Mrs Boyle that Mr Boyle had not in fact made a bust of Mr Fairbairn I

immediately apologised and asked her personally to convey my apologies to her husband.

I again in response to your letter make it clear that I accept that the bust I saw when I visited the Unit on one of my visits was not in fact that of Mr Fairbairn and I again apologise for any embarrassment this may have caused Mr Boyle. . .'

25th April '81

After my run round the football field today I spoke to Jinksy, a lifer just four years into his sentence. He is seeing the prison psychiatrist. Jinksy told me he's read a magazine giving schizophrenic symptoms and told me that every one of them fit him to a 'T'. I told him he is at a critical stage in his sentence and it could be this. He said it isn't this. He went on to tell me how Sarah is brainy and how he would like to write out what he is feeling for me to give her. He said he could answer any questions Sarah wrote out and he would do this truthfully. He said he doesn't want to go to the doctor here as he can't stand marching in and trying to talk while standing to attention. He is also afraid of getting largactil and other crappy drugs.

7th May '81

This morning when walking through 'B' Hall on my way to the reception to go out to Wester Hailes I met Jinksy. He was standing in the toilet area stripped to the waist. He told me not to contact his parents to say he cut his wrists. He had sent word through with another prisoner asking me to do this. I asked him how he felt, realising that it would be difficult for him to 'save face'. His right wrist was badly cut with two lines of stitches. Clearly he had made a serious attempt. I left him with the words, 'Stay strong, fight it'.

I met a Principal Officer who told me he had been to see Jinksy* (earlier in the week I had spoken to him about Jinksy asking if he would recommend him for the Special Unit). He told me Jinksy would be returned to his old Hall. He said he doubts if he will be put on a disciplinary report as they intend to waive this incident. I was puzzled at this and asked what he meant. He told me that anyone doing this is usually charged with causing self-inflicted wounds.

There are moments in here when thinking makes me shudder!

*Jinksy eventually hanged himself in his cell.

9th May '81

I have a shower then lie on top of my bed till 2pm. A voice shouts 'Visits'. Going down to the Hall desk I join others.

Two of us are taken along the corridor to the other side of the prison. We sit in a small side room. There are eleven prisoners in all. Looking round their faces there is tension as some wonder if their visitors will come. If they don't it usually means having to trudge back along the corridor – a humiliating experience. It means having to make excuses to their escort and prisoner mates as to why their visitor didn't turn up. A member of staff comes to the door with visiting slips in his hand and calls out the names. I am first and walk to the door to be searched. I walk into the visit room with my jacket on my arm. The room is vast with tables and chairs spread over it. Prison officers stand against the wall watching. I see Sarah sitting at one of the tables and walk over. My stomach is churning and I want privacy. I lean over and kiss her. 'Happy Birthday,' she says. Sitting at the table we hold hands tightly and look at each other. We talk about this and that, we look, smile, occasionally kiss. . .

Around us prisoners sit with their families. Children race all over the room with toys. . .

A voice shouts 'Time up' after an hour. This is hard and yet it is a relief. We embrace and tell each other of our love. We hug each other tightly before parting. We trudge back along the corridor after yet another search. Sunlight streams through gaps in the enclosed space. I think of Sarah entering her car in the car park. I look around me and feel like weeping.

24th June '81

I was sitting speaking to young Robert this morning. He talked about being home on an SEL. He was in a terrible state and shattered by it. I asked him why this was. He replied that he felt so distant from his family and finds it difficult to speak to them. We talked about him being away from them for five and a half years and how it will never be the same again. He was filled with anger and resentment.

He said he had befriended a guy in prison and he was at his house when he went home. He said he had more in common with this guy than with his family. We talked about this and what prison does to people. In the afternoon Robert came in looking much better. He said the talk we had this morning had done him a power of good... No one at an official level tries to help these guys understand what they are going to come up against at a domestic and social level when released. No wonder many of them fall at the first hurdle.

28th June '81
Big Humph, a prisoner, approached me this evening. He wants to see the Inspector of Prisons to lodge a complaint. He was scheduled to go on his SEL two weeks ago but it was cancelled. I asked him why.

He said on the Hall Notice Board it states that prisoners going on SELs must save £1 from their weekly prison earnings and have it transferred to their personal cash property before going. The night before his SEL he was informed that he was twenty-six pence short. He told the officer that he had this much credit on his wages card so would he transfer it. He was told it was too late. As a result his family expecting him home the following day were disappointed. No one informed them.

10th July '81
(Stolen time): This is my first summer in open space for fourteen years. Leaving the prison in the morning I walked along a small lane. Birds were singing and chirping but the thickness of the greenery amazed me. I've walked this path in the winter when it's bare but the change of seasons has put splendid clothes on it.

Today I went right out into the country and seaside. Sarah was with me and so it was lovely sharing this experience together. The sun shone brightly in North Berwick. Again, the rolling laid-back countryside was stunning. It seemed to go on forever. On a quiet beach I undressed putting on my swimming trunks and like a puppy rushed into the water. It was cold, very cold. Sarah watched, laughing. I waded in smelling the tang of the salt, feeling the hardness of the water, the softness of the sand. I plunged into the shallows. Only the icy water could have matched the intensity of my feelings I had to be as extreme as the experience.

Together we ran across the sand leaving our footprints embedded. Sarah found a jellyfish. We watched as the waves lapped it further on to the beach. My first jellyfish in fourteen years. He was no ordinary jellyfish, he was special! Together we walked to a point in the distance, a soft green downy part that allowed us to lie down. Sarah snuggled up to me, we kissed, we embraced and looked into the distance as the sun cast a beautiful light on the water. It was so peaceful.

To think that all of this will be accessible to me in the freedom of my lifetime, to imagine the rest of my life looking at this natural beauty.

12th July '81

The guy who smashed his cell furniture the other week didn't do it as a result of a direct domestic problem. This is what I first heard. Having probed to find out why, as he seemed such a stable guy, I was informed he wasn't right after his SEL. Apparently he has told guys close to him that being out was a pure 'wind up'. Like most guys he went out with the expectation that all would be well once he was back with his family. In fact it hit him like a ton of bricks that he had changed. He had been living on memories of all those years, keeping it alive, reminding himself what it was before he came in, but time had passed.

Now, having heard this a few times I've brought the subject up with a few guys and am surprised to find quite a lot aren't taking SELs even though they have been eligible for years. I asked why and they all reply that it means going round having to ask screws only to be rejected; and then going home for a few hours. They couldn't handle this they said. It would be too much for them. This flies in the face of the assumption that guys will do anything to get out of prison for a few hours.

Another guy went home on his SEL last week to find that his family didn't come to meet him. This was a bitter disappointment. The member of staff took him for a meal.

The pain that is locked up in this building where I sit can be felt. Behind each cell door is someone aching like an open wound. Each is just a human being needing to be treated as such. This dinosaur of a system is tearing them apart emotionally. What do I mean by this?

I can perhaps illustrate this by giving insight to my feelings at this moment. I have this tight knotted feeling in my stomach, this jealousy in my heart that my wife is with someone else. I pick up small things said during the week and let them magnify out of all proportion in here. I know that when out during the week and stealing time with her she will alleviate these feelings in me. We will have the good fortune of being able to talk about it. The reason I feel this is because sitting here locked in this cell I feel totally devalued. I therefore wonder why anyone could possibly love me or stay with me. It strikes at the very root of my potency. I want to be with her badly but can't. So, I distort this feeling of wanting to be with her on to her wanting to be with me and seeking a substitute. It is completely irrational but stems from being locked in this small cell with my thoughts. What I have that the others don't is the ability to articulate it, to write it out and to meet Sarah mid-week. They don't and it is for these reasons that guys smash up their cells, explode violently, attempt to succeed in suicide.

14th July '81
Arriving back in prison tonight after my day at Wester Hailes, the duty Chief Officer was waiting at the gate. He told me the stepfather of my son called to say James is causing problems – not serious – but was about to be put into a place of care.

He said that normally he wouldn't tell someone news like this at this time of night but I'm a pretty level-headed type and he knows I can cope with it. He spoke to the Assistant Governor who told him I have access to a phone at my work so can phone from there tomorrow.

16th July '81
This morning I called John, my son's stepfather. He explained to me that James is going from bad to worse, that he is glue-sniffing and lately he's had to be carried home suspected of taking heroin. He is only fifteen years old. He said police suspected this and know that heroin is being 'pushed' from the local community centre in the Gorbals and that lots of young girls are taking it.

John said the situation has reached a critical stage and he would like to talk to me about it and we agreed to meet. He came to Edinburgh. One of the problems is that James is put on a pedestal because he is my son. His pals treat him as a hard man but he isn't. All James really knows about me is what he reads, hears and sees in the film. He's really confused as to who and what his father is. The social worker, his mother, and John all agree that I am the only hope for the boy. John wanted to give James over to me this afternoon but I had to explain my circumstances.

18th July '81
The Governor and his Assistant are not at all happy about the

situation concerning James. It is clear they don't want me participating extensively in helping the boy. They have stated that I cannot assume any responsibility for the boy in my present situation. Also, that my access to him must be very limited. All of us are quite shocked at this. . . I hate being in a position where I have to ask them. I made this clear to them.

25th October '81
This morning the clocks were turned back to signify the end of summertime. For some it meant an extra hour in bed. For me it was an extra hour pacing the floor.

Although I still have a year to go in prison this is my last night locked in a traditional cell. Tomorrow I will be allowed five days Home Leave and then go on to what is officially called Training For Freedom. Moving from this rigid penal system I go to a more relaxed setting. However, I am realistic enough to know it is a continuance of my futile confinement. What is momentous is my having five days away with Sarah.

When I wakened the cell was dark. Getting out of bed I put on my trousers and looked out of the window. Frost covered the grass outside. It was cold. I walked up and down the floor. Pacing this floor I carried – wrapped in this body of mine – a messy paradox of human emotion. On the one hand there is the pleasure-filled adrenalin of expectation of being outside, on the other there is a fearful anxiety about a last-minute hitch preventing it. Even with barely twenty-four hours to go I raise the wearying question, 'Am I ever going to make it?'

Walking in this space I told myself it was coming to an end. There are two hours till this door is unlocked. Being in this space means I don't have the basic freedom to switch off the light, go to the toilet, or have a drink of fresh water. After today all of this will be changed. With this perspective I can't help but get vivid images of tomorrow night when tasting freedom with Sarah. I will be able to go for a walk, shop, switch on the TV, walk in the rain, open the door and go into the street. . . As though to act as a balance part of me intrudes to remind me not to be too confident as nothing has happened yet.

I am so distrustful of the authorities. I feel there is still a chance they may want to get back at me. I know they don't like the way I have challenged the system. They don't like to see me leaving a winner. At the same time I don't want to dwell on these negative feelings; I've had enough of those in my lifetime. With these powerful emotions in my mind and body I am having to ease the see-sawing of their movements; and yet I know there is a part of me colluding with this. There is a part of me wanting to experience all the emotional trauma of this situation so that I have *lived* it. This moment in time has been a long time coming so I want to taste it to the full – the good and the bad.

26th October '81
Stepping across the gate into Sarah's arms. We embrace and kiss. So lovely to touch in legitimate time. We waste no time jumping in the car and heading into the distance.

Accumulated thoughts: I am wondering what it will be like to sleep together, having known each other for four years and been married almost two. Up the long winding roads the scenery was spectacular. Sitting there with Sarah at my side, the prison far behind and the wonders of the Scottish Highlands all around me I felt stunned with pleasure. . . How can I possibly explain this experience to anyone after fourteen years in prison. Every fibre was open and alert to this vast mountain scenery. Finally we reached our caravan situated high up on the hillside with a wide and full view of the valley. It was getting quite dark though still enough light for us to see our view from the caravan. Sheep were all around us. We looked down the valley to a spattering of cottages and farmhouses. The visual images are overwhelming. The night was spent in a small double bed with me always aware of Sarah next to me. I was restless. It will take some getting used to after fourteen years of sleeping alone. . . It's the first time in years I've slept on a mattress.

27th October '81
Here we are with each other throughout the day and seeing each other as we waken in the morning. It's gonna take some time for us to adjust to . . . mind you we made the most of it.

Outside I am greeted by snow-capped mountains, jagged skylines and paintbox splashes of Autumn colouring. Nearby there are rushing streams and rivers. . . As I write this I'm still tired and not really able to express fully all the thoughts and feelings which were racing through me all night. This freedom is so precious that I'm scared to sleep in case I miss any of it. I was full of stresses and strains from the sudden change in my situation.

29th October '81
In the morning I was up early and out exploring the landscape with all my senses. Sarah by my side was monitoring a stable influence and steady hand to my almost uncontrollable desire for more. It was thrilling to stand in the silent morning and look to the distance without any man-made structure obstructing the view as in prison. The ever-changing light here is so dramatic; one can imagine any aspiring film technician being inspired by nature's ability to create the most powerful theatrical setting in this landscape.

There are moments when Sarah and I speak but lots of the time is spent in silence, in just being with each other.

30th October '81
Sarah brought me to the prison gate and we parted. . . I was swallowed up by the surrounding wall. Back in here again, it felt as though I had never been away. This place has a way of crushing one's good feelings. The Training For Freedom hostel is secluded in a corner of the prison. On entering the voice shouted, 'Boyle for TFF'. I walked to a small door that was opened by a uniformed prison officer. He escorted me to the small building. He is the duty officer and has a colleague who shares hostel duty with him.

He tells me the Governor has left orders that I've to remain in the prison till such times as I start my work on Monday. He apologises saying he would have let me out on the three hours church parole on Sunday but for some reason the Governor has stated that I've not to go out. In taking my particulars I told him that come Monday I start a community job at Wester Hailes and will be employed by them. He informs me that I will have to bring my weekly wage to him or his colleague who will give me weekly expenses and £3 pocket money. Another £3 will go into my savings for release.

He tells me that each week I'll be given twelve hours free time and every third weekend I'll get forty-eight hours home leave. Each Sunday morning we get three hours Church parole!

Upstairs, blazoned in red print behind the door, was a notice warning all prisoners not to drink alcohol when out on parole. It says this will be considered a breach of the hostel rules and liable to punishment.

Some of the other guys come to greet me. I know them from the old system. They show me to my bed in a dormitory. It is filthy. There are approximately twelve beds. We sit speaking and they tell me what a dump it is. One describes this particular part of the sentence as 'running the gauntlet'. He expands on this saying that if a few minutes late on returning, or smelling of drink, you get thrown in the punishment cells. He described one occasion when it happened to him. He arrived back after a couple of pints but took some mints to cover the smell. They took him to the prison medical officer to verify he had been drinking. He said he hasn't had as much as a wine gum. They took him to the punishment cells and kept him there overnight. In the morning he went before the Governor and was found guilty. They told me how on occasions they've been in a pub and a prison officer has walked in and they've all ducked under the table. One said if any of them are with a girl it is embarrassing.

When talking about their work, one or two described how the prison is tied to two industries, the Fruitmarket, which those working there describe as 'brutal exploitation' and another place where guys do some painting which is considered okay. They say that I am fortunate to be working in the Community. There is another guy doing similar work and one other working in a hospital.

They get their food from the main prison kitchen. They can bring in odd bits and pieces. One of the guys took me to his room. I asked him about this and he informed me that one gets promoted to one of these six small rooms from the dormitory. The door is left unlocked but there is a heavy grill on the window. He told me we can all sit in a small room watching TV and have an electric kettle to make coffee and tea. We are locked in this second floor together from 9.30pm to the following morning.

2nd November '81
First day out from TFF but wasn't allowed out till 9.45am. It's great to see everyone again. They all wanted to know how the five days went. I could tell they were very pleased for us. We have made so many good friends here that it's magic to be back with them. In a way they are our point of sanity with this system we are having to deal with. I spent the day putting myself about, particularly among the younger people. Now that I have more time I can connect with them at a deeper level.

16th November '81

This morning I was taken from the hostel to the social work unit in the prison. The social worker sat as though not knowing what to do. It soon became apparent that he had no papers or anything on me. I explained to him how this is the first social worker I've had in fourteen years. He said this is most unusual as one normally gets a social work report when the Parole Application is being compiled, and that contact is essential when someone is going on to TFF. He said how difficult it will be to get a social worker who can cope with me on a supervisory basis. I asked him the procedure for selecting one. He said it's a team decision in the Office catchment area where my home is. I told him that I hoped they picked someone reasonable as an idiot would be pointless. He said perhaps I could bring an idiot on.

23rd November '81

This morning the social worker came across again. He informed me that he has passed my request for a social worker on to my local office. He said they feel it is a long way off therefore will take some time. I said it was immaterial to me. He's a rather placid guy and carries keys to lock and unlock doors. In many ways he seems like a prison officer, the better type perhaps. I find this sort of meeting has little value. There is a piece in *The Scotsman* quoting the prison governor, Mr Hills: 'While people must be controlled in custody they must also be given the freedom to respond and to be treated decently. To achieve that state of affairs, a prison must demonstrate a reasonable justice, recognise the formal rights of a prisoner, and have contact with and be involved with the community.'

5th December '81

On returning from work this afternoon I met with the prison officer on duty. He said I may be in trouble. I asked what for and he replied that I shouldn't be working on a Saturday. He walked me to the Governor's office telling me to keep my cool.

The Training Governor was with an assistant governor. The former asked what I was doing working on a Saturday? I asked what he meant as I've been working every Saturday morning since coming on to TFF. He then told me my maximum hours of work are fifty per week. He said I have to work within these hours. He said he has been on to Mr Hills, who has instructed that I haven't to go out. I reminded him that I have twelve hours free time and have arranged to meet my wife shortly.

He said it has been specifically laid down that I don't work at the weekends. I told him that I haven't been told this and pulled out my licence:

1) You will obey such instructions as you may receive from the Governor with regard to the hours which you may be absent from the prison each day: *09.45 hrs – 21.00 hrs.*

I was asked to leave the room, the prison officer escorting me to do likewise. Some minutes later I was called back in and told that Mr Hills has instructed (on the phone from his home) that I write in my own handwriting what I thought my working hours to be. He also instructed that I won't be going anywhere till my employer is contacted.

I wrote:

Dear Sir,
The agreement in which I was out was as per Parole Licence. The licence states that I will be absent from the prison each day: 09.45 hrs. – 21.00 hrs. I have been asked to write this statement and I have no idea what I am really expected to write.

J. Boyle

On returning to the Governor's office the Training Governor told me I will get my twelve hours this weekend but I won't be going to work on Monday or Tuesday till this matter is cleared up.

I spoke to the duty hostel officer who told me the whole thing is being blown out of all proportion because it is Jimmy Boyle. He said some of the other prisoners are going out in hours far in excess of mine. He told me of one of the guys who is going off to Celtic Park today and is off somewhere else tomorrow. He said the staff he has spoken to are saying that I have been pretty good, causing no problems for them.

We talked for a bit and he said he's read my history on file, that the early years were bad but in the past ten years I have been faultless. He said one of the problems about here is that the Governor is insisting that I am the same as any other prisoner when I'm not. He notices this with basic Parole Forms as mine are more restrictive than everyone else's. I have a different one from everyone else in the hostel.

10th December '81
There's been considerable upheaval over the Xmas leave for us all on TFF. I was told the dates had come through 24th – 27th Dec. This is only four days whereas in other hostels it's five days. We were informed that all paroles stop between 1st – 4th January. There are no local paroles either (twelve hours are local paroles). I said the rules in this place could be sold as antiques.

We intend taking the matter to the Visiting Committee.

15th December '81
This morning the prison officer told me the Training Governor wanted to see me, and then Mr Hills would see me. I was to stay in from work.

The passman (cleaner) prisoner told me that the Training Governor was upset at me yesterday. When doing his inspection of the Hostel he noticed some pennies and a broken watch on top of my locker and stated I shouldn't be leaving 'valuables' lying around. I counted the pennies; they amounted to 37 pence. The watch was valued at four quid! Surely this isn't why he wants to see me?

Another prisoner informed me that my Trust Fund (set up through royalties from *A Sense of Freedom*) was on TV last night. It gave a good account of the people who have benefited from it. I was pleased to hear this.

By 11am I was an hour late for work and asked the prison officer when the Governors were going to see me. He went to the phone and returned embarrassed saying: a) The Training Governor isn't on duty today and b) Mr Hills has left. The staff member remarked, 'They couldn't organise a piss up in a brewery'.

19th December '81
This morning I sat waiting for the Governor to see me. All the while I was conscious of a drug meeting I had to organise in the community. I sat around till 10.45am, got my jacket and asked a prison officer painting the hostel to let me out. The duty hostel officer came in then. He said the Training Governor has instructed that I stay in till he completes the Governor's Orderly Room. I asked the officer to phone my work and say I won't make the meeting. I sat till 11.40am and was taken to the Governor's office. The Training Governor said Mr Hills wasn't present but he under-

stood I had asked to see him. I stood there feeling extremely angry. There is no sensitivity to the work I am doing outside or the people waiting for me there. This is nothing but gross discourtesy and completely irresponsible.

Putting my best face on I explained yes, I wanted to ask why our Christmas leave had been cut from five to three days. The Training Governor was quite friendly in his attitude saying he doesn't understand why it is so restricted. He asked the duty hostel officer who said it is normal procedure. I explained to him how in Perth Prison the hostel people there are getting from the 24th – 28th. On top of this our local twelve hours parole is restricted from 30th Dec. to 4th Jan. He said he would take it up with Mr Hills. He said he personally thinks it absurd. He mentioned Northern Ireland saying people get out all the time over this period.

22nd December '81
The Assistant Governor has been over seeing the guys individually to tell them they can have their Christmas leave extended to the 29th if they want. It will mean bringing one of their forty-eight paroles forward. I told him I would take it but it is disgraceful we have to use our ordinary paroles to make up the extension.

24th December '81
This morning started with me writing a petition to the Secretary of State for Scotland to complain about the shortage of Christmas leave for prisoners on the TFF. I have asked that the Inspector of Prisons review the situation in the hostel as there seems some confusion as to whether it is a hostel or part of the prison. When I returned to the prison after work the duty officer was disagreeing about the time on our licences. It stated 2pm and he thought it should be 3.30pm. We all felt like tearing his head off. He kept us to the last minute before signing it. I queried mine which said I should return at 6pm on the 27th instead of the 29th. He said I would have to stay back while he checked it with the Governor. This further enraged the prisoners who thought he was 'winding me up'.

Still dressed in my working clothes I walked into the rain wearing my wellies. Sarah was there with Laurence. He drove us to the airport and we flew to London. Heathrow is magic, all nationalities melting into this one pot. The weather here isn't so bad so I look out of place in my wellies. My freedom is such that this means nothing to me.

We arrive and go to Peter McDougall's... Jeremy, John McKenzie, some actors and actresses are there... It's great. We celebrate the coming of Christmas. Sarah and I go off to St Martin-in-the-Fields in Trafalgar Square for mass. The singing and spirit of Christmas is soaking into me. My first one on the outside...

Christmas Day '81
The spiritual quality of the night before combined with waking beside Sarah gave this Christmas morning a very special imprint. Sleepily we smiled and kissed each other. Our being together at nights still doesn't have natural fluency simply because we are in an on/off situation. This didn't detract from what we felt now.

Both of us got dressed, made breakfast then sat with our presents and some champagne. We toasted this special day. If I had a dream it would be this moment in freedom with Sarah.

Opening our gifts was such fun. I had some lovely presents; a jumper, some books and a lovely collage of us. Sarah was equally delighted with her presents from me.

We visited her Dad, who greeted us with warm hugs and kisses. He said to me, 'At long last we've met.' This is something both of us were looking forward to. The atmosphere in the house couldn't have been better. His wit and intellect were sharp, his recall quite amazing. He did not look a man of seventy-eight. I remember this man from every time I went to the movies. As film censor, his name would be scribbled on the certificate.

1st January '82
I sat with George in his small room in the hostel. He completes his life sentence in July. He spoke with strong anger and conviction when he said he couldn't do to anyone what the authorities have done to him; put him away for all these years for something he did when only a sixteen-year-old boy. Although he couldn't articulate this too well he was in effect saying that society allows people to live in sub-standard conditions. In doing so they have to live by a different set of values from the more affluent sections. But when kids like George get caught up in gangs and someone dies as in George's case then the full weight of the authorities falls on him. The same authorities turn a blind eye to all the other equally horrific problems of his lifestyle which are not labelled

'criminal'. This is the world he was born into. There is a burning resentment in him as he speaks.

During our conversation he remarked that both of us have done our time differently. He tells me he has played the system and never got on the wrong side of the screws or Governors. He doesn't mind falling out with the odd screw but not anyone higher up as that could harm his chances of freedom. He said that I have beaten the system by taking them on and he loves this.

George began to open up and tell me ways that he has beaten them. He explained how as a young offender they were allowed parcels at Christmas time. On his way out of the Xmas visit with his parcel he stuck a lump of cannabis under his tongue and when reaching the screws the junior looked to the senior to ask if he should search. The senior replied, 'It's only wee George and he's okay; let him through.'

George pointed to a small bottle of aftershave on his table and explained to me that when returning to the prison tonight he stole it out of a drunk man's pocket. He says he knows he is taking a risk and that his freedom is at stake but he wants to tell himself that they haven't changed him. He talked about his work at a local hospital and resents the fact that the Governor has initiated this to make a name for himself as a liberal humanitarian. George says this is all part of the prison game. He said when the Governor is mentioned it's always in a good light. George says they should judge him on what is happening on the inside.

Another prisoner joined us. We continued this dialogue and it was good. The bells rang us into 1982. I kissed my marriage ring and silently wished Sarah a Happy New Year. The three of us wished each other all the best. I excused myself from them and sat reading a letter Sarah had given me to open at the New Year.

15th January '82
I returned to the prison tonight and spent some time speaking to George and another prisoner. We discussed the problems of adjusting to society after a long time away. Both of them agreed that the hostel is good in that it does give them a chance to sort themselves out although they both think that it should be done long before this.

They discuss the gap between them, their families and friends. They both talk at length and in some depth about the difficulties of adjusting to outside life and the particular frustration of having to deal with Governors who only see prisoners' problems in the context of them wanting extra hours outside.

25th January '82
The duty officer informed me that I must return to the prison at 3pm to go in front of the Visiting Committee. I lay thinking of the VC and decided if I go in with a heavy staff escort surrounding me then I will withdraw from the proceedings and take my case elsewhere. Another prisoner told me this happened to him recently.

When I got there I was made to stand outside the Governor's office. Wattie, a prisoner at my table when in C Hall, was surrounded by prison staff. He was waiting to go in. He looked pale and shaken. I remembered the last time I saw him he was full of tension waiting on a reply from the Parole Board. He has since slashed a prisoner for no apparent reason. He seemed to be in deep trouble now. He told me he is waiting to go to the High Court for it. I felt for him.

Another life prisoner came out from the Visiting Committee. He had been complaining about only being able to hand out three handicraft objects a year. He won and this was increased to six a year.

I walked in without an escort. Governor Hills sat at the top of the table with two male members of the Visiting Committee. A female member sat nearby. The Chief Officer was present.

I explained that I had written a petition asking the new Chief Inspector of Prisons to look into the Training For Freedom hostel. I was asking them to forward this on to him. I explained that I wanted him to look into the whole running of the TFF hostel, the social and employment matters. Mr Hills fumbled about in his desk for my original petition. He said he didn't have a copy. He stated that he understands the new Inspector of Prisons doesn't look into individual cases. I said there was absolutely nothing in the rule book about what this man does, therefore, I could only recall his original appointment and thought he said he would look into individual cases. Mr Hills again fumbled around looking for something on this man's brief. He stated that I could see the Departmental Inspector of Prisons. I said the significant difference between them was, my request was for the one who is 'independent'. It turned out that Mr Hills had nothing on this man's brief. The Chairman of the VC agreed that the Governor should get his information to him and he would let me know. . .

I returned to Wester Hailes and my work.

7th March '82
The weekend with Sarah has softened me. I feel warm and relaxed, my mind at ease with the world. The experience of being together, lying on the bed in each other's arms, the closeness, the love . . . ahh the love. Such beauty in our shared experience! All of this comes to an end as I return to prison. The gate with its studded bolts of rusted metal remind me of rotting teeth in a gaping mouth. The rancid stench, the fear, the acute pain of having to step over the threshold grips me like an iron fist. I walk into the darkness of its throat and feel as though I've been swallowed up. My being here has reduced the flame of our love.

A guard stands looking at me. His eyes are empty, his face expressionless. The neat black moustache sits stiffly on his tight, thin lips. No word is exchanged between us. He stretches a bony hand to take my licence. I walk past him and the door slams closed behind me. The crunch of the keys, the grating of metal grind into my eardrums. I feel a lump of defeat fall heavily within me. The flame, the flame of our love flickers to counter all that surrounds me.

Other prisoners are clustered in the television room. They are locked into it as television is a necessary drug to escape the present situation. I leave them to sit in my small cell. I will get through this experience, I will.

8th March '82
This morning I went down to go for my usual run around the small compound immediately surrounding the hostel. The duty officer informs me that as from today no hostel prisoner will be allowed outside this door unescorted. The reason for this is that the Chief Officer suspects drugs have been smuggled into the prison through the hostel. I explained that I appreciate their concern about drugs but I need my morning run. I reminded him that I abhor the use of drugs and feel that this restriction on the hostel prisoners is in no way going to prevent drugs getting into the prison. I also reminded him that my two years in the main prison have let me see how extensively drugs are used by prisoners. He acknowledged this saying in his experience this prison has been particularly bad for it over the past three or four years. He

then told me there are plans to secure our windows so drugs cannot be thrown over the wall to a nearby working party in the main prison. I told him that I find all of this pretty incredible and would like to see the Governor about it. There is no doubt that the drugs problem in the main prison has reached an alarming level.

10th March '82
Billy is the new prisoner. He has just come from five days Home Leave. He told me the five days blew his head. He said he has done some community work in Dungavel, in a Children's Home. He said unlike other prisoners he didn't have regular outside visitors and so had no idea what to expect outside.

He was thrown on to the streets with a tenner and hadn't a clue what to do, he could have been a raving loony for all they knew. He said they told him to report to Saughton and this hostel for TFF. He has never been in Edinburgh before; he comes from Glasgow.

27th March '82
The prisoner passman approached me to say that Billy is acting strange and resisting any friendliness. He mentioned Billy having been in Carstairs State Hospital and so maybe his behaviour is related to his 'illness'. I said I would have a chat with him as a few guys have mentioned this to me recently.

I approached Billy and asked how he was doing. I presented a very friendly face and was warm towards him. He was tight and remarked that he was okay. I asked if things were difficult and he replied he was okay. His wall of resistance was fighting off my wave of friendliness. He walked away not wanting to take it any further.

28th March '82 (12.30am)
I left the TV room shortly after 10pm to go to my bed. Billy followed me and asked to speak to me. He remarked very seriously that he knows what is going on in here and what we are doing to him. I said that I know he is going through a bad time. I invited him in to sit down and closed the door. He then told me his food is being tampered with and that he will cause trouble if it happens again. I couldn't quite believe my ears. I asked him to explain and he said he was in agony as someone had put something into

his food. He then told me that today he had seriously considered smashing a broken bottle into my face. I could see this guy was frighteningly disturbed. I looked him straight in the eyes and told him in a stern tone of voice not to think I'm a mug because I talk in gentle tones. He immediately pulled back from his frightening stance.

I then asked him what it was all about. Billy then told me everything has been going haywire since he arrived here. He said he was out for a drink on Wednesday and that night after he had eaten his food in the hostel he started sweating and feeling bad. He said it could only have been the food. He then told me that this was the same pattern as Perth, prior to his smashing a bottle into a screw's face. He said he had it all sussed out and as I was a very influential person I must know about it. He said today when I asked if he was having a hard time that this confirmed it. I then explained to him why I had done this. I told him I have done the same for others having problems here.

Billy said he walks to work in the morning with that bastard (another prisoner) so could blow him away no bother. He mentioned George as another little bastard and another prisoner. He said he thinks it is these three who are putting the passmen prisoners up to it. Billy said he could get a mob through to do anyone and he wouldn't need to lift a finger. I told him that I am not in the least impressed or intimidated by this talk. I said I really don't know him but that what he says makes me not want to trust him. He said he went through to Glasgow today and told his brother this. He drove him back through here and contacted an ex-prisoner.

The ex-prisoner told them I wouldn't do anything like that, 'Jimmy would rather do you a good turn than a bad one'. This is why he came to speak to me tonight. He said that he is going off his head in this place. I told him it's going to be very difficult for me to change his mind but I want to tell him that the other guys here are only interested in getting their time done and getting out. They are not into poisoning food. I told him they wouldn't even jeopardise their provisional release dates by complaining when the Governor cut short their Christmas leaves. So, there's no chance of them considering poisoning his food.

I asked him what had happened in Perth. He told me he got into conflict with a group of prisoners, 'the poison' he kept calling it. He said they kept 'winding him up' but when the screw did it he stuck the bottle in his face. Two detectives charged him and he was sent to Carstairs State Hospital without going to trial. He had served six and a half years of his sentence. The day after he was in Carstairs he felt great away from that 'poison in Perth'. The man in Carstairs stated he would like him to stay there a few years and as he is just starting a life sentence he will have some years to do anyway. Billy says he was quite happy to do this as it kept him away from the poison. He told me his brother will come to the prison tomorrow morning at church parole time with the ex-prisoner I know. He would like us all to have a talk and sort this thing out.

I told him that if we are going to talk then I have to be straight and tell him this is all in his head. I reminded him that prior to talking to me I was the one putting everyone else up to poisoning him. This has now shifted from me to the other three guys. Billy replied saying it must be one of them. I told him he should speak to them in the way he is to me. He was quick to reject this saying he would never speak to anyone about the food being tampered with. I reminded him that these guys only want to do their time and get out. He said that is all he wants to do. . .

The common denominator between the Perth incident and what he feels here is his taking drugs (in Perth) and drink here. He said he won't touch drink again and will see this never happens. If the food is tampered with after this then he will go for someone. I advised him to buy his own food as I don't eat here but not for the same reasons as him; after fourteen years of eating prison food I don't want another drop. I sat for over two hours with Billy and finally told him I was going to bed. He left. By the end of our conversation he became easier, laughing and so on, so I hope this has a good effect on him. Clearly, he benefited from speaking to someone. At the same time what emerged is that this guy is badly disturbed and showed to me quite definite signs of blowing up. I know that I will put a chair in front of my door just in case. I do not trust this guy. He kept saying he will not get caught if he strikes. By this I take it he will do it when people are in their beds. I will take personal precautions.

28th March '82 (7.43am)
I wakened from a tense sleep, looking at the chair against the door and immediately criticised myself for being selfish and perhaps melodramatic. The former because other guys slept open and

unknown of the danger of the troubled Billy in their midst. On thinking about the melodramatic part I consider this not to be the case. I can see Billy will be an unpredictable and dangerous quality.

Later:
On the church parole I walked with Billy, in front of the others, to where his brother's car sat. I asked them to move to a spot where we could watch for Sarah coming to pick me up, away from the prying eyes of the prison.

I spoke to them briefly saying Billy and I had a talk last night, mentioning his feelings, etc. I cautioned them on his paranoia saying the guys in the hostel wouldn't consider poisoning his food. I outlined to them the danger of Billy's condition and how there may be a guy come into the hostel who will react to his paranoia and though Billy may be the victor in that he'll physically beat the guy with the broken bottle, ultimately he will be the loser as he will do many more years inside. Surely he hasn't come this far in his sentence for this to happen? Billy asked pointedly why it is he feels better now. I replied its because he has had the opportunity to speak about it and not keep it pent-up in his own head. A problem shared is a problem halved.

Sarah came along and we hailed her. She turned her car to stop behind us. I left them to join her. The ex-prisoner followed us and with a straight face said the wee guy (Billy) is bonkers. . .

Sarah and I went for a walk in one of Edinburgh's natural walkways and discussed all of this. She thought it appalling that someone in Billy's condition should be left like this. Sarah said if there weren't so many complications she would write a letter to the medical side condemning them for this. She suggested that if Billy's behaviour deteriorates then I should speak to the prison psychiatrist. The complications referred to are related to Billy's release date as this would simply be taken away from him and only set him back further. We agreed that I give him some support meantime but monitor the situation very carefully.

29th March '82
This morning I did my exercises and was having a shower when the prison passman remarked that Billy was in a bad state. It seems he has made it known that people had better not mess him around or he will crash an iron bar over their heads. The passman

said he spoke to guys who were in Perth with Billy and they say he is much worse. The picture emerging is that everyone in the hostel is afraid that Billy will crack up while they are sleeping and do one of them an injury. The passman said he keeps a chair behind his door to prevent anyone getting in. The guys sleeping next to him in the dormitory are afraid. What is amazing here is that these guys despite their fears won't go to the authorities. They would rather live with Billy. It isn't that they are afraid of being caught 'grassing', simply that to do so would be to harm him – his provisional release date would be taken away from him. The authorities would react in a punitive and inhumane way and most know Billy wouldn't survive this.

I stood at the door waiting to get out at 10.30am as I had lots of work on. The only way I would get through it was on a well-disciplined schedule. The duty staff officer told me the Governor wanted to see me. Eventually I was called to the office and the Governor spoke to me. He said the police wanted to speak to me about two youngsters who had absconded from List 'D' School. He asked me about it. I informed him that two youngsters approached me led by one of their older brothers. I was told they had run away from this institution and they were looking for advice. I advised them to return and do their time. I thought that by running away they were leaving themselves open to further offences and court appearances. In my experience this usually led to Borstal and then prison. They agreed to return. I called the head of the School and he agreed to come and pick them up. I would have taken them to the meeting place with the head of the school myself but I had other commitments. The elder brother agreed to go with them.

Within a few minutes two uniformed policemen came in. The senior, a Chief Inspector, did most of the talking. He said depending on the way I answered his questions there was a possibility of charges being made against me. The charge being, harbouring two List 'D' absconders. He then told me that he understood I knew the whereabouts of the two youngsters and did from last Tuesday. I informed him of what I had told the Governor. The policeman then told me that the youngsters, including their brother, had become involved in a serious fight with the police resulting in injuries to his men. Apparently the police tried to arrest them at the place where they were meeting the head of the school and wouldn't believe them when they said they were handing themselves in. He asked if I had ever thought of calling the police and I told him no, not in order to deceive them but the head of the school was handling it.

The inspector in telling of the damage they have done to his men and police vehicles said he has known the brothers for four years and knows more about them than I ever could. He was rather dull and authoritarian with no understanding of the pressures on youngsters living in these areas. He did, however, accept my story. It was well supported by the head of the school.

31st March '82
This morning on leaving the hostel the duty officer mentioned Billy to me. He said he had spoken to him but that Billy expressed difficulty when out shopping. This seemed to alleviate the anxieties of the duty officer. He took the view that it is a difficult period of adjustment. I could suss that he was groping in my direction. I asked him why Billy had been sent to Carstairs. He said it was a fixation, more an obsession and persecution complex that others were trying to poison him. I remarked that Billy has stopped eating. The officer's face fell. He said with some trepidation, that he hopes it isn't returning again. He said the Assistant Governor had asked how Billy is doing.

Billy is now bringing in fish suppers to eat at night. He doesn't eat in the place. . .

My visit to the local children's hostel was the highlight of their day to most of the kids. A good percentage asked me if I knew their Dads either in Perth, Saughton or Peterhead Prisons. Their Dads or uncles all knew me and were good fighters. My heart goes out to these babes, what chance have they got in life. . .

16th April '82
This morning the talk in the hostel centred round two things: 1) George being seen in a pub last night. A prison officer saw him. George was taken aside by the duty officer on return and told next time he would be put in the solitary cells. 2) Another prisoner was given the sack at the Fruitmarket because of bad communications between the prison and his boss. The prison are going to try and get him reinstated.

26th April '82
This morning the senior social worker collected me from the TFF

hostel. We sat in his office. He said he didn't know why he had brought me across as he has nothing to tell me. I asked him if there had been any progress on getting me a social work supervisor yet? He replied that it is a bit soon yet and no one ever has one this soon. I told him this is inconsistent with the facts as other guys have theirs. He said this is true but normally for those having problems. . . He hoped that I would have one within the next month. I told him I don't want any last-minute hitches.

We then sat speaking in a stilted way. He asked me how I would handle the amount of publicity I'm likely to face when released. I told him that I have no fears. He said there would be good publicity but how would I handle it if someone wanted to have a go at me. I told him I didn't understand. He said some of my old enemies. I told him that I usually see some of my old friends when visiting my family in the Gorbals. To date they've tried to smother me in kindness.

I moved from this to talking about the TFF and why the Social Work Unit are not more involved there as some guys are really struggling. I knew I had hit a bull's eye with this. He readily acknowledged the failure in this area. He said the TFF Hostel is badly needing re-vamping as it is run on criteria that are long out of date and irrelevant to today's situation. He said he had to be careful about tackling this as 'they' would accuse him of 'airy fairy' ideas. He said change is slow in coming, citing the example of an assistant governor he knew who has twelve years in the system who said he never has enough time to tackle new issues. His work is basically geared to keeping the present rusting system going along. He said these guys are so swamped in other things that their priorities are other things. Innovation is low in their priority. I gave him another example of many assistant governors who had come into the Unit while working in Barlinnie main prison. They largely complained of being treated as glorified message boys and being given little responsibility.

He then talked about Mr Hills saying that most of his time is taken up in trying to educate the public about prisons and in making offenders more acceptable to the community. He said he can hardly fault this as it is a job needing to be done. I said the problem is that his energy is geared to this at the expense of the internal running of the prison. He agreed.

He said he would push to get me a social worker. I asked him what sort of restrictions are liable to be placed on me when released. He said they are standard and advised me to ask what the conditions of release would be around September. He said he didn't know whether I would have any special conditions and gave a wry smile. This smile is about his knowing they have already given me a special licence of conditions on TFF. I asked him what restrictions there would be on travel. He said they aren't too happy at ex-prisoners travelling overseas in case they cause diplomatic hassle. I looked at him saying this hardly applies to guys like me. Perhaps ex-President Nixon's men but not me as I am hardly known outside Scotland. He said I am very modest, that I am an international figure.

Listening to guys like him makes me want to puke. In all probability this guy looks on himself as pretty progressive whereas I see him as a wizened thirty-eight-year old bureaucrat upholding the system. He is the definition of social control in the long-running debate of Care/Control within social work. Back in the hostel I was told the Training Governor wanted to see me. . . I told him about the senior social worker and his statement about a social worker only being necessary at the end of my sentence. Both of them (escorting hostel officer) disagreed with this saying it's much better if I have a social worker early on. The Training Governor said a social worker would ideally be given prior to the five days home leave. The officer made a pertinent observation that I am the only one in the hostel without a social work supervisor.

5th May '82
The war between Britain and Argentina is beginning to result in high casualties. I want to record my feelings about this. First, I would prefer for there to be no conflict (military) whatsoever.

What I find interesting within me is that a strong part wants to see Britain being defeated and humiliated. Obviously this would result in a high loss of life. I am trying to be honest with what is going on inside me as this contradiction is difficult to work out. Perhaps it relates to my past, and the fact that the Junta is being accused of having no consideration for human rights in their country. Whilst this may be true there is this deep part of me that wants people to know that there is a gross negligence of human rights in this country. I think this is the thread of discontent in me. I am firmly behind Tony Benn and his supporters in their uncompromising stance to call a halt to the violence in the

South Atlantic. The thought of two right-wing leaders in Britain and Argentina clinging to their political lives by sending people to be killed is nauseating. Equally, to see the saturation coverage the media is spouting on a KILL, KILL, KILL basis is nauseating. At this moment of writing I have the vivid image of young boys in their teens now reduced to dead bodies and thrown about by the heaving seas with no future left. They are but memories to their relatives, cut off from their future prematurely. In thinking about the conflict I am forcing myself to look at the personal side of it in this way. I don't want to be told through the lifeless monotone of a Ministry of Defence spokesman who sits there devoid of all emotion, sombre in his account of the affair, all of which is calculated to reduce public reaction. I want to lower myself into the freezing cold water and feel the reality of these young lives; dying, so we are told, in a cause of principle.

There can be no victors in this affair now that a life has been lost. The fact that hundreds have been killed renders it a tragedy without due cause or reason. I want to register my protest at this war and say that I condemn it, totally and unequivocally.

17th May '82
This morning George returned from a few days' leave to visit his dying father in Crewe. We talked about it. He said his father is near to death and all the family are down there with him. George described moments when at the bedside he humorously told his father to hold on for two weeks till he is out. George said he has always dreaded losing someone when he is in prison. It hasn't happened yet. The prison authorities have told him he can have another few days at his father's bedside. George said he approached the Governor to ask the Parole Board to release him two weeks early but the Governor refused.

At the Quarry hut (where I work) I watched two young guys play pool. We talked about Argentina. One was filled with exultation as he watched the news on the TV. He talked with full anger and conviction saying we should blow these Argie bastards out of the island. He said we have the power to crush these bastards and should do so. Heatedly he remarked that he would go and fight in a minute. On this issue he was excessively patriotic. He told me he would vote for Margaret Thatcher now as she is the right leader to deal with this. He called Labour a bunch of weak bastards as they want to talk and bring back the Task Force.

This youngster said he keeps all the newspaper clippings on the war and videotapes all the TV items on it. He said any soldier or military man must expect to die if he joins up. He repeated that he would join to fight for his country. He said this is the greatest thing ever to happen in his lifetime as it has brought everybody together to fight these bastards.

This is the frightening part of this situation. I meet so many like him. The anger and aggression in his voice is frightening. Ironically, his present situation is terrible. Along with his imprisonment, his wife and child have been thrown out of the house. They are virtually homeless. I find it difficult to comprehend that this young guy talks so patriotically about his country and the need to fight and die for it when it can't even provide him with the basic protection for his wife and child – a roof over their heads. As though to reinforce the distorted influences in his life, although homeless, he has a TV and video recorder which is a pretty expensive commodity!

18th May '82
. . . This morning I was introduced to my social work supervisor.

19th May '82
On going into the hostel kitchen two new instructions were on the wall 'No unauthorised cooking allowed' and 'All meals must be eaten in the dining hall'. . .

21st May '82
Wattie, who previously worked in the Fruitmarket and was subsequently sacked when the prison dentist kept him back from work for dental treatment, is still unemployed. The prison admits negligence in not informing the Fruitmarket, which means no blame can be laid at the feet of Wattie.

However, the duty officers in the hostel are far from happy at him hanging around all day. No one has approached him to ask about another job or would consider letting him go out and search for one. In fact, noises are being made that he be taken back to 'closed conditions'. In response to this Wattie is saying he doesn't care what happens so long as 'they' don't touch his release date.

Last week he was growing a beard and had a few days' growth. The duty officer told him to get it off as he hasn't had permission from the Governor to grow one. Wattie said he was thinking of taking it off anyway. He said this rather than confront the officer knowing that it is deliberate pressure being put on him.

23rd May '82
On entering the prison gates tonight I was taken aside by the Assistant Governor who then walked with me to the hostel. He informed me that there had been some trouble in the hostel as money had been stolen and staff were in searching the place. They have left my cell closed till I returned from local parole leave. He said if the money is found in my cell I won't be in trouble as it was stolen during the period I was out. At this point I thought one of the prisoners had their money stolen.

On entering the hostel all the prisoners were congregated in the kitchen area while staff searched. One of them told me that all the prisoners' expenses – £150, had been stolen from the office.

When the prisoners were together I made my views clear by stating that whoever did it must be a nutcase, putting his life on the line for a measly £150. Also that it will mean a severe tightening up of the place and perhaps someone being made a scapegoat. The worrying thing is that some staff are going round saying 'the party is over'. They are clearly implying there will be repercussions. When on our own some of the prisoners stated that it was great that someone had done the bastards. I broke this vicious circle of hate breeding hate by letting them know that some innocent person could fall victim to a retaliatory measure. Some of the guys found the strength to give alternative views. Others, of course, carried on with their anti-authority hatred.

24th May '82
One of the guys told me that staff found two knives when searching the hostel for the stolen cash. This has raised lots of anxiety in the place. Those prisoners in the hostel, when it went missing, have been kept off work. The Governor came in and spoke to them saying that investigations are continuing and they will be kept in till such time as they are cleared. Most of them suss they will get out tomorrow.

What worries me is that Billy is now back eating prison food as he is one of those being kept in. . .

25th May '82
Tonight I spoke to the Governor after having arranged to meet

him earlier. I explained to him that I was concerned about an issue in the hostel but was apprehensive about speaking to him as prison authorities tend to be punitive in approach.

I explained in detail the problems surrounding Billy, saying he needed help. After listening he agreed. He told me that he didn't know about the knives being found in the hostel. He said he was pleased that we had spoken so frankly as we do have a duty to the community outside and Billy could do a lot of damage to someone. I told him I had spoken to Peter Whatmore about it, that I called him to ask what was the right thing to do. Mr Hills said he was 'surprised' as Whatmore hadn't said a word to him. I told him the problem for me speaking truthfully to him is that he starts pointing the finger at Peter Whatmore or people like him. I explained how everyone in the Hostel realised how precious a provisional release date was and as a result they were protective of Billy. I mentioned how guys are lying in fear at nights, and the passman, with the chair against the door. Mr Hills said morale must be low if the staff aren't picking this up.

I returned to the hut wondering, have I done the right thing, what way will he respond to this? On the one hand I don't want Billy doing any more damage and on the other he can't be allowed to do something and end up in a worse situation. If that happened they would say it was his own fault, that he was given every support and help when in fact he wasn't. He would be the real victim.

1st June '82
I went in front of the Deputy Governor on request this morning. I explained that I had been refused permission to run in the Edinburgh Marathon and wanted to know why. He said the reason is that Younger's Brewery is sponsoring the competition and this alone should be enough to deter me from running. I replied this was a poor excuse for stopping me. He said that in discussions they felt it would be embarrassing if on coming through the tape I was offered a drink. He said they had refused five other 'D' categories for the same reason. I told him this was unacceptable though I would have to go along with it. He asked if I had been in Skye during my last weekend home. I told him I was. He asked what I was doing there? I replied that I didn't see any reason for not being there. He said I should know better. I asked what he meant. He said this distance is unacceptable. I reminded him that

I have been in Dunbar and in Glasgow in other weekends home. He said they were acceptable distances but if anything had happened in Skye I could have been in trouble. I told him I was more likely to be in trouble if something happened in Glasgow!

I explained to him that we are getting to a ridiculous stage with all of this. He replied that this is embarrassing to the Governor and I could at least phone the Governor and say where I am. I told him this is a new rule he is making up. He said it isn't a new rule and went on to say other prisoners can do what they want in this respect as they won't be recognised by people. Also, I should know better!

All of this was discussed with me made to stand in front of him whilst his henchmen stood at his side. I felt a deep anger in me. I felt that in being treated this way it is difficult to maintain any good feelings towards these people.

7th June '82
This morning I enquired about bringing my bicycle into the prison when I returned from work but was told it wouldn't be allowed. I was told that on a previous occasion when a prisoner tried this he was given two reasons: 1) It could be used as a means of transport for someone escaping. 2) It could be a security risk. I was incredulous at this, though found the former extremely funny. I have this image of someone stopping to haul my bike over the wall in order to cycle to freedom. . .

14th June '82
This morning the remaining prisoner working in the Fruitmarket was sacked. It seems his boss was upset at him arriving in three minutes late. . .

9th July '82
Free from the prison, Sarah and I zoomed home to complete our packing before heading to the airport. The hustle and bustle of people moving around, the tannoy system alerting us to which passengers were leaving at what time. This is magic! Soon Sarah and I will be completely free to go to those far-off places. . . Getting our tickets we checked in. Passing machines that sift the gun-men from the innocent passengers we waited with the other shuttlers. It was crowded with people drinking and talking. Sarah whispered in my ear, 'George Younger is over there'. Looking

across the room I could see the Secretary of State for Scotland with his wife. I felt an excitement and knew this was good luck. Looking across the room I could see this little man standing there away from the trappings of office and asked myself, what is this all about? He would be jostled and pushed like everyone else on the way to the plane. At the same time I was aware that the hand holding the drink could sign my freedom tomorrow. As we stood there I could see one or two businessmen approach him to introduce themselves, perhaps putting in a good – grovellers – word for the Government and the benevolence to industry, rightly or wrongly. It was all so sycophantic. The flight passengers were called and we walked to the plane. As we approached his seat he looked up and smiled. We occupied the seats immediately behind which I'm sure must have made him feel uncomfortable. He turned to talk to me about the weather and how 'muggy' it was, saying it was more so in London. I introduced him to Sarah and then we settled in. He sat reading the *Daily Mail* as I read *Confessions of a Justified Sinner*. I couldn't help thinking of how, from the prison situation I am in, access to the Secretary of State for Scotland is non-existent as there are layers and layers of bureaucracy. And yet, here I am sitting here beside him. . . The flight was quick though bumpy. While waiting to leave the plane he took the initiative in asking Sarah about mutual friends. His wife joined in. We eventually parted with him wishing us a pleasant weekend. . .

14th July '82
This morning a prison officer came into the hostel to escort me back into the prison as I was to have 'mug shots' taken. I had to sit before a screen while the lights flashed my profile. I felt queasy about this though didn't allow myself to be taken down by it. Afterwards, while waiting on the officer, I looked in another room to see two guys playing chess. On looking closer the chess men were all askew. Both men were stoned out of their heads. One of them eventually looked my way. I could see immediately that he was gone. He tried to speak to me but couldn't. He approached, giving me a postcard to post for him. He was too far gone for me to caution. I looked in to where the staff sat and they were sitting quite the thing. There is such a division between staff and prisoners that they just don't see this guy stoned. Perhaps this is one of the good reasons for keeping the dividing line. . .

20th July '82
Billy and another prisoner due for release have been told they can have their three days Home Leave any time between now and when they are released in September.

28th August '82
Tam, serving 10 years for seriously assaulting his wife, came on to TFF last week. He is a first offender and has served four years of his sentence. He comes from a small village, so Edinburgh is a strange new world to him. Today was his first six-hour parole since arriving here. He wants to use six today and six tomorrow as his wife has come down to join him. They are having a go at making it up. She has paid an extortionate sum to get a flat for the weekend. Rates are at a premium due to the Edinburgh Festival. They spent a nice six hours with each other and left the flat to return to the prison on time. However, not knowing Edinburgh they took a wrong turn and ended up in the opposite direction. Eventually they arrived at the prison gate 20 minutes late. On entering Tam was immediately taken to task by the officer and told he was on a disciplinary report and would go before the Governor on Monday. This, in effect, meant that Tam would not see his wife on his remaining six-hour parole tomorrow. He was shattered. He asked John, another TFF prisoner, to speak to his wife when she came to meet him in the morning.

29th August '82
On going out for our three-hour church parole Sarah was waiting. We passed John waiting for Tam's wife to arrive. I told Sarah about it and as I did so Tam's wife passed us beaming with happiness on her way to the prison. It really is disgraceful. There was no consideration given to Tam's wife, her position or the financial outlay to see her husband. . . I spoke to John afterwards. He said Tam's wife was terribly angry and left on her own in this city with no opportunity to speak to her husband.

30th August '82
Tam is downstairs as I write this. He said staff are going to forget the incident and not put him in front of the Governor. He is relieved at this. I am appalled by it. The person most affected and harmed is Tam's wife and through the dynamics of the prison game the prison staff are making themselves goodies by not going

through with the disciplinary report when the real damage has been done.

31st August '82
This morning on going downstairs I noticed one of the three guys scheduled to be released tomorrow as he stood at the cooker. I could see at a glance the full depth of the despair he is feeling. Despite this he is trying to keep up a front. These three guys are expecting to go out tomorrow but no governor has come to speak to them. It is an atrocious state of affairs. On going out to work I bumped into Malcolm Rifkind (Local MP and Under Secretary of State) as he was being shown round the workshop. He came across and we shook hands. He asked how things have been here and I told him it has been an invaluable placement for me. I told him I had nine weeks to go before being released. He was pleased to hear this. He asked if I would be leaving the Community Workshop in November? I told him yes, that Sarah and I want a break but we have made many friends here so will keep our ties with the place. He asked what I was intending to do on release? I explained that Sarah and I intended opening a centre here in Edinburgh. It will be a place offering support to ex-prisoners and mental patients on release. Also, it will be a place where we will campaign for change inside these institutions. He said this is needed. . . Back in the hostel two of the three due to be released were told they would be released on 7th Sept. They were shattered. Billy, who was one of them, has his family coming to meet him at the gate in the morning. The third was told there is no date for his release yet. It may come in the second or third week of the month. The cruelty of doing this to guys who expected to be released tomorrow is crushing to all of us. These people are playing with our minds.

7th September '82
(6.30am) All night I've been restless. Inside me the adrenalin has been pumping, making me aware of something bigger and more important than sleep. Outside my door – across the narrow corridor – I can hear the muffled sounds of movement. I feel a wrenching pain inside. I'd have preferred to have slept. Footsteps and whispered voices can be heard with more muffled activity. The morning light is dull outside the window. My day will come. A stab of fear objects to this confident thought – as real as the

walls around me. My head tells me to be careful, to live for the moment, but my drum-beating heart wants to disregard it and make merry with wild anticipation. The muffled sounds now slip through my window. They are outside. I don't know what will become of Billy in the future but I am in dread for him. They sneak out and through the gate. All of this with regard to those of us left behind. They know what it feels like. Lying here I imagine their stifled joy. Pulling the blankets over my head I try to blank the pain of my confinement and the joy of their freedom. The mainstreet of my mind projects images of them crossing the threshold to freedom. I can see them shake hands with glowing faces as they walk down the prison driveway. Freedom when it comes will be held precious by me.

1st October '82
The Governor asked me to return to the prison at 2.30pm. He was most amiable saying he wanted to write a final report on me. He said he doesn't want to get caught up in the conflict of my being sent here. He prefers to ask how this particular period here went. He wanted to know about my Community placement. I told him the Wester Hailes people and the work was demanding but rewarding as I had made many friends there. He asked if this sort of work would be of benefit to other prisoners. I said yes. He said he feels the scope of my placement may have been too loose. I said it was difficult for me working with many other people's problems and handling a lot of responsibility only to return here to be treated like a child. He said he would never take any one on such a lengthy programme again as he doesn't believe it is good.

He asked about the TFF hostel. I told him the weekend leaves are atrocious, that after such a long period of confinement the simple example of getting used to sharing a bed with someone is in itself a traumatic experience. That once every three weeks is disruptive. He replied that having to live on three different levels must be difficult. I commented on the 9.30pm deadline saying the return time while trying to establish a social life was difficult. Most people only begin their evening entertainment then. He replied that this is because the hostel is within the prison walls. In all, this meeting was amiable and the best I've had with the Governor. In answer to my enquiries he said they had been given an assurance by the Department that my licence will be through early and he sees no problems with my getting out on 1st November.

9th October '82
Last night I went to bed feeling tired and hoping for a good sleep. Three times during the night I wakened – the cold image of steel bars illuminated by the lights stabbed their impression into my consciousness. Each time I hoped for immediate sleep. The 'gate fever' has me gripped in its nightmare fist. It's bad enough coping with it in daytime without doing a nightshift!

Leaving the prison into the dull grey Edinburgh morning I felt good at being outside. Heading into the city centre I walked through the west end full of the agonies of my 'gate fever'. Here I am with three weeks to go and having to drag myself through days that seem to span a week of time. I am very suspicious and paranoid in case someone tries to do something and prevent my release. I have this image of a monster-sized accusing finger pointing my way. My time is dragging. In marathon terms, I've hit the wall.

As I walked along the street wrapped up in a heavy jacket and trying to alleviate the anxieties in my head I recognised something familiar about the small, dapper figure coming my way. He was an old man, smartly dressed with a pink, well-cared-for face. He looked at me with puzzled recognition. I suppose both of us were used to being recognised in the streets. At nose distance and almost upon each other we reached out to shake hands smilingly. It was Lord Cameron! He recognised who I was. Extraordinary! Both of us started, automatically shook hands and began blustering amiably before saying goodbye. I was shocked. Here is this man who sentenced me to spend the past fifteen years of my life in prison and we meet on the street like this. What powerful force of destiny places me in bizarre situations like this? It's incredible to think I am in the throes of anguish while walking the streets, that sleeplessness and pressures of impending release are biting into me at the moment he appears. Looking back on it I feel this is the sort of experience one could easily imagine. Inside me when speaking to him I felt a deep tension and anger at the old bastard for having subjected me to this. Another reasoning part sees him as a minute part of the 'system', whilst a small vocal noise cried from deep inside 'Aye, but it's what he represents'. I couldn't help but wonder, where has he been these past fifteen years? I don't know any other prisoner who has come up against the extremes I have on the way to freedom.

20th October '82
I returned to the prison early to meet with an Assistant Governor. He came into the TFF hostel and spoke to me in the office there.

I was informed that the papers he was carrying were my Conditions of Licence – my release papers. The tension in my entire body was tremendous. I have waited fifteen years to sign these and for many of those years thinking that I would never do so.

The A.G. sat down and began to read out the conditions. I wasn't really listening '. . . your supervisor. . .' He ran through each of these conditions with a speed and flatness that vastly underplayed their significance to me sitting opposite. I was shaking with excitement. Having completed them he went on to say, 'Good luck for your future', in a voice as unfeeling and as mechanised as when he read out the conditions. He had at least six copies of the Licence which I had to sign and date. They already had the signature of R. C. Allan. The papers said I would be released on 1st November.

I took six of my local twelve-hour parole hours to get out and see Sarah. We shared this wonderful moment together. It was infectious and such a relief to know the exact date. I am still trying to contain it though as there are ten slow days to go.

Almost on cue, and with uncanny timing, two journalists arrived on our doorstep to ask for an interview. They wanted an Exclusive. We informed them that an official gag is on me till I'm released. I am not allowed to talk to the media till after the 1st Nov.
1.20am: The 'gate fever' has hit me. Sitting here wide awake I find it difficult to sleep. Almost neurotically I worry that something will go wrong over the next ten days and I won't be released. I know all of this is irrational but the adrenalin surging through my body at this moment is difficult to control. I haven't met one person approaching release who hasn't been subjected to this.

25th October '82
The tension is mounting and I feel it with one week to go. Last night I slept pretty soundly, this being a result of my arduous physical exercise routine. Instead of the feelings in me being joyous and bubbling with happiness I am filled with anxiety. I

look round at the walls containing me and know I distrust them so much. I have had to contend with them over the past fifteen years and have become so conditioned to living with them that I cannot imagine life without them.

In a physical sense I am experiencing severe pains of tension in my neck and back. These are symptoms of the situation. Yesterday I felt myself break free from this acute pain when I went for a lengthy run. I could feel all the tension evaporate. It was as though the 'burn' from the run channelled the energy. There is no doubt that throughout the coming week I'll have to push myself into these hard physical areas to ensure my being worn out. I have to ward off the wakeful darkness of the nights. I know that ultimately I can cope with it as I've shown over the years. However, I do know what *the feeling of confinement* is like in the silence of night. I would prefer not to have this.

27th October '82
The stress is considerable. . . The night-time hours are particularly hard as the silence of night cuts a wedge deep into me. Flashing thoughts collide in my head as the final day approaches. It is these newly-released thoughts that knock me punch-drunk and cross-eyed through these final days. . . I leave the prison for work aware that these hours on the outside are bliss from the dreaded 'gate fever'. There are many distractions on the outside, away from the self-penetration of being alone in a cell. . .

31st October '82
The last day! How can I possibly trust it to be? *Every* morning for the past 15 years I've wakened to these surroundings. This morning is no different except for the underlying feeling of excitement.

I am gaining first-hand experience of the process of freedom. Inside I am aware that many things are going on. There is a part that wants to be joyous about it all but another seemingly stronger part stopping this as something may go wrong at the last minute. This is a sort of 'defence mechanism' that has taken me through less joyful experiences. If I were to go over the top with good feeling and it went wrong then I would be devastated. Recovery would be very difficult. What could go wrong now? I have experienced enough to know that the prison authorities are capable of anything. I distrust them considerably.

Sitting here at this moment I can say there isn't lots of good feeling in me. Many people would find this hard to believe but it's exactly my experience as I sit here. I am filled with stress and strain in these last hours. I know that this time tomorrow having stepped across the ugly prison doorstep for the last time I can afford to let my feelings go.

Having said that, I am aware that there is massive media interest in my release. So, immediately I'll be on stage. For the first time I'll be free to speak to them. These past years they have followed my life and I haven't been able to say anything. The gag will be off. However, the point of it is that their presence will be an intrusion in my feelings. An intrusion in something Sarah and I would like to share ourselves.

I know life for us both will take some adjusting to. We have lived an unreal married life for so long. My fifteen years have been spent in prison surroundings therefore dominated by a strict order and authority. It will take some getting used to on the outside.

There are two other guys here in the hostel going out the same time as me. They too are fraught with all the same anxieties. They are two brothers and will vanish into anonymity. The others remaining must feel as I have in the past. The whole thing about confinement is that one is always under the control of someone else. As a result there is uncertainty and dread as anything one may want to do must first be looked at through the eye of authority so inevitably one doesn't have any choice. It is little wonder that many prisoners on release head straight for drugs or drink. It must be a reaction to the whole process of confinement but particularly the last strenuous days. The freedom to do what has been for so long forbidden must be such a powerful force. The tendency to go for drugs or drink has a double attraction in that it immediately reduces all the tensions one has been living under. The authorities are so strict on the inside that it is also looked on as a real symbol of freedom. The sad thing is that lots of guys lose control when under the influence and are no sooner out than in.

There has to be change in all of this. The authorities must be more civilised in their approach. I know that I have a lot going for me on release, just in having a stable relationship and home. The anxieties I experience do not have the sharp edge of despair that others will have. Most are going out to the unknown. Most have no one or nothing to go out to.

Church Parole: In the house Sarah and I have breakfast. Sarah is feeling it very much. She says she too has 'gate fever'. She cried and we held each other. Matters weren't helped much by a phone-in programme. Two calls commenting on my release state their opinions about it. One guy says he knows of hundreds of enemies going to do me in. He advises I take a plane out of the country. The latter is a woman I've helped recently. She says I'm a magic guy. We both laugh at this.

1st November '82
12.01am: Sitting here awake I am feeling okay. I will rest for the day ahead as it will be heavy going. I find it hard to grasp that this is my last night in a prison cell.

With freedom, Sarah and I will have an opportunity to work at our marriage and relationship. Another aspect to be attended to once the 'media circus' is over will be my exploring the pain of my confinement. Locked inside me is a tremendous amount of pain which I've had to hold in over the years. It will take many years for me to untie the knots inside. In Sarah I couldn't have a better partner to share this with.

5.45am: . . . getting dressed I was told by the duty officer that the media are lining the drive in front of the prison. Looking out the small window I could see across the barbed-wire fence. They were assembling.

I was taken with the two others due to be released into the reception area. We signed out release papers and collected our personal belongings. The brothers agreed to stay behind while the media caught hold of me. They preferred the anonymity.

I was taken to the gate where I waited for Sarah. These were the longest minutes of all. The gate officer said Mr Hills had called to say he was coming in. I stood on edge. Mr Hills drove in the gate. He didn't look at me. He didn't speak. Sarah arrived. Mr Hills gave the signal and the duty officer opened the gate. I stepped over to Freedom.